STOICISM
IN
EARLY
CHRISTIANITY

STOICISM
IN
EARLY
CHRISTIANITY

Edited by
Tuomas Rasimus,
Troels Engberg-Pedersen,
and Ismo Dunderberg

Baker Academic
a division of Baker Publishing Group
Grand Rapids, Michigan

© 2010 by Tuomas Rasimus, Troels Engberg-Pedersen, and Ismo Dunderberg

Published by Baker Academic
a division of Baker Publishing Group
P.O. Box 6287, Grand Rapids, MI 49516-6287
www.bakeracademic.com

Printed in the United States of America

All rights reserved. No part of this book may be reproduced or transmitted in any form or by any means, electronic or mechanical, including photocopying, recording, or by any information storage and retrieval system, without permission in writing from the publisher.

Library of Congress Cataloging-in-Publication Data
Stoicism in early Christianity / edited by Tuomas Rasimus, Troels Engberg-
    Pedersen, and Ismo Dunderberg.
        p. cm.
    Includes bibliographical references and indexes.
    ISBN 978-0-8010-3951-5 (alk. paper)
    1. Stoics. 2. Philosophy and religion—Rome. 3. Church history—Primitive
and early church, ca. 30–600. 4. Bible. N.T.—Philosophy. I. Rasimus,
Tuomas. II. Engberg-Pedersen, Troels. III. Dunderberg, Ismo.
    BR128.A2.S76 2010
    261.2—dc22   2010021683

10 11 12 13 14 15 16   7 6 5 4 3 2 1

In keeping with biblical principles of creation stewardship, Baker Publishing Group advocates the responsible use of our natural resources. As a member of the Green Press Initiative, our company uses recycled paper when possible. The text paper of this book is comprised of 30% post-consumer waste.

Contents

Preface   vii

Abbreviations   ix

1. Setting the Scene: Stoicism and Platonism in the Transitional Period in Ancient Philosophy   1
   Troels Engberg-Pedersen

2. Stoicism as a Key to Pauline Ethics in Romans   15
   Runar M. Thorsteinsson

3. Stoic Law in Paul?   39
   Niko Huttunen

4. Jesus the Teacher and Stoic Ethics in the Gospel of Matthew   59
   Stanley K. Stowers

5. An "Emotional" Jesus and Stoic Tradition   77
   Harold W. Attridge

6. The Emotional Jesus: Anti-Stoicism in the Fourth Gospel?   93
   Gitte Buch-Hansen

7. Stoic Physics, the Universal Conflagration, and the Eschatological Destruction of the "Ignorant and Unstable" in 2 Peter   115
   J. Albert Harrill

8. The Stoics and the Early Christians on the Treatment of Slaves   141
   John T. Fitzgerald

9. Facing the Beast: Justin, Christian Martyrdom, and Freedom of the Will   176
   Nicola Denzey

10. A Stoic Reading of the *Gospel of Mary*: The Meaning of "Matter" and
    "Nature" in *Gospel of Mary* 7.1–8.11   199
    Esther de Boer

11. Stoic Traditions in the School of Valentinus   220
    Ismo Dunderberg

12. Critical Reception of the Stoic Theory of Passions in the
    Apocryphon of John   239
    Takashi Onuki

13. Stoic Ingredients in the Neoplatonic *Being-Life-Mind* Triad: An Original
    Second-Century Gnostic Innovation?   257
    Tuomas Rasimus

Index of Modern Authors   275

Index of Subjects   281

Index of Ancient Sources   288

Preface

What was the earliest Christian interaction with Greco-Roman philosophy like? And how early did it begin? The story has often been told of the engagement with Middle Platonism of the Greek and Latin church fathers up until Origen. Over the last few decades, however, attempts have been made to take the role of philosophy in early Christianity further back into the first century. Here the potential role of Stoicism has also been variously explored. Faced with this new scholarly situation, the three editors of this volume decided that the time was ripe for an investigation into the earliest Christianity and its relationship to Stoicism.

The volume that has come out of this venture is exploratory in nature. In no way did we attempt to cover the whole field. The possible interaction of Stoicism and Platonism in early Christian texts is also not a primary concern in this volume. However, we wanted the volume to address the following question head-on: To what extent are distinctly Stoic ideas useful for illuminating the meaning of Christian texts from the first and second centuries? We suggest that early Christians—the authors of New Testament writings, those of noncanonical early Christian writings, and some early apologists—adopted philosophical ideas in the first and second centuries, and that it was specifically Stoicism that influenced their views, often to a degree greater than Middle Platonism. In this way, an entirely new light can be thrown on the relationship between philosophy and religion at the birth of Christianity.

The essays are arranged in a roughly chronological order. After an introductory chapter by Troels Engberg-Pedersen that sets the scene, there is, first, a series of essays on New Testament authors and Stoicism by Runar M. Thorsteinsson (Romans), Niko Huttunen (Paul and the law), Stanley K. Stowers (Gospel of Matthew), Harold W. Attridge (Gospel of John), Gitte Buch-Hansen (Gospel of John), and J. Albert Harrill (2 Peter). Then follow essays by John T. Fitzgerald (Christians and Stoics on slavery) and Nicola Denzey (Stoics, Justin, and martyrdom). Finally, the presence of Stoic ideas in other early Christian evidence from the second century is explored by Esther de Boer (*Gospel of Mary*), Ismo Dunderberg (Valentinianism), Takashi Onuki (*Apocryphon of John*), and Tuomas Rasimus (Sethianism and Stoicizing Platonism).

It remains to thank everybody involved in bringing off this project, which began during conversations at the Society of Biblical Literature annual meeting in

Washington, D.C., in November 2006. In particular, we would like to thank each of the contributors, who not only accepted our invitation to participate but also delivered what we were after. We would also like to thank Hendrickson Publishers, which has been uncommonly forthcoming in the preparation of this project. Finally, we wish to express our gratitude to Margot Stout Whiting, who has helped improve the English of several non-English-speaking contributors. It is our hope that this volume will help to strengthen a field of study where so much more remains to be done.

Just before the publication of this volume, the editors heard of Esther de Boer's premature and tragic death on July 6, 2010. We are grateful to be able to publish her essay here in her memory.

Tuomas Rasimus
Troels Engberg-Pedersen
Ismo Dunderberg

Abbreviations

Abr.	*De migratione Abrahami (On the Migration of Abraham)*
Abst.	*De abstinentia (On Abstinence)*
Acad. post.	*Academica posteriora (The Later Academics)*
Adv. Ar.	*Adversus Arium (Against Arius)*
Adv. haer.	*Adversus haereses (Against Heresies)*
Aet.	*De aeternitate mundi (On the Eternity of the World)*
Agr.	*De agricultura (De re rustica) (Agriculture)*
Ann.	*Annales (Annals)*
ANRW	*Aufstieg und Niedergang der römischen Welt: Geschichte und Kultur Roms im Spiegel der neueren Forschung.* Edited by H. Temporini and W. Haase. Berlin, 1972–
Ant.	*Antiquitates judaicae (Jewish Antiquities)*
Anth.	*Anthologium (Anthology)*
Ap. John	The *Apocryphon of John*
Apol.	*Apologia (Apology)*
1 Apol.	*Apologia i (First Apology)*
2 Apol.	*Apologia ii (Second Apology)*
ASV	American Standard Version
BDAG	Bauer, W., F. W. Danker, W. F. Arndt, and F. W. Gingrich. *Greek-English Lexicon of the New Testament and Other Early Christian Literature.* 3d ed. Chicago, 1999
Bell. civ.	*Bellum civile (Civil War)*
Ben.	*De beneficiis (On Favors)*
BG	*Berolinensis Gnosticus* (= Berlin Codex 8502)
BGU	*Aegyptische Urkunden aus den Königlichen Staatlichen Museen zu Berlin, Griechische Urkunden.* 15 vols. Berlin, 1895–1983
Carn. Chr.	*De carne Christi (The Flesh of Christ)*
Cat. Maj.	*Cato Major (Cato the Elder)*
CCSL	*Corpus Christianorum: Series latina.* Turnhout, 1953–
Cels.	*Contra Celsum (Against Celsus)*
Char.	*Characteres (Characters)*
Cher.	*De cherubim (On the Cherubim)*
CIL	*Corpus inscriptionum latinarum.* Leipzig and Berlin, 1893–

Civ.	*De civitate Dei* (*The City of God*)
Claud.	*Divus Claudius* (*The Deified Claudius*)
CLE	*Carmina latina epigraphica.* F. Bücheler and E. Lommatzsch, eds. 3 vols. Leipzig, 1895–1926
Clem.	*De clementia* (*On Clemency*)
Cohib. ira	*De cohibenda ira* (*On the Control of the Anger*)
Comm. not.	*De communibus notitiis contra Stoicos* (*On Common Conceptions*)
Comm. Phlm.	*Commentariorum in epistulam ad Philemonem liber* (*Commentary on Philemon*)
Comm. 1 Tim.	*Commentariorum in epistulam i ad Timotheum liber* (*Commentary on 1 Timothy*)
Conf.	*De confusione linguarum* (*On the Confusion of Tongues*)
Congr.	*De congressu eruditionis gratia* (*On the Preliminary Studies*)
Const.	*De Constantia sapientiis* (*On Constancy*)
Cont.	*Controversiae* (*Controversies*)
CSEL	*Corpus scriptorum ecclesiasticorum latinorum*
Deipn.	*Deipnosophistae* (*Philosophers at Dinner*)
De mens.	*De mensibus* (*On the Months*)
De princ.	*De principiis* (*On the First Principles*)
Deus	*Quod Deus sit immutabilis* (*That God Is Unchangeable*)
Dial.	*Dialogus cum Tryphone* (*Dialogue with Trypho*)
Diss.	*Dissertationes* (*Discourses*)
Ebr.	*De ebrietate* (*On Drunkenness*)
El. theol.	*Elementa theologiae* (*Elements of Theology*)
Ench.	*Encheiridion* (*Manual*)
Enn.	*Ennead*
Ep.	*Epistulae morales* (*Moral Epistles*)
Epict. diss.	*Epicteti dissertationes* (*Discourses of Epictetus*)
ET	English translation
Eth. nic.	*Ethica nichomachea* (*Nicomachean Ethics*)
Exc. Theod.	*Excerpta ex Theodoto* (*Excerpts from Theodotus*)
Ex. mart.	*Exhortatio ad martyrium* (*Exhortation to Martyrdom*)
Fat.	*De fato* (*On Fate*)
Fin.	*De finibus* (*On Ends*)
Fuga	*De fuga et inventione* (*On Flight and Finding*)
GCS	*Die griechischen christlichen Schriftsteller der ersten* [*drei*] *Jahrhunderte.* Leipzig: Hinrichs, 1897–
Gen. corr.	*De generatione et corruptione* (*Generation and Corruption*)
Gos. Mary	The *Gospel of Mary*
Gos. Phil.	The *Gospel of Philip*
Gos. Truth	The *Gospel of Truth*
Helv.	*Ad Helviam* (*To Helvia*)
Herc. fur.	*Hercules furens* (*The Madness of Hercules*)
Herc. Ot.	*Hercules Oetaeus* (*Hercules on Mount Oeta*)

Hist. eccl.	*Historia ecclesiastica (Ecclesiastical History)*
Hist. phil.	*Historia philosophiae (History of Philosophy)*
Hist. Rom.	*Historia Romana (Roman History)*
Hom.	*Pseudo-Clementine Homilies*
Hom. 1 Cor.	*Homiliae in epistulam i ad Corinthios (Homilies on First Corinthians)*
In Ar. Phys.	*In Aristotelis physica paraphrasis (On Aristotle's Physics)*
In categ.	*In Aristotelis categorias commentarium (Commentary on Aristotle's Categories)*
In Metaph.	*In Aristotelis Metaphysica commentaria (Commentary on Aristole's Metaphysics)*
Interpr. Know.	*Interpretation of Knowledge*
In Tim.	*In Platonis Timaeum commentaria (Commentary on Plato's Timaeus)*
Ira	*De ira (On Anger)*
L.A.E.	*Life of Adam and Eve*
Laps.	*De lapsis (The Lapsed)*
LCL	Loeb Classical Library
Leg.	*De legibus (On Laws)*
Leg. all.	*Legum allegoriae (Allegorical Interpretation)*
L-S	Long, A. A., and D. N. Sedley. *The Hellenistic Philosophers*. 2 vols. Cambridge, 1987
LSJ	Liddell, H. G., R. Scott, and H. S. Jones. *A Greek-English Lexicon*. 9th ed. with revised supplement. Oxford, 1996
LXX	Septuagint
Mand.	*Mandate*
Marc.	*Ad Marciam de consolatione (On Consolation to Marcia)*
Mart.	*Ad martyras (To the Martyrs)*
Mart. Pol.	*Martyrdom of Polycarp*
Math.	*Adversus mathematicos (Against the Mathematicians)*
Mem.	*Memorabilia (Recollections)*
Metam.	*Metamorphoses*
Mixt.	*De mixtione (On Mixture)*
Mor.	*Moralia (Morals)*
Mos.	*De vita Mosis (On the Life of Moses)*
MT	Masoretic Text
Mur.	*Pro Murena (For Lucius Murena)*
Nat.	*Naturales quaestiones (Natural Questions)*
Nat. d.	*De natura deorum (The Nature of the Gods)*
Nat. hist.	*Naturalis historia (Natural History)*
Nat. hom.	*De natura hominis (On the Nature of Man)*
NHC	Nag Hammadi Codex
NIV	New International Version
NJPS	*Tanakh: The Holy Scriptures: The New JPS Translation according to the Traditional Hebrew Text*

Noct. att.	Noctes atticae (Attic Nights)
NRSV	New Revised Standard Version
Oct.	Octavius
Oec.	Oeconomicus (The Economist)
Off.	De officiis (On Duties)
Opif.	De opificio mundi (On the Creation of the World)
Otio	De otio (On Leisure)
OTP	Old Testament Pseudepigrapha. Edited by J. H. Charlesworth. 2 vols. New York, 1983
Pan.	Panarion (Medicine Chest)
Perpetua	Passion of Perpetua
PG	Patrologia graeca [= Patrologiae cursus completus: Series graeca]. Edited by J.-P. Migne. 162 vols. Paris, 1857–1886
Phaedr.	Phaedrus
Philops.	Philopseudes (The Lover of Lies)
PHP	De placitis Hippocratis et Platonis (On the Doctrines of Hippocrates and Plato)
Plant.	De plantatione (On Planting)
Plat. Theol.	Theologia Platonica (Platonic Theology)
P.Lond.	Greek Papyri in the London Museum
Pol.	Politica (Politics)
Polyb.	Ad Polybium de consolatione (To Polybius on Consolation)
P.Oxy.	Oxyrhynchus Papyri
Praep. ev.	Praeparatio evangelica (Preparation for the Gospel)
Princ.	De principiis (First Principles)
Prov.	De providentia (On Providence)
P.Ryl.	Greek and Latin Papyri in the John Rylands Library
Pyr.	Pyrrhoniae hypotyposes (Outlines of Pyrrhonism)
Pyrrh.	Pyrrhus (Life of Pyrrhus)
QE	Quaestiones et solutiones in Exodum (Questions and Answers on Exodus)
QG	Quaestiones et solutiones in Genesin (Questions and Answers on Genesis)
Rec.	Pseudo-Clementine Recognitions
Ref.	Refutatio omnium haeresium (Refutation of All Heresies)
Rep.	Republic
Resp.	De republica (On the State)
Saty.	Satyricon
SC	Sources chrétiennes. Paris: Cerf. 1943–
Sent.	Sententiae ad intelligibilia ducentes (Sentences)
Sib. Or.	Sibylline Oracles
Somn.	De somniis (On Dreams)
Spec.	De specialibus legibus (On the Special Laws)
Spect.	De spectaculis (The Shows)
Steles Seth	The Three Steles of Seth

Stoic. rep.	*De Stoicorum repugnatiis (On Stoic Self-contradictions)*
Strom.	*Stromata (Miscellanies)*
SVF	*Stoicorum veterum fragmenta.* H. von Arnim. 4 vols. Leipzig, 1903–1924
T. Dan	*Testament of Dan*
Tim.	*Timaeus*
T. Job	*Testament of Job*
TNIV	Today's New International Version
Tranq.	*De tranquillitate animi (On the Tranquility of Mind)*
Tri. Trac.	The *Tripartite Tractate*
Tusc.	*Tusculanae disputationes (Tusculan Disputations)*
Virt.	*De virtutibus (On Virtues)*
Virt. mor.	*De virtute morali (On Moral Virtue)*
Vit. auct.	*Vitarum auctio (Philosophies for Sale)*
Vit. beat.	*De vita beata (On the Happy Life)*
Vit. phil.	*Vitae philosophorum (Lives of Eminent Philosophers)*
Vit. Plot.	*Vita Plotini (Life of Plotinus)*
W-H	Wachsmuth, C. and O. Hense. 1974–1975. *Ioannis Stobaei: Anthologium.* 3d ed. 5 vols. Berlin: Weidmann

1

SETTING THE SCENE: STOICISM AND PLATONISM IN THE TRANSITIONAL PERIOD IN ANCIENT PHILOSOPHY

Troels Engberg-Pedersen
University of Copenhagen

The centuries immediately following the end of the Hellenistic age remain a murky area in the history of philosophy. While a great deal of work has been done in recent years to rehabilitate Hellenistic thought itself from the generally negative assessment of the nineteenth century, the thesis that later philosophy traces a decline into "eclecticism" . . . retains a programmatic hold over studies of the period. Three centuries of intellectual activity are held to mark out a kind of philosophical no man's land between the earlier systems from which they are taken to derive their material, and the glories of "Neoplatonism" to which they look forward.

Thus George Boys-Stones began his intriguing book from 2001, *Post-Hellenistic Philosophy*, subtitled *A Study of Its Development from the Stoics to Origen*.[1] The period that he identified in this way was roughly 100 B.C.E.–200 C.E. This was also the period in which Greco-Roman philosophy began to make a serious impact on Jewish and early Christian thinking, as is documented by the essays in this book. In this introductory essay I will present some of the main features of this period, focusing on the interaction between the various philosophical schools and trying to understand the precise character of that interaction. Since at the beginning of the period Stoicism was the leading philosophical school but had been displaced as such at the end of the period by Platonism, I will also focus on trying to understand the development that resulted in this change. Traditionally, the period has been studied—at least by scholars interested in Platonism and its impact on Jewish and early Christian thinking—under the rubric "Middle Platonism."[2] Scholars have identified two forms of Stoicism in it: so-called Middle Stoicism for the hundred years running approximately from 150 B.C.E. to 50 B.C.E. and so-called Late

---

[1] Boys-Stones 2001, v.
[2] The classic treatment is Dillon 1996b.

Stoicism or Neostoicism for the two first centuries C.E.[3] However, for the purposes of understanding both the interaction between Stoicism and Platonism (and in principle other philosophies) in the whole period and also the relationship of either with early Jewish and Christian thought, it is preferable to identify the period, as is proposed here, as the "Transitional Period" of ancient philosophy.[4]

1. Basic Changes During the Transitional Period

A number of momentous events directly relevant to the development of philosophy took place during the Transitional Period in the political and more broadly cultural fields of the ancient world.[5] While philosophy previously had been something of a Greek specialty focused on Athens, the Romans now began to make their presence felt. In Greece itself, the first representative of Middle Stoicism, Panaetius of Rhodes (ca. 185–109 B.C.E.), who had stayed in Rome in the 140s, maintained close contacts with high-level Romans when he became head of the Stoic school in Athens from 129 until his death. Even more importantly, as a result of the so-called First Mithradatic War (89–85), in which Athens had sided with King Mithradates of Pontus in Asia Minor against the Romans, the four schools of philosophy that had been operating in Athens since the beginning of the Hellenistic period were closed down by the Romans after Sulla had captured the city in the year 86. Philosophy now became homeless and had to go into exile. Even before that, however, the second main representative of Middle Stoicism, Posidonius of Apamea (ca. 135–51), who had studied with Panaetius at Athens, founded his own school of Stoicism in Rhodes. Posidonius, too, had close contacts with high-level Romans. In short, Athens was no longer *the* center of philosophy.

In Rome itself, the new superpower made itself felt in several ways in relation to philosophy. Around 50 B.C.E., Cicero wrote philosophical treatises on the main topics in philosophy—epistemology, physics and theology, ethics—in which he set forth the main positions adopted by the three schools that were recognized as the most important ones at the end of the Hellenistic period: Stoicism, Epicureanism, and the skeptical "New Academy" (which had developed the nondogmatic side of Plato's philosophy), though also with some input from the Peripatetic school derived from Aristotle.[6] Two editorial undertakings had immense influence on the further development of philosophy. Sometime around the mid-first century B.C.E. in Rome, Andronicus of Rhodes produced an edition of Aristotle's works,

---

[3] For excellent overviews, see Sedley 2003 and Gill 2003, respectively.
[4] Compare at least the title of Berchman 1984, *From Philo to Origen: Middle Platonism in Transition*.
[5] Since it is not my aim in what follows to discuss each individual person or event that is mentioned, I have refrained from giving detailed references for the underlying evidence. Many of those references may be found in, for instance, André 1987; Gill 2003; Sedley 2003.
[6] The most important among these treatises are *Academica* (epistemology), *De Finibus Bonorum et Malorum* (ethics), *Tusculan Disputations* (moral psychology), and *De Natura Deorum* (ontology and theology).

including the so-called esoteric ones, which are those that have come down to us and that were to make a huge impact on philosophizing in the centuries to come. About seventy-five years later, the court astrologer of the emperor Tiberius in Rome, Tiberius Claudius Thrasyllus (who notably came from Alexandria), produced what was probably a new edition of Plato's writings, in which he apparently introduced the division of the dialogues into tetralogies that is still in use.

Back in the first century B.C.E., Alexandria in Egypt had come into its own as a place where dogmatic, nonskeptical Platonism began to develop into Middle Platonism. Eudorus of Alexandria, who flourished around 25 B.C.E., "seems to have turned the very Stoicized Platonism of [the dogmatic apostate from the nondogmatic Platonic New Academy] Antiochus of Ascalon in a more transcendental direction, under the influence of Neopythagoreanism."[7] This statement made by an authority on Middle Platonism, John Dillon, points to our theme: the relationship between Stoicism in the Transitional Period and a newly conceived Platonism, which eventually led to the final victory of Platonism over Stoicism both in Neoplatonism (third century) and in Christian thought that is contemporary with Neoplatonism. Witnesses to this victory are two more, later and Christian Alexandrians: Clement of Alexandria (ca. 150–215 C.E.) and the great Origen (184/185–254/255 C.E.). But into this development we should also fit yet another Alexandrian (on whom Clement drew heavily): the Jewish Platonist Philo of Alexandria, back around the birth of Christ (ca. 20 B.C.E.–45 C.E.), who played an important, if somewhat enigmatic, role in the development of Middle Platonism.[8] Dillon's comment also points to the elusive role played at the beginning of this whole development by the "new Academician turned Stoic" Antiochus of Ascalon (ca. 130–69/68 B.C.E.), who had studied in Athens with the last representative of the New Academy, Philo of Larissa (159/158–84/83 B.C.E.), had then founded his own school in the same city, but also maintained extensive contacts with high-level Romans in whose company he even visited Alexandria. We will come back later to Antiochus, who is a characteristic representative at an early stage of the change in the relationship between Stoicism and Platonism that we will consider.

What we have, then, is a move away from Athens as the philosophical center to Rhodes, Alexandria, and Rome; a summary by Cicero in Rome around 50 B.C.E. of Hellenistic philosophy as it more or less appeared before the developments that inaugurated the Transitional Period (though Cicero does make relatively much of the novelties introduced by Antiochus of Ascalon);[9] developments in Alexandria throughout the first century B.C.E. that contributed to creating the form of Platonism known by modern scholars as Middle Platonism (and here we may specifically note the extensive amount of Platonism to be found in the Jewish philosopher Philo of Alexandria); and finally, the fact of major editorial undertakings in Rome of the writings of Aristo-

---

[7] Dillon 1996a.
[8] John Dillon's perceptive discussion of Philo (Dillon 1996b, 139–83) shows the extent to which Philo was influenced by Alexandrian Platonism. His influence on later Platonists seems to have been negligible, however, until one reaches the Christian Clement of Alexandria.
[9] This comes out very clearly in the excellent overview of Antiochus in Dillon 1996b, 52–106.

tle and of Plato. Even as described in these broadly cultural terms, philosophy looked very different in the first century B.C.E. compared to previous centuries.

The changes in the social practices of doing philosophy that took place during the first century B.C.E. and were quite often in one way or another connected with the presence of the Romans laid the ground for a period that runs to the end of the second century C.E. During this period, the development in philosophy gradually changed the overall philosophical landscape rather drastically. Both Epicureanism and Stoicism were still around during the whole period, the latter in the form of Late Stoicism or Neostoicism as represented by, among others, the Roman philosopher and statesman Seneca (ca. 1–65 C.E.); the Roman knight (who wrote in Greek) Musonius Rufus (ca. 30–100); the Roman (but originally Greek) slave (who also taught in Greek) Epictetus (ca. 50–120); and finally the Roman emperor Marcus Aurelius (121–180), who also wrote in Greek. But alongside these two schools, Aristotelianism (the Peripatetics) came into its own as a very important intellectual presence in philosophy, as is witnessed by the extensive amount of commentaries that began to be written on Aristotle's texts—for instance, by the great Alexander of Aphrodisias (ca. 200 C.E.). Similarly, Platonism in the new form that it had achieved during the first century B.C.E. eventually became *the* reigning type of philosophy, which would then also, from the latter half of the second century onwards, exercise a profound influence on Christian theologians such as the Christian Alexandrians noted earlier. This is the period of a number of main representatives of Middle Platonism: Plutarch (ca. 50–120) and a number of figures from the second century C.E. such as Albinus (ca. 150), Alcinous (second century), Apuleius (ca. 125–170), Atticus (ca. 150–200), and Numenius (second century). At a specific point in time at the end of the Transitional Period, in 178 C.E., the emperor Marcus Aurelius sealed the intervening development by setting up four new chairs of philosophy in Athens, which thereby reasserted—if not in actual fact, at least in appearance—the role it had had until the Romans closed the schools in 86 B.C.E. Where Cicero had focused on three philosophies—Epicureanism, Stoicism, and the skeptical New Academy (though also with some input from specifically Aristotelian philosophy)—Marcus Aurelius now installed chairs for the four philosophies that were henceforth to be *the* four philosophies of the ancient world: Epicureanism, Stoicism, Aristotelianism, and dogmatic Platonism. However, and most importantly, by this time both Epicureanism and Stoicism were for all intents and purposes basically extinct, only to be rediscovered at a far later period in the history of European thought, after the Renaissance. The two philosophies that were alive and influential were Aristotelianism and Platonism, with the latter being the leading force.

2. The Problem

With this brief overview in place, we may raise the question of a deeper understanding of some of the changes noted above. One thing particularly striking about the Transitional Period is that almost all philosophers within the period to some degree adopted ideas from philosophies other than their own. In the context of the present book and the overall change from Stoicism to Platonism as the leading force, we will focus particularly on these two schools. What we find is that many philosophers who were basically Stoics, and who saw themselves as such, also drew on ideas that had a specifically Platonic pedigree. Conversely, many philosophers who were basically Platonists, and who saw themselves as such, also drew on ideas that had a specifically Stoic pedigree. Traditionally, as Boys-Stones noted in the quotation with which we began, this phenomenon has been identified as a matter of "eclecticism." More recently, however, this category has been called seriously into question.[10] As John Dillon concludes his analysis of the phenomenon, "*Eclecticism* has for too long been used as a term of contempt in the area of later Greek philosophy. As such, let us have done with it."[11] But then, how should we understand the fact itself of the existence of various types of blending of philosophies in our period? For of course, the fact itself does not go away by calling into question our way of categorizing it.

This question becomes even more serious when one notes that the very same philosophers who in this or the other area engaged in a blending exercise also quite often had very strong opinions about the inadequacy of the philosophy as a whole from which they nevertheless drew certain ideas. At least, while there is a certain openness toward input from Plato, as we will see, in certain Stoics during our period (beginning with Panaetius and extending from him over Posidonius and Seneca to Marcus Aurelius), the Platonists, on their side, wrote explicitly against Stoicism while also adopting Stoic ideas in a number of places. How is that apparent paradox to be understood and explained? Can we find a way of understanding the character of philosophy itself in our period that will also explain and dissolve the paradox?

Before addressing this question, we should note that the question is directly relevant to the issue being discussed in the present book. It is well known, and we have already noted the fact, that from a certain point in time onward, namely, toward the end of the second century C.E., the kind of philosophy that influenced Christian thought was basically that of Platonism. Before that, however, the situation was far less clear-cut. In early Christian texts from the New Testament and well into the second century, one may in fact find traces of Platonism. But one may also find traces of Stoicism. Indeed, some (including the writer of these pages) have argued that at least in the thought of the apostle Paul the Stoic component is far more extensive than normally admitted.[12] But then, since no early Christian writer was either a Platonist or a Stoic per se (rather, they had their own worldview, focused on Christ), how should one understand this adoption of either Platonic or Stoic ideas? And indeed, how may one and the same Christian writer adopt both Platonic and Stoic ideas if that is in fact the case? In order to answer these questions we must obtain a better grasp of the interaction between Platonism and Stoicism during our period in philosophy proper, outside the Christian context.

---

[10] The classic discussion is Dillon and Long 1988.
[11] Dillon 1988, 125.
[12] See Engberg-Pedersen 2000.

3. Attempts at a Solution

Important steps have been taken in recent scholarship to find a solution to the apparent paradox of the copresence of, for instance, Platonism and Stoicism in philosophers who saw themselves as belonging to one of the two schools only and were even highly critical of the school from which they did incorporate certain ideas.

In his excellent overview of "Les écoles philosophiques aux deux premiers siècles de l'Empire," Jean-Marie André spoke of a "cultural integration" of the philosophical schools into society in the way their dogmatic positions had become part of "the encyclopedia of antiquity."[13] That explains Marcus Aurelius's installation of the four chairs of philosophy at the end of our period, but hardly the blending exercise that also took place throughout the period. More recently, in an epilogue to the *Cambridge History of Hellenistic Philosophy*, Michael Frede focused, in a manner that I have basically adopted above, on the change in the role of Athens at the beginning of our period, which saw what David Sedley has also called "the great philosophical exodus from Athens" around 86 B.C.E.[14] When the Athenian schools went out of existence, says Frede, there was no longer any "scholarch to define the philosophical position of the school. It was no longer relatively clear what the position of a school was on a particular question at a particular time."[15] "This vagueness and indefiniteness about what it is to belong to a certain school must have reinforced greatly the process by which the founders of a school turned into *authorities* and their writings became *authoritative texts* that to some extent defined the school."[16] The importance of Frede's emphasis on the turn toward "authoritative texts" as a characteristic feature of our period can hardly be overstated. But again, while it certainly adds to one's understanding of the ossification of the four philosophical schools with their four authoritative founding fathers, the turn does not, of course, explain the blending exercise that gave rise to the old characterization of our period as one of eclecticism.

In a more recent study, David Sedley, who has long been working on the character of philosophy itself in the Hellenistic period, has developed Frede's picture further by speaking of a "new pattern of philosophical teaching" arising from the demise of the Athenian schools, a pattern that involved "the scholarly study of school texts" as a way of "recovering, understanding, and living the wisdom of the ancients."[17] But Sedley also suggests a way of understanding the other side of the paradox in his remarks about the main representatives of Middle Stoicism, Panaetius and Posidonius. Although these two philosophers, Sedley argues, belonged "firmly within the main current of Stoic debate" (i.e., they were Stoics), they also "made regular use of early Peripatetic as well as Platonist writings,"[18] thereby bring-

---

[13] André 1987, 75.
[14] Sedley 2003, 27.
[15] Frede 2005, 792.
[16] Ibid., 793 (my italics).
[17] Sedley 2003, 29. Sedley's earlier work that I hinted at is Sedley 1989.
[18] Ibid., 24.

ing about a "pooling of philosophical resources among what could be seen as three branches of the Platonist tradition: early Platonism, Aristotelianism, and Stoicism."[19] Sedley also speaks of this strategy as being one of "syncretism," but what he actually shows is that such syncretism should be understood not as an act of blending or bringing ideas together in a great melting pot, but in a rather more specific manner as a strategy of "reclaiming" or "absorbing" ideas from a philosophy other than one's own into one's own philosophy. The syncretism does not erase the differences between any two philosophies. Nor does it in any way imply that a given philosopher is no longer either a Stoic or a Platonist (or again, a Christian). On the contrary, it is precisely while being either this or that that one may also "reclaim" or "absorb" foreign ideas into one's own philosophy.

If Panaetius and Posidonius are in this way an example of Stoics who also "syncretized" certain Platonic ideas into their own Stoicism, Sedley shows how Posidonius's contemporary Antiochus of Ascalon, whom I mentioned earlier, fits the opposite bill of being a Platonist who incorporated a huge amount of Stoicism into what he himself took to be the authentic form of Platonism. Antiochus's case is intriguing in a number of ways.[20] His position constituted a break with the skeptical New Academy of his teacher Philo of Larissa, a break that Antiochus marked by speaking of his own position as articulating that of the "Old Academy." In itself, that move is perhaps not so surprising, since epistemological and ontological skepticism surely does not cover everything to be found in Plato. What is more surprising is that, apparently, Antiochus took over from the Stoics a number of ideas in physics that the Stoics themselves had articulated in direct opposition to Aristotelianism and Platonism. When Antiochus insisted, on the basis of his contention that "the doctrines of the Stoics were present already in Plato,"[21] that talk of an immaterial substance (like the Platonic ideas) was "unintelligible," and that he saw "no possibility . . . of anything immaterial, transcendent or external to the material universe,"[22] then certainly he was taking up a basically Stoic position. But how he could also claim that this particular Stoic doctrine was already present in Plato remains a mystery.

It is a very instructive mystery, however. For it shows how far it was apparently possible to go in the direction of reclaiming alien material for one's own philosophy as long as one was able to convince oneself that one remained loyal to the founder of that philosophy—in the present case, Plato.

We should conclude that the paradox identified here—philosophers who both emphasized the differences between the various main types of philosophy and also produced philosophies of their own that look like an amalgam of several types—can be resolved when one sees the whole set of operations as part of a strategy of creating a philosophical identity of one's own. That identity was defined by the founding father with whom one identified. But it also allowed one to bring in

---

[19] Ibid., 22.
[20] A probing account is Barnes 1989.
[21] The quotation is from Sextus Empiricus. See Dillon 1996b, 59n3.
[22] The quotation is from Cicero, *De Finibus*. See Dillon 1996b, 84.

extraneous ideas that might fill in gaps in the thought of the founding father or develop it further in any direction that seemed called for, as long as one might claim (rightly or wrongly) that those ideas in fact belonged to the founding father himself. This is the operation of "reclaiming" or "absorbing" extraneous ideas into the thought system of one's own preferred philosophy as defined by its relation to its postulated founding father. Instead of speaking of "eclecticism" (as if philosophers just picked up a little from here and there as they saw fit and with no systematic concerns), and instead of speaking of "syncretism" (as if philosophers sought to meld together different philosophies into a single blend), we should speak of the underlying philosophical strategy during the Transitional Period as being one of "absorption" into one's own preferred philosophy of alien ideas that one claimed to be actually one's own. This was true of the Stoics Panaetius and Posidonius at the beginning of the period and of the Platonist Antiochus of Ascalon at the same time. And it remained true throughout the period. Seneca, the Stoic, was not averse to absorbing Platonic ideas into his Stoicism.[23] Epictetus, the Stoic, made an Aristotelian concept, *prohairesis*, the fulcrum of his Stoicism.[24] Plutarch, although an avowed Platonist and anti-Stoic, absorbed a number of Stoic ideas that he saw as actually belonging to his own Platonism.[25]

4. Implications

The proposed solution to the initial paradox has an important implication for the proper way of understanding the mix of philosophies to be found in almost all philosophers of the Transitional Period. This implication also shows why it was not in fact quite wrong to speak of "eclecticism" and "syncretism" in the first place. We may give two examples of the implication that pertain directly to the role of Greco-Roman philosophy within early Jewish and early Christian thought.

The implication I have in mind is this: If the proposed solution given above is on the right track, then it becomes understandable why a philosopher who considers himself a Stoic may absorb into his own thinking elements from Platonic thought without necessarily understanding those elements in the exact Platonic way; conversely, a Platonist may absorb into his own thinking elements from Stoicism without necessarily understanding those elements in the exact Stoic way. For what mattered most was the underlying, basic allegiance. If that was to Stoicism, then elements that might be taken over from Platonism might well be reinterpreted in accordance with one's basic allegiance, and vice versa. In short, elements from alien philosophies that were absorbed into one's own need not be understood in exactly the way they were understood as part of the philosophy from which they were taken.

This, I would argue, is what we find in the Jewish philosopher Philo of Alexandria and in the Christian apostle Paul of Tarsus. Philo was a Platonist but also,

---

[23] For this, see below.
[24] On Epictetus, Long 2002 is already a classic.
[25] The classic treatment is Babut 1969.

of course, a Jew. However, in his account of the so-called sublunar world (and also in many other places) he also took over ("absorbed") Stoic ideas into his own philosophy. For instance, the central Stoic notion of the material πνεῦμα ("spirit") that pervades everything in the world and holds it together and directs it underlies much of Philo's description of the sublunar world. To a certain extent, Philo was also able to take over the specifically Stoic claim that the πνεῦμα was in fact a material entity.[26] In spite of this, however, Philo stayed with the basic worldview that he had adopted from Plato, to the effect that the material world was only one half of the cosmos, with the other half consisting of what was immaterial and accessible only through thought. Seen from a Stoic point of view, however, such a combination was meaningless.[27] But Philo probably did not care, precisely because his basic perspective was and remained that of a Platonist.

The converse situation is to be found, I believe, in Paul's thought. I have argued elsewhere that his account of the resurrection in 1 Cor 15 presupposes a basically Stoic understanding of the πνεῦμα that will eventually transform human bodies of flesh and blood into "pneumatic bodies"—that is, into material bodies that are now made up by πνεῦμα instead of flesh and blood.[28] On such an understanding, Paul, whose general worldview was evidently very different from a Stoic one because it was focused on Christ, nevertheless had "absorbed" a great deal of the fundamental Stoic worldview into his own. Apparently, it helped him to articulate something that he needed to articulate as part of his own "philosophy."

However, in 2 Cor 4:16–5:5 Paul also speaks of the relationship between the human presence on earth and in heaven in terms that appear to have strongly Platonic connotations—for instance, when he contrasts "what can be seen" with "what cannot be seen" (4:18). I have argued, though, that he in fact maintains the basically Stoic picture throughout this passage, but also that one can understand the rhetorical purpose of bringing in a bit of "Platonism."[29] Here, then (if I am right), it is the basically Stoic material perspective that stays in place. The absorption of a bit of "Platonism," which would in itself trade on the difference between the material world and an immaterial one, does not take over the full Platonic meaning of the incorporated material.

In the light of these two examples, one can easily understand why scholars have spoken of "eclecticism" and "syncretism." If looked at in the abstract or from the perspective of philosophical systems as independent, abstract entities, one does find signs that something has been "chosen" here, something else there, or that ideas from different systems have to some extent "grown together" in a given philosopher. I have argued here for a better understanding, however, which

---

[26] The classic treatment of Philo on the πνεῦμα is Leisegang 1919.
[27] "Plato and his successors had tended to assign ontological primacy to the intelligible over the sensible. In making corporeality the hallmark of existence . . . the Stoics are in a way reverting to popular ontology. The philosophical grounds for this reversion . . . are extremely powerful" (Long and Sedley 1987, 1:163).
[28] See Engberg-Pedersen 2009; 2010, ch. 1.
[29] See Engberg-Pedersen 2010, ch. 2.

emphasizes the individual identity of the given thinker and his allegiance to this or the other authority in the past as what defines his own position. As part of that position, there is plenty of room for reclaiming or absorbing ideas from other systems into one's own. Still, it is the preferred position that governs how much of the alien position is incorporated into one's own. Understood in this way, the practice of the thinkers that constitute the Transitional Period in ancient philosophy reflects genuine creativity rather than the opposite: an attempt to incorporate the best from other philosophies into one's own.

5. From Stoicism to Platonism

The picture that I have developed of the exact character of the interaction of different philosophies—in particular, Stoicism and Platonism—during the Transitional Period only constitutes one half of what needs to be said here about the period. The other half concerns the change in what constituted the reigning philosophy during the period. To begin with, it was Stoicism. At the end, it was Platonism. How is that change to be understood and explained? And how does it impinge on the interaction of early Jewish and early Christian writings with Greco-Roman philosophy?

The facts themselves are not so controversial. The Middle Stoics Panaetius and Posidonius had remained Stoics while also opening up, to a greater or lesser degree, to incorporating ideas derived from Plato into their own Stoic position. Antiochus of Ascalon, on the other side of the divide, had developed his own Platonic position in a dogmatic direction by bringing in substantial parts of Stoicism that fitted his dogmatic intentions. Both positions show that at the beginning of the Transitional Period it was Stoicism that had the upper hand.

If we then move forward in time to Neostoicism, what we find is basically an attitude comparable to that of Panaetius and Posidonius. In Seneca's writings, for instance, there is a certain interest in Platonic ideas. In two of his letters he discusses basic Platonic ontological categories (*Ep.* 58) and compares the Stoic with the Platonic and Aristotelian understanding of causality or cause (*Ep.* 65). However, Seneca's attitude toward these alien ideas probably is conciliatory rather than negative.[30] In another letter, Seneca recounts a lovely dream he has had of life after death, when he will have left behind the "heavy and earthly prison" in which he is at present detained (*Ep.* 102.22). Throughout his description Seneca conveys an atmosphere that seems genuinely "Platonizing." Apparently, however, Seneca did not see any strong contrast here with his self-professed Stoicism.

Similarly, although Epictetus appears to have had little interest in ideas derived from a Platonizing metaphysics, his attitude toward the human body, that worthless "flesh" (σαρκίδιον), fits a Platonizing sensibility well. In addition, he clearly drew on Plato's account of Socrates, who was a main paradigm of true

---

[30] This is argued in Sedley 2005. In an unpublished article, George Boys-Stones has argued for the contrary view.

wisdom for Epictetus.³¹ Finally, Marcus Aurelius shows an openness to a Platonizing sensibility with regard to the human body that he probably had learned directly from Epictetus. Neither philosopher, however, betrayed his fundamental allegiance to Stoicism.³²

Thus, we find in both Middle- and Neostoicism an openness to certain sides of Platonism that these philosophers felt able to absorb into their own Stoicism without compromising their own philosophy, but admittedly also without taking those Platonic ideas in the full and exact Platonic way. In this, all of them fit easily into the picture developed above of "absorption of what is alien." Also, if I am right that in certain respects the worldview of the apostle Paul was basically a Stoic one, then his use of Platonic-sounding ideas in 2 Cor 4–5 fits very easily into the same picture. In addition, we may note that none of the Middle- or Neostoics went directly out of their way to attack the alien philosophy from which they did take over certain ideas.

The situation is quite different when we look at the Platonists in the same period. They did take over ideas from Stoicism, but they also attacked Stoicism on a number of points. From this side a war was being waged about which philosophy should be the reigning one. By noting some of the specific points in Stoicism that the Platonists would regularly attack, we may perhaps also come to understand better the driving force behind the overall change from Stoicism to Platonism during the period.

A good example is another Jewish, quasi-philosophical writing (in addition, i.e., to Philo of Alexandria), Wisdom of Solomon, which has much to say about what was at stake.³³ This treatise, which may be dated around 30 B.C.E. and located in Alexandria, starts out describing its main theme, Lady Wisdom herself, in terms that derive from the Stoic doctrine of the πνεῦμα. Gradually, however, more Platonicizing terms begin to creep in. And eventually it is (almost) explicitly stated that this is because a Stoicizing account cannot do justice to the character of God that this Jewish writer favors. This suggests, as was already indicated in the quotation above from John Dillon on one of the founders of Middle Platonism, Eudorus of Alexandria, that one point of contention of the Platonists vis-à-vis the Stoics was the Stoic material conception of God. Or to put it in more positive terms, the Platonists were after some form of "transcendence" in the picture of God that they did not find clearly enough in Stoicism. Here, Platonism, with its distinction between material and immaterial parts of the world, did much better.

Exactly the same move can be found in the other Alexandrian Jew, Philo. Moreover, just as the author of Wisdom of Solomon had done, Philo went out of his way explicitly to attack the Stoics for their materialistic conception of God.³⁴

That, then, was one point of attack in the war against Stoicism waged by Platonists: the materialist understanding of God, which did not fit their sense of

---

[31] This is a main point in Long 2002.
[32] On Marcus Aurelius, see Engberg-Pedersen 1998; Gill 2007.
[33] See the analysis in Engberg-Pedersen 2010, ch. 1.
[34] See ibid.

God's "transcendence." However, was that not just a Jewish specialty? Did other, non-Jewish (and non-Christian) thinkers have the same complaint? They did. Plutarch is a case in point. In Plutarch, too, a sense of the "transcendence" of the divine is very strong.[35]

Plutarch also provides evidence of another Platonist complaint against the Stoics, which turns on the issue of freedom and determinism. The Stoics were famous for being determinists. They also strove valiantly to retain enough freedom in the field of human action for the traditional moral system to make sense. The Platonists, however, were unimpressed, and here, too, they felt that the fundamental dualism of Platonism was better able to account for human freedom than the monistic materialism of the Stoics.

One could go on like this. Moreover, one *should* go on in this way were one to articulate a full and comprehensive understanding of why Stoicism lost out in the battle waged against it by Platonists (and Aristotelians, too).[36] What one would then gain is a sense of the fundamental philosophical issues that were at stake in the development of philosophy from the beginning of the Transitional Period to its end, no matter whether one would also end up being more convinced by the Stoics or by their attackers.

That whole project cannot be properly engaged in here. What matters for the profile of the present book is rather the point that for a considerable part of the Transitional Period—say, up until the time of Plutarch—it was Stoicism rather than Platonism that was the reigning Greco-Roman philosophy, a fact that also accounts for all the attacks on Stoicism found throughout the period. This point is of rather great importance when one considers the earliest Christian writings from the two first centuries C.E. For it means that if a Christian writer felt the need to articulate and buttress his own message in philosophical terms, then for the author of the earliest among such Christian writings it would be more natural to look to Stoicism as the best vehicle. By contrast, for an author of later Christian writings, though still pre-200 C.E., it would gradually become more and more natural to look to Platonism for input to help articulate one's own message. Still, even then, as we saw, there would be ample room for "absorbing" Stoic ideas into one's basically Platonic framework.

6. Conclusion

This sets the scene for the essays contained in this book. We have seen that within the field of Greco-Roman philosophy itself the Transitional Period was characterized by a flexible relationship between the different schools that allowed philosophers to have an identity of their own, as defined by their allegiance to an authoritative founding father, at the same time as it also made it possible for them to absorb alien material from other philosophies into their own. We have also

---

[35] See the discussion in Dillon 1996b, 199–225.
[36] An excellent example of this is Alexander of Aphrodisias, *De fato*.

seen that the same pattern immediately fits the way in which Jewish or Christian writers (themselves of a more or less philosophical bent) might make use of material drawn from Greco-Roman philosophy. In addition, we have seen that within this comprehensive pattern there was an actual, though only gradually developing, change from a stage when the reigning philosophy was Stoicism to a stage when Platonism had conquered that position. It is within this subtle and flexible picture of philosophy in the Transitional Period as a whole that the explorations presented in the essays of this book should be seen. They address the potential role of Stoicism in Christian writings that belong both to the earlier period of the New Testament and also to the later period of the second century. It seems fair to say, in light of the overall picture of the whole period presented here, that this issue has been unduly neglected for far too long.

Bibliography

André, J.-M. 1987. "Les écoles philosophiques aux deux premiers siècles de l'Empire." *ANRW* 36.1:5–77. Part 2, *Principat*, 36.1. Edited by H. Temporini and W. Haase. Berlin: de Gruyter.

Babut, D. 1969. *Plutarque et le stoïcisme*. Paris: Presses universitaires de France.

Barnes, J. 1989. "Antiochus of Ascalon." Pages 51–96 in *Philosophia Togata: Essays on Philosophy and Roman Society*. Edited by M. Griffin and J. Barnes. Oxford: Clarendon Press.

Berchman, R. M. 1984. *From Philo to Origen: Middle Platonism in Transition*. Brown Judaic Studies 69. Chico, Calif.: Scholars Press.

Boys-Stones, G. R. 2001. *Post-Hellenistic Philosophy: A Study of its Development from the Stoics to Origen*. Oxford: Oxford University Press.

Dillon, J. M. 1988. "'Orthodoxy' and 'Eclecticism': Middle Platonists and Neo-Pythagoreans." Pages 103–25 in *The Question of "Eclecticism": Studies in Later Greek Philosophy*. Edited by J. M. Dillon and A. A. Long. Berkeley: University of California Press.

———. 1996a. "Eudorus." Page 565 in *The Oxford Classical Dictionary*. Edited by S. Hornblower and A. Spawforth. Oxford: Oxford University Press.

———. 1996b. *The Middle Platonists: 80 B.C. to A.D. 220*. Rev. ed. London: Duckworth.

Dillon, J. M., and A. A. Long, eds. 1988. *The Question of "Eclecticism": Studies in Later Greek Philosophy*. Berkeley: University of California Press.

Engberg-Pedersen, T. 1998. "Marcus Aurelius on Emotions." Pages 305–37 in *The Emotions in Hellenistic Philosophy*. Edited by J. Sihvola and T. Engberg-Pedersen. New Synthese Historical Library 46. Dordrecht: Kluwer.

———. 2000. *Paul and the Stoics*. Louisville: Westminster John Knox Press.

———. 2009. "The Material Spirit: Cosmology and Ethics in Paul." *New Testament Studies* 55:179–97.

———. 2010. *Cosmology and Self in the Apostle Paul: The Material Spirit*. Oxford: Oxford University Press.

Frede, M. 2005. "Epilogue." Pages 771–97 in *The Cambridge History of Hellenistic Philosophy*. Edited by K. Algra et al. Cambridge: Cambridge University Press.

Gill, C. 2003. "The School in the Roman Imperial Period." Pages 33–58 in *The Cambridge Companion to the Stoics*. Edited by B. Inwood. Cambridge: Cambridge University Press.

———. 2007. "Marcus Aurelius' *Meditations*: How Stoic and How Platonic?" Pages 189–207 in *Platonic Stoicism, Stoic Platonism: The Dialogue between Platonism and Stoicism in Antiquity*. Edited by M. Bonazzi and C. Helmig. Ancient and Medieval Philosophy 1/39. Leuven: Leuven University Press.

Leisegang, H. 1919. *Der Heilige Geist: Das Wesen und Werden der mystisch-intuitiven Erkenntnis in der Philosophie und Religion der Griechen*. Leipzig: Teubner.

Long, A. A. 2002. *Epictetus: A Stoic and Socratic Guide to Life*. Oxford: Clarendon Press.

Long, A. A., and D. Sedley, eds. 1987. *The Hellenistic Philosophers*. 2 vols. Cambridge: Cambridge University Press.

Sedley, D. 1989. "Philosophical Allegiance in the Greco-Roman World." Pages 97–119 in *Philosophia Togata: Essays on Philosophy and Roman Society*. Edited by M. Griffin and J. Barnes. Oxford: Clarendon Press.

———. 2003. "The School, from Zeno to Arius Didymus." Pages 7–32 in *The Cambridge Companion to the Stoics*. Edited by B. Inwood. Cambridge: Cambridge University Press.

———. 2005. "Stoic Metaphysics at Rome." Pages 117–42 in *Metaphysics, Soul and Ethics: Themes from the Work of Richard Sorabji*. Edited by R. Salles. Oxford: Oxford University Press.

2

STOICISM AS A KEY TO PAULINE ETHICS IN ROMANS

Runar M. Thorsteinsson
Lund University

1. The (Lack of) Scholarly Discussion of Stoicism in Romans 12-15

Those who wish to learn something from the standard commentaries about potential Stoic allusions or analogies in Paul's letter to the Romans almost certainly will be disappointed.[1] The disappointment culminates when one reaches the discussion of the letter's "ethical" part proper, chapters 12-15. Even with respect to Paul's moral teaching in the letter, the long and influential commentary tradition is largely silent on possible parallels to the prevailing ethical theory of the first century C.E.[2] To be sure, now and then commentators observe that there are indeed some Stoic echoes to be found in Rom 12 in particular, but such observations commonly turn out to be little more than stock expressions dragged from one commentary to another without further reflection.[3] The implications of such

---

[1] This study was financed by the Lars Hierta Memorial Foundation (*Stiftelsen Lars Hiertas minne*), the Harald and Tonny Hagendahl Memorial Foundation (*Stiftelsen Harald och Tonny Hagendahls minnesfond*), and the Erik and Gurli Hultengren Foundation for Philosophy (*Erik och Gurli Hultengrens fond för filosofi*). I am deeply grateful for their generous support.

[2] See, for example, the influential, if outdated, International Critical Commentary by Sanday and Headlam, at the outset of which the authors note that it is "of extreme significance" for the understanding of the growth of Roman Christianity that "it was Seneca also [in addition to the emperor Nero] who was ruling in Rome when St. Paul wrote to the Church there" (Sanday and Headlam 1902, xvii). And yet, neither Stoicism nor individual Stoics, such as Seneca himself, get any further mention in the rest of the commentary.

[3] For example, Lietzmann notes the relevance of Late Stoicism, especially Seneca, for Paul's terminology in Rom 12:1-2 (Lietzmann 1971, 108-9) but makes no further reference to Stoicism in his discussion of Rom 12-15. Käsemann speaks of the Stoic and popular philosophical ("stoisch-popularphilosophische") background to Paul's λογικὴ λατρεία ("reasonable worship") in Rom 12:1 (Käsemann 1974, 316) but says little of Stoicism beyond that. See also Zahn 1910; Dodd 1932; Barrett 1957; Schlier 1977; Michel 1978; Cranfield 1975-1979;

analogies are rarely considered, and when they are, they tend to be quickly dismissed as somehow self-evidently irrelevant to Paul's text. Correspondingly, some commentators simply ignore the Stoic echoes in Rom 12-15 altogether.[4] Exceptions to such silence are rare.[5] It is true that in recent years there has been some increase in the publication of commentary-like monographs on Romans in which the question of Stoic analogies has at times been raised,[6] but the works (monographs) in which this question is seriously addressed remain very few.[7]

The present essay attempts to give some balance to the issue by assessing the extent and nature of Stoic allusions or analogies in Rom 12-15. At the same time, the aim is to provide the reader with a collection of examples of such analogies from the Stoic authors. But first it is necessary to discuss briefly the character and historical setting of the Stoic sources to which I wish to call attention as an important fund of comparative material for studies of Paul's letter to the Romans. I will also explain why I find these particular sources so important in this respect.[8]

Stuhlmacher 1989; Ziesler 1989; Wright 2002. Dunn pays some attention to Stoic influences/analogies in the earlier parts of Romans, but his discussion of similar features in Rom 12-15 is mostly limited to 12;1-2 (Dunn 1988, 2:711-14) and does little more than pass on the standard statements from the commentary tradition. On p. 714 Dunn compares Paul's use of the concept of νοῦς with uses in Stoicism (and elsewhere), but he ends up misrepresenting the Stoic notion of the νοῦς (there is no "mind/body dualism" in Stoicism, as Dunn implies; see Aune 1994, 292-97; Stowers 2003, 527-29). The recent socio-rhetorical commentary by Witherington (2004) pays more attention to Stoic philosophy than many of its kind (see especially the discussion on pp. 305-6 of Seneca's *De clementia* in relation to Rom 13:1-7), but even in this work the treatment is quite superficial, transmitting in passing the standard commentary expressions. For Jewett 2007, see n. 5 below.

[4] For example, Fitzmyer, who, as far as I can see, mentions the Stoics merely once in relation to Rom 12-15, and then only to give an inaccurate view of Stoicism by speaking of its "passive resistance to hostility" (Fitzmyer 1993, 658 [on Rom 12:20]). Epictetus is referred to several times in Fitzmyer's commentary (though nowhere in the discussion of Rom 12-15), but Seneca receives no mention at all.

[5] A welcome exception is the new Hermeneia commentary by Jewett (2007), who is unusually sensitive to the Greco-Roman milieu of Paul's letter, including its philosophical context.

[6] For example, Esler 2003a. Unlike many commentators on Romans, Esler refers to the Stoics only in relation to Rom 12-15. However, whenever he mentions Stoicism in his work, Esler refers (in the endnotes) to his own article (Esler 2004), but that article is marked by a number of misreadings of the Stoics (see my critique in Thorsteinsson 2006; see also Engberg-Pedersen 2005).

[7] The most notable exception is Engberg-Pedersen 2000. As will be clarified below, the present essay differs from Engberg-Pedersen's approach in the choice of primary Stoic sources. Also, there is a considerable lack of references to Stoic texts in his discussion of Paul's moral teaching in Rom 12-15 (pp. 261-92). It may be noted that although the recent study by Lee (2006) on Paul, the Stoics, and the "body" metaphor does not address Rom 12-15 directly (she focuses on 1 Corinthians), it does have a bearing on Paul's use of this metaphor in Rom 12. Earlier, more or less outdated, works on Paul and the Stoics include, for example, Bonhöffer 1911; Sevenster 1961 (see p. 1 for a list of other [earlier] works).

[8] Unless otherwise noted, translations of classical texts are from the LCL. As for Musonius Rufus (not in the LCL), translations are from Lutz 1947 (referred to by discourse, page[s], line[s]). Translations of Pauline texts are usually my own, with some aid from the NRSV.

2. Sources for Stoic Ethics in First-Century Rome: Seneca, Musonius, Epictetus

Several sources are available for Stoic ethics. When comparing the Stoic writings with the texts of the New Testament, some scholars choose to focus on the sources for the earliest phase of the philosophy as they are preserved in Book 7 of the *Lives of Eminent Philosophers* (*Vitae philosophorum*), by Diogenes Laertius (ca. 200–250 C.E.).[9] Others prefer the *Epitome of Stoic Ethics*, collected by Stobaeus in the early fifth century C.E. and attributed to Arius Didymus (late first century B.C.E.).[10] Still others take Book 3 of *On the Ends of Goods and Evils*, by Cicero (106–43 B.C.E.), as a point of departure in their comparison of Stoicism and Paul.[11] The differences between these sources are many (as are the similarities),[12] but common to them all is their secondary nature—that is, their nature of being individual efforts to epitomize what had been written or said earlier by other authors about Stoic ethics. Not all these epitomizers were (professed) Stoics themselves (Cicero, Diogenes),[13] and one of them was actually attempting to give a summary of philosophical theories uttered some four to five hundred years earlier (Diogenes). In addition, the authorities for two of these sources are not entirely clear (Cicero, Arius).[14] This secondary nature of the sources is significant for the present discussion, for while the texts of Cicero, Arius, and Diogenes certainly belong to our most important sources on Stoicism before the beginning of the common era, none of them expresses the actual views of first-century C.E. Stoics.

---

[9] Book 7 covers the key figures of the Stoic school from Zeno (d. 262 B.C.E.) to Chrysippus (d. 206 B.C.E.), including Cleanthes (d. 232 B.C.E.).

[10] Stobaeus, *Anth.* 2.7.5–12 (= 2.57.13–116.18 W-H) = Arius Didymus 7.5–12 (ed. Pomeroy 1999). The work bears the title Ζήνωνος καὶ τῶν λοιπῶν Στωικῶν δόγματα περὶ τοῦ ἠθικοῦ μέρους τῆς φιλοσοφίας. The "other Stoics" are, in addition to Cleanthes and Chrysippus, Diogenes of Seleucia (Babylon), Antipater of Tarsus, Archedemus of Tarsus, and Panaetius of Rhodes (all from the second century B.C.E.); see Pomeroy 1999, 10–11, with n. 1.

[11] The Latin title of Cicero's work is *De finibus bonorum et malorum* (*De finibus*). It was composed in 45 B.C.E.

[12] For a comparison of the three sources, see Long 1996.

[13] Although Cicero clearly was eclectic in his philosophical orientation and was much attracted by Stoic ethics, he remained a professed adherent of the (New) Academy (see, e.g., *Off.* 2.1–8; cf. the useful discussion in Colish 1985, 65–79). Diogenes Laertius, on the other hand, was no philosopher at all (he was "merely a nitwit," according to Brennan [2005, 19]). As for Arius Didymus, it is likely that his contemporaries, at least, regarded him as a Stoic. However, several factors suggest a "considerable philosophical tolerance" on his part (Pomeroy 1999, 3). "His very aim of offering a clear outline of Stoic principles probably means that he harmonized conflicting theories in earlier Stoic thought in order to create logical consistency. It is also likely that he incorporated syncretizing elements from other systems where this assisted his aim" (ibid.).

[14] On Arius, see Long 1996, 130. As for Cicero, Engberg-Pedersen considers it most likely that the source for Stoic ethics in *Fin.* 3 goes back to Antipater of Tarsus (d. ca. 130 B.C.E.) (Engberg-Pedersen 2000, 46). Some scholars believe that Cicero's main authority was Diogenes of Babylon (d. ca. 152 B.C.E.); see Rackham 1931, xvii.

In his recent work *Paul and the Stoics*, Troels Engberg-Pedersen opts for Cicero's text as the primary source for Stoic ethics, with which he then compares the writings of Paul (mainly Philippians, Galatians, and Romans).[15] In the present essay, which focuses specifically on Paul's letter to the Romans, I wish to suggest a different approach to the Stoic sources. This is not to say that Cicero has little or no value for our knowledge of Roman Stoicism, for there can be no doubt that he was a crucial figure in the history of Stoicism in Rome. It was he who introduced Stoicism systematically—in a Latin dress—to the Romans, and it was mainly thanks to his introduction of it that the Stoic tradition became so well established in Rome that already by the turn of the first century B.C.E. it enjoyed the position of being the most favored philosophical school in the city.[16] However, Cicero would not have described himself as a Stoic, and, for present purposes, it matters less how Stoicism had been formulated, say, in the first or second century B.C.E. (or earlier) than how it was understood and experienced in the mid- and late-first century C.E. The latter is the period in which Paul penned his letter and sent it to Rome, and the period in which Paul's Roman addressees received the letter and read and heard it for the first time(s).

Hence, my suggestion is that in addition to Cicero's important account in *De finibus*, the Stoic sources that are most properly to be compared with Paul's moral teaching in Romans are the writings of the Roman Stoics—that is, Seneca (ca. 1–65 C.E.), Musonius Rufus (ca. 25–100 C.E.), and Epictetus (ca. 55–135 C.E.).[17] These are the best sources available for Stoic ethics as it was understood, interpreted, and experienced by the Stoics themselves in the city of Rome from the middle of the first century C.E. to the beginning of the second century. While it is true that the Roman Stoics were very much dependent on the earlier stages of the Stoic philosophy, an important shift of priorities occurred in this third and last stage of the Stoic school. Stoicism traditionally had divided philosophy into the three realms of logic, physics, and ethics, but by the first century C.E. ethics had become the primary subject of the discipline.[18] Moreover, the Roman Stoics appear to have shown less speculative interest in ethics per se than did their predecessors.[19] Like many other philosophical schools at the time, they were primarily concerned with

---

[15] According to Engberg-Pedersen, Cicero's *Fin.* 3 is "the best systematic statement of Stoic ethics that we have" (Engberg-Pedersen 2000, 46). Interestingly, Long insists that it is rather the treatise attributed to Arius Didymus, which "contains the longest and most detailed surviving account of Stoic ethics" (much of which, according to Long, actually corresponds closely to both Cicero and Diogenes [see Long 1996, 107]).

[16] On Cicero's Latinization and introduction of Stoicism to the Romans, see *Fin.* 3.3–5, 40. On the popularity of different philosophical schools in Rome, see the fine discussion in Griffin 1989.

[17] Although Marcus Aurelius (121–180 C.E.) certainly belonged to the Roman Stoics, I exclude him here for the simple reason that his *Meditations* were written at a considerably later date.

[18] In fact, already in Cicero's account ethics is viewed as "the highest branch of philosophy" (*Fin.* 3.6).

[19] See Colish 1985, 12–13.

the practical application of ethics.[20] There is therefore good reason not to take their writings as simple imitations of early Stoicism,[21] but rather to read them in their own terms as expressions of how Stoicism was specifically construed and lived in first- and second-century Rome.

The setting of Paul's letter itself is of great significance here, with respect both to the social setting of the audience and to the chronological and spatial framework. To begin with, the people whom Paul addressed lived in a city in which the most prominent teaching on ethics and morality was precisely that of Stoicism. It may be assumed that the Stoic teaching as such would have been known primarily among the educated minority in Rome, but it may also be expected that a teaching of such prominence would, in one form or another, have reached and influenced the lower classes as well.[22] After all, morality certainly was no trivial thing in the eyes of the Romans, who were almost obsessed with it.[23] As for chronology and space, the sources of Seneca, Musonius, and Epictetus are closely related to Paul's letter both in time and place. All of these Stoics were or had been active in the city of Rome, and one of them, Seneca, was an exact contemporary of Paul, while Musonius and Epictetus were close enough contemporaries to be of direct relevance to the subject. When Paul wrote his letter to Christ-believers in Rome (sometime in 55–58 C.E.), Seneca was acting as an imperial counselor and was highly influential as such.[24] In fact, it was precisely at this point in time that Seneca's sociopolitical power was at its greatest, and scholars agree that the "good period" of Nero's reign (the so-called *quinquennium Neronis*) was when the young emperor was still under Seneca's influence.[25] As a philosopher, Seneca wrote extensively on ethics, before, during, and after his service to the emperor; so much did he write that his works make up the largest collection of Stoic writings that we have.[26] Musonius Rufus was a teacher of philosophy whose lectures and teachings were preserved by his students and followers and by Roman historians. Although he did not write anything himself (as far as we know),[27] the first-century C.E. Roman setting of his lectures makes them both relevant and important for the present discussion, for Musonius was a key figure in late Stoicism and seems to have been a true social

---

[20] "The early Stoics had intended their philosophy to form a guide to life, but the very nature of the evidence makes them appear as theoreticians. Many of the later Stoics were practical men of action and one can see the relevance of their beliefs to their doings. Even those who were primarily teachers were mainly concerned with the practical problems of life which faced them and their pupils" (Sandbach 1989, 19).

[21] As implied by Engberg-Pedersen (2000, 46). His focus, we should add, is aimed at "the basic structure of Stoic ethics" (which he finds primarily in the Chrysippean ethics of Cicero's *De finibus*).

[22] I discuss this more closely in Thorsteinsson 2010.

[23] See the discussion in Edwards 1993.

[24] See Tacitus, *Ann.* 13.2. Cf. Dio Cassius, *Hist. Rom.* 61.3–4; Seneca, *De clementia*. On the life of Seneca, see especially Griffin 1976. See also Abel 1985.

[25] See, for example, the discussion in Griffin 1984, 67–82.

[26] Despite the fact that a number of his works are either fragmentary or entirely lost.

[27] See Geytenbeek 1963, 7–9.

and political provocateur.[28] Epictetus, too, apparently wrote nothing himself, but most scholars agree that his *Discourses* (*Dissertationes/Diatribai*), written down by his student Arrian, are more or less stenographic records of his lectures.[29] It is therefore quite appropriate to take the *Discourses* as a primary source for Roman Stoicism. Epictetus was a former slave and a former student of Musonius, and although his lectures date from the early second century C.E. and were delivered not in Rome but in Nicopolis in western Greece, the first-century Roman roots of his moral teaching are strong and clear.

In what follows, I will compare Paul's moral teaching in Rom 12–15 with the ethics of (roughly) contemporary Stoics in Rome, focusing on the question whether the latter may function as a hermeneutical key to a proper reading and understanding of the former. Before I address this particular question, however, some preliminary remarks about Paul's letter are in order.

3. An Outline of Paul's Moral Teaching in Romans 12–15

With his letter to the Romans, Paul sets out to proclaim (his version of) the εὐαγγέλιον (the "good news") to Christ-believers in Rome. A decisive aspect of this εὐαγγέλιον is its moral or ethical part, to which the apostle turns in chapters 12–15. Moral issues certainly are addressed elsewhere in the letter, especially in chapters 1–2, 6–7, but mainly and most explicitly in chapters 12–15. Indeed, if there is such a thing as "Pauline ethics,"[30] it is most clearly found here, in Rom 12–15. This does not mean that in this text Paul presents, as it were, a moral package that he considers applicable in every detail at every time and location. Rather, in Rom 12–15, Paul sets forth his moral teaching as a general tenet for Christ-believers but modifies certain aspects of it with reference to the local situation in Rome. The text constitutes a sketch of his community-forming ethic, which he no doubt planned to elaborate upon and supplement on his future arrival in Rome (see Rom 15:23–29) or by way of further correspondence (as, e.g., in 1 Corinthians).

Elsewhere I have argued that Paul's formulaic request in Rom 12:1–2, παρακαλῶ οὖν ὑμᾶς, ἀδελφοί . . . ("Therefore I urge you, brothers . . ."), can and should be taken as the letter's center in terms of its epistolary structure.[31] Paul's

---

[28] On the life of Musonius, see especially the important work of Lutz 1947.

[29] See Long 2002, 38–43. The *Manual* or *Handbook* (*Encheiridion*), however, owes more to Arrian.

[30] Esler has criticized the use of the term "ethics" (and "morality") in relation to New Testament texts, partly because of the term's rooted connection with the philosophical tradition, and partly because of its modern connotations (Esler 2003b, 52). (In a subsequent article, Esler himself nevertheless uses the term in relation to Stoic ethics "as a matter of convenience" [Esler 2004, 107n7].) Esler's warning against the careless use of terminology is something to consider (although his definition of "ethics" may be questioned), but I agree with Horrell (2005, 95–97) that it is quite unnecessary and hardly more useful simply to discard the term "ethics" altogether (except, of course, when "convenience" allows its use!).

[31] See Thorsteinsson 2003, 47–54.

request not only alludes to and rests on the previous discourse (i.e., Rom 1–11 as a whole), but also points forward and forms a synoptic account of the subsequent text. It is programmatic, so to speak, for the text to come, a function that is clearly marked by the appropriate epistolary convention, presumably recognized as such by Paul's audience. When Paul exhorts the addressees to respond to God's εὐαγγέλιον by presenting their "bodies" as a "living sacrifice" and by "renewing" their minds, he alludes to his earlier description of the sinful (Gentile) world (Rom 1:18–32) and totally reverses that description.[32] According to Paul, in contrast to their earlier behavior and the conduct of "this world," the addressees' proper, "rational" or "reasonable worship" (λογικὴ λατρεία) should consist in remodeling their disposition and way of thinking in toto in accordance with God's will (as explained by Paul), and in using their bodies accordingly. These two aspects go hand in hand in the letter's moral teaching. The proper worship is both mental and corporeal; it is spiritual as well as physical.

In Rom 12:3–15:14,[33] Paul explains more specifically how the audience's "reasonable worship" should be carried out. In moral terms, this worship involves showing mutual love, respect, and adaptability. That is the basic message of Rom 12–15. While chapters 12–13 speak both of in-group and out-group relations—that is, how the Christ-believers should treat one another and how they should behave toward nonbelievers and the outside world at large—chapters 14–15 are exclusively concerned with the question of proper relationships within the Christ-movement. It is important to notice, however, that not all of chapters 12–13 addresses both questions simultaneously. Contrary to common opinion, Paul does not advocate an ethic of "universal love" in Romans.[34] In 12:3–12 he clearly is concerned solely with the Christ-believing community, and probably in 12:13 as well. In 12:14, on the other hand, he turns to people who almost certainly are outsiders, namely, those who (may) "persecute" (διώκειν) the Christ-believing addressees. In 12:16, then, Paul refers again to in-group relations (cf. εἰς ἀλλήλους),[35] whereas in 12:17–18 he suddenly extends the reference to "all people" (πάντες ἄνθρωποι), presumably also including the Christ-believers. In 12:19–21 attention is again paid to outside groups only (cf. ὁ ἐχθρός σου in v. 20), and the discourse in 13:1–7 continues this specific focus on outsiders, in this case the Roman authorities. In 13:8–10, however, the apostle turns exclusively to relations within the group of Christ-believers, and very explicitly so: "Owe no one anything [μηδενὶ μηδὲν ὀφείλετε], except to love one another [ἀλλήλους]." For Paul, the concept of "love" (ἀγάπη) is an in-group term, and the act of "loving" is an in-group act. In

---

[32] See Stowers 1994, 317–23.

[33] Commentators normally assume that the passage closes with 15:13 (cf. the 27th ed. of the Nestle-Aland Greek text), but, as Glad has convincingly argued, it probably is more accurate to take v. 14 as forming the closure (Glad 1995, 213–35, esp. 217, 232–33).

[34] Nor does he do so in any other letter. See Thorsteinsson 2006, 144–46; see also Engberg-Pedersen 2000, 265–69, 276–77, 287–89; 2005, 58. I discuss this question in more detail in Thorsteinsson 2010.

[35] As for v. 15, the question is more difficult, but Paul probably has in-group relations in mind there as well.

other words, the highest form of virtue, ἀγάπη, is called for and exercised among Christ-believers, and within that group alone. What this means in practice is developed more fully in Rom 14–15.

Since in Rom 14–15 Paul is solely concerned with in-group relations, the issues addressed here are naturally of a more specific kind than those discussed earlier in chapters 12–13. Basically, the passage in 14:1–15:14 lists some of the ways in which the Roman addressees can and should actualize the love called for in 13:8–10 and the community-oriented ethic outlined in 12:3–8 in particular. For that purpose, Paul gives several potential examples of proper and improper attitudes and types of behavior within the Christ-believing community. Rhetorically, these examples are brought to life through personification of certain "weak" and "strong" characters (14:1; 15:1). Scholars often take Paul's personification here quite literally and see in it a description of actual groups of people in Rome, namely, "Jewish Christians" and "Gentile Christians," who are represented, it is thought, by the "weak" and the "strong" respectively. But the text itself gives little support for such a reading.[36] Rather, as part of his general moral teaching in the letter, Paul here portrays a spectrum of moral dispositions, each pole of which is represented by the "weak" and the "strong" respectively. In other words, "Paul's description of people as 'weak' and 'strong' is an attempt at character portrayal, where typical characteristics of certain dispositions and character types are given voice and dramatized."[37] In this way, Paul invites his addressees to identify themselves with certain roles within the community of believers and exhorts them to sympathize with, and adapt to, the needs of those fellow believers who are more vulnerable in terms of certain practical aspects of their faith. He shows the Roman audience a way to love their neighbors. And he does so without passing judgment himself on anyone in particular (cf. 14:13: μηκέτι οὖν ἀλλήλους κρίνωμεν). That is, instead of addressing any "weak" person directly, Paul approaches the addressees as if all of them were "strong" in order not to dishonor and "judge" anyone openly. Moreover, when Paul states in 15:1 that "we the strong [ἡμεῖς οἱ δυνατοί] are obliged to bear the weaknesses of those without strength [τὰ ἀσθενήματα τῶν ἀδυνάτων]," this is his rhetorical means to lead (some of) the audience toward an imitation of himself as "strong," particularly those who are (yet) "weak" in one way or another but may eventually become "strong(er)." The implication is that each and every Christ-believer should, if not actually become "strong," at least continually strive to be so. What will help the believers to concentrate on that goal is, of course, Paul's teaching in the letter, but also their own mutual guidance based on that teaching (cf. 15:14). Paul wants them to keep reminding each other of the

---

[36] Paul nowhere identifies the "weak" and the "strong" as "Jewish Christians" and "Gentile Christians" (or the like). The descriptions given in Rom 14 of different attitudes toward the issues of eating, drinking, and judging days do not prove that a comparison is being made between Jewish and Gentile attitudes (as argued by, e.g., Watson 2007, 175–82). For arguments against that claim, see Meeks 1987, 291–93; Stowers 1990, 276–86; Reichert 2001, 271–333, esp. 323–25. See also my discussion in Thorsteinsson 2003, 92–97, with further references.

[37] Glad 1995, 329.

fact that although the ideal disposition certainly is the "strong" one (cf. 14:14, 17, 20), there will always be members of the community who are "weak" in one way or another. According to the apostle, it is of crucial importance for the upbuilding and unity of the movement (cf. 14:19; 15:5-7) to show full respect for the "weak" members and to adapt to their needs whenever necessary. In short, Rom 14–15 exemplifies how Christ-believers can and should "put on" the Lord Christ himself (13:14)—that is, how they should imitate Jesus Christ and his love of others. Their "reasonable worship" is largely a moral one.

4. Roman Stoic Ethics as a Key to Paul's Moral Teaching in Romans 12–15

Having considered the general outline of Rom 12–15, we are better prepared to address in more detail Paul's moral teaching and to assess the nature and extent of Stoic allusions and analogies in the text. We need to have two basic questions in mind when we meet such (potential) allusions or analogies: First, do they tell us anything about Paul's own philosophical context? Second, how would the Roman addressees, most of whom no doubt had been exposed to Stoic ethics and morality in one way or another, have responded to such allusions/analogies—what implications would these allusions/analogies have had for their reading and understanding of Paul's moral teaching as a whole? The two questions are closely connected, but here I will focus on the latter of the two—that is, on the reading and reception of Paul's text in first-century Rome.[38]

As we saw above, Rom 12:1–2 sets the stage for the moral teaching as a whole. And here we find clear allusions to standard Stoic terminology. To begin with, when Paul uses the word λογικός to define the addressees' proper way of serving God, their λογικὴ λατρεία,[39] he is alluding to a well-known philosophical concept particularly favored among Stoics in their attempts to describe the relationship between human beings as λογικοί and God as λόγος.[40] Epictetus, for instance, states that, as λογικοί, humans do well to worship God through hymns and songs: "If I were a nightingale, I should be singing as a nightingale; if a swan, as a swan. But as it is, I am a rational being [λογικός εἰμι], therefore I must be singing hymns of praise to God ... and I exhort [παρακαλῶ] you to joint [sic] me in this same song."[41] But for Epictetus and his fellow Stoics, the most important way to serve God was

---

[38] For the former question, see the brief discussion in Gibson 2000.

[39] This is the only instance of the adjective λογικός in Paul's letters. Elsewhere in the New Testament it occurs only in 1 Pet 2:2. For λατρεία and cognates in Paul, see Rom 1:9; 9:4; Phil 3:3.

[40] See, for example, Diogenes Laertius, Vit. phil. 7.87–88, 134, 147; Stobaeus, Anth. 2.7.6 (= 2.75.7–78.17 W-H); Epictetus, Diss. 1.3.1–3; 2.8.2–3, 11–14; 3.1.25; Marcus Aurelius, Meditations 4.4; 5.27. For Latin equivalents, see also, for example, Cicero, Nat. d. 1.39; Manilius, Astronomica 2.82–83, 105–127; Seneca, Ep. 66.12; 76.9–10; 92.1–2, 27; 124.23; Nat. 1, Pref. 14.

[41] Epictetus, Diss. 1.16.20–21. See also Diss. 1.16.15–19; 3.26.29–30.

to seek and pursue the morally good. The proper worship means that one continually strives to follow and imitate God, the λόγος, as the ultimate moral being[42] and to obey God's law, which is "most good and most just."[43] Or as Musonius puts it, "The law of Zeus bids man be good."[44] Paul describes this very service to the deity as presenting one's "body" as a "living sacrifice, holy and acceptable to God." This is precisely the "sacrifice" of which Paul's contemporary Seneca spoke, namely, that of wholly devoting oneself to a particular way of life and disposition:

> The honour that is paid to the gods lies, not in the victims for sacrifice, though they be fat and glitter with gold, but in the upright and holy desire of the worshippers [*recta ac pia voluntate venerantium*]. Good men, therefore, are pleasing to the gods with an offering of meal and gruel; the bad, on the other hand, do not escape impiety although they dye the altars with streams of blood.[45]

When Paul implies that a particular way of life can count as a proper and sufficient worship of the deity, some of his addressees may very well have associated his words with parallel statements made by contemporary philosophers.[46] Seneca himself had also stated that "[while] precepts are commonly given as to how the gods should be worshipped . . . God is [only] worshipped by those who truly know Him." For "although a man hear what limit he should observe in sacrifice . . . he will never make sufficient progress until he has conceived a right idea of God." "Would you win over [*propitiare*] the gods?" he asks. "Then be a good man [*bonus*]!" is the answer. "Whoever imitates them, is worshiping them sufficiently."[47] According to Seneca, then, the proper worship consists not in cultic ceremonies but rather in a "will that is reverent and upright" (*pia et recta voluntate*).[48] Similarly, in Rom 12:1, Paul's Roman addressees get to hear that their proper worship of God involves not a literal sacrifice of their bodies but rather an embodiment of God's will and directions through a particular way of life.

The other side of the coin, according to Paul, is the audience's appropriate way of thinking. In Rom 12:2, he urges the readers to let themselves be transformed or "metamorphosed" (μεταμορφοῦσθαι) by the renewing (ἀνακαίνωσις) of the mind (νοῦς), so that they may discern (δοκιμάζειν) what is the will of God. They must learn what exactly counts as "good, acceptable, and perfect" (τὸ ἀγαθὸν καὶ εὐάρεστον καὶ τέλειον) in the eyes of God, and in order to be able to do so they must reverse their way of thinking in total contrast to the sinful attitude and

---

[42] Epictetus, *Diss.* 1.30.4–5; 2.14.12–13; 2.17.23–25; 2.19.26–27; 3.24.65, 95–102, 110; 3.26.29; 4.7.20. Cf. Seneca, *Ep.* 16.5; *Vit. beat.* 15.5; Musonius Rufus, *Diss.* 8.64.14; 17.108.8–18; Cicero, *Fin.* 3.22.

[43] Epictetus, *Diss.* 1.29.13: ὁ τοῦ θεοῦ νόμος κράτιστός ἐστι καὶ δικαιότατος. Cf. *Diss.* 1.13.5; 1.25.3–6; 1.29.4; 2.16.27–28; 3.24.42; 4.3.12; 4.7.17.

[44] Musonius Rufus, *Diss.* 16.104.35–36: ἀγαθὸν εἶναι κελεύει τὸν ἄνθρωπον ὁ νόμος ὁ τοῦ Διός.

[45] Seneca, *Ben.* 1.6.3.

[46] See Behm 1965, 186–89.

[47] Seneca, *Ep.* 95.47–50. Cf. Seneca, *Ben.* 4.25.1; Epictetus, *Diss.* 2.18.19–21. Cf. also Marcus Aurelius, *Meditations* 2.5.

[48] Seneca, *Ep.* 115.5.

behavior described in Rom 1:28-31 (1:28: καὶ καθὼς οὐκ ἐδοκίμασαν τὸν θεὸν ἔχειν ἐν ἐπιγνώσει, παρέδωκεν αὐτοὺς ὁ θεὸς εἰς ἀδόκιμον νοῦν, ποιεῖν τὰ μὴ καθήκοντα).[49] As the "corrupted mind" (ἀδόκιμος νοῦς) is a fundamental hindrance to the proper way of life, the addressees' intellectual "metamorphosis" is a prerequisite for their λογικὴ λατρεία. Some in the audience may have recognized here Paul's close proximity to basic theories of the philosophical schools. Some may even have related Paul's words specifically to the Stoic idea of "the transformation of the mind."[50] As Seneca states, "One who has learned and understood what he should do and avoid, is not a wise man until his mind [*animus*] is metamorphosed [*transfiguratus est*] into the shape of that which he has learned." "You must learn first, and then strengthen your learning by action," he explains.[51] In line with the heavy emphasis put on practical application of the ethical theories by the Romans, Seneca shows that the intellectual aspect of learning was never understood apart from its practical end by the Roman Stoics.[52] Paul also wants his readers to undergo an intellectual metamorphosis, but, precisely as in Seneca, the ultimate purpose is broader: it is to effect a total moral transformation, physical as well as intellectual, of the "body" (σῶμα) as well as the "mind" (νοῦς). And to both Paul and Seneca, moral instruction is essential for that purpose.

Is it possible that Paul's Roman audience would have understood his synoptic account in Rom 12:1-2 as presupposing a specifically Stoic framework? With respect to the prominent position of Stoicism in Rome and the text's strong allusions to popular Stoic terminology, that is quite possible. The question of whether or not that may also be judged likely and whether or not such (potential) associations would have continued as the reading of Paul's text proceeded depends on the language and content of the subsequent discourse. If the following text completely lacks any Stoic allusions or analogies, it seems reasonable to infer that the connections that the readers potentially made to Stoicism were likely to (gradually) fade away. Conversely, if there is a continuation of such allusions/analogies in the subsequent text, it is equally reasonable to infer that at least some in Paul's audience would have interpreted the moral teaching in Rom 12-15 as a whole in a Stoic light.

What kind of terminology does Paul choose as he continues his moral teaching? Does he move away from or resume the use of philosophical language? In fact, already in Rom 12:3 the apostle makes use of popular philosophical terminology when he alludes to current discussions of the moral virtues. He urges the addressees "not to think highly" (μὴ ὑπερφρονεῖν) of themselves "beyond what

---

[49] Romans 1:28: "And since they did not see fit to acknowledge God, God gave them over to a corrupted mind, to do things that should not be done." Note that in Stoic ethics, τέλειον καθῆκον is a complete and appropriate moral act, in contrast to an act παρὰ τὸ καθῆκον, which is ἁμάρτημα. See further Rist 1969, 97-98.

[50] See Betz 1991, 338n87, with further references. For discussion of potential parallels in Aristotle, see Johnson 2003.

[51] Seneca, *Ep.* 94.47-48. Cf. Seneca, *Ep.* 6.1-3; Epictetus, *Diss.* 3.21.1-7.

[52] See Seneca, *Ep.* 6.5; 20.2; *Ben.* 7.1.3; Musonius Rufus, *Diss.* 5.50.32-52.4; Epictetus, *Diss.* 2.11.24-25.

[they] ought to think" (παρ' ὃ δεῖ φρονεῖν), but instead to "think" (φρονεῖν) "so as to mind a proper moderation" (εἰς τὸ σωφρονεῖν). Paul here engages in a wordplay on the root φρον-, doubtless knowing that the virtue of φρόνησις was one of the four cardinal virtues in Greco-Roman thought. As a rule, the Stoics adhered to the four traditional virtues—φρόνησις (*prudentia*, "prudence"), σωφροσύνη (*temperantia*, "moderation" or "self-control"), δικαιοσύνη (*iustitia*, "justice"), and ἀνδρεία (*fortitudo*, "courage")—but to most Stoics (as to other philosophical schools),[53] the first one was the preeminent virtue on the basis of which the other three were determined.[54] Paul's audience would hardly have missed so transparent an allusion to the cardinal virtue φρόνησις,[55] but in that case the reference to σωφροσύνη (through the verb σωφρονεῖν) would have helped further to direct their thoughts toward the traditional virtues of Greek philosophy and Greco-Roman society. By using the verbs φρονεῖν and σωφρονεῖν in Rom 12:3, Paul thus solidly reinforces the associations triggered by vv. 1–2 to Greco-Roman philosophy, Stoic in particular.

Τὸ φρονεῖν εἰς τὸ σωφρονεῖν ("think with proper moderation") is the first example presented by Paul of the moral transformation called for in Rom 12:1–2. This example, in which he makes use of two of the traditional cardinal virtues, is also programmatic for the entire community-forming ethic in Paul's discourse.[56] It is important to notice that Paul's presentation of ὑπερφρονεῖν as an antithesis to (φρονεῖν εἰς τὸ) σωφρονεῖν suggests that he wants to underline the social aspect of the cardinal virtues. For, as becomes clear in the subsequent text, σωφρονεῖν primarily defines how to behave toward other people.[57] Paul clearly shares with first-century moralists the view that right behavior is an outcome of right perception. But his focus on σωφροσύνη as moderation in interpersonal dealings appears to reflect the earlier, classical understanding of this virtue.[58] That Paul is calling for a certain "social moderation" in the Christ-believing community is confirmed (1) by the reference to μέτρον ("measure, limit") in the following clause, which for Paul is defined by "faith" (cf. μέτρον πίστεως), (2) by his use of the metaphor of the "body" in 12:4–5, and (3) by the emphasis in 12:6–8 on various roles and functions within the community. According to the apostle, no Christ-believer should think too highly of himself or herself, regardless of position. It is true, says Paul, that Christ-believers have received different "gifts" (χαρίσματα) from God, and that they therefore really are differently positioned within the community, but no "gift" has been given solely to the owner of that particular gift. Everything is meant for

---

[53] See the helpful discussion in Annas 1993, 73–84.

[54] See, for example, Stobaeus, *Anth.* 2.7.5a–5b7 [= Arius Didymus 5a–5b7]; 2.31.123 (= 2.57.18–65.6; 2.235.23–239.29 W-H); Plutarch, *Stoic. rep.* 1034C; *Virt. mor.* 440E–441D; Musonius Rufus, *Diss.* 4.44.10–35; 4.48.1–14; Seneca, *Ep.* 85.2; 90.46; 120.11.

[55] "There are frequent examples of this particular wordplay in Greek literature, so that Paul's formulation would have evoked delight and immediate comprehension in his hearers" (Jewett 2007, 739).

[56] So also Johnson 2003, 221.

[57] See Moxnes 1994, 219–23.

[58] See Jewett 2007, 739–42, depending on the thorough treatment of the virtue of σωφροσύνη in Greek literature by North (1966).

the benefit of the whole. Paul demonstrates the concern for the community as a whole, rather than single individuals within it, with a metaphor: just as the human body (σῶμα) has many members (μέλη) that have different functions (πράξεις), so Christ-believers, many though they be, form one "body" in Christ (οἱ πολλοὶ ἓν σῶμά ἐσμεν ἐν Χριστῷ) and are members one of another (ἀλλήλων μέλη). Each and every member of the Christ-movement has his or her own particular function within the whole, and each and every member must view his or her position with proper moderation in relation to the others.

The social dimension of ethics was important, too, in Roman Stoicism. Seneca, for instance, placed great weight on virtues such as *humanitas* and *clementia*, both of which corresponded closely to the Greek φιλανθρωπία, although "some have suggested that by the late first century AD [*humanitas*] may have conveyed the idea of a warm, human sympathy for the weak and helpless in a measure which *philanthropia* never did."[59] In one of Seneca's letters, *humanitas* occurs together with two of the cardinal virtues, *temperantia* (= σωφροσύνη) and *fortitudo* (= ἀνδρεία), as well as *fides* (= πίστις, "loyalty"). Seneca defines *humanitas* as follows: it "forbids you to be over-bearing towards your associates [*superbum esse adversus socios*], and it forbids you to be grasping."[60] What we see here is, as in Paul's text, an appeal to a certain social moderation. To Seneca, the primary purpose of philosophy is to lead people toward the virtuous path of unity and mutual care, for "the first thing which philosophy undertakes to give is fellow-feeling with all men [*sensum communem*]; in other words, sympathy and sociability [*humanitatem et congregationem*]."[61] According to him, "man is a social creature [*hominem sociale animal*], begotten for the common good [*communi bono genitum*]."[62] Hence Seneca's advice to the newly enthroned Nero in 55/56 C.E.: "To his fellow-countrymen [*civibus*], to the obscure [*ignotis*], and to the lowly [*humilibus*] he [i.e., the emperor] should show the greater moderation [*moderatius agendum est*]."[63] Moreover, "in a position of unlimited power," *clementia vera* ("true mercy") is "in the truest sense self-control [*temperantia*] and an all-embracing love of the human race as of oneself [*humani generis comprendens ut sui amor*]."[64] To illustrate this point, Seneca portrays Nero as the "head" (*caput*) and "soul" (*animus*) of the state, and the state as his "body" (*corpus*), and declares that "even reprobate citizens should have mercy as being the weak members of the body."[65] Elsewhere Seneca describes the history of the past in these (somewhat idealized) terms: "Not yet had the stronger [*valentior*] begun to lay hands upon the weaker [*infirmiori*]; ... each cared as much for his neighbour as for himself [*par erat alterius ac sui cura*]."[66] According to his fellow Stoic Epictetus, every human being is so created that, if detached

---

[59] Hands 1968, 87.
[60] Seneca, *Ep.* 88.29–30.
[61] Seneca, *Ep.* 5.4.
[62] Seneca, *Clem.* 1.3.2.
[63] Seneca, *Clem.* 1.21.4.
[64] Seneca, *Clem.* 1.11.2. See also *Clem.* 1.13.4; 1.19.6.
[65] Seneca, *Clem.* 1.4.3; 1.5.1. Cf. *Clem.* 2.2.1.
[66] Seneca, *Ep.* 90.40. See also *Ep.* 95.51–52; *Ben.* 4.3.1.

from society, he or she can no longer fulfill the "profession" (ἐπαγγελία) assigned to the "citizen of the world" (πολίτης τοῦ κόσμου), which is "to treat nothing as a matter of private profit, not to plan about anything as though [s]he were a detached unity, but to act like the foot or the hand, which, if they had the faculty of reason [λογισμός] and understood the constitution of nature, would never exercise choice or desire in any other way but by reference to the whole."[67] Sociability belongs to Reason itself, the Roman Stoics claim,[68] and God has greater concern for humanity as a whole than for single individuals.[69]

The metaphor of the "body" was both widely used and widely known in Greco-Roman antiquity, and it was particularly favored by the Stoics.[70] Seneca used it in his famous attempt to lay down a "rule" (*formula*) for everyone's duties in human relationships: "All that you behold, that which comprises both god and man, is one—we are the parts of one great body [*membra sumus corporis magni*]."[71] The metaphor illustrates that the whole is dependent upon its parts, and that all the parts are necessary, though differently positioned, if the whole is to function properly. Seneca writes,

> What if the hands should desire to harm the feet, or the eyes the hands? As all the members of the body are in harmony with another because it is to the advantage of the whole that the individual members be unharmed, so mankind should spare the individual man, because all are born for a life of fellowship, and society can be kept unharmed only by the mutual protection and love of its parts.[72]

The underlying thought here is the Stoic principle of universal humanity, which teaches that every human being is sacred as such,[73] because all have equal share in the divine and all-pervading λόγος (or *ratio*). As one scholar rightly points out, "In practical terms, this doctrine gives Stoic ethics an inescapable social dimension."[74] Morality is simply rooted in the order of Nature itself. As Epictetus explains, every individual is from the very beginning a social and affectionate being (φύσει κοινωνικὸς καὶ φιλάλληλος).[75] It lies in the very nature of humans to do good (εὖ ποιεῖν), to work together (συνεργεῖν), and to pray for each other's well-being (ἐπεύχεσθαι).[76] Hence, a work that is ἀνθρωπικόν is something beneficent (εὐεργετικόν), of common utility (κοινωφελές), and noble (γενναῖον).[77] Similarly,

---

[67] Epictetus, *Diss*. 2.10.4.
[68] See Reydams-Schils 2002; 2005, 53–82. Note also Marcus Aurelius, *Meditations* 11.1 (ἴδιον δὲ λογικῆς ψυχῆς καὶ τὸ φιλεῖν τοὺς πλησίον ["a property (too) of the Rational Soul is the love of our neighbour"]); 7.55; 8.12.
[69] Seneca, *Prov*. 3.1; *Ben*. 7.19.9. Cf. Cicero, *Fin*. 3.64.
[70] See the discussion in Lee 2006, esp. 29–102.
[71] Seneca, *Ep*. 95.51–52. See also Cicero, *Fin*. 3.62–63.
[72] *Ira* 2.31.7: "Quid si nocere velint manus pedibus, manibus oculi? Ut omnia inter se membra consentiunt, quia singula servari totius interest, ita homines singulis parcent, quia ad coetum geniti sunt, salva autem esse societas nisi custodia et amore partium non potest."
[73] See Seneca, *Ep*. 95.33: "Homo, sacra res homini . . ."
[74] Colish 1985, 38.
[75] Epictetus, *Diss*. 3.13.5.
[76] Epictetus, *Diss*. 4.1.122.
[77] Epictetus, *Diss*. 4.10.12. Cf. *Diss*. 1.19.13; 2.10.23.

Seneca declares, "Nature begot me loving all people,"[78] reflecting the optimistic view, shared by his fellow Stoics, of the human capability for living virtuously. As Musonius formulates the point, there is an "innate inclination of the human soul toward goodness and nobleness [καλοκἀγαθίαν]," and there are "seeds of virtue [σπέρμα ἀρετῆς] in each one of us."[79] This does not mean that every person, as it were, automatically possesses virtue itself. Rather, according to the Stoic teaching, every individual has a natural disposition to virtue. While it is impossible to be wholly without fault (ἀναμάρτητος), it is possible "ever to be intent upon avoiding faults" (πρὸς τὸ μὴ ἁμαρτάνειν τετάσθαι διενεκῶς), as Epictetus explains.[80] It is the will and intention that counts—a characteristically Stoic stance.[81]

In Rom 12:9–21, Paul gives various instructions about proper morality. As we saw above, some deal with in-group relations, while others focus on attitudes and behavior toward out-groups (as well). As for the latter, Paul makes a rather radical demand in 12:14 in urging his addressees to "bless those who persecute you" (εὐλογεῖτε τοὺς διώκοντας ὑμᾶς).[82] Although Paul does not advocate any "love of enemies" here,[83] his demand is nevertheless quite striking, and it may have sounded odd to many in the ancient world. But it certainly would not have sounded odd to those acquainted with Stoic teaching. Founding their ethics on the principle of universal humanity, all Roman Stoics stress the importance of treating one's enemies well and helping them as much as possible. Most radical in this respect is Epictetus, who calls for a sort of "love of enemies": the sage (i.e., the ideal philosopher and human being) "must needs be flogged like an ass, and while he is being flogged he must love [φιλεῖν] the men who flog him, as though he were the father or brother of them all."[84] Somewhat similar to Paul (cf. also Rom 12:20a), but much more clearly and forcefully, Musonius argued against the widely fostered "eye for an eye" attitude in this respect:

> To share the common notion that we shall be despised by others if in every way we do not strive to harm the first enemies [ἐχθρούς] we meet is the mark of mean-minded and ignorant men. For we [commonly] say that the despicable man is recognized among other things by his inability to harm his enemies, but actually he is much more easily recognized by his inability to help them [ὠφελεῖν].[85]

---

[78] Seneca, *Ep.* 102.18: "Natura me amantem omnium genuit" (my translation; the LCL translation reads, "I am naturally born to love all men"). Cf. Seneca, *Ep.* 48.2; *Clem.* 1.3.2; *Ben.* 7.1.7. See also Cicero, *Fin.* 3.65.

[79] Musonius Rufus, *Diss.* 2.38.12–14. Cf. 2.38.1–3; 17.108.8–18; Epictetus, *Diss.* 1.19.12–13; 1.23.1; 2.10.23; 2.20.6; 3.7.27; 3.13.5; 3.24.12; 4.7.8; 4.10.12; 4.11.1.

[80] Epictetus, *Diss.* 4.12.19.

[81] See, for example, Seneca, *Ben.* 1.6.1–3; 2.17.4; 3.18.2.

[82] Followed by εὐλογεῖτε καὶ μὴ καταρᾶσθε. Some important MSS omit ὑμᾶς, including $\mathfrak{P}^{46}$ and B, as well as the latter εὐλογεῖτε ($\mathfrak{P}^{46}$).

[83] Contrary to the popular opinion. But the issue in this verse is not *love*; a *blessing* is required, which is not the same thing. Cf. also the discussion in Wilson 1991, 165–71; Engberg-Pedersen 2000, 266–69, 276–77, 288; and the conclusion in Reiser 2001, 426.

[84] Epictetus, *Diss.* 3.22.54. Cf. *Diss.* 3.24.64–65.

[85] Musonius Rufus, Fragment 41.136 (cf. Epictetus, Fragment 7, in the LCL). See also Seneca, *Otio* 1.4; 8.2; *Vit. beat.* 20.5; *Ben.* 7.31.1, 5; *Ira* 2.28.4; *Ep.* 120.10.

Similar points emerge when we compare the subsequent verses in Paul's text with the Stoic sources. The exhortation in Rom 12:17 not to repay evil with evil matches the Stoic demand that it can never be right to correct wrongdoing by doing wrong: "non oportet peccata corrigere peccantem" (Seneca); τὸ μὲν σκοπεῖν, ὅπως ἀντιδήξεταί τις τὸν δακόντα, καὶ ἀντιποιήσει κακῶς τὸν ὑπάρξαντα, θηρίου τινός, οὐκ ἀνθρώπου ἐστίν (Musonius).[86] There is a certain universal thought in 12:17b, but it does not involve "universal love" or anything of that sort;[87] rather, it concerns the audience's noble appearance in the sight of all people (προνοούμενοι καλὰ ἐνώπιον πάντων ἀνθρώπων). This is confirmed by the following verse, in which Paul insists that the addressees do their best to "be at peace with all people" (μετὰ πάντων ἀνθρώπων εἰρηνεύοντες); that is, they should endeavor to avoid any unnecessary conflict with the outside world, a concern that he takes up and develops further in 13:1–7. Interestingly, Epictetus uses almost exactly the same words in exhorting his interlocutor to "be at peace with all people" (εἰρήνην ἄγεις πρὸς πάντας ἀνθρώπους).[88] The difference between the arguments of the two moral instructors is that whereas Paul is careful to add the condition "if possible for your part" (εἰ δυνατὸν τὸ ἐξ ὑμῶν), Epictetus includes no such condition but states, quite to the contrary, that the peace demand is absolute: "no matter what they do" (ὅ τι ἂν ἐκεῖνοι ποιῶσι). Again, the principle of universal humanity is consistently applied by the Stoics.

A further difference between Paul and the Stoics can be seen in Rom 12:19. Having repeated his warning against retaliation (μὴ ἑαυτοὺς ἐκδικοῦντες), Paul nevertheless assures the audience that even though they should never apply the "eye for an eye" principle, God will do so in their stead (δότε τόπον τῇ ὀργῇ): "'Vengeance is mine! I will repay!' says the Lord."[89] There seems to be no comparable justification for retaliation in the writings of the Roman Stoics, even where the doer is divine. But an audience familiar with traditional views from the Jewish writings and/or Greco-Roman society may not have found the thought of a revenging god totally foreign. Paul's main point, however, concerns nonretaliation rather than the opposite. Thus, in 12:20 he reinforces his earlier statement about the proper attitude toward evildoers and enemies (cf. 12:14), now adding that one should even give aid to an enemy in need, for (γάρ) by so doing one may drive the enemy to repentance.[90]

---

[86] Seneca, *Ira* 1.16.1 ("It is not right to correct wrong-doing by doing wrong"); Musonius Rufus, *Diss.* 10.78.26–28 ("To scheme how to bite back the biter and to return evil for evil is the act not of a human being but of a wild beast"). Cf. Seneca, *Ira* 1.14.3; Epictetus, *Diss.* 4.1.122, 167; *Ench.* 43.

[87] As implied in, for example, Schrage 1961, 252, 266; Wilson 1991, 198–99; Söding 1995, 241–50. Furnish claims that Rom 12:17b "reveals Paul's conviction that the gospel ethic summons up and clarifies the deepest and best moral instincts of man: one should 'take thought for what is noble in the sight of all'.... The universalism of the Pauline love ethic is very clear in vs. 18" (Furnish 1972, 106–7). However, Paul does not at all speak of "love" in these verses.

[88] Epictetus, *Diss.* 4.5.24.

[89] Here Paul is citing Deut 32:35, but apparently from a version of the LXX that is unavailable to us (it also differs slightly from the MT); see the discussion in Dunn 1988, 2:749–50.

[90] Paul's point in this last part of Rom 12:20 is somewhat unclear and disputed by scholars. For an overview, see Dunn 1988, 2:750–51; Fitzmyer 1993, 657–59.

We see similar concerns in the writings of the Roman Stoics. In addition to urging people to help their enemies (see above), Musonius states, "To accept injury not in a spirit of savage resentment and to show ourselves not implacable toward those who wrong us, but rather to be a source of good hope to them [αἴτιον εἶναι αὐτοῖς ἐλπίδος χρηστῆς] is characteristic of a benevolent and civilized way of life [ἡμέρου τρόπου καὶ φιλανθρώπου ἐστίν]."[91] And Seneca writes, "We shall never cease to work for the common good [*communi bono*], to help each and all, to give aid even to our enemies [*inimicis*] when our hand is feeble with age."[92] Seneca also declares, "How much more human [*humanius*] to manifest toward wrong-doers [*peccantibus*] a kind and fatherly spirit, not hunting them down [*persequi*] but calling them back [*revocare*]!"[93] Every wrongdoing must be met and treated with its opposite, with good.[94] There is little doubt that a "Stoically prepared" audience would have nodded approvingly at Paul's exhortation in Rom 12:21 that evil must be overcome with good (νίκα ἐν τῷ ἀγαθῷ τὸ κακόν). The audience would have recognized here the same principle as the one recommended by Roman moralists like Seneca: "Persistent goodness wins over bad men, and no one of them is so hardhearted and hostile to kindly treatment as not to love [*amet*] a good man even while they wrong him."[95]

Nor would Paul's audience have been surprised by his argumentation in Rom 13:1–7, which, in essence, dwells on the thought of 12:21 and develops it further, now with respect to the Christ-believers' behavior in society at large and their stance toward the Roman authorities. Paul argues from current ideas of civic authorities as God's instruments on earth in upholding good behavior. Such ideas "writers could take for granted and presuppose in what else they had to say. Indeed, they could appeal to it as something that would not be questioned—and could then move on from there to make whatever other points they were bent on making."[96] Paul's main point in Rom 13 is not that the Christ-believers are to show obedience to the Roman emperor and his agents, a point that he and his audience (can) take for granted, but rather that this is not what really matters. Obedience to earthly rulers is actually an *adiaphoron*[97]—a decidedly Stoic argument (see below). What really matters, according to Paul, is the addressees' attitude and behavior toward each other (13:8–10) and their "putting on" Jesus Christ at the arrival of their salvation (13:11–14). At the same time, however, in 13:1–7 Paul relates to his earlier words about proper behavior toward outsiders in general: to "take thought for what is noble in the sight of all" (12:17) and to "be at peace with all" (12:18),[98] thus implying that the Christ-believers should avoid drawing unnecessary attention to

---

[91] Musonius Rufus, *Diss.* 10.78.31–33.
[92] Seneca, *Otio* 1.4.
[93] Seneca, *Ira* 1.14.3.
[94] See, for example, Seneca, *Ira* 2.10.6–7; 2.28.4; 2.32.2; 2.34.5; 3.27.1, 3; *Ep.* 66.21.
[95] Seneca, *Ben.* 7.31.1.
[96] Engberg-Pedersen 2006, 168, reading Rom 13:1–7 in the light of Seneca's *Clem.* 1.1–4.
[97] This is well argued in Engberg-Pedersen 2006, esp. 169–72.
[98] Cf. εὐσχημόνως περιπατήσωμεν in Rom 13:13, which is "a Greco-Roman moral concept concerning the avoidance of public shame by outwardly conforming to accepted standards" (Jewett 2007, 825).

themselves on behalf of the authorities and try to "fit" into society as much as possible (εἰ δυνατὸν τὸ ἐξ ὑμῶν). Romans 13:1-7 therefore also underlines that Christ-believers should be tactful and wise in their dealings with civic authorities and Roman society at large.

Returning to Paul's teaching about in-group relations, we can see a certain difference between Paul and the Stoics when he in Rom 12:15 exhorts the Christ-believers to "rejoice [χαίρειν] with those who rejoice" and "weep [κλαίειν] with those who weep." Few Stoics, at least in theoretical contexts, would have spoken of passions (πάθη) such as joy (χαρά) and grief (normally λύπη) in such positive terms,[99] although there certainly seem to have been exceptions to the rule.[100] Some members of Paul's audience may have recalled theories of that sort, promptly comparing his message with the prevalent Stoic teaching. At any rate, the subsequent repetition of the root φρον- (v. 16: φρονοῦντες . . . φρονοῦντες . . . φρόνιμοι), which alludes to 12:3 and points again to the importance of this concept in Paul's moral teaching, would almost certainly have (re)directed their thoughts to the Greco-Roman cardinal virtues, especially, of course, the prominent virtue of φρόνησις.

In Rom 13:8-10, Paul finally turns to the central position of "love" (ἀγάπη) in his moral teaching. To be sure, he had already mentioned "love" in 12:9, but only in passing,[101] as one among many examples of virtues and virtuous dispositions, including φιλαδελφία, φιλοστοργία, and τιμή (12:10).[102] Both passages concern in-group relations, and in-group relations only, but it is not until 13:8-10 that Paul distinctly presents his teaching about "love" as the Christ-movement's own "cardinal virtue": "Owe no one anything, except to love one another" (μηδενὶ μηδὲν ὀφείλετε εἰ μὴ τὸ ἀλλήλους ἀγαπᾶν). Quoting Lev 19:18, Paul explains that the Jewish law as a whole—every single moral demand in the law—is indeed "summed up" in this one commandment: "Love your neighbor [τὸν πλησίον σου] as yourself."

The Roman Stoics probably would have agreed wholeheartedly with Paul about the significance of love. For example, Seneca teaches that one must live for one's neighbor, if one would live for oneself (*alteri vivas oportet, si vis tibi vivere*), for Nature engendered in human beings a mutual love (*amorem mutuum*).[103] Human life is therefore "founded on kindness [*beneficiis*] and concord [*concordia*], and is bound into an alliance for common help, not by terror, but by mutual love [*mutuo amore*]."[104] The purpose of Seneca's moral teaching was in fact to lead

---

[99] Cf. Seneca, *Clem.* 2.6.2-3; *Tranq.* 16.4; Epictetus, *Diss.* 3.24.22-24. Note, however, that χαρά is a εὐπάθεια ("good feeling") in Stoic theory; see Engberg-Pedersen 2000, 73.

[100] Cf. Musonius Rufus, *Diss.* 14.94.5-8, praising marriage and the mutual love of the married couple: "Who is so longed for when absent as a husband by his wife, or a wife by her husband? Whose presence would do more to lighten grief [λύπη] or increase joy [χαρά] or remedy misfortune?" Also Epictetus, *Diss.* 2.5.23: ὅπου γὰρ τὸ χαίρειν εὐλόγως, ἐκεῖ καὶ τὸ συγχαίρειν.

[101] See Thorsteinsson 2006, 144-46.

[102] On φιλοστοργία, see Epictetus, *Diss.* 1.11 (Περὶ φιλοστοργίας).

[103] Seneca, *Ep.* 48.2; 95.52.

[104] Seneca, *Ira* 1.5.3.

people to an "all-embracing love [amor] of the human race even as of oneself."[105] Of course, Paul's focus in Romans is aimed not at the human race as a whole, but at a very specific portion of it, namely, the followers of and believers in Jesus Christ.

And so his focus is in Rom 14–15. Paul here relates how the addressees may and should "put on" (ἐνδύεσθαι) Jesus Christ (13:14) in their dealings with one another—that is, how they are to strive to imitate his person and way of life. In Stoic terms, Paul wants them to become, or, rather, strive to become "wise (wo)men" in their moral actions. To the Stoics, as to many others, Socrates was a person to "put on," or, as Epictetus says, a person whom one should consistently attempt to imitate: "Even if you are not yet a Socrates, still you ought to live as one who wishes to be a Socrates [ὡς Σωκράτης γε εἶναι βουλόμενος ὀφείλεις βιοῦν]."[106] Paul's Stoically informed readers would easily have recognized the parallel between "putting on Jesus Christ" and "living as one who wishes to be a Socrates." The definite prerequisite (in both cases) is the kind of transformation or "metamorphosis" spoken of in Rom 12:2.[107]

In Rom 14–15, Paul pays particular attention to the relationship between the "strong" (οἱ δυνατοί) and the "weak in faith" (ὁ ἀσθενῶν τῇ πίστει), and especially the duty of the former to respect and adapt to the needs of the latter. As Paul summarizes in 15:1, "We who are strong are obliged to bear [βαστάζειν] the weaknesses of those who are without strength [τὰ ἀσθενήματα τῶν ἀδυνάτων], and not to please ourselves [μὴ ἑαυτοῖς ἀρέσκειν]." In other words, all relationships within the Christ-believing community are to be characterized by the ethic of adaptability. Clothed with Christ, each believer should please his or her neighbor for the purpose of the good (εἰς τὸ ἀγαθόν), which aims at nothing but building up (πρὸς οἰκοδομήν) (15:2). A Stoic reader of Paul's text would have felt very much at home in this argument, as the topic of adaptability was a very common theme in Greco-Roman texts, including Stoic ones.[108] Paul's subsequent wish in 15:5 that the addressees will τὸ αὐτὸ φρονεῖν ἐν ἀλλήλοις ("be of the same mind one with another" [ASV]), which, once again, recalls his allusion to the cardinal virtue of φρόνησις in 12:3 (cf. 12:16; 14:6), would only have strengthened such a link with Stoicism.

Moreover, a major component in Paul's case for adaptability is the argument involving things indifferent. According to him, people may differ in their ritual observance and in their attitudes toward it, some being quite rigid concerning certain foods or days, whereas others pay no attention whatsoever to such things (14:2, 5). However, although those who share the rigid attitude (the "weak") certainly are wrongly disposed (14:14, 20), all these things, says Paul, are of no real consequence in the bigger picture. For "the kingdom of God is not food and drink [or days] but righteousness and peace and joy in the Holy Spirit" (14:17). It is precisely because these things are totally indifferent that the "strong" can and should

---

[105] Seneca, *Clem.* 1.11.2. See also 2.5.3; Musonius Rufus, *Diss.* 14.92.29–33; Epictetus, *Diss.* 3.22.54; 3.24.64.

[106] Epictetus, *Ench.* 51.3.

[107] On the link between Rom 12:1–2 and Rom 13:11–14, see Thompson 1991, 151–53.

[108] For a general overview (with examples from the Stoics), see Glad 2003. On the ethic of adaptability in Rom 14–15, see especially Glad 1995, 213–35.

disregard their own convictions and adapt to the needs of the "weak," all for the purpose of peace, unity, and mutual upbuilding in the community (cf. 14:19; 15:2, 5–6). Otherwise, the "strong" are "no longer walking in love" (14:15: οὐκέτι κατὰ ἀγάπην περιπατεῖς).

This aspect of Paul's argumentation closely resembles the characteristic Stoic doctrine of "indifferent things," *adiaphora* (ἀδιάφορα, *indifferentia*)—that is, the things that are neither good nor evil and thus of no real consequence.[109] Paul takes great care to explain this aspect of his moral teaching to the audience, perhaps expecting that a knowledge of the Hebrew Bible or the Septuagint alone would provide limited help to fully grasp his message. But to a Stoically informed reader, we may presume, the Stoic theory of *adiaphora* would have served well as a heuristic tool toward that end, namely, for the purpose of discerning what is "good, acceptable, and perfect" in the eyes of God (12:2).

5. Conclusion

In this essay I have argued that the best Stoic sources available for comparison with Paul's moral teaching in Romans are the writings and lectures of the Roman Stoics Seneca, Musonius Rufus, and Epictetus, all of whom exemplify how Stoicism was interpreted, understood, and experienced in the city of Rome in the middle and latter part of the first century C.E. Not only are these Stoics exact or close contemporaries of Paul, but also their ethics represents the prominent moral teaching in Rome at the time.

Following a general outline of Paul's moral teaching in Rom 12–15, I assessed the extent and nature of some of the Stoic allusions and analogies in this passage. The basic question was how Paul's Roman addressees would have read and responded to such allusions and analogies. Thus, the main concern in this essay was the way in which Stoicism could have served as a heuristic key for the audience to properly understand Paul's message—and therefore also, we may add, the way in which Stoicism may serve as a useful tool in our own interpretation of that message.[110]

I identified a number of possible allusions to Stoicism in Rom 12–15, not least in the programmatic opening of the passage. These potential allusions and/or analogies suggest that knowledge of the basic elements of Stoic ethics would have been of much help to Paul's readers to understand his message. Such knowledge may, in other words, have served as an important hermeneutical key to unlock that message.[111] This is not to say that every detail of Paul's text would or

---

[109] See, for example, Cicero, *Fin.* 3.50–58; Seneca, *Ep.* 82.10–12; 92.11; Epictetus, *Diss.* 1.30; 2.6; 2.9.15; 2.19.13. For a general discussion and further examples, see Long and Sedley 1987, 1:354–59; Pohlenz 1948, 121–23. For examples of (Stoic) *adiaphora* in Paul's letters, see Deming 2003. Deming mentions Rom 14:5, 6–8, 14–17, 20 as potential cases of *adiaphora* (p. 398).

[110] For a similar approach, see Engberg-Pedersen 1995, 277–78.

[111] See also Thorsteinsson 2008, in which I discuss some of the ways in which Stoicism may have paved the way for the rise of Christianity in the ancient world.

could have been interpreted in a Stoic fashion by the Roman audience. Rather, this essay suggests that the basic framework of Paul's moral teaching in Rom 12-15 as well as many details of that teaching may well have been understood in a Stoic light—and still can.

Bibliography

Abel, K. 1985."Seneca: Leben und Leistung." *ANRW* 32.2:653-775. Part 2, *Principat*, 32.2. Edited by H. Temporini and W. Haase. Berlin: de Gruyter.
Annas, J. E. 1993. *The Morality of Happiness*. New York: Oxford University Press.
Aune, D. E. 1994. "Human Nature and Ethics in Hellenistic Philosophical Traditions and Paul: Some Issues and Problems." Pages 291-312 in *Paul in His Hellenistic Context*. Edited by T. Engberg-Pedersen. Studies of the New Testament and Its World. Edinburgh: T & T Clark.
Barrett, C. K. 1957. *A Commentary on the Epistle to the Romans*. Black's New Testament Commentaries. London: Black.
Behm, J. 1965. "θύω κτλ." Pages 180-90 in vol. 3 of *Theological Dictionary of the New Testament*. Edited by G. Kittel and G. Friedrich. Translated by G. W. Bromiley. Grand Rapids: Eerdmans.
Betz, H. D. 1991. "Christianity as Religion: Paul's Attempt at Definition in Romans." *Journal of Religion* 71:315-44.
Bonhöffer, A. 1911. *Epiktet und das Neue Testament*. Religionsgeschichtliche Versuche und Vorarbeiten 10. Gießen: Töpelmann.
Brennan, T. 2005. *The Stoic Life: Emotions, Duties, and Fate*. Oxford: Clarendon Press.
Colish, M. L. 1985. *Stoicism in Classical Latin Literature*. Vol. 1 of *The Stoic Tradition from Antiquity to the Early Middle Ages*. Studies in the History of Christian Thought 34. Leiden: Brill, 1985.
Cranfield, C. E. B. 1975-1979. *A Critical and Exegetical Commentary on the Epistle to the Romans*. 2 vols. International Critical Commentary. Edinburgh: T & T Clark.
Deming, W. 2003. "Paul and Indifferent Things." Pages 384-403 in *Paul in the Greco-Roman World: A Handbook*. Edited by J. P. Sampley. Harrisburg, Pa.: Trinity Press International.
Dodd, C. H. 1932. *The Epistle of Paul to the Romans*. Moffatt New Testament Commentary. London: Hodder & Stoughton.
Dunn, J. D. G. 1988. *Romans*. 2 vols. Word Biblical Commentary 38A, 38B. Dallas: Word Books.
Edwards, C. 1993. *The Politics of Immorality in Ancient Rome*. Cambridge: Cambridge University Press.
Engberg-Pedersen, T. 1995. "Stoicism in Philippians." Pages 256-90 in *Paul in His Hellenistic Context*. Edited by T. Engberg-Pedersen. Studies of the New Testament and Its World. Edinburgh: T & T Clark.
———. 2000. *Paul and the Stoics*. Edinburgh: T & T Clark.

———. 2005. "The Relationship with Others: Similarities and Differences Between Paul and Stoicism." *Zeitschrift für die Neutestamentliche Wissenschaft* 96:35–60.
———. 2006. "Paul's Stoicizing Politics in Romans 12–13: The Role of 13.1–10 in the Argument." *Journal for the Study of the New Testament* 29:163–72.
Esler, P. F. 2003a. *Conflict and Identity in Romans: The Social Setting of Paul's Letter*. Minneapolis: Fortress.
———. 2003b. "Social Identity, the Virtues, and the Good Life: A New Approach to Romans 12:1–15:13." *Biblical Theology Bulletin* 33:51–63.
———. 2004. "Paul and Stoicism: Romans 12 as a Test Case." *New Testament Studies* 50:106–24.
Fitzmyer, J. A. 1993. *Romans: A New Translation with Introduction and Commentary*. Anchor Bible 33. New York: Doubleday.
Furnish, V. P. 1972. *The Love Command in the New Testament*. Nashville: Abingdon.
Geytenbeek, A. C. van. 1963. *Musonius Rufus and Greek Diatribe*. Translated by B. L. Hijmans Jr. Rev. ed. Wijsgerige teksten en studies 8. Assen: Van Gorcum.
Gibson, R. J. 2000. "Paul and the Evangelization of the Stoics." Pages 309–26 in *The Gospel to the Nations: Perspectives on Paul's Mission*. Edited by P. Bolt and M. Thompson. Downers Grove, Ill.: InterVarsity Press.
Glad, C. E. 1995. *Paul and Philodemus: Adaptability in Epicurean and Early Christian Psychagogy*. Supplements to Novum Testamentum 81. Leiden: Brill.
———. 2003. "Paul and Adaptability." Pages 17–41 in *Paul in the Greco-Roman World: A Handbook*. Edited by J. P. Sampley. Harrisburg, Pa.: Trinity Press International.
Griffin, M. T. 1976. *Seneca: A Philosopher in Politics*. Oxford: Clarendon Press.
———. 1984. *Nero: The End of a Dynasty*. London: Batsford.
———. 1989. "Philosophy, Politics, and Politicians at Rome." Pages 1–37 in *Philosophia Togata: Essays on Philosophy and Roman Society*. Edited by M. Griffin and J. Barnes. Oxford: Clarendon Press.
Hands, A. R. 1968. *Charities and Social Aid in Greece and Rome*. Ithaca, N.Y.: Cornell University Press.
Horrell, D. G. 2005. *Solidarity and Difference: A Contemporary Reading of Paul's Ethics*. London: T & T Clark.
Jewett, R. 2007. *Romans: A Commentary*. Hermeneia. Minneapolis: Fortress.
Johnson, L. T. 2003. "Transformation of the Mind and Moral Discernment in Paul." Pages 215–36 in *Early Christianity and Classical Culture: Comparative Studies in Honor of Abraham J. Malherbe*. Edited by J. T. Fitzgerald, T. H. Olbricht, and L. M. White. Supplements to Novum Testamentum 110. Leiden: Brill.
Käsemann, E. 1974. *An die Römer*. 3d ed. Handbuch zum Neuen Testament 8A. Tübingen: Mohr Siebeck.
Lee, M. V. 2006. *Paul, the Stoics, and the Body of Christ*. Society for New Testament Studies Monograph Series 137. Cambridge: Cambridge University Press.
Lietzmann, H. 1971. *Einführung in die Textgeschichte der Paulusbriefe: An die Römer*. 5th ed. Handbuch zum Neuen Testament 8. Tübingen: Mohr Siebeck.
Long, A. A. 1996. "Arius Didymus and the Exposition of Stoic Ethics." Pages 107–33 in *Stoic Studies*. Berkeley: University of California Press.

———. 2002. *Epictetus: A Stoic and Socratic Guide to Life*. Oxford: Oxford University Press.
Long, A. A., and D. N. Sedley. 1987. *The Hellenistic Philosophers*. 2 vols. Cambridge: Cambridge University Press.
Lutz, C. E. 1947. "Musonius Rufus: 'The Roman Socrates.'" *Yale Classical Studies* 10:1–147.
Meeks, W. A. 1987. "Judgment and the Brother: Romans 14:1–15:13." Pages 290–300 in *Tradition and Interpretation in the New Testament: Essays in Honor of E. Earle Ellis for His 60th Birthday*. Edited by G. F. Hawthorne and O. Betz. Grand Rapids: Eerdmans.
Michel, O. 1978. *Der Brief an die Römer*. 14th ed. Kritisch-exegetischer Kommentar über das Neue Testament 4. Göttingen: Vandenhoeck & Ruprecht.
Moxnes, H. 1994. "The Quest for Honor and the Unity of the Community in Romans 12 and in the Orations of Dio Chrysostom." Pages 203–30 in *Paul in His Hellenistic Context*. Edited by T. Engberg-Pedersen. Studies of the New Testament and Its World. Edinburgh: T & T Clark.
North, H. 1966. *Sophrosyne: Self-Knowledge and Self-Restraint in Greek Literature*. Ithaca, N.Y.: Cornell University Press.
Pohlenz, M. 1948. *Die Stoa: Geschichte einer geistigen Bewegung*. Vol. 1. Göttingen: Vandenhoeck & Ruprecht.
Pomeroy, A. J., ed. 1999. *Arius Didymus: Epitome of Stoic Ethics*. Society of Biblical Literature Texts and Translations 44, Graeco-Roman Religion Series 14. Atlanta: Society of Biblical Literature.
Rackham, H. 1931. "Introduction." Pages xi–xxxi in *Cicero: De finibus bonorum et malorum*. 2d ed. Loeb Classical Library. Cambridge, Mass.: Harvard University Press.
Reichert, A. 2001. *Der Römerbrief als Gratwanderung: Eine Untersuchung zur Abfassungsproblematik*. Forschungen zur Religion und Literatur des Alten und Neuen Testaments 194. Göttingen: Vandenhoeck & Ruprecht.
Reiser, M. 2001. "Love of Enemies in the Context of Antiquity." *New Testament Studies* 47:411–27.
Reydams-Schils, G. 2002. "Human Bonding and *Oikeiōsis* in Roman Stoicism." *Oxford Studies in Ancient Philosophy* 22:221–51.
———. 2005. *The Roman Stoics: Self, Responsibility, and Affection*. Chicago: University of Chicago Press.
Rist, J. M. 1969. *Stoic Philosophy*. Cambridge: Cambridge University Press.
Sanday, W., and A. C. Headlam. 1902. *A Critical and Exegetical Commentary on the Epistle to the Romans*. 5th ed. International Critical Commentary. Edinburgh: T & T Clark.
Sandbach, F. H. 1989. *The Stoics*. 2d ed. London: Duckworth.
Schlier, H. 1977. *Der Römerbrief*. Herders theologischer Kommentar zum Neuen Testament 6. Freiburg: Herder.
Schrage, W. 1961. *Die konkreten Einzelgebote in der paulinischen Paränese: Ein Beitrag zur neutestamentlichen Ethik*. Gütersloh: Mohn.

Sevenster, J. N. 1961. *Paul and Seneca*. Supplements to Novum Testamentum 4. Leiden: Brill.
Söding, T. 1995. *Das Liebesgebot bei Paulus: Die Mahnung zur Agape im Rahmen der paulinischen Ethik*. Neutestamentliche Abhandlungen 26. Münster: Aschendorff.
Stowers, S. K. 1990. "Paul on the Use and Abuse of Reason." Pages 253–86 in *Greeks, Romans, and Christians: Essays in Honor of Abraham J. Malherbe*. Edited by D. L. Balch, E. Ferguson, and W. A. Meeks. Minneapolis: Fortress.
———. 1994. *A Rereading of Romans: Justice, Jews, and Gentiles*. New Haven: Yale University Press.
———. 2003. "Paul and Self-Mastery." Pages 524–50 in *Paul in the Greco-Roman World: A Handbook*. Edited by J. P. Sampley. Harrisburg, Pa.: Trinity Press International.
Stuhlmacher, P. 1989. *Der Brief an die Römer*. Das Neue Testament Deutsch 6. Göttingen: Vandenhoeck & Ruprecht.
Thompson, M. 1991. *Clothed with Christ: The Example and Teaching of Jesus in Romans 12.1–15.13*. Journal for the Study of the New Testament: Supplement Series 59. Sheffield: JSOT Press.
Thorsteinsson, R. M. 2003. *Paul's Interlocutor in Romans 2: Function and Identity in the Context of Ancient Epistolography*. Coniectanea biblica: New Testament Series 40. Stockholm: Almqvist & Wiksell.
———. 2006. "Paul and Roman Stoicism: Romans 12 and Contemporary Stoic Ethics." *Journal for the Study of the New Testament* 29:139–61.
———. 2008. "The Role of Morality in the Rise of Roman Christianity." Pages 139–57 in *Exploring Early Christian Identity*. Edited by B. Holmberg. Wissenschaftliche Untersuchungen zum Neuen Testament 226. Tübingen: Mohr Siebeck.
———. 2010. *Roman Christianity and Roman Stoicism: A Comparative Study of Ancient Morality*. Oxford: Oxford University Press.
Wachsmuth, C., and O. Hense. 1974–1975. *Ioannis Stobaei: Anthologium*. 3d ed. 5 vols. Berlin: Weidmann.
Watson, F. P. 2007. *Judaism and the Gentiles: Beyond the New Perspective*. Revised and expanded edition. Grand Rapids: Eerdmans.
Wilson, W. T. 1991. *Love without Pretense: Romans 12.9–21 and Hellenistic-Jewish Wisdom Literature*. Wissenschaftliche Untersuchungen zum Neuen Testament 46. Tübingen: Mohr Siebeck.
Witherington, B., with D. Hyatt. 2004. *Paul's Letter to the Romans: A Socio-Rhetorical Commentary*. Grand Rapids: Eerdmans.
Wright, N. T. 2002. "The Letter to the Romans: Introduction, Commentary, and Reflections." Pages 395–770 in vol. 10 of *The New Interpreter's Bible*. Edited by L. E. Keck. Nashville: Abingdon.
Zahn, T. 1910. *Der Brief des Paulus an die Römer*. Kommentar zum Neuen Testament 6. Leipzig: Deichert.
Ziesler, J. 1989. *Paul's Letter to the Romans*. TPI New Testament Commentaries. London: SCM Press; Valley Forge, Pa.: Trinity Press International.

3

STOIC LAW IN PAUL?

Niko Huttunen
University of Helsinki

1. Stoicism—Neglected but Important

Following on E. P. Sanders's epochal *Paul and the Palestinian Judaism* (1977), a majority of biblical scholars have accepted covenantal nomism and the so-called new perspective on Paul. Today, the debate is about questions such as how far covenantal nomism describes Jewish thinking and to what extent Paul is using its categories in his treatment of the Torah.[1] This debate has continued for over thirty years, and it is likely that the best and most solid results have already been reached. Now it is time to discover other perspectives, not in order to supersede the earlier view but rather to complement it.[2]

No one claims that the context of Paul's thinking is only Palestinian Judaism. His roots are in the Diaspora, if we can believe what Luke has him saying in Acts (21:39; 22:3). Although this report can be doubted, Paul's epistles, which are written in Greek, unequivocally betray his close contacts with Gentiles outside of Palestine. Several scholars have taken this fact seriously and have depicted Paul and his thinking from the Greco-Roman perspective.[3] Despite this intense scholarly work, Paul's teaching on law has been left practically untouched from this perspective. On the one hand, those who study Paul in his Greco-Roman context have shown little interest in his teaching on law; on the other hand, those who study his teaching on law have not been interested in the Greco-Roman context apart from a concern with purely linguistic matters. Only a few scholars have even noticed this gap in Pauline studies.[4]

---

[1] For the history of research, see Westerholm 2004.
[2] This essay is based on Huttunen 2009.
[3] For example, Malherbe 1989; Seeley 1990; Glad 1995; Martin 1990; 1995; Engberg-Pedersen 2000.
[4] Jones 1987, 94; Downing 1998, 57.

But is it not the Jewish law, the Torah, that Paul is speaking of? How would the Greco-Roman perspective enrich our understanding of his treatment of this Jewish issue? First, it is well known that Jews in the Diaspora interpreted the Torah in philosophical categories.[5] Anyone acknowledges this fact when reading, say, Philo's treatises, where the Torah, like anything else, is interpreted in philosophical categories. It is a priori unlikely that Paul was an exception among Diaspora Jews. It is quite to be expected, moreover, that Greco-Roman interpretations were not alien to the apostle whose liberal views of the inclusion of Gentiles tested the boundaries of Judaism. Second, Paul is not always speaking of *the* law. We cannot straightforwardly assume that Paul is always using the Greek expressions for "law," "commandment," or "ordinance," and so on to denote the Torah and its regulations. Heikki Räisänen has shown that in some Pauline passages it is difficult to interpret ὁ νόμος as the Torah.[6] In these cases, Paul's Greco-Roman background would provide an alternative interpretive option to be explored in more detail.

Since Paul was a Diaspora Jew, it might seem reasonable to compare his views with those of other Diaspora Jews. However, I avoid this kind of comparison for methodological reasons. A comparison with Diaspora Jews would always lead to the question of whether the similarities between potentially compared parts were due to the shared Judaism or to the shared Greco-Roman background. If Paul and another Diaspora Jew put forward similar views, the easiest interpretation for the similarities would be the shared Jewish background, not the Greco-Roman one. Such an explanation is precluded, however, if we compare the views of Paul and a pagan thinker. In this case, the reason for the similarities can be found not in Judaism but, evidently, in the shared Greco-Roman background.

In this essay I compare Paul's sayings about law to those of the Stoic Epictetus (ca. 50–130 C.E.). Epictetus's thoughts are like a window to the intellectual milieu of the first centuries C.E., when Late Stoicism flourished and influenced society in general. For example, shortly after Epictetus, Marcus Aurelius tried to combine the role of a Roman emperor with that of a Stoic philosopher. But Stoicism was not only a philosophy of the aristocracy, since the lower ranks knew of it through Cynicism, a close philosophical relative of Stoicism.[7] Interestingly enough, Epictetus himself was situated between social classes. He was not only a professional philosopher with a school of his own in Nicopolis of Epirus, but also a former slave who consciously treated everyday life from a philosophical point of view. His vernacular language was quite close to that of Paul.[8] Epictetus knew of Christians, but they were not of any deeper interest to him (*Diss.*

---

[5] See, for example, Weber 2000.
[6] Räisänen 1992, 48–94.
[7] We should maintain a difference between Stoics and Cynics (Malherbe 1989, 11), though the difference between Stoics and Cynics is not always very clear (Cicero, *Off.* 1.128). Roman Stoicism, however, had close contacts with Cynicism (Pohlenz 1948, 279).
[8] For the language, see, for example, Bultmann 1984; Stowers 1988; Malherbe 1989, 25–33.

2.9.19-21; 4.7.6).⁹ It is a matter of consensus that Christianity did not influence Epictetus's philosophy.[10]

I will discuss two Pauline passages on law in which the Greco-Roman context is highly important (1 Cor 7:17-24; Rom 1:18-32). I begin both analyses with a brief presentation of the Pauline passage and the issues on which Epictetus's texts may shed some light. Then I analyze the Epictetan texts, return to Paul, and highlight the Pauline issues presented at the beginning of the analyses. My purpose is to show that Paul's treatment of law carries more, and deeper, Stoic components than has earlier been thought.

2. Commandments and Paul's Christian Stoicism

2.1. The Problem of Commandments

In 1 Cor 7:17-24, Paul admonishes Christians to remain in their present social position and claims that circumcision and uncircumcision are nothing, while "obeying the commandments of God [τήρησις τῶν ἐντολῶν τοῦ θεοῦ] is everything" (1 Cor 7:19).[11] This latter expression is reminiscent of Wis 6:18 and Sir 32:23, where similar expressions denote the need to obey the Torah.[12] But if Paul is thinking of the Torah, how could he say that circumcision "is nothing" (οὐδέν ἐστιν)? It is well known that in Judaism circumcision was one of the main expressions of obedience to the Torah. Unlike the so-called allegorists (Philo, *Abr.* 89-93), Paul makes no spiritual reinterpretation of circumcision. Had he meant this, circumcision would be not nothing but something, namely, something spiritual—for example, similar to the circumcision of the heart (Rom 2:28-29). But here Paul maintains that circumcision is simply nothing.

Another interpretive option is to understand the commandments as a reference to the love command (Lev 19:18). For Paul, the command to love is the crystallization of the Torah (Rom 13:9; Gal 5:14). Even this option is not very reliable, however, since it is difficult to think that a plural ("commandments") would refer to the singular (the love command).[13] Moreover, "love" is not mentioned in the passage at all. Rather, I think that we should understand "obeying the commandments

---

⁹In *Diss.* 4.7.6, Epictetus speaks of Galileans, and in principle one can question whether he means Christians at all. Yet, it is a common assumption that these Galileans are Christians. A more ambiguous case is *Diss.* 2.9.19-21. In this passage Epictetus compares counterfeit Jews and real Jews who are baptized. Scholars usually assume that Epictetus is speaking of God-fearers (counterfeit Jews) and proselytes (Jews), but this interpretation is based on an unsupported textual emendation. In an earlier article (Huttunen 2007), I assume that Epictetus's words reflect a Christian supersessionist theology where Christians are the real Jews.

[10] For example, Bonhöffer 1911, 4-81; Sharp 1914; Long 2002, 35. Few scholars have held the opposing view (see Spanneut 1962, 630).

[11] Unless otherwise indicated, translations of biblical quotations are from the NRSV.

[12] Lang 1986, 96; Räisänen 1987, 68.

[13] Lindemann 2000, 171.

of God" in its textual context, where Paul discusses social positions. We would expect that "the commandments" have something to do with them. Many scholars have noted resemblances between Stoicism (or "popular philosophy") and Paul's teachings on social positions.[14] I claim that Stoicism sheds light on what Paul says about "the commandments of God."

2.2. Epictetus: God's Command to Use Indifferent Things

The *Encheiridion* is a short summation of Epictetus's philosophy.[15] It begins with the fundamental division between the things that are our own and under our control and the things that are not our own (ἀλλότρια) and not under our control. "Under our control are conception, choice, desire, aversion, and, in a word, everything that is our own doing; not under our control are our body, our property, reputation, office, and, in a word, everything that is not our own doing" (*Ench.* 1.1).[16] The things that are not our own and not under our control have several names in Epictetus's *Discourses*, such as "external things" (τὰ ἐκτός) or "materials" (ὕλαι) (*Diss.* 1.29.2).

According to Epictetus, "materials are indifferent [ἀδιάφορα]" (*Diss.* 2.5.1). What makes the difference are our conceptions, choices, desires, and so forth. These are mental operations that result in value judgments (δόγματα) on external things. It is Epictetus's basic conviction that external things per se are indifferent, and only our judgments make them good or bad. In other words, that which is good or bad lies not in external things but solely in our judgments. This is his Stoic theory of value.

The aim of Epictetus's philosophy is a serene life. If external things are indifferent, they cannot disturb us. "What, then, are the things that weigh upon us and drive us out of our senses? Why, what else but our judgements" (*Diss.* 2.16.24). For example, we can feel free in front of a tyrant despite the fact that the tyrant can imprison, behead, or exile us. All these tyrannical operations threaten external things, and they do not disturb one's composure "if I feel that all this is nothing to me" (*Diss.* 1.29.5–7).

One may wonder why Epictetus continued to live, eat, and teach in his school despite the fact that all these are indifferent external things. Epictetus would answer that indifference to external things does not determine the use of those things. "Materials are indifferent, but the use [χρῆσις] which we make of them is not a matter of indifference" (*Diss.* 2.5.1). In *Diss.* 2.16 Epictetus presents the right use of external things as a law of God. The starting point is the fundamental division between the things that are our own and those that are not.

---

[14] For example, Bonhöffer 1911, 171; Jones 1987, 37, 53; Vollenweider 1989, 211, 241; Deming 1995, 159; Dautzenberg 2001, 61–62.

[15] For Epictetus's philosophy in general, see Long 2002; also Bonhöffer 1890; 1894. The two studies by Bonhöffer are still highly regarded and worth consulting regardless of their age. Long's immensely learned study is the first comprehensive survey since Bonhöffer.

[16] Unless otherwise indicated, translations of Epictetus are from Oldfather 1995–1996.

And what is the law of God [ὁ νόμος ὁ θεῖος]? To guard [τηρεῖν] what is his own, not to lay claim to what is not his own, but to make use [χρῆσθαι] of what is given to him, and not to yearn for what has not been given; when something is taken away, to give it up readily and without delay, being grateful for the time in which he had the use [ἐχρήσατο] of it. (*Diss.* 2.16.28)

One should guard (τηρεῖν) what the law of God commands—that is, one's judgments. We should be content with the things that God has given us on loan, make use (χρῆσθαι) of them, and give them away if it is God's will (see *Diss.* 2.5.22; *Ench.* 11). Social position is one of the external things of which people should make use. This is expressed in an exemplary prayer: "Wouldst Thou have me to hold office, or remain in private life; to remain here or go into exile; to be poor or be rich? I will defend all these Thy acts before men" (*Diss.* 2.16.42). It does not matter what the social position is. What makes a difference is the careful use of the position that God has given.

Epictetus expresses a similar attitude toward social positions in *Diss.* 3.24, where he also speaks of God's commands. Epictetus says that a good and excellent man fills his place (χώρα) "with due obedience to God" until it is time to depart (*Diss.* 3.24.95–97).

"How do you depart?" "Again [πάλιν], as Thou didst wish it, as a free man [ἐλεύθερος], as Thy servant [ὑπηρέτης], as one who has perceived Thy commands and Thy prohibitions [ὡς ᾐσθημένος σου τῶν προσταγμάτων καὶ ἀπαγορευμάτων]. But so long as I continue to live in Thy service, what manner of man wouldst Thou have me be? An official or a private citizen, a senator or one of the common people, a soldier or a general, a teacher or a head of a household? Whatsoever station and post [χώραν καὶ τάξιν] Thou assign me, I will die ten thousand times, as Socrates says, or ever I abandon it."[17] (*Diss.* 3.24.98–99)

The departure from life should "again" happen according to God's "commands and prohibitions," which is a Stoic definition of law.[18] The word "again" points out that God's law belongs not only to the "art of dying" but also to life, which is discussed before *Diss.* 3.24.98. One should live and die obeying God's law, but, as Epictetus's wording makes plain, as a free person or as a free servant (ὑπηρέτης), not as a compelled slave (δοῦλος).[19] Epictetus emphasizes this freedom many times—for example, "I am a free man and a friend of God, so as to obey Him of my own free will. No other thing ought I to claim, not body, or property, or office, or reputation. . . . I cannot transgress any of His commands [τῶν ἐντολῶν]" (*Diss.* 4.3.9–10). Later in *Diss.* 3.24 Epictetus explains that in difficult and changing circumstances one is a witness in the service of God. He argues that social positions are indifferent, while obedience to God's commands is everything:

---

[17]This may be a paraphrase of Plato, *Apol.* 28E–29A (cf. Epictetus, *Diss.* 1.9.23–24; 3.1.19–20).
[18]Bonhöffer 1911, 231; *SVF* 3.314.
[19]For the difference between ὑπηρέτης and δοῦλος, see Rengstorf 1974, 532–33.

When I have been appointed to such a service, am I any longer to take thought as to where I am, or with whom, or what men say about me? Am I not wholly intent upon God, and His commands and ordinances [πρὸς τὸν θεὸν τέταμαι καὶ τὰς ἐκείνου ἐντολὰς καὶ τὰ προστάγματα]? (*Diss.* 3.24.114)

With 1 Cor 7 in mind, it is interesting to note that according to Epictetus, God summons witnesses. An exemplary person is "a witness summoned by God" (μάρτυς ὑπὸ τοῦ θεοῦ κεκλημένος), and one should not disgrace "the summons which He gave you" (τὴν κλῆσιν ἣν κέκληκεν) (*Diss.* 1.29.46, 49; cf. 2.1.39).

2.3. Paul's Christian Stoicism

So, what are "the commandments of God" in 1 Cor 7:19? If Paul is referring to the commandments of the Torah, his idea is totally blurred, as is evidenced by the indifference that he shows toward circumcision. If he held such a blurred idea, it does not explain what the content of the "commandments" would be. In the context, however, Paul speaks not of the Torah, but of social positions. Epictetus's Stoic philosophy aids in understanding what the commandments in Paul's text are.

In 1 Cor 7:17–24, Paul stresses that God calls (καλέω, κλῆσις) each person in his or her social position. The position, however, is indifferent as such: circumcision and uncircumcision are nothing, and a slave has no reason to be concerned about his or her lower status. It is logical that one should not be concerned about statuses, since such things are indifferent. Paul's metaphors also point in the direction that social positions are indifferent. He says that slaves are freedmen of the Lord, while free persons are the Lord's slaves. This status reversal does not indicate any real reversal. It is a metaphor that Paul can easily change by saying that all Christians are slaves bought (ἀγοράζω) by the Lord.[20] The changing metaphors only illustrate the indifference of social positions. Paul clearly shares the Stoic theory of value: external things are indifferent.

It may seem paradoxical that Paul strongly stresses that Christians should remain in their social positions. If social positions are indifferent, why should anyone pay attention to them? Epictetus's philosophy makes this paradox understandable: external things are indifferent, but their use (χρῆσις) is not. This idea makes both Paul and Epictetus emphasize that one should remain in one's position. It is noteworthy that Paul even uses the Stoic technical verb χρῆσθαι in 1 Cor 7:21.

It is well known that 1 Cor 7:21 can be interpreted in different ways. There are two standard options: Paul admonishes slaves either to remain in slavery or to gain their freedom. Both interpretations can be understood along the lines of Stoic philosophy. When pondering the interpretative options, we should note that the choice between freedom and slavery was officially always in the hand of the owner, not in the hand of the slave.[21] If Paul wanted to admonish one to remain in slavery,

---

[20] The Greek verb denotes the buying of a slave for service, not a payment for freedom (Jones 1987, 31; Martin 1990, 63). Cf. 1 Cor 6:19–20.

[21] Bartchy 1973, 106–9. Bartchy himself tries to interpret the verse in a third way: Paul admonishes manumitted slaves to remain Christians.

he means that slaves should not make any unofficial petitions to their owners. This kind of petition usually expresses a striving for an external social position that Stoics could not accept. Since social freedom is indifferent, it is not worth striving for. We can, however, imagine the type of situation where the owner just asks what the slave would like to happen. In this case, there is no striving, and Stoics surely would admonish the slave to gain his or her freedom.[22]

Both interpretations of 1 Cor 7:21 can be read along the lines of Stoic philosophy. This is not to say that it must be read in this way, but the context makes the Stoic reading very probable. The passage reflects a Stoic theory of value and Stoic-sounding admonitions to remain in one's social position. Moreover, Paul uses here the Stoic technical verb χρῆσθαι. In the last analysis, it is quite unimportant whether or not Paul admonishes us to make use of freedom or slavery. What is quite probable is that Paul has the Stoic idea that one should make use of indifferent things—whatever they are.

The philosophical idea of the use of indifferent things can also be presented in theological terms. As we saw, Epictetus utters prayers in which he declares his loyalty in any social position. The loyalty is based not on the value of those social positions, but on God's will. Epictetus remains in his position because God prefers such conduct. One should boldly remain anywhere and in any social position, and remain God's witness. God summons or calls (καλέω, κλῆσις) us to be his witness. God's call is also a central idea in Paul's text, and his teaching on this issue differs little from that of Epictetus. For Paul, God's call has a double meaning: it is simultaneously a call to remain in a social position and to become a Christian.[23] For Epictetus, the connection between the call and the social position is more vague. God calls us to be his witness, and this witnessing activity is performed in some social position. Although Epictetus does not explicitly say that God calls us into a certain social position, it is clear that these positions are given by God. Thus, the difference between Paul and Epictetus is quite small, and it does not diminish the general similarity. God's call occurs in the Stoic philosophy, and Paul seems to adjust it in the context of a Stoic theory of value.

The Stoic context, therefore, must be taken into account when we interpret the commandments of God in 1 Cor 7:19. Here again Paul uses a term that sounds Stoic. The word τήρησις reminds us of τηρέω, which Epictetus used in speaking of the divine law (*Diss.* 2.16.28). The law stressed the importance of the Stoic theory of value and admonished one to make use (χράομαι) of any external thing that God has given. We saw that Epictetus uses the word "command" (ἐντολή) and similar expressions when speaking of social positions. This is part and parcel of his theological formulation of the Stoic theory of value. We have also found this theory in 1 Cor 7:17–24 together with several other Stoic features. It is quite natural to think that the commandments of God refer in this passage to the different social positions. The fact that each position imposes different demands explains the plural form.

---

[22] Bonhöffer 1911, 170–72.
[23] Plank 1987, 26; Schrage 1995, 137.

The Stoic interpretation of "the commandments of God" makes excellent sense in the context of 1 Cor 7:17–24. It is much more difficult to interpret the commandments as referring either to the love command or to Mosaic commandments in general. The context does not speak of love or the Torah. It is true that Paul can blur the line between the Stoic natural law and the Torah (cf. Rom 2:14), but if this happens in 1 Cor 7:19, the reference to the Torah is purely superficial. The actual content of the commandments is derived from the Stoic philosophy.

This is not to say that Paul's thinking is fully Stoic in 1 Cor 7:17–24. There is one point that is absolutely alien to Stoicism: Christ. For Paul, Christ secures the indifference of social positions. In addition, there is an equality between Christians in different statuses, not between all people, as Epictetus thinks. This is why Paul's reasoning is not pure Stoicism but rather a Christian adaptation of it.

3. Gentile Lapse, God's Decree, and Stoic Natural Law

3.1. Towards a More Precise Understanding of Stoicism in Romans 1

Standard exegetical commentaries nearly always refer to the possibility that there are philosophical strains in Rom 1–2.[24] What is usually at stake is natural theology in Rom 1:19–20 and natural fulfillment of the Torah in Rom 2:14–15. It is, however, a quite general claim that some strains in this passage are philosophical. To prove this, we should show that Paul's teaching is related to certain philosophical ideas. Scholars usually have assumed that Paul has adapted Stoic ideas in Rom 1–2, but this is not self-evident. At first sight, the division between that which is visible and that which is invisible (Rom 1:19–20) resembles Platonic philosophy.[25] Another matter concerns natural law, which we meet already in Plato (*Leg.* 890D). Is it, then, the Stoic or the Platonic natural law that Paul is speaking of?

I propose that Rom 1:18–32 is the key to understanding the idea of natural fulfillment of the law in Rom 2:14. If Rom 1 is clearly Stoic, it is probable that Rom 2:14 should be interpreted in a Stoic sense as well. It is also worth noting that Rom 2:14 is not the first verse in Romans where Paul sets up a relation between the Gentiles and law. In Rom 1:32, he already spoke of a knowledge of God's decree (τὸ δικαίωμα τοῦ θεοῦ) among Gentiles. He says that according to the decree, previous vices (Rom 1:29–31) result in death. The problem, as C. E. B. Cranfield points out, is that "many things listed in vv. 29–31 could not conceivably carry a death penalty in any code." Cranfield therefore pursues a spiritual understanding of death, which is the "ultimate penalty of sin."[26] Other scholars connect this spiritual understanding to the death with which God threatened the first humans in paradise: "In the day that you eat of it you shall die" (Gen 2:17).[27]

---

[24] For example, Kuss 1963, 73; Cranfield 1975, 115; Wilckens 1978, 133–35; Dunn 1988, 57–58; Moo 1996, 124.
[25] Pohlenz 1949, 71–72.
[26] Cranfield 1975, 134.
[27] Dunn 1988, 69, 76; Moo 1996, 121.

In this interpretation, "the decree" that Paul mentions is either the Torah or God's threat in the story of the fall. This is, however, far from evident. Paul is speaking not of the fall, but of Gentile lapse after the fall. If we believe Paul, death has been the lot of humankind since Adam (Rom 5:12). Thus, death as a result of vices cannot be the death caused by the fall. What, then, would death mean?[28]

The problem with earlier studies on Rom 1 is that Stoicism usually is seen as delivering unconnected excerpts in the story line. Only recently has Engberg-Pedersen noted that "there is much more of a theory involved in such a passage as 1:18–32 than is usually recognized."[29] Actually, the whole story of the Gentile lapse is colored by Stoic ideas. This context must be taken into account when interpreting God's decree in Rom 1:32. Romans 1, then, gives us the perspective to decide whether natural law in Rom 2:14 is the Stoic or the Platonic natural law.

Stanley Stowers has shown that in Rom 1 Paul utilizes a fixed Greco-Roman tradition of the myth of the primeval Golden Age and later degeneration. Philosophers used these myths to illustrate their philosophical ideas. For example, the Stoic Posidonius told a story of decline (Seneca, *Ep.* 90).[30] Jewish authors coined their own versions of these myths, by means of which they explained the origins of pagan cults and criticized them (e.g., Wis 13–14). Both elements are also present in Rom 1. The strong emphasis on fulfilling God's will in deeds fits well with Jewish covenantal nomism.[31] Paul's Jewish accent, however, does not rule out philosophical components in the narrative, since Jewish and philosophical components are combined. Next, we will look at some topics in Epictetus's philosophy in order to realize the philosophical components in Paul's narrative. Epictetus also provides us with a point of reference that enables us to determine whether these components are Stoic or Platonic.

3.2. Intellectual Lapse, Vice Lists, and Homosexuals in Epictetus

In *Diss.* 1.12.1–7, Epictetus presents five views of the existence of the gods and their relation to the universe. He ponders the five alternatives and concludes that the gods exist and that they take care of each person. The conclusion runs as follows:

> The good and excellent man must, therefore, inquire into all these things, before he subordinates his own will to him who administers the universe, precisely as good citizens submit to the law of the state [καθάπερ οἱ ἀγαθοὶ πολῖται τῷ νόμῳ τῆς πόλεως]. (*Diss.* 1.12.7)

The analogy between the state and the universe was a natural one for Epictetus to draw, since he understood the state as a miniature copy of the universe (*Diss.* 2.5.26). It is noteworthy that in the analogy God, "who administers the universe,"

---
[28] For the different interpretations of "death," see Kuss 1963, 55–56.
[29] Engberg-Pedersen 2000, 211.
[30] Stowers 1994, 85, 97–100.
[31] For the Jewish background of Rom 1–2, see, for example, Sanders 1983, 123–35.

is compared to state law. This betrays something of Stoic theology. Stoics usually are labeled as pantheists who saw God or the gods as an impersonal power or law of the universe. But this is not exactly true, as Keimpe Algra has recently noted. There were monotheistic and polytheistic elements in Stoic theology,[32] and this holds true for Epictetus.[33] At the same time, we should not deny that there are pantheistic elements in Stoic theology. These elements make understandable the equation between God and the law of the universe.

In accordance with the pantheistic elements of Stoic theology, Epictetus thought that God is omnipresent in the universe. This becomes clear when he ridicules the desire to see a statue of Zeus in Olympia: "Yet when there is no need to travel at all, but where Zeus is already, and is present in his works [πάρεστιν τοῖς ἔργοις], will you not yearn to behold these works and know them [θεάσασθαι καὶ κατανοῆσαι]?" (*Diss.* 1.6.24). People, however, need a comprehensive view of things and a sense of gratitude (τὸ εὐχάριστον) in order to come to the point of praising God (*Diss.* 1.6.1). Especially gratitude is often connected with theology in Epictetus's texts (e.g., *Diss.* 1.4.32; 1.12.32; 1.16.7).

It is reasonable that theology and ethics are closely connected, since God also constitutes the natural law. Where the existence of God is denied, all types of vices fill the void. Epictetus ironically praises the view that God, piety, and sanctity are lies told by legislators to restrain evildoers. What follows is the loss of righteousness, reverence, and family ties. "Well done," he sarcastically comments (*Diss.* 2.20.23-25). For Epictetus, the denial of God's existence is also a denial of God's moral law.

The decisive factor in Epictetus's ethics, as we saw in the previous section, is the theory of value. One should understand what is indifferent and what is not. The basic mistake is to revere and be in awe of something that is of no worth. A wrong judgment on the value of externals is followed by passions (πάθος), which the Stoics divided into four main categories: wrong desire (ἐπιθυμία), pleasure (ἡδονή), fear (φόβος), and grief (λύπη).[34] Keeping Paul in mind, we should make a note on wrong desire. We can say that the wrongness of a desire is defined by the wrong object of a desire. The wrong desire arises when we think that some external thing, which is always indifferent in Epictetus's philosophy, is good and therefore we begin to desire it. Thus, a wrong desire is a result of a wrong value judgment, which, in turn, is an intellectual operation. The origin of a wrong desire (as well as of all other passions) is an intellectual lapse.

For Epictetus, passions are mental vices that contain their own punishments. This becomes clear in his vice lists. In *Diss.* 3.24, for example, Epictetus reproaches one of his students for homesickness when he claims that it is pleasurable to be at home. Pleasure is one of the main categories of the passions. Epictetus thus labels the student as an adherent of a philosophy of pleasure—that is, an adherent of the

---

[32] Algra 2003, 165-67.
[33] Bonhöffer 1894, 80; Long 2002, 153-56.
[34] For passions in Stoicism, see, for example, Nussbaum 1994, 386; Brennan 1998, 30-31.

Epicureans (paragraph 37). Epictetus concludes that the student only pretends to be a Stoic, and that his punishment will be just as severe as that of those who falsely claim to be Roman citizens (paragraph 41). Indeed, this implies that the punishment could be death in the worst case (Suetonius, *Claud.* 25). Then Epictetus continues with a list of vices that are comparable to this severe punishment.

> The divine and mighty and inescapable law is the law which exacts the greatest penalties from those who are guilty of the greatest offences. Now what are its terms? "Let him who makes pretence to things which in no wise concern him be a braggart, let him be a vainglorious man; let him who disobeys the divine governance be abject, be a slave, suffer grief, envy, pity,—in a word, be miserable and lament." (*Diss.* 3.24.42–43)

The student pretends to be a Stoic and thus becomes a braggart and a vainglorious man. In a word, the punishment for a wrong deed is that one becomes a wrongdoer.[35] Moreover, when thinking that home is something good, the student has disobeyed the divine governance of which we should be content instead of yearning after things that we do not have. Yearning is a mental state that inescapably contains painful passions that also serve as punishments. This inescapable punishment can also be expressed in terms of wrath: "Let us obey God, that we rest not under His wrath [μὴ θεοχόλωτοι ὦμεν]" (*Diss.* 3.1.37; cf. 2.8.14; 3.22.2). Wrath denotes the punishments, and it should not be taken literally as though God felt it. It would be an impious idea for a Stoic that God is wrathful, since wrath is a passion in Stoic philosophy.[36]

Epictetus's vice lists contain mainly passions, but the lists are by no means strict and systematic, which can be seen when they are compared to some other Stoic lists (*SVF* 3.412–416 [Chrysippus]). For example, lamentation in *Diss.* 3.24.43 is not a passion but rather a wrong deed in Epictetus's philosophy. This shift from passions to wrong deeds is understandable because the former generate the latter. A smooth shift from passions to deeds should not blur the basic distinction between the intellectual stage and that of deeds. Epictetus programmatically distinguishes between the two. The intellectual stage has to do with value judgments and passions, while at the stage of deeds one can distinguish between a wrong deed (παρὰ τὸ καθῆκον) and a right deed (καθῆκον).[37] Actually, Epictetus also distinguished a third stage, that of right and wrong knowledge, but it has only minor relevance for the comparison with Paul, and so I leave it aside.[38]

What, then, gives us guidelines for right judgments and right deeds? Nature. It is well known that the Stoics invoked the natural law, though the idea was not exclusively Stoic. "We must do what nature demands," says Epictetus, and "observe what is in accordance with nature [τὸ κατὰ φύσιν]" (*Diss.* 1.26.1–2). In *Diss.*

---

[35] Bonhöffer 1894, 9; 1911, 310.
[36] Bonhöffer 1911, 248–49. Cf. Cicero, *Off.* 3.102.
[37] The Stoics also operated with a κατόρθωμα, which is a right deed done out of a purely right conviction (Rist 1969, 97–111; Forschner 1995, 196–211). Epictetus was, however, quite free with his terminology, and he used καθῆκον in the sense of κατόρθωμα (Bonhöffer 1894, 198–200).
[38] For the three stages, see, for example, Dobbin 1998, 92–94; Long 2002, 112–18.

2.10, Epictetus says that a citizen should understand "the constitution of nature" (παρακολούθουν τῇ φυσικῇ κατασκευῇ) in order to live properly (paragraph 4). Epictetus continues a little later that in a homosexual relationship both the passive and the active partner destroy their own manhood (paragraph 17). In this case, the moral guideline is manhood, namely, the nature of a man. In *Diss.* 1.6.9, Epictetus presents the heterosexual relationship as a piece of evidence for the existence of providence. This contains an idea of manhood and womanhood that functions as a moral guideline for sexual relations.

> And the male and the female [τὸ δ'ἄρρεν καὶ τὸ θῆλυ], and the appetite [ἡ προθυμία] of each for intercourse with the other, and the faculty which makes use of the organs which have been constructed for this purpose, do these things not reveal their artificer either? (*Diss.* 1.6.9 [translation slightly revised])

Epictetus seeks to show that several components cohere so harmoniously that providence must exist. There are two sexes, "the faculty which makes use of the organs," the construction of the "organs" and sexual appetite. Besides the physical characteristics, there is also a mental factor, namely, sexual appetite. It is not a wrong desire (ἐπιθυμία), but a natural desire (προθυμία). Whereas a wrong desire is based on a voluntary but mistaken value judgment, a natural desire is involuntary and good.[39]

Epictetus's praise of the heterosexual relationship makes it evident why he condemned the homosexual one. The difference between the sexes and natural desire are without purpose in a homosexual relationship. In this light, homosexual desire has a wrong object, and it is not a good and natural προθυμία but rather an unnatural ἐπιθυμία. Thus, in Epictetus's philosophy, homosexual practice is not "in accordance with nature" (κατὰ φύσιν). Like any vice, homosexual practice contains its own punishment: it destroys manhood in the sense that it is deprived of a purpose.

For Epictetus, the origin of transgression is at the mental stage. Transgressing people have lost their grateful attitude toward God, who can be grasped as a natural part of the universe. They have also made wrong value judgments that are concretized at the stage of deeds. God's law punishes mental lapse by painful passions, and wrong deeds stigmatize people as wrongdoers. According to Epictetus, punishment thus is part of the vices themselves.

3.3. Paul's Stoic Narrative of Gentile Lapse

Natural theology was already known in the Jewish Scriptures (e.g., Pss 19; 29), which speak of God's voice in nature. Paul's natural theology is based on seeing, which is central in Greek philosophical views (Xenophon, *Mem.* 1.4; 4.3; Plato, *Tim.* 47B–C). Plato understood seeing in a metaphorical sense, since God belongs

---

[39] For the Stoic and Epictetan terminology, see Bonhöffer 1890, 233–49, 278–84; Sorabji 2000, 52–53.

to the invisible world of ideas. Ideas are understood, not seen in the world (Plato, *Rep.* VI.507B). Paul speaks about seeing the invisible (Rom 1:20), which, however, is only partly a metaphor. For he thinks that God's invisible attributes are seen through his works (τοῖς ποιήμασιν)—that is, through the world.[40] This means that God's attributes are somehow present in the universe. Concrete seeing with understanding (νοούμενα) can grasp God.

From such a perspective, Paul's natural theology resonates strongly with Stoic theology.[41] According to Epictetus, Zeus is present in his works and can be seen and understood (*Diss.* 1.6.24). In contrast to Plato, the theologies of Paul and Epictetus are not based only on understanding but also presuppose concrete seeing. It is also interesting that Paul connects gratitude with the right understanding of God's existence (Rom 1:21). This is a connection that we have already encountered in Epictetus's texts.

Epictetus understood God's wrath not literally but rather as a metaphor for punishments that are included in the vices. It is very easy to get a similar impression of God's wrath in Rom 1:18, as Cranfield points out.[42] God's wrath took place when God abandoned the Gentiles. It is difficult to imagine why God would have given them up, except because of the wrath they incurred by their own idolatry and vices. The abandonment means that God's wrath becomes concrete in the idolatry and vices in and of themselves. Paul affirms this openly by condemning male homosexuals who "received in their own persons [ἐν ἑαυτοῖς] the due penalty for their error" (Rom 1:27). "In their own persons" expresses reciprocality that is also in other respects present in Paul's sentence on penalty.[43] It remains unclear, however, what the exact penalty is; possibly it is the degrading of bodies (Rom 1:24). However, what is clear is that the penalty is included in the vice itself, and this idea is also reflected in Epictetus.

There is no narrative of mass decline in Epictetus's texts. Paul's narrative, however, has one central feature that was important to Epictetus as well: a division between a lapse at the mental stage and at that of deeds. This becomes clear in the process of decline that is described three times (Rom 1:21–24, 25–27, 28–32). The first description is the most complete, and it presents two stages both in the theological and ethical fields. A theological lapse occurs when the right understanding of God's existence is darkened (vv. 21–22). This, then, results in idolatrous deeds (v. 23). The theological lapse is followed by an ethical one. God gives over Gentiles to their lusts, which result in shameful deeds (v. 24). The second description

---

[40] Balz and Schneider 1991, 226 (s.v. καθοράω).

[41] Fridrichsen 1994; *pace* Pohlenz (1949, 71–72), who understands Paul in the Platonic sense.

[42] Cranfield 1975, 109–11. Surprisingly, Cranfield rejects this interpretation in favor of his idea of the gospel of wrath, which would be the counterpart to the gospel of righteousness in the previous verses. There is, however, no indication of any such gospel of wrath, and Dunn (1988, 54–55) rightly accepts the interpretation rejected by Cranfield.

[43] The expression cannot mean "personally," since that is self-evident: penalty cannot be suffered impersonally. The reflexive pronoun can be understood in terms of reciprocality. For other reciprocal elements in the sentence, see Dunn 1988, 65.

contains idolatrous deeds (v. 25), leading the Gentiles to passions (v. 26) and shameful deeds (vv. 26–27), while the third description contains an intellectual lapse in theology (v. 28), leading them to a debased mind (v. 28) and shameful deeds (vv. 28–31).

It is noteworthy that Paul correlates lusts and passions with the debased mind. In the first and the second descriptions, shameful deeds follow lusts or passions; in the third description, these deeds follow the debased mind. Paul seems to think, like Epictetus, that lusts and passions are intellectual fallacies. This is important to note, and it points to the fact that Paul's philosophical background is Stoic, not Platonic. In Platonic anthropology, passions and lusts have their origin in the lowest part of the human soul. Accordingly, the ethical question is how much one can or should resist these impulses of the lowest part (Plato, *Rep.* IV.434D–441C; *Phaedr.* 253C–256D). For mainstream Stoics such as Epictetus, there is only one part in the soul. Passions and lusts are fallacies of the intellectual calculation.[44] Paul seems to follow the Stoic line rather than the Platonic one. In Rom 1, he betrays no hint of separate parts in the human soul.[45]

Paul's list of vices (Rom 1:29–31) contains mainly deeds, not mental vices, which play the main role in Epictetus's lists.[46] This difference, however, does not mean that Paul's list is philosophically deviant from Epictetus's Stoicism. Vis-à-vis Epictetus's point of view, Paul rightly places his list in the division between the stages of intellectual operations and of deeds. The list is clearly meant to be a list of deeds, as is indicated by the verbs ποιέω and πράσσω (vv. 28, 32). Moreover, Paul introduces the list of vices with the words "things that should not be done" (τὰ μὴ καθήκοντα). The word καθῆκον denoted appropriate deeds also in Epictetus's Stoic philosophy. It is true that the word is not distinctively Stoic (cf., e.g., Exod 5:13; 36:1 LXX), and that Paul's negation is technically wrong from the Stoic point of view.[47] However, although the right negation was παρὰ τὸ καθῆκον, Epictetus's teacher Musonius Rufus used exactly the same formula as Paul (Fragment 32).[48] If a professional Stoic philosopher could do this, why not a Christian apostle? We have seen that Paul's narrative of decline is structured by Stoic philosophy, and this context makes it quite probable that τὰ μὴ καθήκοντα indicates Stoic influence on Paul.

Stoic influence is also to be seen in the way that Paul condemns homosexual practice, which, as he says, is contrary to nature. However, it was not the Stoics but rather Plato who first introduced nature as a basis for criticism against homosexual conduct (*Leg.* 636C; 836C–841D). What sets the Stoics apart from the views of Plato is not the use of nature as an ethical principle but rather their understanding of nature. According to Plato, homosexual practice goes beyond the limits of natural pleasure: people fall into homosexual deeds because of their incapacity to restrain pleasure (*Leg.* 636C). This view is based upon Plato's psychological theory

---

[44] Bonhöffer 1890, 86–94; Gill 1983, 138–39; Long 2002, 163–66.
[45] The Stoic psychology becomes even clearer in Rom 7. See Huttunen 2005.
[46] See Schmithals 1988, 81.
[47] Bonhöffer 1911, 157–58.
[48] Fragment 32 = Lutz 1957, 133.

of the lower part of the human soul. Epictetus's criticism of homosexuals is not based on this kind of psychology. For him, the human soul is unified, and every passion (πάθος) and every wrong desire (ἐπιθυμία) is a mistaken value judgment. Epictetus thinks that those who have homosexual desires have valued things that should not be valued. In other words, they have changed a right sexual object for a wrong one.

It is easy to see that a change of sexual object is a key motif in Paul's criticism. Dishonorable passion (πάθος) and lusts (ἐπιθυμίαι) are concretized in the change of the heterosexual relationship in favor of the homosexual one. This idea of change links Paul to the Stoic tradition. Therefore, Paul's "nature" should also be interpreted in the Stoic manner. It is interesting that Paul and Epictetus present physical characteristics as guidelines for natural sex. Both speak of "male" and "female" (ἡ θήλεια, ὁ ἄρσην and τὸ ἄρρεν, τὸ θῆλυ) instead of using the more common terms "man" and "woman." "Male" and "female" emphasize the particular characteristics of the sexes, including their physical features.[49] The homosexual practice, thus, seems to be something that is contrary to bodily nature, as Paul claims that Gentiles degrade their bodies (Rom 1:24). Epictetus claims that we should act in full understanding of the constitution of nature (παρακολούθουν τῇ φυσικῇ κατασκευῇ) (Diss. 2.10.4). No doubt, the natural constitution also covers "the organs which have been constructed" (δύναμις ἡ χρηστικὴ τοῖς μορίοις τοῖς κατασκευομένοις) for sex (Diss. 1.6.9). This is quite close to what Paul meant by natural sex (ἡ φυσικὴ χρῆσις) (Rom 1:26–27).

Romans 1 contains so many Stoic features and its ideological structure is so deeply Stoic that we must ask whether "God's decree," mentioned in Rom 1:32, also bears Stoic connotations. We must again note that there is a Stoic division between the intellectual lapse and the lapse of deeds. The aorist participle ἐπιγνόντες shows that Gentiles knew God's decree before they committed vices. This temporal sequence is the same as earlier in Rom 1, where it mirrored the Stoic theory of a mistaken intellectual calculation as an origin of vice. In this light, we must conclude that Paul's idea was that Gentiles once knew God's decree and their conduct was sound, but then they lost their knowledge of this decree, vicious conduct commenced, and, according to Paul, it still continues.

What, then, is the content of God's decree in Paul's theology? This content is expressed by a clause beginning with ὅτι: those who commit the vices listed in earlier verses and other similar vices (τοιαῦτα) deserve death. We have seen at the beginning of this section that this type of content makes it difficult to identify "God's decree" with the Torah or with any other existing code. We also saw that the decree is not the same threat of death as in the story of the fall, since Paul's narrative of decline is no variant of this biblical story.

In Rom 1, Paul claims that vices somehow contain God's punishments. This is also a Stoic idea. It is quite clear that a conduct that is "full of murder" (Rom 1:29) involves death, but this conclusion is less clear as regards many other vices in the list. How, for example, do foolishness and faithlessness (Rom 1:31) involve death?

---
[49] Kuss 1963, 50; Cranfield 1975, 125; Dunn 1988, 64.

Epictetus's text, however, shows us a way out. In *Diss.* 3.24.41–43, he claims that those who pretend to be Stoics are punished similarly to those who pretend to be citizens, namely, by death at worst. This is clearly an exaggeration. The following list of vices includes such punishments as to be a braggart, to be a vainglorious person, to be abject, to be a slave, and so forth. There is no hint of death. Paul seems to make a similar exaggeration. He claims that all vices involve their own punishments, but he implies that these punishments are more lenient than the full condemnation of death. God's wrath appears in lusts and passions, in bodies that people themselves degrade, and in the chaotic flood of people's vices. Death is an exaggeration. A similar exaggeration is present in Gal 5:15, where Paul claims that the Galatian Christians should keep the love command as their guideline to Christian life. He warns that fighting would result in their entire destruction. The imagery Paul uses is that of animal fights. Read literally (εἰ + present tense), it gives a real possibility that Galatians would kill each other like animals in life-and-death fights. This is, however, a clear exaggeration,[50] and this also seems to be the case in Rom 1:32.

Finally, Paul's argumentation poses the question how Gentiles knew of God's decree before they lost this knowledge. The answer lies ready at hand. The whole narrative of decline claims that the origin of all iniquity is the theological lapse: the vices emerged as the Gentiles ceased to honor God. We must conclude that the knowledge of God is somehow connected with the knowledge of God's will. This is also indicated by a parallel between Rom 1:28 and 1:32. In Rom 1:28, Paul claims that the theological lapse of the Gentiles happened because they "did not see fit to acknowledge [ἔχειν ἐν ἐπιγνώσει] God"; in Rom 1:32, he says that Gentiles knew (ἐπιγνόντες) God's decree before (aorist participle) they started to commit vices. Those who knew God also knew God's decree.

In the light of Stoic theology, it is quite understandable that the knowledge of God is at the same time knowledge of God's law. We saw that Epictetus equated God and the law of the universe. The idea is close to pantheism, though the Stoics were not unequivocally pantheists. Because Paul exploited this tradition, his words also acquired a kind of pantheistic ring. This does not mean that Paul was a pantheist, but that his words betray the Stoic tradition that he used.

In the Stoic tradition, knowledge of God and God's law is reached in the very same way, namely, by observing the universe and human nature. It is just this kind of natural theology that Paul presumes as a background to knowledge of God. It is also reasonable to think that Paul even understood God's decree as being part of the universe and thus also present in human nature. Paul's criticism of homosexual practice points in just this direction: the standard of sexual morality is already expressed in concrete nature, and nature is represented in a Stoic, not a Platonic, manner. As a result, we can say that God's decree seems to be something quite close to Stoic natural law. A natural understanding of law is explicitly mentioned in Rom 2:14, and in the light of Rom 1, what Paul has in mind is most probably Stoic natural law.

---

[50] Betz 1979, 267–68; Longenecker 1990, 244.

4. Conclusion

I have discussed two passages, 1 Cor 7 and Rom 1, in which an approach from the Stoic point of view is decisive. I have argued that we neglect something very important if we do not see how essentially Stoic ideas form the background of Paul's thinking in these passages. In 1 Cor 7, it seems very probable that the commandments of God contain the Stoic idea that God has commanded a certain social position for every person, and that this social position should be maintained, but not because of the value of those positions. In themselves, these positions are indifferent and contain no value. The positions should be maintained because one is obliged to use things that are indifferent in themselves. The way the things are used is important, not the things that are used. Epictetus can also formulate this duty to use indifferent things in theological terms: one's social position should be maintained because God has commanded it. Paul utilizes this theological formulation, but clearly he presupposes the philosophical background, namely, the Stoic theory of value. The relationship between the commandments of God and the Torah remains unclear in Paul. Possibly, he thinks that the Stoic ideas that he presents can somehow be drawn from the Torah. If this is the case, he provides a very philosophical interpretation of the Scriptures. What is clear is the Stoic content of the commandments.

In 1 Cor 7:19, Stoicism explains Paul's way of speaking about "the commandments of God" much better than distinctive Jewish categories do. Rom 1:18–32, in turn, has clear ties with Jewish covenantal nomism. In a traditional Jewish way, the passage presents Gentiles and their idolatry as being opposite to the chosen people and their piety. That this piety is questioned in Rom 2 is another matter. Romans 2 does not change the fact that in Rom 1 Paul draws a very traditional, Jewish picture of Gentiles. Despite the ties with covenantal nomism, Rom 1 also has clear ties with Stoicism. The narrative of decline cannot be rightly understood without the knowledge of Stoic philosophical principles—for example, natural theology and ethics, the intellect/deeds division, and the idea that vices involve their own punishments. In this context, it is difficult to understand God's decree in Rom 1:32 as a real or a spiritual sentence of death. The death of which the decree speaks is more easily understood as a rhetorical exaggeration of the more lenient punishments involved in vices.

Romans 1 shows that the Stoic features do not rule out covenantal nomism, but the two can easily be present, side by side. "Paul represented a fascinating hybrid of Judaism and Stoicism," Bruce Chilton claims.[51] The question is not whether the background of Paul's thinking is either Stoicism or covenantal nomism. It is, rather, one of degree: how much did Paul depend upon Stoicism, and to what extent did he think in categories of covenantal nomism? The latter part of his thinking has been studied for decades. Now it may be time to explore more fully the role of Stoicism.

---

[51] Chilton 2004, 216.

Bibliography

Algra, K. 2003. "Stoic Theology." Pages 153–78 in *The Cambridge Companion to the Stoics.* Edited by B. Inwood. Cambridge: Cambridge University Press.
Balz, H., and G. Schneider, eds. 1991. *Exegetical Dictionary of the New Testament.* Vol. 2. Grand Rapids: Eerdmans.
Bartchy, S. S. 1973. *ΜΑΛΛΟΝ ΧΡΗΣΑΙ: First-Century Slavery and the Interpretation of 1 Corinthians 7:21.* Society of Biblical Literature Dissertation Series 11. Missoula, Mont.: Society of Biblical Literature.
Betz, H. D. 1979. *A Commentary on Paul's Letter to the Churches in Galatia.* Hermeneia. Philadelphia: Fortress.
Bonhöffer, A. 1890. *Epictet und die Stoa: Untersuchungen zur stoischen Philosophie.* Stuttgart: Enke.
———. 1894. *Die Ethik des Stoikers Epictet: Anhang: Exkurse über einige wichtige Punkte der stoischen Ethik.* Stuttgart: Enke.
———. 1911. *Epiktet und das Neue Testament.* Religionsgeschichtliche Versuche und Vorarbeiten 10. Gießen: Töpelmann.
Brennan, T. 1998. "The Old Stoic Theory of Emotions." Pages 21–70 in *The Emotions in Hellenistic Philosophy.* Edited by J. Sihvola and T. Engberg-Pedersen. New Synthese Historical Library 46. Dordrecht: Kluwer.
Bultmann, R. 1984. *Der Stil der paulinischen Predigt und die kynisch-stoische Diatribe.* Forschungen zur Religion und Literatur des Alten und Neuen Testaments 13. Göttingen: Vandenhoeck & Ruprecht.
Chilton, B. 2004. *Rabbi Paul: An Intellectual Biography.* New York: Doubleday.
Cranfield, C. E. B. 1975. *A Critical and Exegetical Commentary on the Epistle to the Romans.* Vol. 2. International Critical Commentary. Edinburgh: T & T Clark.
Dautzenberg, G. 2001. "Freiheit im hellenistischen Kontext." Pages 57–81 in *Der neue Mensch in Christus: Hellenistische Anthropologie und Ethik im Neuen Testament.* Edited by J. Beutler. Quaestiones disputatae 190. Freiburg: Herder.
Deming, W. 1995. *Paul on Marriage and Celibacy: The Hellenistic Backround of 1 Corinthians 7.* Society for New Testament Studies Monograph Series 83. Cambridge: Cambridge University Press.
Dobbin, R. F. 1998. *Epictetus: Discourses, Book I.* Clarendon Late Ancient Philosophers. Oxford: Clarendon Press.
Downing, F. G. 1998. *Cynics, Paul, and the Pauline Churches: Cynics and Christian Origins II.* London: Routledge.
Dunn, J. D. G. 1988. *Romans 1–8.* Word Biblical Commentary 38A. Dallas: Word Books.
Engberg-Pedersen, T. 2000. *Paul and the Stoics.* Edinburgh: T & T Clark.
Forschner, M. 1995. *Die Stoische Ethik: Über den Zusammenhang von Natur-, Sprach- und Moralphilosophie im altstoischen System.* Darmstadt: Wissenschaftliche Buchgesellschaft.
Fridrichsen, A. 1994. *Exegetical Writings: A Selection.* Edited by C. C. Caragounis and T. Fornberg. Wissenschaftliche Untersuchungen zum Neuen Testament 76. Tübingen: Mohr Siebeck.

Gill, C. 1983. "Did Chrysippus Understand Medea?" *Phronesis* 28:136–49.
Glad, C. E. 1995. *Paul and Philodemus: Adaptability in Epicurean and Early Christian Psychagogy.* Supplements to Novum Testamentum 81. Leiden: Brill.
Huttunen, N. 2005. "The Human Contradiction: Epictetus and Romans 7." Pages 324–33 in *Lux Humana, Lux Aeterna: Essays on Biblical and Related Themes in Honour of Lars Aejmelaeus.* Edited by A. Mustakallio et al. Publications of the Finnish Exegetical Society 89. Göttingen: Vandenhoeck & Ruprecht.
———. 2007. "Stoalaisfilosofi Epiktetoksen näkemys kristityistä." *Teologinen aikakauskirja* 112:387–403.
———. 2009. *Paul and Epictetus on Law: A Comparison.* Library of New Testament Studies 405. London: T & T Clark.
Jones, F. S. 1987. *"Freiheit" in den Briefen des Apostels Paulus: Eine historische, exegetische und religionsgeschichtliche Studie.* Göttinger Theologische Arbeiten 34. Göttingen: Vandenhoeck & Ruprecht.
Kuss, O. 1963. *Der Römerbrief.* Vol. 1. 2nd ed. Regensburg: Pustet.
Lang, F. 1986. *Die Briefe an die Korinther.* Das Neue Testament Deutsch 7. Göttingen: Vandenhoeck & Ruprecht.
Lindemann, A. 2000. *Der erste Korintherbrief.* Handbuch zum Neuen Testament 9/1. Tübingen: Mohr Siebeck.
Long, A. A. 2002. *Epictetus: A Stoic and Socratic Guide to Life.* Oxford: Clarendon Press.
Longenecker, R. N. 1990. *Galatians.* Word Biblical Commentary 41. Dallas: Word Books.
Lutz, C. E. 1947. "Musonius Rufus: 'The Roman Socrates.'" *Yale Classical Studies* 10:1–147.
Malherbe, A. J. 1989. *Paul and the Popular Philosophers.* Minneapolis: Fortress.
Martin, D. B. 1990. *Slavery as Salvation: The Metaphor of Slavery in Pauline Christianity.* New Haven: Yale University Press.
———. 1995. *The Corinthian Body.* New Haven: Yale University Press.
Moo, D. J. 1996. *The Epistle to the Romans.* New International Commentary on the New Testament. Grand Rapids: Eerdmans.
Nussbaum, M. C. 1994. *The Therapy of Desire: Theory and Practice in Hellenistic Ethics.* Martin Classical Lectures, New Series 2. Princeton, N.J.: Princeton University Press.
Oldfather, W. A. 1995–1996. *Epictetus: The Discourses as Reported by Arrian, the Manual, and Fragments.* 2 vols. Loeb Classical Library. Cambridge, Mass.: Harvard University Press.
Plank, K. A. 1987. *Paul and the Irony of Affliction.* Society of Biblical Literature Semeia Studies. Atlanta: Scholars Press.
Pohlenz, M. 1948. *Die Stoa: Geschichte einer geistigen Bewegung.* Vol. 1. Göttingen: Vandenhoeck & Ruprecht.
———. 1949. "Paulus und die Stoa." *Zeitschrift für die Neutestamentliche Wissenschaft* 42:69–104.
Räisänen, H. 1987. *Paul and the Law.* 2nd ed. Wissenschaftliche Untersuchungen zum Neuen Testament 29. Tübingen: Mohr Siebeck.

———. 1992. *Jesus, Paul and Torah: Collected Essays.* Translated by D. E. Orton. Journal for the Study of the New Testament: Supplement Series 43. Sheffield: JSOT Press.
Rengstorf, K. H. 1974. "ὑπηρέτης κτλ." Pages 530–44 in vol. 8 of *Theological Dictionary of the New Testament.* Edited by G. Kittel et al. Grand Rapids: Eerdmans.
Rist, J. M. 1969. *Stoic Philosophy,* Cambridge: Cambridge University Press.
Sanders, E. P. 1977. *Paul and Palestinian Judaism: A Comparison of Patterns of Religion.* London: SCM Press.
———. 1983. *Paul, the Law, and the Jewish People.* Philadelphia: Fortress.
Schmithals, W. 1988. *Der Römerbrief: Ein Kommentar.* Gütersloh: Mohn.
Schrage, W. 1995. *Der Erste Brief an die Korinther.* Vol. 2. Evangelisch-katholischer Kommentar zum Neuen Testament 7/2. Solothurn: Benziger; Neukirchen-Vluyn: Neukirchener Verlag.
Seeley, D. 1990. *The Noble Death: Graeco-Roman Martyrology and Paul's Concept of Salvation.* Journal for the Study of the New Testament: Supplement Series 28. Sheffield: JSOT Press.
Sharp, D. S. 1914. *Epictetus and the New Testament.* London: Kelly.
Sorabji, R. 2000. *Emotion and Peace of Mind: From Stoic Agitation to Christian Temptation.* Oxford: Oxford University Press.
Spanneut, M. 1962. "Epiktet." Pages 599–681 in vol. 5 of *Reallexikon für Antike und Christentum.* Edited by T. Klauser et al. Stuttgart: Hiersemann.
Stowers, S. K. 1988. "The Diatribe." Pages 71–83 in *Greco-Roman Literature and the New Testament: Selected Forms and Genres.* Edited by D. E. Aune. Society of Biblical Literature Sources for Biblical Study 21. Atlanta: Scholars Press.
———. 1994. *A Rereading of Romans: Justice, Jews, and Gentiles.* New Haven: Yale University Press.
Vollenweider, S. 1989. *Freiheit als neue Schöpfung: Eine Untersuchung zur Eleutheria bei Paulus und in seiner Umwelt.* Forschungen zur Religion und Literatur des Alten und Neuen Testaments 147. Göttingen: Vandenhoeck & Ruprecht.
Weber, R. 2000. *Das Gesetz im hellenistischen Judentum: Studien zum Verständnis und zur Funktion der Thora von Demetrios bis Pseudo-Phokylides.* Arbeiten zur Religion und Geschichte des Urchristentums 10. Frankfurt am Main: Lang.
Westerholm, S. 2004. *Perspectives Old and New on Paul: The "Lutheran" Paul and His Critics.* Grand Rapids: Eerdmans.
Wilckens, U. 1978. *Der Brief an die Römer.* Evangelisch-katholischer Kommentar zum Neuen Testament 6/1. Zürich: Benziger.

4

JESUS THE TEACHER AND STOIC ETHICS IN THE GOSPEL OF MATTHEW

Stanley K. Stowers
Brown University

The author of the Gospel of Matthew did not identify himself as a Stoic, but that writer understood Stoic ethics and freely adapted elements of Stoic thought in creating his picture of Jesus the moral teacher. This holds especially for the so-called Sermon on the Mount, but it may apply more broadly. I have arrived at this conclusion by asking what is distinctive about Matthew's depiction of Jesus as a teacher of ethics. Scholarship on Christian ethics often has characterized it as a combination of the ethics of divine law and of virtue. If I am correct, this combination can be pushed back further than usually thought to the Gospel of Matthew.

It will be helpful to review what are taken as basic facts in Gospel studies and studies of the earliest traditions about Jesus. In the earliest sources, the only sources that precede and are not definitively shaped by the Roman destruction of the Judean temple and Jerusalem, one cannot even determine that Jesus was a teacher of ethics.[1] If Paul knew that Jesus was such a teacher, he does not use either the teachings or the idea that Jesus was a teacher of ethics, even though the teachings from the later Matthew and Luke would be very relevant and overlap with his own teachings. In the Gospel of John, Jesus teaches, but those teachings are about himself (e.g., "I am the light of the world" [John 8:12]), and there are no teachings that might be considered broadly moral teachings beyond the saying that his disciples should love one another (John 15:12). This brings us to Matthew's primary source, the

---

[1] Paul's letters do have two "commands of the Lord" (1 Cor 7:10; 9:14), but 1 Thess 4:15 and other considerations make it likely that these were prophetic commands of the risen Lord. Even if Paul is referring to the historical Jesus, the commands do not provide enough of a picture to determine that Jesus was a great teacher rather than one who had given a few pronouncements. Paul does not speak of Jesus as a "teacher" or of his "teaching." The command in 1 Cor 7:10 comes closest to being an ethical teaching, although this would be slim evidence for concluding that Jesus had been a teacher of ethics, were it our only information. The highly anachronistic "command" about preaching the gospel in 1 Cor 9:14 is only marginally "ethical" at best. One cannot rule out that Jesus' teachings about divorce in the Synoptic Gospels came from Paul's comment.

Gospel of Mark, which Matthew almost entirely reproduces as a basis for his own major additions and transformations. Mark presents Jesus as a teacher of mysterious teachings about the coming kingdom of God, a mystery so obscure that none of Jesus' disciples are able to understand it. Jesus in Mark is about as remote from a guide about how one ought to live day to day as one can imagine. Luke's and, above all, Matthew's idea that Jesus was centrally a great ethical teacher, offering definitive interpretation of Jewish Scripture, owes something, perhaps much, to their use of the sayings source Q. The question of what Q was and whether it preserves quite early materials is a set of issues that is best to bracket here. But clearly, the author of Matthew exploited Q in the process of developing its distinctive portrait of Jesus' moral teachings. Even with the debt to Q, however, what is distinctive about the ethical teachings of Jesus in Matthew clearly belongs to that writer and appears in additions to and reinterpretations of Q and Mark.

A "Stoic reading" of Matthew could easily be a monograph.[2] At the risk of being superficial, I will limit the study to a few of the most distinctive ideas: the idea of a universal ethic for individuals based on divine law; the demand for perfection; and the so-called criterion of "interiority" or "intention." If the logic of these notions does indeed have a Stoic inspiration, however, it will be difficult to isolate these from other moral concepts. Stoicism is and was famous for its systematic coherency, even if many critics charged that its central notions were counterintuitive and its demands impractical.[3]

Jesus' teachings in Matthew present themselves as an interpretation of Judean law that authoritatively reveals its true meaning. Stoic thought presented its ethical theory as the universal law of Zeus or God. I suggest that this conjunction of ethics and law in Stoic thought made it congenial for the writer of this Gospel to attribute his Stoically inflected teachings to Jesus the Judean sage. Although New Testament scholarship typically describes Stoicism as pantheistic, it was in fact a combination of theism and pantheism.[4] God is both the active organizing principle of the universe and the mind that is the author and administrator of each recreation of the universe after the dissolution of the former age.[5] Stoicism denied

---

[2] Erin Roberts is currently writing a dissertation at Brown University entitled "Anger, Emotion and Desire in the Gospel of Matthew," which will include consideration of Stoicism.

[3] Plutarch, *De Stoicorum repugnatiis (On Stoic Self-contradictions)*; Cicero, *Mur.* 61; Horace, *Epistulae* 1.1.106–108; *Satirae* 1.3.76–142; 2.3.40–46. To objections like Plutarch's and Cicero's that Stoic teachings contradicted common sense and experience, one might add charges that the Stoic teachings about the emotions would lead to bad consequences (e.g., Cicero, *Tusc.* 4.43–57) and charges that Stoic ideas were inhumane (e.g., Cicero, *Tusc.* 3.12–13). Lucian's *Hermotimus* seeks to make absurd the Stoic notion of progress. Finally, going back at least to the Academic Carneades was the charge that Stoicism took sensible doctrines and clothed them in extreme terminology that made them seem absurd (Cicero, *Fin.* 3.41; 4.20.72; 5.20, 74; *Tusc.* 5.32, 120).

[4] For good recent discussions of Stoic theology with bibliography, see Long 2002, 142–79; Algra 2003; Thom 2005.

[5] Matthew adopts at least elements of this Stoic doctrine in speaking of heaven and earth passing away (5:18; 24:35) and in using the technical Stoic term for the re-creation (παλιγγενεσία) in 19:28.

that God had a humanlike form, but it accommodated traditional Greek thought about Zeus and the gods as symbolic. My point is not that Matthew adopted Stoic conceptions of the divine, but only that there was enough similarity between Stoic and Judean conceptions—the latter being extremely diverse and untheorized—that a Judean thinker could find adapting some Stoic thought to his own purposes possible and congenial. And this is exactly what we find other Jewish writers doing, most notably Philo and the author of Wisdom of Solomon.

Chrysippus wrote a treatise, *On Law*, which begins with a paean to the law and speaks of it as right reason and the will of Zeus (Diogenes Laertius, *Vit. phil.* 7.87–88; *SVF* 1.555). Cleanthes' famous *Hymn to Zeus*, which a number of scholars have compared to the Lord's Prayer, speaks of Zeus as "first cause and ruler of nature, governing everything with your law."[6] Moreover, "it is right for all mortals to address you: for we have our origin in you, bearing a likeness to God." After praising God's kingly rational rule of the universe, the hymn turns to human rebellion: "This all mortals that are bad flee and avoid, the wretched, who though always desiring to acquire good things, neither see nor hear God's universal law, obeying which they could have a good life with understanding." Instead, these people pursue glory, wealth, and indulgence in pleasure (24–29). Cleanthes prays for Zeus to "deliver human beings from their destructive ignorance" (33). Replace "Zeus" with "the God of Abraham, Isaac, and Jacob," and Matthew agrees with all of this, including the emphasis on understanding. The law is a manifestation of divine wisdom, and Jesus an embodiment.[7]

The law that humans ought to follow in their actions and feelings, and that the sage always obeys, does not consist of a set code of specific laws like that of the laws of cities and peoples. Rather, obeying this law is following right reason in each circumstance of life as willed by Zeus.[8] So how might a Jewish writer relate Judean law to Stoic thought about divine law? One could do this by borrowing from Stoicism a structure that distinguished and related the common ordinary human law and morality manifested in particular societies from the conditions of character required for obeying those laws correctly. This distinction appears in the concepts of the καθήκοντα, variously understood as proper or natural functions, appropriate actions, the befitting, and so on, and the κατορθώματα, understood as right or perfect actions.[9] Everything that a sage does is an appropriate action and a perfect action, but non-sages, all of whom are wicked and fools, perform appropriate actions depending upon their degree of progress toward virtue (= wisdom). They never perform a perfect action. So, for example, the ordinary person and the sage might both perform exactly the same external act in honoring parents, but the action of the non-sage will be vicious and the action of the sage virtuous. The

---

[6] Translation, Thom 2005. On the hymn and the Lord's Prayer, see Thom 2001, 493–95.

[7] Much has been written on this. A standard is Suggs 1970, although he may have overstated his case.

[8] A now classic discussion of this Stoic theory is Inwood 1985.

[9] An appropriate action or proper function is a condition or behavior that is natural to a plant or animal and is rational in that sense, even if only the perfected human follows right reason. See Long and Sedley 1987, 1:359–68.

difference is that the sage performs the act from a virtuous or wise character. The act is thus qualitatively different. Merely performing the right action does not suffice for moral goodness and for obeying the commands of God. The right action must be performed in the right way, meaning with the right disposition of character that is wisdom.

Especially later Stoics and those of the Roman period emphasized that the καθήκοντα corresponded to what was commonly agreed upon across the laws and moral codes of human cultures. All the things that cultures agreed upon as actions and habits of good people were appropriate acts because that agreement reflected natural human moral development. Thus Cicero's *De officiis* (*officia* being his translation for καθήκοντα) is based on the Stoic Panaetius's *Concerning Appropriate Acts*, but highly adapted to Roman moral sensibilities and featuring *praecepta*, moral rules. *Praecepta* enjoin "appropriate actions." Both Philo and Paul know the term τὰ καθήκοντα and use the concept for moral teachings from the law such as indicated in the Ten Commandments.[10]

This, however, is not the whole story. Ultimately, there is only one way to know what is the right thing to do in a particular circumstance or what Zeus requires: consult a sage. According to circumstances, the sage might even go against what convention and local law deemed to be appropriate actions in order to perform an appropriate and perfect action. The sage's action, obedient to reason/Zeus, ultimately defines what constitutes a perfectly appropriate action in any particular circumstance.[11] On this view, moral authority requires a perfect moral expert. Only the sage, then, stands as an authoritative interpreter of these common norms, codes, and local laws. This made the sage into a rather formal concept for ethical thinking, since Stoics either doubted that a sage had ever lived or thought that maybe one or two had existed—perhaps Socrates, Heracles, or the earliest humans. Philo of Alexandria makes Moses into such an authority, a sage who embodies the law. I suggest that Matthew's Jesus, who, unlike the traditional Judean experts on the law, interprets the law with total authority and embodies God's own wisdom, is a figure shaped by the Stoic idea of the sage. Of course, there are also many non-Stoic elements in Matthew's Jesus, including the Jesus of Mark, whom Matthew had inherited and had to accommodate.[12]

Because Stoic ethics began with the idea of common ordinary morals natural to humans as a foundation for complete human development, Stoics used the language of "the perfect" and "perfection" when they talked about that full potential for humans. Archedemus (second century B.C.E.) even formulated the human end as "to perfect all appropriate actions in one's life."[13] Stoics defined the kind of action that a sage performed, a κατόρθωμα, as a perfectly appropriate action

---

[10] For example, Philo, *Cher.* 14–15; Rom 1:28.

[11] Cicero, *Leg.* 1.6.18; see Brennan 2005, 191–94.

[12] Some caution is due here. Stoicism and the figure of the sage were so pervasive in the eastern Mediterranean that in a more general way than the one for which I am arguing regarding Matthew, the idea of the sage was likely to have already shaped the picture of Jesus in Q and Mark.

[13] Diogenes Laertius, *Vit. phil.* 7.88.

(τέλειον καθῆκον).[14] Discussion of Matthew's use of perfection will also, I believe, clarify the Stoic conception.

Matthew 5:48 is a good place to begin: "Therefore you be [ἔσεσθε] perfect [τέλειοι] as your heavenly father is perfect [τέλειος]."[15] The idea that humans ought to be morally perfect and have a kind of perfection that they share with the divine is odd and at odds with Jewish traditions that posit a great difference between God and very fallible humans.[16] The Gospel may be playing on "You shall be holy, for I the LORD your God am holy" (Lev 19:2; cf. 20:26), but Matthew's concept of perfection is quite different from holiness.[17] More speculatively, the author may have been encouraged in the direction of a Stoic interpretation by taking Noah, Abraham, and Job as ancient Jewish sages because Scripture sets them apart by calling them blameless or perfect (*tāmîm*).[18] The contradiction to normal Jewish and, I would argue, human moral thought more generally in demanding perfection has often been seen as a puzzle. That this counterintuitiveness comes from an adaptation of Stoic theory is suggested by the structure of thought in much of the Sermon on the Mount.

What God requires for righteousness is not simply the performance of actions that in themselves are generally accepted as morally good, but rather that such actions be done with the right moral disposition that is the equivalent of doing God's will.[19] That in having the right disposition (based on wisdom) the sage was like God and imitating Zeus was basic to Stoic thought.[20] Stoicism had only two categories of people: sages, who were perfect, and non-sages, who were wicked and foolish. The actions of all but the sage are errors (ἁμαρτήματα [*SVF* 3.661]). According to Matt 7:24, those who do what Jesus teaches will become like a "wise man,"[21] a sage, whose good is indestructible. Matthew adds this statement as an explanation of the story of the builder taken from Q, which Luke (6:46–49) tells without the reference to the wise man. Jesus as depicted in the Matthean Sermon

---

[14] Diogenes Laertius, *Vit. phil.* 7.107; Arius Didymus in Stobaeus, *Anth.* 2.7.8 (= 2.85.13–86.4 W-H).

[15] I see no good reason for construing ἔσεσθε as an indicative rather than an imperative. Unless otherwise indicated, translations are my own.

[16] The "image of God" motif in Jewish traditions could conceivably be interpreted in a Stoic fashion with humans sharing God's reason.

[17] Olyan 2000, 15–27.

[18] "Noah was a righteous man. He was perfect in his generations. He walked with God" (Gen 6:9); "I am El Shadday. Walk before me and be perfect" (Gen 17:1); "That man was perfect and righteous and a fearer of God who turned away from evil" (Job 1:1).

[19] So, for instance, Matthew adds 7:21–23 to the following material (vv. 24–27) that it shares with Luke. What they share teaches the lesson that one must actually do what Jesus teaches, but vv. 21–23 add a different and more radical notion that even seemingly good actions, including miracles of the kingdom of God, are wicked unless they are a result of doing the will of God. But what could that be if not doing things that clearly are a result of God's power? They must also be done righteously, a matter of a particular quality of character. Not even the ability to perform a miracle guarantees righteousness.

[20] Cicero, *Leg.* 58–59; Epictetus, *Diss.* 3.14.11–13; see Thom 2005.

[21] The adjective is φρόνιμος, used by Stoic writers as a synonym for σοφός (*SVF* 3.157–158; Long 2002, 37).

on the Mount not only calls for perfection but also treats those whom he addresses with his teachings as wicked: "If you then who are evil [πονηροί] know how to give good gifts to your children, how much more will your Father in heaven give good things to those who ask him" (7:11). The next verse connects this perfection to the law: "In everything do to others as you would have them do to you; for this is the law and the prophets" (7:12).[22] But there are few who are virtuous: the wide road leads to destruction, and few make it on the hard road through the narrow gate (7:13). Earlier Jesus had said that he had come not to do away with the law, but rather to fulfill it (5:17–20). Every bit of it must be done. A person cannot enter the kingdom of heaven without possessing righteousness that "excessively exceeds" that of the recognized moral and religious exemplars, the scribes and the Pharisees (5:20). The pleonasm, I suggest, indicates that the righteousness of which Matthew speaks is to be understood qualitatively and in a way similar to virtue or wisdom in Stoicism. The scribes and the Pharisees can do everything that the law requires yet not be righteous. They merely seem to be righteous. Righteousness is a particular qualitative state of the soul.[23]

At first, the story of the rich young man in Matt 19:16–22 might seem to belie this conclusion: if the man just keeps one more commandment, he will be perfect. Acquiring perfection seems to be incremental:

> "Teacher, what good should I do so that I might have eternal life?" Jesus said to him, "Why do you ask me about the good? One is good. If you want to enter into life, keep the commandments." He said to him, "Which ones?" Jesus said, "You shall not kill; you shall not commit adultery; you shall not steal; you shall not witness falsely; honor your father and mother; and you shall love your neighbor as yourself." The young man said to him, "I have kept all of these things. What do I still lack?" Jesus said to him, "If you want to be perfect, go sell your possessions and give them to the poor, and you will have a treasure in the heavens, and come follow me." When the young man heard the reasoning [word/speech], he went away grieving because he had many possessions.

Matthew bases the story on Mark 10:17–31, but he shapes it according to his own agenda, including the addition of Jesus' words about becoming perfect and appending the commandment to love one's neighbor (Lev 19:18). In Mark, instead of

---

[22] The translation of 7:11–12 is from the NRSV.

[23] I am not arguing on narrowly philological grounds about the meaning of δικαιοσύνη ("righteousness"), but I believe that a study of the term would support my thesis of Matthew having a concept similar to virtue in Stoicism. I find Przybylski's conclusions highly anachronistic. He concludes (1980, 119–23) that righteousness is "a Jewish concept" that Matthew uses as a provisional transitional concept to be replaced by the "Christian concept" of the will of God. Three uses in the Sermon on the Mount (5:6, 10; 6:33) directly support my claim, as do 5:20; 6:1, which contrast genuine righteousness with false or seeming righteousness. The other two instances (3:15; 21:32) have John giving support to Jesus, who exemplifies righteousness (27:19). The case of δίκαιος ("righteous") is similar but a bit more complex. The fact that Mark uses the term twice and Matthew seventeen times is a witness to the importance of the concept for Matthew. The concepts are, of course, Jewish, and they are also Greek. Matthew certainly draws on Jewish discourses in using the terms. It is simply ideological to place the Jewish and the Greek into opposition here.

asking what the good is that he must do, the man (not a "young man") runs up, kneels before Jesus, and calls him "good teacher."[24] Jesus rebukes him and says that only God is good. The verse, together with the versions in Matthew and Luke, caused fits for theologians in the fourth and fifth centuries who were constructing the orthodox christological and trinitarian doctrines. But Matthew is unaware of any of these issues.

Rather, he has reshaped Mark in a way that echoes the structure of Stoic thought about value and moral development. A fragment preserved in Stobaeus makes a good point of departure for analysis: "Chrysippus says: 'The man who progresses to the furthest point performs all proper functions without exception and omits none. Yet his life,' he says, 'is not yet happy, but happiness supervenes on it when these intermediate actions acquire the additional properties of firmness and tenor and their own particular fixity'" (5.906.18–907.5).[25] The person who has made the furthest progress toward wisdom/happiness/virtue will be doing all of the appropriate actions, exactly the things and kinds of things that Jesus lists, and still not be wise, happy, or good. Jesus' call for the young man to give up his possessions is not a call to keep yet another commandment. There is no such commandment. Rather, it is like a Socratic bit of questioning. The challenge reveals that the young man does not possess the good/wisdom/happiness that Matthew calls "righteousness" even if he does all of the expected righteous acts.

A Stoic would analyze the situation like as follows. Outwardly, the young man does all of the things that a wise or righteous person does, but his system of values does not cohere into the qualitative whole (i.e., Chrysippus's firmness, tenor, and fixity). The man's constitution is so structured that he thinks that wealth is a good rather than an indifferent that the sage will skillfully deploy depending upon circumstances with virtues such as justice and love of others. The young man does not understand that if he loses or gives away the wealth, it will not affect his goodness, happiness, or wisdom.

Attention to Matthew's use of Mark shows the moral structure of the former's reshaping. Commentators assimilate Matthew's "One is good" to Mark's (and Luke's, following Mark) "No one is good except God." But why would Matthew, who is notorious for trying to explain and make Mark clear, change the unambiguous reference to God into "One is good" ("one" is εἷς, a masculine adjective)? Furthermore, Matthew changes the issue from one about Jesus being good to a question about the nature of good in a moral sense. The writer seems to be playing on the Socratic and philosophical idea of the good by introducing a reference to "the good" and by creating ambiguity. This ambiguity that could refer to both divine and human character makes sense for an author who thinks that humans ought to have a perfection like God's (Matt 5:48). I tentatively suggest that Matthew's reinterpretation of the story alludes to the Stoic doctrine of the unity of virtue.[26] The virtues entail each other, and one must have them all as a unity to

---

[24] Matthew's "young man" clearly seems also to be a play of contrast on "perfect" as in mature.

[25] *SVF* 3.510 (translation, Long and Sedley 1987).

[26] Perhaps the best discussion of the topic is Schofield 1984.

have virtue at all. For Stoics, there is no such thing as possessing some of the virtues and not others. Matthew's version of the story goes on to show that the young man does appropriate acts but not perfectly appropriate acts due to his lack of wisdom, indicated by false values regarding the good.

But why did Matthew add the love command? For his Stoically shaped interpretation to work, he must make clear reference to virtue or a virtue appropriate to the context. Matthew has made it clear in his larger narrative that for him love is the master virtue. In Stoic thought, the virtues add the adverbial element that is central to their ethic. Virtues are the moral skills of the sage. Honoring parents, being a monogamous husband, and having wealth are, for the Stoics, in the category of indifferents. Such things that constitute the appropriate acts have value and are to be sought, but they do not involve virtue (and the good) until the adverbial aspect is added. Acting as a child toward parents, acting as a husband, or using possessions involve virtue and perfectly appropriate acts when these things are done justly, courageously, wisely, lovingly, and so on.[27] The addition of the love command makes it clear that giving to the poor, if done lovingly, would entail the perfection of the young man's appropriate acts/keeping of the commandments. Then he would be a follower of Jesus.

If this Stoically inflected reading of Matthew makes sense, then it helps to explain the Gospel's so-called emphasis on intention or interiority that has puzzled and distinctively shaped Christian ethics throughout history. This tendency is clear and well known in the Beatitudes. Broad scholarly agreement holds that Luke follows Q, and that Matthew's dramatic changes and additions reflect its own preoccupations.[28] So Luke makes it clear that the blessing to come in the kingdom of God is pronounced on actual poor, hungry, and oppressed people (6:20–26). Matthew changes "blessed are you poor" to "blessed are the poor in spirit [πνεύματι]," meaning something like "those who know that they lack strength of pneumatic stuff."[29] Πνεῦμα, of course, plays a central role in Stoic thought.[30] Among other things, it is the active material of one's mind, soul, and character. Whether or not Matthew's πνεῦμα has a Stoic shaping, it is clear that the writer has shifted the blessing's meaning from referring to a class of people to a quality of character. Instead of blessing people who lack food, Matthew pronounces happiness in the kingdom on "those who hunger and thirst after righteousness." I have already suggested that righteousness, for Matthew, is something like virtue, for Stoics. Matthew also adds blessings for mercifulness, purity of heart, and peacemaking (5:7–9).[31] Luke's Jesus announces a mission directed at the poor and the oppressed. Matthew's Jesus teaches about a rigorous quality of character that is the goal of his ethic and that will characterize the winners in the future kingdom.

---

[27] For example, Diogenes Laertius, *Vit. phil.* 7.103; Seneca, *Ep.* 118.11. The adverb expresses what depends solely on the person's character, what is "up to one's self."

[28] Stanton 1992, 285–300.

[29] "Spirit" here is typically given what I take to be an anachronistic modern understanding as a reference to one's subjective interiority or essential self.

[30] Engberg-Pedersen 2006.

[31] Concepts for which there is arguably something similar in Stoicism.

Even more important for the moral thought of Christendom are Matthean teachings in negative formulation that have been taken on one extreme as indicating a radical asceticism and on the other as implying that the law is impossible to keep and that Jesus is cleverly abrogating it.³² To be angry at someone is as morally evil as murder (5:21–22) and to desire someone's wife sexually is as bad as, and equivalent to, the act of adultery (5:27–28). Thus soon-to-be president Jimmy Carter confessed that he had committed adultery many times.³³ But perhaps the teachings are better understood through the lens of Stoicism. Cato, representing the Stoic position in Cicero's *On Ends*, says,

> Whatever takes its start from wisdom must be immediately perfect in all of its parts. For in it is situated what we call "desirable." Just as it is wrong to betray one's country, to show violence to one's parents, to steal from temples, actions which consist in bringing about certain results, so even without any result it is wrong to fear, to show grief, or to be in a state of lust. As the latter are wrong not in their after-effects and consequences but immediately in their first steps, so those things which take their start from virtue are to be judged right from their first [moral psychological] undertaking and not by their accomplishment.³⁴

This ethic derives from a highly technical Stoic theory of action that resulted in making people morally responsible for their emotions and not just actions motivated by emotion (e.g., anger leading to murder). What matters ethically about any action—and Stoics treated emotions like actions—is the mental event that initiates the action. The mental event is a kind of assent that something is appropriate. For walking to be an action, as opposed to an accidental stumbling forward, it must involve assent to the impression that walking is appropriate at this moment.³⁵ Unlike in much thought in the Cartesian tradition, the mental event need not be, and was usually not thought to be, conscious. Stoics emphasized that the things to which people assented involved values (i.e., beliefs), and that most of the time these reflected one's habits of thought and dispositions—that is, character. Stoics analyzed anger as assent to the false belief that someone has caused you harm and the desire for revenge with an accompanying psychophysical upheaval.³⁶ If one held to the correct value that only one's virtue/character/righteousness was a good and that it could not be harmed by others, then one could not assent as in the case above and have anger. A Stoic inspiration makes good sense of Matthew's Jesus teaching that the moral error in anger and sexual desire are matters of initiating mental events and not simply the final actions. In a similar way, Matt 5:33–37 forbids oaths. The taking of oaths was one of the most important mercantile/economic, political and religious practices in antiquity. The reason given for the prohibition is that what

---

³² Allison 1999, 1–5.
³³ Scheer 1976, 86: "I've committed adultery in my heart many times."
³⁴ Cicero, *Fin.* 3.32 (translation, Long and Sedley 1987 [I have changed "concupiscence" to "lust" and added the words in the brackets]).
³⁵ I borrow the example from Graver 2007, 27.
³⁶ Thus, anger is a species of desire, desire for revenge. See Graver 2007, 56–57.

will happen in the future is beyond a person's control. One has control only over one's own character, whether it is truthful and trustworthy or not.[37]

It is important to understand Stoic thinking here in order to distinguish it from modern, often Kantian ethical theories that make morality depend upon the agent's intentions, and the appeal to good intentions sometimes in instances of ancient moral thinking. The point is not that the sage did not have the right intentions, but that the more restricted modern focus misses the larger point that the Stoics wanted to make. It is not that the sage needs to have thoughts about virtue or acting virtuously or altruistically or to will that the principle guiding one's action apply to all humans. Both a sage and a wicked person can borrow money from a friend with exactly the same intention to pay it back, but the sage acts virtuously and the non-sage with moral error. The sage will, of course, characteristically have altruistic thoughts and motivations, but the sage's character organized around the knowledge that virtue is the only good so as to choose and act skillfully in everyday life, not correct thoughts as an ethical subject, is what makes the difference.[38] For Matthew, I suspect that righteousness involves a character that is constituted by total commitment and obedience to God and his law in a way that is similar to the Stoic conception. Perhaps even closer to Stoic formulation, Matthew holds that righteousness, like virtue, is the consistent expertise in discerning and obeying God's will amidst the details of everyday life. Righteousness is the only good for humans, and Jesus is the only one in the Gospel to display that quality of character.

A Stoic-like conception of righteousness would explain why only Matthew of the Synoptic Gospels develops the concept of "the will of God."[39] As John Cooper says of Stoicism, "even fully virtuous persons (so-called sages) experience virtuous action as something imposed on them by Zeus," and even though one cannot know all the reasons why things happen, one knows that there are divine reasons, which "gives emphasis to the idea that in living virtuously one lives in obedience ... or by the will of Zeus."[40] Whereas obedience to the commandments of the Mosaic law might be seen to concern particular matters, obeying the will of God and being righteous are comprehensive. The two concepts give a distinctive shape to Jesus' teachings in Matthew.

The other side of righteousness as a matter of character in Matthew is the hard polemic against the hypocrisy of those who are outwardly doing the right things but lack the right inner formation. Immediately after the exhortation to be perfect like God comes a series of warnings against seeming to be altruistic and pious in

---

[37] DesRosiers 2007.

[38] I am taking sides here on some basic issues in the interpretation of Stoicism and am persuaded by scholars who hold that virtue is knowledge of indifferents and skillful sensitivity in assessing these relative values and handling them. This is without motivational reference to the good beyond the knowledge that virtue is the only good and without action guiding rules of virtue. I take this to be probably the dominant view among specialists on Stoicism. For a lucid account of this position, see Brennan 2003.

[39] "Will of God" occurs only once in Mark, twice in Luke, but five times in Matthew (6:10; 7:21; 12:50; 18:14; 26:42).

[40] Cooper 1996, 276–77.

order to win honor and good reputation when one is not truly altruistic and pious (6:1–17). God is able to see one's true inward character and will reward and punish (6:18).[41] The theme is prominent outside of the Sermon on the Mount in Matthew and focuses on the scribes and Pharisees. Matthew 23 is an extremely harsh and extensive polemic against them. Matthew borrows a much less extensive hypocrisy theme from Mark and Q, but he develops the theme that the scribes and Pharisees only seem to be righteous, since they possess vices such as vanity, greed, and lack of self-mastery (23:5–6, 25) and are deficient in virtues such as justice, mercy, and trustworthiness (23:23).[42]

Returning to Matt 5:48, we should note that although scholars widely agree that the call to perfection is a general moral principle for Matthew, the immediate context is the call to love one's enemies. "Love your enemies and pray for those who are persecuting you, so that you may be sons of your father in the heavens. For he makes his sun rise on the evil and the good and makes it rain on the righteous and the unrighteous. For if you love those who love you, what reward do you have? Even the tax collectors do the same, do they not?" (Matt 5:44–46). The command to imitate God in this respect is central to the thought of the sermon as a whole. God's love is for all. Much has been made of Lev 19:18 in Matt 5:43, but no Jewish text interprets it as commanding the love of enemies, and scholars usually admit that the idea is not present there in Leviticus.[43] When one looks for both the idea of love or benevolence toward enemies and the kind of reasoning that supports the idea here, the evidence for this odd idea strongly points to Stoicism.

A scholar writing explicitly from inside Christian tradition about love of enemies in antiquity has concluded that "only Socrates and Roman Stoics recommended never taking revenge," and that Jesus was "the first to have understood Lev 19:18 in this sense."[44] Epictetus (according to Arrian, *Epict. diss.* 3.22.54) says that a true philosopher if flogged "must love the ones who flog him as if he were their father or brother." And Seneca says, "Someone gets angry at you? In return, challenge him with kindness" (*Ira* 2.34), and, "Stoics say . . . we shall never quit working for the common good, helping everyone, even our enemies, until our helping hand is feeble with age" (*Otio* 1.4). For Stoics, the idea of following or imitating God (e.g., Seneca, *Vit. beat.* 15; *Ep.* 16.5; Epictetus, *Diss.* 1.30; Marcus Aurelius, *Meditations* 7.31) means caring for the creation and, above all, fellow rational animals in the way that divine providence administers the common good.[45] Matthew 5:45 almost sounds like an echo of Seneca, *Ben.* 4.26: "If you are imitating the gods, you say, 'Then give benefits also to the ungrateful, for the sun rises also upon the wicked, and the sea stands open to pirates.'" Matthew 7:25–34 (also 10:29–31) develops the theme of God's providential care for the universe, teaching,

---

[41] The first part of this is also Stoic. Epictetus, for example, says (*Diss.* 2.14.11) that Stoics hold that God not only cares for the world but also sees "not only what a person does, but also what one intends and thinks."
[42] For the chaos of source and composition theories, see Newport 1995, 15–56.
[43] Reiser 2001, 420–23.
[44] Ibid., 411.
[45] Reydams-Shils 2005, 73.

in service of an exhortation to refrain from being anxious, that God takes care of birds and flowers and humans alike. What people are to do instead of worrying is strive to have "God's righteousness" (Matt 6:33). A Stoic would say that instead of treating the necessities of food and clothing as genuine goods and their lack as evils, those who are progressing toward virtue ought to realize that they share what is truly good with God, and that they ought to pursue that reason/wisdom/virtue. Foremost of the eupathic emotions (good emotions) of the sage was joy, and sources give one of the subspecies of joy that would characterize the sage as εὐθυμία, defined in one source as "joy at the management of the universe."[46]

Again there is detailed technical Stoic theory behind their distinctive attitude toward enemies and love of humanity.[47] In their theory of human moral development (οἰκείωσις), the morally mature human will extend the kind of affection and concern that "good people" have for family and close kin to all humans when called upon to do so by fitting circumstances. Recent scholarship has shown how especially Stoics of the Roman period developed and extended these ideas.[48] But again I want to emphasize the point that Matthew does not have to detail or explicitly appeal to the technical theory in using Stoic thought to construe Jesus and create an ethic for him, especially since he is unlikely to want the connection to be specific and since the form is that of narrative.

I am convinced that the Stoic explanation works well in explaining the materials that I have treated thus far. There is a major problem that challenges my whole enterprise, however.[49] In the Sermon on the Mount, Jesus teaches that any anger at all is wrong, but later in the narrative Jesus seems to attack the money changers in anger (Matt 21:12–13). One scholar has described the episode as Jesus' "temple tantrum."[50] There is indeed a problem of Jesus seeming to blatantly contradict his own teachings. On a broader level, this has long been recognized, so that Hans Dieter Betz, for instance, in his monumental commentary has argued that the Sermon on the Mount was a preexisting moral treatise that Matthew placed in his narrative without fully integrating it by making the whole consistent.[51] Betz's creative idea has not won assent.[52] To continue with examples of contradictions, in Matt 5:22, Jesus teaches that someone who calls another person a fool will be liable to burn in hell. But in Matt 23:17, he calls the scribes and Pharisees fools using exactly the same word. If Matthew had adapted the Stoic position that emotions were moral errors, then we would expect this to apply not only to anger but also to other emotions, such as grief. But Jesus is said to have "grieved and been agitated," and he says, "I am extremely grief-stricken, even to the point of death" (26:37–38). Would a Stoic sage act like that?

---

[46] Pseudo-Andronicus, *On Emotions* 3 (*SVF* 3.432).
[47] On grounds for φιλανθρωπία in late Stoicism and especially theology, see Fiasse 2002.
[48] Banateanu 2001; Reydams-Shils 2005, 53–82.
[49] This problem was first pointed out to me by Erin Roberts.
[50] See, for example, the introduction in Fredriksen 2000.
[51] Betz 1995, 70–88.
[52] See Stanton 1992, 307–25. Stanton critiques articles by Betz that became the basis for his treatment of the thesis in his 1995 commentary.

Is Matthew's Jesus radically inconsistent, or is there another explanation? Any answer must come to terms with that Gospel's use of sources. It closely follows Mark's passion narrative, which is tightly constructed around allusions to and quotations from "the" Greek translation of the Hebrew Scripture. Mark's brilliant creation may have had too much authority by the time Matthew wrote to allow for major changes or changes in key features of the story. So, for example, Mark's "I am extremely grief-stricken even to the point of death," followed by Matthew, is a quotation from Ps 42:6 (41:6 LXX).

I want to suggest that there is a Stoic way to interpret Jesus' behavior. This argument involves two general claims. First, the sage's action, although always following the will of God, the universal law and reason, might in particular circumstances be contrary to what the accepted moral norms of non-sages indicated was right, even for sages. This would go along with the theme, which Matthew borrows from Mark, of Jesus' ability to teach and act with unique authority. Thus, Matthew's narrative gives the sense that only Jesus was rightly able to teach what he taught and act in the often dramatic and unorthodox ways that he acted. Of course, this is because he is the Son of God, the Messiah, and the Son of Man. But to put it in these terms is to be anachronistic and to fail to imagine the possibilities that readers contemporary with the author could have brought to their reading. As is well known and widely accepted in contemporary scholarship, "son of god," for example, was a common expression for individuals thought to have a special relationship with the divine, from King David to Roman emperors and beyond. The Gospels are in the process of inventing the "Christian" idea that the Jews were looking for "the messiah." In order to avoid anachronism, the historian has to ask what culturally available components Matthew drew upon to construct this strikingly new, yet conventional, figure. My claim is that the Stoic sage and aspects of Stoic ethics should be added to the mix.

Second, contrary to popular and scholarly conceptions of the Stoic, the sage was to be a highly "passionate" person who had and expressed strong feelings.[53] Scholars of early Christianity consistently treat Stoic ἀπάθεια as a total lack of emotion like that exhibited by the character Spock in the television show *Star Trek*. But the Stoic teaching was that the sage would have a set of good emotions (εὐπάθειαι) instead of the diseased emotional states of the non-sage. Although certainly wired in a different way, the sage was not without feeling, even intense feeling. In Stoic theory, all impressions involve an act of assent that involves a judgment usually based upon one's preexisting values and therefore entailing moral responsibility for the ensuing mental states. The Stoics taught that in the present cultures deeply corrupted by false values (e.g., wealth is a good, others can truly harm me, prestige and repute are goods), emotions as shaped by these values were moral diseases. The sage, however, would have "emotions" based solely on true values—virtue is the only good, vice the only evil. The evidence, I believe, following recent scholarship, shows that these good emotions might involve intense feeling such as in joy, religious reverence, and even erotic love.[54] A sage would never have grief, anger, or fear.

---

[53] For what follows, see especially Graver 2007.
[54] See ibid., with relevant bibliography.

Matthew seems to present Jesus as sinless, the only living righteous one in the story and the embodiment of God's wisdom.[55] So Jesus can, without hypocrisy, call the Pharisees fools because he knows with certainty that they are fools and he is consistently wise. It is just and righteous censure. The unrighteous, the imperfect, on the other hand, cannot justly censure others in this way. But grief and anger are more difficult. My hypothesis is that the author of Matthew may have conceived of Jesus in a consistent way encouraged by contemporary treatments of God's frequent displays of anger in the Hebrew Scriptures. It is well known that Philo and other Jewish writers denied that God had this emotion, and they claimed that the texts were an accommodating way to express God's just indignation. The episode of Jesus' confrontation with the money changers in the temple does not use the word "anger." A sage, knowing that no other person can truly cause unjust harm to the sage's good (virtue), has no anger. Stoic theory might make it seem that the good emotions would only concern the sage's own good—what was up to him—and for the most part they do. But sources for the subspecies of the good emotions also have good emotions that express concern for the good of others. Pseudo-Andronicus, in *On Emotions* (*SVF* 3.432), for instance, defines good intent (εὔνοια) as "a wish for good things for another for that person's sake." One then might conceive of Jesus' action as an expression of his just indignation that the money changers were causing harm to their good and the good of others by devaluing a place where only the model of God's perfection ought to be exhibited. Instead of fear, the sage was to have an emotion usually translated as caution. Andronicus defines one subspecies, reverence (ἁγνεία), as "caution against misdeeds concerning the gods." These considerations, I think, show that the hypothesis of a consistent Jesus shaped by the Stoic idea of the sage deserves further study.

Matthew could not do much with an inherited episode of Jesus fulfilling Scripture by grieving deeply. Origen, who along with many ancient Christian writers assumed, like the Stoics, that grieving was morally wrong, had an interpretation that may deserve consideration.[56] Origen claims that Matthew wrote "Jesus began to grieve" and uses the Stoic concept of a preemotion to explain that text.[57] Jesus did not have an emotion—that requires assent—but only the initial reaction that the Stoics said was involuntary and natural. Matthew gets "began" from Mark but changes Mark's word ἐκθαμβεῖσθαι, which usually (at least without the prefix) means "to be amazed" in Mark and elsewhere. But translators assimilate the Markan word to Matthew and the psalm and usually render it as "to be distressed." Matthew changes this to the common word for grief that the Stoics used, λυπεῖσθαι, which connects Matt 26:37 to the word for grief in the quotation from Ps 42 [41]. Matthew then can be read in this Stoic way: Jesus had the initial "biting contraction" of grief that is natural to all humans, including sages, accompanied with his proclamation of the Scripture that predicted it, but he never allowed the

---

[55] For some specific statements regarding Jesus' righteousness, see Matt 3:15; 27:4, 19.
[56] My discussion of Origen, Philo, and preemotions is based on Graver 1999; 2007, 102–6.
[57] See Graver 1999.

natural preemotion to develop into an evil and unnatural emotion that construed his impending death as an evil.[58] In Stoic thought, life is a preferred indifferent. Life ought to be desired, pursued, and preserved, but one is not to think that who one truly is and what is truly valuable will be harmed by that natural and universal state of death that is another part of God's plan. In Matthew, the prayers of Jesus that follow can be read as expressing this attitude. At the end of the scene (26:42) that starts with the "pre-grief," he calmly says to God, in effect, "If my death cannot be avoided, then your will be done."

If this reading is correct, then Philo employs the same strategy in treating Abraham's grieving over Sarah (*QG* 1.79). Even though Gen 23:2 says that "Abraham came to mourn for Sarah and to weep," Philo strongly denies that Abraham had the emotion of grief. Margaret Graver shows that Philo's argument uses the Stoic concepts of impression, assent, and preemotion.[59] Abraham had the initial natural pangs of loss, but he did not allow this to develop into the emotion that expresses the judgment that God taking Sarah was a genuine evil. Of surviving Stoic writers, Seneca seems to go the furthest when he grants that the sage will involuntarily weep and shake with sobs at a funeral.[60] The sage will also voluntarily (i.e., in a manner that is constructed with reason) and therefore eupathically weep in a way that involves joy when remembering the goodness and companionship of the loved one. That a major Stoic figure can go this far shows that Matthew's author and ancient readers could quite easily construe Jesus' grieving in a way that would be consistent with the Stoically inflected teachings in the Sermon on the Mount.[61]

The reasons why the author of Matthew drew upon Stoic ethics seem clear. That writer inherited a Jesus who was known as a teacher but had no clear and elaborated ethical teachings that would make him like, or rather, superior to, the other great teachers of the culture. Stoicism was the most prominent and widely respected philosophy of the day. Furthermore, it had a reputation for being both rigorous and popular. It was popular in the sense that it was directed at everyone and focused upon those who were sinners and those who were trying to make moral progress. But it also held up the nearly impossible ideal of the sage and urged people to measure themselves against this model of human perfection. The

---

[58] Sorabji (2000, 346–49) also helpfully discusses Origen's interpretation of Jesus' grief. Against Sorabji, Graver (2002; 2007, 85–108) convincingly argues that Seneca did not invent the preemotions, and that they probably go back to the early Stoa. Graver also convincingly shows against him that the Stoics advocated a rich and strong pattern of feelings with their good emotions.

[59] Following Graver 2007, 103.

[60] Seneca, *Ep.* 99.

[61] A non-Stoic element in the context is the saying in Matt 26:41 that "the spirit [πνεῦμα] is willing, but the flesh is weak." Stoic doctrine rejected an opposition between mind or soul and body such as found in Platonic traditions. However, Stoics in the Roman period, in spite of enunciating the Stoic theory, often used Platonic-sounding dualistic language. This is especially true of Epictetus and Seneca. This seems at least partly due to the fact that Stoic lineage-making had by this time long traced Stoic origins to Socrates, and Epictetus and Seneca took Plato's dialogues to be genuine sources for the founder of Stoicism.

rigor fit well with Matthew's harsh apocalyptic ideas about an exacting and vengeful God who would consign all but a faithful few to eternal torment.[62]

The Matthean Gospel's adaptation of the ethic also helped to solve a huge problem that it had inherited from Mark and Q. How is it that the people of God, the Jews, had been so blind and so evil that God had to destroy the nation and the religion as it had been known? How is it that they could have rejected and killed God's chosen Messiah and been allowed to bear such evil guilt that even their descendants would share it? With resources adapted from Stoicism, Matthew could "argue" that they were evil because in spite of all outward appearance of being good people, they lacked the essential qualitative aspect of character that God had always required and taught through his law: righteousness. The problem that Matthew left for future generations of Christian thinkers was that the rigorous ethical side wedded to an apocalyptic framework with a vengeful God made an ill fit with the love of enemies and the universal providential care of God that the writer also borrowed from Stoicism. This dilemma is, I think, one reason why later Christian thinkers from Origen to Augustine had to add another story about an originary or premundane fall that would provide an explanation in terms of a deep general human recalcitrance that was then read as the backdrop for the stories of Scripture.

Bibliography

Algra, K. 2003. "Stoic Theology." Pages 153–78 in *The Cambridge Companion to the Stoics*. Edited by B. Inwood. Cambridge: Cambridge University Press.

Allison, D. C. 1999. *The Sermon on the Mount: Inspiring the Moral Imagination*. New York: Crossroad.

Banateanu, A. 2001. *La théorie stoïcienne de l'amitié: Essai de reconstruction*. Vestigia 27. Fribourg: Éditions universitaires Fribourg; Paris: Cerf.

Betz, H. D. 1995. *The Sermon on the Mount: A Commentary on the Sermon on the Mount, Including the Sermon on the Plain (Matthew 5:3–7:27 and Luke 6:20–49)*. Edited by A. Y. Collins. Hermeneia. Minneapolis: Fortress.

Brennan, T. 2003. "Stoic Moral Psychology." Pages 257–94 in *The Cambridge Companion to the Stoics*. Edited by B. Inwood. Cambridge: Cambridge University Press.

———. 2005. *The Stoic Life: Emotions, Duties, and Fate*. Oxford: Clarendon Press.

---

[62] Matthew substantially intensifies Mark's apocalyptic severity. For example, Matt 7:13–14 is harsher than the parallel in Luke 13:23–24. The standards for escaping destruction are extremely strenuous (e.g., Matt 7:21–23; 5:20, 22). Future judgment pervades the Sermon on the Mount. Gehenna occurs 7 times in Matthew, but only 3 times in Mark and once in Luke, and Matthew emphasizes the horrible suffering (outer darkness, fire, burning, weeping an gnashing of teeth, etc). Cf. the many references to judgment in 8:12, 29; 10:15, 26–28; 11:20–24; 12:41; 13:42, 50; 18:3, 10; 22:13; 24:51; 25:30. Note also Matthew's redactional additions about the judging of the Son of Man in 3:12 and 16:27. In addition, Matthew stresses fear of destruction as a central motivating force of his ethic (e.g., 10:26–28).

Cooper, J. 1996. "Eudaimonism, the Appeal to Nature, and 'Moral Duty' in Stoicism." Pages 261–84 in *Aristotle, Kant, and the Stoics: Rethinking Happiness and Duty*. Edited by S. Engstrom and J. Whiting. Cambridge: Cambridge University Press.

DesRosiers, N. 2007. "The Establishment of Proper Mental Disposition and Practice: The Origin, Meaning, and Social Purpose of the Prohibition of Oaths in Matthew." Ph.D. diss., Brown University.

Engberg-Pedersen, T. 2006. "A Stoic Understanding of Pneuma in Paul." Pages 101–23 in *Philosophy at the Roots of Christianity*. Edited by T. Engberg-Pedersen and H. Tronier. Copenhagen: University of Copenhagen.

Fiasse, G. 2002. "Les fondements de la philanthropie dans le nouveau stoïcisme, deux cas concrets: l'esclavage et la gladiature." *Les études philosophiques* 63(4):527–47.

Fredriksen, P. 2000. *From Jesus to Christ: The Origins of the New Testament Images of Jesus*. 2nd ed. New Haven: Yale University Press.

Graver, M. R. 1999. "Philo of Alexandria and the Stoic Προπάθειαι." *Phronesis* 44:300–25.

———. 2002. Review of R. Sorabji, *Emotion and Peace of Mind: From Stoic Agitation to Christian Temptation*. *Ancient Philosophy* 22:225–34.

———. 2007. *Stoicism and Emotion*. Chicago: University of Chicago Press.

Inwood, B. 1985. *Ethics and Human Action in Early Stoicism*. Oxford: Oxford University Press.

Long, A. A. 2002. *Epictetus: A Stoic and Socratic Guide to Life*. Oxford: Clarendon Press.

Long, A. A., and D. N. Sedley. 1987. *The Hellenistic Philosophers*. 2 vols. Cambridge: Cambridge University Press.

Newport, K. 1995. *The Sources and Sitz Im Leben of Matthew 23*. Journal for the Study of the New Testament: Supplement Series 117. Sheffield: Sheffield Academic Press.

Olyan, S. 2000. *Rites and Rank: Hierarchy in Biblical Representations of Cult*. Princeton, NJ: Princeton University Press.

Przybylski, B. 1980. *Righteousness in Matthew and His World of Thought*. Society for New Testament Studies Monograph Series 41. Cambridge: Cambridge University Press.

Reiser, M. 2001. "Love of Enemies in the Context of Antiquity." *New Testament Studies* 47:411–27.

Reydams-Shils, G. 2005. *The Roman Stoics: Self, Responsibility, and Affection*. Chicago: University of Chicago Press.

Scheer, R. 1976. "Jimmy Carter: A Candid Conversation with the Democratic Candidate for the Presidency." *Playboy* 23(11):63–86.

Schofield, M. 1984. "Ariston of Chios and the Unity of Virtue." *Ancient Philosophy* 4:83–96.

Sorabji, R. 2000. *Emotion and Peace of Mind: From Stoic Agitation to Christian Temptation*. Oxford: Oxford University Press.

Stanton, G. N. 1992. *A Gospel for a New People: Studies in Matthew*. Edinburgh: T & T Clark.

Suggs, J. M. 1970. *Wisdom, Christology, and Law in Matthew's Gospel*. Cambridge, Mass.: Harvard University Press.

Thom, J. C. 2001. "Cleanthes' Hymn to Zeus and Early Christian Literature." Pages 477–99 in *Antiquity and Humanity: Essays on Ancient Religion and Philosophy Presented to Hans Dieter Betz on His 70th Birthday*. Edited by A. Y. Collins and M. M. Mitchell. Tübingen: Mohr Siebeck.

———. 2005. *Cleanthes' Hymn to Zeus: Text, Translation and Commentary*. Studien und Texte zu Antike und Christentum 33. Tübingen: Mohr Siebeck.

5

AN "EMOTIONAL" JESUS AND STOIC TRADITION

Harold W. Attridge
Yale University

1. The Gospel of John and Ancient Philosophy

Tradition attributes the Fourth Gospel to John, the Theologian,[1] thereby attributing a high level of conceptual sophistication to the author. The lofty prose of the prologue, with its allusion to Greek and Hellenistic-Jewish speculation on the Logos,[2] no doubt reinforced, and perhaps inspired, that assessment of the text. If that traditional suggestion were correct, it might be profitable to explore whether any of the theological claims of the Fourth Gospel are grounded in or in some way at least engaged with the philosophical milieu of the first century. The question has not been at the forefront of Johannine scholarship, which has pursued many other concerns, including the relationship of this Gospel to religious traditions of antiquity, the social location of the Johannine community, and the literary history and dynamics of the text.[3]

The issue has, however, recently been raised anew by a series of sophisticated analyses by young scholars associated with the research project Philosophy at the Roots of Christianity (University of Copenhagen). Connected with that scholarly group is Kasper Bro Larsen (Aarhus University), whose work on the phenomenon of "anagnoresis" or "recognition" in the Fourth Gospel combines conceptual and literary analysis that illuminates how this Gospel plays with the category of "knowledge."[4] If Larsen is correct, then the evangelist, as well as

---

[1] For the traditions about the author, see Culpepper 1994.
[2] The literature is enormous. For analyses of the conceptual world reflected in the prologue, see Borgen 1972; Colpe 1979; Evans 1993; Leonhardt-Balzer 2004; Siegert 2004; Attridge 2005.
[3] The most useful surveys of the range of modern Johannine scholarship are Brown 2003; Ashton 2007. For briefer summaries, see Attridge 2001; 2006a.
[4] Larsen 2008.

being a careful literary artist, is in conversation with first-century discussion of epistemology.[5]

Gitte Buch-Hansen, who defended her dissertation in the fall of 2007 at the University of Copenhagen, focused on the language of "spirit" in the Fourth Gospel and tried to put it in a new conceptual context grounded in Stoicism. Her work, focusing on Stoic physics and metaphysics, rehearses what Stoics thought about πνεῦμα, a material substance that pervades all things and holds them together, something like what modern physicists think of as energy. The Jewish appropriation of that notion is evident in Wisdom of Solomon and in Philo's reflection on the Logos. But Stoics also thought that various kinds of matter could be transformed and all material forms underwent such a transformation in the periodic conflagration that consumed all things and reduced the physical universe to what modern cosmologists might call a singularity from which it would again emerge. For that process, the Stoics used a technical term, ἀναστοιχείωσις, which means something like "resolution of matter into its elements." Philo appropriates these categories with a twist, turning an eschatological category into a useful tool for describing a biblical event. The mysterious departure of Moses at the end of Philo's treatment of Moses (*Mos.* 2.288) is treated by Philo using the language of "anastoicheiosis," an elimination of his fleshy materiality and a transformation into a *pneuma* available to his community in a new way, through Torah.

Buch-Hansen argues that the story of *pneuma* in the Fourth Gospel reflects precisely this kind of appropriation of a Stoic notion, now with a focus on Jesus, not Moses or the Torah. Among other things, the divine πνεῦμα undergoes a process of transformation that explains some of the little narrative conundrums that have always baffled interpreters, such as the famous *noli me tangere* scene in which the resurrected Jesus seems to repulse Mary Magdalene (20:16–17). Jesus, who had already completed the work that he had come to do (chapter 19), apparently has something more to undergo by returning to the Father. The spirit that is breathed out on the cross cannot be breathed into his disciples as a community-forming event until Jesus is well and truly gone, transformed into the new form of existence.[6] There are tropes galore in that famous episode, but the conceptual play on how πνεῦμα operates may well be one important element of the mix. If Buch-Hansen is correct, then the Fourth Gospel knows and uses a piece of technical Stoic theory, albeit one that has already been adapted to religious use by Jewish thinkers.[7]

These studies on the possible traces of technical philosophy, both Platonic and Stoic, lurking within the narrative of the Fourth Gospel call out for further exploration. If there are at least traces of metaphysical and epistemological principles at work, are there other elements of ancient philosophy at work in the text?

---

[5] The combination of literary and conceptual considerations in Larsen's (2008) work is essential for unpacking the complexity of the Fourth Gospel. For an analogous attempt, see Attridge 2006b.

[6] For further reflection on the significance of that scene, see Attridge 2003.

[7] How the technical categories of ancient philosophers were available to the author of the Fourth Gospel remains an intriguing problem. Hellenized Jewish authors such as Philo perhaps were the primary conduit.

An experiment may test whether we can in fact detect further echoes of philosophy: a probe into the ethics of the Fourth Gospel.[8] Some critics might dispute whether this Gospel pays much attention to ethics. Its recommendations seem to boil down to the love command, and that aimed primarily, if not exclusively, at members of the community.[9] Nonetheless, it might be possible to conduct the probe from another angle.

At first glance at least, it appears that certain features of the portrait of Jesus in the Fourth Gospel bear some family resemblance to the Stoic depiction of an ideal "sage," the wise man whose life is totally governed by reason. This ideal figure, a goal to which ordinary mortals aspire and few, if any, ever reach,[10] possessed in truth the status and values to which all aspired. Thus, only the sage was free,[11] only the sage was truly a king. In the words of the summary of Stoicism in Diogenes Laertius:

> They declare that he alone is free and bad men are slaves, freedom being power of independent action, whereas slavery is privation of the same; though indeed there is also a second form of slavery consisting in subordination, and a third which implies possession of the slave as well as his subordination; the correlative of such servitude being lordship; and this too is evil.
>
> Moreover, according to them not only are the wise free, they are also kings; kingship being irresponsible rule, which none but the wise can maintain; so Chrysippus in his treatise vindicating Zeno's use of terminology.[12]

The Johannine Jesus, who solemnly declares that the truth will make one free (8:32) and who stands before the only apparent political power of Rome hinting at his own true royalty (18:33–38), bears at least a family resemblance to this Stoic sage.

Similarly, the generally "high" Christology of the Fourth Gospel, often accused of being a kind of naïve Docetism,[13] might be compatible with what Diogenes Laertius reports of the sage: "They are also, it is declared, godlike; for they have a something divine within them."[14] The Jesus of the Fourth Gospel, in whom there is definitely "something divine," often seems to be quite "above the fray," serenely in control of the situation, unperturbed by the concerns and sufferings around him. The embarrassment of a resource-challenged wedding feast is not his

---

[8] For another parallel probe, see Lang 2004.
[9] See Meeks 1996.
[10] The distinction was clearly drawn by Panaetius, according to Seneca, *Ep.* 116.5. See Long 1986, 215. Note also Seneca, *Ira* 2.10.6: The wise person "scit neminem nasci sapientem sed fieri, scit paucissimos omni aevo sapientis evadere, quia condicionem humanae vitae perspectam habet."
[11] Philo's tractate *Quod omnis probus liber sit* (*That Every Good Person is Free*) offers a Jewish appropriation of the trope.
[12] Diogenes Laertius, *Vit. phil.* 7.121–122.
[13] The claim, famously attributed to Ernst Käsemann (1966), surely is overblown. For a critique, see Schnelle 1992.
[14] Diogenes Laertius, *Vit. phil.* 7.119.

concern until his mother nudges him to take the appropriate action (2:3–5). In the face of hostile questions he always seems calm and measured, though his retorts can at times be pointed (8:44; 10:6). Even when about to be stoned, his response is a calm and rational question (10:32), though followed by what would no doubt be considered outrageous claims (10:38).

The depiction of the serene Jesus reaches its culmination on the cross and conforms to other notions of a noble death. In this regard, he seems to conform to the requirements of a Stoic sage: "Now they say that the wise man is passionless, because he is not prone to fall into such infirmity."[15] Even in his passion, Jesus, like the sage, evidences the ideal of ἀπάθεια.

Jesus in the Fourth Gospel also displays a deep sense of duty. His food is to do the will of the one who sent him (4:34; cf. 9:4). Like a good emissary, he does what he is told (5:30) and teaches what he has been taught from on high (7:16; 12:49). There are sheep that he "must" gather (10:16). What is "completed" on the cross (19:30) is, among other things, the mission on which he had been sent, the duty that he had to perform.

There are, to be sure, qualities attributed to the ideal type that do not quite seem to fit the portrait of Jesus. After noting the "divine" quality of the sage, Diogenes Laertius continues:

> The good, it is added, are also worshippers of God; for they have acquaintance with the rites of the gods, and piety is the knowledge of how to serve the gods. Further, they will sacrifice to the gods and they keep themselves pure; for they avoid all acts that are offences against the gods, and the gods think highly of them; for they are holy and just in what concerns the gods. The wise too are the only priests; for they have made sacrifices their study, as also the building of temples, purifications and all the other matters appertaining to the gods.[16]

There may be hints of a paradoxical "priestly" Christology in John,[17] but none that Jesus was an expert in ritual affairs.

Other points of tension might be found between the ideal portraits of a sage and the Johannine depiction of Jesus, but one set of descriptions in particular creates problems for a comparison with Stoic traditions, a set that seems to stand in some tension with the general depiction of the serene and undisturbed Jesus: depictions of his emotions.

2. The Emotions of Jesus

Several passages in the Fourth Gospel, often noted as examples of the true humanity of Jesus, portray him as having what appear to be strong emotions. The narrative does not describe his emotional state during his action in the temple

---

[15] Diogenes Laertius, *Vit. phil.* 7.117.
[16] Diogenes Laertius, *Vit. phil.* 7.119.
[17] See John 17. On such Christologies in general, see Loader 1981.

(2:12–16), but the narrator comments that his disciples later remember words from Ps 69:9: "Zeal for your house will consume me." By implication, Jesus was motivated by "zeal" (ζῆλος [2:17]), which might appear to be something akin to anger.

The clearest examples of what appear to be emotions appear toward the end of Jesus' public ministry. When Jesus comes to deal with the dead Lazarus, he becomes "deeply moved in spirit" and "agitated."[18] The precise nature of this agitation has been the subject of debate. The last phrase, whose verb recurs at 12:27, is clear enough. The first, less common, verb causes some difficulty. The word ἐμβριμάομαι, which can be used of the snorting of horses,[19] appears in Synoptic accounts of exorcism (Matt 9:30; Mark 1:43) where Jesus angrily confronts demons. Some suspect that the evangelist inherited the word from a source.[20] However that may be, the word suggests that the agitation was visible and probably involved more than a hint of anger.[21]

The object of Jesus' anger has been the subject of considerable speculation. Was he upset at being forced by the crowds to perform a miracle,[22] at the Jews and Mary for the faithlessness displayed in their weeping,[23] at the reality of death and the inimical powers that cause it?[24] All are possible; none are explicitly marked in the text.

Jesus then openly displays his grief by weeping (11:35), and when he approaches the tomb, he is again "deeply moved" (ἐμβριμώμενος ἐν ἑαυτῷ [11:38]), presumably by the same emotions to which his tears testified several verses earlier.

It is interesting that chapter 11 offers us other examples of emotions at work, particularly in the picture of Mary, who says little but feels deeply. The surrounding friends who attempt to console her believe that her abrupt departure from the house at the news of Jesus' coming is simply a move toward graveside weeping (11:31). The image is of a woman in deep grief. She also reacts with an extravagant gesture when she encounters Jesus (11:32). Is she demonstrating her devotion or her distress? In any case, there may be a deliberate polarity between her and her sister, with Martha exemplifying a reaction of the head, and Mary a response of a grieving heart.[25]

To return to Jesus, as his "hour" approaches, he is again agitated, this time in "soul" (ἡ ψυχή μου τετάρακται [12:27]). Exactly how Jesus was agitated is not

---

[18] ἐνεβριμήσατο τῷ πνεύματι καὶ ἐτάραξεν ἑαυτόν (11:33). Several witnesses offer a slightly more complex reading: εταραχθη τω πνευματι ως εμβριμουμενος (-μωμενος 𝔓66c Θ l) 𝔓45vid.66 D Θ l *pc* p sa ac2), "he was disturbed in spirit as one agitated." The phrasing perhaps insulates Jesus from real emotion. He only is *like* one who is deeply moved.

[19] See *LSJ* 540b; *BDAG* 322.

[20] See Lindars 1972, 398; 1992, esp. 94–95; Haenchen 1984, 2:66; Story 1991. For a critique, see Thyen 2005, 532–53.

[21] See Barrett 1978, 398–400, relying on the uses of the verb at Dan 11:30 and Lucian, *Menippus* 20. See also Brown 1966, 425–26, 435; Moloney 1998, 330.

[22] Barrett 1978, 399.

[23] Bultmann 1971, 406; Schnackenburg 1980, 2:335–36.

[24] Brown 1966, 435; Haenchen 1984, 2:66.

[25] The two women have garnered a considerable amount of scholarly attention. See Moloney 1994; Stibbe 1994; Kitzberger 1995, 570–78.

specified, but it is hardly unreasonable to suspect that he had at least a slight shudder of fear, dread, or apprehension. That would be particularly true if this brief remark in John is a vestige of or distant cousin to the stories of the prayer of Jesus in the garden of Gethsemane.[26] He later urges his disciples not to let their hearts be agitated (14:1) and, in repeating that injunction, specifies that disturbance is equivalent to fear.[27]

Lurking behind both of the expressions of emotion in chapters 11 and 12 may be the language of the psalms, which readily portray and inspire emotional appeals. Particularly relevant is the combination of Ps 42 and Ps 43—for example, the refrain of 42:5, 11; 43:5: "Why are you cast down, O my soul, and why are you disquieted within me."[28] Whatever the inspiration, the result of the portrait is clear. Jesus seems to share sentiments that would be recognizable to ordinary human beings.

Scholars occasionally note the presence of these apparent emotions as an element that distinguishes the Fourth Gospel from the philosophical tradition.[29] They note passages such as Diogenes Laertius, *Vit. phil.* 7.118: "Nor indeed will the wise man ever feel grief; seeing that grief is irrational contraction of the soul, as Apollodorus says in his *Ethics*." Although scholars wonder about what caused the "anger" of Jesus in John 11, the reality of death or lack of faith, they finally tend to see the emotion as evidence of the humanity of Jesus, marking his solidarity with suffering humanity.[30]

The Fourth Gospel, then, might be seen as either quite divorced from the philosophical tradition in general and from Stoic tradition in particular, or even, perhaps, a bit of "anti-Stoicism," a precursor of the later Augustine.[31] In order to test whether that is so, a bit of background on the Stoic discourse about emotions is needed.

3. The Stoics on Emotions

As we have become acutely aware of in recent decades, emotions were of extreme importance to Stoic ethical theory, a subject of significant reflection within the school in the late Hellenistic and early imperial periods, and a bone of contention between the Stoics and their philosophical rivals.[32] For the Stoics, emotions

---

[26] See Brown 1961, esp. 143–48.
[27] μὴ ταρασσέσθω ὑμῶν ἡ καρδία μηδὲ δειλιάτω (14:27).
[28] See Beutler 1978; Thyen 1979, 533; Daly-Denton 2000, 253–58.
[29] So, for example, Keener (2003, 2:845n98) on John 11:33 and the verb ταράσσω: "A goal of philosophy, by contrast, was to be ἀτάραχον (Epictetus [*Diss.*] 2.5.2; 4.8.27; Diogenes Laertius 10.85; 10.144.17; cf. *T. Dan* 4:7; *T. Job* 36:3/4–5; ἀπαθείας in Crates *Ep.* 34, to Metrocles)." The passages cited by Keener from Diogenes Laertius have to do with Epicurean ideals of tranquility, interesting but not germane to our inquiry into connections with Stoicism, which featured so strongly not only an ideal of "imperturbability" but also a sophisticated analysis of what emotions were and how they worked.
[30] See ibid., 2:845–46.
[31] For an insightful account of Augustine's critique of the Stoic tradition, see Wolterstorff 2008, 180–206.
[32] In general, see Nussbaum 1994, 359–401; Sorabji 2000. For a useful review of the issues involved, see the collection of essays in Sihvola and Engberg-Pedersen 1998.

(πάθη) were inimical to moral flourishing and should be extirpated as far as possible. The ideal human being, the sage, is totally governed by reason, living totally in conformity to nature, in unperturbed harmony. This Stoic position, grounded in the conviction that the soul is unitary and not divided, as Platonists and Peripatetics thought, into three different parts or functions,[33] stimulated severe and constant criticism as being counter to the facts of human experience.[34]

What the Stoics technically meant by "emotion" (πάθος) created some of the difficulty. In the classical theory and throughout the history of Stoicism, emotion involved not just a feeling, but a judgment. The emotion of anger was not simply the physical affect of a reddened face, eyes blazing, and lips quivering—the kind of portrait that Seneca vividly sketches[35]—but a judgment that a certain course of action was to be pursued (e.g., the offending enemy was to be eliminated). The propositional dimension of the emotion, not simply the "excessive" character of the subjective state,[36] was what stood in opposition to reason.

Stoics devoted enormous attention to the emotions (πάθη), not merely their taxonomy, but also the processes for dealing with the impulses that could lead to passions. When they sketched the image of the "sage," there was no room for such misfirings of the soul. But Stoics also were concerned with the training of souls in the pursuit of that ever elusive goal of the wise person's pure rationality. They recognized that even the sage could be stirred in the direction of an undesirable emotion and had to deal with that stirring.

The categories of emotion attributed to Jesus, and by extension to his disciples, would be familiar to anyone steeped in the Stoic tradition. Different mappings of the world of emotion could be made. According to the account of Zeno's *On the Passions* preserved in Diogenes Laertius, *Vit. phil.* 7.111, there were four great classes of emotion: grief or distress (λύπη), fear (φόβος), desire or craving (ἐπιθυμία), and pleasure (ἡδονή).[37] The episodes in the Fourth Gospel that apparently describe how Jesus feels readily correspond to the first two of these overarching categories: grief (chapter 11), fear (chapters 12, 14). Anger, which Jesus apparently experiences in his encounter with Mary and Martha, is a subspecies of the third category.[38]

---

[33] See Brennan 1998.
[34] For reflection on such criticism, see Irwin 1998.
[35] Seneca, *Ira* 1.1.3–4.
[36] The chief characteristics are combined in Stobaeus, *Anth.* 2.7.10–10a (= 2.88.8–90.6 W-H): "They say that passion is impulse which is excessive and disobedient to the dictates of reason, or a movement of soul which is irrational and contrary to nature; and that all passions belong to the soul's commanding faculty" (see Long and Sedley 1987, 1:410; 2:404). The combination of ingredients in the definition reflects some of the tensions in the Stoic discourse about emotions/passions, but the final phrase is important for locating the passion in the function of the ἡγεμονικόν, the controlling element of the soul, where judgments occur.
[37] Stobaeus, *Anth.* 2.7.10–10a (= 2.88.8–90.6 W-H) and Pseudo-Andronicus, *On Emotions* 1 list the same παθή but in a different order. See Long and Sedley 1987, 1:411; 2:404.
[38] According to Stobaeus, *Anth.* 2.7.10b (= 2.90.19–91.9 W-H). See *SVF* 3.394; Long and Sedley 1987, 1:412; 2:406–7.

4. How to Handle Emotions

The ways in which the emotions are treated in the cases of grief, anger, and fear merit attention. The critical point is that even for the sage, the ideal limiting condition of rational humanity, it is not impossible to have what we might call feelings, stirrings of the soul, occasioned by sensory impressions. What made these psychic motions emotions was the judgmental assent to their propositional content by the ἡγεμονικόν, the controlling element of the soul. This assent turned the initial stirring into an impulse (ὁρμή), which could be defined as a proposition with a practical object.[39] What takes place in the case of animals, a sort of stimulus-response that produces action, becomes in the case of human beings a process in which reason intervenes to shape the response.[40] The ideal embodiment of ἀπάθεια will not be devoid of external impressions and stirrings of the soul but will shape them and subject them to rational control. The impressions that become impulses to action will remain in conformity with the dictates of reason/nature and will not interfere with the tranquility of the philosophical mind.

The emotionless sage is a limiting case, defining one end—the most desirable, of course—of human experience. Most people are on a journey toward that limit. In the words of many Stoic moralists, they are "making way" (προκόπτων) toward that goal.[41] Sages in training may experience the emotional tug, the "irrational contraction," but will respond to it with some therapy, an alternative impression, an argument perhaps, convincing themselves that the proposition embedded in or implied by the "contraction" is wrong.

The basic Stoic framework for thinking about emotions—unnatural judgments corresponding to excessive impulses of the soul—was part of the traditional teaching of the school. In the late Hellenistic period there was new emphasis on the first stage of the process, the basic impulse that led to the disordered state that was passion. The influential first-century B.C.E. philosopher Posidonius is credited with breaking with traditional Stoic teaching and rehabilitating the "irrational" dimensions of the soul on which Platonic and Aristotelian rivals insisted.[42] We need not solve the disputed issue of how significant his departures were from traditional Stoicism.[43] The interest of Posidonius in the question of the emotions was shared by Stoics of the Roman period, and their methods for the "therapy" of the soul may be useful to compare with the portrait of Jesus in the Fourth Gospel.

---

[39] So Stobaeus, *Anth.* 2.7.9b (= 2.88.2–6 W-H). See Long and Sedley 1987, 1:197; 2:200.

[40] The overall psychic process is outlined succinctly in Diogenes Laertius, *Vit. phil.* 7.86, culminating in the affirmation that "reason supervenes as the craftsman of impulse" (τεχνίτης γὰρ οὗτος [scil. λόγος] ἐπιγίνεται τῆς ὁρμῆς).

[41] For a sketch of the "one who is making progress," see Epictetus, *Diss.* 1.4; 3.2.

[42] For a general assessment, see Rist 1969, 201–18; and with even more caution about attributing too much influence to Posidonius, Long 1986, 216–22. For a quite different picture of Posidonius, see Gill 2006.

[43] For discussion of the possibilities, see Brennan 1998; Sorabji 1998. For another account of some of the distinctive features of Roman Stoicism, see Reydams-Schils 2005.

The distinction between the initial impressions and the emotions that could flow from them is quite clear in Seneca's treatment of anger:

> Singing sometimes stirs us, and quickened rhythm, and the well-known blare of the War-god's trumpets; our minds are perturbed [*movet mentes*] by a shocking picture and by the melancholy sight of punishment even when it is entirely just; in the same way we smile when others smile, and are saddened by a throng of mourners [*et contristat nos turba maerentium*], and are thrown into a ferment by the struggles of others. Such sensations, however, are no more anger than that is sorrow which furrows the brow at the sight of a mimic shipwreck . . . but they are all emotions of a mind that would prefer not to be so affected; they are not passions, but the beginnings that are preliminary to passions.[44]

> None of these things which move the mind through the agency of chance should be called passions; the mind suffers them, so to speak, rather than causes them. Passion, consequently, does not consist in being moved by the impressions that are presented to the mind, but in surrendering to these and following up such a chance prompting.[45]

> Therefore that primary disturbance of the mind [*illa agitatio animi*] which is excited by the impression of injury is no more anger than the impression of injury is itself anger; the active impulse consequent upon it, which has not only admitted the impression of injury but also approved it, is really anger—the tumult of a mind proceeding to revenge by choice and determination.[46]

How, then, should one deal with these impressions? Seneca suggests that certain principles be kept in mind, principles that will govern and shape the response to the impressions. Remembering human folly will lead one to dispense with anger and to grant indulgence to the wayward.[47] Proper training of the young may counter the effects of natural bodily conditions that may be conducive to anger;[48] for adults, what most often produces anger is an impression of injury (*opinio iniuriae*).[49] Put those opinions in perspective, and the anger will dissipate. A little self-awareness will keep resentments toward others in check.[50] While psychagogy will take various forms in the face of different characters—entreaty, reproof, shame[51]—the fundamental strategy is to have a right assessment of the character of the passion itself.[52] Knowing the truth in various ways is what sets the sage, or the person striving to be one, free from the deleterious passion of anger.

---

[44] Seneca, *Ira* 2.2.4–5. "Sed omnia ista motus sunt animorum moveri nolentium nec adfectus sed principia proludentia adfectibus."
[45] Seneca, *Ira* 2.3.1. "Nihil ex his, quae animum fortuito impellunt, adfectus vocari debet; ista, ut ita dicam, patitur magis animus quam facit. Ergo adfectus est non ad oblatas rerum species moveri, sed permittere se illis et hunc fortuitum motum prosequi."
[46] Seneca, *Ira* 2.3.5.
[47] Seneca, *Ira* 2.9.1–2. "Ne singulis irascaris, universis ignoscendum est, generi humano venia tribuenda est." Cf. Epictetus, *Diss.* 1.18.
[48] Seneca, *Ira* 2.19–21.
[49] Seneca, *Ira* 2.22.2.
[50] Seneca, *Ira* 2.28.5–8.
[51] Seneca, *Ira* 3.1.2.
[52] Seneca, *Ira* 3.5.4.

For Epictetus, full of practical advice for those who are "making progress," the "first and greatest task of the philosopher is to test the impressions [τὰς φαντασίας] and discriminate between them, and to apply none that has not been tested."[53] When impressions that could lead to passions emerge, he suggests that the "polished weapons" that will counter them are right "preconceptions" (πρόληψεις).[54] Against the fear of death stands the understanding that it is inevitable and one must do one's duty.[55] When impressions come along, the like of which later theological traditions would call temptations, one who is progressing in virtue will counter them. Against the impression of a fair youth ready for sex, one will "introduce and set over against it some fair and noble impression, and throw out this filthy one."[56]

When the Johannine Jesus is tugged by the initial stirrings of what a Stoic would call a "passion," he responds in ways that a contemporary Stoic might recognize but also have some doubts about. The pattern is clearest in the case of the fear that Jesus has begun to experience in the face of impending death (12:27). Jesus is portrayed as engaged in a monologue that turns into a prayer. He notes the agitation (ἡ ψυχή μου τετάρακται) and responds with a rhetorical question, asking himself how to respond (καὶ τί εἴπω). The question itself suggests a kind of detachment from the first timorous impression. The response first asks the Father, in a rather non-Stoic way, for deliverance (σῶσόν με ἐκ τῆς ὥρας ταύτης), perhaps reflecting the biblical traditions of lament psalms that possibly lurk in the background of the chapter.[57] But then comes the reaffirmation that duty calls (ἀλλὰ διὰ τοῦτο ἦλθον εἰς τὴν ὥραν ταύτην),[58] a principle (might we call it a πρόληψις?) that runs through the Fourth Gospel.[59] The concluding invocation to glorify the name of the Father and above all the voice from heaven that comes in response to Jesus' prayer (12:28) do not fit comfortably in a Stoic environment. Fear is overcome by a sense of duty, but also by an appeal to and an external affirmation from the One from whom duties flow. A Stoic, such as Cleanthes, might offer his famous hymn to Zeus, but he probably would not expect the kind of response that Jesus receives.

If the Stoic-like pattern of a response to a potentially emotive movement of the soul is discernible in chapter 12, it is less clear within the framework of the narrative of the emotion-laden chapter 11. The stirrings of anger and grief that lead to Jesus' tears (11:33–35) may not be "emotions" in the technical Stoic sense, and the passage from Seneca (*Ira* 2.2.5) about sadness at the sight of mourners not being grief might help one who wants to detect Johannine compatibility with Stoicism

---

[53] Epictetus, *Diss.* 1.20.7.
[54] Epictetus, *Diss.* 1.27.6.
[55] Epictetus, *Diss.* 1.27.7–10.
[56] Epictetus, *Diss.* 1.28.25.
[57] On the allusions to the psalms, see Beutler 1978; Thyen 1979, 533; Daly-Denton 2000, 253–58.
[58] The sources of the Johannine motif of the "sending" of the Son no doubt lie in prophetic christological patterns (on which, see Meeks 1967; Miranda 1977; Boring 1978–1979). Nonetheless, Epictetus would have understood the notion of the philosophical hero, the true Cynic, being on a divine mission (see *Diss.* 3.22.23–25).
[59] See 4:34; 5:23–24, 30, 37; 6:38–39; 7:16, 28, 33; 8:16, 18, 26, 29; 9:4.

here. What we do not find is a narrative of Jesus confronting his impression with a set of principles or practices that would shape the movement of the soul and steer it away from its potentially pathetic path. Instead, the relationship between emotion and action that we find in the final stage of the story is precisely what Stoics would find troubling. Whatever it is that upsets Jesus about the situation, it does appear to be his emotion that at least accompanies and perhaps motivates the action of raising Lazarus (ἐμβριμώμενος ἐν ἑαυτῷ ἔρχεται εἰς τὸ μνημεῖον [11:38]). This could represent the kind of relationship between anger and action that Peripatetics defended and Stoics rejected. For the Aristotelian opponents of the Stoa, moderated emotion properly channeled could have good effects.[60] Alternatively, it might be that the anger remains interior "within himself" (ἐν ἑαυτῷ), where a good Stoic such as Seneca would recommend keeping whatever stirrings there might be. But his weeping (11:35) is an open display of grief.

Although the portrait of Jesus' treatment of his own "emotions" seems to run counter to the general Stoic mold, his interactions with the mourning women in John 11, whatever the subtle differences between them, do suggest a response to their grief that has at least a formal resemblance to Stoic principles. In that response Jesus presents a truth or series of truths that should eliminate the grounds of their grief: Lazarus will rise again (11:23). Martha understands Jesus eschatologically (11:24), but he insists that what he means refers to the present (11:25–26). However we understand the Fourth Gospel's eschatology,[61] the principle is clear that the divine power dramatically encountered in the presence of Jesus banishes fear of death now and forevermore. However the characters in the dramatic setting of the Fourth Gospel may develop, the book as a whole, on this point at least, is engaged in a bit of therapy for its readers, providing them with the principle on which they may escape "fear of death."[62] Stoics might recognize the strategy, though probably they would be unimpressed with the eschatological solution.

5. Positive "Emotion"

Most of the emoting in the Fourth Gospel appears in chapters 11–12, as the public ministry of Jesus reaches its conclusion. In what follows, there appear other hints at emotional states that merit brief attention. As his "hour" (12:23) begins, Jesus displays his love for his own as he dines with them (13:1) and teaches them about self-giving love through example (13:15), command (13:34; 15:12), and proverb (15:13).[63] The love that Jesus exemplifies and teaches leads to a relationship between himself and his disciples (15:4) and between all of them and the Father

---

[60] See Seneca's repeated critique of Academic positions in *Ira* 1.9.2; 1.17.1; 2.13.1; 3.3.1. See also Nussbaum 1994, 402–38.

[61] On resurrection in particular, see Attridge 2008.

[62] The dynamics of the treatment of "fear of death" is not unique to the Fourth Gospel. See also, for example, Heb 2:15. For the background to the imagery of that passage, which may also reflect Stoic elements, see Attridge 1990.

[63] See Thyen 1979; Scholtissek 2004.

(14:2), a relationship of mutual indwelling. It is not clear that any of this love is to be considered an emotion, as opposed to a willing commitment of the self to others and to the community that they form. The relationship does, however, produce one other apparent emotion, a fulfilled joy (χαρά [15:11]). Grief (λύπη) and joy are also paired in a prediction of what the disciples will experience in the future, as they lament the departure of Jesus, over which the world will rejoice. Reversal will occur, however, and the disciples' grief will be turned to lasting joy (16:20–23).[64]

With these passages one might be tempted to compare the Stoic reflections on the "positive emotional states," the *eupatheiai*. Diogenes Laertius provides a handy summary:

> Also they say that there are three emotional states which are good, namely, joy [χαρά], caution [εὐλάβεια], and wishing [βούλησις]. Joy, the counterpart of pleasure, is rational elation; caution, the counterpart of fear, rational avoidance; for though the wise man will never feel fear, he will yet use caution. And they make wishing the counterpart of desire (or craving), inasmuch as it is rational appetency.[65]

Whether the "joy" envisioned by the Fourth Gospel is what the Stoics had in mind is hardly clear, and there may be some reason to doubt that it is. Like so much else in the vocabulary of Stoicism, this common word has a technical meaning. Martha Nussbaum captures its flavor nicely, discussing whether her fictive young woman philosopher, Nikidion, would have accepted the Stoic line as articulated by Seneca:

> But I believe that we should not be lulled by this sort of Stoic rhetoric into thinking that extirpation will leave much of Nikidion's happiness where she is accustomed to find it, while merely getting rid of many difficulties and tensions. The state that Seneca describes is indeed called joy. But consider how he describes it. It is like a child that is born inside of one and never leaves the womb to go out into the world. It has no commerce with laughter and elation. For wise people, we know, are harshly astringent, *austēroi*, intolerant of idle pleasure in themselves and in others.[66]

Seneca's joy, like that promised by Jesus, may be never failing,[67] but it is a "stern matter" (*res severa*), and it is a rather restrained joy (*gaudio . . . blando*) that fills the heart. Nussbaum again summarizes nicely:

> But we can see already that the change to Stoic joy from Nikidion's own is vast. It is the change from suspense and elation to solid self-absorption; from surprise and spontaneity to measured watchfulness; from wonder at the separate and external to security in that which is oneself and one's own.[68]

---

[64] As in the case of Jesus' fear and grief, there are no doubt other echoes of biblical motifs. On sadness turned into joy, see Isa 66:5–14, complete with the illustration of the woman in childbirth. So commentators regularly note. See Barrett 1978, 493; Keener 2003, 2:1045; Thyen 2005, 673.
[65] Diogenes Laertius, *Vit. phil.* 7.116.
[66] Nussbaum 1994, 400, referring to Diogenes Laertius, *Vit. phil.* 7.117.
[67] Seneca, *Ep.* 23.4 ("numquam deficiet, cum semel unde petatur inveneris").
[68] Nussbaum 1994, 401.

However much liberating truth plays a role in the soteriology of the Fourth Gospel, what finally causes the disciples' joy does not seem to be the calm assurance that one is, according to the basic Stoic formula, "living in conformity" with nature. It is rather the joy that arises from the intimacy of personal relation, the fellowship of Father, Son, and Spirit-guided believers. It is a joy that appears in the narrative when the disciples come to see the resurrected one (20:20). The relationship may lack what the Stoics called passions, but it displays an intimate interpersonal dimension and suggests an intensity that the Stoics might have found problematic.

6. Summary

The effort to test the hypothesis that the Fourth Gospel is in some conversation with Stoic traditions has yielded decidedly mixed results. Some elements of the portrait of the serene and detached Jesus echo aspects of the ideal Stoic sage. The portrait of the "emotions" of Jesus does not immediately remove Johannine narrative from the realm of possible Stoic discourse. Stoics recognized that "impressions" had to be tamed by reason lest they become problematic "emotions." The Fourth Gospel does provide means for dealing with what are like "impressions" in the Stoic system, and those means do on occasion seem to have a formal resemblance to the way Stoics exercised their "therapy of desire." Yet the resemblance remains formal. If the evangelist has any relationship to Stoic notions of the passions and their healing, he invests them, as he does in so many other cases, with a new meaning.[69] The principles by which one overcomes the stirrings of grief and fear, and on which positive emotions are based, are ultimately not abstract theories about the simple truth that virtue is the only good and all else is indifferent. Those principles are relationships, with the one who is "the way, and the truth, and the life" (14:6) and with all those who find Spirit-guided access to the Father through him.

Bibliography

Ashton, J. 2007. *Understanding the Fourth Gospel*. 2nd ed. Oxford: Clarendon.
Attridge, H. W. 1990. "Liberating Death's Captives: Reconsideration of an Early Christian Myth." Pages 103–15 in *Gnosticism and the Early Christian World: In Honor of James M. Robinson*. Edited by J. E. Goehring et al. Forum Fascicles 2. Sonoma, Calif.: Polebridge Press.
———. 2001. "Johannesevangelium." Pages 551–62 in vol. 4 of *Religion in Geschichte und Gegenwart: Handwörterbuch für Theologie und Religionswissenschaft*. Edited by H. D. Betz et al. 4th ed. Tübingen: Mohr Siebeck.
———. 2002. "Genre Bending in the Fourth Gospel." *Journal of Biblical Literature* 121:3–21.

---

[69] See Attridge 2002.

———. 2003. "Don't Be Touching Me: Recent Feminist Scholarship on Mary Magdalene." Pages 140–66 in vol. 2 of *A Feminist Companion to John*. Edited by A.-J. Levine with M. Blickenstaff. Feminist Companion to the New Testament and Early Christian Writings 5. London and New York: Sheffield Academic Press.

———. 2005. "Philo and John: Two Riffs on One Logos." *Studia Philonica Annual* 17:103–17.

———. 2006a. "Johannine Christianity." Pages 125–44 in *Origins to Constantine*. Vol. 1 of *The Cambridge History of Christianity*. Edited by M. M. Mitchell and F. M. Young. Cambridge: Cambridge University Press.

———. 2006b. "The Cubist Principle in Johannine Imagery: John and the Reading of Images in Contemporary Platonism." Pages 47–60 in *Imagery in the Gospel of John: Terms, Forms, Themes, and Theology of Figurative Language*. Edited by J. Frey et al. Wissenschaftliche Untersuchungen zum Neuen Testament 200, Tübingen: Mohr-Siebeck.

———. 2008. "From Discord Rises Meaning: Resurrection Motifs in the Fourth Gospel." Pages 1–19 in *The Resurrection of Jesus in the Gospel of John*. Edited by C. R. Koester and R. Bieringer. Wissenschaftliche Untersuchungen zum Neuen Testament 222. Tübingen: Mohr Siebeck.

Barrett, C. K. 1978. *The Gospel According to John: An Introduction with Commentary and Notes on the Greek Text*. 2nd ed. Philadelphia: Westminster.

Beutler, J. 1978. "Psalm 42/43 im Johannesevangelium." *New Testament Studies* 25:33–57.

Borgen, P. 1972. "'Logos Was the True Light': Contributions to the Interpretation of the Prologue of John." *Novum Testamentum* 14:115–30.

Boring, M. E. 1978–1979. "The Influence of Christian Prophecy on the Johannine Portrayal of the Paraclete and Jesus." *New Testament Studies* 25:113–23.

Brennan, T. 1998. "The Old Stoic Theory of Emotions." Pages 21–70 in *The Emotions in Hellenistic Philosophy*. Edited by J. Sihvola and T. Engberg-Pedersen. New Synthese Historical Library 46. Dordrecht: Kluwer.

Brown, R. E. 1961. "Incidents That Are Units in the Synoptic Gospels but Dispersed in St. John." *Catholic Biblical Quarterly* 23:143–60.

———. 1966. *The Gospel According to John (I–XII)*. Anchor Bible 29. Garden City, N.Y.: Doubleday.

———. 2003. *An Introduction to the Gospel of John*. Edited by F. J. Moloney. Anchor Yale Bible Reference Library. New York: Doubleday.

Bultmann, R. 1971. *The Gospel of John: A Commentary*. Translated by G. R. Beasley-Murray. Oxford: Blackwell.

Colpe, C. 1979. "Von der Logoslehre des Philo zu der des Clemens von Alexandrien." Pages 89–107 in *Kerygma und Logos: Beiträge zu den geistesgeschichtlichen Beziehungen zwischen Antike und Christentum; Festschrift für Carl Andresen zum 70. Geburtstag*. Edited by A. M. Ritter. Göttingen: Vandenhoeck & Ruprecht.

Culpepper, R. A. 1994. *John the Son of Zebedee: The Life of a Legend*. Studies on Personalities of the New Testament. Columbia: University of South Carolina Press.

Daly-Denton, M. 2000. *David in the Fourth Gospel: The Johannine Reception of the Psalms*. Arbeiten zur Geschichte des antiken Judentums und des Urchristentums 47. Leiden: Brill.

Evans, C. 1993. *Word and Glory: On the Exegetical and Theological Background of John's Prologue.* Journal for the Study of the New Testament: Supplement Series 89. Sheffield: Sheffield Academic Press.
Gill, C. 2006. *The Structured Self in Hellenistic and Roman Thought.* Oxford: Oxford University Press.
Haenchen, E. 1984. *John: A Commentary on the Gospel of John.* 2 vols. Hermeneia. Philadelphia: Fortress.
Irwin, T. H. 1998. "Stoic Inhumanity." Pages 219–41 in *The Emotions in Hellenistic Philosophy.* Edited by J. Sihvola and T. Engberg-Pedersen. New Synthese Historical Library 46. Dordrecht: Kluwer.
Käsemann, E. 1966. *Jesu letzter Wille nach Johannes 17.* Tübingen: Mohr Siebeck.
Keener, C. S. 2003. *The Gospel of John: A Commentary.* 2 vols. Peabody, Mass.: Hendrickson.
Kitzberger, I. R. 1995. "Mary of Bethany and Mary of Magdala—Two Female Characters in the Johannine Passion Narrative: A Feminist, Narrative-Critical Reader Response." *New Testament Studies* 41:564–86.
Lang, M. 2004. "Johanneische Abschiedsreden und Senecas Konsolationsliteratur: Wie konnte ein Römer John 13,31–17,26 lesen?" Pages 365–412 in *Kontexte des Johannesevangeliums: Das vierte Evangelium in religions- und traditionsgeschichtlicher Perspektive.* Edited by J. Frey and U. Schnelle. Wissenschaftliche Untersuchungen zum Neuen Testament 175. Tübingen: Mohr Siebeck.
Larsen, K. B. 2008. *Recognizing the Stranger: Recognition Scenes in the Gospel of John.* Biblical Interpretation Series 93. Leiden: Brill.
Leonhardt-Balzer, J. 2004. "Der Logos und die Schöpfung: Streiflichter bei Philo (Op 20–25) und im Johannesprolog (Joh 1,1–18)." Pages 295–320 in *Kontexte des Johannesevangeliums: Das vierte Evangelium in religions- und traditionsgeschichtlicher Perspektive.* Edited by J. Frey and U. Schnelle. Wissenschaftliche Untersuchungen zum Neuen Testament 175. Tübingen: Mohr Siebeck.
Lindars, B. 1972. *The Gospel of John.* New Century Bible. London: Oliphants.
———. 1992. "A New Analysis of the Lazarus Story of John 11." *New Testament Studies* 38:89–104.
Loader, W. 1981. *Sohn und Hoherpriester: Eine traditionsgeschichtliche Untersuchung zur Christologie des Hebräerbriefes.* Wissenschaftliche Monografien zum Alten und Neuen Testament 53. Neukirchen: Neukirchener Verlag.
Long, A. A. 1986. *Hellenistic Philosophy: Stoics, Epicureans, Sceptics.* 2nd ed. Berkeley: University of California Press.
Long, A. A., and D. N. Sedley. 1987. *The Hellenistic Philosophers.* 2 vols. Cambridge: Cambridge University Press.
Meeks, W. A. 1967. *The Prophet-King: Moses Traditions and the Johannine Christology.* Supplements to Novum Testamentum 14. Leiden: Brill.
———. 1996. "The Ethics of the Fourth Evangelist." Pages 317–26 in *Exploring the Gospel of John: In Honor of D. Moody Smith.* Edited by R. A. Culpepper and C. C. Black. Louisville: Westminster John Knox Press.
Miranda, J. P. 1977. *Die Sendung Jesu im vierten Evangelium: Religions- und theologiegeschichtliche Untersuchungen zu den Sendungsformeln.* Stuttgarter Bibelstudien 87. Stuttgart: Katholisches Bibelwerk.

Moloney, F. J. 1994. "The Faith of Martha and Mary: A Narrative Approach to John 11,17–40." *Biblica* 75:471–93.

———. 1998. *The Gospel of John*. Sacra Pagina 4. Collegeville, Minn.: Liturgical Press.

Nussbaum, M. 1994. *The Therapy of Desire: Theory and Practice in Hellenistic Ethics*. Martin Classical Lectures 2. Princeton, N.J.: Princeton University Press.

Reydams-Schils, G. 2005. *The Roman Stoics: Self, Responsibility, and Affection*. Chicago: University of Chicago Press.

Rist, J. M. 1969. *Stoic Philosophy*. Cambridge: Cambridge University Press.

Schnackenburg, R. 1980. *The Gospel According to John*. 3 vols. New York: Seabury.

Schnelle, U. 1992. *Antidocetic Christology in the Gospel of John: An Investigation of the Place of the Fourth Gospel in the Johannine School*. Translated by L. M. Maloney. Minneapolis: Fortress.

Scholtissek, K. 2004. "'Eine grössere Liebe als diese hat niemand, als wenn einer sein Leben hingibt für seine Freunde' (Joh 15,13)." Pages 413–42 in *Kontexte des Johannesevangeliums: Das vierte Evangelium in religions- und traditionsgeschichtlicher Perspektive*. Edited by J. Frey and U. Schnelle. Wissenschaftliche Untersuchungen zum Neuen Testament 175. Tübingen: Mohr Siebeck.

Siegert, F. 2004. "Der Logos, 'älterer Sohn' des Schöpfers und 'zweiter Gott': Philons Logos und der Johannesprolog." Pages 277–94 in *Kontexte des Johannesevangeliums: Das vierte Evangelium in religions- und traditionsgeschichtlicher Perspektive*. Edited by J. Frey and U. Schnelle. Wissenschaftliche Untersuchungen zum Neuen Testament 175. Tübingen: Mohr Siebeck.

Sihvola J., and T. Engberg-Pedersen, eds. 1998. *The Emotions in Hellenistic Philosophy*. New Synthese Historical Library 46. Dordrecht: Kluwer.

Sorabji, R. 1998. "Chrysippus — Posidonius — Seneca: A High-Level Debate on Emotion." Pages 149–70 in *The Emotions in Hellenistic Philosophy*. Edited by J. Sihvola and T. Engberg-Pedersen. New Synthese Historical Library 46. Dordrecht: Kluwer.

———. 2000. *Emotion and Peace of Mind: From Stoic Agitation to Christian Temptation*. Oxford: Oxford University Press.

Stibbe, M. W. G. 1994. "A Tomb with a View: John 11.1–44 in Narrative-Critical Perspective." *New Testament Studies* 40:38–54.

Story, C. I. K. 1991. "The Mental Attitude of Jesus at Bethany." *New Testament Studies* 37:51–66.

Thyen, H. 1979. "Niemand hat grössere Liebe als die, daß er sein Leben für seine Freunde hingibt." Pages 467–81 in *Theologia Crucis, Signum Crucis: Festschrift für Erich Dinkler zum 70. Geburtstag*. Edited by C. Andresen and G. Klein. Tübingen: Mohr Siebeck.

———. 2005. *Das Johannesevangelium*. Handbuch zum Neuen Testament 6. Tübingen: Mohr Siebeck.

Wolterstorff, N. 2008. *Justice: Rights and Wrongs*. Princeton, N.J.: Princeton University Press.

6

THE EMOTIONAL JESUS:
ANTI-STOICISM IN THE FOURTH GOSPEL?

Gitte Buch-Hansen
University of Copenhagen

1. The Emotional Jesus

Knowing everything that is about to happen, the anointed Son of Man proceeds through the first ten chapters of the Fourth Gospel in a lofty—we may even say, almost Stoic—manner.[1] However, the description of Jesus changes as he sets out for Jerusalem the last time. When the betrayal by one of his own disciples draws near, Jesus is repeatedly seized by emotional upheavals. In this Gospel, in which Jesus' heavenly origin as the eternal λόγος is most perceptible, he is also portrayed as a more emotional character than in the Synoptics. This tension has serious consequences for our approach to the Fourth Gospel. John's concept of πνεῦμα—his pneumatic theology (4:24) and his pneumatic anthropology—invites us to a Stoic interpretation of the Gospel, but Jesus' emotions challenge the Stoic ideal of ἀπάθεια and a priori seem to rule out any attempt to situate the Gospel in the prevailing philosophy of its age.[2] The aim of this essay is to demonstrate that this need not be the case. But let us first look at the way that our problem presents itself in John.

1.1. The Johannine Jesus and His Emotions—A Challenge to Stoic Values?

Provoked by Jesus' statement that he and the Father are one, the Jews of Jerusalem had attempted several times to stone Jesus (5:18; 8:59; 10:31). During the

---

[1] It was this loftiness that led Käsemann (1971, 26) to characterize the Johannine Jesus as a divine stranger. The depiction of Christ as an "über die Erde schreitender Gott" (Käsemann 1971, 62) was symptomatic of the naïve Docetic Christology of the Fourth Gospel. Similarly, Stibbe notices that up to this point, apart from an isolated reference to Jesus' tiredness in 4:7, "Jesus has not been portrayed as a man with obvious weaknesses, needs and emotions" (1994, 44).

[2] In this essay, translations of the Fourth Gospel are my own. Unless otherwise indicated, translations of Greek and Latin texts are from the editions listed in the bibliography.

Feast of Tabernacles, the conflict aggravates and forces Jesus to leave Jerusalem. Jesus withdraws with his disciples to point zero, the place on the other side of the Jordan where John had been practicing his baptism (10:40) and where he had himself gathered his first followers. While staying there, Jesus is informed about the illness of his beloved friend Lazarus,[3] who lives with his two sisters in Bethany, a village near Jerusalem (11:3). Knowing that this illness will not lead to death but serves the glory of God, Jesus waits two days before he with his disciples heads for Bethany (11:4–6). The wait, however, causes Lazarus to die before Jesus reaches the village. The sisters of Lazarus lament Jesus' delay; they believe that if he had been there, he would have prevented their brother from dying (11:21, 32). Meanwhile, several Jews have arrived from Jerusalem at the family's house in order to console the bereaved sisters. When Jesus meets Mary and the Jews and sees them crying, he is strongly affected by the situation (11:33). He asks Mary to take him to the place where Lazarus is buried (11:34), whereupon he bursts into tears (11:35). The Jews interpret Jesus' tears as a sign of his loving affection for Lazarus (11:36). As the crowd approaches Lazarus's grave, Jesus is once more upset (11:38). In spite of Martha's protest that since her brother has been dead for four days there will be a stench, Jesus orders that the stone be removed from the entrance to the grave and commands Lazarus to leave the cave, which he does. The returning Jews bring the message of Lazarus's resurrection to Jerusalem. This piece of information aggravates the conflict between Jesus and the authorities in Jerusalem, and the enigmatic hour of the Son of Man's glorification draws near (12:23). Again, Jesus is emotionally overwrought by the situation, and his soul is troubled (12:27). Only on one further occasion is Jesus seized by an emotional upheaval, and that is when, during the last common meal, he is about to reveal the identity of his betrayer (13:21). Having received the bread, Judas immediately leaves the disciples' company and disappears into the night (13:30). From that moment on, Jesus appears totally dedicated to his appointed task and is no longer disturbed by any emotions.

Different expressions are employed to describe Jesus' (and his disciples') emotional behavior:

11:33: [Jesus] ἐμβριμήσατο τῷ πνεύματι καὶ ἐτάραξεν ἑαυτόν

11:35: ἐδάκρυσεν ὁ Ἰησοῦς

11:38: Ἰησοῦς οὖν πάλιν ἐμβριμώμενος ἐν ἑαυτῷ

12:27: νῦν ἡ ψυχή μου [Jesus'] τετάρακται

13:21: ταῦτα εἰπὼν [ὁ] Ἰησοῦς ἐταράχθη τῷ πνεύματι

14:1, 27: μὴ ταρασσέσθω ὑμῶν [the disciples'] ἡ καρδία

The anthropology of the evangelist seems to be hidden in these idioms. The Fourth Gospel describes the emotional experience physically, associates it with the

---

[3]The Greek term for "illness" here is ἀσθένεια (11:2, 3, 4, 6), the literal meaning of which is "weakness." The term was used by the Stoics for weakness of will, which was their version of ἀκρασία.

spirit, and locates it in the soul and in the heart. Although such emotional experience does not immediately fit the Stoic idea of ἀπάθεια, the description has several features in common with the Stoic theory of emotions. According to the Stoics, an emotional judgment coexisted with moderations in the tensional pattern of the πνεῦμα of the leading part of the soul (τὸ ἡγεμονικόν), which had its place in or around the heart (ἡ καρδία). It was these physiological changes in the πνεῦμα that engendered the feeling or psychological awareness of being emotionally affected.[4] As just noted, this approach to Jesus' emotions raises more problems than it solves because Jesus' emotional upheaval challenges the Stoic ideal of freedom from passion.[5] If it is philosophical at all, the ideal embodied by the crying Savior seems closer to the Peripatetic idea of μετριοπάθεια than the Stoic ἀπάθεια. Aristotle and the Peripatetics valued the emotions as a source for interpersonal identification and as the basis for social life. Consequently, their ideal was the moderation of passions, not their extinction.[6] Does the Fourth Gospel in fact side with the Aristotelians in the discussion of the value of emotions? Do Jesus' tears reflect the charge of inhumanity so often leveled against the Stoic sage in antiquity?

I will argue that Jesus' emotional outbursts do not have to reflect an anti-Stoic stance on John's part. In order to substantiate this claim, I will look at the early reception of the Gospel in Origen's *Commentary on St. John's Gospel*. Here this otherwise Platonic philosopher and exegete offers an interpretation of Jesus' emotional behavior that accords well with the Stoic theory of emotions, especially in the revised version that we find in Seneca's *On Anger* (*De ira*). However, the philosophical reception of Jesus' emotions only sharpens the problem with which we are wrestling: maybe Origen's exposition of Jesus' emotional upheavals is the interpreter's apologetic attempt to justify an embarrassing Johannine fact. Once more we must ask: if the evangelist had any sympathy with Stoic theory, why did he not depict Jesus as a lofty sage throughout his Gospel? A suitable answer may be found with help from the Jewish philosopher and exegete Philo, or, more precisely, from Philo's reworking of the Stoic doctrine. Since Philo approves of the Stoic ideal of ἀπάθεια, he is forced by the continuous crying of his biblical heroes to adjust the Stoic theory of emotions. His solution is to develop the Stoic doctrine of legitimate and virtuous emotions, the εὐπάθειαι. Seemingly, Philo invents a fourth εὐπάθεια corresponding to pain, of which two subspecies exist: the virtuous teacher may be subjected to pain when his disciples turn away from the truth, and the disciples

---

[4] The locus classicus in the Stoic corpus for the heart as the place of emotional awareness was Galen's quotation in *De placitis Hippocratis et Platonis* (De Lacy 1978) of Chrysippus's theory: "They [the Stoics] say that distress and anxiety and suffering are not pains . . . that arise in some region other than *the governing part* (of the soul) [τόπῳ ἢ τῷ ἡγεμονικῷ]. We shall say the same also about joy and good cheer, which reveal their origin in the area of the *heart* [περὶ τὴν καρδίαν]" (*PHP* 3.7.3 [my italics]). See also Frede 1986, 102.

[5] This point is repeated several times in Stephen Voorwinde's book on Jesus' emotions in the Fourth Gospel: "Although John records no Gethsemane scene he hardly portrays a Jesus who conforms to the Stoic ideal of *apatheia* or to the Hellenistic Jewish ideal of devout reason" (2005, 194–95).

[6] See, for example, Dillon 2000, sect. VIII. See also Nussbaum 1994, chs. 2–3.

may be in a true and legitimate kind of pain when they recognize their failure and regret it. A similar idea seems to be at work in 2 Corinthians, in Paul's account of an earlier letter that has come to be known as the Letter of Tears (see 2 Cor 2:3-4). The idea of virtuous pain may in this way have entered intellectual Jewish Christian circles. In conclusion, a Stoic reading of the Fourth Gospel is not a priori ruled out because of Jesus' tears.

Before we turn to our ancient sources from Origen, Seneca, Philo, and Paul, we will take a brief look at the reception of Jesus' emotions in modern exegesis.

1.2. Jesus' Emotions in Modern Exegesis

A survey of the scholarly reception of John 11 reveals two opposing tendencies.[7] A predominantly German tradition emphasizes Jesus' anger on the basis of 11:33. Schnackenburg's translation of the Greek text, which follows Luther's, is typical of the German tradition: "When Jesus saw the way she and her fellow Jews cried, indignation and irritation seized him."[8] In contrast, the Anglo-American tradition highlights 11:35, in which Jesus features as a compassionate being, deeply moved by the situation. As a representative of the latter tradition, Raymond Brown translates: "Now when Jesus saw her weeping, and the Jews who had accompanied her also weeping, he shuddered, moved with the deepest emotions."[9]

The contrasting interpretations reflect an exegetical problem: when read against the background of classical and biblical usage, the verb ἐμβριμᾶσθαι unequivocally denotes the display of strong, even aggressive excitement.[10] However, when this aggression is transposed to the Fourth Gospel and 11:33, 38 are seen as displays of anger, it disturbs the immediate context, where Jesus is himself moved to tears (11:35) by the grief of Mary and her Jewish neighbors (11:33).[11] Jesus' crying is understood by the Jews as a sign of his loving affection for Lazarus (11:36). Their interpretation accords with the sisters' description of the relation (κύριε, ἴδε ὃν φιλεῖς ἀσθενεῖ [11:3]), the narrator's summary of the situation (ἠγάπα δὲ ὁ Ἰησοῦς τὴν Μάρθαν καὶ τὴν ἀδελφὴν αὐτῆς καὶ τὸν Λάζαρον [11:5]), and Jesus' own statement about the relation (Λάζαρος ὁ φίλος ἡμῶν κεκοίμηται [11:11]). We may conclude that the interpretive problems arise from the fact that the lexical meaning of the idiom in 11:33 is on a collision course with the text's unanimous statements about Jesus' relation to his beloved friend.

Both interpretations attempt to do away with the tension between the idiom and the context. The German tendency seeks a plausible explanation of Jesus' anger

---

[7] See Lindars 1992, 90.
[8] My translation of Schnackenburg 1971, 419.
[9] Brown 1966, 421.
[10] The classic example to which the commentators refer is Aeschylus's *Seven against Thebes*, where the "mares" are "snorting [ἐμβριμώμενας] in the bridles" as they are led to their appointed places in the ambush outside the city gates. The breath whistling in the horses' nostrils demonstrates their physical excitement. See Lindars 1992, 92.
[11] Lindars says that it "makes havoc of the context" (1992, 90).

vis-à-vis, first, the tears of Mary and her mourning Jewish neighbors and, second, Jesus' own tears. The solution is that Jesus' emotional reaction is dissociated from the grief of the mourners; Jesus' tears represent an anger directed at what their tears signify, namely, a continuous disbelief in spite of Jesus' teaching about the resurrection. The differentiation between Jesus' tears and those of the mourners is supported by the choice of different words for the emotions of the characters in the story: κλαίειν for the mourners (11:33), δακρύειν for Jesus (11:35). Jesus cries in indignation, not in compassion. Some interpretations are able to maintain Jesus' lexical anger and still make sense of the context. Raymond Brown, for instance, suggests that the anger is directed at Satan as the demonic and destructive power of death who has brought sin and sorrow into the world and who now, through Judas, is the ultimate agent behind Jesus' death (13:2).[12] In this way, opposing emotions may be present simultaneously. Jesus' anger is directed at Satan, while he shares his love and compassion with the victims of death.

Whether Jesus reacts out of anger or compassion, his emotions are seen by modern readers as an adequate and theologically meaningful response to the situation. The Stoic ideal of ἀπάθεια is seldom discussed. In general, modern commentaries do not attempt to situate their more positive evaluation of Jesus' anger or compassion in the discourse of emotions so prominent in Hellenistic philosophy. In contrast with modern exegesis, Origen's explanation of Jesus' emotions cannot be understood apart from that ancient discourse.

2. Origen's Interpretation of Jesus' Emotions

In Origen's *Commentary on St. John's Gospel*,[13] Jesus' emotional reactions to the death of Lazarus (John 11), to his own impending death (John 12), and to Judas's betrayal (John 13) are interpreted in light of one another.[14] Unfortunately, most of the books with Origen's comments on the Lazarus story have been lost; Book 28, which we have, begins with 11:39.[15] Fragments on 11:34 and 11:35 (Fragment 83) and on 11:38 (Fragment 84) exist, but no specific comments have survived on the difficult verse 11:33. However, 11:33 is discussed in relation to the comments on 11:38 (Fragment 84) and 13:21 (Fragment 100). Fortunately, Book

---

[12] Brown finds inspiration for his interpretation of Jesus' anger in the Synoptic tradition: a better explanation of it "would be the reason offered for similar displays of anger in the synoptic tradition, namely, that he was angry because he found himself face to face with the real power of Satan which, in this instance, was represented by death" (1966, 435). Brown's appeal to Satan seems to be inspired also by Origen's reading of John.

[13] Analyses of Origen's reading of the Lazarus story are found also in Story 1991; Lindars 1992.

[14] Text from Brooke 1896.

[15] Books 19–20 comment on John 8; Books 21–27 are lost; Book 28 begins with John 11:39 and finishes the comments on John 11; Books 29–31 are lost; Book 32 covers John 13 but ends with 13:33. An English version of the books is found in Heine 1993. Since Heine does not translate the fragments, the translations presented in this essay are my own.

28 on the final part of the Lazarus story provides us with a proper context for our understanding of the various fragments. Also the book on John 12 is lost, but a fragment on 12:27 has survived (Fragment 88). Book 32, the last book in the commentary and probably also the last that Origen wrote on John, comments on John 13. We also have a fragment on 13:21 (Fragment 100); parts of it are found in Book 32, other parts probably belong to the lost books. When the surviving fragments and books are read together, we get a coherent picture of how Origen understood Jesus' emotions.

The tension between Jesus' anger and his tears, with which modern exegesis wrestles, is solved by Origen through his interpretation of the ultimate cause of Jesus' anger, fear, and lament. In order to explain Jesus' tears, Origen has recourse to an allegorical/anagogic interpretation of Lazarus's death. In Fragment 83, Origen comments on Jesus' request to know where the mourning Jews have placed Lazarus (11:34). Of course, the heavenly λόγος cannot be without this knowledge, Origen states; consequently, the Savior's question must be interpreted allegorically. The request should be understood as a divine command concerning the disciples' relation to their own mortal bodies: they themselves are to leave their corpses behind.[16] Origen, somewhat enigmatically, explains, "If anyone ignores that he belongs to God, he will be ignored himself."[17] In order to understand Origen's argument in the fragment, Book 28 in which the allegorical meaning of Lazarus's death is discussed must be consulted: "The anagogical sense concerning the passage is not difficult. . . . For he asked that the one who had sinned, after becoming his friend, and has become dead to God return to life by divine power."[18] When Jesus calls Lazarus forth from the cave, the Jews gathered at the grave marvel "that someone who had become foul-smelling from sins to death and was dead to virtue, should return to virtue."[19] Origen summarizes his exegesis of Lazarus's death by drawing an exhortative conclusion:

> Now, we ought to be aware that there are some Lazaruses even now who, after they have become Jesus' friends, have become sick and died, and as dead persons they have remained in the tomb and the land of the dead with the dead.[20]

When in Fragment 83 Origen stated, "But if it should happen that someone among his beloved remains in the grave, Jesus cries,"[21] it is this kind of psychological death that Origen allows Jesus to lament.[22] In particular, beginners in faith

---

[16] Fragment 83 (Brooke 1896, 2:292, lines 3–4): ὥς γε τοῖς μαθηταῖς ἐντέλλεται ἀφιέναι τοὺς νεκρούς.

[17] Fragment 83 (Brooke 1896, 2:292, lines 1–3). Origen quotes 1 Cor 14:37-38.

[18] Book 28 (Heine 1993, §49; Brooke 1896, 2:115, lines 23-28).

[19] Book 28 (Heine 1993, §50; Brooke 1896, 2:115, lines 28-32).

[20] Book 28 (Heine 1993, §54; Brooke 1896, 2:116, lines 20-25).

[21] Fragment 83 (Brooke 1896, 2:292, lines 4–5): δακρύει δὲ ὁ Ἰησοῦς ἐάν τις αὐτοῦ τῶν φίλων ἐν μνημείῳ γένηται.

[22] Origen's allegorical interpretation may be justified by the fact that the word used for Lazarus's illness in John 11:2, 3, 4, 6 is ἀσθένεια, which was the Stoic term for moral weakness. As we noted in an earlier footnote, the term was used by the Stoics for weakness of will, which was their version of ἀκρασία.

are in danger of this moral death. "I think," Origen says, "that the choice of those still advancing is changeable and susceptible to willing the opposite to what it formerly preferred."²³ Because the disciples are aware of this danger, they look at one another with uncertainty when Jesus reveals that one among them is going to betray him. Origen explains their reaction: "Since they have learned with what powers we wrestle, they were cautious [εὐλαβοῦντο] because of the uncertainty in men, lest perhaps they be overcome and take upon themselves even the betrayal of their teacher."²⁴

Origen inquires how this change of attitude may occur. The danger resides with the body-bound passions: in order to enter the human heart and disturb the sound choices of the soul, Satan makes use of the passions. Satan is, Origen claims, "the ruler of passion in the time of salvation."²⁵ The case of Judas is a vivid example of how Satan affects human beings. Due to his love of money, Judas's heart became susceptible to the satanic powers of evil thoughts and wicked choices.²⁶ In order to make Judas a warning example and invest his story with a moral point, Origen emphasizes that Judas did not begin as a wicked person. In fact, it was the other way around: "Judas was holy and changed for the worse."²⁷ When Jesus states that "one of you will betray me," it is, according to Origen, "said marvelously with the following meaning: he who betrays me is not alien from my disciples, and he is not even one of the many disciples, but he is one of the apostles honored by my choice."²⁸ After all, only a person fully acquainted with Jesus' great and numerous teachings would be capable of betraying Jesus in his true greatness.²⁹

The anger that Jesus demonstrates on his way to Lazarus's grave, when he ἐνεβριμήσατο τῷ πνεύματι (11:33), and also later when he faces the coming of Judas's betrayal and is troubled in his spirit (13:21) emerges from his knowledge of the confrontation with the evil one who is in wait. Although Jesus "is momentarily stuck with fear due to the excessiveness of the wickedness that has caught Judas's character,"³⁰ his anger is ultimately directed at Satan and the destructive passionate powers that "in the time of salvation wage war against the Savior."³¹ In spite of the fact that anger and fear trouble Jesus' soul "in a human manner,"³² his fear is not caused by the prospect of dying. The Savior fears only "that he himself would not be

---

²³Book 32 (Heine 1993, §255; Brooke 1896, 2:187, lines 1-4): ἐμέμνηντο γὰρ, οἶμαι, ἄνθρωποι ὄντες, ὅτι τρεπτή ἐστιν ἡ προαίρεσις τῶν ἔτι προκοπτόντων καὶ ἐπιδεχομένη τὰ ἐναντία θέλειν οἷς πρότερον προέθετο.
²⁴Book 32 (Heine 1993, §256; Brooke 1896, 2:187, lines 4-7).
²⁵Fragment 88 (Brooke 1896, 2:294, lines 23-24—295, line 1): Πᾶσα ἡ τοῦ Σατανᾶ δύναμις ἅμα τοῦ αὐτῆς ἡγεμόνος κατὰ τὸν καιρὸν τοῦ σωτηρίου πάθους ἐπεστράτευσε τῷ σωτῆρι.
²⁶Book 32 (Heine 1993, §244; Brooke 1896, 2:185, line 28): φιλάργυρος.
²⁷Book 32 (Heine 1993, §247; Brooke 1896, 2:186, line 11): ὅτι ἅγιος ὢν μεταπέπτωκεν.
²⁸Book 32 (Heine 1993, §235; Brooke 1896, 2:184, lines 11-14).
²⁹Book 32 (Heine 1993, §237; Brooke 1896, 2:184, lines 19-22).
³⁰Fragment 100 (Brooke 1896, 2:305, lines 14-17).
³¹Fragment 88 (Brooke 1896, 2:294, lines 23-24—295, line 1).
³²Fragment 88 (Brooke 1896, 2:295, lines 1-2): ἡ τοῦ σωτῆρος ψυχὴ ἀνθρωπίνως ἐταράττετο.

the weaker one."³³ "In order that he may become the cause of an everlasting salvation for those who are obedient to him,"³⁴ Christ is going to surrender himself to the evil one and his power, but he fears that, due to his personal strength, the confrontation with Satan will be so short that the salvation will be without the intended effect in the end. According to Origen, it is this fear that causes Jesus to pray in John 12:

> But see if not [John 12:27-28], he also prays himself that—although the struggle against those evil forces that wage war against him will not be of long duration, but finished in a moment—this will suffice for Jesus' soul to conquer every force of the evil one.³⁵

The prospect of a confrontation with Satan left Jesus' soul in distress and troubled it in "a human manner." Nevertheless, Origen claims, "the disturbance was not in the manner, when someone is subdued by the trouble and accepts it; it was only of a momentary character."³⁶ Jesus only experiences a sting of anger and fear, and then the feeling is over and gone; Origen's Jesus is capable of mastering his emotions. The different wordings with which the evangelist describes Jesus' upheavals in 11:33 and 11:38, respectively, demonstrate Jesus' ability to handle his emotions. When Jesus is still at a distance from Lazarus's grave, he is in a state in which he ἐνεβριμήσατο τῷ πνεύματι (11:33), but later, when Jesus draws near to the grave, the evangelist tells us that he is ἐμβριμώμενος ἐν ἑαυτῷ" (11:38). The meaning of those idioms is discussed by Origen in his comments on 11:38, in which he notes,

> Now when he [Jesus] approaches the dead, he no longer ἐμβριμᾶται τῷ πνεύματι. Instead, the ἐμβρίμησις is within himself [ἐν ἑαυτῷ].... Therefore, he says: Ἐμβριμώμενος ἐν ἑαυτῷ ἔρχεται εἰς τὸ μνημεῖον. Thus, he once more rebukes [ἐπιτιμᾷ] the passion [πάθει].³⁷

When Jesus approaches Lazarus's grave, his emotional upheaval changes from being displayed outwardly to being kept within himself—that is, in check. Nevertheless, the outward display of the emotion also has a purpose. Origen understands the idiom ἐνεβριμήσατο τῷ πνεύματι as synonymous with the rebuke or censure of emotions (ἐπιτιμᾷ πάθει).³⁸ Jesus condemns, first outwardly then inwardly, the weapon that Satan uses to conquer the human soul and influence their choice, namely, the passion.

Here I summarize. According to Origen, Jesus' display of emotions serves several purposes. First, it is so that "we may learn that he [Jesus] has been gener-

---

³³Fragment 88 (Brooke 1896, 2:295, lines 2-3): οὐ τὸν θάνατον δειλιῶσα, εἰ καὶ τοῦτο ἀνθρώπινον, ἀλλὰ τὸ μὴ ἡττηθῆναι.
³⁴Fragment 88 (Brooke 1896, 2:295, lines 4-5): καὶ ἐπείπερ ἔμελλε τοῖς ὑπακούουσιν αὐτῷ αἴτιος σωτηρίας αἰωνίου γίνεσθαι.
³⁵Fragment 88 (Brooke 1896, 2:295, lines 9-13).
³⁶Fragment 88 (Brooke 1896, 2:295, lines 5-8): διὰ τοῦτο περὶ τούτων ἐλυπεῖτο αὐτοῦ ἡ ψυχὴ, καὶ ἐταράττετο, οὐχ ὡς ἄν τις νομίσειεν ὑπὸ τῆς ταραχῆς κατακρατούμενος, ἀλλ' ἀκαριαίως.
³⁷Fragment 84 (Brooke 1896, 2:292, lines 6-11).
³⁸This is also the conclusion of Lindars (1992, 95).

ated human ... just like us."[39] The sudden occurrence of an emotion testifies to the true humanity of the divinely begotten Son. Second, Jesus warns his disciples (and Origen's) against the satanic passion that is the cause of his friends' psychological death. Instead of being obedient to the will of God, they have become obedient to the desires of their bodies; they ignore God, and so they will be ignored.[40] Soon the satanic power will also be the cause of Jesus' own physical death. When in Fragment 83 Jesus summons his disciples to leave the corpses behind, this is probably a request to live as if the body with its desires was already dead.[41] Finally, by his own behavior Jesus provides his own and the Gospel's audience with an example of emotional management that ought to be followed.

Origen succeeds in giving an account of the Johannine Jesus' emotions that solves the tension between Jesus' display of anger (11:33) and his crying (11:35). By his allegorization of Jesus' tears, Origen steers free of the impression that Jesus might have submitted to a grief that would, first, be at odds with his display of anger, but also with the behavior expected of a Stoic sage. Origen's identification of the cause of Jesus' anger accords with the condemnation of the passions that we find in Hellenistic moral philosophy. Throughout the Fourth Gospel, Jesus' emotional upheavals are caused by the prospect of a confrontation with the evil powers of Satan.

At first glance, Raymond Brown's interpretation of Jesus' emotions resembles Origen's, but in Origen's interpretation there is no room for grief, no room for compassion. Origen's Jesus only experiences emotions that comply with the purpose of his sending, namely, to deliver the fallen souls from the grasp of bodybound passions and to reestablish them in their former contemplation of God. Jesus' emotional reactions, however short they may be, are measurements of his success or failure as Savior.

To a modern reader, Origen's exegesis of Jesus' emotions may seem unnecessarily complicated, strained, and in any case apologetic. In order to grasp Origen's ideas better, his interpretation must be placed in its proper context: the Stoic doctrine of emotions.

3. The Stoic Doctrine of Emotions

The charge against the Stoic sage of lack of humanity reflects the fact that then, as now, the Stoic aspiration to ἀπάθεια has often been understood exclusively in psychological terms: ἀπάθεια is identified with the so-called Stoic attitude of lofty calmness and an absence of all feelings. The Stoics were famous for their

---

[39] Fragment 84 (Brooke 1896, 2:292, lines 10–11): ἵνα μάθωμεν ὅτι ἄνθρωπος γέγονεν ἀτρέπτως, ὡς ἡμεῖς.

[40] Fragment 83 (Brooke 1896, 2:292, line 2): εἰ δέ τις ἀγνοεῖ ἀγνοεῖται.

[41] In ancient philosophy, the attempt to transcend the desires that originated in the fleshly body was seen as an anticipation of the death when the eternal soul was separated physically from the body. See the discussion of *commentatio mortis* (μελέτη θανάτου) in Aune 1995, 305–12.

provocative and paradoxical statements that pushed the doctrine to extremes. The scandalous Stoic attitude was captured perfectly in the words with which, according to Cicero, the Stoic sage would receive the message of a child's death: "I was already aware that I had begotten a mortal."[42] The paradoxes, however, were invitations to engage in an inquiry into Stoic theory that would in the end explain, illuminate, and justify the enigmatic statement. The Stoic calmness was not the goal of the detachment from passions, but rather was a secondary and, indeed, welcome side effect. Grief, for instance, was problematic because in all its various subspecies it was "rasping and hindering us from viewing the situation as a whole."[43] Calmness was to be pursued only for the sake of the virtuous life—that is, a life lived in accordance with nature.[44] It is when the Stoics' notion of ἀπάθεια is isolated from their physics that it becomes an inhumane way of relating to one's fellow beings.[45] Consequently, the proper context of the doctrine of emotions was neither ethics nor logic, but physics.

Apart from the aspiration to ἀπάθεια, there is yet another aspect of the Stoic doctrine of emotions that has puzzled and provoked scholars: the claim of the Old Stoa that an emotion was throughout a rational phenomenon. Chrysippus (280–206 B.C.E.) identified the emotion with the propositional judgment that (1) evaluated the situation as personally choiceworthy (or the opposite) and, consequently, (2) called for an appropriate action in order to reach or maintain the good (or to shun the bad). To moderns used to the post-Kantian divide between reason and emotion, the claim appears nonsensical. To the ancients, the reduction of emotions to value judgments appeared to contradict common sense. Everyday experience taught that some kind of impulse beyond rational control must be involved in the development of an emotion. Crying against one's will and the abatement of emotions in the course of time were singled out as cases against Chrysippus's definition.[46] But the Old Stoa insisted on the sufficiency and necessity of the judgment for an emotion to develop. It was in this functional and formal sense—that is, as a linguistic proposition—that the emotion was claimed to be a rational phenomenon. However, since the Stoics valued knowledge as the one and only good, the emotions were, from a normative point of view, false evaluations of the situation and thus viewed as irrational responses.[47]

---

[42] Cicero, *Tusc.* 3.30.
[43] Diogenes Laertius, *Vit. phil.* 7.112.
[44] Diogenes Laertius, *Vit. phil.* 7.87.
[45] And even a "stingy" way of relating to one's fellow beings, as claimed by Nussbaum in her analysis of Plato's *Phaedrus*: "For the non-lover of 'Lysias,' though he did make a claim based on *arête*, offered no clear picture of a vision or understanding of the world towards which he would intend to lead his beloved. *He has Stoic apatheia without Stoic physics, and that can indeed seem a cramped and stingy sort of union.* The Stoic, by contrast, offers an understanding of life so awe-inspiring in itself that it claims to transcend the merely personal; inhabiting it, both lovers will feel reverence and awe for the *logos*, and that, they claim, is more exhilarating than feeling it for one another" (Nussbaum 1998, 97 [my italics]).
[46] For the Stoic discussion of Chrysippus's theory, see Gill 1998; Sorabji 1998.
[47] Brennan (1998, 23–24) speaks of the minimal sense in which the emotion as a linguistic proposition is rational and the maximal sense in which it is irrational due to the fact

3.1. The Doctrine of Emotions—and Stoic Physics

The fundamental idea in Stoic physics is the understanding of cosmos as one organic being organized by one continuous, dynamic pneumatic body.[48] Everything that comes into being is part of this coherent whole, variously called the All, Nature, or even God. What we perceive as distinct beings are just parts—that is, analytically and artificially separable entities of the whole.[49] This, of course, pertains to the human being as well. The individual person denotes a region of cosmic matter that is organized by a relatively stable, but continuously fluctuating, pattern of tensional movements in the unified πνεῦμα. It is by the aid of the tensional movements in the surrounding pneumatic continuum that one perceives and communicates, being affected, at least theoretically, by every happening in space and time, while every one of his actions affects the All.

The idea of the dynamic continuum has important implications for the Stoic understanding of the human soul. As part of the dynamic continuum of the All, the microcosmos of the human soul follows the rules of mutual interaction. In opposition to Plato's tripartition of the soul, and Aristotle's differentiation within the soul between a rational wishing part and an irrational desiring one, the Stoics insisted on the unity of the soul and on the mutual interaction between the different faculties of the soul. The two higher faculties of the soul—the divine reason (λόγος) and the animal faculty of sense perception and impulsive movements (ψυχή)—were unified in the leading part of the soul (τὸ ἡγεμονικόν), which was throughout a rational unit.[50] Accordingly, activity in one faculty of the soul was immediately reflected in the other(s). When sense perception gave rise to an impression, the appearance (φαντασία) was immediately presented to the reasoning faculty. Here the impression was verbalized as a proposition and subjected to a scrutiny that evaluated the belief and negotiated the action that was implied by the impression. If reason assented (συνκατάθεσις) to the appearance, the impulse (ὁρμή) was immediately present in the ψυχή, and the action was carried out by the body. In his essay *De virtute morali*, Plutarch summarizes the psychology of the passions perfectly:

---

that the emotion pursues a false goal. Gill (1998, 116–17), operating with the same classification, uses the terms "functional" and "normative."

[48] Christensen (1962) perfectly captures the way that Stoics' thinking hinges on their physics. Samburksy (1959) also makes physics the starting point of Stoic philosophy.

[49] Diogenes Laertius, *Vit. phil.* 7.87–88D: "as Chrysippus says in the first book of his *De finibus*; for our individual natures are parts of the nature of the whole universe [μέρη γὰρ εἰσιν αἱ ἡμέτεραι φύσεις τῆς τοῦ ὅλου]. And this is why the end may be defined as life in accordance with nature [διόπερ τέλος γίνεται τὸ ἀκολούθως τῇ φύσει ζῆν]."

[50] Long (1996, 234–39) argues that in the case of animals, the Stoics made a distinction between soul in a general and a specific sense. In the general sense, soul denotes all the pneumatic bodies that pervade a region of matter and provide it with form, from the cohesive force to the specific intelligible power of higher beings. In the specific sense, soul designates the two higher powers alone, and it is opposed, as the commanding center or governing part (τὸ ἡγεμονικόν), to the body shaped by the two lower powers of cohesion (ἕξις) and growth (φύσις). Without compromising their monism, the Stoics operated in practice with a dualism of body and soul.

Yet all of these men . . . think that the passionate and irrational part of the soul is not distinguished from the rational by any difference or by its nature, but is the same part, which, indeed, they term intelligence and the governing part [ἡγεμονικόν] . . . it contains nothing irrational within itself, but is called irrational whenever, by the overmastering power of our impulses, which have become strong and prevail, it is hurried on to something outrageous which contravenes the convictions of reason. Passion, in fact, according to them, is a vicious and intemperate reason, formed from an evil and perverse judgment which has acquired additional violence and strength.[51]

It was the collapse of the partition of the Academic and Peripatetic soul that caused the Stoics to displace the charge of moral failure from the outer action to the approved inner belief. The assent to a passionate belief was itself the beginning of an action that would be carried through to the end unless another and competing belief happened to impede it. The inner passionate impulse was the "birth" of an action, the outer action nothing but its "afterbirth."[52]

We are now in a position to understand why the notion of ἀπάθεια obtained such a central position in Stoic philosophy. The correct framework of the doctrine of emotions is the physics of the dynamic continuum and the ethical claim that it subsequently engenders. Whereas children and animals followed nature instinctively, human adults were required to use their reasoning potential.[53] The person who reasoned rightly and virtuously adapted his or her self to the All—that is, to Nature. Passionate beliefs were failures to comply with the natural development and destination of the human being. What was wrong was first and foremost the understanding of the self that was to benefit from the action and subsequently the value ascribed to the pursued phenomenon. Only a body-bound understanding of the self would value externals as something choiceworthy. The doctrine of emotions was a "theory of the motivations of vicious behaviour," and in the ideal state of mind, these motivations would, of course, be extinguished.[54]

3.2. Seneca and the Preemotion

On the face of it, the Stoic doctrine of emotions has no room for a figure like the Johannine Jesus momentarily seized by anger (11:33, 38), prone to tears (11:35), and caught in emotional despair (12:27; 13:21). Yet, according to Seneca, the sage may pale at an apparent danger, shed tears when seeing others crying, and be aroused sexually without being subjected to the corresponding emotions.[55]

In *De ira*, Seneca discusses whether anger is an instinctive reaction in which the conscious self is carried away by the emotion, or whether it is a willful and calculated response to an unjustified offense.[56] In his analysis of the development of

---

[51] Plutarch, *Virt. mor.* 441B–D (translation, Helmbold 1957).
[52] Cicero, *Fin.* 3.32.
[53] Diogenes Laertius, *Vit. phil.* 7.86: "For reason supervenes to shape impulse scientifically" (τεχνίτης γὰρ οὗτος ἐπιγίνεται τῆς ὁρμῆς).
[54] Brennan 1998, 33.
[55] Seneca, *Ira* 2.3.1–2.
[56] Seneca, *Ira* 2.4.1–2.

an emotion, Seneca distributes the analytical elements of Chrysippus's emotion—appearance (φαντασία), assent (συγκατάθεσις), and impulse (ὁρμή)—along a temporal axis as three successive steps. Seneca discusses how the emotion arises (first step: *incipiant*), grows (second step: *crescant*), and finally, as a full-blown emotion, dispenses with reason (third step: *efferantur*). The initial sting (*primus motus*) in the soul, which is caused by the presentation of the situation to the mind, is a spontaneous response accompanied by physical reactions such as paling, crying, and the blushing of excitement. These reactions constitute the beginning of an emotion, but neither the first appearance nor the physical reaction should be taken as a proper emotion. The preemotional response, which is shared by nonrational animals, prerational children, and rational grown-ups alike, is inaccessible to rational argument, but the strength of the response may be influenced, Seneca suggests, by good habits and continuous psychological awareness.

In the second step, the belief and the action implicit in the appearance—for example, the inappropriateness of the offense and the appropriateness of revenge—are subjected to the mind's conscious deliberation. The secondary move, which is the result of reflection, can also be dissolved by reflections (*iudicio nascitur, iudicio tollitur*). The deliberative gap between the preemotion and the full-blown emotion makes therapeutic intervention possible. But when the mind has finally assented to the belief that is immanent in the appearance, the emotion is once more physically beyond control, and the implied action will be carried out.

According to Seneca, it is the character of the deliberation that decides at what price an action will be carried out. If the person's beliefs concerning the right thing to do are weak, he or she soon gives in to the desired object of the preemotion, and the inner preemotion is turned into an outwardly reacting act. If the truth in the person's mind is well-founded and strong, the preemotion is quickly extinguished. The momentary unrest is nothing but a scar from the person's former prerational state of being. In the case of an intermediate person, deliberation keeps the preemotion alive, and he or she oscillates between the desire of the preemotion and the conviction that giving in is not the right thing to do. Prolonged deliberation leaves the person in a vulnerable situation, and the final choice is left to chance.

Seneca's interpretation of the doctrine of the Old Stoa and his introduction of the preemotion accounted for the irrational element that common sense felt was involved in emotions. He did that without compromising the rationality that was claimed to be involved in the (full) emotion.

3.3. Origen, Seneca, and the Tears of the Sage

To a certain extent, Seneca's theory of preemotions may prove illuminating to Origen's exegesis of Jesus' emotional reactions. It explains why the emotional upheaval may be seen as specifically human: the preemotion is a scar of the childish, prerational mode of relating to the world. It may also explain why the emotional disturbance is over in a moment. Jesus recognizes the anger, but he does not assent to it; he senses the fear, but he is not carried away by it; in other words, the disturbance passes away like a preemotion. In spite of the fact that Jesus' emotions are directed at a true evil—Satan and his demonic powers—the upheaval is kept in check and only lasts long enough for the warning to be registered by others. Even Jesus' crying might have been explained by the theory of the preemotion: Seneca points to the spontaneous crying in reaction to others' tears as an example of the prerational preemotions. But according to Origen, Jesus' tears are not mimetic; Jesus laments the psychological and moral death of his beloved friends brought about by Satan and his powers. In his interpretation of Jesus' emotional behavior, Origen, on the one hand, situates the Johannine Jesus in the tradition of Hellenistic ethics derived from Plato's *Republic* in which the emotions were seen as disturbances of the soul that impaired a correct evaluation of the situation.[57] On the other hand, by accepting Jesus' crying, Origen has added a foreign element to that tradition. Let us therefore turn to a philosopher who, seemingly without giving up the Stoic ideal, allowed his biblical heroes to cry out of true and genuine emotion: Philo of Alexandria.

4. Εὐπάθειαι in Stoicism, in Philo, and in Paul

The fact that the Israelites' mourning, crying and tears pervade the pages of Scripture—the virtuous Moses being no exception—seems to have provoked Philo to develop the Stoic doctrine of emotions. He understands the biblical lament or crying as a rational kind of pain that aspires to the position of the fourth type of right sensibility (εὐπάθεια) that is missing in the Stoic theory.

4.1. Εὐπάθειαι in Stoic Theory

The idea of right sensibilities (εὐπάθειαι) can be seen as one of the strategies used by the Stoics to counter the accusation of inhumanity against their sage.[58] Hellenistic expositions of Stoic theory repeatedly stressed that the sage's ἀπάθεια was not to be confused with the apathy of the fool. In his *Vitae philosophorum* (*Lives of Eminent Philosophers*), the doxographer Diogenes Laertius (ca. 200 C.E.) reports the Stoic view that whereas the wise person is passionless because of not being prone to false and passionate beliefs, the absence of feelings in the fool takes the form of "callousness and relentlessness."[59] Also, Plutarch quotes sources in his *De virtute morali* that insist that the state of ἀπάθεια should not be mistaken for insensibility: ἀπάθεια does not destroy the emotional life of temperate persons, but rather puts their emotional life in order. Instead of insensibility, the state of ἀπάθεια denotes the right sensibility represented by the εὐπάθειαι of joy (χαρά), volition (βούλησις), and precaution (εὐλάβεια).[60] For his own part, Plutarch does not find the Stoic theory of sage's ἀπάθεια convincing; he sees the εὐπάθειαι and

---

[57] Plato, *Rep.* II–III. See also the analysis of Plato's *Republic* in Nussbaum 1993, 104–8.
[58] For a discussion of the accusation, see Irwin 1998.
[59] Diogenes Laertius, *Vit. phil.* 7.117.
[60] Plutarch, *Virt. mor.* 449B.

the preemotions as linguistic categories invented to explain away the fact that ἀπάθεια was an unattainable ideal even for the sage.

> But my opponents... yet persist in calling shame "modesty" [αἰδεῖσθαι τὸ αἰσχύνεσθαι], pleasure "joy" [τὸ ἥδεσθαι χαίρειν], and fears "precautions" [τοὺς φόβους εὐλαβείας]. No one would blame them for this euphemism if they would but call these same emotions by these soft names when they attach themselves to reason, and call them by those harsher names when the emotions oppose and offer violence to reason. But when, convicted by their tears and tremblings and changes of colour, in place of grief and fear they call these emotions "compunctions" and "perplexities" [δηγμούς τινας καὶ συνθροήσεις] and gloss over the desires with the term "eagernesses" [προθυμίας τὰς ἐπιθυμίας ὑποκοίζωνται], they seem to be devising casuistic, not philosophic, shifts and escapes from reality through the medium of fancy names.[61]

In the Stoic doctrine, the definition of the right sensibilities mirrored the four standard types of emotions: pleasure (ἡδονή), desire (ἐπιθυμία), fear (φόβος), and pain (λύπη). The sage feels joyful and elated when he knows that something is happening that is truly good—that is, something good that concerns the All. The fool feels elated, too, when judging, however falsely, that the pleasure personally experienced should be pursued as something good.[62] The sources agree that a εὐπάθεια corresponding to pain (λύπη) does not exist. Cicero states it clearly:

> The wise man, however, is not subject to the influences of present evil.... And consequently the first definition of distress is that it is shrinking together [LCL note: *contraction*... answers to Greek συστολή] of the soul in conflict with reason. Thus there are four *disorders*, three *equable states* [LCL note: εὐπάθειαι in Greek], since there is no equable state in opposition to distress.[63]

Tad Brennan, a modern scholar of Stoic emotions, summarizes the argument in the following way: "So by definition, the Sage could never have the knowledge that some evil was present to him; thus, there can be no fourth *eupatheia*."[64] The unanimity with which the absence of a fourth εὐπάθεια corresponding to pain is stated by the ancient sources challenges a philosophical interpretation of Jesus' crying in John 11 and in turn of a Stoic interpretation of the Fourth Gospel.

4.2. Philo and the Fourth Εὐπάθεια

In order to evaluate Philo's interpretation of the Israelites' and Moses' crying, I wish to draw attention to the fact that in Philo's writings we find no polemical attitude against the Stoic theory of emotions. Philo supplements the theoretical doctrine by including the Aristotelian idea of μετριοπάθεια as a pragmatic step

---

[61] Plutarch, *Virt. mor.* 449A (translation, Helmbold 1957).
[62] For expositions of the Stoic εὐπάθειαι, see Frede 1986; Nussbaum 1987; 1994; Engberg-Pedersen 1990; Brennan 1998; Strange 2004; Graver 2007.
[63] Cicero, *Tusc.* 4.6.14 (translation, King 1971 [my italics]). See also Diogenes Laertius, *Vit. phil.* 7.118.
[64] Brennan 1998, 35.

on the way to virtue, but still the ideal of ἀπάθεια is maintained as the ultimate goal of intellectual development. Whereas Aaron is a representative of the case of μετριοπάθεια, ἀπάθεια is reserved for the virtuous Moses.[65]

Scholars such as John Dillon and Margaret Graver are convinced that Philo was acquainted with the Stoic theory of the εὐπάθειαι,[66] and they draw attention to the allegorical exegesis in QG 2.57 of Gen 9:3, in which Philo provides an answer to the question "Why does [Scripture] say, 'Every reptile that lives shall be to you for food'?" Dillon and Graver also agree that the Armenian source to QG 2.57 is fraught with problems that make our understanding of the text difficult. Dillon has suggested the following translation of the text:[67]

> The nature of reptiles is twofold. One is poisonous, and the other is tame. . . . This is the literal meaning. *But as for the deeper meaning the passions resemble unclean reptiles, while joy (resembles) clean (reptiles). For alongside the passion of Pleasure there is Joy. And alongside Desire there is Will.*[68] *And alongside Grief there is Compunction.*[69] *And alongside Fear*[70] *there is Caution.* Thus, these passions threaten souls with death and murder, whereas joys are truly living as He Himself has shown in allegorizing, and are the causes of life for those who possess them.

The structure of the text leaves us with the impression that Philo operates with four εὐπάθειαι. In fact, this was Dillon's conclusion in his first draft of the "Note on Quaes Gen 2.57." Dillon suggested that the origin to "this fourth εὐπάθεια" could be found with "the Stoicizing Platonists, i.e. Platonists who, while in general siding with the Stoa on ethical questions against Aristotle, were moved, in this case, to soften the rough edges of the Stoic ideal by allowing for a rational form of Grief."[71] Dillon takes Philo as a representative of this new tradition and locates it in Alexandria. But in an appendix added later to the "Note on Quaes Gen 2.57" he withdraws his first conclusion and now refers it to "an ad hoc development by Philo to produce symmetry in this passage. Philo is loose enough elsewhere in his use of technical terminology to be open to suspicion here."[72] Nevertheless, by

---

[65] Philo, *Leg. all.* 3.134.

[66] See Dillon and Terian 1976–1977; Graver 1999.

[67] Dillon and Terian's argument involved in the restoration of the text is technically complicated and will not be considered here.

[68] Dillon and Terian 1976–1977, 19. So far, Dillon and Terian follow the translation of the LCL edition.

[69] The LCL edition reads, "And alongside grief there is remorse and constraint." Dillon and Terian (1976–1977, 17) and Graver (1999, 317) agree that this interpretation goes beyond the textual evidence. Instead of Dillon and Terian's "compunction," Graver suggests that "biting and contraction" may be a better and more literal translation of the Armenian text. Graver refers to Dillon and Terian's own argument: the two words of the Armenian equivalent to "grief" correspond to derivates of the Armenian word that in other translations of Philo's Greek text correspond to δηγμός (Dillon and Terian 1976–1977, 18)—that is, the physical reaction involved in passionate pain and its corresponding *propatheia*.

[70] Textual problems are also involved in the reconstruction and translation of this sentence. See Dillon and Terian 1976–1977, 18.

[71] Ibid., 20.

[72] Ibid., 21–22.

coupling "biting" with passionate pain or grief, Philo is at one with contemporary sources. We saw how Plutarch blamed the Stoics for explaining away the sage's anger by renaming it and reducing it to the physical constituent of the emotion. We also saw, in the text from Cicero, that the physical element was said to constitute "the first definition [*prima definitio*] of distress" or pain. In Graver's argument that the idea of preemotions predates Seneca's analysis in *De ira*, precisely these three texts—Philo, Plutarch, and Cicero—are featured.[73] The three sources accord with general Stoic theory; although no pain is found in the sage, the sage may still experience the physical sting of a preemotion.

In *Leg. all.* 3.211, however, we find an example in which Philo treats the intensive and excessive pain (σφοδρὰ καὶ ἐπιτεταμένη λύπη) expressed in groaning (στεναγμός) as at least a kind of εὐπάθεια. Here, Philo juxtaposes the vicious and virtuous aspects of the emotion:[74]

> One kind [of groaning] is found in men who desire and long for opportunities of wrongdoing and cannot get them, and this a bad kind. Another kind is that which is seen in those who repent and are vexed over their defection in former days and cry: "Hapless we, how long a time had we, as is now evident, been ill all unaware of it with the illness of folly and senselessness and unrighteousness in our conduct" .... When wickedness has died, he that seeth God groans over his failure, "for the children of Israel groaned by reason of their material and Egyptian works" (Exod 2:23).[75]

In *Stoicism and Emotion*, Graver draws attention to the challenge, theoretically as well as pragmatically, that the tears of Alcibiades in Socrates' lap in Plato's *Symposium* contributed to the Stoic theory of emotion.[76] Alcibiades lamented his present vices: his vanity, his pleasure in his beauty and wealth. But how should Alcibiades' dismay be classified Stoically? Although he himself is unwise, the impression of his own situation that triggers off his emotional reaction is true. Alcibiades' tears became a paradigm of the remorse and pain that accompany moral progression. Graver describes these cases of "progressor-pains" as yet another Stoic intermediary phenomenon:

> Even those who are not wise will sometimes respond affectively to integral objects—that is, to features of our own character or conduct. When we do this, it certainly seems possible within Stoic theory that our responses are at least sometimes generated on the basis of true beliefs. These would then have the same status as our other actions have when premised on true beliefs about appropriateness; that is, the status of *kathēkonta*.[77]

Philo's evaluation of the Israelites' groaning fits in with the Alcibiades paradigm. In his *Commentary on St. John's Gospel*, Origen describes the pain involved in repentance as a divine kind of pain and, consequently, as more in line with a

---

[73] Graver 1999.
[74] Philo here employs a style that we also find in Diogenes Laertius, *Vit. phil.* 7.117: "The wise man is said to be free from vanity ... there being another who is also free from vanity ... the bad man."
[75] Philo, *Leg. all.* 3.211–213 (translation, Colson and Whitaker 1956).
[76] Graver 2007, 191–211.
[77] Ibid., 210–11.

true εὐπάθεια. Although a divine remedy, the teacher must be aware that the pain involved in remorse is inflicted only on the repentant soul with utmost care:

> We must reply that just as we must not apply to all people nor always the sorrow that is according to God [τὴν κατὰ θεὸν λύπην], which works repentance without regrets unto salvation, but only to that one and everyone who has done things worthy of such sorrow and who changes his mind in relation to them, and we must apply it with due limit and not excessively lest in excessive sorrow he be swallowed by Satan.[78]

Seemingly, Origen has upgraded the intermediary remorse to the status of a right sensibility. Although Dillon withdrew his thesis of a special development of the Stoic doctrine within the Alexandrian milieu, there still seems to be something in it: remorse functions as the fourth εὐπάθεια.

Of course, repentant groaning will never befall the sage, but Philo allows his devotees of virtue to bewail the presence of vice and ignorance among their fellow human beings. Whereas Philo's sage rejoiced when "good ... befell your neighbour for his own sake,"[79] he also was pained by and lamented the evil and vice that were present with his friends. The various attitudes mirror different relations to the same desired object. The sage is even prone to shed tears when facing the misfortune of the unwise:

> And yet indeed it is not unusual for the devotees of virtue themselves to be much moved and to shed tears [ἀλλὰ γὰρ καὶ τοῖς χορευταῖς ἀρετῆς σφαδᾴζειν καὶ δακρύειν ἔθος], either when bemoaning the misfortunes of the unwise owing to their innate fellow-feeling and humaneness [ἢ τὰς τῶν ἀφρόνων ὀδυρομένοις συμφορὰς διὰ τὸ φύσει κοινωνικὸν καὶ φιλάνθρωπον], or by reason of being overjoyed.[80]

To Philo, this lament represented an attitude of fellow-feeling (κοινωνία) and humaneness (φιλανθρωπία), which were generally acknowledged as core Stoic virtues.[81] The fact that the sage was naturally made for society ultimately rested on the idea of the sage's physically extended self.

In conclusion, in spite of the fact that Philo does not explicitly speak of virtuous lament as the fourth and missing εὐπάθεια, it functions in this way, and we should recall that Philo called the "biting and contraction" involved in pain a εὐπάθεια. We may also supplement Philo's exposition by referring to the Stoic fact that the self of the sage is an extended self that potentially encompasses the All. Seen in this light, it becomes difficult to uphold the argument that the sage "by definition ... could never have the knowledge that some evil was *present to him*,"

---

[78] Book 28 (Heine 1993, §26; Brooke 1896, 2:111, lines 10–21).

[79] Philo, *Plant.* 106. Philo quotes the Stoic definition of goodwill, a subspecies of the rational wish, almost verbatim. In his treatise *On Emotions* 6 (Περὶ παθῶν), Pseudo-Andronicus describes goodwill (εὔνοια) as the common denominator of the subspecies of βούλησις: "εὔνοια is the rational wish that good things may happen to others *for their own sake*" (*SVF* 3.432 [my translation and italics]).

[80] Philo, *Abr.* 156 (translation, Colson and Whitaker 1958).

[81] Whereas, according to Cicero, misanthropy characterizes the unwise (*Tusc.* 4.11.25), Diogenes Laertius describes the sage as "naturally made for society" (*Vit. phil.* 7.123: κοινῶνικος γὰρ φύσει καὶ πρακτικός).

and that, accordingly, there could "be no fourth *eupatheia*."[82] The self of the sage includes the sage's fellow citizens. In the end, Philo's virtuous lament appears to be more consistently Stoic than the Hellenistic doxographers' (and their modern interpreters') exposition of Stoic theory.

4.3. Paul and the Letter of Tears

Philo's introduction of a virtuous kind of pain finds a parallel in Paul's second letter to the Corinthians (2 Cor 2:1–11). In Paul's description of his relation to the Corinthians, the emotions of pain (λύπη) and happiness (χαρά) are intimately intertwined with tears (δάκρυα). The Corinthians' behavior has caused Paul pain (2:5), and if he had visited them as originally planned, he would have ended up causing them pain too (2:1–2). Instead, he has in tears written a letter to them (2:3–4). The purpose of this letter is to remove the cause of pain and prepare the Corinthians for a visit in which the pain that Paul and the Corinthians now share (2:5) will be replaced by happiness. In spite of the fact that Paul emphatically denies that the purpose of the Letter of Tears was to cause the Corinthians pain, this is probably what the letter was intended to do.

Just as a desired object may give rise to various passions—pleasure (ἡδονή) when the object is present, pain (λύπη) when absent, fear (φόβος) in the prospect of losing it—so the εὐπάθειαι of happiness and virtuous pain also correspond: χαρά rejoices by the gain of virtue, λύπη laments its loss, φόβος shivers at the prospect of its absence. Accordingly, pain is depicted in 2 Cor 2:1–11 as the absence of happiness, and vice versa. To Paul, happiness prevailed when believers progressed in Christ; pain was predominant when they did not; "being in Christ" was the object on which Paul's right sensibilities hinged.

Paul's personal pain and tears resemble the emotions that characterize Philo's devotees of virtue, and the pain that the Letter of Tears was intended to inflict upon the Corinthians reminds us of the repentant pain or remorse among Philo's disobedient Israelites. Since the ultimate purpose of the Letter of Tears was to resettle the Corinthians in Christ, they should conceive of Paul's harsh letter as yet another expression of his love for the community. To summarize, Philo's attempt to define a place for virtuous crying within Stoic theory finds an analogy in the way that Paul relates pain to happiness in 2 Corinthians.[83]

5. Conclusion

In exploring the question whether the Johannine Jesus' emotional upheavals reflected an anti-Stoic stance, I have shown how Origen's interpretation of Jesus'

---

[82] Brennan 1998, 35 (my italics). See Cicero, *Tusc.* 4.14; Diogenes Laertius, *Vit. phil.* 7.118.
[83] In his monograph *Paul and the Stoics* (2000), Troels Engberg-Pedersen argues that scholarly acknowledged problems in Philippians, Galatians, and Romans may be solved when the letters are read within a Stoic perspective. The tentative analysis of Paul's appeal to emotions that I have made here suggests that this may also hold true for the Corinthian correspondence.

emotions rested firmly on Stoic ground. Origen's exposition of Jesus' emotional upheavals perfectly matches the Stoic theory of the preemotion. Jesus' anger is also justified by the negative evaluation of the emotions in Stoic theory: although Jesus' anger is directed against Satan, it is Satan's passionate affliction of the human soul that is the ultimate cause of the problem. The exposition that we find in Origen's exegesis of John 11–13 wholly accords with Philo's attempt to reconcile biblical crying with Stoic theory. Philo understands the excessive pain of groaning involved in sincere remorse as a Stoic intermediary, and he counts the pain of the devotee of virtue, who laments the misfortune of unwise fellow citizens, among the right sensibilities. Philo develops a εὐπάθεια corresponding to passionate λύπη. I have also emphasized that Philo's innovation was in full accordance with the Stoic idea of the sage's extended self. In a manner that resembles Philo's ideas, Paul too plays with the various forms of virtuous pain in his reflections on his own motive when he was writing his Letter of Tears. In Paul's case, λύπη refers to the kind of virtuous pain that characterizes Philo's devotees of virtue; in the case of the Corinthians, it is the "progressor-pain" or remorse that is intended by the letter. A link between Philo's innovation and the New Testament thinking is thus established.

In conclusion: Before John, in Philo's Jewish circles and in Pauline Christianity, lament and crying were not seen as incompatible with the image of the Stoic sage; after John, in Origen's reception of John, Jesus' emotional upheavals were justified by their Stoic character. Although, we will never know what the writer of the Fourth Gospel had in mind when portraying Jesus as an emotional figure, these emotions do not a priori rule out an interpretation of this Gospel from a Stoic perspective.

Bibliography

Aune, D. E. 1995. "Human Nature and Ethics in Hellenistic Philosophical Traditions and Paul: Some Issues and Problems." Pages 291–312 in *Paul in His Hellenistic Context*. Edited by T. Engberg-Pedersen. Minneapolis: Fortress.

Brennan, T. 1998. "The Old Stoic Theory of Emotions." Pages 21–70 in *The Emotions in Hellenistic Philosophy*. Edited by J. Sihvola and T. Engberg-Pedersen. New Synthese Historical Library 46. Dordrecht: Kluwer.

Brooke, A. E. 1896. *The Commentary of Origen on S. John's Gospel*. 2 vols. Cambridge: Cambridge University Press.

Brown, R. E. 1966. *The Gospel According to John (I–XII)*. Anchor Bible 29. Garden City, N.Y.: Doubleday.

Christensen, J. 1962. *An Essay on the Unity of Stoic Philosophy*. Scandinavian University Books. Copenhagen: Munksgaard.

Colson, F. H., and G. H. Whitaker. 1956. *Philo in Ten Volumes (and Two Supplementary Volumes)*. Vol. 1. Loeb Classical Library. Cambridge, Mass.: Harvard University Press.

———. 1958. *Philo in Ten Volumes (and Two Supplementary Volumes)*. Vol. 4. Loeb Classical Library. Cambridge, Mass.: Harvard University Press.

De Lacy, P. 1978. *Galen: On the Doctrines of Hippocrates and Plato*. Corpus medicorum graecorum. Berlin: Akademie-Verlag.

Dillon, J. M. 2000. *The Golden Chain: Studies in the Development of Platonism and Christianity*. Collected Studies Series 333. Aldershot: Variorum, 1990. Repr., Aldershot: Ashgate.

Dillon, J. M., and A. Terian. 1976–1977. "Philo and the Stoic Doctrine of Εὐπάθειαι: A Note on Quaes Gen 2.57." *Studia Philonica* 4:17–24.

Engberg-Pedersen, T. 1990. *The Stoic Theory of Oikeiosis: Moral Development and Social Interaction in Early Stoic Philosophy*. Studies in Hellenistic Civilization 2. Aarhus: Aarhus University Press.

———. 2000. *Paul and the Stoics*. Edinburgh: T & T Clark.

Frede, M. 1986. "The Stoic Doctrine of the Affections of the Soul." Pages 93–111 in *The Norms of Nature: Studies in Hellenistic Ethics*. Edited by M. Schofield and G. Striker. Cambridge: Cambridge University Press.

Gill, C. 1998. "Did Galen Understand Platonic and Stoic Thinking on the Emotions?" Pages 113–48 in *The Emotions in Hellenistic Philosophy*. Edited by J. Sihvola and T. Engberg-Pedersen. New Synthese Historical Library 46. Dordrecht: Kluwer.

Graver, M. R. 1999. "Philo of Alexandria and the Origins of the Stoic Προπάθειαι." *Phronesis* 44:300–325.

———. 2007. *Stoicism and Emotion*. Chicago: University of Chicago Press.

Heine, R. E. 1993. *Origen: Commentary on the Gospel According to John Books 13–32*. Fathers of the Church 89. Washington, D.C.: Catholic University of America Press.

Helmbold, W. C. 1957. *Plutarch's Moralia in Sixteen Volumes*. Vol. 6. Loeb Classical Library. Cambridge, Mass.: Harvard University Press.

Irwin, T. H. 1998. "Stoic Inhumanity." Pages 219–41 in *The Emotions in Hellenistic Philosophy*. Edited by J. Sihvola and T. Engberg-Pedersen. New Synthese Historical Library 46. Dordrecht: Kluwer.

Käsemann, E. 1971. *Jesu letzter Wille nach Johannes 17*. 3rd ed. Tübingen: Mohr Siebeck.

King, J. E. 1971. *Cicero: Tusculan Disputations*. Rev. ed. Loeb Classical Library. Cambridge, Mass.: Harvard University Press.

Lindars, B. 1992. "Rebuking the Spirit: A New Analysis of the Lazarus Story of John 11." *New Testament Studies* 38:89–104.

Long, A. A. 1996. *Stoic Studies*. Berkeley: University of California Press.

Nussbaum, M. C. 1987. "The Stoics on the Extirpation of the Passions." *Apeiron: A Journal for Ancient Philosophy and Science* 20/2:129–78.

———. 1993. "Poetry and the Passions: Two Stoic Views." Pages 97–149 in *Passions and Perceptions: Studies in Hellenistic Philosophy of Mind; Proceedings of the Fifth Symposium Hellenisticum*. Edited by J. Brunschwig and M. C. Nussbaum. Cambridge: Cambridge University Press.

———. 1994. *The Therapy of Desire: Theory and Practice in Hellenistic Ethics*. Princeton, N.J.: Princeton University Press.

———. 1998. "Eros and the Wise: The Stoic Response to a Cultural Dilemma." Pages 271–304 in *The Emotions in Hellenistic Philosophy*. Edited by J. Sihvola and T. Engberg-Pedersen. New Synthese Historical Library 46. Dordrecht: Kluwer.

Sambursky, S. 1959. *Physics of the Stoics*. London: Routledge.

Schnackenburg, R. 1971. *Das Johannesevangelium: II. Teil: Kommentar zu Kap. 5–12*. Freiburg: Herder.

Sorabji, R. 1998. "Chrysippus—Posidonius—Seneca: A High Level Debate on Emotions." Pages 149–70 in *The Emotions in Hellenistic Philosophy*. Edited by J. Sihvola and T. Engberg-Pedersen. New Synthese Historical Library 46. Dordrecht: Kluwer.

Stibbe, M. W. G. 1994. "A Tomb with a View: John 11.1–44 in Narrative-Critical Perspective." *New Testament Studies* 40:38–54.

Story, C. I. K. 1991. "The Mental Attitude of Jesus at Bethany: John 11.33,38." *New Testament Studies* 37:51–66.

Strange, S. K. 2004. "The Stoics on the Voluntariness of the Passions." Pages 32–51 in *Stoicism: Traditions and Transformations*. Edited by S. K. Strange and J. Zupko. Cambridge: Cambridge University Press.

Voorwinde, S. 2005. *Jesus' Emotions in the Fourth Gospel: Human or Divine?* Library of New Testament Studies 284. London: T & T Clark.

7

STOIC PHYSICS, THE UNIVERSAL CONFLAGRATION, AND THE ESCHATOLOGICAL DESTRUCTION OF THE "IGNORANT AND UNSTABLE" IN 2 PETER

J. Albert Harrill
Indiana University

Apocalyptic scenarios of eschatological destruction and renewal appear in many early Christian writings as a commonplace for God's final judgment.[1] For example, the apostle Paul declares the wrath of the Day of the Lord (1 Thess 1:10; 4:13–5:10; cf. 2 Thess 2:1–12) and the ultimate transformation of "all creation" (Rom 8:18–25). The Gospel of Mark promises its audience that heaven and earth "will pass away" (παρελεύσονται) in the imminent end times (13:24–31; cf. Matt 5:18; Luke 16:17; Isa 13:9–13). The seer of Revelation envisages the cosmos literally collapsing in upon itself (6:13–14) and a "new heaven and a new earth" replacing "the first heaven and the first earth," which "had passed away" (ἀπῆλθαν) (21:1). The Gospel of Matthew speaks of a "renewal of all things" (παλιγγενεσία) following the final judgment (19:28). And the *Didache* warns its audience about "the fire of testing" (ἡ πυρὰ τῆς δοκιμασίας) into which all human creation will soon enter (16.5). Yet, compared with these early Christian texts, only 2 Peter invokes the particular eschatology of a total conflagration of the heavens and the earth:[2]

---

[1] Previous versions of this essay were presented in various forums: an interdisciplinary conference, "The End of Everything: Catastrophe and Community in the Ancient Mediterranean and Near Eastern Worlds," sponsored by the Indiana University Program in Ancient Studies, Bloomington, Ind., October 2007; the annual meeting of the Society of Biblical Literature (Hellenistic Moral Philosophy and Early Christianity Section), San Diego, Calif., November 2007; and the annual meeting of the Society of Biblical Literature (Corpus Hellenisticum Novi Testamenti Consultation), Boston, Mass., November 2008. Stalnacker (2008, 431–33, 438) kindly references the paper as a case study on the problem of comparative ethical judgment. I thank Elizabeth Asmis, David Brakke, Troels Engberg-Pedersen, Christopher Gill, A. A. Long, Dale B. Martin, and Aaron Stalnacker for their critical responses and suggestions. All faults that remain are my own.

[2] The letter of 2 Peter is pseudonymous, dating to the first quarter of the second century C.E. (a few scholars prefer an earlier dating of 80–90 C.E.). It uses the letter of Jude as a

They deliberately ignore this one fact, that by the word [λόγος] of God heavens existed long ago and earth was formed out of water and by means of water, through which the world of that time was deluged with water and perished. But by the same word [λόγος] the present heavens and earth have been reserved for fire, being kept until the day of judgment and destruction of the godless.... For the day of the Lord will come like a thief. Then the heavens will pass away [παρελεύσονται] with a roar; the elements [στοιχεῖα] will be burned up and dissolved [καυσούμενα λυθήσεται]; and the earth and all its works will be found out [εὑρεθήσεται]. Since all these things will be dissolved [λυομένων] in this way, what sort of people ought you to be in leading lives of holiness and godliness as you await and hasten the coming of the Day of God, when the heavens will be set on fire [πυρούμενοι] and dissolved [λυθήσονται] and the elements [στοιχεῖα] burned and melted [καυσούμενα τήκεται]? According to his promise, we await "new heavens and a new earth," where righteousness will dwell. (2 Pet 3:5-7, 10-13)[3]

The author of 2 Peter responds to opponents within his congregation who argue against eschatological belief and divine providence. Those "scoffers" (ἐμπαῖκται), who see unfulfilled the promise of the Lord's coming, ridicule the very idea of cosmic eschatology (3:3-4).[4] The author presents this "letter," the apostle Peter's farewell address and last testament, as a response (1:12-15; 3:1-2). "Peter" assures the congregation that the cosmic end will (eventually) come and brands the scoffers as "the ignorant and unstable" (οἱ ἀμαθεῖς καὶ ἀστήρικτοι). They will undo themselves ("twist to their own destruction") in a process of physical self-destruction, which the author declares is as certain and real as the impending total conflagration of the universe itself (3:7, 10-12, 16). The author then imagines salvation of the Christian self (soul) at the total conflagration (3:13-14). Here lies the exegetical puzzle: how could a self "be found" in the end times if, in the end times, the universal conflagration dissolves "all things" with fire (3:10-11)? The apparent paradox prompts various attempts to extract acceptable sense from the crux.[5] One influential solution, for example, proposes that 2 Peter refers not to a "burn up" but rather a "melt down," evoking the principle of "refinement" from ancient metallurgy—the faithful in the letter will "be found" more pure than the sinful opponents[6]—an idea that repeats early Christian apology.[7]

---

source, copying much of it word for word. For a general introduction, see Elliott 1992, 282-87. Biblical scholars recognize that its eschatology of a universal conflagration is unique in the New Testament (see Bauckham 1983, 300).

[3] Translation, Neyrey 1993 (altered).
[4] In my view, the best discussion of the opponents is Neyrey 1980. Neyrey argues convincingly that the author of 2 Peter characterizes the "scoffers" as teachers within the congregation who voice conventional Epicurean polemic against divine providence (with formal similarities to the Epicurean polemic to which Plutarch responds in *Mor.* 548B-568A, *On the Delays of the Divine Vengeance*). See also Adams 2005b; Caulley 2008.
[5] Lenhard 1961; 1978; Danker 1962; Wenham 1987.
[6] Wolters 1987 (by parallel to 1 Pet 1:7; Mal 3:2-4; *Barn.* 21.6; *2 Clem.* 16.3); van der Horst 1998, 289n69. Wolters critiques a standard hypothesis that interprets εὑρεθήσεται to mean simply the Old Testament theme of "will be judged" (Bauckham 1983, 303, 318-21; cf. the "forensic investigation of the heart" interpretation in Neyrey 1993, 243-44). On the metaphor of fire meaning a "smelting" (purification) process in early Christian literature, see Milavec 1995. See also Adams 2007, 225-29.
[7] See Mansfeld 1983; Murphy 1983.

Previous scholars debate whether the elements of the scenario in 2 Peter come from ancient Stoic eschatology, in which the entirety of the universe erupts into fire (ἐκπύρωσις).⁸ By suggesting the emendation of ἐκπυρωθήσεται ("will be burnt to ashes") for εὑρεθήσεται ("will be found"), Frank Olivier, professor of Latin language and literature at the University of Lausanne, famously wrote the parallel directly into the text of 2 Peter itself (3:10).⁹ Current commentary rightly rejects that ingenious conjecture as lacking any manuscript support and favors εὑρεθήσεται as the *lectio difficilior*.¹⁰ The passage thus reads, "Then the heavens will pass away [παρελεύσονται] with a roar; the elements [στοιχεῖα] will be burned up and dissolved [καυσούμενα λυθήσεται]; and the earth and all its works will be found out [εὑρεθήσεται]" (3:10). While probably a case of *lectio difficilior*, the preferred reading nonetheless fits logically. The author envisions a juridical procedure through which what is now present on earth, including "earthly deeds" (ἔργα), will "be found (out)." The saved will also be burnt (καυσούμενα, "reserved for fire") but plucked from the ashes (3:7), a theme proverbial, and familiar, from Paul's letters (1 Cor 3:15).¹¹

In any event, finding support in the rejected emendation of ἐκπυρωθήσεται, many commentators after Olivier dismiss completely the parallel to Stoicism for any meaningful interpretation of 2 Peter. They protest that the parallel is not exact, common terminology notwithstanding, because the "Hellenistic" doctrine of ἐκπύρωσις affirms a perpetually repeated cycle of destruction and creation, whereas 2 Peter transmits the "Jewish" (or "biblical") tradition of a one-time eschatology, the final judgment¹²—an argument that (again) repeats early Christian apology.¹³ Such biblical scholars find Stoic influence on 2 Peter unlikely and urge instead the distinctiveness of early Christianity against its Hellenistic ("pagan") environment, a distinctiveness that it allegedly shared with ancient Israel.¹⁴ This

---

⁸On Stoic ἐκπύρωσις and its association with the Near Eastern cycles of the "Great Year" and alternating aquatic κατακλυσμοί (not attested before Seneca the Younger), see Collins 1974, 101–15; Mansfeld 1979; Hahm 1997, 185–99; Long 2006. For a general introduction, see Furley 1999; Gourinat 2002; White 2003; Adams 2007, 114–29. Most of the primary sources are anthologized in Long and Sedley 1987, 1:274–79 (translations); 2:271–77 (texts and commentaries).
⁹Olivier 1963.
¹⁰Εὑρεθήσεται, implying that the earth (γῆ) will not be destroyed, lies in tension with the previous statement that the heavens and the earth will melt in fire; but it is in the oldest witnesses and best explains the origin of the other readings. See Kelly 1969, 364–66; Neyrey 1993, 243–44; Metzger 1994, 636–37; van der Horst 1998, 288–89.
¹¹On "plucked from the ashes," see Conzelmann 1975, 77; Fee 1987, 143–44.
¹²The most detailed discussion is Gerdmar 2001, 163–65, 185–206, and *passim*. See also Chaine 1937; Glasson 1961, 79; Testa 1962; Vögtle 1970, 121–42; Fuchs and Reymond 1988, 134–36; Sim 1993, 6–7; Russell 1996, 194; Gilmour 2002, 65. On the approach generally, see Kee 1985.
¹³See Origen, *Cels.* 4.68–69. Other early Christian apologists praised the Stoic idea of the final conflagration to show its imperfect understanding of the truth, but not to reconcile Christianity to Greek philosophy (Justin Martyr, *1 Apol.* 60.8–9); see Droge 1989, 52–53.
¹⁴Thiede 1986; rightly criticized in van der Horst 1998, 278n28. See also Mayer 1956, 124–25; Green 1968, 131–33; Riesner 1984, 139–40; Paulsen 1992, 162; Arichea and Hatton 1993, 150; Starr 2000, 153–54. Assuming the letter to be authentic, one earlier scholar

"biblical theology" approach is unhelpful, however, because its totalizing interpretative framework sets up "Judaism" and "Hellenism" as code words masquerading as fixed historical entities, which are then said to be capable of "interacting" with each other.[15] A few scholars, therefore, continue the hypothesis that the author of 2 Peter borrows the precise imagery of Stoic ἐκπύρωσις for the sake of his argument, albeit adapted from apocalypticism.[16] The present essay deepens and expands this line of interpretation.

I aim to shift the current debate over the Stoic "influence" on and "origins" of the eschatological ideas in 2 Peter to the cultural diffusion of Stoic ideas for an ancient audience.[17] This methodology is concerned less with where a particular eschatological idea came from and more about the content of the logic (often unspoken).[18] Seeking the distant "origins" of an eschatological idea does not explain its meaning or purpose in the Petrine congregation. A better approach offers a more contextual analysis of the work in its contemporaneous culture, which leads to a closer reading of the text than what is currently available in the commentary literature.

The history of research reveals a further, hermeneutical problem. Both sides on the scholarly debate share an unexamined historical presupposition: in the exegesis of 2 Peter "the facts" of the religious and philosophical traditions are clear, whereas "the meaning" of the text is uncertain. This presupposition overlooks the need to investigate the Hellenistic and Roman thought about ἐκπύρωσις before drawing any exegetical conclusions about its relevance for interpreting 2 Peter. This is no easy task. The primary evidence for ἐκπύρωσις is fragmentary, mostly excerpted by authors hostile to the concept, and constructs propositions conceived in a polemical context of powerful alternatives offered by rival philosophical schools (Peripatetics and Epicureans).[19] Any interpretation of 2 Peter must attend to the debate in Hellenistic and Roman thought, the diffusion of ἐκπύρωσις

---

assures Bible readers that the Stoic doctrine is "too scientific for St. Peter" (Bigg 1922, 294–97). On the false scholarly opposition of the Greek "circular" conception of time against the biblical "linear" one, see Feeney 2006, 3, and the literature there cited.

[15] On the problem generally, see Martin 1995, xiii–xiv; Meeks 2001, 21; 2005; Harrill 2006, 2. To be sure, any project of comparison must attend also to the distinctive differences with the Hellenistic material (Collins 1974, 209n9).

[16] The best discussion is van der Horst 1998, 289, and *passim*. An encyclopedic attempt to make a similar thesis is Adams 2007, 200–235. See also von Allmen 1966, 260–64; Fornberg 1977, 66–67 (cf. Bauckham 1988, 3732); Neyrey 1993, 241; Dupont-Roc 1994; Charles 1997, 92, 107–8, 121, 155; Downing 2000, 177–78; Pearson 2001.

[17] On the methodological importance of analyzing diffusion rather than seeking "influence," see Graf 2004, 5.

[18] See Martin 1995, xii–xiii, xiv–xv.

[19] The longest extant discussion is Philo, *Aet*. 8–9, 83–103, 120–129, which excerpts divergent opinions by the Skeptic technique of διαφωνία to reveal Gentile philosophical ignorance on the topic and ends with a promise to give a reply in a (nonextant) future work. For analogies of the scheme, and so models of what that lost work would have likely argued—the truth lies in Moses' Torah, which affirms creation but not destruction—see Philo, *Plant*. 140–177; *Ebr*. 1–3, 198–205. See Runia 1981. Arguments against the Philonic authorship of *De aeternitate mundi*, based on purported contradictions with Philo's *De opi-*

as a cosmology in ancient culture, and the various opinions about the concept even among the Stoics themselves.[20]

The present essay traces a specific theme of ἐκπύρωσις that 2 Peter evokes. The Stoic philosophy of the wise having a holistic, and stable, self, which was widely diffuse in Hellenistic and Roman culture, is a more plausible context in which to read the argument of 2 Peter.[21] The core of my thesis pertains to the survival of "the stable" (the wise) until the total conflagration. A discussion of the stable self and its eschatology in light of Stoic conflagration physics occupies the first section below. A second section applies these findings to an exegesis of 2 Pet 3. The author of 2 Peter assumes that knowing the physical properties of the universe, the cosmic bonds and their eschatology of dissolution, leads a believer toward a higher morality, and that such knowledge stabilizes the self for survival at the universal conflagration—to "be found" by the Lord and to experience "the new heavens and the new earth" (3:13–14).

1. The Stable (Holistic) Self and Its Eschatology in Stoic Conflagration Physics

My term "stable (holistic) self" identifies an ancient philosophical idea that correlated one's ethical character (virtue and vice) and one's physical state (order and disorder) directly. Body and psyche were seen as a single, consubstantial entity. The Stoics (and Epicureans) developed this idea from previous thinkers, such as Plato and Aristotle, but modified it to their physical worldview. The idea contested core-centered and part-based psychologies, such as the Platonic tripartite soul having the reasoning (λογιστικόν), spirited (θυμοειδής), and appetitive (ἐπιθυμητικόν) faculties. Rather than presenting the soul as having "parts," each with primary desires pulling in opposite directions, the Stoic model of the soul presented a person, like other animals, as a psychophysical whole. There is no idea in Stoicism that the soul contains independent and potentially opposing sources of motivation; there is no "irrational" part of the soul. The "self" is a rational and unified consciousness, the ruling principle in a soul, the so-called ἡγεμονικόν ("mind"), whose proper functioning is virtue. The structural soundness and physical stability of the self depend upon its degree of internal tension (τόνος). The

---

ficio mundi, do not take sufficient account of the ancient techniques of excerpting or the overarching διαφωνία pattern, and so they remain unpersuasive. *Contra* Fuglseth 2006.

[20] Totalizing generalizations about Stoicism and ἐκπύρωσις make problematic the recent study of Adams 2007.

[21] For the Stoic idea, see Gill 2006; 2007. I favor "stable (holistic) self" over Gill's "structured self" in order to avoid confusion with Platonic and Aristotelian discourses of the soul, which can also be interpreted as "structured" (e.g., Hart 2002). But Gill uses the term "structured self" as an umbrella notion for the psychophysical holism, psychological holism, and "Socratic" ethical claims about the sage in Stoic (and Epicurean) thought. For critical reviews of Gill 2006, which have been largely positive, see Berryman 2007; Boys-Stones 2007, 133–34; Inwood 2007; Konstan 2007.

peculiarly Stoic idea of τόνος thus denotes the "sinewy" cohesion in a body, which maintains its shape, firmness, and overall character according to the bonds of its essential πνεῦμα ("breath"). Πνεῦμα names a physical substance mixed into and being continuous throughout the entire cosmos that connects everything into an integrated system, or "structure"; λόγος is the cognitive character or quality of that substance. The vocabulary draws on common parlance in contemporary Hellenistic medicine (particularly after the scientific discoveries of the vascular and nervous systems), which used πνεῦμα to define the soul both as a form of the body and as distributed in a single system.[22]

The Stoic account of human psychology diagnoses madness (μανία) as the instability of weak pneumatic tension (ἀτονία) throughout one's whole body and the cognitive condition of the ignorant. Conversely, the wise display the stability of strong (healthy) tension (εὐτονία). The sharp contrast of the ignorant (unstable) and the wise (stable) evokes a famous tenet of Stoic teaching, and a version of its "Socratic" ethical claims, that only the wise are psychologically coherent, and structured, in accord with nature. The model described human personality in nearly architectural language, as Margaret Graver explains:

> A number of texts express the notion of determination by character by speaking of assent as either "strong" or "weak". . . . The usage is related to that in which knowledge (the epistemic condition of the wise) is linked to high levels of "tension" or "tensile strength" in the *pneuma*. A tight internal structure, with many correct beliefs linked to each other in coherent logical relations, is proof against the most plausible-seeming falsehood. A close paraphrase of Chrysippus in the Latin author Aulus Gellius draws the contrast between strong and weak assent in terms that sound almost architectural. Minds which are "constructed by nature" in a healthy way are able to let a misleading impression pass through them without being damaged, but those minds that are "rough, unlearned, crude, and not shored up by the supports of education" offer "obstruction" to the impression, rather like loose boards to a gale. Thus they are liable to "collapse," and when they do so the fault will rest with "their own crookedness and voluntary impulse."[23]

In Stoic philosophy, therefore, the virtues are physical as well as moral states. As A. A. Long puts it,

> It follows that no clear distinction can be drawn in Stoicism between physics and ethics, between factual and moral statements. The virtues are physical states of the *hegemonikon*, and statements about them are objective: they refer to actual or possible states of affairs, the mind of God or the mind of a sage. The command to the bad man, "become good" is a command to effect a physical alteration of his disposition, to become healthy instead of sick, stable instead of vacillating.[24]

The Stoic connection between physics and ethics proposes that the ignorant are unstable selves.

---

[22] Primary sources: Gould 1970, 126–37; Long and Sedley 1987, 1:290–94; Annas 1992, 7, 14, 20–26, 46–47, 68–70, 204; von Staden 2000, 96–105; Reydams-Schils 2005, 15–52.
[23] Graver 2007, 65 (citing Aulus Gellius, *Noct. att.* 7.2.6–7).
[24] Long 1996, 103.

To be sure, the Stoics shared with the Aristotelians a strongly cognitive view of the emotions. Yet, while an Aristotelian or a Platonist could have described bad people as ignorant and uncontrolled, the specific link of cognitive failure and psychophysical instability was particular to the Stoics. For example, Aristotle considered vice to be stable, the habituation of bad character (e.g., *Eth. nic.* 3.5 [1114A12–21]). The Stoics disagreed, seeing vice as fundamentally unstable (a form of madness), as Arius Didymus reports in his *Epitome of Stoic Ethics*:

> Furthermore they [the Stoics] say that every worthless person is mad, as he is in a state of ignorance about himself and his affairs, which is madness. But ignorance is the opposite vice to self-restraint. And this, when providing unstable and agitated impulses in relation to something else, is madness. Hence they describe madness in this manner: as agitated ignorance.[25]

Important for my interpretation of 2 Peter is this precise Stoic topos that links "the ignorant" and "the unstable" in a psychophysical whole. Indeed, much Stoic thinking on the passions associates ignorance, madness, and instability as manifestations of a single phenomenon: an unstable self with a defective bodily architecture. The topos depicts folly to be not the active rule of "irrational part" of the soul over the better parts, as in Platonic psychology, but the structural collapse of the whole self. For the Stoics, the opposite of self-control is chaos and thus the eschatological destruction of the self.[26]

The Stoic psychophysical combination of the "ignorant and unstable" also unites microcosm and macrocosm in a biological, rather than a mechanistic, worldview. As in a human body, so also in the cosmos, believed to be a massive organism, the permeation of πνεῦμα creates the tension (τόνος) that holds the All (τὸ πᾶν, the universe) in its living coherence (συμπάθεια). Just as the release of sensory tension in the human body occasions death, so also the release (ἀνάλυσις) of the universal pneumatic tension, which dissolves all bonds in a total conflagration (ἐκπύρωσις), occasions the death of the universe. The subsequent regeneration of all pneumatic bonds in a cosmic rebirth (παλιγγενεσία) resets the cosmic lifespan until the next ἐκπύρωσις, a cycle endlessly repeated (at least in theory) in most Stoic cosmologies.[27] The main authority for this idea was Chrysippus of Soli (ca. 280–207 B.C.E.), who succeeded Cleanthes as head of the Stoic school in 232. In a series of motifs derived from daily life—the "weaving together" of fate and its "chain" of interlocked material causes—Chrysippus made the Stoic cosmology a well-argued position and intelligible to students.[28]

---

[25] Arius Didymus, *Epitomai*, in Stobaeus, *Anth.* 2.7.5b13 (= 2.68.18–23 W-H) (Pomeroy 1999, 27). Arius Didymus (first century B.C.E.) was an Alexandrian philosopher and advisor to the Roman emperor Augustus; for a questioning of this identity, however, see Göransson 1995, 203–18.

[26] Long and Sedley 1987, 2:410–11 (§65A), 412–14 (§§65G, J), 417–18 (§65R); Hershkowitz 1998, 7–8; Tieleman 2003, 112–13, 184–97; Gill 2006, esp. 244–66; see also 29–46, 74–100, 127–66, 460, and *passim*; Graver 2007, 109–32; Wasserman 2008, 397–98.

[27] Lapidge 1989, 1383; White 2003, 133.

[28] Lapidge 1979, 346–49; 1989, 1381–85.

Later Stoic thinkers held diverse views on ἐκπύρωσις. A few rejected its cosmology, and others largely neglected its details. For example, Panaetius of Rhodes (ca. 185–110 B.C.E.) denied the idea of an endless cycle of ἐκπύρωσις/ παλιγγενεσία, Boethus of Sidon (*floruit* second century B.C.E.) abandoned it as untenable, and Diogenes of Babylon (head of Stoa in early to mid-second century B.C.E.) is said to have had doubts about the conflagration.[29] But whether Stoic thinkers overall took an interest in cosmology is a separate question. To be sure, the later Hellenistic heads of the Stoa may not have placed such an emphasis on cosmology as Chrysippus did.[30] But Posidonius of Apamea (ca. 135–50 B.C.E.), Panaetius's student, had great interest in the science of cosmology, as did Cleomedes in the second century C.E.[31] And Seneca's *Natural Questions* is our longest surviving text on natural phenomena. This evidence for a continuity of interest in cosmology, even if some Stoic thinkers did not share this interest, makes a connection between 2 Peter and ἐκπύρωσις more plausible than previous studies have allowed.[32]

Stoic cosmology fed the Roman cultural imagination in many and creative ways, in part because the Stoics reformulated popular religious myths into a rational, scientific framework.[33] Evidence for the widespread treatment of Stoic cosmological motifs appears across the board, in genres as diverse as philosophy, rhetoric, and poetry to biography, satire, scientific handbook compendia, and tragedy; apparently, ἐκπύρωσις even inspired a cosmological dance.[34] Educated writers and their audiences of the first and second centuries C.E. would, therefore, have been familiar with the (Chrysippean) imagery of Stoic ἐκπύρωσις, if not the details of the theory that underlay it.[35]

---

[29] Philo, *Aet.* 76–77; Cicero, *Nat. d.* 2.118–119.

[30] I qualify Lapidge 1979, 349–51.

[31] Cleomedes' pedagogical treatise *The Heavens* (ca. 200 C.E.) maintained Chrysippus's cosmological theories; see Bowen and Todd 2004. On the date, see also Jones 2003, 333.

[32] For a review of the Stoa in the Roman imperial age, challenging many received views about it, see Gill 2003, 38–40.

[33] Whether the Stoic language had become a "dead metaphor" is debated; see Todd 1989, 1369–70; Crowley 2005, 378.

[34] Philosophy: Cornutus, *Epidrome* 17.2–4 (Hays 1983, 78–79); Cicero, *Resp.* 6.23–24; *Nat. d.* 2.19–92; Arrian, *Epict. diss.* 3.13.4–5; Seneca, *Ep.* 9.17; 71.12–14; 91.1–21; *Clem.* 1.4; *Ben.* 4.6.2–3, 6.21–22; *Polyb.* 1.1–2; *Marc.* 26.5–7; Marcus Aurelius, *Meditations* 3.3.1; 10.7.2; Plutarch, *Mor.* 389C; 415F–416A; 926D–928D; 950D–951B; 955E–F; 1052C–1053E; 1074E–1076A; 1077A–E; Sextus Empiricus, *Pyr.* 1.212. Rhetoric: Dio Chrysostom, *Orationes* 1.42–49; 36.40–61. Poetry: Lucan, *Bell. civ.* 1.71–84; 2.4–11; 5.75–96, 176–182; 6.611–616; Ovid, *Metam.* 1.253–261; 2.201–234; Manilius, *Astronomica* 1.121–146; 2.63–81; cf. Lucretius, *De rerum natura* 1.215–250. Biography: Diogenes Laertius, *Vit. phil.* 7.133–143, 156–157; 9.7–9, 33. Satire: Lucian, *Vit. auct.* 14. Scientific handbook compendia: Pliny, *Nat. hist.* 2.240–241; 7.73; Seneca, *Nat.* 3.13, 27–30; see also Pliny, *Epistulae* 6.20.15 (Sherwin-White 1966, 380). Tragedy: Seneca, *Thyestes* 789–884; *Herc. fur.* 940–952; *Herc. Ot.* 1101–1127 (see Volk 2006, esp. 185–94). The dance: Athenaeus, *Deipnosophistae* 14.629F.

[35] Lapidge 1979, 350.

Many testimonies and compendia cite the imagery in debates on the soul's postmortem survival.[36] According to Arius Didymus, "the soul ... does not perish immediately when freed from the body, but abides for some time by itself; the soul of the good [wise] until the resolution of all things to fire, but the souls of the foolish for certain periods of time."[37] A similar Stoic excerpt appears in the patristic writers Epiphanius, *De fide* 9.40 (GCS 37/3:508), and Theodoret of Cyrus, *Graecarum affectionum curatio* 5.23–24 (SC 57/1:233) (= Pseudo-Plutarch, *Placita philosophorum* 4.7.3), the common source of which Hermann Diels ascribed to a certain Aëtius of the first century C.E. (who is an otherwise unknown author).[38] The compendium of Diogenes Laertius reports that while all Stoics infer that the soul "is a body" who "survives death," Cleanthes, on the one hand, allows all souls to survive until the total conflagration, and Chrysippus, on the other hand, limits that eschatological survival to "only the souls of the wise";[39] in any case, the Stoics consider heroes to be "the souls of the righteous left behind" after death.[40] And an inscription of Diogenes of Oenoanda, the Epicurean (2nd century C.E.), criticizes the idea publicly:

> The Stoics, however, wishing here also to say something stranger than other people, absolutely deny that souls are indestructible, but then go on to say that the souls of the foolish perish immediately after the dissolution of the body whereas those of the virtuous survive, and then they also perish in time. See how manifestly unconvincing their doctrine is; they make their assertion as though the wise and the nonwise are not subject to the same mortality even if they do differ in intelligence. But I am more surprised at their restraint, why, if once the soul is going to be able to exist part from the body—even, we might say, for the least amount of time—(they do not allow it to last for ever).[41]

But one of the best examples of the theme from a Roman Stoic source directly appears in a moral epistle by Seneca the Younger. In *Ep.* 91, Seneca consoles his friend over the news of a recent catastrophic fire that had burned down the Roman colony of Lyons (ancient Lugdunum), the "pride of Gaul."[42] To make sense of the loss, Seneca imagines future cataclysm—the end of everything—by invoking a traditional, and paradigmatic, motif of his worldview, the total conflagration (ἐκπύρωσις). Using the category of catastrophe as a vehicle to "think with," the

---

[36] See, for example, Plutarch, *Mor.* 1107B; Cicero, *Tusc.* 1.77–78; Tacitus, *Agricola* 46; Sextus Empiricus, *Math.* 9.70–74, 78–85. General surveys: Bonhöffer 1890, 54–67; Hoven 1971, 54–67; Annas 1992, 67–68; Gill 2006, 80–81.

[37] Arius Didymus, *Epitomai, apud* Eusebius, *Praep. ev.* 15.20.6 (SC 338:326) (translation, Gifford 2002). See Hahm 1990, 3015–29; Lewis 1995, 97–98.

[38] Diels 1958, 393; Runia 1989, 248–49, 259; Mansfeld 1992; Crego 1993, 224; Lachenaud 1993, 149; Williams 1994, 650; Mansfeld and Runia 1997, 1:121–68.

[39] Diogenes Laertius, *Vit. phil.* 7.156–157.

[40] Diogenes Laertius, *Vit. phil.* 7.151.

[41] Diogenes of Oenoanda, Fragment 3 (Chilton 1967, 60–62; translation, Chilton 1971). See Hoffman 1977, 1:369–72; Mansfeld 1990, 3154–57.

[42] On this letter, see Rosenmeyer 1989, 148–49; Kee 1985, 140 (incorrectly cited as Seneca, *Ep.* 73.16).

Stoic philosopher turns the news of the provincial disaster into an opportunity to teach the need for perspective. Seneca exhorts his friend, a wealthy citizen of Lyons, to deduce from the disaster the value of mental (bodily) fortitude, which only comes from seeing the big picture: "We ought to bear with level-headed [stable] minds [*aequus animus*] the destruction of cities. They stand but to fall! This doom awaits them, one and all."[43] For Seneca, natural laws do not merely describe the cosmic rational order; they constitute actual moral imperatives that Nature (the divine) issues to all humanity.[44] "If this inevitable law is binding upon the highest and lowest alike," Seneca counsels, "be reconciled to this fate, by which all things are dissolved [*a quo omnia resolvuntur*]."[45] But, to the idea of cosmic dissolution, Seneca adds a moral hope: "Perhaps [the Roman colony's] destruction has been brought about only that it may be raised up again to a *better* destiny."[46] Rather than referencing every detail of the cosmological system to which the motif belongs, namely, a replicated recurrence (παλιγγενεσία, as writers in Greek called it), Seneca suggests a material improvement, and progressive change, to arise from the conflagration of physical entities such as praiseworthy Lyons. Adapting the motif of ἐκπύρωσις to his genre of consolation, Seneca does not speculate on pure cosmology or worry about getting technical details of the theory "right."[47]

Seneca offers a similar therapy in his consolation to an aristocratic woman, Marcia, mourning the death of her young son Metilius after having already lost her own father, Cremutius Cordus, to suicide during an imperial proscription. Seneca asks Marcia to imagine Cremutius, together with Metilius, numbered among the "blessed souls" (*felices animae*) in the high heaven and so flourishing.[48] From "the free and boundless spaces of eternity," the rhetorical personification of Marcia's dead father describes the fated cycles of earthquakes, eruptions, tidal waves, floods, and, ultimately, the final conflagration. The prosopopoetic father exhorts:

> "Now I may have the view of countless centuries, the succession and train of countless ages, the whole array of years: I may behold the rise and fall of future kingdoms, the downfall of great cities, and the new inundations of the sea. For, if the common fate can be a solace for your yearning, know that nothing will abide where it is now placed, that time will lay all things low and take all things with it. And not simply people will be its sport—for how small a part are they of fortune's domain!—but places, countries, and the great parts of the universe. It will level whole mountains, and in another place will pile new rocks on high; it will drink up seas, turn rivers from their courses, and, sundering the communication of nations, break up the association and society of the human race; in other places it will swallow up cities in yawning chasm, will shatter them with earthquakes, and from deep below send forth a pestilential vapor; it will

---

[43] Seneca, *Ep.* 91.11–12.
[44] On natural laws as ethical commands in Stoicism, see DeFilippo and Mitsis 1994, 253–54; Inwood 2005, 224–48.
[45] Seneca, *Ep.* 91.15–16.
[46] Seneca, *Ep.* 91.13 (my italics).
[47] On Seneca's idea of progressive change, see Motto 1984, 232. On Seneca's therapy of consolation, see Wilson 1997.
[48] Seneca, *Marc.* 25.1–2.

cover the floods with the face of the inhabited world, and, deluging the earth, will kill every living creature, and in huge conflagration [*ignis vastus*] it will scorch and burn all mortal things. And when the time shall come for the world to be blotted out in order that it may begin its life anew, these things will destroy themselves by their own power, and stars will clash with stars, and all the fiery matter of the world that now shines in orderly array will blaze up in a common conflagration [*unus ignis*]. Then also the souls of the blest, who have partaken of immortality, when it shall seem best to God [Zeus] to create the universe anew—we, too, amid the falling universe, shall be added as a tiny fraction to this mighty destruction, and shall be changed again into our former elements." Happy, Marcia, is your son, who already knows these mysteries![49]

The passage literally ends with a bang. Thus Seneca delivers a happy lesson of Stoic cosmology and its eschatology of the holistic, and stable, self. The general and periodic catastrophes of the earth's surface, and even of the very cosmos, show Marcia that she has no reason to suppose her family's exemption from Nature's law of universal mortality. Premature death often follows the virtuous. The fortitude of her Stoic father, and that of her son, bring a superior existence, everlasting (*aeternus*) among the wise ("blessed souls"), in the highest pneumatic tension and the highest hierarchical region of the cosmos. For Seneca, "we" blessed souls will be holistic, and thus stable, enough to survive until the ἐκπύρωσις, which lies in the remote future. To be sure, Seneca's consolation does follow traditional Stoic teachings. But it is imprecise, without apparent concern over either the theoretical inconsistencies or details, and adapted to the *consolatio* genre.[50]

Another good example comes from Seneca the Younger's nephew Lucan.[51] This Stoic-influenced author applies the motifs of ἐκπύρωσις to his subject without apparent concern over whether they match all the detailed speculations of (what modern scholars reconstruct as) the pure theory. Lucan's *Civil War* (*Bellum civile/ Pharsalia*) deals with bonds of all sorts—familial, social, political, cosmic—and describes their dissolution in the Roman civil wars of Julius Caesar with the Stoic language of universal conflagration:

> My spirit leads me to reveal the causes of such great events, and an immense task is opened up—to tell what drove a maddened people to war, to tell what cast out peace from the world. It was the envious chain of destiny, impossibility of the very high standing long, huge collapses under too much weight, Rome's inability to bear herself. So, when the final hour brings to an end the long ages of the universe, its structure dissolved, reverting to primeval chaos, then fiery stars will plunge into the sea, the earth

---

[49] Seneca, *Marc.* 26.5-7 (translation, Basore 1979).
[50] See Manning 1981, 150-52; Dunn 1987. Seneca's consolation to Marcia echoes Cicero's "Dream of Scipio" (Cicero, *Resp.* 6.9-26) and thus employs several Platonic themes. It also offers a mythical, rather than philosophical, presentation. But, in the end, Seneca adapts the Platonic and mythical themes to a particularly Stoic eschatology; see Reydams-Schils 2005, 35-36.
[51] Scholars debate whether Lucan's poem supports or undermines Stoic philosophy; see D'Alessandro Behr 2007, 171-78, and *passim*; Long 2007. My investigation does not depend on either side of this debate for its argument, only on the thesis that the poem clearly adapts Stoic tenets.

will be unwilling to stretch flat her shores and will shake the water off, Phoebe will confront her brother and for herself demand the day, resentful of driving her chariot along its slanting orbit, and the whole discordant mechanism of the universe torn apart will disrupt its own laws. Mighty structures collapse on to themselves; for prosperity the powers have set this limit to growth.[52]

The Stoic motifs of ἐκπύρωσις tell the disastrous and nefarious effects of the Roman civil wars on the stability of the state. As the character Cato the Younger laments,

> Who would wish to watch the stars and universe collapsing, free from fear himself? to fold his arms and keep them still when ether rushes from on high and earth shudders beneath the weight of the condensing universe?[53]

Cato, like the narrator, imagines how Stoic ἐκπύρωσις would appear from the earth: as the highest cosmic layer of ether (fire) consumes the upwardly expanding lower layers, the stars would appear to be falling (but in fact the earth would be rising up to the stars). Lucan adapts the clearly Stoic imagery to his own end by omitting certain theoretical details unhelpful to his theme, which his audience must also forget in order to apprehend the universal doom and full horror of the civil wars. The madness (*furor*) of Caesar dissolves (*soluere*) the entire structure of the once-glorious Roman republic, down through the cosmic frameworks and bonds (*compages, foedera mundi*). The readers see that arbitrary human *furor* ("rage"), not the *fatum* ("will") of divine λόγος ("reason"), causes the catastrophe. Furthermore, Lucan's own imagery of ἐκπύρωσις does not contain the Stoic norm of a subsequent regeneration (παλιγγενεσία). This absence is conspicuous because Lucan, in his first two books, emphasizes Roman history as a cyclical pattern, generation after generation experiencing the same burst of internecine bloodshed.[54] Lucan thus knows about the Stoic cyclical time but avoids the idea in his particular motifs of ἐκπύρωσις. The full horror of Lucan's poem is its nihilistic finality: it offers nothing but a vision of irreparable cosmic destruction.[55] Lucan's modification of Stoic conflagration imagery into a one-time ἐκπύρωσις, however, is not unique to ancient literature. The variation appears also in Hellenistic Jewish writings such as *Sibylline Oracles*—and, I argue, in 2 Peter—which helpfully complicates the question of what is "Jewish" and what is not.[56]

---

[52] Lucan, *Bell. civ.* 1.67–81 (translation, Braund 1991).

[53] Lucan, *Bell. civ.* 2.289–292 (translation, Braund 1991).

[54] See Leigh 1997, 299–300. The sole, and tantalizing, reference to cosmic παλιγγενεσία that I could find in the poem is the scene of sand settling after a desert storm on the Libyan plain: "And now for him [Cato] the dust started to congeal more and more and Libya thickened and began to turn into earth again" (Lucan, *Bell. civ.* 9.942–945). But this language belongs to the wider description of the Stoic sage's capacity to maintain local stability amid the chaos swirling around him (on Cato, see below).

[55] A point stressed in Schotes 1969, 25; Sklenář 2003, 68–69; 1999, 282–84, 290, and *passim*. See also Lapidge 1979, 359–62; 1980, 281; 1989, 1408; Most 1989, 2055; George 1991, 252.

[56] See Josephus, *Ant.* 1.70; *L.A.E.* 49.3 (*OTP* 2.292); *Sib. Or.* 3.75–92 (*OTP* 1.363–64); 5.515–531 (*OTP* 1.405); Collins 1974, 92–93, 103, 112–15; van der Horst 1998, 218–85. My analysis sets the Sibyllina closer to the Roman literary imagination than Collins (1974) suggests. See also Adams 2007, 52–100.

The unshaken Cato in Lucan's *Civil War* illustrates also the eschatological survival of the Stoic holistic (stable) self.[57] Lucan's several descriptions or allusions to the final cataclysm include no fewer than four epic storms.[58] The last two describe dissolutions by water and by fire, the two main phases of Stoic ἐκπύρωσις,[59] in order to develop Cato's characterization. In the dangerous waters of the Syrtes (rocky gulfs off the Libyan coast), a whirlwind smashes a portion of Cato's invasion fleet; the bursting apart of sails, mast riggings, and ship hulls provides the nautical metaphors for ἀτονία.[60] In the desert of Africa, "the burnt-up places of the world," a sandstorm "attacks the Roman army, and the tottering soldiers cannot stand firm on the sands."[61] There, Cato and his army encounter also homicidal snakes on a plain, whose fiery venom kills by liquefaction. Lucan's grotesque diction emphasizes ligament disintegration; each victim literally melts into a pool of his own viscera and blood. The sinewy disintegration of the Roman soldier's body symbolizes national, and cosmic, ἀτονία.[62] Yet, by virtue of his sturdy fortitude, Cato withstands the watery and fiery calamities and inspires his surviving troops toward greater physical and mental stability. An increasingly isolated figure in the poem, the diehard Cato represents the last cognitively stable Republican marching into the ἐκπύρωσις. He is the Stoic sage surviving until the universal conflagration.[63]

Many biblical commentators protest that 2 Peter's imagery of a final conflagration cannot be "Stoic" because the parallel to ἐκπύρωσις is not exact. This protest contains the unexamined presupposition that all possible allusions to Stoic ἐκπύρωσις must refer precisely to every detail of a set of theoretical speculations. The Roman evidence above does not support this "all or nothing" mindset, but rather suggests that the Stoic motifs of ἐκπύρωσις were flexible and were commonly adapted to make a narrative or rhetorical point. Roman literary imagination used the motifs of Stoic ἐκπύρωσις without necessarily meaning also an endless cycle, or even a rebirth (παλιγγενεσία) of the same exact universe. This finding responds to exegetical objections to pursuing a Stoic context for interpreting 2 Peter, thus allowing a better contextualization of the author's cosmic eschatology and argument about the "ignorant and unstable."

---

[57] On the ambiguities of Cato's Stoic ideal in the poem, however, see Hershkowitz 1998, 197-246; D'Alessandro Behr 2007, 113-61; Graver 2007, 229n10; Long 2007.

[58] Lucan, *Bell. civ.* 4.48-120; 5.504-677; 9.319-347, 445-492.

[59] The process of ἐκπύρωσις reabsorbed the elements into fire through phases—earth becoming water, water becoming air, and then air becoming fire. See Colish 1985, 2:25.

[60] Lucan, *Bell. civ.* 9.319-347. The Greek term ἀτονία does not occur in Lucan's Latin text, of course, but the idea is clearly present.

[61] Lucan, *Bell. civ.* 9.381, 463-465.

[62] Lucan, *Bell. civ.* 9.734-838.

[63] See Thomas 1982; Newmyer 1983; Masters 1992, 58-47; Morford 1996, 42-57; Leigh 2000, 95-109. The apotheosis of Pompey after his funeral pyre also evokes this theme (Lucan, *Bell. civ.* 8.777-9.18); see Marti 1945, 373.

2. The "Ignorant and Unstable" and the Cosmic Dissolution in 2 Peter

The Stoic idea of the holistic (stable) self, in which the wise survive until the total conflagration, offers a plausible context in which to interpret the eschatology of 2 Peter. The text's connection is not so much on a technical level but rather on a cultural one: it shares the content of Stoic thinking and its terminology. The ideas come from the common currency of Stoicism in Greco-Roman culture, not from any professional training on the part of the author in Stoicism. The cultural level of discourse that I am describing is analogous to how a modern person might know and use, more or less, some Freudian terms (ego, superego, the subconscious, a "Freudian slip"), picked up from the common currency and authority of such discourse in modern society and not from any actual education in the psychoanalytic theories of Sigmund Freud. To be sure, 2 Peter advances the non-Stoic ideas of an ensuing judgment, the survival of persons after the conflagration, and new heavens and earth. I do not claim that the author of 2 Peter is consistently Stoic, but his insistence that the universe has a physical dissolution into fire, and that moral behavior has physical effects on the self, plausibly reflects the Stoic premise that the sage alone is the holistic, and stable, self who survives until the universal conflagration.

The conceptual connection of 2 Peter to Stoicism begins in the letter's opening testament, in which virtues appear in a list (1:5–7). Most of the terms—"faithfulness" (πίστις), "excellence" (ἀρετή), "knowledge" (γνῶσις), "self-control" (ἐγκράτεια), "endurance" (ὑπομονή), "piety" (εὐσέβεια)—are found also in Stoic texts, while others, such as "brotherhood" (φιλαδελφία) and "love" (ἀγάπη), are not.[64] But the content of the thinking is similar: the wise are moral and stable like the divine. They "become participants [sharers] in the divine nature [θείας κοινωνοὶ φύσεως]" and so "escape from the corruption that is in the world because of lust" (1:4). The ignorant members are immoral and unstable. They "ignore deliberately" the physical knowledge of the universe, how it "was formed" (συνεστῶσα) by the λόγος of God. The author of 2 Peter proposes the divine λόγος as a physical cosmic agent, which "forms" and "keeps" (τηρέω) all there is (3:5–7).[65] Creation is a "binding" (συνίστημι)—a term occuring also in Stoic authors—and destruction is a "dissolution."[66]

The author of 2 Peter calls on fellow Christians to transform their lives in light of the physical principles of the universe. Asserting that the universe is governed by a rational force, the λόγος, which is identical with the will of God, the author

---

[64] The claim by Wibbing (1959, 86), that 2 Pet 1:5–7 echoes a Stoic catalog of virtues, goes too far; see Charles 1997, 121n51; Starr 2000, 144–66. Specifically Stoic virtues tend to appear in a formal list that ascends in a hierarchy; see the examples collected in *SVF* 3.262–272.

[65] The idea of the λόγος as both creator and destroyer is unusual in the New Testament; see Bauckham 1983, 296–97; Neyrey 1993, 234.

[66] On the Stoic sense of συνίστημι, see Fornberg 1977, 67. The deity in 2 Peter is not "transcendent" or otherwise existing outside the universe (*pace* Starr 2000, 149).

claims that the cosmos itself will dissolve materially, into its elemental masses (στοιχεῖα, "building blocks"), in an eschatological purification by the most primary element of all, fire (3:10, 12).⁶⁷ He writes, "By the same word [λόγος] the present heavens and earth are now stored up [τεθησαυρισμένοι] for fire [πυρί], kept for the day of judgment and destruction of the ungodly" (3:7). He thus links the biblical creation of the world "out of and through water" and the eschatological "dissolution into fire" into a divinely appointed cycle, attempting to integrate Gen 1 and Stoic physics.⁶⁸ According to "Peter," such appointed cycles always move towards dissolution, which helps explain the congregation's current factionalism:

> But false prophets also arose among the people, just as there will be false teachers among you, who will secretly bring in destructive opinions [or "factions"; αἱρέσεις]. They will even deny the Master who bought them—bringing swift destruction on themselves. Even so, many will follow their licentious ways, and because of these teachers the way of truth will be maligned. And in their greed they will exploit you with deceptive words. Their condemnation, pronounced against them long ago, has not been idle, and their destruction is not asleep. (2 Pet 2:1–3 NRSV)

Corruption has occurred before, in prophetic times, and it will recur after the apostle's death. Ordinary metaphors intelligible from daily life explain a physics of inevitability and fate. Just as purchased slaves who deny their lawful owner cannot escape a swift punishment, and as the greedy cannot help exploiting victims with deceptive words, so also false teachers inevitably arise among the people "called" by God. Predicting the organic emergence of false teachers in the congregation sets the local conflict into a wider, cosmic cycle of "corruption" (and its containment) that goes back to the primeval and patriarchal eras (fallen angels, Noah, Sodom and Gomorrah) (2:4–10). The author of 2 Peter claims that all community bonds inevitably loosen over time, which would resemble the physics of ἀτονία for an ancient audience familiar with Stoicism.

The exhortation connects physics and ethics into a new synthesis by correlating moral behavior and psychophysical integrity.⁶⁹ Knowledge builds stability, as ignorance produces instability. The author condemns the scoffers for their ignorance and warns believers about the importance of maintaining their own psychophysical integrity: "Beware that you are not carried away by the lawless and lose your own stability" (2 Pet 3:17 NRSV). The author urges moral believers not to fear the end's purge of corruption (3:14), because their physical stability will enable their eschatological survival at the final conflagration, "to the day of eternity" (3:18), even when the end lies in the remote future from a human perspective of time (3:8–9). Important for the community is internal cohesion here and now.

---

⁶⁷ The term στοιχεῖα had a variety of meanings in ancient Greek. For Stoic usages, see Lapidge 1973; Crowley 2005, 367–94. Wigodsky (2007) criticizes scholars such as Crowley (2005) for treating all uses of the term as constituents of one meaning. Cf. Bauckham 1983, 315–17; Neyrey 1993, 243.

⁶⁸ See Adams 2005a.

⁶⁹ Helpful to the formulation of my analysis in this section is Asmis 2008, 141, 156.

Cohesion both personally and communally figures prominently in "Peter's" opening bequest:

> Therefore I intend to keep on reminding you of these things, though you know them already and are established [ἐστηριγμένους] in the truth that has come to you. I think it right, as long as I am in this body, to refresh your memory, since I know that my death will come soon, as indeed our Lord Jesus Christ has made clear to me. And I will make every effort so that after my departure you may be able at any time to recall these things. (2 Pet 1:12-15 NRSV)

The communal bonds of "brotherly love [ἐν τῇ φιλαδελφίᾳ τὴν ἀγάπην]" (1:7) are already "established" (στηρίζειν, "make stable") from knowing the fundamental "truth" (wisdom).[70] Abiding by the prophecy of the author's farewell message keeps "your call and election" (1:10) "more firm" (βεβαιότερον) (1:19). The author thus promises the wise that their cognitive effort toward personal and communal cohesion will overcome congregational agitation and division after the apostle's death, even to the end times.

In these ways, the author urges members of the congregation to conform their individual identities to that of the whole group of the wise, which is similar to what the Stoics called "affinity/appropriation" (οἰκείωσις).[71] The moral world of 2 Peter places the opponents outside the community. The dislocation stresses their sheer emptiness; they are like mists driven by a storm (2:17).[72] "They speak bombastic nonsense [ματαιότης]," the author condemns, "and with licentious desires of the flesh they entice [δελεάζω] people who have just escaped from those who live in error" (2:18 NRSV). The so-called scoffers seduce (unsettle) believers from "Peter's" firm prophecy, threatening the structural bonds of both community and personality. Affective kinship language cultivates the communal cohesion that the author desires: "You therefore, beloved [ἀγαπητοί], since you are forewarned, beware that you are not carried away [συναπαχθέντες] with the error of the lawless and lose your own stability [ἐκπέσητε τοῦ ἰδίου στηριγμοῦ]. But grow in the grace and knowledge of our Lord and Savior Jesus Christ" (3:17-18 NRSV). In this context, the verb συναπάγω is almost a technical term for what happens in πάθος: it "runs out of control."[73] The moral warnings of being "carried away" and losing "your own stability" point precisely to the physical losses that accompany the dissolution of social bonds—ignorance and instability.

In short, the author brands the opponents as unstable (chaotic) selves. "These people," the author declares, "are like irrational animals [ἄλογα ζῷα φυσικά], mere creatures of instinct, born to be caught and killed" because they prey on the insecure members of the congregation (2:12 NRSV). These feral humans return again

---

[70] The term στηρίζειν had technical meaning in ancient cosmology, including that of the Stoics, for the firmness of the *axis mundi*—the celestial pillar symbolizing the cosmic order; see Segal 1997, 144-45.
[71] See Engberg-Pedersen 1990; 2000; Gill 2006, 36-46, 77-79, 129-34, and *passim*.
[72] See Neyrey 1993, 130.
[73] Chrysippus, for example, defined πάθος as "rejection" or "disobedience." On Stoic interpretations of *pathos*, see Gill 1996, 230-31.

and again as dogs to vomit and pigs to mire (2:22).⁷⁴ "They have eyes full of adultery, insatiable for sin. They entice unsteady souls [δελεάζοντες ψυχὰς ἀστηρίκτου]" (2:14 NRSV). This animal invective against the opponents develops the biblical story of Balaam, which was a popular tale of polemic in early Jewish and Christian writings.⁷⁵ In the congregation, the scoffers "have left the straight road and have gone astray, following the road of Balaam son of Bosor, who loved the wages of doing wrong, but was rebuked for his own transgression; a speechless donkey [ὑποζύγιον ἄφωνον] spoke with a human voice and restrained the prophet's madness [ἐκώλυσεν τὴν τοῦ προφήτου παραφρονίαν]" (2:15–16 NRSV). The author uses the story's comic irony—a self-serving prophet shamed by a dumb ass—as a morality tale on the need for self-control and the restraint of "madness." Like Balaam, the opponents are false prophets mad from greed. They are the "ignorant and unstable," who "twist to their own destruction" all the Scriptures upon which the community's foundation rests secure (3:16). The exhortation goes beyond the Balaam story by linking "madness" and "instability" in a topos, presumably obvious to its audience, which is familiar from the wider Hellenistic and Roman discussions on the Stoic stable self. Instead of the "cleverly devised myths" that the scoffers teach (1:16), the author of 2 Peter tries to reformulate early Christian beliefs about the parousia into the rational framework of a scientific eschatology.

3. Conclusion

Stoic conflagration physics, widely diffuse throughout the ancient Mediterranean world, helps to provide an interpretative context for 2 Peter's imagery of a cosmic dissolution and the author's argument about the eschatological destruction of the "ignorant and unstable." Biblical commentators who restrict the meaning to allude only to passages in the "Old Testament" overlook the promising context of Stoicism for this letter's interpretation. In Roman literature, for example, the motifs of the ἐκπύρωσις (total conflagration) were diffuse and did not evoke every detail of previous theoretical speculations, such as the endless or the exact same recurrence (παλιγγενεσία). Prime examples appear in the writings of Seneca the Younger and of his nephew Lucan.

Importantly, the motifs participated in a wider Stoic idea of the stable self. This idea affirmed the corporeal and psychological wholeness of both human personality and the cosmos, integrated by the divine principle of λόγος. The psychophysical model of ethics contrasted the immoral and the moral in a particularly physical way. The Stoic sage had holistic, and a stable, architecture; the

---

⁷⁴On the feral human as a Stoic topos, see Graver 2007, 123.
⁷⁵The original story is in Num 22:21–35, but the author of 2 Peter gets the reference from Jude 11, redacting the parts that suit his polemics; see Neyrey 1993, 73–74, 211–12; Fornberg 2008. Cf. Caulley (2008), who argues that the author of 2 Peter followed the use of the Balaam saga in "Jewish and Christian tradition" generally, as a warning against assimilation to Hellenistic culture.

fool inevitably experienced "dissolution" like a poorly constructed building. The physics of stability and dissolution mirrored that in the cosmos generally, and connected to Stoic eschatology. Because the wise were more stable than the foolish, the self of the wise was believed by some Stoic authors to survive until the total conflagration.

The exhortation in 2 Peter reflects many of these same concepts. The opponents are not merely vicious; they are the "ignorant and unstable" (ἀμαθεῖς καὶ ἀστήρικτοι) (3:16). Those bad members drift like mists in a storm, destined for eschatological destruction (2:17). Believers, in contrast, will survive until and even beyond the end times by virtue of their proper "knowledge" and "stability," which the author defines through the persona of the apostle Peter. These good members await "new heavens and a new earth, where righteousness is at home" (3:13 NRSV). Their eschatological hope is to see the "day of the Lord"—because of which "the heavens will be set ablaze and dissolved, and the elements [στοιχεῖα] will melt with fire" (3:12 NRSV)—no matter how long it takes.

Bibliography

Adams, E. 2005a. "Creation 'out of' and 'through' Water in 2 Peter 3:5." Pages 195–210 in *The Creation of Heaven and Earth: Re-interpretations of Genesis 1 in the Context of Judaism, Ancient Philosophy, Christianity, and Modern Physics*. Edited by G. H. van Kooten. Themes in Biblical Narrative, Jewish and Christian Tradition 8. Leiden: Brill.

———. 2005b. "'Where Is the Promise of His Coming?' The Complaint of the Scoffers in 2 Peter 3.4." *New Testament Studies* 51:106–22.

———. 2007. *The Stars Will Fall from Heaven: Cosmic Catastrophe in the New Testament and Its World*. Library of New Testament Studies 347. London: T & T Clark.

Annas, J. E. 1992. *Hellenistic Philosophy of Mind: Hellenistic Culture and Society*. Berkeley: University of California Press.

Arichea, D. C., and H. A. Hatton. 1993. *A Handbook on the Letter of Jude and the Second Letter from Peter*. United Bible Societies Handbook Series. New York: United Bible Societies.

Asmis, E. 2008. "Lucretius' New World Order: Making a Pact with Nature." *Classical Quarterly* 58:141–57.

Basore, J. W. 1979. *Seneca: Moral Essays*. Vol. 2. Loeb Classical Library. Cambridge, Mass.: Harvard University Press.

Bauckham, R. J. 1983. *Jude, 2 Peter*. Word Biblical Commentary 20. Waco, Tex.: Word Books.

———. 1988. "2 Peter: An Account of Research." *ANRW* 25.5:2713–52. Part 2, *Principat*, 25.5. Edited by H. Temporini and W. Haase. Berlin: de Gruyter.

Berryman, S. 2007. Review of C. Gill, *The Structured Self in Hellenistic and Roman Thought, Journal of the History of Philosophy* 45:324–25.

Bigg, C. 1922. *A Critical and Exegetical Commentary on the Epistles of St. Peter and St. Jude.* International Critical Commentary 42. New York: Scribner.
Bonhöffer, A. 1890. *Epictet und die Stoa: Untersuchungen zur stoischen Philosophie.* Stuttgart: Enke.
Bowen, A. C., and R. B. Todd. 2004. *Cleomedes' Lectures on Astronomy: A Translation of "The Heavens."* Hellenistic Culture and Society 42. Berkeley: University of California Press.
Boys-Stones, G. R. 2007. "Subject Reviews: Philosophy." *Greece and Rome* 54:133–35.
Braund, S. H. 1991. *Lucan: Civil War.* Oxford World's Classics. New York: Oxford University Press.
Caulley, T. S. 2008. "'They Promise Them Freedom': Once Again, the ψευδοδιδάσκαλοι in 2 Peter." *Zeitschrift für die neutestamentliche Wissenschaft* 99:129–38.
Chaine, J. 1937. "Cosmogonie aquatique et conflagration finale d'après la Secunda Petri." *Révue biblique* 46:207–16.
Charles, J. D. 1997. *Virtues amidst Vice: The Catalog of Virtues in 2 Peter 1.* Journal for the Study of the New Testament: Supplement Series 150. Sheffield: Sheffield Academic Press.
Chilton, C. W. 1967. *Diogenis Oenoandensis fragmenta.* Leipzig: Teubner.
———. 1971. *Diogenes of Oenoanda: The Fragments.* London: Oxford University Press.
Colish, M. L. 1985. *The Stoic Tradition from Antiquity to the Early Middle Ages.* 2 vols. Stoicism in Classical Literature 2. Leiden: Brill.
Collins, J. J. 1974. *The Sibylline Oracles of Egyptian Judaism.* Society of Biblical Literature Dissertation Series 13. Missoula, Mont.: Society of Biblical Literature.
Conzelmann, H. 1975. *1 Corinthians: A Commentary on the First Epistle to the Corinthians.* Translated by J. W. Leitch. Hermeneia. Philadelphia: Fortress.
Crego, P. 1993. "A Translation and Commentary of Theodoret of Cyrus (Graecarum affectionum curatio) Book Five: On Human Nature." Ph.D. diss., Boston College.
Crowley, T. J. 2005. "On the Use of Stoicheion in the Sense of 'Element.'" *Oxford Studies in Ancient Philosophy* 29:367–94.
D'Alessandro Behr, F. 2007. *Feeling History: Lucan, Stoicism, and the Poetics of Passion.* Columbus: Ohio State University Press.
Danker, F. 1962. "II Peter 3:10 and Psalm of Solomon 17:10." *Zeitschrift für die neutestamentliche Wissenschaft* 53:82–86.
DeFilippo, J. G., and P. T. Mitsis. 1994. "Socrates and Stoic Natural Law." Pages 252–71 in *The Socratic Movement.* Edited by P. A. Van der Waerdt. Ithaca, N.Y.: Cornell University Press.
Diels, H. 1958. *Doxographi Graeci.* 3rd ed. Berlin: de Gruyter.
Downing, F. G. 2000. "Common Strands in Pagan, Jewish and Christian Eschatologies in the First Century." Pages 169–87 in *Making Sense in (and of) the First Christian Century.* Journal for the Study of the New Testament: Supplement Series 197. Sheffield: Sheffield Academic Press.

Droge, A. J. 1989. *Homer or Moses? Early Christian Interpretations of the History of Culture*. Hermeneutische Untersuchungen zur Theologie 26. Tübingen: Mohr Siebeck.

Dunn, F. M. 1989. "A Prose Hexameter in Seneca? (Consolatio ad Marciam 26.7)." *American Journal of Philology* 110:488–91.

Dupont-Roc, R. 1994. "Le motif de la création selon 2 Pierre 3." *Révue biblique* 101:95–114.

Elliott, J. H. 1992. "Peter, Second Epistle of." Pages 282–87 in vol. 5 of *The Anchor Bible Dictionary*. Edited by D. N. Freedman. New York: Doubleday.

Engberg-Pedersen, T. 1990. *The Stoic Theory of Oikeiosis: Moral Development and Social Interaction in Early Stoic Philosophy*. Studies in Hellenistic Civilization 2. Aarhus: Aarhus University Press.

———. 2000. *Paul and the Stoics*. Louisville: Westminster John Knox Press.

Fee, G. D. 1987. *The First Epistle to the Corinthians*. New International Commentary on the New Testament. Grand Rapids: Eerdmans.

Feeney, D. 2006. *Caesar's Calendar: Ancient Time and the Beginnings of History*. Sather Classical Lectures 65. Berkeley: University of California Press.

Fornberg, T. 1977. *An Early Church in a Pluralistic Society: A Study of 2 Peter*. Coniectanea biblica: New Testament Series 9. Lund: Gleerup.

———. 2008. "Balaam and 2 Peter 2:15: 'They Have Followed in the Steps of Balaam' (Jude 11)." Pages 265–74 in *The Prestige of the Pagan Prophet Balaam in Judaism, Early Christianity and Islam*. Edited by G. H. von Kooten and J. van Ruiten. Themes in Biblical Narrative 11. Leiden: Brill.

Fuchs, E., and P. Reymond. 1988. *La deuxième épître de saint Pierre; l'épître de saint Jude*. 2nd ed. Commentaire du Nouveau Testament, deuxième série 13B. Geneva: Labor et Fides.

Fuglseth, K. 2006. "The Reception of Aristotelian Features in Philo and the Authorship Problem of Philo's De Aeternitate Mundi." Pages 1–11 in *Beyond Reception: Mutual Influences between Antique Religion, Judaism, and Early Christianity*. Edited by D. Brakke, A.-C. Jacobsen, and J. Ulrich. Early Christianity in the Context of Antiquity 1. Frankfurt am Main: Lang.

Furley, D. 1999. "Cosmology." Pages 412–51 in *The Cambridge History of Hellenistic Philosophy*. Edited by K. Algra et al. Cambridge: Cambridge University Press.

George, D. B. 1991. "Lucan's Cato and Stoic Attitudes to the Republic." *Classical Antiquity* 10(2):237–58.

Gerdmar, A. 2001. *Rethinking the Judaism–Hellenism Dichotomy: A Historical Case Study of Second Peter and Jude*. Coniectanea biblica: New Testament Series 36. Stockholm: Almqvist & Wiksell.

Gifford, E. H. 2002. *Eusebius: Preparation for the Gospel*. 2 vols. Oxford: Clarendon Press, 1903. Repr., Eugene, Ore.: Wipf & Stock.

Gill, C. 1996. *Personality in Greek Epic, Tragedy, and Philosophy: The Self in Dialogue*. Oxford: Clarendon Press.

———. 2003. "The School in the Roman Imperial Period." Pages 33–58 in *The Cambridge Companion to the Stoics*. Edited by B. Inwood. Cambridge: Cambridge University Press.
———. 2006. *The Structured Self in Hellenistic and Roman Thought*. Oxford: Oxford University Press.
———. 2007. "Galen and the Stoics: Mortal Enemies or Blood Brothers?" *Phronesis* 52:88–120.
Gilmour, M. J. 2002. *The Significance of Parallels between 2 Peter and Other Early Christian Literature*. Society of Biblical Literature Academia Biblica 10. Atlanta: Society of Biblical Literature.
Glasson, T. F. 1961. *Greek Influence in Jewish Eschatology*. London: SPCK.
Göransson, T. 1995 *Albinus, Alcinous, Arius Didymus*. Studia Graeca et Latina Gothoburgensia 61. Gothenburg: Acta Universitas Gothoburgensia.
Gould, J. B. 1970. *The Philosophy of Chrysippus*. Philosophia antiqua 17. Leiden: Brill.
Gourinat, J.-B. 2002. "L'éternal retour et temps périodique dans la philosophie stoïcienne." *Revue philosophique de la France et de l'étranger* 127(2):213–27.
Graf, F. 2004. "What Is Ancient Mediterranean Religion?" Pages 3–16 in *Religions of the Ancient World: A Guide*. Edited by S. I. Johnston. Harvard University Press Reference Library. Cambridge, Mass.: Belknap Press.
Graver, M. R. 2007. *Stoicism and Emotion*. Chicago: University of Chicago Press.
Green, M. 1986. *The Second Epistle General of Peter and the General Epistle of Jude*. Grand Rapids: Eerdmans.
Hahm, D. E. 1990. "The Ethical Doxography of Arius Didymus." *ANRW* 36.4:2935–3055. Part 2, *Principat* 36.4. Edited by H. Temporini and W. Haase. Berlin: de Gruyter.
———. 1997. *The Origins of Stoic Cosmology*. Columbus: Ohio State University Press.
Harrill, J. A. 2006. *Slaves in the New Testament: Literary, Social, and Moral Dimensions*. Minneapolis: Fortress.
Hart, V. 2002. *Plato on Parts and Wholes: The Metaphysics of Structure*. Oxford: Clarendon Press.
Hays, R. S. 1983. "Lucius Annaeus Cornutus' Epidrome [Introduction to the Traditions of Greek Theology]." Ph.D. diss., University of Texas at Austin.
Hershkowitz, D. 1998. *The Madness of Epic: Reading Insanity from Homer to Statius*. Oxford Classical Monographs. Oxford: Clarendon Press.
Hoffman, G. N. 1977. "Diogenes of Oenoanda: A Commentary." 2 vols. Ph.D. diss., University of Minnesota.
Hoven, R. 1971. *Stoïcisme et Stoïciens face au problème de l'au-delà*. Bibliothèque de la Faculté de philosophie et lettres de l'Université de Liège 197. Paris: Les Belles Lettres.
Inwood, B. 2005. *Reading Seneca: Stoic Philosophy at Rome*. Oxford: Clarendon Press.

———. 2007. Review of C. Gill, *The Structured Self in Hellenistic and Roman Thought*, Philosophical Quarterly 57:479–83.
Jones, A. 2003. "The Stoics and the Astronomical Sciences." Pages 328–44 in *The Cambridge Companion to the Stoics*. Edited by B. Inwood. Cambridge: Cambridge University Press.
Kee, H. C. 1985. "Pauline Eschatology: Relationships with Apocalyptic and Stoic Thought." Pages 135–58 in *Glaube und Eschatologie: Festschrift für Werner Georg Kümmel zum 80. Geburtstag*. Edited by E. Gräßer and O. Merk. Tübingen: Mohr Siebeck.
Kelly, J. N. D. 1969. *A Commentary on the Epistles of Peter and Jude*. Black's New Testament Commentaries. London: Black.
Konstan, D. 2007. Review of C. Gill, *The Structured Self in Hellenistic and Roman Thought*, Journal of Hellenic Studies 127:248.
Lachenaud, G. 1993. *Plutarque: Opinions des philosophes*. 2nd ed. Collection des universités de France. Paris: Les Belles Lettres.
Lapidge, M. 1973. "ἀρχαί and στοιχεῖα: A Problem in Stoic Cosmology." Phronesis 18:240–78.
———. 1979. "Lucan's Imagery of Cosmic Dissolution." Hermes 107(3):344–70.
———. 1980. "A Stoic Metaphor in Late Latin Poetry: The Binding of the Cosmos." Latomus 39(4):817–37.
———. 1989. "Stoic Cosmology and Roman Literature, First to Third Centuries A.D." ANRW 36.3:1379–1429. Part 2, *Principat*, 36.3. Edited by H. Temporini and W. Haase. Berlin: de Gruyter.
Leigh, M. 1997. *Lucan: Spectacle and Engagement*. Oxford Classical Monographs. Oxford: Clarendon Press.
———. 2000. "Lucan and the Libyan Tale." Journal of Roman Studies 90:95–109.
Lenhard, H. 1961. "Ein Beitrag zur Übersetzung von II Ptr 3,10d." Zeitschrift für die neutestamentliche Wissenschaft 52:128–29.
———. 1978. "Noch einmal zu 2 Petr 3,10d." Zeitschrift für die neutestamentliche Wissenschaft 69:136.
Lewis, E. 1995. "The Stoics on Identity and Individuation." Phronesis 40:89–108.
Long, A. 2007. "Lucan and Moral Luck." Classical Quarterly 57:183–97.
Long, A. A. 1996. "Language and Thought in Stoicism." Pages 75–113 in *Problems in Stoicism*. Edited by A. A. Long. London: Athlone Press, 1971. Repr., London: Athlone Press.
———. 2006. "The Stoics on World-Conflagration and Everlasting Recurrence." Pages 256–82 in *From Epictetus to Epicurus: Studies in Hellenistic and Roman Philosophy*. Oxford: Clarendon Press.
Long, A. A., and D. N. Sedley. 1987. *The Hellenistic Philosophers*. 2 vols. Cambridge: Cambridge University Press.
Manning, C. E. 1981. *On Seneca's "Ad Marciam."* Mnemosyne Supplementum 69. Leiden: Brill.
Mansfeld, J. 1979. "Providence and the Destruction of the Universe in Early Stoic Thought." Pages 129–88 in *Studies in Hellenistic Religions*. Edited by M. J. Ver-

maseren. Études preliminaries aux religions orientales dans l'empire romain 78. Leiden: Brill.
———. 1983. "Resurrection Added: The Interpretatio Christiana of a Stoic Doctrine." *Vigiliae christianae* 37(2):218–33.
———. 1990. "Doxography and Dialectic: The Sitz im Leben of the 'Placita.'" *ANRW* 36.4:3056–3229. Part 2, *Principat*, 36.4. Edited by H. Temporini and W. Haase. Berlin: de Gruyter.
———. 1992. "*Physikai doxai* and *Problēmata physika* from Aristotle to Aëtius (and Beyond)." Pages 63–111 in *Theophrastus: His Psychological, Doxographical, and Scientific Writings*. Edited by W. W. Fortenbaugh and D. Gutas. Rutgers University Studies in Classical Humanities 5. New Brunswick, N.J.: Transaction.
Mansfeld, J., and D. T. Runia. 1997. *Aëtiana: The Method and Intellectual Context of a Doxographer*. 2 vols. Philosophia antiqua 73. Leiden: Brill.
Marti, B. M. 1945. "The Meaning of the Pharsalia." *American Journal of Philology* 66:352–76.
Martin, D. B. 1995. *The Corinthian Body*. New Haven: Yale University Press.
Masters, J. 1992. *Poetry and Civil War in Lucan's "Bellum Civile."* Cambridge Classical Studies. Cambridge: Cambridge University Press.
Mayer, R. 1956. *Die biblische Vorstellung vom Weltenbrand: Eine Untersuchung über die Beziehungen zwischen Parsismus und Judentum*. Bonner orientalische Studien 4. Bonn: Selbstverlag des Orientalischen Seminars der Universität Bonn.
Meeks, W. A. 2001. "Judaism, Hellenism, and the Birth of Christianity." Pages 17–28 in *Paul Beyond the Judaism/Hellenism Divide*. Edited by T. Engberg-Pedersen. Louisville: Westminster John Knox Press.
———. 2005. "Why Study the New Testament." *New Testament Studies* 51:155–70.
Metzger, B. M. 1994. *A Textual Commentary on the Greek New Testament*. 2nd ed. Stuttgart: Deutsche Bibelgesellschaft.
Milavec, A. 1995. "The Saving Efficacy of the Burning Process in Didache 16.5." Pages 131–55 in *The "Didache" in Context: Essays on Its Text, History, and Transmission*. Edited by C. N. Jefford. Supplements to Novum Testamentum 77. Leiden: Brill.
Morford, M. P. O. 1996. *The Poet Lucan: Studies in Rhetorical Epic*. 2nd ed. London: Bristol Classical Press.
Most, G. W. 1989. "Cornutus and Stoic Allegoresis: A Preliminary Report." *ANRW* 36.3:2014–65. Part 2, *Principat*, 36.3. Edited by H. Temporini and W. Haase. Berlin: de Gruyter.
Motto, A. L. 1984. "The Idea of Progress in Senecan Thought." *Classical Journal* 79:225–40.
Murphy, F. S. 1983. "Conflagration: The Eschatological Perspective from Origen to John Chrysostom." *Studia patristica* 18(1):179–85.
Newmyer, S. 1983. "Imagery as a Means of Character Portrayal in Lucan." Pages 226–52 in *Studies in Latin Literature and Roman History III*. Edited by C. Deroux. Collection Latomus 180. Brussels: Latomus.

Neyrey, J. H. 1980. "The Form and Background of the Polemic in 2 Peter." *Journal of Biblical Literature* 99:407–31.

———. 1993. *2 Peter, Jude: A New Translation with Introduction and Commentary*. Anchor Bible 37C. New York: Doubleday.

Olivier, F. 1963. "Une correction au texte de Nouveau Testament: II Pierre 3,10." Pages 129–52 in *Essais dans le domaine du monde gréco-romain antique et dans celui du Nouveau Testament*. Université de Lausanne, Publications de la Faculté des lettres 15. Geneva: Librarie Droz. [Reprinted from *Revue de théologie et de philosophie* 8 (1920): 237–78.]

Paulsen, H. 1992. *Der Zweite Petrusbrief und der Judasbrief*. Kritisch-exegetischer Kommentar über das Neue Testament 12/2. Göttingen: Vandenhoeck & Ruprecht.

Pearson, B. A. 2001. "Indo-European Eschatology in 2 Peter 3." Pages 536–45 in *Kontinuitäten und Brüche in der Religionsgeschichte: Festschrift für Anders Hultgård*. Edited by M. Stausberg et al. Ergänzungsbände zum Reallexikon der germanischen Altertumskunde 31. Berlin: de Gruyter.

Pomeroy, A. J., ed. 1999. *Arius Didymus: Epitome of Stoic Ethics*. Society of Biblical Literature Texts and Translations 44, Graeco-Roman Religion Series 14. Atlanta: Society of Biblical Literature.

Reydams-Schils, G. 2005. *The Roman Stoics: Self, Responsibility, and Affection*. Chicago: University of Chicago Press.

Riesner, R. 1984. "Der Zweite Petrus-Brief und die Eschatologie." Pages 124–43 in *Zukunftserwartung in biblischer Sicht: Beiträge zur Eschatologie*. Edited by G. Maier. Wuppertal: Brockhaus; Giessen: Brunnen.

Rosenmeyer, T. G. 1989. *Senecaean Drama and Stoic Cosmology*. Berkeley: University of California Press.

Runia, D. T. 1981. "Philo's De Aeternitate Mundi: The Problem of Its Interpretation." *Vigiliae christianae* 35(2):101–52.

———. 1989. "Xenophanes on the Moon: A Doxographicum in Aëtius." *Phronesis* 34:245–69.

Russell, D. M. 1996. *The "New Heavens and New Earth": Hope for Creation in Jewish Apocalyptic and the New Testament*. Studies in Biblical Apocalyptic Literature 1. Philadelphia: Visionary Press.

Schotes, H.-A. 1969. *Stoische Physik, Psychologie und Theologie bei Lucan*. Habelts Dissertationsdrucke, Reihe klassische Philologie 5. Bonn: Habelt.

Segal, C. 1997. *Dionysiac Poetics and Euripides' "Bacchae."* Expanded ed. Princeton, N.J.: Princeton University Press.

Sherwin-White, A. N. 1966. *The Letters of Pliny: A Historical and Social Commentary*. Oxford: Clarendon Press.

Sim, D. C. 1993. "The Meaning of παλιγγενεσία in Matthew 19.28." *Journal for the Study of the New Testament* 50:3–12.

Sklenář, R. 1999. "Nihilistic Cosmology and Catonian Ethics in Lucan's Bellum Civile." *American Journal of Philology* 120:281–96.

———. 2003. *The Taste for Nothingness: A Study of "Virtus" and Related Themes in Lucan's "Bellum Civile."* Ann Arbor: University of Michigan Press.

Stalnacker, A. 2008. "Judging Others: History, Ethics, and the Purposes of Comparison." *Journal of Religious Ethics* 36(3):425–44.
Starr, J. M. 2000. *Sharers in Divine Nature: 2 Peter 1:4 in Its Hellenistic Context.* Coniectanea biblica: New Testament Series 33. Stockholm: Almqvist & Wiksell.
Testa, P. E. 1962. "La distruzione del mundo per il fuoco nella 2 ep. di Pietro 3,7.10.13." *Rivista biblica italiana* 10(3):252–81.
Thiede, C. P. 1986. "A Pagan Reader of 2 Peter: Cosmic Conflagration in 2 Peter 3 and the Octavius of Minucius Felix." *Journal for the Study of the New Testament* 9:79–86.
Thomas, R. F. 1982. "The Stoic Landscape of Lucan 9." Pages 108–23 in *Lands and Peoples in Roman Poetry: The Ethnographical Tradition.* Proceedings of the Cambridge Philological Society: Supplement 7. Cambridge: Cambridge Philological Society.
Tieleman, T. 2003. *Chrysippus' On Affections: Reconstructions and Interpretation.* Philosophia antiqua 94. Leiden: Brill.
Todd, R. B. 2005. "The Stoics and Their Cosmology in the First and Second Centuries A.D." *ANRW* 36.3:1365–78. Part 2, *Principat*, 36.3. Edited by H. Temporini and W. Haase. Berlin: de Gruyter.
Van der Horst, P. W. 1998. "'The Elements Will Be Dissolved with Fire': The Idea of Cosmic Conflagration in Hellenism, Ancient Judaism, and Early Christianity." Pages 271–92 in *Hellenism, Judaism, Christianity: Essays in Their Interaction.* 2nd ed. Contributions to Biblical Exegesis and Theology 8. Leuven: Peeters.
Vögtle, A. 1970. *Das Neue Testament und die Zukunft des Kosmos.* Kommentare und Beiträge zum Alten und Neuen Testament. Düsseldorf: Patmos.
Volk, K. 2006. "Cosmic Disruption in Seneca's Thyestes: Two Ways of Looking at an Eclipse." Pages 183–200 in *Seeing Seneca Whole: Perspectives on Philosophy, Poetry, and Politics.* Edited by K. Volk and G. D. Williams. Columbia Studies in the Classical Tradition 28. Leiden: Brill.
von Allmen, D. 1966. "L'apocalyptique juive et le retard de la parousie en II Pierre 3:1–13." *Revue de théologique et de philosophie* 99:255–74.
Von Staden, H. 2000. "Body, Soul, and Nerves: Epicurus, Herophilus, Erasistratus, the Stoics, and Galen." Pages 79–116 in *Psyche and Soma: Physicians and Metaphysicians on the Mind–Body Problem from Antiquity to Enlightenment.* Edited by J. P. Wright and P. Potter. Oxford: Clarendon Press.
Wasserman, E. 2008. "Paul among the Philosophers: The Case of Sin in Romans 6–8." *Journal for the Study of the New Testament* 30:387–415.
Wenham, D. 1987. "Being 'Found' on the Last Day: New Light on 2 Peter 3.10 and 2 Corinthians 5.3." *New Testament Studies* 33:477–79.
White, M. J. 2003. "Stoic Natural Philosophy (Physics and Cosmology)." Pages 124–52 in *The Cambridge Companion to the Stoics.* Edited by B. Inwood. Cambridge: Cambridge University Press.
Wibbing, S. 1959. *Die Tugend- und Lasterkataloge im Neuen Testament und ihre Traditionsgeschichte unter besonderer Berücksichtigung der Qumran-Texte.* Beihefte zur Zeitschrift für die neutestamentliche Wissenschaft 25. Berlin: Töpelmann.

Wigodsky, M. 2007. "Homoiotetes, Stoicheia and Homoiomereiae in Epicurus." *Classical Quarterly* 57:521–42.

Williams, F. 1994. *The Panarion of Epiphanius of Salamis: Books II and III (Sects 47–80, "De Fide")*. Nag Hammadi and Manichaean Studies 36. Leiden: Brill.

Wilson, M. 1997. "The Subjugation of Grief in Seneca's 'Epistles.'" Pages 48–67 in *The Passions in Roman Thought and Literature*. Edited by S. M. Braund and C. Gill. Cambridge: Cambridge University Press.

Wolters, A. 1987. "Worldview and Textual Criticism in 2 Peter 3:10." *Westminster Theological Journal* 49:408–13.

8

THE STOICS AND THE EARLY CHRISTIANS ON THE TREATMENT OF SLAVES

John T. Fitzgerald
University of Miami, USA, &
North-West University, South Africa

The issue of how to treat slaves is as old as slavery itself. Furthermore, this issue does not stand alone in a social or intellectual vacuum. It is akin to a host of similar issues regarding how humans ought to treat particular types of people, such as spouses, children, siblings, relatives, friends, neighbors, strangers, and so forth. Implicit in such questions are numerous related issues, such as how slaves are to treat masters, how children are to treat parents, how younger people are to treat older people, how clients are to treat patrons, and, of course, how humans are to treat the gods. For most people in the ancient Mediterranean world, the question of how to treat the gods was essentially a religious question, whereas many of the other issues would have been viewed as moral or social ones. In this regard, slavery usually was considered differently. Although some people did view slavery from a moral and/or theological standpoint, they were the exception rather than the rule. For most people, the treatment of slaves was ultimately a socioeconomic or management issue: how to treat one's slaves so as optimally to achieve one's purposes in owning them.

The following essay comprises four unequal parts. In the first part I provide an overview of slave management in the ancient world, paying particular attention to the use of rewards and punishments to induce slaves to perform their assigned tasks. This overview is intended to lay the foundation for the remaining three parts of the essay. The second part contains introductory comments on Stoics and Christians in regard to slavery. The third part is devoted to a sketch of some Stoic views on slave management, and the fourth part is a discussion of several Christian texts in light of the first three parts of the essay. All four parts of the essay are selective as far as the examination of slavery and slave management is concerned, but that is particularly true of the second, third, and fourth parts. Despite this selectivity, I trust that what is discussed will be suggestive for what a more comprehensive treatment would demonstrate. It is to the ancient topos of slave management that we now turn.

1. Slave Management in the Ancient World

The history of slavery in the ancient Mediterranean world shows that masters managed their slaves in a wide variety of ways, with some masters treating their slaves well and regarding them with affection, and other masters mistreating their slaves and subjecting them to violence. How slaves were treated depended on a daunting variety of factors, including the master's personality, disposition, and management philosophy; the slave's character and conduct; the circumstances under which the slave became the master's property; and the tasks that the slaves were assigned. That masters treated one or more of their slaves well did not necessarily mean that their other slaves received the same kind of treatment. Indeed, as we will see later in this essay, there were often conspicuous disparities in how the same owner treated his or her slaves.

In examining the issue of how slaves were treated, we must remember that ancient slavery, as an institution, was neither static nor monolithic. It changed enormously over time, and it varied a great deal even during particular points in time. In the Greco-Roman world, for example, some slaves were entrusted with middle- and upper-management positions that gave them, in conjunction with their heightened responsibilities, considerable power, authority, and independence. Other slaves lived in houses and performed a variety of domestic tasks. Still others worked on farms and in vineyards, whereas others toiled in mines alongside prisoners of war and hardened criminals. How slaves were treated depended greatly on the kind of work that they were assigned and the means by which their masters elected to motivate them.

In general, Greco-Roman masters used two kinds of incentives to motivate slaves to work: rewards and punishments. Disobedient slaves whose work was slipshod and slovenly were routinely subjected to punishments involving physical pain, whereas obedient slaves who worked conscientiously and meticulously were given various kinds of rewards, with manumission often functioning as the ultimate reward.[1] Although some masters undoubtedly were sadists who enjoyed using physical coercion with their slaves, and a few masters apparently hoped to induce appropriate behavior exclusively through bribes, almost all masters appear to have used both the "stick" and the "carrot" in managing their slaves, choosing whichever method or combination of methods worked best with a given slave. Accordingly, they adjusted the levels of punishment and reward, of physical force and material goods, so as to maximize the slave's obedience and productivity.

Viewed from an economic standpoint, slaves as "human capital" were among the master's financial assets, and masters sought to make an optimal use of those assets. That was essential because masters incurred a number of financial costs in order to acquire and maintain their slaves. Certain kinds of slave labor may have been relatively cheap, but it was never free. In addition to direct costs involving the slave per se (for things such as food, clothing, and housing), masters incurred

---

[1] On manumission among Greeks, see Zelnick-Abramovitz 2005.

other kinds of costs, such as expenditures for the equipment used by slaves, the repair or replacement of property accidentally or deliberately damaged by slaves, medical care for ill and injured slaves, the personnel involved with the training and supervision of slaves (even if the supervisors were themselves slaves), and the recovery of escaped slaves. Economic concerns are particularly conspicuous in a master such as Cato the Elder. He advises masters that when they arrive at the farm for an inspection, they are not to accept lame excuses from the overseer, such as "the slaves have not been well" or "slaves have run away" (*Agr.* 2.2)[2] but they are to teach the overseers what adjustments could and should have been made under those circumstances. "When the slaves were sick," for example, "such large rations should not have been issued" (*Agr.* 2.5). Furthermore, he makes clear that when slaves are perpetually ill or become too old to be productive workers, they should not be maintained. Along with worn-out equipment and other nonessential items, they should be sold: "Sell worn-out oxen, blemished cattle, blemished sheep, wool, hides, an old wagon, old tools, an old slave, a sickly slave, and whatever else is superfluous" (*Agr.* 2.7).

Furthermore, inasmuch as slave labor was largely involuntary, slaves often needed to be induced to work, either to obtain rewards or to avoid painful penalties. "Masters," in short, "must bribe or coerce labor services from their slave stock and this implicitly defines a cost function to the owner of the stock."[3] In this regard, the typical Greco-Roman slave owner appears to have been no different from masters in other time periods.[4] From a historical perspective, the typical master is fundamentally "indifferent as to the combination of force and other incentives received by his slaves. He is concerned only with the problem of minimizing the cost of utilizing his given stock of slave capital."[5] For the same reason, masters as a general rule "will use both pain incentives and ordinary rewards, adjusting their levels until they yield an equal marginal benefit per unit cost."[6]

The use of rewards and punishments as two different incentives in order to achieve a common goal was hardly unique to slave owners in antiquity. Parents and schoolteachers routinely used both methods of motivation with children, and corporal punishment at both home and school was the norm throughout the ancient world.[7] Farmers and generals also used both methods, as Socrates reminds Critobulus:

> Therefore the man who is going to be a successful farmer must make his laborers eager and disposed to be obedient. And the man who leads his men against the enemy must

---

[2] Translations of Cato the Elder's *De agricultura* (= *De re rustica*) are from Hooper and Ash 1954.
[3] Canarella and Tomaske 1975, 623.
[4] For an important recent collection of articles devoted to a comparative study of ancient and modern slave systems, see Dal Lago and Katsari 2008.
[5] Canarella and Tomaske 1975, 624.
[6] Fenoaltea 1984, 637.
[7] On corporal punishment as a routine disciplinary method throughout the ancient Mediterranean world, see Fitzgerald 2008a. On corporal punishment among the Greeks and Romans, see Cribiore 2001; Laes 2005; 2006, 123–31.

contrive to produce the same result by giving gifts to those who behave as brave men should and by punishing those who disobey commands.[8]

In view of this widespread use of rewards and punishments as dual incentives, it is not at all surprising to find Ischomachus, in Xenophon's *Oeconomicus*, telling his wife about her special concerns as manager of the household slaves. Not only will she have the pleasure of taking unskilled slaves and training them so as to make them more valuable, but also she will have it within her power "to reward the helpful and reasonable members of [her] household and to punish any of them who appears to be vicious."[9]

Although rewards and punishments were commonly used, the two methods were quite different psychologically, especially when used by masters to motivate slaves:

> Pain incentives, it would seem, are the more effective in generating effort. The main reason is that effort varies directly with the level of anxiety, and a threat to one's physical integrity produces very high anxiety indeed. A subsidiary reason is that threats can be of immediate pain, while rewards are typically of delayed gratification.... On the other hand, pain incentives are the less effective in generating carefulness. One reason is that the ability to work carefully is enhanced by low levels of anxiety but inhibited by high ones, so that the severe tension produced by pain incentives is counterproductive even if one is doing one's best.[10] Another reason, of course, is that threats tend to cause ill will, and therefore intentional ("malicious") carelessness.[11]

It is highly probable that, in general, the percentage of rewards and punishments used by masters with their slaves varied according to the slaves' skills, the degree of attentive care required to perform tasks, and their ability to work without supervision. Skilled slaves, those entrusted with positions of responsibility, and slaves who could be trusted to work independently were motivated largely by rewards. On the other hand, unskilled slaves, those who were assigned tasks requiring brute strength rather than meticulousness, and slaves who required constant supervision in order to complete their assigned tasks were far more likely to be motivated largely by pain incentives. To give an example, imperial slaves—that is, the members of the *familia Caesaris*—constituted an elite group in the early empire, with an individual *servus Caesaris* ("slave of Caesar") able to acquire wealth, influence, and social status that often were superior to those of a freeborn Roman citizen.[12] They needed no lash to motivate them. The rewards for loyal service were

---

[8] Xenophon, *Oec.* 5.15. See also *Oec.* 9.14, where cities appoint guardians of the laws to "praise the law-abiding and punish the law-breakers." Unless otherwise indicated, all translations of this work are from Pomeroy 1994, sometimes slightly modified.

[9] Xenophon, *Oec.* 7.41.

[10] For an example of fear of punishment being counterproductive, see Aristotle, *Eth. nic.* 7.6.1, where he gives an example of overly eager servants hastening to do the master's bidding without waiting to hear all of the instructions. They rush to obey because they are fearful of arousing the master's anger, yet their haste is counterproductive because they fail to execute the master's actual command.

[11] Fenoaltea 1984, 637.

[12] On the imperial slaves, see Chantraine 1967; Boulvert 1970; Weaver 1972.

self-evident, and the possibility of losing their power and position was a much greater fear than that posed by any whip. Their situation was vastly different from that of the slaves who worked in the mines and the agrarian slaves tasked with the breaking and moving of rocks. With such slaves, the lash was a daily, if not hourly, incentive. Between these two extremes, it was likely that masters' use of pain incentives generally tended to decline and that of rewards increased as the activities required of slaves necessitated greater skills and meticulousness.[13]

Prudent masters preferred to use rewards rather than punishments because doing so not only gave slaves something to hope for but also fostered their loyalty to the master. Xenophon makes both of these points in the *Oeconomicus*. Socrates tells Critobulus, "Slaves need some good thing to look forward to no less, in fact, even more than free men so that they may be willing to stay" on the farm and work (*Oec.* 5.16). The rewards that Xenophon mentions in this treatise include a share in the house's profits (*Oec.* 9.11–13; 12.9, 15), nice clothes and shoes (*Oec.* 13.10), abundant food and drink (*Oec.* 13.9), and permission for procreation (*Oec.* 9.5).[14] Other slave owners would immediately have added a reward that Xenophon fails to mention: manumission. Aristotle, for example, argues that "it is advantageous that all slaves should have their freedom set before them as a reward" (*Pol.* 7.9.9).[15]

But if slaves wanted their master's rewards, masters wanted their slaves' loyalty. Because the loyalty of slaves entailed their goodwill, faithfulness, and obedience, masters sought to instill and cultivate it. If successfully instilled, it ensured that the slave's obedience would be voluntary rather than involuntary, making the lives of masters much more enjoyable.[16] And the best method of accomplishing this didactic purpose was to reward the slaves. This becomes particularly clear in a conversation between Socrates and Ischomachus concerning the crucial and indispensable importance of loyalty. The two men agree completely that the chief lesson that a slave—especially a slave who is to be trained as a foreman—needs to be taught is goodwill (εὔνοια) as manifested by loyalty:

> "First of all," I [Socrates] said, "he [the foreman] should be loyal [εὔνοιαν] towards you and yours if he is to be capable of representing you in your absence. For what is the use of a foreman's having any kind of knowledge at all, if he has no loyalty?"
>
> "None, by Zeus," replied Ischomachus. "So, you see, the first lesson I try to teach him is to be loyal to me and mine."

---

[13] I am dependent here on Fenoaltea (1984, 637–43), who uses economic transaction-costs analysis to develop a continuum model to discuss the use of rewards and pain incentives in motivating slave labor.

[14] See Pomeroy 1994, 256.

[15] Aristotle promises to explain later why this strategy is advisable, but he never does so. Translations of Aristotle usually are from Rackham 1956; 1959, sometimes slightly modified, but occasionally the renderings are my own.

[16] Compare Xenophon, *Oec.* 21.12: "For ruling over willing subjects, in my view, is a gift not wholly human but divine, because it is a gift of the gods. . . . The gods give tyranny over unwilling subjects, I think, to those who they believe deserve to live a life in Hades like Tantalus."

"And how on earth do you teach the man you've chosen loyalty to you and yours?" I asked.

"By Zeus," said Ischomachus, "by rewarding [εὐεργετῶν] him whenever the gods grant us an abundance of some good thing."

"Do you mean to say," I asked, "that by getting some pleasure from your good things, they become loyal to you and want to do some good to you?"

"Yes, Socrates, for I have come to see that this is the best device for securing loyalty." (Xenophon, *Oec.* 12.5–7)

Accordingly, when Ischomachus and his wife appointed a housekeeper, he undertook the task of making her loyal. "We taught her to be loyal [εὐνοϊκῶς] to us," he says, "by giving her a share of our joy when we were happy, and if we had any trouble, we called on her to share it too" (*Oec.* 9.12). Similarly, when Ischomachus told his wife that one of her concerns would involve "nursing any of the slaves who become ill," she replied that she would not mind doing that at all, for "it will be most gratifying if those who are well cared for will prove to be thankful [χάριν] and more loyal [εὐνούστεροι] than before" (*Oec.* 7.37). Properly training and caring for slaves is thus intended to make them not only skilled and thus financially valuable but also faithful (πιστήν [*Oec.* 7.41]). Faithful loyalty is in turn rewarded, making such slaves even more loyal, whereas problematic slaves are denied the privileges that loyal slaves enjoy. That includes the privilege of procreation and having a family. "For, generally, honest slaves become more loyal when they have produced children, but when bad ones mate, they become more troublesome" (*Oec.* 9.5). Alternatively, productive slaves are rewarded with better clothing than that worn by their less productive counterparts. "I make sure," Ischomachus asserts, "that the clothing and the shoes that I must supply for the workers are not identical, but some are of inferior quality, and others superior, so that I can reward the better workers with superior garments and give the inferior ones to the less deserving" (*Oec.* 13.10).

Although prudent masters preferred to use rewards because of the goodwill and loyalty that it produced in the slaves whom they regarded as deserving, they were also quite prepared to punish slaves who were disobedient or careless in discharging their duties. Furthermore, a variety of factors enhanced the likelihood of masters resorting to pain incentives in managing their slaves. In the first place, the relationship between master and slave was asymmetrical, with the master possessing enormous power over the slave. In such a situation, coercion of some kind was almost inevitable when persuasion failed and anger commenced.[17] "For slaves, force is a discommodity. It is applied at the discretion of the master, and slaves are unable to avoid the pain of the lash. . . . Masters can at some cost always apply sufficient force to induce slaves to provide additional labor services."[18]

Second, masters tended to regard slaves collectively rather than individually and thus attributed to them as a group certain negative attributes and charac-

---

[17] See Plutarch, *Cohib. ira* 459B.
[18] Canarella and Tomaske 1975, 626–27.

teristics. Consequently, "slaves were stereotyped as rascally, prone to excesses of drinking and eating, and dumb,"[19] and those stereotypes made it easier for masters to believe that they had to use physical force with their slaves "to whip them into shape." They feared that the character of their slaves would be ruined if they showed them too much forbearance (ἀνεξικακία) and refrained from punishing them.[20]

Third, slaves not only were stereotyped as dumb and morally inferior but also were dehumanized and often conceived of as animals. This dehumanizing and animalizing of slaves began early in Greek thought, with slaves distinguished from other humans and made comparable to animals. Some Greeks argued that slaves were utterly devoid of reason and thus could only be commanded rather than exhorted. Aristotle rejected that idea (*Pol.* 1.5.11), but he stopped short of endowing slaves with full rationality.[21] He says that a natural slave "participates in reason to the extent of understanding it," yet unlike the master, "does not possess it" (*Pol.* 1.2.13). That distinction is crucial, for this cognitive disability means that slaves differ as markedly from humans who do have autonomous rationality—that is, masters and other free people—"as the soul does from the body and the human being from the lower animal" (*Pol.* 1.2.13).[22] Slaves may be extremely intelligent and have considerable technical skill, but their lack of autonomous rationality means, among other things, that they lack the soul's deliberative (βουλευτικόν) part (*Pol.* 1.5.6) and are incapable of making choices based on deliberation (προαίρεσις); as a consequence, they cannot achieve happiness (εὐδαιμονία).[23] It is significant that slaves share this incapacity for *prohairesis* and *eudaimonia* with the lower animals (*Pol.* 3.5.10), so that the hunting of wild animals (θηρία) can be compared to the acquisition of slaves by warfare (*Pol.* 1.3.8). But whether acquired through war, bought in a market, or bred at home, the slave is an "animate article of property" (κτῆμα ἔμψυχον), a living "tool" (ὄργανον) designed for action (πρακτικόν) that the master uses in order to accomplish his purposes (*Pol.* 1.2.4–6). As far as utility (χρεία) is concerned, slaves can again be correlated with animals: "The usefulness of slaves diverges little from that of animals; bodily service for the necessities of life is forthcoming from both, from slaves and from domestic animals alike" (*Pol.* 1.2.14).

Ischomachus is similar in distinguishing slaves from other humans. He notes the way in which "humans" (ἀνθρώπους) can be made more obedient by merely talking to them and contrasts that with the vastly different method by which

---

[19] Garnsey 1997, 160. On stupidity as a characteristic trait of slaves, see Epictetus, *Diss.* 2.26.5.

[20] See Plutarch, *Cohib. ira* 459C. For the second and third points, see also Fitzgerald 2007b, esp. 38–39.

[21] In what follows, I have been particularly influenced by the analysis in Heath 2008.

[22] It should be noted that as negative as these categorizations of slaves are, they pale in comparison to Aristotle's assertion that some remote tribes of barbarians were "irrational [ἀλόγιστοι] by nature and lived solely by sensation [αἰσθήσει]" (*Eth. nic.* 7.5.6).

[23] Note also Aristotle, *Eth. nic.* 10.6: "No one allows a slave any measure of happiness, any more than a life of his own."

"slaves" (δούλοις) are taught obedience.[24] This sociocultural tendency to dehumanize and animalize slaves is recognized in certain early Christian texts, such as *Acts of Thomas*, where slaves are told, "Although you are men they lay burdens upon you, as upon the irrational beasts, because your lords think that you are not men like themselves."[25] As Keith Bradley has concluded, "The ease of association between slave and animal . . . was a staple aspect of ancient mentality, and one that stretched back to a very early period: the common Greek term for 'slave,' *andrapodon* [ἀνδράποδον], 'man-footed creature,' was built on the foundation of a common term for cattle, *tetrapodon* [τετράποδον], 'four-footed creature.'"[26] This animalizing of slaves was reflected even in how one was exhorted to feed them. In his discussion of how to make slaves more obedient, Ischomachus makes the following argument: "But for slaves the method of training that is accepted for wild animals [θηριώδης] is very effective in teaching obedience. For if you gratify their desires by filling their bellies, you may get a great deal out of them" (Xenophon, *Oec.* 13.9). In short, for Ischomachus, household slaves are to be treated just like domestic animals; give them as much food as they want, and they will behave. But what if they do not behave? The implication is clear: just as you reward colts and puppies when they obey you and punish them when they do not, you teach disobedient slaves by punishing them (*Oec.* 13.6–8).

Fourth, the use of rewards and punishments as dual motivations resulted in striking discrepancies in how masters treated individual slaves. Ischomachus is quite explicit in affirming, "I, myself, then, by no means think that better workers should receive the same treatment as worthless ones." Unequal treatment is necessary because "good workers become very discouraged when they see that although they have done all the work, nevertheless those who are unwilling to work or, when necessary, run risks, earn rewards equal to their own" (Xenophon, *Oec.* 13.11–12). Given this philosophy, it was natural for masters to want to make "examples" of both "useful" and "useless" slaves, doing so by heaping praise on the former and by punishing the latter. This modus operandi was consistent with their management philosophy and had a clear didactic purpose. It was not necessary to punish a slave's every failing, but it was useful to make an example of a troublesome slave by applying the whip. "From the master's point of view, the application of force to a single slave has positive externalities," for "slaves are astute enough in avoiding the lash to react to the whipping of a fellow slave by increasing the intensity of their own labor."[27]

When the slave's punishment is viewed as an exemplum, it is irrelevant whether the slave is a fool who refuses to make a change in conduct or is sufficiently sagacious to mend errant ways. If the latter occurs, that outcome is much preferable from the owner's perspective. Indeed, masters believed that slaves remembered the beatings that they had endured, and that those memories served as

---

[24] Xenophon, *Oec.* 13.9.
[25] *Acts of Thomas* 83 (translation, Elliott 1993).
[26] Bradley 2000, 110.
[27] Canarella and Tomaske 1975, 627.

deterrents to a repetition of the actions that had occasioned the blows.[28] Yet even if the punished slave does not learn from the sufferings, the lesson will not be lost on other slaves.[29] This same pedagogical idea appears in the biblical wisdom tradition, where corporal punishment of children is occasionally justified by the rationale that others, observing the beatings, will learn that it is utter folly to resist discipline.[30] "Beat the scoffer and the simple will become clever" (Prov 19:25 NJPS). "In other words, if you smite an impudent lad, not he but others—*even* the callow naïf—will get the point,"[31] and so did slaves who watched as their disobedient or careless colleagues were whipped.

Fifth, ancient laws usually did not protect slaves from masters who beat them, even severely. Indeed, even if the slave was maimed[32] or died[33] or committed suicide[34] as a result of a beating, usually there were no serious legal consequences in Greece and Rome, at least until very late. As Seneca says, "The law allows anything in dealing with a slave" (*Clem.* 1.18.2).[35] For the most part, the main deterrent to severe violence was economic, not legal or moral. The owner who maimed or killed his own slave had damaged his own property. Consequently, if the slave

---

[28] See Epictetus, *Diss.* 3.25.9–10.

[29] Quintus Veranius, the first governor of Lycia-Pamphylia (43–48 C.E.), issued a decree on altering documents that is preserved on a limestone stele from Myra of Lycia (Acts 27:5). In it, he shows how he has dealt with Tryphon, a public slave of the city of Tlos, and how he plans to deal with him in the future, and how that treatment was intended to be educative for Tryphon and paradigmatic for other slaves. Tryphon, he says, "has [not] learned his lesson either from my edicts or threats or from the punishment of slaves who have committed errors of a similar nature, that it is not permitted to receive (for registration in the city archives) documents of the administration that have interpolations and erasures. I have introduced him to the [realization] of my displeasure in such matters by having him lashed with the whip, and I have demonstrated to him by such a method that [if] he is again careless of my orders concerning registration of documents, not only by beatings but also by the supreme punishment will I force the rest of the *public slaves* to forget their former indifference" (translation, Sherk 1988 [no. 48]).

[30] For the recognition by Egyptian scribes and Israelite sages that corporal punishment was not always effective, see Fitzgerald 2008a, 299, 304–5.

[31] Fox 1997, 67. Note also Prov 21:11: "When a scoffer is punished, the simple man is edified" (NJPS). In contrast to the MT, the LXX of Prov 22:3 makes a similar point: "A clever [πανοῦργος] man, seeing an evil [πονηρόν] man severely punished, is himself educated [παιδεύεται], but fools pass by and suffer loss."

[32] An example of a master permanently maiming a slave is the emperor Hadrian, who blinded one of his slaves when he struck him in the eye with a stylus (Galen, *De affectuum dignotione* 1.4).

[33] For an imaginary example of killing a slave by flogging, see Lucian (*Philops.* 20), who has Eucrates report that when a Libyan slave stole offerings made to a curative bronze statue of Pellichos (the Corinthian general), Pellichos himself punished the slave. The latter "got a sound thrashing then, on being caught, and he did not long survive the incident, dying a rogue's death from being flogged, he said, every night, so that welts showed on his body the next day" (translation, Harmon 1960).

[34] The "tactless man" in the *Characters* of Theophrastus "stands watching while a slave is being whipped and announces that a boy of his own once hanged himself after such a beating" (*Char.* 12) (translation, Diggle 2004).

[35] Translation, Basore 1989.

died, the master suffered the loss of the slave as an asset; if the slave survived but was maimed, he suffered a reduction in the slave's economic value. Even in the Hebrew Bible, the situation is not fundamentally different. The Book of the Covenant, for example, mandates the manumission of both male and female slaves in cases where the owner has destroyed the slave's eye or knocked out a tooth (Exod 21:26–27). The owner is punished economically by being deprived of his "damaged property," and the slaves' emancipation as a consequence of permanent bodily harm functions as compensation for their injuries.[36] Again, if a master beats a slave with a stick so severely that the latter dies a day or so later, the master is not punished beyond the economic loss that he himself sustains through his slave's death. The slave is not avenged, and the master, rather than being punished for manslaughter, is fully exonerated. The reason for the exoneration is explicit: the slave is the master's "money"—that is, his "property" (Exod 21:21). The only exception to this rule is when the male or female slave dies "on the spot," which indicates that the slave's death was intentional rather than accidental. In that case, the slave's death is treated as a capital offense (Exod 21:20).[37]

Finally, it should not be forgotten that many slaves were children, and they were set to work at an early age, typically in the Roman world at the age of five.[38] Sometimes these child slaves worked alongside their parents, who were also slaves, but at other times they had no family members or other relatives living with them, having been purchased as an individual commodity from a slave dealer. Child slaves were found wherever adult slaves were found, even in the mines, which were widely regarded as the harshest form of slavery, and in brothels, serving side by side with freeborn children who had been kidnapped and forced into prostitution. Osteological evidence from Herculaneum and Pompeii shows that child slaves were not always exempt from the heavy, continuous manual labor required of many adult slaves, with more than a tenth of the Herculaneum skeletons of those who were fifteen years old and younger exhibiting serious injuries to the costoclavicular ligament. "Severe lesions were found in the skeletons of two children aged 8–9 years, and less severe lesions were seen in younger children, including one who was about 5 years of age."[39] Nor were slave girls exempt from hard labor or given any better care than were boy slaves. The skeleton of a fourteen-year-old slave girl from Pompeii, for example, showed that she had been undernourished (or perhaps severely ill) as an infant, had to have several teeth removed because of abscesses, and had been forced to lift heavy weights on a reg-

---

[36] See also Philo, *Spec.* 3.201–202.

[37] For other suggestions as to "plausible conditions that would bias slave . . . owners toward force intensive management techniques," see Canarella and Tomaske 1975, 626–27.

[38] See Laes 2008, on which I am heavily dependent for my basic understanding of child slavery in the Roman world.

[39] Capasso and Di Domenicantonio 1998. On the skeletons found at Herculaneum as a result of the archaeological excavations of the ancient beach begun in 1982, see Capasso 2000; and especially Capasso 2001, which provides a full discussion of the skeletal remains of 162 "fugitives of Herculaneum."

ular basis.⁴⁰ There was no concept of "child labor" in the ancient Mediterranean world.⁴¹ Children labored alongside adults, and child slaves were rewarded and punished according to the same principles used with adult slaves. They certainly were beaten, at times severely, yet it must be remembered that the master who did so was subjecting them to the same disciplinary measure that he used with his own children at home and that teachers used with all children at school.⁴²

In sum, masters used both rewards and punishments to coax and coerce their slaves' obedience and productivity. Some masters thought that slaves were so devoid of rationality that one could only command them what to do and then beat them if they failed to obey. Other masters, such as Aristotle, believed that slaves were sufficiently rational for masters to appeal to their mind (νοῦς) and be admonished; indeed, he argues that "admonition [νουθετητέον] is more properly employed with slaves than with children" (*Pol.* 1.5.11).⁴³ At their best, the bestowal of rewards functioned to create what Aristotle called "a certain community of interest (συμφέρον) and affection (φιλία) between slave and master." Punishments, on the other hand, entailed the use of force (βιασθεῖσι), and although they may have secured the slaves' obedience, they had the opposite effect as far as mutual advantage and affection were concerned (*Pol.* 1.2.21). And the more painful the master's incentives, the more likely it was that resentment and animosity toward the master would be the outcome for most slaves,⁴⁴ especially if they were punished without being given an opportunity to explain or defend their actions.⁴⁵ As with any system that relies heavily on punitive measures, there was an acute awareness that the extraordinarily great power of masters could be misused, resulting in all kinds of deleterious and dangerous countermeasures by slaves. These included slaves resorting to greater subterfuge in order to keep their wrongdoings hidden from their masters,⁴⁶ slaves stealing goods and absconding with their masters' stolen property,⁴⁷ slaves taking vengeance on their masters by murdering them,⁴⁸ and slave revolts.⁴⁹ The proper treatment of slaves was intended to enhance the efficiency of the slave system not only by encouraging the use of techniques that worked but also by criticizing and eliminating practices that were viewed as abusive, unjust, counterproductive, and dangerous.

---

⁴⁰ Bisel 1986; 1987.
⁴¹ Laes 2006, 194–97.
⁴² On corporal punishment as a routine disciplinary method throughout the ancient Mediterranean world, see Fitzgerald 2008a. On corporal punishment among the Greeks and Romans, see Cribiore 2001; Laes 2005; 2006, 123–31.
⁴³ Pseudo-Demetrius, *Epistolary Types* 7, defines admonition as "the instilling of sense [νοῦν] in the person who is being admonished, and teaching him what should and should not be done" (translation, Malherbe 1988).
⁴⁴ On the theme of animosity, see Fitzgerald, van Rensburg, and van Rooy 2009.
⁴⁵ See Plutarch's caution against depriving slaves of the opportunity to offer a defense or a plea before punishing them (*Cohib. ira* 459E).
⁴⁶ Plutarch, *Cohib. ira* 459D.
⁴⁷ Epictetus, *Diss.* 3.26.1.
⁴⁸ Tacitus, *Ann.* 14.42–45.
⁴⁹ See Urbainczyk 2008.

2. Stoics and Christians on Slavery: Introductory Comments

It is against this general backdrop regarding slave management that Stoic and early Christian statements regarding the treatment of slaves will be examined. Although individual Stoics and Christians criticized aspects of slavery or various abusive practices associated with it, neither group advocated its abolition as a socioeconomic institution. Of the various reasons why neither group sought to abolish slavery, one merits mention here. In the final analysis, both groups, or at least key members of both groups, tended to view institutional slavery as an ἀδιάφορον—that is, an "indifferent," something that, in and of itself, is neither good nor evil but falls in between. As such, it contributes neither to happiness (or salvation) nor to unhappiness (damnation) and thus is not a priority from a philosophical or theological perspective.[50] This is essentially Paul's attitude toward slavery in 1 Cor 7:21–24, the perspective of Theodore of Mopsuestia (ca. 350–428) in commenting on Paul's letter to Philemon,[51] and the sentiment shared by a host of other ancient Christians. For them, freedom in the legal sense was at best a "preferred indifferent," one of the προηγμένα.[52] Spiritual freedom and moral slavery were totally different; the former was a "good" and the latter an "evil," and obtaining "true" freedom was the sine qua non for both Stoics and Christians. But that spiritual focus did not mean that they were intellectually "indifferent" to the physical treatment of slaves, about which they had much to say, both explicitly and implicitly.

In criticizing ancient slavery in both theory and practice, Stoics and Christians were not alone. For example, Aristotle mentions those who "maintain that for one man to be another man's master is contrary to nature [παρὰ φύσιν], because it is only convention [νόμῳ] that makes the one a slave and the other a freeman and there is no difference between them by nature, and that therefore it is unjust [οὐδὲ δίκαιον], for it is based on force [βίαιον]" (*Pol.* 1.2.3).[53] It was, of course, in opposition to such critics that Aristotle asserted that "the household in its perfect [τέλειος] form consists of slaves and free people" and mounted his infamous apology for "natural slavery" (τὸ φύσει δοῦλον), which he considered the most common form of slavery in the Greek world,[54] arguing that it was not only

---

[50] See Diogenes Laertius, *Vit. phil.* 7.104.

[51] See especially Theodore, *Comm. Phlm.* 2:262.25–263.7 (cited according to the volume, page, and line numbers of the critical edition of Swete 1880–1882).

[52] For this and other reasons, I think that Paul's μᾶλλον χρῆσαι in 1 Cor 7:21 should be interpreted in the sense of obtaining freedom if it is possible to do so. Manumission was the quintessential reward for faithful service as a slave, often granted by masters in their wills. It is inconceivable that Paul would refuse to allow a Christian slave to accept a master's testamentary manumission. To refuse such a gift would be the height of ingratitude on the part of the slave. For this interpretation, see especially Harrill 1995.

[53] On the Greek controversy about slavery, see Brunt 1993, 351–56. As he rightly says, "The debate concerned the justice of slavery, not any practical proposal for its abolition" (352).

[54] "Aristotle accepted that most slaves in his own society were natural slaves" (Schofield 1999, 133). For him, most non-Greeks (βάρβαροι) fell self-evidently into this category (Aristotle, *Pol.* 1.1.5; 3.9.3).

"natural" (φύσει) but also "advantageous" (συμφέρει) for the enslaved themselves and therefore "just" (δίκαιον).[55] Some three centuries later, Cicero (*Resp.* 3.37) was to repeat some of Aristotle's arguments and observations, and there was no shortage of defenders of the status quo.[56]

Of the Stoics whose comments on slavery are extant, Seneca is usually credited with making the most damning statements about the abuse of slaves, doing so most famously in *Ep.* 47.[57] Of the Christians, the fiercest attack on slavery was launched by Gregory of Nyssa, who exhorted Christian masters to manumit their slaves.[58] That certain parallels in thought have been discerned between Seneca's letter and Gregory's fourth homily on Ecclesiastes is thus not surprising.[59]

Yet Gregory was not entirely alone in arguing for the manumission of Christian slaves. There were other Christians in the fourth and fifth centuries who argued for the emancipation, not of all slaves, but of particular Christian slaves. But whereas Gregory used exhortations to lobby for manumission, these Christians made demands. Theodore of Mopsuestia refers to them derisively in his commentary on Paul's letter to Philemon as follows:

> But if someone nowadays found such a case [as that involving Onesimus], he would neither entreat nor seek that the slave should be pardoned by his master, but would write with much authority that "a slave joined to us in faith and hastening to true religion [*pietatem*][60] of his own free will ought to be freed from slavery." For there are many people like this at the present time, who want themselves to be seen circumspect by imposing burdensome orders on others. (*Comm. Phlm.* 2:264.8–14)[61]

Theodore never precisely identifies these "many people" who issue such "burdensome orders" (*onerosa imperando*) regarding the emancipation of other people's slaves. Yet it is virtually certain that he is referring to the ecclesiastical debate whether slaves who converted to Christianity had to be emancipated before they were ordained. That debate per se had nothing to do with how Christian masters were to treat their nonemancipated slaves, and so it can be safely left aside here. In what follows, I am concerned not with the manumission of slaves but rather with how masters are to treat their current slaves, regardless of whether the latter are ever manumitted.

---

[55] Aristotle, *Pol.* 1.2.1, 15, 18, 20. Aristotle readily admitted that not all instances of slavery were natural (*Pol.* 1.2.19), but his intention was to defend slavery as a just institution within his own society. On Aristotle's theory of "natural slavery," see Fortenbaugh 1975–1979; Brunt 1993, 343–88; Garver 1994; Schofield 1999; Kraut 2002, 277–305; Heath 2008.

[56] See Raymer 1940.

[57] See Richter 1958; Griffin 1976, 256–85, 458–61; Bradley 2008.

[58] Dennis 1982; Bergadá 1994; Stramara 1997; Hart 2001; Ramelli 2008. I thank Ilaria Ramelli for generously making a copy of her paper available to me prior to its publication.

[59] See Moriarty 1993, 65–66.

[60] *Pietas*, literally, "piety," is often a code word in patristic parlance, as here, for "Christianity."

[61] This rendering is by Rowan Greer, whose translation of Theodore's commentaries on the minor Pauline Epistles is scheduled to appear in the near future in the Society of Biblical Literature Writings from the Greco-Roman World series. I am grateful to Prof. Greer for permitting me to make use of his translation prior to its publication.

As we will see, both Stoics and Christians argued for the humane treatment of slaves, but in doing so they were not alone. Others encouraged masters to do the same and denounced those who operated with purely pecuniary values. Two examples should suffice in this regard.[62] First, Aesop, in the anonymous biography *Life of Aesop*, is an ex-slave and tells his adopted son Helios, "Take care of your slaves, and share what you have with them, so that they may not only obey you as their master but also honor you as their benefactor" (*Life of Aesop* 109).[63] Second, Plutarch was horrified by Cato the Elder's advice to sell old and sickly slaves, and he had this to say about it:

> For my part, I regard his treatment of his slaves like beasts of burden, using them to the uttermost, and then, when they were old, driving them off and selling them, as a mark of a very mean nature, which recognizes no tie between person and person but that of necessity.... I certainly would not sell even an ox that had worked for me, just because it was old, much less an elderly man, removing him from his habitual place and customary life, as it were from his native land, for a paltry price, useless as he is to those who sell him and as he will be to those who buy him. (*Cat. Maj.* 5.1, 5)[64]

Stoics and Christians shared these concerns, but they had other concerns as well, which need to be noted.

3. Stoicism and the Treatment of Slaves

A thorough and comprehensive discussion of Stoic and early Christian views and actions regarding the treatment of slaves—what Seneca referred to as *de usu*

---

[62] Attempts to humanize the institution of slavery were also made in ancient Israel. The Deuteronomic Code reworked the older Covenant Code's laws of manumission and abolished the different treatments of male and female Hebrew slaves (Deut 15:12, 18). It also required that released slaves be given ample supplies so that they did not depart from their masters' houses "empty-handed" (Deut 15:13–14). The "Jubilee" law of the Holiness Code went even further and made perpetual slavery for Hebrews impossible by mandating emancipation and the restoration of patrimony every fiftieth year (Lev 25:8–55). This priestly legislation was intended to prevent latifundia and to bring a periodic end to the exploitation and disenfranchisement that are inevitable in any multiclass society. But even these steps left much unchanged, and the Jubilee's liberation and laudable concern for humane treatment was, unfortunately, restricted to Israelites and did not address the plight of foreigners, who could be owned and bequeathed to heirs as property (Lev 25:44–46).

[63] Translation, Daly in Hansen 1998.

[64] Translation, Perrin 1959 [slightly modified]). Plutarch's argument for the humane treatment of animals is based on χρηστότης ("kindness, goodness"): "When it comes to beneficence and charity, these often flow in streams from the gentle heart, like water from a copious stream, even down to dumb beasts. A kindly [χρηστῷ] man will take good care of his horses even when they are worn out with age, and of his dogs, too, not only in their puppyhood, but when their old age needs nursing" (*Cat. Maj.* 5.2). Of course, kindness is a trait that the New Testament attributes to the divine (Luke 6:35; Rom 2:4; 11:22; Eph 2:7; Tit 3:4; 1 Pet 2:3) and encourages in humans (2 Cor 6:6; Gal 5:22; Eph 4:32; Col 3:12; see also Rom 3:12).

servorum (*Ep.* 47.11)⁶⁵—is far beyond the scope of this essay. As far as the Stoics are concerned, I will limit myself to four major points. First, Stoics completely rejected the Aristotelian notion of natural slavery, both as an idea and as a defense of the institution. Second, Stoics were often so focused on the problem of moral slavery to the passions that they missed opportunities to criticize slave abuse. Yet, by focusing on anger as the impetus for most instances of brutality toward slaves, they were quite likely seeking to reduce the number of instances of aggravated assault on slaves. Third, when they spoke directly on the topic of slave management, they emphasized the humane treatment of slaves. Fourth, despite their pleas for humane treatment, they did not always reject the use of physically painful punishments in dealing with instances of slave misconduct and disobedience. Each of these four points will be briefly illustrated in the following section. For the second and fourth points, I will use two chreiai involving Zeno of Citium that are preserved by Diogenes Laertius in his *Lives of Eminent Philosophers*. Both anecdotes were preserved because of their relation to typical Stoic teaching.

First, Stoics rejected Aristotle's assertion that some humans are slaves by nature. This rejection probably goes back to Chrysippus in the Old Stoa, who was concerned with definitions of slaves.⁶⁶ One such definition was that "a slave is a hired hand [*mercenarius* = μισθωτός] for life,"⁶⁷ which underlies Philo of Alexandria's statement "Masters are to treat the slaves they purchase with silver [ἀργυρωνήτοις] as their hired hands [μισθωτοῖς], not as their slaves by nature [μὴ ὡς φύσει δούλοις]" (*Spec.* 2.122).⁶⁸ Philo's rejection of the idea that purchased slaves should be treated as natural slaves is grounded in his claim that "no person is by nature a slave" (*Spec.* 2.69),⁶⁹ which likely also has Chrysippus as its source.⁷⁰ In any event, the Stoic rejection of natural slavery was well established by the first century C.E. As Miriam Griffin says, "The principal philosophical dogma in Seneca's thought on slavery is that there are no natural slaves: all men share in the divine reason and thus may claim the gods as ancestors."⁷¹ All humans share the same cosmic *pneuma*, and, Seneca says, both master and slave come from the "same seed" (*Ep.* 47.10). The same idea is the basis of these words by Epictetus:

---

⁶⁵ The phrase *de usu servorum* (literally, "concerning the use of slaves") corresponds to the typical Greek formula of πῶς (or τίνα τρόπον) δούλοις χρηστέον. Hierocles, for example, uses such formulations to introduce discussions of the proper manner to treat or behave toward the gods, one's country, and one's relatives. See Hierocles *apud* Stobaeus 1.3.53; 3.39.34; 4.27.23 (1:63.6–7; 3:730.17; 4:671.3 W-H). In *Ep.* 94.1 Seneca treats "how a master should rule his slaves" (*domino quomodo servos regat*) as a topic that is appropriate for the use of precepts.

⁶⁶ See Athenaeus, *Deipn.* 6.267B (*SVF* 3.353).

⁶⁷ *Apud* Seneca, *Ben.* 3.22.1 (*SVF* 3.351).

⁶⁸ *SVF* 3.352b. The Chrysippean basis of *Spec.* 2.122 is rightly noted in Richter 1958, 205n22.

⁶⁹ *SVF* 3.352a.

⁷⁰ Richter (1958, 205n22) doubts this, but Griffin (1976, 459) convincingly argues that this formulation is Stoic in origin and probably goes back to Chrysippus.

⁷¹ Griffin 1976, 257. Griffin also says aptly, "That slavery was not natural was the only view consistent with Stoic physics."

Slave, will you not bear with your own brother, who has Zeus as his progenitor [πρόγονον] and is, as it were, a son [υἱός] born of the same seed as yourself and of the same sowing from above; but if you have been stationed in a like position above others, will you forthwith set yourself up as a tyrant? Do you not remember what you are and over whom you rule—that they are kinsmen [συγγενῶν], that they are brothers by nature [ἀδελφῶν φύσει], that they are the offspring [ἀπογόνων] of Zeus? (*Diss.* 1.13.3-4)[72]

As a result of this divine sowing, all humans are, says Cicero, the god's "offspring" (cf. Acts 17:28-29) and share "the divine gift of mind" (*Leg.* 1.24), and thus they possess autonomous rationality. "All men are united especially by their common share in reason, which they have from god" and have in common with the gods.[73] Whereas Aristotle's natural slaves did not possess reason, for Stoics that is a gift that unites all humans. Consequently, all humans, even masters and their slaves, are, says Epictetus, "brothers by nature" (ἀδελφῶν φύσει), "sons" of a common father and thus "kinsmen" (*Diss.* 1.13.3-4). Nature represents "the laws of the gods," and by those laws no one is a slave by nature; slavery stems from custom, from the laws (νόμους) of dead men, not from the law of the living gods (*Diss.* 1.13.5). According to Seneca, it is not nature but fortune that makes people slaves (*Ep.* 47.1). In staunchly rejecting the idea of natural slaves, Stoics were not alone, being joined by a large number of others who expressed the same views.[74]

Second, the Stoics focused more on moral slavery to the passions than they did on physical slavery, and this focus caused them to miss opportunities to criticize the abuse of slaves. To illustrate this point, I will use the first of the two chreiai about Zeno to which I referred earlier. It is as follows:

Zeno, on seeing a student's young slave [παιδάριον] bruised from a severe beating [μεμωλωπισμένου], said to his student, "I see the traces [ἴχνη] of your anger [θυμοῦ]."[75]

This chreia is unquestionably related to the theme of the passions (πάθη), with Stoics championing the ideal of ἀπάθεια (freedom from passion, the absence of emotion) and contending that the sage is ἀπαθής, not subject to the tyranny of emotion. Of all the passions, anger was often viewed as the most conspicuous,[76] and it was a particular concern of Stoics from at least the second century B.C.E. onward. Both Antipater of Tarsus (ca. 200–ca. 130 B.C.E.) and Posidonius (ca. 135–ca. 51 B.C.E.) wrote treatises *On Anger* (περὶ ὀργῆς) that consisted of at least two

---

[72] Translations of Epictetus are from Oldfather 1995-1996. For the idea of humans as the seeds sown by the divine, see also Cicero, *Leg.* 1.24.

[73] Dobbin 1998, 146. See Epictetus, *Diss.* 1.3.3.

[74] Note, for example, Albucius *apud* Seneca the Elder, *Cont.* 7.6.18: "No one is naturally free or slave. These are titles imposed later on individuals by fortune" (translation, Winterbottom 1974); Petronius, *Saty.* 71: "A slave is a man and drank his mother's milk like ourselves, even if cruel fate has trodden him down" (translation, Heseltine 1987).

[75] Diogenes Laertius, *Vit. phil.* 7.23 (translation, Hock and O'Neil 1986).

[76] Seneca, *Ira* 1.1.5: "Other vices may be concealed and cherished in secret; anger shows itself openly and appears in the countenance, and the greater it is, the more visibly it boils forth." Unless otherwise indicated, translations of Seneca are from Basore 1989.

books.[77] Following their example, Seneca (ca. 1 B.C.E.–65 C.E.) wrote a work *On Anger* (*De ira*), probably using Posidonius's work as a source.[78] Similarly, Epictetus focused attention on the objects of anger in "That We Should Not Be Angry [χαλεπαίνειν] with the Erring [ἁμαρτανομένοις]" (*Diss.* 1.18) and "That We Should Not Be Angry [χαλεπαίνειν] with People [ἀνθρώποις]" (*Diss.* 1.28). This concern with anger was hardly unique to Stoicism, for it spanned all philosophical schools and was a recurring theme in various kinds of Greek and Roman literature.[79] Inasmuch as it was widely held that "the doctrine of the virtues follows necessarily from the doctrine of the emotions,"[80] no serious moralist could discuss virtue without initially or simultaneously discussing the emotions, especially anger. This includes Jesus as he is depicted in the Sermon on the Mount. When the Jesus of Matthew's Gospel immediately moves from a demand for greater righteousness and justice (δικαιοσύνη [5:20]) to an attack on anger (ὁ ὀργιζόμενος [5:22]), he is making a transition that would have been perfectly logical to any Hellenistic moralist or philosopher.[81]

It is this pervasive concern with anger that accounts for the preservation of the chreia about Zeno and his student. It is important to note that in this particular chreia, Zeno is totally focused on his angry student and exhibits no apparent concern whatsoever for the abused slave. He is concerned here solely with the abusive master's moral slavery to the passion of anger, and he views the battered body of the legal slave as incontrovertible proof of that moral slavery. The student has erred, and the philosopher deals with him without becoming angry himself.[82]

Although the chreia functioned as part of Stoic teaching on the passions and provided an exemplum for how a philosopher should correct an errant student, its lack of explicit concern for the abused slave is especially striking. It aptly illustrates P. A. Brunt's observation that "one constantly feels that the Stoics were concerned rather with the moral evil involved in injustice than with the sufferings of the slaves."[83] Indeed, "on the strict Stoic view, ill-treatment of others harmed the agent who suffered in the soul, rather than the victim."[84] In keeping with the Stoic war on anger, Zeno here focuses on the angry student, not the victim of that anger.

---

[77] For Antipater, see Athenaeus, *Deipn.* 14.643F (*SVF* 3.65); for Posidonius, fragments 36, 155 in Edelstein and Kidd 1972–1979, 1:55, 140.

[78] For a partial list of scholars who view Posidonius as a source for Seneca, especially in *Ira* 2.1.3–4.2; 2.19–21, see Steinmetz 1994, 675.

[79] On the emotions, especially anger, as a common Greco-Roman topic of philosophy and literature, see Fitzgerald 2008b, 10–11.

[80] Galen, *PHP* 5.6.1.

[81] See Fitzgerald 2007a.

[82] See Epictetus, *Diss.* 1.18, "That We Should Not Be Angry with the Erring."

[83] Brunt 1993, 223 (see 210–44). One of Brunt's illustrations involves the famous attack by Musonius Rufus (*Diss.* 12) on masters having sex with their female slaves: "Musonius condemned sexual intercourse between master and handmaiden not out of regard to her feelings but because of his lack of self-restraint" (223).

[84] Ibid., 222.

In this particular incident the victim is a young slave (παιδάριον), and the master, as one of Zeno's students,[85] is likely a teenager. In short, in all likelihood one teenage boy has beaten another boy, who is either the same age or younger. Furthermore, the abuse is not minor. The young slave is not struck lightly or just once, but is severely and repeatedly beaten, and the beating includes places on the body visible to onlookers such as Zeno.[86]

The Greek word that Diogenes Laertius uses here for the abuse is μωλωπίζω, which LSJ (1158) defines as "beat and bruise severely," so that μώλωπες, bruises in the form of "welts," appear on the body.[87] That is clear from Pausanias the Atticist, the second-century C.E. lexicographer, who defines μώλωψ as τὸ ἐκ πληγῆς οἴδημα, "the swelling from a blow."[88] Welts were typically the result of flogging. As Sirach says, πληγὴ μάστιγος ποιεῖ μώλωπα, "The blow of a whip raises a welt" (28:17 NRSV). Whipping slaves was so common in Jewish circles that Sirach can say that "a household slave [οἰκέτης] who is constantly under scrutiny will not lack welts" (23:10). The best-known text in which the noun appears is Isa 53:5 LXX, where it is used quite appropriately of the wounded (ἐτραυματίσθη) slave (δοῦλος/παῖς)[89] by whose "welt" (μώλωπι) one is healed (see also 1 Pet 2:24). In the case of Zeno's student, the welts on the slave's body are like "footprints" (ἴχνη) in the dirt, for they are evidence of the master's anger.[90]

---

[85] The Greek term is γνώριμος, which can mean "acquaintance" and is so rendered in Hicks 1958-1959. But it is also a term used to refer to students (LSJ 355), which often it does in Diogenes Laertius's doxography. He uses it in *Vit. phil.* 1.118 of Aristoxenus's work *On Pythagoras and His Students* (τῶν γνωρίμων), where the reference clearly has to do with Pythagoras's school. Similarly in *Vit. phil.* 2.11, Metrodorus of Lampsacus (the friend and disciple of Epicurus) is called the γνώριμος of the pre-Socratic Anaxagoras, not because they knew one another—Anaxagoras died about one hundred years before Metrodorus was born—but because he defended a thesis that Anaxagoras was the first to advance (and perhaps also because Anaxagoras had died and was buried in Lampsacus). Again, in *Vit. phil.* 2.63, Aristotle is the "single disciple" (γνώριμος) of Aeschines, not his only acquaintance. See also *Vit. phil.* 2.110; 5.35 [bis], 70; 6.5, 73, 75, 77, 78, 80; 7.36, 41, 121; 8.14; 9.67, 106; 10.9 [bis], 12.

[86] Cf. Plutarch, *Cohib. ira* 463A-B: "The tokens of savage and irascible men you will see on the faces of their servants and in the marks branded upon them and their fetters. 'The only music heard within the house' of an angry man 'is wailing cries,' as the stewards are being lashed within and the servant-maids being tortured" (translation, Helmbold 1957).

[87] LSJ 1158, which notes that both the noun and the verb are used by the late first-century C.E. medical writer Herodotus to refer to eruptions resembling mosquito bites. The verb is used by Aquila in his translation of Song 5:7.

[88] The definition is cited by BDAG, 663. On welts (μώλωπες) stinking and festering, see Ps 37:6 LXX (38:5 ET). According to Epictetus, *Diss.* 2.18.11, if people already have welts on their bodies and are again whipped (μαστιγωθείς), "it causes no longer welts but wounds" (οὐκέτι μώλωπας, ἀλλ' ἕλκη ποιεῖ).

[89] In the four so-called Servant Songs of Second Isaiah (42:1-9; 49:1-7; 50:4-11; 52:13-53:12), the servant is called both a δοῦλος (49:3) and a παῖς (42:1; 52:13; see also 43:10; 44:1-2, 21). The latter term was a common way of referring to slaves in the Greek-speaking world, where even an elderly slave could be called "boy" (παῖς).

[90] In *Diss.* 2.18.11, Epictetus uses the two words together, referring to the "imprints and welts" (ἴχνη καὶ μώλωπες) left on the mind by the passions.

In sum, it was not unusual for slaves in the ancient Mediterranean world to have welts on their bodies. These welts not only were evidence of the slave's punishment for some transgression, whether great or small, but also were suggestive of the master's anger when he administered the punishment. The greater the number of welts, the more likely it was to observers such as Zeno that the master had been angry when he punished the slave. Zeno's focus on the master's anger rather than on the slave's welts was typical, not just of Stoicism but of the moralists in general. Yet, at the same time, it does seem probable that Stoics believed that by attacking the problem of the master's anger, they were simultaneously seeking to eliminate the source of the vast majority of cases in which masters had brutally assaulted their slaves.

Third, if the attack on the master's anger was an indirect way in which Stoics dealt with the problem of slave abuse, their counsels regarding slave management show a direct engagement with the issue. It is here that one finds them repeatedly advising masters to be moderate in the exercise of their authority over slaves[91] and to treat their slaves humanely. To give just one example, Hierocles (ca. 150 C.E.), in his *On Appropriate Acts* (Περὶ τῶν καθηκόντων), begins his discussion of duties (καθήκοντα)[92] toward siblings by saying,

> Now, the first recommendation is very clear and quite simple, and besides it is also common. For, for pretty much every role, this argument is sound: that the treatment of anyone is clear from supposing that one is oneself that person and that that person is oneself. For, in fact, a person would treat a slave well, if he considered how he would think the other should behave toward himself, if the other were the master and he himself the slave. And the argument is similar for parents in respect to children and children in respect to parents and, in a word, for all in respect to all.[93]

Hierocles' advice, of course, is nothing other than a Stoic form of the "golden rule" applied to slaves.[94] Seneca's advice to Lucilius is similar: "Treat your inferior just as you would like your superior to treat you" (*Ep.* 47.11).[95] For Stoics, this humane treatment is grounded in doctrines such as συμπάθεια, the bond that unites all humans to one another and enables one to put oneself "in another person's shoes,"[96] and of sociable οἰκείωσις ("appropriation, familiarization"),[97] which

---

[91] Seneca, *Clem.* 1.18.1.
[92] Cicero used the Stoic philosopher Panaetius's Περὶ καθήκοντος as a major source for his *On Duties* (*De officiis*) and translated καθῆκον as *officium* ("duty").
[93] Hierocles *apud* Stobaeus 4.27.20 (translation, Ramelli 2009) (4:660.16–661.6 W-H).
[94] On the golden rule as a widespread ancient moral ideal, see Dihle 1962 (reference to Hierocles, p. 104).
[95] Translations of Seneca's *Ep.* 47 are from Costa 1988. For the thought, cf. Cicero, *Off.* 1.41: "We must remember that justice is to be observed even to the lowliest in society. Slaves represent that lowliest condition and status. The advice of those who recommend that we treat them as hired hands is reasonable enough: make them work, but give them what is their due" (translation, Walsh 2000).
[96] Note Seneca, *Clem.* 1.18.2: "It may be legal to do anything to a slave, but the right shared by all living creatures sets a particular limit on what a human being may suffer" (translation, Davie 2007).
[97] On this highly complex Stoic notion, see Engberg-Pedersen 1990.

"the followers of Zeno treat as the principle of justice."[98] The latter "is the kind of *oikeiōsis* that is not directed toward oneself but toward the others and entails duties or appropriate actions toward them."[99] At its best, this leads to a rejection of the correlation of slaves with animals. Seneca laments the common way that masters mistreat their slaves, saying that "we abuse them, not even as though they were human beings but as if they were beasts of burden" (*Ep.* 47.5), and he praises Lucilius for his enlightened approach with his slaves: "So I feel that your policy is absolutely right in that you don't want your slaves to fear you and you punish them by words only: beatings are for animals" (*Ep.* 47.19).

This last assertion by Seneca leads to the fourth and final point that I wish to make: Seneca's famous rejection of corporal punishment and his endorsement of Lucilius's policy of using only verbal castigation (*verborum castigatione*) in the treatment of slaves cannot be taken as representative of either Stoicism in general or of Seneca's own practice or the counsel he gives elsewhere. What the Stoics, in concert with other Hellenistic moralists, opposed was the penchant of masters to punish their slaves when angry.[100] To punish in anger was viewed as tantamount to punishing excessively, which meant that the angry, punitive master was simultaneously guilty of both injustice and cruelty.[101] Viewed solely in economic terms, the injuries done to slaves, and especially the flights and deaths of slaves that resulted from angry threats or actual punishments, meant that the financial losses were far more serious than the irritating incidents that had occasioned them.[102] Given the high cost of slaves, which had risen steadily during the last two centuries B.C.E. and remained high during the early empire,[103] their flight, death, or permanent injury was no insignificant loss of human capital. Being enslaved to the passion of anger simply made no sense at all, either economically or morally.[104]

---

[98] Porphyry, *Abst.* 3.19 (*SVF* 1.197). See Ramelli 2009, xliii.

[99] Ibid., xlvi.

[100] Despite Plutarch's many disagreements with the Stoics, he shared their conviction that masters should not punish slaves in anger. See *Cohib. ira* 459D–E and the anecdote about him calmly having one of his slaves punished by flogging (Aulus Gellius, *Noct. att.* 1.26.4–9).

[101] See especially Seneca's condemnation of Vedius Pollio's notorious cruelty toward slaves in *Clem.* 1.18.2; *Ira* 3.40.2–5.

[102] Seneca, *Ira* 3.4.4; see also Plutarch, *Cohib. ira* 459A.

[103] Prices for slaves were relatively low in classical Athens and during the early Roman republic, but that began to change during the last two centuries of the Roman republic, when slave prices began to rise steadily and sharply. Slave prices continued to be high during the early principate. See Hopkins 1978, 158–63; Jongman 1988, esp. 195; 2007, 601–2; Scheidel 2005; note Scheidel 2008, 123: "In this environment [Roman Egypt], slaves were luxury items: most households did not own any slaves, and most that did had only one or two." Some Romans, however, paid astronomically high amounts of money for slaves. Whereas the typical price for a slave in Italy under the principate was anywhere from one thousand to a few thousand sesterces (so Jongman 2007, 602), Calvisius Sabinus (a contemporary of Seneca) assembled a group of highly educated slaves at an average cost of one hundred thousand sesterces per slave (Seneca, *Ep.* 27.4–8).

[104] "Bad treatment of slaves was uneconomical" (Raymer 1940, 20).

The proper procedure was for masters to defer punishment until their anger had abated, to the time when the slave's infraction could be assessed dispassionately. At that point, the appropriate punishment for the offense could be determined and administered. If verbal castigation sufficed as a punishment, that was fine; if clemency could or should be shown, that was even better.[105] Yet if corporal punishment was warranted, a beating could justly be administered. Seneca writes,

> An impressive act it would be on our part, no doubt, if we packed off some wretched slave to prison! Why are we in a hurry to flog him on the spot, then promptly to break his legs? We will not lose the power to do this, if we postpone it. Wait for the time to arrive when it will be our own order: at the moment we shall be speaking under anger's command; when it disappears, then we shall see how much value to set on the damage. For in this we are particularly liable to error; we have recourse to the sword, to capital punishment, and with chains, imprisonment, and starvation we punish an offence that should be chastised by a light whipping. (*Ira* 3.32.1–2)[106]

That Zeno was willing to beat slaves is indicated by one of the anecdotes about him:

> Zeno, they say, was whipping [ἐμαστίγου] a slave [δοῦλον] for stealing. When the latter said, "It was decreed by fate [εἵμαρτο] for me to steal," Zeno replied, "And to be beaten [δαρῆναι]."[107]

In this chreia, Zeno's slave is guilty of theft (κλοπῇ), and Zeno punishes him for the crime. The slave does not deny that he is guilty, but he cleverly seeks to evade the flogging by appealing to the deterministic idea of fate (εἱμαρμένη), that he had been "fated" to steal and thus should not be punished for acting according to his fixed destiny. Inasmuch as Stoics championed the idea of fate and held that it was ineluctable,[108] the slave hoped that it might form the basis for Zeno excusing or forgiving his actions. But his ploy fails; instead of viewing fate as the basis for clemency, Zeno uses it to justify the beating, arguing that it too had been determined by the same fate to which the slave had appealed.

As this anecdote suggests, Stoics were not averse to using corporal punishment when they deemed it justified, but the preceding discussion shows that they

---

[105] Seneca, *Ira* 3.24.2: "What right have I to make my slave atone by stripes and manacles for too loud a reply, too rebellious a look, a muttering of something that I do not quite hear? Who am I that it should be a crime to offend my ears? Many have pardoned their enemies; shall I not pardon the lazy, the careless, and the babbler? Let ... a slave be pardoned by the bond of familiarity" (translation, Basore 1989 [modified]). See also Plutarch, *Cohib. ira* 459C–D, where, in contrasting masters who give orders silently with a nod and those who use blows and branding irons, he argues that many slaves respond better to pardon than to punishment.

[106] Translation, Davie 2007. See also *Ira* 3.35.2.

[107] Diogenes Laertius, *Vit. phil.* 7.23 (my translation). The chreia's presupposition that Zeno had at least one slave is shared by Musonius Rufus, who regards a man by the name of Manes as one of Zeno's slaves (*Diss.* 18a [*SVF* 1.287]; cf. Epictetus, *Diss.* 3.26.37). Seneca, by contrast, argues that Zeno did not have any slaves (*Helv.* 12.4).

[108] For a judicious discussion of fate and determinism in Hellenistic philosophy, see Hankinson 1999.

sought, for both moral and economic reasons, to set limits to the practice and to encourage greater moderation and humanity in the treatment of slaves.

4. Early Christianity and the Treatment of Slaves

I will restrict my discussion of early Christian views of slavery and slave management to eight major points. First, the author of 1 Peter is partly accurate in depicting the social reality that whereas some masters were "kind and lenient" (ἀγαθοῖς καὶ ἐπιεικέσιν)[109] in their treatment of slaves, others were "harsh" (σκολιοῖς) (2:18). That is precisely the impression given us in some other Greco-Roman sources,[110] but this simple twofold classification of "good" and "bad" masters masks the reality that the same master could be viewed by some of his slaves as gentle but by others as harsh. As is often the case, social reality is more complex than the simple categories that we use to organize and interpret data, and the New Testament, like the Hellenistic moralists in general, lacks a slave's perspective on the various issues affecting slaves.[111]

Second, the widespread use of rewards, the existence of many masters who endeavored to be as kind and forbearing as possible, and the proliferation of slaves who held positions of power and prestige should not lead us to think that slavery was fundamentally a humane institution at the time of the New Testament.[112] It was not—not by a long shot. Life may have been relatively good for some slaves, but "slavery in the Greco-Roman world remained an often exploitative and humiliating institution in which slaves, though recognized in a sense as human beings, were still property or 'things' (res), and could be beaten, tortured, or even killed by their owners."[113] Both the Stoics and the Christians acknowledged the brutal

---

[109] As I have argued elsewhere, ἐπιείκεια is one of the virtues that create goodwill and make the use of coercion unnecessary; indeed, it is the virtue of those who voluntarily do not make full use of the power that their superior position justly allows. See Fitzgerald 1990, 194n26. On ἐπιείκεια as a virtue, see also Walker 2002.

[110] Bartchy (1973, 67–72) rightly notes that instances of both kindness and cruelty toward slaves are well documented.

[111] A partial exception is Epictetus, who had once been a slave (*Diss.* 1.9.29; 1.19.21) and, according to Celsus, became lame when a cruel master (presumably Epaphroditus, a freedman and secretary in charge of petitions under Nero and Domitian) twisted his leg until it broke (Origen, *Cels.* 7.53). It is debated whether his *Discourses*, delivered at Nicomedia after his emancipation, reflect his experiences as a slave. Geoffrey de Ste. Croix (1981, 142) famously accused Epictetus of being an "ex-slave who had thoroughly acquired the outlook of a master." For a different perspective, see Bradley 1994, 174–78. For other philosophers who were once slaves, see Aulus Gellius, *Noct. att.* 2.18.1–10; see also Rigsby 2008.

[112] The lingering tendency in some academic circles to view ancient slavery as more humane than is assumed and argued in this paper is due largely to the work of Joseph Vogt and his school. See especially Vogt 1975, which was important as a corrective but paints too rosy a picture of slavery.

[113] Hershbell 1995, 188. On slaves as legally both a human being (*persona*) and a piece of property (*res*) according to Roman law, see Kirschenbaum 1987, 15–16. On the torture of slaves as part of the Roman legal system, see especially Brunt 1980. Note also the

way in which many slaves were treated. Seneca, for instance, concedes that "we are extremely arrogant, cruel and insulting" to slaves (*Ep.* 47.11), and that is why an old proverb, "You have as many enemies as you have slaves," was still applicable in his time.[114] As he says in his comment on the proverb, "We don't acquire them as enemies: we make them enemies" (*Ep.* 47.11). As we will see below, the New Testament also reflects the brutal ways in which some slaves were treated.

Third, the ancient slave's fundamental state was one of fear. That emotional state was inextricably linked with the penchant of masters to resort to humiliation and to physically painful measures in punishing slaves. Not all slaves were in fact subjected to corporal punishment, at least not regularly. Yet all slaves were potentially subject to various forms of violence, as well as to countless techniques designed to embarrass and humiliate them. Such punitive measures were an ever-present threat that hung like a dark cloud over the typical slave's head. "Though inhuman exploitation was not the rule, it was always an impending danger."[115]

> The conditions of life which produced fear of their owners in slaves were thus numerous and all-embracing. . . . Slaves were never in a position to predict when the wrath of an owner would descend upon them and their lives were thus conditioned by this perennial fear of physical abuse and maltreatment. Within that element of fear lay owners' capacity for the permanent control of their slaves.[116]

Stoics, Christians, and others knew only too well that the typical slave feared the master, and especially the master's anger. That is why Plutarch says, "Newly purchased slaves inquire about their new master, not whether he is superstitious or envious, but whether he is ill-tempered" (*Cohib. ira* 462A).[117] That is also why Epictetus refers to masters (δεσπόται) as terrifying (φοβεροί) and depicts with penetrating accuracy the fearful anxiety of the runaway slave who is "in a flutter and upset" if someone merely mentions the word "master" (*Diss.* 1.29.59–63). Finally, that is also why in Rom 8:15 Paul can say to the Christ-believers in Rome, "For you did not receive a spirit of slavery [δουλείας] that reduces you again to a state of fear [φόβον]." The apostle here explicitly associates slavery with fear, and he contrasts that fearful condition with the bold liberty that characterizes the adopted children of God. Unlike fearful slaves, who address their owners as "Master," the Christ-believers as God's children call upon him with the words "Abba, Father" (Rom 8:15), an invocation seldom if ever found on a slave's lips when addressing the master.

---

way in which Paul in 1 Cor 9:27 associates slavery (δουλαγωγῶ) with "beating the body" (ὑπωπιάζω τὸ σῶμα). The verb ὑπωπιάζω (literally, "to strike under [the eye]") is especially suggestive of punching someone in the face, so as to give that person a black eye. Note the reference to boxing in 1 Cor 9:26, and see Aristotle, *Rhet.* 3.11.15; Diogenes Laertius, *Vit. phil.* 6.89.

[114] The proverb is also quoted by Sextus Pompeius Festus, a late second-century Roman grammarian, who is important because he summarized Verrius Flaccus's monumental *De verborum significatu* (*On the Meaning of Words*), which dates from the Augustan age. For the proverb, see Lindsay 1913, 314.

[115] Laes 2008, 272.

[116] Bradley 1987, 137.

[117] Translation, Helmbold 1957. Cf. Plutarch, *On Calumny*, fragment 153 (Sandbach 1987).

Fourth, the New Testament often reflects and fully embraces the standard system of rewards and punishments used in the treatment of slaves, yet it does so in a way that Stoics would have found problematic. To illustrate this point, I will discuss three parables told by the Matthean Jesus. In the parable of the three slaves and the talents (Matt 25:14–30), the two good and faithful (ἀγαθὲ καὶ πιστέ) slaves are rewarded with greater responsibilities and granted a share of their master's joy (25:21, 23). These two slaves surely would have regarded this master as good, because he has acted in keeping with all of the principles of sagacious slave management. But the third slave fearfully (φοβηθείς) regards the master as harsh (σκληρός), which foreshadows the way in which the master will deal with this particular slave, whom he regards as evil (πονηρέ), lazy (ὀκνηρέ), and useless (ἀχρεῖον) (25:26, 30). Not surprisingly, this third slave is punished by being cast into the outer darkness, where there will be wailing and gnashing of teeth (25:30).

Similarly, in the parable of the two slaves placed in charge of the household (Matt 24:45–51), the faithful and prudent (πιστὸς καὶ φρόνιμος) slave who discharges his assigned duties is rewarded (μακάριος) and entrusted with even greater responsibilities (24:45–47), whereas the wicked (κακός) slave who abuses his position and fellow slaves is punished severely; indeed, the latter is "dichotomized" (διχοτομήσει), literally, "cut in two," and his portion placed with the hypocrites, where there will be wailing and the gnashing of teeth (24:48–51). The precise meaning of "cut in two" ("cut in half," "cut to pieces") is debated, but clearly it signifies severe punishment of some kind. In view of the explicit harshness of the master in this parable, the implicit savagery of the envisioned action should not be minimized or reduced to a mere metaphor.[118] The slave is viciously attacked and quite likely butchered with a sword, as in 3 Baruch 16.3 (διχοτομήσατε αὐτοὺς ἐν μαχαίρᾳ, "hack them to pieces with a sword") and other texts where the verb διχοτομέω occurs.[119] Seneca mentions a sword as one of the weapons used by masters against slaves (Ira 3.32.2), and that is precisely what one of Galen's friends used to attack two of his slaves:

> He fell into a rage. Since he had nothing else with which to strike the young men, he picked up a good-sized sword in its scabbard and came down on the heads of both of them with the sword—scabbard and all. Nor did he bring down the flat side (for in this way he would have done no great damage) but struck with the cutting edge of the sword. The blade cut right through the scabbard and inflicted two very serious wounds on the heads of both—for he struck each of them twice. (Galen, De affectuum dignotione)[120]

In the real world, any slave cut into pieces would die as a result of a violent, aggravated assault,[121] bringing the punishment to an end. But in the eschatological

---

[118] Like most terms, the verb διχοτομέω can indeed be used figuratively (see LSJ Supplement, 96), but that is hardly the case in Matt 24:51.

[119] In Plutarch, Pyrrh. 24.3, Pyrrhus cuts his barbarian foe in two, from top to bottom, with a sword (ξίφει). Similarly, in Josephus, Ant. 8.31, Solomon orders a member of his bodyguard to draw his sword (μάχαιραν) and to cut the babies of the two prostitutes in half (referring to the famous story in 1 Kgs 3:16–28).

[120] Translation, Harkins 1963.

[121] See 1 Sam 15:33; Heb 11:37; Herodotus 2.139; 3.13; 7.39; Suetonius, Gaius 27.

world of the Matthean Jesus' parables and teaching, the fatal punishment of the butchered slave in this life and his fate in the afterlife are conflated. As a result of this telescoping technique, the parable's lens shifts suddenly and seamlessly from the bloody scene of the master's cleavage of his slave (tantamount to the eschatological last judgment) to a scene in the netherworld, where the slave takes his place with other evildoers. These wretches are doomed to eternal remorse ("wailing and gnashing of teeth" [8:12; 13:42, 50; 22:13; 24:51; 25:30]) for their misdeeds and to eternal punishment (25:46); this is the fate of the punished slave both in this parable (24:51) and in the preceding one (25:30). It should be noted, however, that the savage punishment of the wicked slave in this parable is inflicted by the master himself, who does not delegate the task of inflicting the punishment to another member of his household (contrast 18:34; 25:28–30).[122]

Finally, in the parable of the unforgiving slave (Matt 18:23–35), a king is prepared to sell one of his slaves, along with the slave's wife, children, and possessions, in order to recover some of the money that the slave owes him (18:24–25). When the slave petitions for more time and pledges to repay the entire debt, the king is compassionate (σπλαγχνισθείς) and forgives the entire debt (18:26–27). Yet when the king learns that this pardoned slave has failed to treat one of his fellow slaves with the same mercy (ἠλέησα) that he received from the king (18:28–31), the monarch's compassion turns to anger (ὀργισθείς), the ungrateful slave's massive debt of ten thousand talents is reinstated, and instead of being sold along with his family and possessions (as was the master's original plan), the wicked slave (δοῦλε πονηρέ) is turned over to those who will torture (βασανισταῖς) him until the entire debt is repaid (18:32–34).

When read against the backdrop of discussions of slave management by Stoics and other Hellenistic moralists, two shocking features of this parable stand out. First, the king acts in anger (18:34), which was extremely common in dealing with slaves but violated the counsels of both Stoics and Middle Platonists such as Plutarch, which focused on deferring punishment until anger subsided. Second, the angry master subjects the unforgiving slave to torture (18:34), which not only is a more dire punishment than he originally contemplated (18:25) but also is far more severe than the penalty (imprisonment) to which the unforgiving slave has subjected his fellow slave as debtor (18:30). Without question the slave in this parable is despicable—an ungrateful, vindictive wretch who merits punishment.

---

[122] For another fictional account of a slave in charge of the household dying a gruesome death, see Apuleius, *Metam.* 8.22, where a farm bailiff, who was married to a fellow slave, fell in love with a free woman and made her his mistress. When his distraught wife learned of his affair, "she burned his account-books and all of the contents of his store-room," then killed herself and their child. "Her death so shocked the owner of the farm that he seized the bailiff whose infidelity had provoked it and ordered him to be stripped naked, smeared all over with honey and bound fast to a rotten fig-tree which was swarming with ants inside and out. As soon as the ants smelt the honey they began running over him and with minute but innumerable and incessant bites gradually ate him up, flesh, guts and all. He survived the torture for some time, but in the end there was nothing left of him but his skeleton, picked clean" (translation, Graves 1951).

But any Stoic who read or heard this parable would have raised the issue whether torture was an appropriate punishment, especially since it was decreed in the heat of the master's anger, which, along with sheer depravity, was widely regarded as the prime cause of cruel and excessive punishments. Yet far from raising such questions or from criticizing the master's anger or his use of torture, the Matthean Jesus makes the angry king's torture of his slave analogous to God's future action! Like the king in the parable, God will inflict punishment on all those who refuse to grant others the same forgiveness that they themselves have received (18:35; see also 6:12, 14–15).

In addition to raising moral and theological objections to the actions of the master in the parable of the unforgiving slave,[123] Stoics would likely have questioned whether a useless (ἀχρεῖον) slave who has only cost his master the interest on a single talent should be cast into the outer darkness (25:30). Useless (ἄχρηστον) slaves normally were not punished in perpetuity but rather were sold to someone else.[124] In short, from the perspective of many Stoics, the reactions of masters to their slaves' failures and misdeeds in the Matthean Jesus' parables would have been deemed extreme, resulting in excessive and cruel punishments. In this sense, the New Testament does not simply reflect aspects of social reality. Far more troubling is the fact that it here endorses by divine analogy precisely those abusive aspects of slave management that Stoics sharply criticized.

Fifth, elsewhere, of course, the New Testament does encourage humane treatment of slaves, especially in the *Haustafeln* of Colossians and Ephesians.[125] Masters are exhorted by the Paulinist authors of these writings to treat slaves with justice and fairness (τὸ δίκαιον καὶ τὴν ἰσότητα [Col 4:1]), and to do good (ποιήσῃ ἀγαθόν) to their slaves in the same way that slaves are encouraged to do good their owners (Eph 6:8–9). These are exhortations that Stoics and many others in the Greco-Roman world would have seconded. Implicit in such exhortations is the idea that masters should reward their slaves for their loyal service and be their benefactors. Indeed, it should be recalled that the ideal set forth by Xenophon in the *Oeconomicus* is precisely the idea of mutual euergetism that the author of Ephesians endorses. Ischomachus tells Socrates that he "does good" (εὐεργετῶν) to the slave who is serving as his foreman "whenever the gods grant us an abundance of some good thing." Inasmuch as Ischomachus rewards his slaves by allowing them to share in his good things, they in turn "want to do some good" (ἀγαθόν τί ... βούλονται πράττειν) to him (*Oec.* 12.6–7).[126] Similarly, the kind of loyalty

---

[123] A Stoic reader or any advocate of *apatheia* undoubtedly would have criticized the master for succumbing to the emotion of pity (Matt 18:27). The shift from pity to anger would have constituted evidence that both of the master's decisions regarding the slave's fate were based not on reason, but on emotion, and thus were faulty.

[124] Epictetus, *Diss.* 1.19.22.

[125] For brief introductions to the New Testament household codes and bibliographies of the most important studies, see Fitzgerald 1992; 2000.

[126] Over against those who think that only masters can be benefactors, Seneca argues that slaves can provide benefits to their masters (*Ben.* 3.18–28) and gives an impressive collection of examples in support of his claim (*Ben.* 3.22–27).

(εὔνοια) that Xenophon seeks to foster by rewarding slaves is exactly the kind of service that Ephesians enjoins on slaves (6:7: μετ' εὐνοίας δουλεύοντες). The key difference between Xenophon and Ephesians is that the former is articulating his philosophy of how masters should treat slaves and the response that such treatment should engender from slaves. He is not speaking directly to slaves, whereas Ephesians is giving exhortations to both slaves and masters. This means that even if the Christian masters do follow the instructions of the Paulinists, it does not necessarily mean that the pagan owners of these Christian slaves will act in the same fashion. For that reason, Ephesians assures Christian slaves that the Lord will reward them for their service (6:8) and exhorts them to serve "with loyalty, as to the Lord and not to human (masters)" (6:7).

There is one point at which Eph 6 merits extended comparison with what we find in Seneca, *Ep.* 47. It will be recalled that this is where Seneca rejects corporal punishment as something fitting only for animals and seconds Lucilius's proposal to use only verbal castigation in managing his slaves (47.19). By adopting this radical policy,[127] Lucilius is seeking to have his slaves respect (*colant*) him rather than fear (*timeant*) him (47.17). Seneca explains that "one who is respected [*colitur*] is also loved [*amatur*]" and, in words that bring to mind 1 John 4:18, affirms that "love [*amor*] and fear [*timore*] cannot go together" (47.18). He even defends dining with slaves (*Ep.* 47.2), calls slaves "humble friends" (47.1), and advises Lucilius to hunt for friends among his slaves at home (47.16). "Treat your slave gently, even genially," he tells Lucilius; "let him join in your talk, your plans, and your social life" (47.13).

Yet in all this, he never contemplates the idea of dispensing with verbal castigation. Lashing slaves with the tongue is one form of social control that neither Seneca nor Lucilius is willing to relinquish. What is not so clear is whether Lucilius's verbal castigation includes or excludes the use of threats of bodily harm. It was a standard device to threaten corporal punishment in the hope that one would not have to resort to it, and it would be remarkable if Lucilius was willing to go that far. But that is precisely what the author of Ephesians does in 6:9 when he exhorts masters that they should dispense with the use of "threats" (ἀπειλήν). Inasmuch as threats were a standard means of managing slaves and served as a prelude to actual punishments, this is as close as the New Testament comes to rejecting the use of punishments in the treatment of slaves.[128]

At the same time, the author of Ephesians retains the idea of obeying masters "with fear and trembling" (μετὰ φόβου καὶ τρόμου [6:5]) when addressing Christian slaves. Given that slaves typically lived in fear of masters and their punishments (see above), exhorting them to render fearful obedience to their masters was to state the obvious. But his retention of the idea of servile fear may be because

---

[127] Contrast Cicero, *Off.* 2.24: "Those who by the power of office repress subjects who have been brought low by force must inevitably deal harshly with them, as masters do with their servants if these cannot be controlled in any other way" (translation, Walsh 2000).

[128] To punish without first giving a warning was viewed as utterly inappropriate and unfair.

many of these Christian slaves served pagan masters. Many of these pagan masters, especially those who routinely used threats, intimidation, and beatings to control slaves, would have regarded the exhortation to cease using threats as tantamount to "advocating freedom for slaves" and "undermining the authority of masters," which is how Seneca thought his plea for respect rather than fear would be interpreted by unsympathetic readers (*Ep.* 47.18). It could also reflect a dual strategy by which masters, on the one hand, are exhorted to dispense with threats and punishments, and slaves, on the other hand, are encouraged to live in light of the possibility of masters applying pain incentives to them.

Sixth, some patristic writers, such as Theodore of Mopsuestia, found in Paul's characterization of Onesimus as Philemon's "beloved [ἀγαπητόν] brother" the key not only to the purpose of Paul's letter to this slave owner but also to the entire master-slave relationship. According to Theodore, Paul's primary purpose in writing to Philemon is to persuade him "to pardon Onesimus" and "to take him back in affection" (*Comm. Phlm.* 2:259.2–4; cf. 2:280.8–9). To pardon Onesimus is tantamount to showing him "kindness" (*bonitate* [2:283.16]), which God will reward with a similar kindness toward Philemon (2:283.10). With these words, Paul is encouraging Philemon not simply to take Onesimus back, but also to do so "affectionately" (*affectuose* [2:278.15–16]). Theodore lays enormous stress on "affection," mentioning it nine times in his commentary on the letter.[129] If Philemon regards Onesimus with affection, it means that he will take him back "as more than a slave" (2:281.9) and "exact no reckoning for what the slave had once committed" (2:260.8–10). Furthermore, in commenting on Eph 5:21 (1:182.15–183.21), Theodore makes clear that he regards affection as a mutual obligation of masters and slaves alike, with both the owners and the owned called upon to treat one another affectionately. In terms of slave management, "affection" is the antonym of "fear,"[130] and the ideal master-slave relationship is one characterized by affection rather than fear.

Seventh, it is debated whether οἱ τῆς εὐεργεσίας ἀντιλαμβανόμενοι in 1 Tim 6:2 refers to masters as the recipients of their slaves' benefactions (NRSV, NIV) or as the benefactors who confer benefits on their slaves (TNIV).[131] A full discussion of this debate is impossible here, but it is far more likely on both lexical and contextual grounds that the masters are depicted in this passage as the benefactors. Lexically, the evidence for an active meaning of ἀντιλαμβανόμενοι is overwhelmingly stronger than for a passive meaning (see, e.g., Luke 1:54; Acts 20:35), and the only occurrence of a cognate term in the Pauline corpus is also active in meaning (ἀντιλήμψεις [1 Cor 12:28]). Furthermore, *1 Clement* uses the cognate term ἀντιλήπτωρ ("provider") of God in his role as the master (δέσποτα) who functions

---

[129] Theodore, *Comm. Phlm.* 2:259.4, 260.7, 269.12, 272.7, 273.10, 275.1, 278.15, 17, 281.8. See Fitzgerald 2010, 359.

[130] Cf. Plutarch, *Cat. Maj.* 6.3, where Cato is depicted as being "mild and sparing to those under his authority," yet as displaying "severity" in administering justice. These two different ways of acting created "affection" among the former group and "fear" among the latter.

[131] For the former interpretation, see, for example, Johnson 2001, 284–85; for the latter view, Fiore 2007, 116–17.

as the helper (βοηθόν) and supplier of his servants' needs (59.4). This designation of God as the ἀντιλήμπτωρ who helps, protects, and provides for his people has a firm Septuagint background (2 Sam [Kgdms] 22:3; Ps 3:4 [3:3 ET]; 17:3 [18:2 ET]; 41:10 [42:9 ET]; 45:8 [46:7 ET]) and belongs to depictions of the divine as beneficent and to descriptions of kings and other powerful people as benefactors of their people. In P.Lond. 23 (158 B.C.E.), for example, Ptolemaeus petitions King Ptolemy VII Philometor and Queen Cleopatra II to grant him assistance (βοήθειαν), saying, "I have no means of gaining the necessaries of life except by seeking refuge with you, the most great gods and protectors [ἀντιλήμπτορας]." Later he adds, "Let me partake, if it seems good to you, of the pious protection [ἀντιλήμψεως] that you afford to all people."[132] Similarly, in BGU 4.1138,19 (19/18 B.C.E.), a petitioner invokes a Roman official as "the savior and helper of all" (τὸν πάντ[ων] σωτῆ[ρα] καὶ ἀντιλ[ήμπτορα]). In short, the lexical evidence for οἱ ἀντιλαμβανόμενοι and its cognates strongly supports an active meaning for the term, with τῆς εὐεργεσίας functioning to specify the kind of assistance given. They are masters who "undertake," "engage in," "devote themselves" to "beneficial activity." More concretely, they are masters who "are devoted to the welfare of their slaves" (TNIV).

The contextual evidence points toward the same conclusion. Contextually, the author of 1 Timothy is concerned with slaves having the proper attitude toward masters, not with the benefits that slaves provide masters as a result of their service. Positively, slaves are to regard masters (δεσπότας) as "worthy of all honor" (6:1) and as "beloved" (6:2), and, negatively, they are "not to show contempt" toward them (6:2). In terms of traditional theory of slave management, honor and affection are the consequence of masters rewarding their slaves for good service, and contempt is the result of masters treating slaves cruelly and unjustly. The author of the *Life of Aesop*, for example, urges masters to treat their slaves properly, so that "they may honor you as a benefactor" (ὡς εὐεργέτην τιμῶσιν) (109). Similarly, the author of 1 Timothy presumes that, as Christians, the masters will provide benefits (εὐεργεσίας) in return for their slaves' obedient service (δουλευέτωσαν), and that is precisely why the slaves should regard them with affection (ἀγαπητοί) rather than contempt (καταφρονείτωσαν). Elsewhere in 1 Timothy the author will exhort masters, as the more affluent members of the church, to engage in the kind of good works that he here assumes (6:17–18; see also 2:9–10). That the Christian masters in the Pastoral Epistles are being depicted here as benefactors was recognized by Theodore of Mopsuestia, who says that Christian slaves ought to serve Christian masters more readily because the latter "are masters who use them kindly [*benigne*]" (*Comm. 1 Tim.* 2:174.18–19). Paul means, he says, that the believing masters "are eager to raise them up with benefits [*beneficiis*] for the sake of the true religion they follow" (2:175.1–2). "Therefore, the kindness [*benignitas*] of masters ought not to become an opportunity for the slaves to despise them, but ought all the more bind them with fuller affection [*in affectu ampliori*]" (2:175.2–4).

Eighth, as is well known, only the *Haustafeln* of Ephesians and Colossians address both masters and slaves, whereas the admonitions regarding slaves in the

---

[132] Translation, Hunt and Edgar 1956 (slightly modified).

Pastoral Epistles (1 Tim 6:1–2; Titus 2:9–11) and to slaves in 1 Peter (2:18–25) lack a corresponding direct admonition to masters. This reverses the situation of Seneca, who always speaks to masters (such as Lucilius) and never directly to slaves. That seems to be typical, with current and future masters comprising the bulk of Stoic audiences rather than slaves. But some Stoics, such as Musonius Rufus, did occasionally have slaves among their students and did address them directly. The most famous example is Epictetus, who was still a slave when he studied under Musonius, and the latter would address him regarding his servile condition and the threats that were part and parcel of his existence as a slave (*Diss.* 1.9.29–30).[133]

5. Conclusion

Stoics and Christians shared certain ideas about slavery and slave management. In many cases, their views were identical or similar to those of the majority of people in the ancient Mediterranean world, yet in other cases they held minority viewpoints (such as the conviction that slavery was fundamentally indifferent to one's well-being as a person). Some of their ideas were radical for the time (such as dispensing with the use of threats [Ephesians] and with corporal punishment [Seneca and Lucilius]), whereas others were quite traditional (such as the commonplace that slaves should obey their masters). Needless to say, there was some diversity of thought in both groups. Neither all Stoics nor all Christians had precisely the same ideas on slaves and slave management, and that fact is hardly surprising.

If Stoics and Christians had read one another's documents, they would have discovered how much they had in common, yet also how much they differed, not only on slavery but also on other topics. Neither group attempted to abolish slavery, nor did the early Christians or the Stoics seriously concern themselves with the plight of those who endured the harshest and most degrading forms of slavery, such as those who lived and died in the mines. Unfortunately, some Christians were guilty of abusing their slaves,[134] and doubtless that was also true of those who claimed to be Stoics. Despite these failings, at least some individuals in both groups tried very hard to eliminate the more egregious aspects of ancient slavery and thereby render it more humane, and for their efforts and partial success we should be grateful.

Bibliography

Bartchy, S. S. 1973. *ΜΑΛΛΟΝ ΧΡΗΣΑΙ: First-Century Slavery and the Interpretation of 1 Corinthians 7:21*. Society of Biblical Literature Dissertation Series 11. Missoula, Mont.: Society of Biblical Literature.

Basore, J. W. 1989. *Seneca: Moral Essays*. Vol. 1. Loeb Classical Library. Cambridge, Mass.: Harvard University Press.

---

[133] On this obscure and difficult passage, see Dobbin 1998, 128.
[134] See Fitzgerald 2007b, 40–42.

Bergadá, M. 1994. "La condemnation de l'esclavage dans l'Homélie IV." Pages 185–96 in *Gregory of Nyssa: Homilies on Ecclesiastes*. Edited by S. G. Hall. New York: de Gruyter.
Bisel, S. L. C. 1986. "The People of Herculaneum AD 79." *Helmantica* 37:11–23.
———. 1987. "Human Bones at Herculaneum." *Rivista di studi pompeiani* 1:123–29.
Boulvert, G. 1970. *Esclaves et affranchis impériaux sous Haut-Empire: Rôle politique et administratif*. Biblioteca di Labeo 4. Naples: Jovene.
Bradley, K. R. 1987. *Slaves and Masters in the Roman Empire: A Study in Social Control*. New York: Oxford University Press.
———. 1994. *Slavery and Society at Rome*. Cambridge: Cambridge University Press.
———. 2000. "Animalizing the Slave: The Truth of Fiction." *Journal of Roman Studies* 90:110–25.
———. 2008. "Seneca and Slavery." Pages 335–47 in *Seneca*. Edited by J. G. Fitch. Oxford Readings in Classical Studies. Oxford: Oxford University Press.
Brunt, P. A. 1980. "Evidence Given under Torture in the Principate." *Zeitschrift der Savigny-Stiftung für Rechtsgeschichte* (Romanistische Abteilung) 97:256–65.
———. 1993. *Studies in Greek History and Thought*. Oxford: Clarendon Press.
Canarella, G., and J. A. Tomaske. 1975. "The Optimal Utilization of Slaves." *Journal of Economic History* 35:621–29.
Capasso, L. 2000. "Herculaneum Victims of the Volcanic Eruptions of Vesuvius in 79 AD." *The Lancet* 356(9238):1344–46.
———. 2001. *I fuggiaschi di Ercolano: Paleobiologia delle vittime dell'eruzione vesuviana del 79 d.C.* Bibliotheca archaeologica 33. Rome: "L'Erma" di Bretschneider.
Capasso, L., and L. Di Domenicantonio. 1998. "Work-Related Syndesmoses on the Bones of Children Who Died at Herculaneum." *The Lancet* 352(9140):1634.
Chantraine, H. 1967. *Freigelassene und Sklaven im Dienst der römischen Kaiser: Studien zur ihrer Nomenklatur*. Foschungen zur antiken Sklaverei 1. Wiesbaden: Steiner.
Costa, C. D. N. 1988. *Seneca: 17 Letters*. Warminster: Aris & Phillips.
Cribiore, R. 2001. *Gymnastics of the Mind: Greek Education in Hellenistic and Roman Egypt*. Princeton, N.J.: Princeton University Press.
Dal Lago, E., and C. Katsari, eds. 2008. *Slave Systems: Ancient and Modern*. Cambridge: Cambridge University Press.
Davie, J. 2007. *Seneca: Dialogues and Essays*. Oxford World's Classics. Oxford: Oxford University Press.
Dennis, T. J. 1982. "The Relationship between Gregory of Nyssa's Attack on Slavery in His Fourth *Homily on Ecclesiastes* and His Treatise *De Hominis Opficio*." *Studia patristica* 17(3):1065–72.
Diggle, J. 2004. *Theophrastus: Characters*. Cambridge: Cambridge University Press.
Dihle, A. 1962. *Die goldene Regel: Eine Einführung in die Geschichte der antiken und frühchristlichen Vulgärethik*. Studienhefte zur Altertumswissenschaft 7. Göttingen: Vandenhoeck & Ruprecht.

Dobbin, R. F. 1998. *Epictetus: Discourses, Book 1*. Clarendon Late Ancient Philosophers. Oxford: Clarendon Press.

Edelstein, L., and I. G. Kidd, eds. and trans. 1972–1979. *Posidonius*. 3 vols. Cambridge Classical Texts and Commentaries. Cambridge: Cambridge University Press.

Elliott, J. K. 1993. *The Apocryphal New Testament*. Oxford: Clarendon Press.

Engberg-Pedersen, T. 1990. *The Stoic Theory of Oikeiosis: Moral Development and Social Interaction in Early Stoic Philosophy*. Studies in Hellenistic Civilization 2. Aarhus: Aarhus University Press.

Fenoaltea, S. 1984. "Slavery and Supervision in Comparative Perspective: A Model." *Journal of Economic History* 44:635–68.

Fiore, B. 2007. *The Pastoral Epistles*. Sacra Pagina 12. Collegeville, Minn.: Liturgical Press.

Fitzgerald, J. T. 1990. "Paul, the Ancient Epistolary Theorists, and 2 Corinthians 10–13." Pages 190–200 in *Greeks, Romans, and Christians*. Edited by D. L. Balch, E. Ferguson, and W. A. Meeks. Minneapolis: Fortress.

———. 1992. "Haustafeln." Pages 80–81 in vol. 3 of *The Anchor Bible Dictionary*. Edited by D. N. Freedman. New York: Doubleday.

———. 2000. "Haustafeln." Pages 1485–86 in vol. 3 of *Religion in Geschichte und Gegenwart*. Edited by H. D. Betz et al. 4th ed. Tübingen: Mohr Siebeck.

———. 2007a. "Anger, Reconciliation, and Friendship in Matthew 5:21–26." Pages 359–70, 462–73 in *Israel's God and Rebecca's Children: Christology and Community in Early Judaism and Christianity: Essays in Honor of Larry W. Hurtado and Alan F. Segal*. Edited by D. B. Capes et al. Waco, Tex.: Baylor University Press.

———. 2007b. "Early Christian Missionary Practice and Pagan Reaction: 1 Peter and Domestic Violence against Slaves and Wives." Pages 24–44 in *Renewing Tradition: Studies in Texts and Contexts in Honor of James W. Thompson*. Edited by M. W. Hamilton, T. H. Olbricht, and J. Peterson. Princeton Theological Monograph Series 65. Eugene, Ore.: Pickwick Publications.

———. 2008a. "Proverbs 3:11–12, Hebrews 12:5–6, and the Tradition of Corporal Punishment." Pages 291–317 in *Scripture and Traditions: Essays on Early Judaism and Christianity*. Edited by G. O'Day and P. Gray. Supplements to Novum Testamentum 129. Leiden: Brill.

———. 2008b. "The Passions and Moral Progress: An Introduction." Pages 1–26 in *Passions and Moral Progress in Greco-Roman Thought*. Edited by J. T. Fitzgerald. Routledge Monographs in Classical Studies. London: Routledge.

———. 2010. "Theodore of Mopsuestia on Paul's Letter to Philemon." Pages 333–63 in *Philemon in Perspective: Interpreting a Pauline Letter*. Edited by D. Francois Tolmie. Beihefte zur Zeitschrift für die neutestamentliche Wissenschaft und die Kunde der älteren Kirche 169. Berlin: de Gruyter.

Fitzgerald, J. T., F. J. van Rensburg, and H. F. van Rooy, eds. 2009. *Animosity, the Bible, and Us: Some European, North American, and South African Perspectives*. Society of Biblical Literature Global Perspectives on Biblical Scholarship 12. Atlanta: Society of Biblical Literature.

Fortenbaugh, W. W. 1975–1979. "Aristotle on Slaves and Women." Pages 135–39 in vol. 2 of *Articles on Aristotle*. Edited by J. Barnes, M. Schofield, and R. Sorabji. 4 vols. London: Duckworth.
Fox, M. V. 1997. "Who Can Learn? A Dispute in Ancient Pedagogy." Pages 62–77 in *Wisdom, You Are My Sister: Studies in Honor of Roland E. Murphy, O.Carm., on the Occasion of His Eightieth Birthday*. Edited by M. Barré. Catholic Biblical Quarterly Monograph Series 29. Washington, D.C.: Catholic Biblical Association of America.
Garnsey, P. 1997. "The Middle Stoics and Slavery." Pages 159–74 in *Hellenistic Constructs: Essays in Culture, History, and Historiography*. Edited by P. Cartledge, P. Garnsey, and E. Gruen. Berkeley: University of California Press.
Garver, E. 1994. "Aristotle's Natural Slaves: Incomplete *Praxeis* and Incomplete Human Beings." *Journal of the History of Philosophy* 32:173–95.
Graves, R. 1951. *The Transformations of Lucius; Otherwise Known as The Golden Ass*. New York: Farrar, Straus & Giroux.
Griffin, M. T. 1976. *Seneca: A Philosopher in Politics*. Oxford: Clarendon Press.
Hankinson, R. J. 1999. "Determinism and Indeterminism." Pages 513–41 in *The Cambridge History of Hellenistic Philosophy*. Edited by K. Algra et al. Cambridge: Cambridge University Press.
Hansen, W., ed. 1998. *Anthology of Ancient Greek Popular Literature*. Bloomington: Indiana University Press.
Harkins, P. W. 1963. *Galen: On the Passions and Errors of the Soul*. Columbus: Ohio State University Press.
Harmon, A. M. 1960. *Lucian in Eight Volumes*. Vol. 3. Loeb Classical Library. Cambridge, Mass.: Harvard University Press.
Harrill, J. A. 1995. *The Manumission of Slaves in Early Christianity*. Hermeneutische Untersuchungen zur Theologie 32. Tübingen: Mohr Siebeck.
Hart, D. B. 2001. "The 'Whole Humanity': Gregory of Nyssa's Critique of Slavery in Light of His Eschatology." *Scottish Journal of Theology* 54:51–69.
Heath, M. 2008. "Aristotle on Natural Slavery." *Phronesis* 53:243–70.
Helmbold, W. C. 1957. *Plutarch's Moralia in Sixteen Volumes*. Vol. 6. Loeb Classical Library. Cambridge, Mass.: Harvard University Press.
Hershbell, J. P. 1995. "Epictetus: A Freedman on Slavery." *Ancient Society* 26:185–204.
Heseltine, M. 1987. *Petronius*. Corrected ed. Loeb Classical Library. Cambridge, Mass.: Harvard University Press.
Hicks, R. D. 1958–1959. *Diogenes Laertius: Lives of Eminent Philosophers*. Rev. ed. 2 vols. Loeb Classical Library. Cambridge, Mass.: Harvard University Press.
Hock, R. F., and E. N. O'Neil, eds. 1986. *The Chreia in Ancient Rhetoric*. Society of Biblical Literature Texts and Translations 27, Graeco-Roman Religion Series 9. Atlanta: Scholars Press.
Hooper, W. D., and H. B. Ash. 1954. *Marcus Porcius Cato: On Agriculture*. Rev. ed. Loeb Classical Library. Cambridge, Mass.: Harvard University Press.
Hopkins, K. 1978. *Conquerors and Slaves*. Cambridge: Cambridge University Press.

Hunt, A. S., and C. C. Edgar. 1956. *Select Papyri II: Non-literary Papyri, Public Documents*. Loeb Classical Library. Cambridge, Mass.: Harvard University Press.

Johnson, L. T. 2001. *The First and Second Letters to Timothy*. Anchor Bible 35A. New York: Doubleday.

Jongman, W. 1988. *The Economy and Society of Pompeii*. Dutch Monographs on Ancient History and Archaeology 4. Amsterdam: Gieben.

———. 2007. "The Early Roman Empire: Consumption." Pages 592–618 in *The Cambridge Economic History of the Greco-Roman World*. Edited by W. Scheidel, I. Morris, and R. Saller. Cambridge: Cambridge University Press.

Kirschenbaum, A. 1987. *Sons, Slaves, and Freedmen in Roman Commerce*. Jerusalem: Magnes Press; Washington, D.C.: Catholic University of America Press.

Kraut, R. 2002. *Aristotle: Political Philosophy*. Founders of Modern Political and Social Thought. Oxford: Oxford University Press.

Laes, C. 2005. "Childbeating in Roman Antiquity: Some Reconsiderations." Pages 75–89 in *Hoping for Continuity: Childhood, Education and Death in Antiquity and the Middle Ages*. Edited by K. Mustakallio et al. Acta Instituti Romani Finlandiae 33. Rome: Institutum Romanum Finlandiae.

———. 2006. *Kinderen bij de Romeinen: Zes eeuwen dagelijks leven*. Leuven: Davidsfonds.

———. 2008. "Child Slaves at Work in Roman Antiquity." *Ancient Society* 38:235–83.

Lindsay, W. M., ed. 1913. *Sexti Pompei Festi, De uerborum significatu quae supersunt cum Pauli epitome*. Leipzig: Teubner.

Malherbe, A. J. 1988. *Ancient Epistolary Theorists*. Society of Biblical Literature Sources for Biblical Study 19. Atlanta: Scholars Press.

Moriarty, R. 1993. "Human Owners, Human Slaves: Gregory of Nyssa, *Hom. Eccl.* 4." *Studia patristica* 27:63–69.

Oldfather, W. A. 1995–1996. *Epictetus: The Discourses as Reported by Arrian, the Manual, and Fragments*. 2 vols. Loeb Classical Library. Cambridge, Mass.: Harvard University Press.

Perrin, B. 1959. *Plutarch's Lives in Eleven Volumes*. Vol. 2. Loeb Classical Library. Cambridge, Mass.: Harvard University Press.

Pomeroy, S. B. 1994. *Xenophon's Oeconomicus: A Social and Historical Commentary*. Oxford: Clarendon Press.

Rackham, R. 1956. *Aristotle: The Nicomachean Ethics*. Rev. ed. Loeb Classical Library. Cambridge, Mass.: Harvard University Press.

———. 1959. *Aristotle: Politics*. Loeb Classical Library. Cambridge, Mass.: Harvard University Press.

Ramelli, I. 2008. "Slavery as a Necessary Evil or an Evil That Must Be Abolished? The Patristic Debate on the Institution on Which the Ancient Economy Was Based." Paper presented at the annual meeting of the Society of Biblical Literature. Boston, Mass. November.

———. 2009. *Hierocles the Stoic: Elements of Ethics, Fragments, and Excerpts*. Translated by D. Konstan. Society of Biblical Literature Writings from the Greco-Roman World 28. Atlanta: Society of Biblical Literature.

Raymer, A. J. 1940. "Slavery—The Graeco-Roman Defence." *Greece and Rome* 10:17–21.
Richter, W. 1958. "Seneca und die Sklaven." *Gymnasium* 65:196–218.
Rigsby, K. J. 2008. "Hauranus the Epicurean." *Classical Journal* 104:19–22.
Sandbach, F. H. 1987. *Plutarch's Moralia in Sixteen Volumes*. Vol. 15. Loeb Classical Library. Cambridge, Mass.: Harvard University Press.
Scheidel, W. 2005. "Real Slave Prices and the Relative Cost of Slave Labor in the Greco-Roman World." *Ancient Society* 35:1–17.
———. 2008. "The Comparative Economics of Slavery in the Greco-Roman World." Pages 105–26 in *Slave Systems: Ancient and Modern*. Edited by E. Dal Lago and C. Katsari. Cambridge: Cambridge University Press.
Schofield, M. 1999. "Ideology and Philosophy in Aristotle's Theory of Slavery." Pages 115–40 in *Saving the City: Philosopher-Kings and Other Classical Paradigms*. Issues in Ancient Philosophy. London: Routledge.
Sherk, R. K., ed. 1988. *The Roman Empire: Augustus to Hadrian*. Translated Documents of Greece and Rome 6. Cambridge: Cambridge University Press.
Ste. Croix, G. E. M. de. 1981. *The Class Struggle in the Ancient Greek World: From the Archaic Age to the Arab Conquests*. Ithaca, N.Y.: Cornell University Press.
Steinmetz, P. 1994. "Viertes Kapitel: Die Stoa." Pages 495–716 in *Die hellenistische Philosophie*. Vol. 4.2 of *Die Philosophie der Antike*. Edited by H. Flashar. Basel: Schwabe.
Stramara, D. F., Jr. 1997. "Gregory of Nyssa: An Ardent Abolitionist?" *St. Vladimir's Theological Quarterly* 41:37–60.
Swete, H. B., ed. 1880–1882. *Theodori Episcopi Mopsuesteni in epistolas B. Pauli commentarii*. 2 vols. Cambridge: Cambridge University Press.
Urbainczyk, T. 2008. *Slave Revolts in Antiquity*. Berkeley: University of California Press.
Vogt, J. 1975. *Ancient Slavery and the Ideal of Man*. Translated by T. Wiedemann. Cambridge, Mass.: Harvard University Press.
Wachsmuth, C., and O. Hense. 1974–1975. *Ioannis Stobaei: Anthologium*. 3rd ed. 5 vols. Berlin: Weidmann.
Walker, D. D. 2002. *Paul's Offer of Leniency: Populist Ideology and Rhetoric in a Pauline Letter Fragment*. Wissenschaftliche Untersuchungen zum Neuen Testament 2/152. Tübingen: Mohr Siebeck.
Walsh, P. G. 2000. *Cicero: On Obligations (De Officiis)*. Oxford: Oxford University Press.
Weaver, P. R. C. 1972. *Familia Caesaris: A Social Study of the Emperor's Freedmen and Slaves*. Cambridge: Cambridge University Press.
Winterbottom, M. 1974. *The Elder Seneca: Declamations in Two Volumes*. Vol. 2. Loeb Classical Library. Cambridge, Mass.: Harvard University Press.
Zelnick-Abramovitz, R. 2005. *Not Wholly Free: The Concept of Manumission and the Status of Manumitted Slaves in the Ancient Greek World*. Mnemosyne Supplements 266. Leiden: Brill.

9

FACING THE BEAST: JUSTIN, CHRISTIAN MARTYRDOM, AND FREEDOM OF THE WILL

Nicola Denzey
Harvard University & Brown University

> *God has deemed us worthy instruments of his purpose to discover how much human nature can endure.*
> —Seneca, *De providentia* 4.12

Sometime during the reign of the emperor Antoninus Pius (138–160 C.E.), a young man named Justin arrived from Asia Minor to explore the schools of philosophy catering to members of Rome's elite: young, aimless men well schooled in the traditions of their fathers.[1] In his *Dialogue with Trypho*, Justin describes his long process of education and conversion to Christianity.[2] Searching for a deeper meaning in his life, the young Justin had, like many of the educated young men of his age, approached the schools of philosophy active in second-century Rome. His first foray into philosophy, so he informs us, brought him to the Stoics.[3] Justin, who already knew at least the basic tenets of various Greek philosophical schools operating in his day, was aware that the idea, for example, of the *logos*—so prominent in the Gospel of John—was as much a Stoic tenet as it was Christian. He admired the Stoics for their understanding that the penetrative *logos* had entered "into every race of humans."[4]

But Justin quickly became disillusioned with the Stoics—or so he tells us. There were certain things, he insisted, that they had gotten completely wrong. The first was the idea of the ἐκπύρωσις, the periodic universal conflagration that eventually would completely consume the cosmos.[5] That the world could be created,

---

[1] Justin draws his theological vocabulary directly from Greco-Roman philosophy and remains intellectually indebted to it. For studies of Justin's philosophy, see Barnard 1967; van Winden 1971, esp. 7–53 on Stoicism; Lyman 1993; Allert 2002.

[2] The best new Greek critical edition of Justin's *Dialogue with Trypho* is Marcovich 1997; for a recent English edition, see Falls 2003.

[3] Justin, *Dial.* 2.1–2.

[4] On Justin's view of Stoicism, see Montini 1985.

[5] Justin, *1 Apol.* 19.5; 20.1–2, 4; *2 Apol.* 8.3; cf. *Dial.* 1.5.

destroyed by fire, then recreated in an undying cycle contradicted both Jewish and Christian notions of a created world existing within linear time. Justin reserved his most caustic criticism, however, for the Stoic position on free will. Stoics were, he asserted, firm believers in astral fatalism; human will remained powerless in the face of higher cosmic forces. Justin attributed to Stoic philosophy the view that humans could do or suffer nothing contrary to fate.[6] In his critique of this position, Justin adopted a stance, ironically, that could have come directly from the mouth of a Roman Stoic such as Seneca: "But neither do we affirm that it is by fate [καθ' εἱμαρμένη] that people do what they do or suffer what they suffer," he claimed in his *Second Apology*, "but that each person by free choice [προαίρεσις] acts rightly or sins."[7]

This essay explores some articulations of Stoic philosophical positions on determinism and the human capacity for free choice as made by the Roman Stoic philosopher, statesman, and playwright Lucius Annaeus Seneca (4 B.C.E.–65 C.E.), on the one hand, and Christian martyrs, including Justin, in the second century of the Common Era, on the other.[8] I argue that Christians pursued a complex relationship with Stoic philosophy, rejecting it overtly while nevertheless embracing elements of it in a complicated pattern of rebuttals, refutations, and ultimate assimilation of Stoic ideals, even while deliberately repudiating them. To say that there were significant continuities between pagan and later Christian philosophies is an argument both unoriginal and obvious;[9] I part with the work of my predecessors here in locating different reasons for these continuities. Although current studies of Christianity, particularly Christian martyrdom, frequently emphasize the countercultural, antisocial elements of Christian behaviors in the face of Roman hegemony, I see many Christians of the second-century drawing actively, even ironically, on Stoic ideas in order to gain a precious social commodity: respectability. I draw on the works of Seneca in this essay because they represent the touchstone of Roman Stoic articulations.[10] Senecan Stoicism also reveals intriguing points of contact between traditional Roman ways of thinking about determinism and free choice and Christian teachings on the same issues. Thus, it is no wonder that Tertullian called Seneca "our Seneca," or that there circulated in antiquity pseudepigraphical correspondence between the contemporaries Seneca and Paul, or that Jerome and Augustine quoted Senecan works freely.[11] Still,

---

[6] Justin, *2 Apol.* 7.
[7] Justin, *2 Apol.* 7 (translation, Barnard 1997). For the Greek text, I use the critical edition Munier 2006.
[8] The standard modern biography of Seneca is Griffin 1976; more recently, Veyne 2003. All quotations of Seneca's works here are from the Loeb Classical Library editions: Basore 1928–1935; Gummere 1917–1925.
[9] For engagement with Stoicism in the early Christian tradition, see Spanneut 1957; for the first-century evidence, Seeley 1990.
[10] See Inwood 2005. Also significant as a Roman Stoic innovator is Epictetus, but he was far less popular than Seneca in early Christian and patristic writings. For Epictetus on moral freedom and the issues explored in this essay, see Bobzien 1998, esp. chapter 7.
[11] For the patristic references, see Spanneut 1957; for an edition of the fourteen letters attributed to Seneca and Paul, see Berry 1999.

the focus of this essay is not comparative philosophy but one specific element of Christian praxis: martyrdom. The phenomenon of martyrdom, I argue, becomes a place where Christian rhetoric of anti-Stoicism sits in an uncomfortable disjuncture with Christian practices of the philosophy of emotional experience. Nowhere do we experience this disjuncture more acutely than in the rhetoric and behavior of the martyrs. The theme of moral free choice (προαίρεσις, *voluntas*) and freedom (ἐλευθερία, *libertas*) resolves or reconciles this tension, both in the Roman Stoic perspective and in early Christian writings on martyrdom.

1. Justin the Stoic

To those who specialize in Greek philosophy, Justin's critique of ostensibly Stoic positions on determinism is revealing in its naiveté; for in his assertion that Stoics were thoroughgoing determinists, Justin failed entirely to appreciate the subtleties of Stoic philosophy—subtleties that would hardly have been lost on a highly educated Roman intellectual such as Seneca. Seneca may have known, for instance, that the ancient Stoic sources themselves never reveal a single instance of a radical ethical or ontological determinism.[12] But Justin had received Stoic teaching with far less finesse than Seneca, apparently staying among the Stoics only long enough to discover that their teachings could not offer him the type of life philosophy that he sought. It is difficult to know how long this might have been, or indeed, if Justin really seriously studied Stoicism at all. His intellectual odyssey may well have been mostly fabricated, a sort of conceit in self-representation that formed the core of Christian conversion narratives. The theme of a young student disillusioned with philosophical παιδεία who converts to Christianity had become, by Justin's time, common enough to be a literary trope. To give another example, the young hero of the third-century *Pseudo-Clementine Recognitions* joins different philosophical study groups before he is converted to Christianity through his compatriot Barnabas's earnest assessment of various Greek philosophical positions: "Some Greeks have brought in fate . . . contrary to which no one can do or suffer anything." Barnabas ponders the ethical pitfalls of this type of fatalism before rejecting it outright: "When someone believes that one can do nothing and suffer nothing contrary to fate, it is easy to be ready to sin."[13]

For the newly Christian Justin, Stoic determinism was a plainly erroneous concept, another example of how pagan philosophers had failed to perceive the cosmic οἰκονομία. And like Justin, many Christians of the second century apparently maintained that the belief that astral fate controlled all human activity could lead to a slippery slope of vice and degradation. In truth, God, by his providence,

---

[12] The extant primary evidence is gathered in von Arnim 1964. For a study, see Salles 2005. Generally, on the Stoics, see the essays in Inwood 2003, especially Frede 2003. On the tendency of Romans to mischaracterize and misrepresent Greek Stoic determinism, see Rist 1969, 123–32.

[13] *Rec.* 12.3–4 (translation, Schneemelcher 1992, 2:521 [with modifications]).

had ensured that all people were able to make their own choice to behave ethically: "Each person by free choice [προαίρεσις] acts rightly or sins" was Justin's version of the Christian free-choice argument. If this were not the case, after all, then God would be responsible for human vice. At the same time, the term προαίρεσις was technical vocabulary drawn directly from Stoicism, thus the position is not distinctively Christian but rather a direct parroting of Roman Stoic ethics.

Are we masters of our own destiny? In an important sense, this was the question underlying Justin's pronouncement that humans possessed a free will that should guide them in the direction of a life lived "rightly." His was one answer—and certainly not one antithetical to Roman Stoic teachings—to this question that hung in the air, catching pagans and Christians alike into furious debate. At the heart of the issue lurked the complex and confusing relationship between God's providential care and human free will. The matter had originated in the halls of the Stoa and had rankled for centuries to emerge again full force in the first and second centuries of the Common Era.[14] During this period, the otherwise distinct concepts of freedom and "what depends on us" came to be linked. Freedom (ἐλευθερία), which had predominantly political associations in Greek and early Roman discourse, could be defined as internal freedom from drives and desires rather than from political tyranny; it could then be associated with "free will" (προαίρεσις) and set against cosmic determinism.[15] We find, then, all these philosophical terms freely negotiated within Roman Stoicism, developing within Christianity into discourses on the place of Christian free will against both the desires and appetites of the body and against the tyranny of the state.

2. Masters of Destiny

In the second century, Roman contempt for the perceived limitations of classical Stoic "determinism" grew, not just within Christian circles. We find the same perspective among those who affiliated themselves with Platonism. Like Christians, most Middle Platonists were quick to criticize Stoic determinism for what they argued were its significant philosophical limitations. Because the early Stoics had been unwilling to assign to God anything other than the good, any evil that befell humans could not be reconciled with an essentially beneficent cosmic οἰκονομία. First-century Roman Stoics such as Seneca and Epictetus wrestled with this problem of evil, emphasizing its origins in human emotions and actions. Middle Platonists adopted this same strategy, although they conveniently distanced it from "true," that is to say, "classical" Stoicism. Responsibility for evil lay not within fate, they taught, but within human action and responsibility, for the "human will is autonomous."[16]

---

[14] For a classic study of the development of free will in classical antiquity, see Dihle 1982, esp. 1–19, where he contrasts Greco-Roman notions of human free choice against a more biblically derived notion of "will."

[15] For *libertas* in Roman political thought, see the classic study Wirszubski 1950.

[16] Dillon 1986, 225.

Plutarch, like Justin, attributed to Stoicism the generalization that fate is "invincible, not to be overpowered, and victorious over everything."[17] But fate, he believed, could be contrasted, even bested, by τὸ ἐφ' ἡμῖν, "that which is in our power."

Epictetus, a slave for much of his life to the wealthy freedman Epaphroditus, spoke of προαίρεσις, moral choice, which was a matter of human will. Προαίρεσις was predicated by διαίρεσις, the ability to distinguish between what is under one's control and what is not.[18] The paradox of a slave advocating a doctrine of freedom defined and delimited by moral choice rather than by ontological or social status nicely captures the complex thought world of early second-century Rome. On a purely social level, opportunities to acquire wealth and prestige provided even enterprising slaves with the chance for social advancement, even if one were likely to suffer the profound contempt and discrimination that surely would follow any low-born individual who was able to buy oneself out of the limitations of his de-based birth status. Still, Epictetus's example reminds us that on another level, the harsh and unspoken fixity of an individual's social status stood as rarefied in Rome, disconnected from a higher and more sublime level of cosmic order: whatever one's social caste, an individual who was properly aligned internally could attain a freedom of choice, but one construed ethically as well as ontologically.

In fact, in late first-century and early second-century Rome, there was not yet such a philosophical construction as ontological freedom; the only, true choice was whether one would serve one's master willingly or not. We find this idea in the very earliest of Christian writings. In Rom 7:3; 8:1–2, for example, Paul contends that the Christian is free from bondage to sin and death, as well as bondage to the law. Nevertheless, in his extant corpus of writings, Paul relatively infrequently uses the noun ἐλευθερία or its verbal form ἐλευθερόω, most likely because he simply did not imagine that ontological or spiritual "freedom" was an attainable state. Rather, Paul asserts that humans, by their very nature, must remain in service to something. The choice lay in which power to serve: "Do you not know," Paul informs his community in Rom 6:16, "that if you yield yourselves to any one as obedient slaves, you are slaves of the one whom you obey, either of sin, which leads to death, or of obedience, which leads to righteousness?" The members of his community thus become, in his eyes, "slaves of righteousness" (Rom 6:18) or "slaves of God" (Rom 6:22). Becoming a Christian, then, was not precisely freedom; it was the free decision to serve a higher master and a willingness to participate fully and joyfully in that servitude.[19]

Paul's teachings on servitude and the limits of human freedom aligned him well with Stoic teachings. Epictetus, who was in his youth when Paul was writing, expresses a similar conviction: even a free person is a slave, if seen in a broad enough context.[20] The attitude was a common one within Roman Stoicism. In one

---

[17] Plutarch, *Stoic. rep.* 1056D.

[18] Epictetus, *Diss.* 2.6.24.

[19] On Paul's notion of freedom and its Stoic roots, see the incisive essay Engberg-Pedersen 2006.

[20] Epictetus, *Diss.* 4.7.

of his dialogues, Epictetus's student Arrian has his philosopher protagonist dress down a too haughty Roman aristocrat:

"You are just as much a slave yourself as those who have been thrice sold."

"How can I be a slave, . . . my father is free, my mother is free, no one has bought me. . . ."

"Does it seem to you slavery to act against your will, under compulsion and with groaning?"

"I grant that, . . . but who can compel me except Caesar, who is lord of all?"

"Why, then, your own lips confess that you have one master. . . . You are a slave in a large household."[21]

Even a pagan aristocrat in the first century balanced on a knife's edge, rendering to Caesar what was Caesar's, and to God what was God's. But the recognition that one was bound in an inevitable servitude *to something* was not merely relentless determinism; that would be to fundamentally distort the Stoic message. Rather, the point was to fully understand the nature of one's own servitude and to work to realign oneself into a position of ethical freedom—then to assent to this servitude willingly and joyfully.

To what, or whom, was an individual indentured? More often than not in Roman pronouncements, the human condition is one of servitude to a bitter or capricious Fortune. Pliny the Elder, for example, expresses the predicament in a famous passage from his *Natural History (Naturalis historia)*:

Throughout the whole world, at every place, every hour, by every voice Fortune alone is invoked and her name spoken; she is the one defendant, the one culprit, the one thought in people's minds, the one object of praise, the one cause. She is worshipped with insults, counted as fickle and often blind, wandering, inconsistent, elusive, changeful and a friend of the unworthy. . . . We are so much at the mercy of chance that Chance is our god.[22]

Similar views on Fortuna perdured through the life of the empire.[23] Apuleius, in the second century, also terms Fortuna "blind" (*caeca*) and "cruel" (*nefaria*).[24] The same language figures prominently on funerary epitaphs from the high empire.[25] Fate, or "blind" Fortuna, was a powerful goddess, terrifying in her arbitrariness, the Fates or *Moirai*—the triumvirate of Atropos, Klotho, and Lachesis—a

---

[21] Arrian, *Epict. diss.* 4.1.6–14.
[22] Pliny the Elder, *Nat. hist.* 2.22.
[23] On the Roman cult of Fortuna, see the monumental work Champeaux 1982–1987; also Arya 2002.
[24] Apuleius, *Metam.* 11.15.
[25] See the collection in Lattimore 1962, §36, 154–58. For specific references to Fortuna as *maligna, laeva, atrox, improba,* and *caeca,* see *CLE* 506, 980, 1065, 1485, 1952, 404, 1171, 1187, 1226, 1252, 515, 521, 530, 569, 814, 1019, 1136, 1290, 1610, 1788, 2149, 110, 373, 376, 456; *CIL* 8.5498. Lattimore (1962, 156n123) points out, interestingly, that the mention of Fortuna in epitaphs seems confined to Rome and North Africa. This seems to me an indication of a fashion rather than of any true sentiment.

combined symbol of human dread. From a Roman perspective, it was Fortuna who hammered humans into confrontation with unspeakable humiliation, pain, and the shocking recognition that one was destined to face a death both premature and violent.

Seneca provides our most penetrating Roman perspective on Fortuna's craft. "Death is the ultimate threat," he writes, "and injustice and the most cruel tyrants have nothing beyond death with which to threaten us. Death is Fortune's final expenditure of energy."[26] Seneca's sagest advice was therefore to meet Fortune willingly, as the only possible antidote to death's cruel caprice:

> And so if we accept death with a calm and steadfast mind and we realize that it is not an evil and therefore not even an injury, we will much more easily endure other things—losses and insults, humiliations, exiles, bereavements, and separations.[27]

Seneca views death not as malevolent but as one of the Stoic *indifferentia*; like sickness or pain, death was morally neutral, providing us with the opportunity to build and display virtue by exercising mastery over our own fear of annihilation. Seneca thus advocates seeing even misfortune as a training exercise:

> Why are you surprised if God tests noble spirits harshly? The proof of one's *virtus* is never an easy thing. Fortune beats and lashes us; we should patiently endure. This is not cruelty, but a contest, and the more often we enter into it, the stronger we will be. . . . By enduring Fortuna, we may be hardened by her.[28]

Note the triumphalism of this passage; nowhere is the sense that Seneca advocates acquiescence to Fortune's hold. Rather, the rhetoric of a blind Fortuna does not mark an existential (or nihilistic) worldview, but is instead an extended metaphor for internal struggle; it is also a necessary prolegomenon for a potent doctrine of facing death virtuously—that is, "like a man." From this "contest," the *sapiens* emerges victorious—free, and with honor restored. As Seneca himself states, it is when you understand Fortuna that she ceases to have power over you.[29]

Seneca's concern with dying "like a man" is evident in his extant work, from the *Epistulae morales*, a collection of short pieces arranged in the form of 124 letters addressed to his friend Lucilius that he penned toward the end of his life—over half of which contain references to death—to short moral essays such as *On Constancy* (*De Constantia sapientiis*) and *On the Tranquility of Mind* (*De tranquillitate animi*). Forced to commit suicide by Nero's order in 65 C.E., Seneca had the opportunity to make true his assertion that one must understand that one is dying every day (*se cotidie mori*).[30] Emulating the death of Socrates, he surrounded himself with his philosopher friends. Their dialogue, at least as Tacitus tells it, was not merely academic and abstract; like a good Christian martyr, Seneca also avails himself of the opportunity to denounce the emperor. His death therefore encapsulates virtue,

---

[26] Seneca, *Const.* 8.3.
[27] Seneca, *Const.* 8.3; cf. 5.4.5.
[28] Seneca, *Prov.* 4.12–13; see also Seneca, *Ep.* 2.4.
[29] Seneca, *Ep.* 51.9.
[30] Seneca, *Ep.* 1.2.

indifference to suffering and death, and political rebellion or resistance at once. His death itself, too, is every bit as agonizing as those of the later Christian martyrs. The severing of his veins—first in his arms and then his legs—brings only a slow ooze of blood; Seneca orders poison, and then a steam bath, to hasten his demise.[31]

Seneca's ghastly death provided the opportunity for the philosopher to self-actualize. Here are his own words, composed much earlier:

> I was born for a greater destiny than to be the slave of my body. I consider my body as nothing else but a chain that restricts my freedom. And therefore I set my body as an obstacle to Fortune; on it she may make assaults; but I will not allow any wound to penetrate through the body to the real me. My body is the only part of me which can be injured; but within this fragile dwelling-place lives a soul that is free. And never will that flesh drive me to feel fear, or to a role that is unworthy of a good man. Never will I lie for the sake of this silly little body. Whenever it seems to be the right time, I will sever this partnership with the body. Even now, while we are still bound together, we will not be partners on equal terms, because the soul will assume all authority. Contempt for one's body is absolute freedom.[32]

In Roman Stoicism, freedom was attainable—almost ironically—through self-discipline and self-mastery. Control of the passions ensured the necessary emotional detachment of the *sapiens*. And yet Seneca pursues this line further: the antidote to Fortuna's control is a measured and controlled death: "Whenever it seems the right time, I will end my partnership with the body."

Seneca's teachings on death—specifically, on conquering the fear of death and on the utility of suicide—reveal a sangfroid familiar to those of us who read Christian martyr acts, just as it teaches us much about Roman attitudes toward the capacious limits of human free will. To begin with, as the classicist Catherine Edwards has pointed out, death can have social and political value only when it is a public act of communication performed before an audience.[33] Second, controlling death defines *virtus* in the Roman context; the word *virtus* itself embraces notions of bravery while facing down death with steely emotional control. Third, death is both participational (in that the *sapiens* welcomes it actively) and oppositional (in that it crystallizes a nexus of oppositional encounters: human will against Fortune or Death; honor and freedom against the tyranny of the state). In all these ways, the death of the Christian martyr mirrors or refracts the death of the Stoic philosopher, reduplicating its image rather than merely turning away.

3. The Gladiator and the Philosopher

The Stoic sage represented one living model for confronting death publicly and virtuously. But there was another, perhaps more immediate: the gladiator. "We are wont to see the gladiator and the martyr operating in mutually exclusive

---

[31] Tacitus, *Ann.* 15.60–64.
[32] Seneca, *Ep.* 65.21–22.
[33] Edwards 2007, 144, 159.

emotional spheres," comments classicist Carlin Barton.[34] In fact, it is the solemn commitment to honorable death—itself a product of Stoic philosophy—that binds the two, as the work of Carlin Barton and Catherine Edwards has so impressively demonstrated.[35] There is no wonder that the image and example of the gladiator emerges so frequently in both Seneca's works and our extant Christian martyrologies.

Philosopher and gladiator shared contempt for death. In Book 2 of his *Tusculan Disputations*, Cicero draws on his Stoic training to present the gladiator as a philosopher/soldier, who through his unflinching courage in the face of death brings honor to the shame of slavery.[36] Cicero admires the gladiator for his collusion with his own fate, his recognition of his own powerlessness in the face of a larger order of causality: "What even mediocre gladiator ever groans, ever alters the expression on his face?"[37] Seneca models the *sapiens* or sage after the gladiator in his essay *On the Tranquility of Mind*:

> When [the sage] is bidden to give up his life, he will not quarrel with Fortuna, but will say "I give thanks for what I possessed and held. I have managed your property to great advantage, but, since you order me, I give it up, I surrender it gratefully and gladly."[38]

Then, further, here speaking to Nature:

> "Take back the spirit that is better than when you gave it. I do not quibble or hang back; of my own free will I am ready for you to take what you gave me before I was conscious—away with it."[39]

Most modern studies of martyrdom have predicated themselves upon the notion that Christians' defiance in the face of death in the amphitheater is best understood as a desperate act of social subversion and political rebellion.[40] Recently, the influential work of Michel Foucault encouraged a conceptualization of martyrdom as actively participating in a broader discourse of power, characterized by resistance to a dominant, hegemonic order.[41] Indeed, our extant martyr accounts work well for Foucauldian analysis. They show us, for instance, that those compelled to participate in the trial process leading up to facing the beasts adopted a position of defiant self-negation vis-à-vis Rome's carefully constructed scaffolding of social identities; disparities and differences in class and gender were erased by

---

[34] Barton 1994, 41.

[35] Beyond their work that I have cited so far, mention must be made of Barton's masterful monograph *The Sorrows of the Ancient Romans: The Gladiator and the Monster* (Barton 1993); as well as Edwards's essay "The Suffering Body: Philosophy and Pain in Seneca's Letters" (Edwards 1999).

[36] Cicero, *Tusc.* 2.17.41.

[37] Cicero, *Tusc.* 2.17.41.

[38] Seneca, *Tranq.* 11.1–6.

[39] Seneca, *Tranq.* 11.1–6.

[40] See, for instance, Riddle 1931; Ste. Croix 1963; Frend 1965; Bowersock 1995; Fox 1995, esp. 419–92. For a revisionist study that rejects old tropes without examining Stoic backgrounds for martyrdom, see Castelli 2004.

[41] See, generally, Foucault 1980.

their defiant cry "Christianus sum!" ("I am a Christian") when individuals were compelled under torture to identify themselves by name.[42] In the case of the martyrs, resistance was indeed power.

Foucault himself barely addressed the phenomenon of Christian martyrdom, but he was much concerned with Christian ἄσκησις as an emergent "technology of the self" drawn primarily from Stoic concepts of self-fashioning.[43] As Elizabeth Castelli observed in her masterful *Martyrdom and Memory*, Christian martyrdom would have proved fertile ground for Foucault's analysis.[44] Still, what is most remarkable to me about Foucault's work is that it develops Christian notions of resistance to Roman power within the framework of Stoic articulations of self. He sees this development not as oppositional, but rather as a direct and logical progression; early Christians engaged the same ethical problematics that Romans and Greeks before them faced. Of course, Foucault was no historian, but the ancient sources themselves do not need to be massaged to reveal such a provocative *mise-en-place* of Christian emotional theory.

The argument that Christian martyrdom is best understood as resistance, then, is to substantially oversimplify the case. To give only a minor example at this point, Robin Lane Fox, a historian of ancient Rome, argued that the heavenward gaze of Christians in the amphitheater would have been interpreted, following Roman physiognomic handbooks, as "a sign of impudence."[45] Yet there was more to it than that; this "impudent" gaze was also a means of demonstrating free will, particularly for those bound or otherwise unable to speak.[46] The gaze therefore encapsulates the concept of "resistance" while also drawing on semiotic discourses of power already well known; it was not merely impudent to look at one's enemy in the amphitheater, it was to participate in a language whose rules Roman Christians did not seek to alter.

Through Stoic lenses, the desperate acts of will exercised by the martyrs might be viewed differently. That martyrs welcomed torture and public execution fearlessly, even joyfully, becomes a stock element in martyr *exempla*; indeed, it is remarkable to note in the martyrologies of Justin and others in the second century the marked emphasis on dying "willingly" or of one's "own free will." Ignatius of Antioch, facing the long journey to Rome to be put to death, wrote ahead to the Christians there, "I am writing to all the Churches and state emphatically to all that I die willingly for God, provided you do not interfere. . . . Suffer me to be the food of wild beasts."[47] Almost exactly a century later, in Carthage in 203, the Roman matron Perpetua uses similar language: "We came to this of our own free will, that our freedom should not be violated."[48] Then, continues the anonymous writer of

---

[42] The cry is standard in extant martyr acts. See *Perpetua* 6.4; *Mart. Pol.* 10.1; *Passion of the Scillitan Martyrs*; *Martyrs of Lyons and Vienne* 3–6.
[43] Foucault 1994.
[44] Castelli 2004, 70–77.
[45] Fox 1995, 422.
[46] Barton 1994, 48.
[47] Ignatius, *To the Romans* 4. See Tanner 1985.
[48] *Perpetua* 18.5.

the epilogue to her journal describing the details of Perpetua's martyrdom, "she and her fellow Christians got up and went to the place reserved for throat-slitting of their own accord"; and later, "Perhaps such a great woman, who was so feared by the unclean spirit, could not be killed unless she herself willed it."[49] Cyprian reports that Christians during the Decian persecution of 250 C.E. "ran to the marketplace of their own accord; they hastened to death of their own will."[50] Origen, commenting on the Maccabean martyrs, placed special emphasis on the voluntary nature of their sacrifice: "Who would be so rightly praised as the person who died of his own accord. . . ? This is what Eleazar was like, who, welcoming death with honor rather than life with pollution, went up to the rack of his own accord."[51]

On one hand, writers of martyr acts and attendant literature depict "freedom" from the world as far preferable to subjection to an essentially demonic regime.[52] But there is more to it than that. First is the deeply ingrained notion that proper suffering—that is, facing suffering deliberately with active will—elevated the sufferer. As Carole Straw notes, "Because suffering was so contemptible when imposed against one's will, it became all the more glorious and stunning when embraced actively with the will."[53] Seneca would have concurred: "Good men are not dragged by Fate," he writes, "they follow it and keep in step." Invoking one of his favorite moral exemplars, Demetrius the Cynic *sapiens*, he continues,

> Demetrius said, "I am not being forced into anything and I am not putting up with anything against my will. I do not submit to God; I agree with him, and I strongly agree with him because I know that all things happen according to a law which is valid and established for eternity."[54]

In his studies of Christian martyrdom, Arthur Droge argues that Christians drew their ideas of an ideal, willing death from two sources.[55] On one level, Christ provided a model of directed, intentional suffering that at once encapsulated a steely, silent resistance to Roman hegemony and a willingness to submit to the inexorable unfolding of God's plan. Christian martyrs lived out Christ's defiant words in John 10:18: "No one takes [my life] from me, but I lay it down of my own free will. I have power to lay it down, and I have power to take it again." Thus, in the Decian-era *Martyrdom of Pionius*, the heroic Pionius confides to his fellow Christians: "What these people forget is that this criminal, Christ, departed his life at his own choice [ὁ ἰδίᾳ προαιρέσει ἐξάγων ἑαυτὸν τοῦ βίου]."[56] On another level, Plato's account of the death of Socrates placed Christian notions of conscious death within the broader framework of the ideal death expected of a philosopher. Droge

---

[49] *Perpetua* 20.7; 21.8–10.
[50] Cyprian, *Laps.* 8.
[51] Origen, *Ex. mart.* 22; cf. 2 Macc 6:18–28.
[52] The connection between martyrdom and the language of freedom and free will has been noted by Droge and Tabor 1992, 2; Droge 1995.
[53] Straw 2002, 40.
[54] Seneca, *Prov.* 5.4.6.
[55] Droge 1995, 157.
[56] *Martyrdom of Pionius* (Musurillo 1972, 152–53).

urges us to hear the "echo of Plato's *Phaedo* still being heard six centuries later."[57] Still, by late antiquity, Socrates' death was not so much an exemplar as something that Christians had already outdone in their virtuous displays; John Chrysostom argues that martyrs were superior to Socrates because "not against their will did the martyrs endure, but of their will, and being free to suffer," whereas Socrates had had no choice in his death.[58]

Those who were forced to face the beasts had no "free choice" about their fate. And yet the issue of choice, the question of acquiescence, remained central. This decision to face death willingly, even joyfully, hinged upon potent Stoic concepts of human autonomy in relation to higher, universal mechanisms. The spectacle or stage of the games was itself only a window of opportunity to participate in a higher reality. It was, to employ a metaphor from Buddhist thought, the finger pointing to the moon, not the moon itself. Those Christians whom circumstance or Fortuna had set on the clotted sand floor of the arena were "free" to the extent that they were able to craft for themselves their own response to the death that they inevitably would meet. Witness the words of the martyr Flavian: "We conquer death and are not conquered by it"; and Cyprian: "[Martyrs] cannot be conquered, ... they are able to die, and ... they are invincible because they do not fear to die."[59] To conquer death itself was the ultimate triumph of the will.[60] It was also to align oneself with God's will: "Blessed indeed and noble are all the martyrdoms that took place in accordance with God's will. For we must be very careful to assign to God a providence over them all," cautions Evarestus in *Martyrdom of Polycarp*.[61]

The problem with the theory that martyrdom was (merely) political rebellion was that in the violent world of second-century Rome, even God was understood to have had a taste for human blood. "How beautiful a spectacle for God," writes Minucius Felix, "when a Christian comes into close quarters with pain, is matched with threats and punishments and tortures, confronts with a laugh the din of death and the hideous executioner."[62] For Tertullian, God was the *agonothetes*—the one who produced the games.[63] Cyprian too plays with the image, claiming that martyrs delighted the Lord with "the sublime, the great, the acceptable spectacle" of the games, the "flow of blood which quenches the flames and fires of hell by its glorious gore."[64] Christianity itself thus becomes the *editor* of the games, demonstrating its status and power with a titillating display. Again, the motif is Stoic: human volitional suffering is transcendent; it provides the opportunity not (just)

---

[57] Droge 1995, 259.

[58] John Chrysostom, *Hom. 1 Cor.* 4.7 (on 1 Cor 1:25).

[59] *Martyrdom of Montanus, Lucius and Flavian* 19.6 (Musurillo 1972, 232); Cyprian, *Epistle* 60.2.3 (CCSL 3C:376).

[60] Straw (2002) argues eloquently, and rightly, that Christians claimed to conquer death in a way that the pagans did not; the promise of the resurrection made concrete and visceral the claim. It was not merely about conquering one's fear of death; death itself was vanquished by God's promised gift of eternal life.

[61] *Mart. Pol.* 2.1.

[62] Minucius Felix, *Oct.* 37.1–2.

[63] Tertullian, *Mart.* 3.

[64] Cyprian, *Epistle* 10.2–3.

to exercise obstinacy in the face of political hegemony but also to impress through heroic feats of self-control (what was "in one's power") in the face of what was simply not in one's power. In his essay *On the Tranquility of Mind*, Seneca envisions Fortuna in the same role of *agonothetes*: "'Why should I save you,' she said, 'weak and quivering beast? All the more will you be mangled and stabbed because you do not know how to offer your throat.'"[65] A trained, disciplined gladiator did indeed know how to offer his throat. Christians—at least in our extant martyr acts—knew how, too. Consider the climax of the *Passion of Perpetua*:

> The others, without moving and in silence, received the sword, especially Saturus, who was the first to ascend the platform, and the first to give up his spirit. For he was there to sustain Perpetua. Perpetua, however, had to taste more pain yet. She screamed out in agony as she was struck on the bone. Steadying the quivering hand of a novice gladiator, she guided it to her throat.[66]

The equanimity of the martyrs was not lost on some; to a Roman audience, it marked them publicly as philosophers, not criminals. Marcus Aurelius's personal physician, Galen, considered Christianity nothing more than a "third-rate" philosophy. But he admired Christian martyrs for their σοφροσύνη and contempt for death: "They also number individuals who, in self-discipline and self-control in matters of food and drink, and in their keen pursuit of justice, have attained a pitch not inferior to that of genuine philosophers."[67] In the Roman purview, Christians who faced the beasts with equanimity were not gladiators; they were true Stoics.

4. Status Inconsistency, Respectability, and the Performance of Death

In his *Ep.* 70, Seneca tells Lucilius that the ability to escape Fortuna through the exercise of will is not limited to the educated, elite sage. Even a prisoner of war can act freely in the face of death:

> There is no reason why you should think that only great men have had the strength necessary to break the chains of human bondage. . . . Men of the lowliest rank have escaped to safety through their own heroic impulse. Even when they were not allowed to die at a time of their own convenience, even when they were not allowed a choice in the means of their death, they snatched whatever opportunity was at hand and by sheer force made for themselves lethal weapons from objects which are not by nature harmful.[68]

He then proceeds to relate two remarkable accounts. In the first, a German prisoner of war compelled to fight the beasts withdraws to the lavatory, where he takes a wooden stick and attached sponge used to wipe away human excrement

---

[65] Seneca, *Tranq.* 11.5; see Barton 1993, 23n42.
[66] *Perpetua* 21.9–10.
[67] Walzer 1949, 14–15.
[68] Seneca, *Ep.* 70.

and stuffs it down his throat, choking to death. "From his example," Seneca concludes, "you, too, can learn that the only thing which makes us hesitate to die is the lack of will." In Seneca's second account, a man destined for the amphitheater sticks his head between the spokes of a cart wheel "and remained calmly in his seat until his neck was broken."[69] To a modern audience, these are chilling tales of desperation, but from a Roman philosophical perspective, these were tales of triumph; those forced to face death prematurely by the potent combination of human appetites and sheer bad luck from a cosmic point of view gained the upper hand, if only by choosing one's own moment and mode of death. Historian Carole Straw puts it succinctly: "By definition, whatever one willed freely was honorable—even, and especially, degradation."[70] To die at the end of an excrement-covered stick was not abasement but rather a wry and desperate victory.

Christians in the empire shared with Seneca's German prisoner of war the choice of voluntary death over a compelled death, just as they shared his social standing that made such acts of self-will particularly noteworthy from an elite Roman standpoint. In the Roman empire of the second century, being Christian ensured status paralysis at best, a profound social debasement at worst.[71] There was no prestige to be gained from openly confessing one's belief in Christ—only contempt, suspicion, hostility, or, occasionally, worse. Tertullian notes that by the second century, Christians daily endured the cry "To the lions!"[72] Being openly Christian did not lead to certain death in the amphitheater—one had to work diligently to meet such a fate—but it secured individuals an existence as marginal as it was inexorable.

Christians combated status paralysis or debasement with a number of strategies. First, one could invert or reject traditional, entrenched Roman social values. Thus, the Christian rhetorical strategy of claiming equality in Christ Jesus (as Paul writes of in Gal 3:28) translated into a social macrocosm of inverted statuses: Christians, whether initially slave or freeborn, whether male or female, endeavored to treat one another as equals. Women chose to forgo the social inevitability of marriage and childbirth in order to teach and lead their communities; slaves could regard their owners as brothers, not masters. The result was the construction of liminal communities, communities on the margins necessarily at odds with the values and mores of the Roman state.

Those living in liminal communities had a choice: to break further from mainstream society, or else to embark upon a public relations campaign in order to lessen the conceptual difference between themselves and others. It is fair and accurate to say, generally, that many Christians of the second century walked both paths, choosing either cultural accommodation/assimilation or self-imposed cultural isolation. Indeed, it is also fair and accurate to say that such choices were

---

[69] Seneca, *Ep.* 70.19–21, 23.
[70] Straw 2002, 40.
[71] On Christian social status in the first three centuries, see the classic study Meeks 1992; more recently, Knust 2005; for earlier sociological studies of early Christians, see Gager 1975; Meeks 1983; on status paralysis, Stark 1996.
[72] Tertullian, *Spect.* 27.

rarely so simple; a community might accommodate at times, or to degrees, while seeking to distance or distinguish themselves at other times. Individuals likewise could be inconsistent; thus it was with Justin Martyr, who rejected the trappings of Greco-Roman culture while appearing in public in the rough cloak (τρίβων) of the philosopher.

Christian status inconsistency could also provoke strenuous attempts to gain respectability. To be successful, this respectability had to be performed publicly, before a labile audience likely to be impressed and even profoundly changed by its performance. Martyrdom became the ultimate opportunity to perform this spectacle of respectability. The rules and overall shape of this spectacle, moreover, were necessarily well constrained and delineated by Greco-Roman παιδεία. Catherine Edwards notes that in Roman declamation schools, the "Death of Cato" and other *exempla* of heroic Roman and Greek suicides were "performed" regularly.[73] Whether by the example of the philosopher or the gladiator, when it came to facing death, Christians followed cultural scripts already over a century old. These scripts, furthermore, were immediate, visual, and visceral. In essence, performance of these scripts marked their performers not just as brave or honorable—though the performance of such valued virtues were sure to make an impression on an audience; they were also to elevate the social status of performers as participants in a higher, more rarefied discourse from which, as Christians, they were otherwise excluded.

In the hot sand and stench of blood, Justin watched as Christians stood before the beasts and sung hymns of triumph. They faced death with the steady gaze of those who had accepted their fate with dignity and forbearance. This death, in which the ideal death of the gladiator was identical to the ideal death of the philosopher, greatly impressed Justin, recalling his philosophical training. The resonances between the noble death of the Christian martyr and the death of Socrates ("who was accused of the very same crimes as ourselves") were not lost on Justin.[74] But it was not only the injustice of being persecuted, or worse, that struck Justin; it was, above all, the Christians' preternatural calm and sense of control, of utter freedom or lack of participation in a regime they found to be demonic, that Justin found the most moving. These *living* philosophers—not the schoolhouse wiseacring of the Platonists, Stoics, Cynics, or Epicureans—inspired Justin to face life as a Christian.[75] This control of the passions was "right behavior" at its most sublime. "Fearless of death," they cultivated in Justin an appetite that still confounds us: after witnessing their suffering, Justin knew that he too desired to someday face the beast.

The mastery of the passions—so evident in the steadfast martyrs in the arena who had compelled Justin to embrace the "true" philosophy—was purely Stoic.[76] Carole Straw parses it out for us:

---

[73] Edwards 2007, 156. See also Griffin 1986.
[74] Justin, *2 Apol.* 10.5.
[75] Justin, *2 Apol.* 12.1.
[76] As David Aune (1994) has ably demonstrated, before Christian martyrdom the Jews under Antiochene domination had similarly drawn on the doctrine of controlling the passions, even in the hour of their martyrdom.

The martyr loves honor (*philotimea*). He has generosity (*liberalitas*), freedom (*libertas, eleutheria*), self-control (*sophrosyne*), and the confidence of speaking freely (*parrhesia*). His acts are freely chosen—voluntarily and deliberately (*proairesis, autoproairetos, thelesis*). The martyrs' deeds become noble examples of courage and manliness (*andreia, virtus, fortitudo*).[77]

These are Stoic virtues, and Christian martyrs aimed to create a potent and lasting display of virtuous behavior that their audience would read as such. What remains remarkable is that Justin explicitly rejects Stoic philosophy of the schoolroom as empty philosophizing while being profoundly moved by "lived" Stoic philosophy in Christian guise; performance distinguishes these two facets of παιδεία (though only partly, as public declamations on the "Death of Cato" prove). Here Justin misleads us, since the Christian performance of martyrdom is not quintessentially and uniquely Christian at all, but is merely a Christian enactment of Roman cultural values. That he is moved to "convert" by witnessing Christian control of the passions is ironic.

Like the Stoic *sapiens*, the Christian martyr was a paradigm of ἀπάθεια. Again, Seneca presents the power of the *sapiens* in similar terms:

> *Virtus* is free, inviolable, immovable, unshaken, and so steeled against the blows of chance that it cannot even be bent, much less toppled. It looks straight at the instruments of torture and does not flinch; its expression never changes, whether adversity or prosperity comes into its view.[78]

Both Stoics and Christians could exhibit joy in the face of certain death. The *Passion of Perpetua* emphasizes the joyous assent with which Christians faced their death; Perpetua and her fellow Christians enter the arena singing hymns of triumph.[79] Eusebius's martyrs receive "with joy, laughter and much rejoicing the final sentence of death."[80] Christians embraced the opportunity to showcase their own mastery of the passions, their replacement of vice with virtue. This attitude of "inverse exaltation" would not necessarily have shocked an audience. To the contrary, meeting one's death willingly and joyfully actually reinforced a deeply constructed Roman cultural identity.

5. The Noble Suicide

To end one's life by one's own hand was, in a Roman context, an undeniably estimable display of courage and will. Yet, classical Stoic positions eschewed suicide as imposing one's will against the higher will of Fortuna; one should wait for Nature to release an individual from life.[81] Seneca pushed against this idea,

---

[77] Straw 2002, 44.
[78] Seneca, *Const.* 5.
[79] *Perpetua* 6.1; see also Lactantius, *Inst.* 6.17.
[80] Eusebius, *Hist. eccl.* 8.9.5.
[81] Griffin 1976, 375.

insisting that death provided the "opportunity to withdraw" (*libertas recedendi*).⁸²
In the classical Stoic sense of the word, "freedom" (*libertas*, ἐλευθερία) connoted
freedom from the passions and wrong desires; for Seneca, however, freedom and
death are synonymous: "'Think on death': one who says this instructs us to think
on freedom."⁸³ To those philosophers who reject suicide as contrary to nature,
Seneca comments, "One who says this does not see that he is shutting the gate
to freedom" (*hoc qui dicit, non videt se libertatis viam cludere*), and "One who
has learned to die has unlearned slavery" (*qui mori didicit, servire dedidicit*).⁸⁴ As
Brad Inwood observes, Seneca connects freedom and death through the concept
of agency.⁸⁵ Voluntary death or suicide (*voluntaria mors*) allows the exertion of individual agency even against misfortune: the opportunity to shape, confront, and
withstand an individual's last encounter with pain, suffering, and extinction.

Seneca's emphasis on the free agency of suicide manifests itself in his marked
preoccupation with the death of the statesman and fellow Stoic Cato the Young-
er.⁸⁶ Cato's decision to end his life rather than live under conditions inimical to
his political values struck Seneca as the ultimate valorous death. Early Christian
writers appear to have inherited Seneca's characterization of voluntary death as the
highest form of freedom. As Catherine Edwards observes, Christian martyrdom
would not have developed as it did without the Senecan "turn" toward the idea of
suicide as freedom, nor without the Roman glorification of noble suicide.⁸⁷ Latin
apologetic literature invoked pagan examples of fortitude as inspirational *exempla*
of ideal Christian martyrdoms. Again and again, Christians looked not just to earlier Christians to set examples of "right behavior," but to the virtuous suicides of
pagan "martyrs."⁸⁸ Tertullian lauds the heroic self-sacrifices of men such as Mucius
Scaevola, Heraclitus, Peregrinus, and Regulus, and women such as Dido, Lucretia,
and Cleopatra.⁸⁹ Clement of Alexandria adds to these courageous women Leaena,
Telesilla, and Alcestis.⁹⁰ Seneca, too, favored these *exempla*, drawing on them often
in his work.⁹¹

Although Christian authors deployed such examples of pagan fortitude predominantly to demonstrate how Christian martyrs outdid them, they concurred
with pagans that any voluntary acceptance of death was both virtuous and a stunning display of free agency. Carlin Barton observes,

---

⁸²Seneca, *Ep.* 22.5–6.
⁸³Seneca, *Ep.* 26.10.
⁸⁴Seneca, *Ep.* 70.14; 26.10. One wonders if Seneca is influenced here by Roman law that terms forced suicide *liberum mortis arbitrium*, "Free choice of the form of death."
⁸⁵Inwood 2005, 306.
⁸⁶See, for instance, Seneca, *Prov.* 2.10.
⁸⁷Edwards 2007, 209.
⁸⁸See, besides the examples given here, Minucius Felix, *Oct.* 37.3–6 (CSEL 2:52); Augustine, *Civ.* 5.18; 15–24. On this matter, see Carlson 1948.
⁸⁹Tertullian, *Mart.* 4.1.4–9; *Apol.* 50.7–8.
⁹⁰Clement, *Strom.* 4.19 (GCS 15:300–303).
⁹¹See, for example, *Prov.* 3.9 for the example of Regulus, whom Seneca calls a *documentum fidei* and *documentum patientiae*.

The Romans, like the Greeks, believed that life was a treasure that retained value or power only when expended. . . . The Chosen Death, the generous death, was the extreme renunciation that put a high charge on life; it was the renunciation that enhanced the value of the thing renounced. Moreover, the Chosen Death "sacralized," "electrified," empowered the person or thing or value on which it was spent.[92]

The litany of pagan examples of suicide could be altered at will so as to emphasize different virtues, from manly courage to feminine *pudor*. Note this story from Eusebius, where the death of Lucretia lurks behind Christian women's choice to die rather than to face sexual defilement:

> She exhorted both herself and her daughters that they ought not to submit to listen to even the least whisper of such a thing, and said that to surrender their souls to the slavery of demons was worse than all kinds of death and every form of destruction. So she submitted that to flee to the Lord was the only way of escape from it all. And when they had both agreed to her opinion, and had arranged their garments suitably around them, on coming to the middle of their journey they quietly requested the guards for a little time for retirement, and threw themselves into the river that flowed by. Thus they became their own executioners.[93]

The lesson is clear: as Carole Straw notes, no one is forced to die who dies voluntarily.[94] She observes, "In all these expressions of ultimate commitment, a series of equations exists: volition = honor = death = proof of authenticity."[95] At least in the second century, martyrdom as suicide maintained its connotations of heroic self-sacrifice to one's ideals.[96] Only later, through the influence of Augustine, would suicide become sinful.

6. Conclusion

If we understand Christian martyrdom simply as the desperate last acts of political and social rebellion within the most public of possible forums, we overlook Christians' essential conservatism from the perspective of Roman attitudes toward death. As "children of choice and knowledge," the martyrs of the second century had, in fact, galvanized an essentially philosophical position concerning human freedom in the face of cosmic determinism—humans are essentially free and not subject to the vicissitudes of fate—onto the level of action: they were free enough to recognize that they were not to be conquered by a contingent and imperfect cosmic οἰκονομία, though it could still hold in thrall the bulk of the inhabitants of the empire.

Christians chose martyrdom not because (or not only because) it was rebellion against the state; from another perspective, going peacefully to one's fate was

---

[92] Barton 1994, 47.
[93] Eusebius, *Hist. eccl.* 8.12.3–4.
[94] Straw 2002, 41.
[95] Ibid., 46.
[96] Amundsen 1996, 70–126.

to ultimately accommodate to philosophies of self-control, which themselves had Stoic foundations. Thus, to show control in the amphitheater was to own and embody deeply ingrained Roman models of emotional continence. The martyrs were not only political rebels; they were philosophers, and gladiators, at once. Even the choice to rebel against the empire was, in a sense, scripted and overdetermined. To "rebel" against the extravagant displays of a "demonic" empire, the Christians of our extant martyr acts chose the path of virtue. Yet, those models of virtue open to them were themselves Roman, traditional, and conservative.

Christians chose voluntary death to rebel against empire because such a death was already the way by which a good citizen registered nobility of spirit against the tyranny of the state. Given that most martyrs were not even citizens, a public encounter with pain and death earned them symbolic enfranchisement; there was much to be gained. Gaining status and respectability through voluntary death gave second-century Christians much-needed cultural capital. Not only did martyrdom prove an effective "recruiting" tool, as we have seen in the case of Justin, but also it could potentially garner the very social respectability that Christianity lacked. We should not underestimate the considerable surplus of respectability that came with the assessment from a highly placed Roman, Galen, of Christians as "in self-discipline and self-control . . . not inferior to that of genuine philosophers."[97] At the same time, the danger in martyrdom as a spectacle of respectability is that Christians might go overboard; although σωφροσύνη in the arena could be a dazzling display of virtue, those who zealously rushed headlong toward death displayed a rashness that rendered the inherent nobility of voluntary death merely a vulgar, self-aggrandizing display. Thus, Marcus Aurelius, himself a Stoic, heaped scorn upon Christians who sought a showy and pointless death in the amphitheater.[98] The effectiveness of emotional control in the amphitheater as respectability-building or as cultural capital depended, then, on how successfully a martyr followed Stoic rules of engagement.

So let us return, in the end, to Justin. His eagerness for martyrdom becomes more understandable if we acknowledge the degree to which he felt disaffected with the world around him, a participant within a new order of freedom. He and his contemporaries boasted that they had become citizens in a higher, heavenly world; they no longer needed to be bound by the demonic ties of empire.[99] They belonged to a heavenly πολίτευμα, a word that, as Wayne Meeks notes, was used not for an organized body of citizens but rather for resident aliens lodged in an unaccommodating, hostile society.[100] Justin appealed to Antoninus Pius and Marcus Aurelius as the "truest philosophers" to recognize that they themselves were not masters of their own minds, but had haplessly given in to demonic forces. With his bold statements, he knew that he himself faced arraignment and condemnation *ad bestias*. His attitude was sanguine: "You can kill us," he boasts to Antoninus

---

[97] Galen, as cited by an anonymous Arabic chronicler; see Walzer 1949, 15.
[98] Marcus Aurelius, *Meditations* 11.3.
[99] Justin, *1 Apol.* 11; *Diognetus* 5–6; see also Phil 3:20.
[100] Meeks 1992, 13.

Pius, "but you cannot hurt us."[101] Still, even in the Roman Empire, death did not necessarily come easily to dissenters. It took Justin fifteen years of formal, public grievances before the emperor considered Justin as much of a threat to the stability and peace of the empire as Justin did the emperors.

In the end, Justin got his wish—at least, Christian tradition preserves for us both his unofficial title, "Justin Martyr," and three slightly differing accounts of his martyrdom. Like the other martyrologies of the empire, their value for us as modern readers lies not in their historicity but rather in what in them was imagined by early Christian readers to be an ideal life and death. In some of these accounts, Justin is not beheaded, but like Socrates, he meets his death surely by his own hand—with a draught of hemlock.[102]

Bibliography

Allert, C. D. 2002. *Revelation, Truth, Canon, and Interpretation: Studies in Justin Martyr's Dialogue with Trypho.* Supplements to Vigiliae christianae 64. Leiden: Brill.

Amundsen, D. W. 1996. *Medicine, Society, and Faith in the Ancient and Medieval Worlds.* Baltimore: Johns Hopkins University Press.

Arya, D. 2002. "Fortuna in Imperial Rome: Cult, Art, Text." Ph.D. diss., University of Texas at Austin.

Aune, D. E. 1994. "Mastery of the Passions: Philo, 4 Maccabees, and Earliest Christianity." Pages 125–58 in *Hellenization Revisited: Shaping a Christian Response within the Greco-Roman World.* Edited by W. E. Hellerman. Lanham, Md.: University Press of America.

Barnard, L. 1967. *Justin Martyr: His Life and Thought.* Cambridge: Cambridge University Press.

———. 1997. *Justin: The First and Second Apologies.* Ancient Christian Writers. New York: Paulist Press.

Barton, C. 1993. *The Sorrows of the Ancient Romans: The Gladiator and the Monster.* Princeton, N.J.: Princeton University Press.

———. 1994. "Savage Miracles: the Redemption of Lost Honor in Roman Society and the Sacrament of the Gladiator and Martyr." *Representations* 45:41–71.

Basore, J. W. 1928–1935. *Seneca: Moral Essays.* 3 vols. Loeb Classical Library. London: Heinemann.

Berry, P. 1999. *Correspondence Between Paul and Seneca, A.D. 61–65.* New York: Mellen.

Bobzien, S. 1998. *Determinism and Freedom in Stoic Philosophy.* Oxford: Oxford University Press.

---

[101] Justin, *1 Apol.* 1.
[102] *The Martyrdom of the Holy Martyrs Justin, Chariton, Charites, Pæon, and Liberianus, Who Suffered at Rome* has Justin beheaded; according to Dods (1969), the tradition that Justin took hemlock is Greek.

Bowersock, G. W. 1995. *Martyrdom and Rome*. Cambridge: Cambridge University Press.

Carlson, M. L. 1948. "Pagan Examples of Fortitude in the Latin Christian Apologists." *Classical Philology* 43:93–104.

Castelli, E. A. 2004. *Martyrdom and Memory: Early Christian Culture Making*. New York: Columbia University Press.

Champeaux, J. 1982–1987. *Fortuna: Recherches sur le culte de la Fortune à Rome et dans le monde romain des origines à la mort de César*. Rome: École française de Rome.

Dihle, A. 1982. *The Theory of Will in Classical Antiquity*. Berkeley: University of California Press.

Dillon, J. M. 1986. "Plutarch and Second Century Platonism." Pages 214–29 in *Classical Mediterranean Spirituality: Egyptian, Greek, Roman*. Edited by A. H. Armstrong. World Spirituality: An Encyclopedic History of the Religious Quest 15. New York: Crossroads.

Dods, M. 1969. "Introductory Note to the Martyrdom of Justin Martyr." Page 303 in vol. 1 of *The Ante-Nicene Fathers*, edited by A. Roberts and J. Donaldson. Buffalo, N.Y.: Christian Literature Publishing Company, 1885. Repr., Grand Rapids: Eerdmans.

Droge, A. J. 1995. "The Crown of Immortality: Toward a Redescription of Christian Martyrdom." Pages 155–69 in *Death, Ecstasy, and Other Worldly Journeys*. Edited by J. J. Collins and M. Fishbane. Albany: State University of New York Press.

Droge, A. J., and J. Tabor. 1992. *A Noble Death: Suicide and Martyrdom among Christians and Jews in Antiquity*. San Francisco: HarperSanFrancisco.

Edwards, C. 1999. "The Suffering Body: Philosophy and Pain in Seneca's Letters." Pages 252–68 in *Constructions of the Classical Body*. Edited by J. I. Porter. Ann Arbor: University of Michigan Press.

———. 2007. *Death in Ancient Rome*. New Haven: Yale University Press.

Engberg-Pedersen, T. 2006. "Self-Sufficiency and Power: Divine and Human Agency in Epictetus and Paul." Pages 117–39 in *Divine and Human Agency in Paul and His Cultural Environment*. Edited by J. M. G. Barclay and S. J. Gathercole. Library of New Testament Studies 335. London: T & T Clark.

Falls, T. 2003. *Justin Martyr's Dialogue with Trypho*. Washington, D.C.: Catholic University of America Press.

Foucault, M. 1980. *Politics, Philosophy, Culture: Interviews and Other Writings, 1977–1984*. Edited by C. Gordon. Translated by A. Sheridan et al. New York: Pantheon.

———. 1994. "Technologies of the Self." Pages 223–51 in *Ethics: Subjectivity and Truth*. Edited by P. Rabinow. Essential Works of Foucault 1. New York: New Press.

Fox, R. L. 1995. *Pagans and Christians*. San Francisco: HarperSanFrancisco.

Frede, D. 2003. "Stoic Determinism." Pages 179–205 in *The Cambridge Companion to the Stoics*. Edited by B. Inwood. Cambridge: Cambridge University Press.

Frend, W. H. C. 1965. *Martyrdom and Persecution in the Early Church: A Study of Conflict from the Maccabees to Donatus*. Oxford: Oxford University Press.

Gager, J. G. 1975. *Kingdom and Community: The Social World of Early Christianity.* Englewood Cliffs, N.J.: Prentice-Hall.
Griffin, M. T. 1976. *Seneca: A Philosopher in Politics.* Oxford: Clarendon Press.
———. 1986. "Philosophy, Cato and Roman Suicide." *Greece and Rome* 33:64–77, 192–202.
Gummere, R. M. 1917–1925. *Lucius Annaeus Seneca: Moral Epistles.* 3 vols. Loeb Classical Library. Cambridge, Mass.: Harvard University Press.
Inwood, B., ed. 2003. *The Cambridge Companion to the Stoics.* Cambridge: Cambridge University Press.
———. 2005. *Reading Seneca: Stoic Philosophy at Rome.* New York: Oxford University Press.
Knust, J. W. 2005. *Abandoned to Lust: Sexual Slander and Ancient Christianity.* New York: Columbia University Press.
Lattimore, R. 1962. *Themes in Greek and Latin Epitaphs.* Urbana: University of Illinois Press.
Lyman, R. 1993. *Cosmology and Christology.* Oxford: Clarendon Press.
Marcovich, M., ed. 1997. *Iustini Martyris dialogues cum Tryphone.* Patristische Texte und Studien 47, Berlin: de Gruyter.
Meeks, W. A. 1983. *The First Urban Christians: The Social World of the Apostle Paul.* New Haven: Yale University Press.
———. 1992. *The Origins of Christian Morality: The First Two Centuries.* New Haven: Yale University Press.
Montini, P. 1985. "Elementi di filosofia stoica in S. Giustino." *Aquinas* 28:457–76.
Munier, C. 2006. *Saint Justin: Apologie pour les chrétiens.* Paris: Cerf.
Musurillo, H. 1972. *The Acts of the Christian Martyrs.* Oxford: Clarendon Press.
Riddle, D. W. 1931. *The Martyrs: A Study in Social Control.* Chicago: University of Chicago Press.
Rist, J. M. 1969. *Stoic Philosophy.* Cambridge: Cambridge University Press.
Salles, R. 2005. *The Stoics on Determinism and Compatibilism.* Burlington, Vt.: Ashgate.
Schneemelcher, W., ed. 1992. *New Testament Apocrypha.* Rev. ed. 2 vols. Louisville: Westminster John Knox Press.
Seeley, D. 1990. *The Noble Death: Graeco-Roman Martyrology and Paul's Concept of Salvation.* Journal for the Study of the New Testament: Supplement Series 28. Sheffield: JSOT Press.
Spanneut, M. 1957. *Le Stoïcisme des pères de l'église de Clément de Rome à Clément d'Alexandrie.* Patristica Sorbonensia 1. Paris: Seuil.
Stark, R. 1996. *The Rise of Christianity: A Sociologist Reconsiders History.* Princeton: Princeton University Press.
Ste. Croix, G. E. M. de. 1963. "Why Were the Early Christians Persecuted?" *Past and Present* 26:6–38.
Straw, C. 2002. "'A Very Special Death': Christian Martyrdom in Its Classical Context." Pages 39–57 in *Sacrificing the Self: Perspectives in Martyrdom and Religion.* Edited by M. Cormack. Oxford: Oxford University Press.
Tanner, R. G. 1985. "Martyrdom in Saint Ignatius of Antioch and the Stoic View of Suicide." *Studia patristica* 16:201–5.

Van Winden, J. C. M. 1971. *An Early Christian Philosopher: Justin Martyr's Dialogue with Trypho*. Philosophia Patrum 1. Leiden: Brill.
Veyne, P. 2003. *Seneca: The Life of a Stoic*. New York: Routledge.
von Arnim, H. F. A., ed. 1964. *Stoicorum Veterum Fragmenta*. 4 vols. Leipzig: Teubner, 1903–1924. Repr., Stuttgart: Teubner.
Walzer, R. 1949. *Galen on Jews and Christians*. London: Oxford University Press.
Wirszubski, C. 1950. *Libertas as a Political Ideal at Rome during the Late Republic and Early Principate*. Cambridge: Cambridge University Press.

10

A STOIC READING OF THE *GOSPEL OF MARY*: THE MEANING OF "MATTER" AND "NATURE" IN *GOSPEL OF MARY* 7.1–8.11

Esther de Boer
Theological University of Kampen

The second-century *Gospel of Mary* is generally believed to belong to a Gnostic context, in which Christians were convinced that they must be freed from their attachment to the material world to be able to open up to the divine.[1] At first, scholars simply assumed the Gnostic character of the *Gospel of Mary*, since it was found in a codex that contained other Gnostic writings.[2] Later scholars have employed more specific arguments in favor of a Gnostic character of the *Gospel of Mary*. They refer to, for instance, the postmortem ascent of the soul beyond archontic powers, the dissolution of matter, the idea of being ill, of the Son of Man inside, of being made human, of Mary not being shaken, of silence and rest as purposes, of the liberation from the fetter of sleep, and of the putting on of the perfect human being.[3]

A number of scholars, however, reject the Gnostic character based on the view that all these elements occur also in the broader context of Hellenism, and that the central feature of Gnosticism—the view that the cosmos is created by an evil or

---

[1] I wish to express my special gratitude to Paula Pumplin for her comments on my use of the English language.

[2] For a first overview of scholarly research on the *Gospel of Mary*, see Tardieu and Dubois 1986, 99–107. Thus far, two third-century Greek papyri have been found (P.Ryl. 263; P.Oxy. 3525) that contain some parts of the *Gospel of Mary*. A late fourth- or early fifth-century Coptic version of nineteen pages, from which the pages 1–6 and 11–14 are missing, was found in a codex (BG 8502) that also contains the *Apocryphon of John*, the *Sophia of Jesus Christ*, and the *Act of Peter*. For a discussion of the nature of the four writings, see de Boer 2004b, 52–56. Photos of the Greek and Coptic texts of the *Gospel of Mary* as well as a critical edition can be found in Tuckett 2007, 86–118. For other critical comments on the texts, see Till and Schenke 1972; Wilson and MacRae 1979; Pasquier 1983, 30–47; Lührmann 1988; Mohri 2000, 253–65.

[3] See Marjanen 1996, 94n1; Petersen 1999, 60, 134n194; Hartenstein 2000, 132–33.

ignorant demiurge—is missing.[4] Some of them would not characterize the *Gospel of Mary* as Gnostic because of the conviction that there was "no such thing as Gnosticism."[5] Others argue that the *Gospel of Mary* must be situated in the gray zone between Christianity and Gnosticism[6] or in the prophetic and ascetic movement of the early church.[7]

In the debate about the character of the *Gospel of Mary*, one thing is widely taken for granted: underlying this text are a strong dualism of spirit and matter as well as a Gnostic or Middle Platonic view of the utter transcendence of the supreme God. In this essay, I argue that this interpretation does not fit *Gos. Mary* 7.1–8.11, and I explore the possibility that the *Gospel of Mary*'s use of the words "matter" and "nature" is at home in a more monistic Stoic and Jewish context, in which there is one God, who is the benevolent creative power that shaped the world.

1. "Matter" and "Nature" in the *Gospel of Mary*

The words "matter" and "nature" occur on the first two extant pages of the *Gospel of Mary* (7.1–8.11). On these pages the Savior answers the disciples' questions about the fate of matter and the sin of the world. The context of these questions is unclear because the introductory pages of the *Gospel of Mary* are missing and the first extant question is in the seventh page. Here follows a translation of the Coptic text. Italics are used to show how the words "matter" and "nature" occur.

> [...] will *[mat]ter* then be de[stroy]ed or not?" The Savior said, "*All nature*, all that has been moulded, all that has been brought into being exists in and with each other, and will be unloosened again up to their own root, since the *nature of matter* is unloosened up to what belongs to *her nature* alone. He who has ears to hear, let him hear." Peter said to him, "Since you have told us everything, tell us this also: What is the sin of the world?" The Savior said, "Sin does not exist, but you are the ones who sin when you do things which are like the *nature of adultery*: that is called sin. Because of this the Good came into your midst, to those who belong to *all nature*, in order to restore *nature up to her root*." Then he continued and said, "That is why you become sick and die, for [...]. [He who] understands, let him understand. *[Mat]ter* [brought forth] passion that, since it proceeded from *something contrary to nature*, has no form. From then on confusion exists in the whole body. That is why I said to you, 'Be fully assured and do not

---

[4] De Boer 1997, 93; 2004a; 2004b, 27–35. Marjanen (1996, 94n1) once held that the *Gospel of Mary* is a Gnostic text, but later (2002, 32n3) he changed his mind. Tuckett (2007, 146), however, comparing *Gos. Mary* 8.1–6 with the *Apocryphon of John*, concludes that the *Gospel of Mary* does contain "cryptic references" to a Gnostic version of a creation myth. Tuckett (2007, 175–80) also suggests that the powers that the soul encounters in *Gos. Mary* 15.1–17.7 show similarities with powers belonging to Yaldabaoth.

[5] King 2003b, 156 (cf. King 2003a). King (1994, 629n10) originally argued that because there is no evidence of a fully developed Gnostic myth behind the text, the *Gospel of Mary* should be interpreted without importing Gnostic myth.

[6] Schröter 1999, 178–88, esp. 178n2, 186–87, based on an interpretation of the "Son of Man" imagery in the *Gospel of Mary*.

[7] Morard 2001, 155–71, esp. 160, 171, based on *Gos. Mary* 9.13–19.

be persuaded, since you are already persuaded in the presence of the *various forms of nature*. He who has ears to hear, let him hear.'" (*Gos. Mary* 7.1–8.11 [my translation])

Through the threefold repetition "He who has ears/he who understands/he who has ears . . . let him hear/let him understand/let him hear," the author urges the reader not to give up, but really try to understand. The author seems to be aware that the text is relating something new and unexpected ("he who has ears/he who understands": do we have ears, do we understand?) and at the same time emphasizes the importance of understanding (beware: do hear, and do understand).

Apart from difficulties in translation,[8] the main problem in the text is the exact meaning of "nature." The word appears eight times. There is "nature" and "something contrary to nature"; "nature" has a root; "nature" has various forms; one can speak of "all nature" mixed with everything that exists and "all nature" to which the disciples belong; and there is "the nature of adultery" and "the nature of matter."

What is one to make of this? And what does this teaching reveal about the *Gospel of Mary*'s view on "matter"?

2. Anne Pasquier on Gnostic Myth and Stoic Language

In an article on *Gos. Mary* 7.1–8.11 published in 1981, Anne Pasquier argues that by the repetition of the word "nature," the author obliges the reader to put the use of the word in relief and to understand the new paradigm that the author is offering.[9] She suggests that the *Gospel of Mary* uses three different meanings of "nature": (1) nature as a created entity (all nature, everything that exists); (2) nature as essence (the nature of matter and of adultery); (3) most importantly, nature as a superior principle (all nature to which the disciples belong, nature up to her root, something contrary to nature and various forms of nature).[10]

In Pasquier's view, nature as a superior principle is contrasted to the nature (the essence) of matter. Those in whom the superior principle of nature is present are dominated by their mixture with the material world. Although mixture is the only form of existence in the material world, for those who belong to the superior principle of nature, this mixture is equivalent to adultery. Originally androgynous, the soul prostitutes itself by entering into the body. This adultery is contrary to nature and causes passion and confusion. The Good has come to separate the superior principle of nature from the material world and to enable those who belong to the superior principle of nature to find their original unity with their spiritual images (the forms of nature).

Pasquier's complicated and ingenious reading of *Gos. Mary* 7.1–8.11 is based on the general conviction that the *Gospel of Mary* is a Gnostic writing. The great merit of her view is that she endeavors to explain in detail the use of the word

---

[8] For instance, the translation of *Gos. Mary* 8.7–10. For a discussion of the various possibilities that are suggested, see de Boer 2004, 35–49.

[9] Pasquier 1981, 390.

[10] Ibid., 397.

"nature" in *Gos. Mary* 7.1–8.11. In order to understand the use of the word "nature" in *Gos. Mary* 7.1–8.11, she argues, one must detect the author's own particular Gnostic language.[11] According to Pasquier, the author of the *Gospel of Mary* uses traditional materials (New Testament and philosophical language) and artistically reorganizes them in order to reveal to the reader a new way of thinking: a specifically Gnostic cosmology and eschatology.[12]

The most important contribution of Pasquier's article is that she points to Stoic philosophy as a means to understand the language of *Gos. Mary* 7.1–8.11. In Pasquier's view, the author of the *Gospel of Mary* uses in particular the Stoic categories of the Good/the Logos and of the superior principle of nature to be able to write about the Gnostic Savior, whose role is to liberate the divine sparks of the transcendent God from their imprisonment in the material world.[13]

Following Pasquier's article and later commentary,[14] most scholars writing about the *Gospel of Mary* acknowledge in one way or another the use of Stoic language in the first extant part of the *Gospel of Mary*, especially in the discussion about matter and dissolution.[15] Thanks to Pasquier, I have become convinced that the author of the *Gospel of Mary* indeed uses the Stoic concept of nature to reveal a new paradigm. But what is this paradigm?

3. Two Problems

One must agree with Pasquier that all eight uses of the word "nature" in the *Gospel of Mary* cannot have the same meaning. At least in the expression "the nature of adultery" it might refer to essence. I am not convinced, however, by her interpretation of the expression "every nature" (ϕycic nim) in *Gos. Mary* 7.3, 18–19.

The first occurrence of the expression is in *Gos. Mary* 7.3, in the Savior's answer in about the fate of matter.[16] Most commentators, and with them Pasquier, believe that ϕycic nim here is referring to the material world in contrast to the spiritual one. When the words ϕycic nim occur again in *Gos. Mary* 7.18–19, where the Savior assures his disciples that the Good came into their midst, "to those who belong to ϕycic nim, in order to restore ϕycic up to her root," the same commentators who interpret the first ϕycic nim as referring to matter interpret the second ϕycic nim as referring to spiritual nature.[17]

---

[11] Ibid., 391.
[12] Ibid., 390–91.
[13] Ibid., 397–99.
[14] Pasquier 1983. Most scholars react to her commentary, which does not treat *Gos. Mary* 7.1–8.11 in as much detail as her article does.
[15] King 1994, 603; 2003, 44; Tuckett 2007, 137–40.
[16] See Till and Schenke 1972, 27; Pasquier 1981, 391–92; 1983, 50; Tardieu 1984, 226; King 1995, 603; 2003, 45–46; Tuckett 2007, 142–43.
[17] Till and Schenke 1972, 27, 63; Pasquier 1981, 391–93; 1983, 53; Tardieu 1984, 226; King 1995, 604; 2003, 50–51; Tuckett 2007, 140, 142–43.

In addition, Pasquier, as most other scholars, interprets "nature" in the expression "nature of matter" and "her nature alone" as essence.[18] She says that the expression "nature of matter" in the sense of "essence of matter" represents substance.[19] Christopher Tuckett, who finds Pasquier's discussion of the two natures "broadly convincing," adds that in addition to the various meanings of the word "nature," the word "root" is used in different ways.[20] In the first occurrence it is a plural, and in the second occurrence a singular form of the word. The translation of *Gos. Mary* 7.3–7 and 7.18–20 would then be:

> *All nature*, all that has been molded, all that has been brought into being exists in and with each other, and will be unloosened again up to *their own roots*, since the *essence of matter* is unloosened up to what belongs to *her essence alone*. (*Gos. Mary* 7.3–8)

> The Good came into your midst, to those who belong to *all nature*, in order to restore nature up to her root. (*Gos. Mary* 7.18–20)

In this interpretation, the two instances in which "all nature" occurs seem to speak about two different worlds: the world of matter and the world of nature.

Although most scholars interpret or translate the first occurrence of "root" as a plural, in both cases it is, grammatically speaking, a singular noun.[21] Pasquier explains her interpretation by arguing that the first ⲫⲩⲥⲓⲥ ⲛⲓⲙ must be interpreted in a material way because the question is about matter alone ("will matter then be destroyed or not?"), and because in the answer, all that has been formed (ⲡⲗⲁⲥⲙⲁ ⲛⲓⲙ) and all that has been brought into being (ⲕⲧⲓⲥⲓⲥ ⲛⲓⲙ) also refer to the material world.[22] This explanation, however, does not justify the contradictory interpretation. Clearly, the question is about matter, but is that also the case with the answer? The Savior's answer to a question can be quite unexpected, as can be seen on the same page, when the second question is about the content of the sin of the world and the Savior answers that sin does not exist (*Gos. Mary* 7.12–13).

When one translates "nature" as nature and "root" as root and then again examines the two instances where the expression "all nature" occurs, they do not seem to contradict each other.

> *All nature*, all that has been molded, all that has been brought into being exists in and with each other, and will be unloosened again up *to their own root*, since the *nature of matter* is unloosened up to what belongs to *her nature alone*. (*Gos. Mary* 7.3–8)

> The Good came into your midst, to those who belong to *all nature*, in order to restore nature up to her root. (*Gos. Mary* 7.18–20)

If one interprets nature in these sentences in all five instances as the superior principle of nature, then there are not two contradictory worlds. On the contrary,

---

[18] Pasquier 1981, 397.
[19] Pasquier 1983, 51.
[20] Tuckett 2007, 142n20.
[21] See Till 1978, 100. Tuckett (2007, 142n20) argues that ⲧⲟⲩⲛⲟⲩⲛⲉ also, grammatically speaking, means "their roots." However, "their roots" more likely would have been ⲛⲟⲩⲛⲟⲩⲛⲉ.
[22] Pasquier 1983, 50n7.

the two instances where "all nature" occurs seem to complement each other. In both instances the emphasis is on the fate of all nature and the root of nature; nature will be unloosened/restored up to her root.

Why, then, speak of two contradictory worlds? What is the underlying argument for such a translation? There is only one argument: the presupposition that the text must reveal a Gnostic view on the material world. There is one major objection: why translate the same expression "all nature" in closely connected sentences in totally contradictory ways, when a more straightforward reading also seems possible?

Although Karen King does not presuppose a Gnostic myth behind the *Gospel of Mary*, she nevertheless also interprets the expression "all nature" in a contradictory way and distinguishes between the spiritual and the material worlds. She does so because of her conviction that *Gos. Mary* 7 is about Platonic thought. Referring to the Platonic view as described by Cicero, she argues that in the first sentences of *Gos. Mary* 7 the Platonic character of thinking in the *Gospel of Mary* is already evident.[23] Cicero writes,

> But they [the Platonists] hold that underlying all things is a substance called "matter," entirely formless and devoid of all "quality" ... and that out of it all things have been formed and produced, so that this matter can in its totality receive all things and undergo every sort of transformation throughout every part of it, and in fact even suffers dissolution, not into nothingness, but into its own parts. (*Acad. post.* 1.27)[24]

In this quotation Cicero recounts Varro's discussion of the book of Antiochus of Ascalon on physics. Anthony Long, in his study on Hellenistic philosophy, especially Stoicism, describes Antiochus's particular stance on Platonism. Although Antiochus claimed to be an Academic, most of his doctrines conform to Stoic thought, which Antiochus viewed as only a correction on Platonism, not a new system.[25] When Long writes that "Antiochus' philosophy of nature is more Stoic than anything else," he refers to exactly the same passage as King does.[26]

Clearly, the contradictory interpretation of "all nature" in the *Gospel of Mary* is not forced on us: *Gos. Mary* 7.1–19 might be neither Gnostic nor necessarily Platonic. Nor is the text meant to be confusing or esoteric and to be understood only by insiders. This is clear from the emphasis in the *Gospel of Mary* on the importance of the proclamation of the gospel (*Gos. Mary* 8.21–22; 18.14–21).[27] Mary also willingly shares with the others what she alone knows (*Gos. Mary* 10.8). When the text is meant to be understandable, one would expect ⲫⲨⲤⲒⲤ ⲚⲒⲘ in both instances so intimately connected to mean the same.

Another problem in Pasquier's article on *Gos. Mary* 7.1–8.11 is the interpretation of *Gos. Mary* 8.1–4. Most commentators insist that matter is the cause of

---

[23] King 1994, 603; 2003, 45.
[24] Translation, Rackham 1979.
[25] Long 1974, 222–29.
[26] Long 1974, 224. Long refers to Cicero, *Acad. post.* 1.26–30.
[27] De Boer 2004, 56–57.

passion.[28] In this reading of *Gos. Mary* 8.2-4, ⲟⲩⲡⲁⲣⲁⲫⲩⲥⲓⲥ in 8.4, which can be translated as an adjective (something contrary to nature) as well as a noun (an opposite nature), explains the nature of ⲑⲩⲗⲏ ("matter") in 8.2. In this reading, because matter has brought forth passion, and passion proceeds from "something contrary to nature," matter and this "something contrary to nature" must be one and the same in both instances. And, indeed, in a Middle Platonic and Gnostic dualistic view, the material world is contrary to the spiritual world. In this view, whereas the union with the spiritual world brings forth the good, the union with the material world brings forth the bad. In such an interpretation of *Gos. Mary* 8.2-4, the disciples must be freed from their attachment to the material world (*Gos. Mary* 7.13-16).

A more straightforward reading of *Gos. Mary* 8.2-4, however, seems to be that matter brings forth passion because passion has been generated by "something contrary to nature." Matter is acted upon by "something contrary to nature" and thus brings forth passion. Pasquier solves this problem by adding an extra word, "union": "matter has brought forth a passion which has no Image, since it has come from a (union) contrary to nature."[29] In Pasquier's view, matter as such is not contrary to nature, but the union between spirit and matter is. However, the word "union" is not found in the Coptic text.

Is it possible to find an interpretation of "nature" and "matter" that would fit the more straightforward readings of both *Gos. Mary* 7.3, 18-19 and *Gos. Mary* 8.2-4? I believe that there is, if one adheres to the view that the *Gospel of Mary* uses not only Stoic language, but Stoic philosophy as well.

4. Stoic Philosophy on Matter, Nature, Mixture, and Dissolution

In Stoic philosophy there is no contrast between the spiritual world and the material world. Everything that exists has a body, but although matter is the substance of the entire cosmos, it does not exist in itself. Calcidius explains:

> Zeno says that this very substance is finite and that it is the one common substance of everything which exists. It is also divisible and continuously subject to change. Its parts are changed, but they do not perish so as to be destroyed from existing into nothing. But as the case with the innumerable different shapes of wax as well, so he thinks there will be no form or shape or any quality at all intrinsic to the matter which is the basis of all things; yet it is always united and inseparably connected with some quality or other. And since equally without origin or perishing, because it does not arise from

---

[28] Till and Schenke 1972, 27; Pasquier 1983, 54; Tardieu 1984, 76, 227; King 1995, 362; 2003, 50-51; Marjanen 1996, 94n1; Hartenstein 2000, 129.

[29] Pasquier 1981, 390; Pasquier 1983, 33, 54: "La matière engendre une passion qui ne possède pas l'Image puisqu'elle est issue d'une (union) contre nature." Tuckett (2007, 146), although he states that passion came forth from something or someone contrary to nature, also speaks of "an act that is out of keeping with the proper ordering of existence," referring to the Gnostic motif of Wisdom bringing forth an offspring without the consent of her consort.

something non-existent and will not perish into nothing, it does not lack breath and vitality from eternity, to set it in motion rationally, sometimes in its entirety, at other times in respect of its parts. (Calcidius, *In Timaeum* 292)[30]

Matter is always intertwined with a pneumatic force ("breath and vitality from eternity").[31] This pneumatic force is called Pneuma, Logos, Zeus, but also Nature, since in Stoicism God and the divinity of Nature are one and the same. Nature is not a mere mechanical force, but rather a living and leading deity, a shaping power in the cosmos as well as in human lives.[32]

As Seneca says, "Matter is inert, a thing which is available for everything, but which will be dormant unless something moves it." The active principle is the pneumatic force identified as "reason which shapes matter and moves it whithersoever it wishes and fashions from it products of different kinds" (*Ep.* 65.2).[33]

It is through mixture that reason, Nature, creates and arranges all for the good of the whole: the pneumatic force is mixed with matter and is the seminal principle in the world using matter for the successive stages of creation.[34] It brings about the coherence of a stone, the structure of a plant, the soul of an animal as well as the mind of human beings.[35] They all have their own "nature," but related to and governed by Nature itself.[36]

The idea that Nature as an intelligent entity governs the cosmos is a fundamental concept in Stoic philosophy. To this philosophy also belongs the antithesis of living according to Nature and living contrary to Nature. Humankind is endowed with reason in order to choose life according to Nature over and above life contrary to Nature.[37]

Finally, to Stoic philosophy belongs the thought that at certain moments everything that exists dissolves again into Nature, the designing fire.[38] The conflagration is activated by the sun and brings a state of rest. As Seneca says, "At the time when the world is dissolved and the gods have been blended into one, when nature comes to a stop for a while; he [Zeus] reposes in himself given over to his thoughts" (*Ep.* 9.16).[39]

---

[30] Translation, Long and Sedley 1987, 269.

[31] Long 1974, 147–54. The Stoics are, however, not to be seen as "materialists." Long argues that "Stoics are better described as vitalists" (1974, 154). Matter and the active shaping principle can be drawn apart only for the purpose of conceptual analysis (Steinmetz 1994, 686; Long and Sedley 1987 1:271).

[32] For example, Diogenes Laertius, *Vit. phil.* 7.135.

[33] Quoted in Long 1974, 154.

[34] For example, Diogenes Laertius, *Vit. phil.* 7.135–136, 142; Aëtius, *De placita* 1.7.33; Alexander of Aphrodisias, *Mixt.* 225.1–2. See Long and Sedley 1987 1:270–74; also Todd 1976, 36–49, 70–72.

[35] Long 1974, 156, referring to *SVF* 2.441, 448, 716.

[36] Long 1974, 148, referring to *SVF* 2.937, 549, 1211, 1132–1133, 913; *SVF* 1.158, 176; *SVF* 3.323.

[37] Long 1974, 182, referring to *SVF* 1.566 and Seneca, *Ep.* 120.4.

[38] For example, Eusebius, *Praep. ev.* 15.14.2; 15.18.2. See Long and Sedley 1987, 1:275–79.

[39] See ibid., 1:277.

All these notions—the divinity of Nature, the mixture of Nature and matter as the essence of the harmonious cosmos, one's potential to act according to or contrary to Nature, and the expected dissolution of the world—are important parts of Stoic philosophy.

5. Only a Resemblance to Stoic Philosophy?

Although the elements of matter, nature, mixture, and dissolution as well as the antithesis between nature and contrary to nature are present in *Gos. Mary* 7.1–8.11, Pasquier argues that the *Gospel of Mary* uses Stoic language in a way that allows only a vague resemblance with Stoic philosophy.[40] In Pasquier's opinion, it is clear from the very beginning of *Gos. Mary* 7 that there is a major difference with Stoicism, because in *Gos. Mary* 7 there is a material world that will dissolve and a spiritual world that will be saved by "the Good."

Pasquier acknowledges that Nature in Stoicism was equated with divinity, and that, being identical with the Good and the Logos, it holds the cosmos together.[41] Yet, in the *Gospel of Mary*, Pasquier does not equate "nature," but only "the Good," with the Stoic Logos.[42] In the *Gospel of Mary* this Logos does not have the task of keeping the whole cosmos together, as Logos/Nature has in Stoic philosophy.[43] In the *Gospel of Mary* the Good/the Logos exclusively liberates the superior principle of nature, because only this nature originally belongs to the heavenly Good.[44] Also, as we have seen, according to Pasquier and others, the mixture of things in the *Gospel of Mary* is viewed as a mixture of material elements in contrast to spiritual nature. This is very different from a Stoic mixture of Nature and matter. In this Gnostic interpretation, the Savior in the *Gospel of Mary* has come to save not all (material) nature (*Gos. Mary* 7.3), but rather all (spiritual) nature (*Gos. Mary* 7.18–19).[45]

But what if a contemporary reader of the second-century *Gospel of Mary* was steeped in the thoughts of Stoic philosophy? What if the mixture of things in the *Gos. Mary* 7.1–5 was interpreted in a Stoic way as a harmonious mixture of Nature and matter? What if a reader believed that matter does not exist alone but is inert and changes only when acted upon by Nature? In a Stoic interpretation "all nature" would in both instances (*Gos. Mary* 7.3 and 7.18–19) refer to Nature as intertwined with matter. Furthermore, in Stoic philosophy it is obvious that

---

[40] Pasquier 1981, 397.
[41] Ibid.
[42] Ibid., 394–95.
[43] For an understanding of the relation between Logos and Nature, see Long 1974, 148–49. As the governing principle of all things, Nature is equivalent to Logos. But, although all things are mixtures of nature and matter, only human beings possess reason (Logos) as a natural faculty.
[44] As a consequence, in contrast to Long 1974, Pasquier never writes "nature" with a capital letter, but only the Good and the Logos. See Pasquier 1981, 394, 395, 397, 399, 400.
[45] Pasquier 1981, 394.

passive matter does not bring something forth by itself but must be acted upon by an active principle (*Gos. Mary* 8.2–4). Hence, the two problems resulting from a Gnostic or Middle Platonic interpretation mentioned above would be avoided.

The question inevitably arises whether a Stoic interpretation also creates new difficulties. The most serious problem is the fact that the Savior presents the cosmos not as a harmonious unity but rather as a "whole body" in confusion (*Gos. Mary* 8.2–6). In a Stoic context, "body" refers to the human body as well as the cosmos. For a reader acquainted with Stoic thought, a cosmos in confusion would be a foreign concept, as would be the belief that a Savior is needed, since in the Stoic view the cosmos is in harmony, and in the Stoic dissolution of things the world dissolves through Nature's cessation.

Also new is the concept of following the nature of adultery (*Gos. Mary* 7.15–16) instead of the Stoic concept of living contrary to Nature. Clearly, the *Gospel of Mary* is not a Stoic document. I agree with Pasquier that the author uses traditional Stoic views to reveal a new insight, but it may be that this insight is different from the one that she and others presuppose.

Although the idea that the whole cosmos is in confusion is definitely a non-Stoic notion, passion bringing about confusion (*Gos. Mary* 8.2–7) is a very familiar Stoic idea. Passion is an important cause of misjudgments, and misjudgments are at the heart of the Stoic explanation of the experience of evil versus the belief in the cosmos as being harmonious and arranged all through for the good of the whole. The experience of both cosmic and moral evil, according to the Stoics, is essentially based on misjudgments. Even passion itself is seen as a misjudgment.[46] In this Stoic concept the origin of evil remains an embarrassing problem.[47]

It should be noted that passion in Stoic philosophy is not to be confused with sexual desire or with emotions. Passion is, instead, a general, overpowering, unhealthy state of mind. It is the source of all unhappiness, the four primary passions being appetite, pleasure, fear, and distress.[48] Seneca asserts that floods of tears, sexual arousal, heavy breathing, and the like are but bodily drives. Passion consists of surrendering one's mind to these drives and allowing oneself to assent to them.[49] The Stoic reader recognizes this in the *Gospel of Mary* when the disciples cry and give in to their fear (*Gos. Mary* 9.6–11). They allow passion to take over. Mary also starts to cry, but instead of giving in to her emotional reaction to Peter, she tries to bring him to reason (*Gos. Mary* 18.1–5).

---

[46] Pasquier (1981, 400n41) refers to Aëtius 1.3.25 (*SVF* 1.85, which she quotes as von Arnim I, 24, 11) for the view that, according to Stoic philosophy, matter is the cause of passion (αἴτιος τοῦ πάσχειν). But Tuckett (2007, 143n26) rightly argues that the verb here refers not to passion but rather to the passive role of matter, in contrast to the active role of god (αἴτιος τοῦ ποιεῖν). The same contrast occurs in the parallel quotation of Diogenes Laertius, *Vit. phil.* 7.134.1, in which god is said to be active (τὸ ποιοῦν) and matter to be passive (τὸ πάσχον). See also the translation of this text in Long and Sedley 1987, 1:268.

[47] Kidd 1971, 206.

[48] See, for example, Stobaeus, *Anth.* 2.7.10b (= 2.90.19–91.9 W-H) as quoted in Long and Sedley 1987, 1:412. For an overview of Stoic thought on passion, see Long and Sedley 1987, 1:410–23.

[49] Seneca, *Ira* 2.3.1–2.4.

According to Stoic philosophy, sickness is one of the things that occur when one allows passion to take command of one's lifestyle.[50] In the *Gospel of Mary* the occurrence of sickness is explained not by passion but rather by following "the nature of adultery." This may remind the Stoic reader of the notion of living contrary to nature.

Posidonius, and also Epictetus and especially Roman Stoics of his time, refer to a divine power within, a strength that enables one to choose daily for reason over passion.[51] The Stoic reader recognizes this in the *Gospel of Mary* when the Savior asserts that the Son of Man is within (*Gos. Mary* 8.15–19), and that the disciples can bring forth his peace, in contrast to the confusion that passion brings. The Stoic reader would, however, detect a non-Stoic explanation of the origin of passion.

6. The Origin of Passion in the *Gospel of Mary*

Whereas Nature has forms, passion, according to the *Gospel of Mary*, has no form. The Savior explains this by pointing to passion's origin: matter has brought forth passion. A Stoic reader would not interpret these words in the sense that matter by itself brought forth passion, since matter is passive and inert. According to Stoic philosophy, matter is changed into various forms by the pneumatic power of Nature. In the *Gospel of Mary* matter brings forth something that is without form: passion. Passion is without form because it does not originate in divine Nature.

As we saw earlier, the straightforward reading of *Gos. Mary* 8.2–4 points to a combination of matter and "something contrary to Nature" as responsible for the birth of passion, resulting in an unstable cosmos. In this reading of *Gos. Mary* 8.2–4, matter and "something contrary to Nature" are not one and the same thing, as most scholars argue; rather, "something contrary to Nature" is a separate entity.

In a metaphorical sense, matter, like a mother, has given birth (ⲭⲡⲟ) to a child called "passion." As we already noted, in Stoic philosophy God/Nature is compared to a sperm. He/it is the seminal principle of the world, making matter serviceable to himself/itself for the successive stages of the harmonious and orderly creation. By contrast, in the *Gospel of Mary*, passion brings confusion in the whole body since the origin (ⲉⲓ ⲉⲃⲟⲗ ϩⲛ) of this product is "something contrary to Nature," instead of Nature.[52]

In the Stoic monistic view there is no cosmic power contrary to Nature.[53] Nature alone exists. In Stoic philosophy one can only act contrary to Nature. Allowing oneself to be guided by passion is, for instance, acting contrary to nature

---

[50] For example, Stobaeus, *Anth.* 2.7.10e (= 2.93.1–13 W-H).

[51] For Posidonius, see Galen, *PHP* 448.11–12; Epictetus, *Diss.* 2.8.11–14; Seneca, *Ep.* 41.2. See also Sandbach 1975, 174; Sharples 1996, 128–29.

[52] For ⲭⲡⲟ in the sense of "giving birth," see Crum 1939, 779a. The male origin of a child is mostly described as ⲉⲓ ⲉⲃⲟⲗ ϩⲛ †ⲡⲉ ("coming out of the loins of" [cf. Heb 7:10]). I thank Jan Helderman for this observation.

[53] See Long 1968, 335–36.

(παρὰ φύσιν). Whereas in mainstream Stoic philosophy passion is a result of false judgments and "a movement of soul which is irrational [ἄλογος] and contrary to nature [παρὰ φύσιν],"[54] the *Gospel of Mary* declares that there is a cosmic power contrary to Nature, which, by acting upon matter, has produced passion.

Thus, the *Gospel of Mary* introduces a new concept, a cosmic power contrary to Nature, which, by infecting the harmonious mixture of Nature and matter, disturbs the original cosmic harmony. According to the *Gospel of Mary*, the ultimate cause of passion lies in this cosmic power contrary to Nature. This power is the origin of the disturbing confusion that came into the whole cosmos.

In a Stoic reading, the mixture and dissolution in *Gos. Mary* 7.3–8 seem to be about the harmonious mixture of Nature and matter that will cyclically dissolve and retreat in what belongs to Nature alone. A Stoic reader of the rest of *Gos. Mary* 7 would wonder about the necessity of a Savior, but in *Gos. Mary* 8.2–6 it becomes clear that a non-Stoic view is added, which explains the presence of a Savior. This non-Stoic view relates to the Stoic question of evil.

When reading again about the mixture mentioned in *Gos. Mary* 7.4, a Stoic reader of *Gos. Mary* 8.2–6 will now see that the Savior is not talking about a harmonious mixture of Nature and matter, but is referring to the world as it has become: a disturbing and inharmonious mixture of Nature and something contrary to Nature, both acting upon matter.

7. The Effect of the Power Contrary to Nature and How to Handle Its Influence

Later in the *Gospel of Mary*, when Mary relates the words that the Savior revealed to her alone, a Stoic reader would detect what this power contrary to Nature brings about (*Gos. Mary* 15.1–17.9). In Mary's account, when the Savior tells about the ascent of the soul, the four powers that the soul encounters are arranged according to the figures four and seven in such a way that the fourth power, which is closest to heaven, manifests itself in seven forms. According to Stoics, the cosmos, and thus also the human body, consist of the four elements of earth, water, air, and fire. The human soul consists of seven faculties. These are the five senses, the power of speech, and growth, which is necessary for the body. They receive the impressions that the human body experiences from its environment. The capacity to order these impressions, the ruling mind, is akin to the fourth element, the designing fire, and is located in the chest, whereas the seven faculties are spread throughout the body.[55]

The powers that, according to the Savior, lay siege to the soul thus are analogous to the elements that, for the Stoics, make the body and the cosmos what they are. It seems likely that the Savior is in this way defining more precisely exactly what the power contrary to Nature has caused by acting upon matter, and thus

---

[54] Stobaeus, *Anth.* 2.7.10 (= 2.88.8–10 W-H) (Long and Sedley 1987, 1:410 [65A1]).

[55] See, for example, Diogenes Laertius, *Vit. phil.* 7.135.6; Aëtius, *De placita* 4.21.1–4; see also Long and Sedley 1987, 1:275, 315; Sharples 1996, 67.

generating the birth of passion. Mary reveals that he told her about what the confusion means for the individual. Apparently, the body, being endowed with the natural elements of earth, water, air, and fire with its seven faculties for the soul, has come under the siege of the antinatural vices of darkness, desire, ignorance, and anger with its seven appearances. Redemption consists of being freed from the grip of these powers, which are contrary to Nature.

In the *Gospel of Mary*, the ruling mind has the task of controlling bad influences in a Stoic way. The Son of Man, who can be found and followed by those who seek him, is the divine power that lives in the mind in order to enable people to choose reason over passion.[56] The Son of Man, who lives in the disciples' minds, seems to be the same as the Good within to which Mary turns the disciples' attention in order to enable them to overcome and reject their grief and instead discuss the content of the gospel (*Gos. Mary* 9.21–23). The Good within is a divine power because it originates in the Good, which is God (*Gos. Mary* 7.17).[57]

According to the Stoics, impressions must be examined in order to understand whether they are true or false. Impressions that include false propositions must be rejected by using true propositions.[58] This is what happens in the discussion of the soul with the powers (*Gos. Mary* 15.1–17.7). In the *Gospel of Mary*, the soul through its right judgment can conquer the false reasoning of darkness, desire, ignorance, and anger. Similarly, thanks to her right judgment, Mary Magdalene understands, in contrast to the anxious disciples, the joy brought forth by the gospel.[59]

It is interesting to see in a Stoic light the male discussion about whether one should listen to Mary's teaching (*Gos. Mary* 17.10–15). According to the Stoics, the capacity for right reason was present in women as well as in men. Since they were equal in this respect, women and men should receive the same philosophical schooling and intellectual training.[60] But within Stoicism there were different interpretations of what this meant for male and female social behavior. The tendency seems to be that women should use their intellectual training to become better helpmates at home, while their husbands held public offices outside the home.[61]

A similar ambiguity is felt in the *Gospel of Mary* in the discussion about Mary's role. Her equal intellectual capabilities are implied. Peter even acknowledges that Mary would know more than the other disciples. Yet as a woman, is she to have authority, even over men? When Peter unexpectedly does not want to listen to Mary as a woman, although earlier he had been the one to ask her to share her

---

[56] *Gos. Mary* 10.14–23; 9.20–23 (where P.Oxy. 3525.13 has "mind" [*nous*] instead of "heart"); 8.15–21.

[57] See King 2003b, 37–38. For a discussion on the identity of the Son of Man and the Good, see de Boer, forthcoming.

[58] See Epictetus, *Diss*. 1.1; 2.8; 3.3, 8, 12; on the importance of fighting false impressions in order to remain free from passions, chief of which are desire and anger, see Long 2002, 214–20.

[59] On the importance of right judgment and false reasoning in the *Gospel of Mary*, see de Boer 2004, 85–86, 92–93.

[60] Asmis 1996.

[61] Engel 2003.

knowledge with the others, it becomes clear from Levi's answer that Peter's refusal is influenced by the power of anger. In the *Gospel of Mary*, the ambiguity over a specific female role of Mary as a woman is due to the power contrary to Nature. The right judgment, in response to the false reasoning of her brothers brought about by the powers of passion, is articulated by Mary when speaking about the Son of Man: "He made *us* Human Being" (*Gos. Mary* 9.20 [my italics]). With regard to the discipleship of the Son of Man, there are no specific male and female roles. Those who argue differently are not adhering to Nature but rather are allowing the power contrary to Nature to take over.

The occurrence in the *Gospel of Mary* of a non-Stoic power contrary to Nature explains the expression "following the nature of adultery." The disciples must choose to either follow Nature, to which they originally belong, or follow this power contrary to Nature. Following the latter, in a metaphorical sense, is adulterous behavior. In this new paradigm of the origin of evil, the disciples do not act contrary to Nature in a Stoic sense, but when obeying the power contrary to Nature, they act adulterously and betray Nature, to which they belong.

Thus it also becomes clear why in the *Gospel of Mary*'s view a Savior is needed. In the Stoic view, Nature causes the coming into existence of the universe, and all by itself the universe will dissolve into Nature again. In the *Gospel of Mary*, the Good brought the harmonious mixture of Nature and matter into existence, but somehow "something contrary to Nature" has interfered. Nature is no longer on its own, is no longer its harmonious self, but must be saved from this power contrary to Nature. The Good/the Son of Man has come to rescue Nature and, with Nature, the entire originally harmonious cosmos.

8. A Jewish View

A parallel to the specific cosmology in the *Gospel of Mary* can be found in the works of the Jewish exegete Philo of Alexandria.[62] There are a number of similarities between Philo's exegesis of the Torah and the *Gospel of Mary*:

- God is called the Good, and passion is called formless,[63] whereas all other things are formed;[64]

---

[62] Morris (1987, 872) argues that Philo could be called a Platonist, but just as well a Stoic or a Pythagorean. This is why Dillon (1977, 139-83) calls him a Middle Platonist. Morris (1987, 873-80) emphasizes that Philo was first of all a Jew, since he regarded the Torah of Moses as the supreme authority. Furthermore, Philo does not present his thoughts systematically, but rather in conjunction with Old Testament texts. Thus, for Morris (1987, 880), it is better to call Philo an exegete than a philosopher. For this view, see also Runia 1990, 189.

[63] For the Greek text and a translation of Philo's works, see Colson and Whittaker 1929-1962. For God as the Good, see, for example, Philo, *Spec.* 2.53. For passion as formless, see Philo, *Conf.* 85.

[64] Philo, *Fuga* 12. For Philo's use of the expressions "formless passion" and "the forms of Nature," see de Boer 2004, 45-46.

- the Good finds its home in the sovereign part of the soul, which is the reasoning faculty;[65]
- life on earth ceased to be Paradise and became harsh because of passion;[66]
- the soul overcomes passion through its reasoning faculty, which enables the soul to ascend to God, which Philo, like the *Gospel of Mary*, describes as an experience of rest;[67]
- like the Savior in the *Gospel of Mary*, Philo speaks about the relation of *pneuma*, *nous*, and *psychē*,[68] about being steadfast when drawn near to God and irresolute through passion and a lack of knowledge,[69] and about people being made "human" by a divine intervention.[70]

In addition, Philo's concept of Logos seems to be close to the *Gospel of Mary's* concept of Nature. According to Philo, God does not enter in a direct contact with matter, but rather employs his Logos as an architect or a cutter to perform the task of creation. David Runia concludes about Philo's view of the Logos: "Through the doctrine of the Logos God can be said to be immanent in the universe which he created without the affirmation of his transcendence put at risk."[71] The same may apply to the Stoic concept of Nature in the *Gospel of Mary*. By means of his Nature, God created the world and thus is present in the world and at the same time beyond it.

Philo admonishes his readers that they are not to regard God as the cause of evil. At least in one writing he explains evil by describing the cosmos as a mixture of two contrary powers.[72] These are the salutary and beneficent power and the opposite one, the unbounded and the destructive.[73] According to Philo, the heavens and the entire world have received this mixture. All that exists, however, is created in accordance with the better part of these, "namely when the salutary and

---

[65] Philo, *Virt.* 187–188. See also *Gos. Mary* 9.20–23, where P.Oxy. 3525.13 has "mind" (*nous*) instead of "heart."
[66] Philo, *Opif.* 151–156. See Runia 2001, 359–61.
[67] *Gos. Mary* 15.1–17.7; Philo, *Conf.* 84–103; *Deus* 151–167; *Somn.* 2.228.
[68] *Gos. Mary* 10.20–21; Philo, *Leg. all.* 1.31–32, 37–38.
[69] *Gos. Mary* 9.16; 10.13; Philo, *Congr.* 60; *Somn.* 2.228; *Abr.* 148–150.
[70] *Gos. Mary* 9.20; Philo, *Somn.* 2.267. See Leisegang 1967, 85–88.
[71] Runia 1986, 450.
[72] Philo, *QE* 1.23. Philo suggests different solutions as to what is the cause (see Runia 2003). Close to the view of two contradictory powers is Philo, *Opif.* 72–75: creatures of a mixed nature, which admit opposite characteristics (good deeds and evil deeds), cannot have been created by God alone; their evil part must have been created by others who are subordinate to him.
[73] Runia (1986, 282) argues that the unbounded power must be identified as matter, since Philo describes matter as unbounded too. Matter, however, is not a power but rather a passive substance devoid of all quality (see, e.g., *Fuga* 9). I agree instead with Marcus (1953, 2:32m) that the two opposing powers as Philo distinguishes them correspond to good and evil cosmic powers identified with good and bad angels (or demons). Philo adds that this view is also held by others.

beneficent (power) brings to an end the unbounded and destructive nature."[74] In his view, the mixture of the two opposing powers within humans is not ontologically fixed, but instead depends on behavior. Thanks to the Divine, in Philo's view, the prudent and noble soul receives the better power and is protected against the destructive one.

Against this background, the Savior's encouragement in the *Gospel of Mary* not to be persuaded does not sound strange (*Gos. Mary* 8.8). Although the text does not explain by what the disciples are not to be persuaded, with Philo in mind one may understand that the disciples are warned not to be persuaded by the power contrary to Nature. In the end, the salutary power is more powerful than the destructive one. Likewise, the Savior's encouragement to be fully assured (*Gos. Mary* 8.7) that his disciples are already persuaded "in the presence of the various forms of Nature" (*Gos. Mary* 8.9–10) does not sound strange when we recall Philo's view that although the mixture of the cosmos is a mixture of two opposing powers, all that exists is created in accordance with the better part.

In order to be able to adhere to the Jewish belief of the good creator who did not bring evil into the world, Philo, like the *Gospel of Mary*, developed a dualism of two contradictory powers, which is not a Gnostic or a Middle Platonic one of a good spirit and evil matter. This, in combination with the similarities between the *Gospel of Mary* and Philo's exegesis of the Torah, suggests that the *Gospel of Mary* came into being in a Jewish Greco-Roman context.

9. A Contemporary Early Christian Parallel

An interesting early Christian parallel to the *Gospel of Mary*'s view of the good creator, the role of passion, and the role of the Savior can be found in the discussion by Clement of Alexandria about the true interpretation of the words spoken to Salome in the *Gospel of the Egyptians*. Jesus says to her, "I have come to destroy the works of the female." When Salome asks, "How long will human beings go on dying?" he answers, "As long as women give birth."[75]

Clement refutes the interpretation of "those who attack God's creation"[76] according to which the Savior has come to destroy desire, in the sense of the works of birth and decay, and thus the material world. Instead, according to Clement, the cosmos is beautiful, and creation has come into being through the holy demiurge, who is the one and only almighty God.[77] Birth and decay as such, the union of soul and body and their dissolution, belong to a divine arrangement. Clement also asserts that the flesh is not at enmity with the soul, and that the Savior has come to heal body and soul alike from the influence of passions.[78]

---

[74] Philo, *QE* 1.23.
[75] Clement, *Strom.* 3.63.1; 64.1 (translation, Ferguson 1991). Text in PG 8:1165–1168.
[76] Clement, *Strom.* 3.63.1 (translation, Ferguson 1991).
[77] Clement, *Strom.* 3.45.1.
[78] Clement, *Strom.* 3.104.4.

Clement argues that the Lord indeed has come to destroy desire, but that "desire" should be interpreted not as the works of birth and decay but rather as the works of desire in the sense of passion, which are "the love of money, or winning, or glory, craziness over women, a passion for boys, gluttony, profligacy and the like."[79] Clement thus interprets the word "desire" as referring to passion in a Stoic way. According to Clement, the true interpretation of the phrase "I have come to destroy the works of the female" is that the Lord has come to annihilate these works of passion. Against the view that birth as such brings the decay of the world, Clement asserts that the birth of the works of desire in the sense of passion brings the decay of the soul.

Clement's discussion shows that a Stoic reading was used to defend the material world as a divine creation, against a more negative worldview.[80] Thus, what we have here is a contemporary interpretation of sayings of Jesus that, in contrast to a Gnostic or encratic approach, tries to stay close to a more positive, more Jewish, evaluation of the creation through a Stoic approach.[81] The role of the Lord in Clement's argument is close to the role of the Savior in the *Gospel of Mary*. He has come not to destroy or dissolve the material world, but to annihilate the works of passion.

10. Conclusion

On the basis of the two exegetical problems in the Gnostic or Middle Platonic interpretation of *Gos. Mary* 7.1–8.11 discussed in this essay, I cannot support the view that according to the *Gospel of Mary*, evil originates in mixing with the material world and attachment to the material world must be avoided. Instead, I suggest that in the *Gospel of Mary* the world was created by the Good through Nature acting upon matter, just as in Stoic philosophy matter is acted upon by Nature, resulting in a harmonious and stable cosmos. In the *Gospel of Mary* the cosmos is unstable and confused because matter is also acted upon by "something contrary to Nature."

This reading strongly contrasts with the view on matter, sin, and salvation held by the Gnosticizing and Platonizing interpreters of the *Gospel of Mary*. In the Stoic reading suggested in this essay, it is not the material world that is to be avoided, but rather the power of "something contrary to Nature," which causes passion. The Savior has come not to destroy or dissolve the material world or to rescue Nature from its mixture with matter, but to liberate the world from the grip of passion. He has come to restore Nature from the mixture with "something contrary to Nature" in order to restore Nature to its root, which is the Good.

This interpretation generates a straightforward and consistent reading of *Gos. Mary* 7.1–8.11. Furthermore, it helps to clarify other parts of the *Gospel of Mary*.

---

[79] Clement, *Strom.* 3.63.1.
[80] On Clement of Alexandria's Stoic view of the cosmos, see Spanneut 1957, 368–70.
[81] Van Unnik (1950) argues about a similar Stoic approach of Clement of Rome in *1 Clement* 20, that Clement of Rome uses Stoic language to clarify the Jewish view of creation.

Moreover, the similarities between the *Gospel of Mary* and Philo's view on the Good, passion, and evil and Clement of Alexandria's view on the good creation, passion, evil, and the role of the Lord strengthen the view that the *Gospel of Mary* belongs to an early Christian context in which Hellenistic and especially Stoic philosophy was used to explain the origin of evil within the Jewish belief in one God, who is the good creator of a good creation.

I hope that the discussion presented in this essay will further the debate about the *Gospel of Mary*'s view on matter and nature. This is important not only for the study of the beliefs of those in early Christianity who claimed to follow Mary Magdalene, and for the quest of a more historical view on the development of early Christian beliefs, but also for the study of how early Christians understood Jesus' Jewish gospel in a Greco-Roman Hellenistic context. The *Gospel of Mary* is not just another Gnostic writing; rather, it seems to present unique testimony to the early effort to understand the meaning of Jesus' gospel in contemporary popular Stoic categories.

Bibliography

Asmis, E. 1996. "The Stoics on Women." Pages 68–94 in *Feminism and Ancient Philosophy*. Edited by J. K. Ward. London: Routledge.

Colson, F. H., and G. H. Whitaker. 1929–1962. *Philo in Ten Volumes*. Loeb Classical Library. London: Heinemann.

Crum, W. E. 1939. *Coptic Dictionary*. Oxford: Clarendon Press.

De Boer, E. A. 1997. *Mary Magdalene: Beyond the Myth*. Translated by J. Bowden. Harrisburg, Pa.: Trinity Press International.

———. 2004a. "A Gnostic Mary in the Gospel of Mary?" Pages 695–708 in *Coptic Studies on the Threshold of a New Millennium: Proceedings of the Seventh International Congress of Coptic Studies, Leiden, 27 August–2 September, 2000*. Edited by M. Immerzeel and J. van der Vliet. Orientalia lovaniensia analecta 133. Leuven: Peeters.

———. 2004b. *The Gospel of Mary: Beyond a Gnostic and a Biblical Mary Magdalene*. Journal for the Study of the New Testament: Supplement Series 260. London: T & T Clark International.

———. Forthcoming. "Followers of Mary Magdalene and Contemporary Philosophy: Belief in Jesus according to the *Gospel of Mary*." In *Jesus in Apokryphe Evangelien*. Edited by J. Frey and J. Schröter. Wissenschaftliche Untersuchungen zum Neuen Testament. Tübingen: Mohr Siebeck.

Dillon, J. M. 1977. *The Middle Platonists: A Study of Platonism 80 B.C. to A.D. 220*. London: Duckworth.

Engel, D. M. 2003. "Women's Role in the Home and the State: A Stoic Theory Reconsidered." *Harvard Studies in Classical Philology* 101:267–88.

Ferguson, J. 1991. *Clement of Alexandria: Stromateis 1–3*. Fathers of the Church 85. Washington, D.C.: Catholic University of America Press.

Hartenstein, J. 2000. *Die Zweite Lehre: Erscheinungen des Auferstandenen als Rahmenerzählungen frühchristlicher Dialoge.* Texte und Untersuchungen zur Geschichte der altchristlichen Literatur 146. Berlin: Akademie-Verlag.

Kidd, I. G. 1971. "Posidonius on Emotions." Pages 200–15 in *Problems in Stoicism.* Edited by A. A. Long. London: Athlone.

King, K. L. 1994. "The *Gospel of Mary.*" Pages 601–34 in *A Feminist Commentary.* Vol. 2 of *Searching the Scriptures.* Edited by E. Schüssler Fiorenza. London: SCM Press.

———. 2003a. *What Is Gnosticism?* Cambridge, Mass.: Belknap Press.

———. 2003b. *The Gospel of Mary of Magdala: Jesus and the First Woman Apostle.* Sonoma, Calif.: Polebridge Press.

Leisegang, H. 1967. *Die vorchristlichen Anschauungen und Lehren vom Pneuma und der mystisch-intuitiven Erkenntnis.* Vol. 1.1 of *Der heilige Geist: Das Wesen und Werden der mystisch-intuitive Erkenntnis in der Philosophie und Religion der Griechen.* Leipzig: Teubner, 1919. Repr., Darmstadt: Wissenschaftliche Buchgesellschaft.

Long, A. A. 1968. "The Stoic Concept of Evil." *Philosophical Quarterly* 18:329–43.

———. 1974. *Hellenistic Philosophy: Stoics, Epicureans, Sceptics.* New York: Scribner.

———. 2002. *Epictetus: A Stoic and Socratic Guide to Life.* Oxford: Oxford University Press.

Long, A. A., and D. N. Sedley. 1987. *The Hellenistic Philosophers.* 2 vols. Cambridge: Cambridge University Press.

Lührmann, D. 1988. "Die griechischen Fragmente des Mariaevangeliums P Ox 3525 und P Ryl 463." *Novum Testamentum* 30:321–38.

Marcus, R. 1953. *Philo: Supplement.* 2 vols. Loeb Classical Library. London: Heinemann.

Marjanen, A. 1996. *The Woman Jesus Loved: Mary Magdalene in the Nag Hammadi Library and Related Documents.* Nag Hammadi and Manichaean Studies 40. Leiden: Brill.

———. 2002. "The Mother of Jesus or the Magdalene? The Identity of Mary in the So-Called Gnostic Christian Texts." Pages 31–42 in *Which Mary? The Marys of Early Christian Tradition.* Edited by F. S. Jones. Society of Biblical Literature Symposium Series 19. Atlanta: Society of Biblical Literature.

Mohri, E. 2000. *Maria Magdalena: Frauenbilder in Evangelientexten des 1. bis 3. Jahrhundert.* Marburger theologische Studien 63. Marburg: Elwert.

Morard, F. 2001. "L'Évangile de Marie, un message ascétique." *Apocrypha* 12:155–71.

Morris, J. 1987. "The Jewish Philosopher Philo." Pages 809–89 in vol. 3.2 of Emil Schürer, *The History of the Jewish People in the Age of Jesus Christ (175 B.C.–A.D. 135).* Revised and edited by G. Vermes, M. Goodman, and F. Millar. Edinburgh: T & T Clark.

Pasquier, A. 1981. "L'Eschatologie dans l'Évangile selon Marie: Étude des notions de nature et d'image." Pages 390–404 in *Colloque International sur les textes de Nag Hammadi (Québec 22/8–25/8 1978).* Edited by B. Barc. Bibliothèque copte de Nag Hammadi, Section "Études" 1. Québec: Presses de l'Université Laval; Leuven: Peeters.

———. 1983. *L'Évangile selon Marie: Texte établi et présenté.* Bibliothèque copte de Nag Hammadi, Section "Textes" 10. Québec: Presses de l'Université Laval; Leuven: Peeters.

Petersen, S. 1999. *"Zerstört die Werke der Weiblichkeit!": Maria Magdalena, Salome und andere Jüngerinnen Jesu in christlich-gnostischen Schriften.* Nag Hammadi and Manichaean Studies 48. Leiden: Brill.

Rackham, H. 1979. *Cicero: De Natura Deorum; Academica.* Loeb Classical Library. Cambridge, Mass.: Harvard University Press.

Runia, D. T. 1986. *Philo of Alexandria and the Timaeus of Plato.* Philosophia antiqua 44. Leiden: Brill.

———. 1990. *Exegesis and Philosophy: Studies on Philo of Alexandria.* Collected Studies Series 332. Aldershot: Variorum.

———. 2001. *Philo: On the Creation of the Cosmos According to Moses.* Philo of Alexandria Commentary Series 1. Leiden: Brill.

———. 2003. "Theodicy in Philo of Alexandria." Pages 576–604 in *Theodicy in the World of the Bible.* Edited by A. Laato and J. C. De Moor. Leiden: Brill.

Sandbach, F. H. 1975. *The Stoics.* London: Chatto & Windus.

Schröter, J. 1999. "Zur Menschensohnvorstellung im Evangelium nach Maria." Pages 178–88 in *Schrifttum, Sprache und Gedankenwelt.* Vol. 2 of *Ägypten und Nubien in spätantiker und christlicher Zeit: Akten des 6. Internationalen Koptologenkongresses Münster, 20–26 Juli, 1996.* Edited by S. Emmel et al. Sprachen und Kulturen des christlichen Orients 6. Wiesbaden: Reichert.

Sharples, R. W. 1996. *Stoics, Epicureans and Sceptics: An Introduction to Hellenistic Philosophy.* London: Routledge.

Spanneut, M. 1957. *Le Stoïcisme des pères de l'église: de Clément de Rome à Clément d'Alexandrie.* Patristica Sorbonensia 1. Paris: Seuil.

Steinmetz, P. 1994. *Die Stoa.* Vol. 2 of *Die Hellenistische Philosophie.* Edited by H. Flashar. Grundriss der Geschichte der Philosophie: Die Philosophie der Antike 4. Basel: Schwabe.

Tardieu, M. 1984. *Écrits gnostiques: Codex de Berlin.* Sources gnostiques et manichéennes 1. Paris: Cerf.

Tardieu, M., and J.-D. Dubois. 1986. *Collections retrouvées avant 1945.* Vol. 1 of *Introduction à la littérature gnostique.* Initiations au christianisme ancien. Paris: Cerf.

Till, W. C. 1978. *Koptische Grammatik (Saïdischer Dialekt): Mit Bibliographie, Lesestücken und Wörterverzeichnissen.* Leipzig: Verlag Enzyklopädie.

Till, W. C., and H.-M. Schenke. 1972. *Die gnostischen Schriften des koptischen Papyrus Berolinensis 8502.* Texte und Untersuchungen zur Geschichte der altchristlichen Literatur 60. Berlin: Akademie-Verlag.

Todd, R. B. 1976. *Alexander of Aphrodisias on Stoic Physics: A Study of the "De Mixtione" with Preliminary Essays, Text, Translation and Commentary.* Philosophia antiqua 28. Leiden: Brill.

Tuckett, C. M. 2007. *The Gospel of Mary*. Oxford Early Christian Gospel Texts 1. Oxford: Oxford University Press.

Van Unnik, W. C. 1950. "Is 1 Clement 20 Purely Stoic?" *Vigiliae christianae* 4:181–89.

Wilson, R., and G. W. MacRae. 1979. "The Gospel according to Mary." Pages 453–71 in *Nag Hammadi Codices V,2-5 and VI with Papyrus Berolinensis 8502,1 and 4*. Edited by D. M. Parrott. Nag Hammadi Studies 11. Leiden: Brill.

11

STOIC TRADITIONS IN THE SCHOOL OF VALENTINUS

Ismo Dunderberg
University of Helsinki

Hippolytus of Rome is known for his attempt to connect all early Christian heretics with particular strands of ancient philosophy.[1] Although his efforts in this field are strained in most cases,[2] few would disagree with his claim that Valentinus, Heracleon, Ptolemaeus, and "their entire school" were "disciples of Pythagoras and Plato."[3] In fact, all those early Christians who distinguished between the perfect God and an inferior creator god were heavily indebted to Platonic philosophy. The Platonic influence can be seen, above all, in their teaching that the world is an inferior copy of the eternal realm.[4]

Nevertheless, there is reason to believe that other philosophical currents, including Stoicism, had impact on these Christians as well. Ideas stemming from ancient schools of thought have been especially traced in recent studies on the Sethian *Apocryphon* (or *Secret Book*) *of John* (NHC II,1; III,1; IV,1; BG 8502,2). Takashi Onuki sees in this text signs of a critical dialogue with Stoicism,[5] Gerard Luttikhuizen emphasizes affinities between the *Apocryphon of John* and Aristotelianism,[6] and Zlatko Pleše recently has demonstrated that there are hints at all kinds of philosophical currents, including Stoicism, in this text.[7]

---

[1] In addition to the two other editors of this book, I wish to thank Niko Huttunen and Risto Auvinen for their careful reading of, and helpful comments on, an earlier draft of this essay.
[2] See Mansfeld 1992.
[3] Hippolytus, *Ref.* 6.29.1. Hippolytus makes this claim repeatedly in his account of Valentinian theology (*Ref.* 6, *praef.*; 6.21.1-3; 6.22.1-3; 6.37.1, 5-6). Links between Valentinians and Plato were already created by Irenaeus (*Adv. haer.* 2.14.3-4; 2.33.2), and Tertullian designated Valentinus "the apostate, and heretic, and Platonist" (*Carn. Chr.* 20).
[4] Some of these Christians also adopted the Platonic designations of the body as "prison" and "cave" from which one's true self should be liberated; see Williams 1996, 116–21, with references to the Sethian *Ap. John* (NHC II,1) 21; 31.
[5] Onuki 1989 (see also Onuki's essay in the present volume); for other scholars who have seen affinities between Stoics and Sethians, see ibid., 4–5.
[6] Luttikhuizen 2006.
[7] Pleše 2006; for Stoic ideas in the *Apocryphon of John*, see esp. 58–59, 95–105, 199.

While Einar Thomassen has made a strong case for the influence of Neopythagorean theories on Valentinian myths of origin,[8] the relationship between Valentinians and Stoics has attracted less attention.[9] One noteworthy exception is Bentley Layton's suggestion that the Valentinian *Gospel of Truth* (NHC I,3) draws upon Stoic ideas:

> The basic world view of [the *Gospel of Truth*] is not simply Platonist. Rather, the cosmological model of [the *Gospel of Truth*] is provided by Stoic pantheistic monism and by astronomy. God (the father) is held to be uncontained and to contain all things. Individuals within him are also said to contain god: thus god permeates, or can permeate, all individual things.[10]

Layton adds that there are also some striking differences between the *Gospel of Truth* and Stoicism: "Unlike Stoic cosmology, the system of [the *Gospel of Truth*] is strongly antimaterialist, even illusionist, as regards the reality of material structures."[11] Unfortunately, Layton offers no detailed argumentation in support of his Stoic reading of the *Gospel of Truth*. The problem with his proposal as it now stands is that the Stoic ingredient described therein is not distinct enough. The notion that God is uncontained but contains, or encircles, everything was commonplace among ancient philosophers of all different types since the pre-Socratics.[12] That God "permeates, or can permeate, all individual things" may sound more unmistakably Stoic, but this statement is not explicitly made in the *Gospel of Truth*; rather, it is Layton's own inference from the text.

I will discuss in this essay four cases in which we may be entitled to see Valentinian adaptations of ideas stemming from Stoic philosophy. My initial working hypothesis was cautious: I assumed that such cases be attributed to the relatively broad dissemination of Stoic ideas in the Greco-Roman intellectual world.[13] In consequence, even if certain details in Valentinian sources ultimately go back to Stoicism, this does not have to mean that Valentinian teachers or their audiences were immersed in Stoic philosophy.

Yet, as the result of my analysis, I am inclined to state my case more forcefully: my claim is that the audiences with knowledge of Stoic philosophy were in a better position to understand Valentinian teachings than those who lacked this knowledge. Hence, I am no longer content with the idea that hints at Stoic thought in Valentinian sources were merely due to freely floating traditions with philosophical flavor that Valentinians used simply because they happened to be available.

---

[8] Thomassen 2006, 270–312.
[9] For a brief analysis devoted to this issue, see Sagnard 1947, 579–85.
[10] Layton 1987, 250.
[11] Ibid.
[12] For analogies derived from Aristotle, Philo, Hermetists, and the Shepherd of Hermas (*Mand.* 1.1), see Schoedel 1979, 75–76; 1980, 380–81. This was also one of the points that Irenaeus and his Valentinian opponents agreed upon. Irenaeus used this theologumenon to rebut the Valentinian idea of the void outside the divine realm. For analysis and discussion, see Greer 1980.
[13] For example, Lapidge (1989) shows that in the Roman era, Stoic cosmological views were well known to, and often adopted by, non-Stoics.

I rather take these hints as invitations to recognize how Valentinian teachers, through adoption, selection, and modification, made creative use of ideas borrowed from Stoic philosophy.

1. Condensation and Dissolution

One of the few surviving fragments of Valentinus's own works is a poem entitled *Harvest*.[14] It eloquently describes a cosmic chain that reaches from "flesh" to "aether" and is held together by the Spirit:

> I see that all is suspended by the Spirit,
> I understand that all is carried by the Spirit:
> flesh, hanging from soul,
> soul, <depending on> air,
> air, hanging from aether,
> fruits borne from the depth,
> a babe brought forth from the womb.

In affirming that all things are "suspended by the Spirit" (κρεμάμενα πνεύματι) and "carried by the spirit" (ὀχούμενα πνεύματι), Valentinus clearly alludes to the Stoic doctrine of the all-pervasive spirit (or "breath," πνεῦμα), which holds together the entire universe.[15]

It is possible that Valentinus was also familiar with allegorical interpretations of the traditional lore of Zeus hanging a golden cord from heaven to encircle all other gods and goddesses (*Iliad* 8.19). This story was often explained as referring to cosmic structures, or to all kinds of bonds that are keeping the universe from falling apart.[16]

In particular, the golden cord of Zeus was connected with the Stoic theory of four elements (fire, air, water, earth) and their mutual relationships. The fact that Valentinus mentions four items in the cosmic chain may thus be indicative of his indebtedness to Stoic physics. In addition, like Stoics (but unlike Aristotelians), Valentinus includes "aether" in the group of four elements.[17] For Stoics, "aether" was synonymous with "fire." The distinctive characteristic of this substance is hotness, whereas "air" was considered to be the cold element, "water" the moist one, and "earth" the dry one.[18]

Stoics called these four substances "elements" (στοιχεῖα) because everything else emerges from them. In consequence, it was assumed that some or all of the

---

[14] Hippolytus, *Ref.* 6.37.7. The subsequent commentary explaining the poem in terms of full-blown Valentinian theology can be set aside here because practically all interpreters agree that it comes not from Valentinus but rather from his later followers.

[15] See Markschies 1992, 240–41.

[16] Ibid., 233–37.

[17] Aristotelians regarded "aether" as the fifth, divine, element distinct from, and outside the system of, the four basic elements. For this difference between Aristotelian and Stoic physics, see Long and Sedley 1987, 1:286–87.

[18] Diogenes Laertius, *Vit. phil.* 7.137.2 (L-S 47B).

four elements (τὰ τέσσαρα στοιχεῖα) are present in all things. While earthly things consist of all four elements, the moon was regarded as a compound only of fire and air, and the sun as "pure fire."

The Stoic theory held that the elements can, and constantly do, change into other ones in two ways: by condensation and dissolution. The more subtle elements can turn into coarser ones (fire → air → water → earth) by acquiring a greater degree of density (κατὰ σύστασιν).[19] A reversed process of transformation from the coarse to the subtle elements (earth → water → air → fire) takes place by liquefaction and evaporization.[20]

An obvious point of difference between Valentinus and the Stoic theory of the elements is that, instead of water and earth, Valentinus mentions "flesh" and "soul" as the two lowest items in the cosmic chain. The shift from the physical theory to anthropological concepts suggests that Valentinus was more preoccupied with the human condition than with theoretical discussion about natural science.

Valentinus's choice of the terms "soul" and "flesh" probably goes back to Paul.[21] This, however, does not resolve the question of how Valentinus conceived of the relationship between the four "elements" mentioned in *Harvest*. The link between flesh and soul, on the one hand, and that between air and aether, on the other, may have seemed self-evident to most ancient readers, but the link between the soul and air requires a closer analysis.

Christoph Markschies suggests that the four items in *Harvest* imply a dichotomy between the upper (air/aether) and the lower (soul/flesh) world.[22] What makes this explanation problematic is that no clear distinction between the two worlds is indicated in the poem itself. Valentinus uses a similar language of dependence in describing the relationships between all four "elements." There is no greater rupture between "air" and "soul" than there is between "soul" and "flesh."

My suggestion is that the hierarchy of the four elements in *Harvest* reflects the Stoic theory of the transformation of the elements and the ways this theory was applied to the human soul. A popular ancient etymology for the Greek word for "soul" (ψυχή) was that it is related to, or derives from, the Greek words meaning "cold" (ψῦχος, ψυχρός), "cooling" (ψῦξις), and "to make cold" (ψύχω). This etymology called forth philosophical and theological speculation about the soul's nature and fate.

Leaning on the Stoic conception of air as the cold element, Philo of Alexandria explained how the soul could be envisioned as having undergone "cooling down" in the air. In this process, "the warm nature within us" (i.e., mind, νοῦς) was strengthened by the cold air in the same manner as hot iron is hardened by plunging it into cold water.[23] The soul, thus, is the result of the cooling down of the mind in the air.

---

[19] For the word σύστασις in the sense of "density" and "degree of solidity," see LSJ s.v., B 3.
[20] Stobaeus, *Anth.* 1.10.16c (= 1.129.2–130.13 W-H) (L-S 47A).
[21] See Markschies 1992, 239.
[22] Ibid., 240.
[23] Philo, *Somn.* 1.31.

Origen shared Philo's idea of the soul as a chilled mind[24] and saw in it justification for his theory of the fall of preexistent souls. Origen also resorted to this idea to explain the differences between angels, astral souls, and humans: the souls of humans are inferior to those of other beings with souls because human souls have cooled down more than the souls of other intellectual beings.[25]

These Jewish and Christian variations on the idea that the soul emerged as the result of the mind's chilling in the cold air provide the intellectual framework in which the shift from "air" to "soul" in Valentinus's *Harvest* becomes reasonable: Valentinus can say that the soul "depends" on the air because he thought that the soul came into being when the divine essence was mixed with the cold air. What is more, the placement of the soul between air and the flesh implies that, for Valentinus, the soul is the penultimate state in the process of condensation of the divine essence. The ultimate state of this process is, by consequence, "flesh."

This reading of *Harvest* implies that Valentinus did not conceive of the soul and the flesh as morally "neutral" elements in the cosmic chain.[26] For the gradual condensation of the divine element also marks increased alienation from one's original state. It should be noted that, according to Valentinus, the flesh will not be saved.[27] Therefore, we are entitled to assume that he found a reverse process of dissolution—from flesh to soul to air to aether—necessary for salvation.

This interpretation is clearly attested in the Valentinian *Gospel of Truth*. Its author makes use of the Stoic theory of condensation and evaporation in describing the transformation of believers.[28] The author calls the children of the Father his "fragrance" (ⲥⲧⲁⲓ) and describes how this fragrance "grew cold in psychical form [ⲟⲩⲡⲗⲁⲥⲙⲁ ⲙ̄ⲯⲩⲭⲓⲕⲟⲛ]."[29] There is no doubt that this passage evokes the idea of the soul having come into being as a result of the chilling of the divine essence.

The Stoic theory of the constant transformation of elements was particularly adaptable for theological interpretation because of the two directions it involved: there was a downward movement (condensation from subtle to coarse) and an upward movement (diffusion from coarse to subtle). Just as Jewish and Christian

---

[24] Origen, *Princ.* 2.8.3; see Strutwolf 1993, 250.

[25] Ibid., 251–53.

[26] In fact, it would be very surprising if Valentinus had regarded the soul as a completely neutral element, since he was inspired by Paul, who used the term "soul" as denoting either limited understanding or complete lack thereof. Paul insisted that "a psychic person [ψυχικὸς ... ἄνθρωπος] cannot understand that which pertains to God's spirit," while "the spiritual person [ὁ ... πνευματικός] examines all things" (1 Cor 2:14–15). In the same vein, Valentinus's followers saw the "psychic persons" (ψυχικοί) as forming the middle ground between the truly spiritual ones and those people who are completely material (see below). Although there is no clear evidence for this tripartite anthropology in the Valentinian fragments, his view of the soul as belonging to the lower levels of the cosmic ladder may have paved the way for that theory.

[27] Valentinus, Fragment 11 = Hippolytus, *Ref.* 10.13.4. Markschies (1992, 278–80) remains undecided on the authenticity of this fragment, but in my opinion it fits well with the picture that we get from other fragments by Valentinus (see Dunderberg 2008, 66–67).

[28] See Strutwolf 1993, 250.

[29] *Gos. Truth* 34.

interpreters were able to explain the fall of the souls in terms of condensation, the theory of diffusion provided a suitable framework for their understanding what takes place in spiritual progress.

Both aspects are present in the *Gospel of Truth*. Its author not only compares the offspring of the Father to "cold water" sunk on earth (condensation), but also explains how "the water evaporates when the wind draws it up, and it becomes warm" (evaporation). "Wind" (ⲛⲓϥⲉ) is an especially appropriate metaphor here because it also evokes the idea of the divine breath warming up the chilled souls.[30] In the author's application, faith is defined as leading to "the warm fullness of love," which entails complete absence of coldness.[31]

Similar imagery is attested in the Valentinian *Gospel of Philip* (NHC II,3). In one passage, which may be an excerpt from baptismal catechesis, it is affirmed that when "the spirit of the world ... blows, winter comes. When the Holy Spirit blows, summer comes."[32] In another passage, "this world" is compared to "winter" and the eternal realm to "summer."[33] In both passages it is implied that "winter" and "summer" denote the two states into which the soul can change: it can either cool down more and more and become "worldly" (or "fleshy"), or it can allow the Holy Spirit to warm it up.[34] There is a practical application for this theory: the latter passage in the *Gospel of Philip* ends with the warning that "we should not pray in winter." By implication, the right ("warm") condition of the soul is a prerequisite for an effective prayer.[35]

2. Emotions

In his essay in the present volume, Takashi Onuki discusses the way the Stoic theory of emotions is appropriated in the Sethian *Apocryphon of John*. This text follows a distinct Stoic tradition not only in naming the four basic emotions (delight, desire, distress, fear), but also in specifying their subcategories.[36] This text

---

[30] The author of the *Gospel of Truth* here plays intertextually with the description of God's spirit moving above the primeval water in Gen 1:2.

[31] *Gos. Truth* 34–35 (translation, Thomassen in Meyer 2007, 44).

[32] *Gos. Phil.* §109 (NHC II, p. 77) (translation, Meyer in idem 2007, 180).

[33] *Gos. Phil.* §§7–8 (NHC II, p. 52).

[34] For similar ideas in other Valentinian texts, see Valentinus, Fragment 2 (= Clement, *Strom.* 2.114.3–6); Hippolytus, *Ref.* 6.34.6. Valentinus compared the heart to an inn because it is either inhabitated by demons or it will be purified and made holy by God. In the Valentinian interpretation recorded by Hippolytus, the soul is likewise compared to an inn: the soul can stand completely alone, but it can also be a dwelling place either for divine "words" (λόγοι) or for demons.

[35] I see here a connection to the caution made in the *Gospel of Philip* (§59 [NHC II, p. 64]) that it is possible to become baptized "without receiving anything," even if the initiated says, "I am a Christian." Only one who has received the Holy Spirit is entitled to this name "as a gift." In other words, the ritual is effective only for those whose inner condition is up to it.

[36] *Ap. John* NHC II, p. 18.

links the emotions with "the four chief demons" engaged in creation of the soul of the human being.

Emotions also play a crucial role in Valentinian myths of origin, but they occur in a different context. Instead of being linked with primeval demons, emotions loom large in Valentinian tales of the divine Wisdom (Σοφία), whose ill-advised action in the divine realm led to the creation of the visible world. In different versions of the Valentinian myth, it is variably described how Wisdom, unlike other divine beings, could not control her desire; how she—or the emotional part of her—experienced distress and fear after being deported outside the divine realm; how her emotions were healed by Christ visiting her from the divine realm; and how her misery and joy contributed to the structure of the world. Valentinians even used the tale of Wisdom entangled in emotions to explain the origins of certain natural phenomena (such as the seas, the springs, and the rivers, which they maintained stem from the tears of the abandoned Wisdom).[37]

Such details may easily be mistaken for being poetic embellishments of a mythic story, but a closer look at them shows that more is at stake.[38] The story of Wisdom, who was fully entangled in emotions and then healed by Christ, was clearly of paradigmatic value to Valentinian Christians. Not only was Christ the healer of Wisdom's emotions, but he also is portrayed as the healer of *our* emotions in Valentinian sources.[39]

The Valentinians' stories of Wisdom and Christ, thus, show how important a notion the therapy of emotions was for them. At this point, their interests coincided with those of ancient philosophers who advised their students both in theory and in practice how to cope with emotions pestering them.[40] The question that needs to be addressed here is whether there are any specific links between the Valentinian Wisdom myth and Stoic theories about emotions.

The case is less clear than in the *Apocryphon of John*. In Valentinian descriptions of Wisdom's sufferings outside the divine realm, four emotions are customarily mentioned, just like in Stoic sources. However, only two of them, distress (λύπη) and fear (φόβος), are the same as in the Stoic analysis, whereas the other two Stoic main categories of the emotions, desire (ἐπιθυμία) and delight (ἡδονή), are not mentioned in Valentinian accounts of Wisdom. Instead of desire and delight, we encounter in Valentinian sources a number of other mental states that Wisdom was subject to: "perplexity" (ἀπορία), "ignorance" (ἄγνοια), "consternation" (ἔκπληξις), "entreaty" (δέησις, ἱκετεία), and "to be distracted" (ἐκστῆναι).[41]

It is striking that the two Stoic emotions not mentioned in Valentinian sources are those that, according to the Stoic analysis, involve a belief that something good

---

[37] Irenaeus, *Adv. haer.* 1.4.3.
[38] This part of my essay builds upon my more thorough analysis of Valentinian views about emotions in Dunderberg 2008, 95–118.
[39] Clement, *Exc. Theod.* 67.2.
[40] See Nussbaum 1994. For emotions in Greco-Roman philosophy, see also Knuuttila 2004 and the articles in Sihvola and Engberg-Pedersen 1998.
[41] Irenaeus, *Adv. haer.* 1.2.3; 1.4.1; Hippolytus, *Ref.* 6.32.5; for a synopsis, see Dunderberg 2008, 112.

is present (delight) or within one's reach in the future (desire). The two emotions retained in the Valentinian accounts of Wisdom are the ones that involve a belief that something evil is present (distress) or to be expected in the future (fear). Other Valentinian qualifications of Wisdom's mental state, putting additional emphasis on her anxiety (perplexity and consternation), seem like expansions of distress and fear.[42]

The difference between the Valentinian and the Stoic classifications of emotions does not necessarily disprove a link between these two strands of thought. The difference indicates that Valentinians refocused the discussion about emotions. For them, delight and desire were less pertinent problems than anxiety and ignorance. The latter two are especially important because what the Valentinian teachers had to offer were counterparts to these mental states. First, as the counterpart of "anxiety," Valentinians promoted "the gospel of truth," which brings about "joy."[43] The fact that "joy" is mentioned as the consequence of the proclamation of the gospel creates yet another link to the Stoic analysis of emotions in which "joy" was one of the three "good emotions" (εὐπάθειαι). Second, as the counterpart of ignorance, Valentinians emphasized the importance of "knowledge," which, together with baptism, should bring about freedom.[44]

Moreover, in Valentinian theology, ignorance not only constitutes the human condition after creation, but it is already present in the divine realm. One version of the Valentinian myth describes how Wisdom was first filled with love toward the Father of All, which then turned to agony when she realized that the Father is inscrutable.[45] What is noteworthy in this portrayal is that Wisdom differs from other eternal beings in the divine realm not because of her desire to know the Father, but rather because she yielded to this desire. It is described how all eternal beings "quietly" wanted to see the Father, but it is said of Wisdom that she "drove herself exceedingly far ... and experienced a passion."[46]

This brief passage recalls three essential aspects of the Stoic theory of emotions: (1) passion results from an excessive impulse (ὁρμή πλεονάζουσα) that a person (erroneously) believes to be something that cannot be avoided; (2) assent to that impulse leads the soul into movement (κίνησις ψυχῆς) that can no longer

---

[42] Of these emotions describing Wisdom's anxiety, "consternation" (ἔκπληξις) may have been derived from Stoic tradition where it was allocated as a subcategory of fear (*SVF* 3.407–409 = Diogenes Laertius, *Vit. phil.* 7.112; Stobaeus, *Anth.* 2.7.10c (= 2.92.1–6 W-H); Pseudo-Andronicus 3; see Onuki 1989, 38).

[43] *Gos. Truth* 16.

[44] Clement, *Exc. Theod.* 78.2.

[45] Irenaeus, *Adv. haer.* 1.2.2. The Greek version of this passage, stemming from Epiphanius's lengthy quotation of Book 1 of Irenaeus's work (*Pan.* 31.9–32), uses the word ἀγών, which means "struggle," for the mental state of Wisdom; the word has also the sense of "a mental struggle, anxiety." Nevertheless, it is possible that the word used in the original Greek version was ἀγωνία ("agony, anguish"), since this Greek word occurs in the Latin translation of *Adv. haer.* 1.2.2 ("in magna agonia"). While the word ἀγών does not appear in Stoic catalogs of emotions, ἀγωνία is listed in them as a subspecies of fear (*SVF* 3.407–409 = Diogenes Laertius, *Vit. phil.* 7.112; Pseudo-Andronicus 3; Stobaeus, *Anth.* 2.7.10c (= 2.92.1–6 W-H).

[46] Irenaeus, *Adv. haer.* 1.2.1.

be stopped;[47] (3) even truly wise persons are subject to "stings of passion"—that is, preliminary physical states that may lead to emotions. Yet, the wise persons recognize these states before they develop into full-blown emotions, and thus they are able to resist the impulse inherent in these "pre-passions."[48] The Valentinian portrayal of the eternal beings who wanted to know the Father can be understood as a reflection of this last aspect: all eternal beings were subject to "stings of passion" in that they had the wish to know the Father, but it is only Wisdom who yielded to that impulse, lost control, and acted to fulfill her wish. When these things happen, therapy of emotions is needed.

The healing of passion is offered at different points in the subsequent story of Wisdom and her role in the creation of the worlds. First, it is related how a new eternal being, called "Limit" (ὅρος), was created to teach Wisdom that the Father cannot be understood. What takes place at this stage of the myth is extirpation of emotions: the heavenly Christ visits Wisdom and supplies her with complete lack of passion (ἀπαθῆ κατεσκεύασεν),[49] which makes Wisdom able to abandon the passion that followed from her misguided intention.[50] This part of the Valentinian myth, thus, shares the essentially Stoic ideal of *apatheia*.[51]

However, the Valentinian myth does not completely subcribe to the Stoic standard of *apatheia*. As the story goes on, it becomes clear that the emotions extirpated from the heavenly Wisdom did not simply disappear; they had to be removed from the divine realm. The expelled passions of Wisdom are personified in Valentinian myth as a lower Wisdom, also called "Achamoth" (derived from the plural *ḥākmôt* of the Hebrew word *ḥokmâ*, "wisdom"). This Wisdom outside the divine realm is now "completely entangled" in the emotions mentioned above (distress, fear, perplexity, etc.). For example, she feels distress due to her inability to understand the light that the heavenly Christ left behind, and she is afraid of death.[52] Again, an account of healing of emotions follows: the eternal beings in the divine realm send the Savior down to the lower Wisdom, and he "provided the cure of passions by extirpating them" and by turning them into "incorporeal matter [ὕλη]."[53]

Physics and the theory of passions are at this point combined in a manner that may have seemed odd to those familiar with Stoic philosophy, not least because the Stoics taught that matter is eternal, having neither a beginning nor an end. No less suprising for learned audiences would have been the claim that matter stems from emotions. On the other hand, such audiences may have realized that the way

---

[47] Stobaeus, *Anth.* 2.7.10–10a (= 2.88.8–90.6 W-H) (L-S 65A); for the aspect of movement, see also Seneca, *Ira*, 2.3.1–2 (L-S 65X).

[48] See Epictetus, Fragment 9 (L-S 65Y).

[49] Clement, *Exc. Theod.* 45.1–2.

[50] Irenaeus, *Adv. haer.* 1.2.2.

[51] Strikingly, the same set of ideas recurs in a Valentinian description of how the heavenly Christ raised the dead body of Jesus after it "had put off emotions" (Clement, *Exc. Theod.* 61.7).

[52] Irenaeus, *Adv. haer.* 1.4.1.

[53] Irenaeus, *Adv. haer.* 1.4.5; cf. Hippolytus, *Ref.* 6.32.5–6.

Valentinians told the story adds to the urgency of the theme of emotions: if the "stuff" from which the world was created stems from emotions, the consequence is that this world is in its entirety wound around with passion. It may be difficult to see how this view contributes to discussions about physical theory, but the claim inherent in it, that passion is not just an individual problem but is one with cosmic dimensions, certainly lends additional weight to the Valentinians' message that people need to be set free from passion by Christ.[54] Another possible function of the juxtaposition of passion and matter in the Valentinian myth of Wisdom is that this combination explained why passions drag people downward, toward material things, and thus stand in the way of their upward movement.

However that might be, the Valentinian view that matter consists of passion is clearly different from the Stoic view that matter is what God acts upon, or mixes with, in creating and sustaining the world.[55] Matter is not linked with passions in Stoic natural philosophy as it is in Valentinian myth. Thus, if we assume that Valentinians were familiar with Stoic teaching about emotions, as I think we can do, we should also see how bold they were in bringing together these theories with elements of physical theory, all discussed in a mythic framework.

3. Moral Progress

One key claim in Irenaeus's campaign against Valentinians was that they considered themselves "the spiritual ones" (οἱ πνευματικοί), whereas they relegated all other Christians to an inferior category of those whose essence is determined by the soul (οἱ ψυχικοί), and non-Christian humankind into the lowest category of "the material ones" (οἱ ὑλικοί). According to Irenaeus, Valentinians thought that they will be saved "not because of what they do but because they are spiritual beings by nature," whereas faith and good conduct were required of other Christians.[56]

Irenaeus describes the Valentinian distinction between the two classes as predetermined and fixed: there was no danger of being downgraded for the spiritual ones, no matter what they did, and there was no prospect of promotion for other Christians. However, Irenaeus paints the fixed picture of Valentinian anthropology for a reason. This picture serves his attempt at preventing his audience from joining the Valentinians: there would obviously be little point in joining a group that does not grant newcomers full membership, nor even a prospect of it!

Other sources suggest that Valentinian anthropology was more flexible, more aimed at the transformation of the soul, and more concerned with good conduct than Irenaeus was willing to admit. My suggestion is that Valentinian theories of two kinds of Christians can be better understood in light of Stoic theories about

---

[54] Clement, *Exc. Theod.* 67.2.
[55] See Seneca, *Ep.* 65.2 (L-S 55E); Alexander of Aphrodisias, *Mixt.* 225.1 (L-S 45H).
[56] Irenaeus, *Adv. haer.* 1.6.1–2. For the accusation that Valentinians claimed for themselves the status of spiritual beings, saved by nature, see also Clement, *Strom.* 2.10.2; *Exc. Theod.* 56.

"the wise person" and moral progress than in terms of a predetermined distinction between two real-life groups of Christians.

Stoics made a strict distinction between the sage (σοφός), who was "the perfect one" (ὁ τέλειος), and "fools," that is, all other humans regardless of how morally advanced they might be.[57] The wise person "does everything well," since this person accomplishes "everything in accordance with right reason and in accordance with virtue"; on the other hand, "the inferior man does everything that he does badly and in accordance with all the vices."[58] In other words, there is an essential gap between the wise and the fools, just as there is between virtue and vice. You either have all virtues or you have none of them.[59] For this reason, even the "progressing ones" (οἱ προκόπτοντες),[60] who "are getting close to virtue, are no less in a state of vice as those who are far from it"; they "remain foolish and vicious right up to their attaiment of virtue."[61]

Yet another point of difference between the wise and the fools in Stoic analysis is that doing the right thing comes naturally and effortlessly to the wise, whereas the fools need someone telling them what to do and what to avoid. Precepts and injunctions are effective because they strengthen one's natural character, which "is concealed and weighed down." This kind of instruction is needed until the person finally becomes capable of judging reliably and independently what "he should do in every matter."[62] It should be added that becoming "the perfect one" was a theoretical option rather than a realistic goal for Stoics. There may have been no more than "one or two good men" who have attained this level of perfection.[63] In practice, all humans belong to the inferior group of fools.

From this perspective, the Valentinian distinction between the spiritual ones, who are not in need of any ethical guidance, and all other Christians, who are "uncultured and ignoramuses,"[64] looks very similar to the Stoic distinction between the wise and the fools. What is more, just as the Stoics affirmed that wise persons are very rare, Valentinians are on record as stating that there are only a few spiritual persons.[65]

It is less clear what ethical implications Valentinians drew from their distinction between two kinds of Christians. Irenaeus claims that they took gross liberties

---

[57] My analysis of Stoic theories of the "perfect human" and moral progress is in particular indebted to Engberg-Pedersen 2004; for an incisive application of these views to the Gospel of John, see Buch-Hansen 2010. For my suggestion that these distinctions may be useful also for understanding the *Gospel of Judas*, see Dunderberg 2009.

[58] Stobaeus, *Anth.* 2.7.5b10 (= 2.66.14–67.4 W-H) (L-S 61G).

[59] See Plutarch, *Stoic. rep.* 1046E–F (L-S 61F).

[60] Plutarch, *Comm. not.* 1063B (L-S 61T).

[61] Plutarch, *Comm. not.* 1063A–B (L-S 61T). Stoic philosophers and those writing under their influence apparently used the words ὁ προκόπτων and προκοπή as technical terms in moral discourse; see, for example, Epictetus, *Diss.* 1.4 (entitled "Of Progress"); Philo, *Leg. all.* 3.159.

[62] Seneca, *Ep.* 94 (L-S 66I).

[63] Alexander of Aphrodisias, *Fat.* 199.14–22 (L-S 61N).

[64] Irenaeus, *Adv. haer.* 1.6.4.

[65] Clement, *Exc. Theod.* 55–56.

due to their self-understanding as the spiritual Christians: they unscrupulously ate food offered to idols, attended gladiatorial shows, and, most alarmingly, seduced and defiled Christian women—the wives of rich Christians were especially in danger. At the same time, the Valentinians demanded of other Christians "continence and good conduct."[66]

However, Irenaeus's description of Valentinians behaving badly certainly is biased, and there is much evidence to refute it.[67] It is not even clear that all Valentinians claimed the status of "the spiritual ones" for themselves (although some of them may have done so). The Valentinian *Interpretation of Knowledge* (NHC XI,1), addresses the situation of a rift in a community between those who have "the spiritual gift" and those who have not. Strikingly, it is those who belong to the former group who are said to "make progress in the Word" (ϥⲡⲣⲟⲕⲟⲡⲧⲉ ϩⲙ ⲡⲗⲟⲅⲟⲥ).[68] In Stoic discourse, the verb προκοπτείν was a technical term applied to those seriously seeking moral improvement.[69] The use of this verb in the *Interpretation of Knowledge* suggests that its author was familiar with the Stoic distinction between the wise person and "the progressing ones," who have not yet attained perfection.

One consequence of this affinity is that we should not be too hasty to identify "the advancing ones" mentioned in the *Interpretation of Knowledge* with "the spiritual ones" mentioned in other sources of Valentinian theology. It is true that in the *Interpretation of Knowledge* "the advancing ones" form a privileged group, for only they are entitled to speak in the community's gatherings.[70] Nevertheless, the instruction that the author of this text addresses to his entire audience[71] shows that even those belonging to this superior group are not yet the perfect ones who would know how to do the right thing without any guidance from others.

To sum up, it seems possible that Valentinians understood the category of "spiritual ones" as the ultimate goal of moral progress in the same manner as Stoics used the category of "the wise person." Like the Stoic sage (or Isaac and Moses in Philo's works), the Valentinian "spiritual one" no longer needs precepts, instruction, or even reflection to do the right thing. This person acts in the right manner (i.e., in the way best suited to each particular situation) spontaneously, due to his or her very nature—hence Irenaeus's polemical allegation that Valentinians disregarded all rules.

However, those on the lower steps of the moral ladder need deliberation, admonition, precepts, and rehearsal—hence Irenaeus's claim that all other Christians needed "good works" to be saved. Irenaeus claims that Valentinians regarded

---

[66] Irenaeus, *Adv. haer.* 1.6.3; cf. 1.13.5.3–5 (on Marcus).

[67] Most strikingly, Irenaeus himself admits that there were Valentinians whose moral conduct was irreproachable (*Adv. haer.* 3.15.2)!

[68] *Interpr. Know.* 16.32.

[69] As I mentioned in a note above, Stoic philosophers and those writing under their influence apparently used the words ὁ πρόκοπτων and προκοπή as technical terms in moral discourse; see, for example, Epictetus, *Diss.* 1.4 (entitled "Of Progress"); Philo, *Leg. all.* 3.159.

[70] See *Interpr. Know.* 16.34–35.

[71] See, for example, the author's summary of the Savior's ethical instruction in *Interpr. Know.* 9.27–37.

themselves as the spiritual ones and felt recklessly free from all codes of decent behavior, but the *Interpretation of Knowledge* demonstrates that, just like the Stoic Seneca, Valentinians rather saw themselves as belonging to the category of the advancing ones who still needed instruction and practice in doing the right thing.

This interpretation finds support in Ptolemaeus's interpretation of the ritual laws in the Hebrew Bible. His *Letter to Flora* is addressed to a novice in Valentinian theology, but in detailing "the spiritual sense" (τὸ πνευματικόν) of the ritual law, he constantly refers to an in-group ("us").[72] That is, Ptolemaeus does not claim that the in-group members no longer need any rules of behavior. Moreover, "the spiritual sense" for Ptolemaeus is all about lifestyle: "offerings" become realized in worship, in fellowship with others, and in good deeds; "keeping the Sabbath" means withdrawal from evil works; and the true, or spiritual, fasting means abstinence from bad deeds.[73] "The spiritual sense" of Scripture outlined by Ptolemaeus is, thus, entirely practical: it becomes realized in one's way of life. Ptolemaeus's approach is squarely opposed to what we read in Irenaeus, who accused Valentinians of using their spiritual status as an excuse for moral indifference, but it is in keeping with the ethical orientation of all ancient schools of thought.

4. Blending

Valentinians probably shared common ground with Stoics also in theories of mixture.[74] This issue was a matter of special interest to Chrysippus, one of the founding figures of Stoicism. He distinguished between three different kinds of mixtures: juxtaposition (παράθεσις), fusion (σύγχυσις), and blending (κρᾶσις).

Chrysippus's category of "blending" seems very similar to the compound of the "psychic" and the "spiritual" essences in Valentinian analysis.[75] In Chrysippus's theory, "blending" differs from the two other forms of mixture insofar as in this particular form the original substances are completely mixed with each other and "pass through one another, so that no part among them fails to participate in everything contained in such a blended mixture." Blending, however, differs from a complete fusion in that "the original substances and their qualities [are] preserved" in blending,[76] whereas they disappear completely in fusion. Since the distinct

---

[72] I take this in-group to be Christians in general, not Valentinian Christians in particular. Ptolemaeus obviously has in mind a broader group of people with different lifestyles, as can be seen in his reference that "there are also some among us who practice visible fasting" (*Flora* [apud Epiphanius, *Pan.*] 33.5.13).

[73] *Flora* 33.5.10–12.

[74] See L-S 48A–F. It was the fine summary by Buch-Hansen (2010, 75–84) of the Stoic theory of blending that drew my attention to this issue and made me think of the potential ramifications of this theory for Valentinian theology.

[75] For the possible impact of the Stoic theory of blending on the views of Sethians, see Pleše 2006, 265–66.

[76] As Risto Auvinen remarked in his comments on a previous draft of my essay, this point makes the Stoic theory of blending different from Aristotle's. Aristotle argued that both constituents change in blending, becoming "that which is intermediate and common"

properties of the constituents are preserved in blending, the obvious implication is that the constituents of blending can also be separated from each other.[77]

For Stoics, the soul, conceived of as pervading the whole body and yet preserving its own substance, constituted a prime example of the type of mixture that blending involves.[78] For my analysis below, it is also important to note that Stoics used the language of blending and repose in connection with eschatological events: Seneca describes how Zeus "reposes in himself," when the world, after the conflagration, "is dissolved and gods have been blended together into one."[79]

Unlike some other parts of Stoic physics (such as the Stoic view of conflagration), the Stoic theory of blending was not commonly accepted by ancient philosophers of other persuasions.[80] Therefore, if it can be shown that Valentinians made use of this theory, this could be an instance of a more specific affinity between their teaching and Stoic traditions.

We can be sure that blending was discussed by some Valentinians, since Clement attributes to them the teaching that "Jesus, the church and Wisdom form a powerful and complete blending of bodies [κρᾶσις τῶν σωμάτων]." It is quite clear that these Valentinians knew ancient philosophical theories about blending, since they illustrated their view with the mixture of water and wine,[81] which was a classic example in philosophical discussions of blending, attested both in Aristotle[82] and in Stoic sources.

There are three other cases in Valentinian data in which theories of blending seem operative. All three instances are related to the distinction between the spiritual and the psychic essence. First, Valentinians taught that the spiritual substance "cannot take on corruption."[83] This teaching is clarified with comparison to gold, which, even when it lies in mud, "does not lose its beauty, but preserves its own nature."[84] This implies that Valentinians conceived of the spirit's presence

---

(Aristotle, *Gen. corr.* I 10.328a29–31 [Wolfson 1956, 375]). Wolfson (1956, 381) points out that "according to Aristotle, the resultant mixture is a *tertium quid*, which is neither one nor the other of its constituent parts."

[77] See Long and Sedley 1987, 1:293. The Stoics and Aristotle agreed on this point; Aristotle also maintained that the constituents of a blending can be resolved to their original natures (*Gen. corr.* I 10.327b [Wolfson 1956, 376]).

[78] Alexander of Aphrodisias, *Mixt.* 216.14–218.6 (L-S 48C).

[79] Seneca, *Ep.* 9.16 (L-S 46O). I assume that Seneca here speaks of the gods' blending (instead of fusion) with each other, since he presupposes that the gods preserve their distinct natures even in the state of repose and can be again separated from each other when the new cosmic cycle will start all over again after the conflagration.

[80] For critics of the Stoic theory of blending, see Plutarch, *Comm. not.* 1078B–D (L-S 48E); Themistius, *In Ar. Phys.* 104.9–19 (L-S 48F).

[81] Clement, *Exc. Theod.* 17.1.

[82] For Aristotle, see *Gen. corr.* I 5.321a–312b, 322a; 10.328a (Wolfson 1956, 377–78); for Stoics, see the examples collected in L-S 48A–D (Diogenes Laertius, *Vit. phil.* 7.151; Plutarch, *Comm. not.* 1078E; Alexander of Aphrodisias, *Mixt.* 216.14–218.6; Stobaeus, *Anth.* 1.17.4 (= 1.155.5–11 W-H).

[83] Irenaeus, *Adv. haer.* 1.6.2. I take the following comment ("regardless of what practices they may have engaged in") to be Irenaeus's own comment.

[84] Irenaeus, *Adv. haer.* 1.6.2.

in humans in a way similar to Stoics thought of blending: although the spirit permeates the whole body (cf. Valentinus's teaching discussed above), this does not change the spirit into something else, as would happen in fusion or in "Aristotelian" blending, but rather it retains its own distinct nature.[85]

The second case of blending in Valentinian sources comes from the *Tripartite Tractate* (NHC I,5). It contains a lengthy account of how two different orders of powers came into being as the result of Word's (unintended) break with the divine realm and his conversion.[86] As the two orders were then engaged in a struggle for power, they became completely intermingled with each other. In the battle, even the more virtuous of the two parties became infected by the lust for power, which was characteristic of the inferior party to begin with. As the result of this cosmic battle, those belonging to the more virtuous party became as ignorant of the true divinity as those against whom they were fighting.[87] Nevertheless, the mixture of the two orders is only temporary. For when the divine Son appears to both groups "like a flash of lightning" (good Barthian imagery!), their responses are divided. Those belonging to the superior order "greeted his revelation and bowed down before him," whereas those in the inferior one only became frightened, without showing any signs of true conversion.[88]

The *Tripartite Tractate* describes here a mixture that Stoics probably would have defined as blending (rather than juxtaposition or fusion): there are two constituents that are, at one point, completely intermingled with each other, and yet they preserve their distinct natures. This can be seen in the fact that they can be separated from each other at any given point. What gives this description a characteristically Valentinian twist is the idea that it is the Son's revelation that affects the separation and make one's true nature known.[89] This case, however, is not as clearly "Stoic" as the first one, for the blending of the better and the worse party in the *Tripartite Tractate* results in a tertium quid, which was the characteristic feature of the Aristotelian theory of blending: the better party took over some features of the other constituent and thus became something new in the mixture.

My third case is a famous *crux interpretum* of Valentinian scholarship. Clement of Alexandria reports that Valentinians waited for an eschatological wedding banquet to which two kinds of souls—the souls of spiritual beings and the "other faithful souls" (αἱ ... ἄλλαι πισταὶ ψυχαί)—will be summoned. In the wedding feast, the distinction between the spiritual and the psychic souls will disappear:

---

[85] Alexander of Aphrodisias also mentions gold as an example in his discussion of the Stoic theory of blending (L-S 48C), but he does so in a way that is completely different from the Valentinian teaching reported by Irenaeus. There is, thus, no reason to suppose that the Valentinian saying concerning gold in mud was inspired by Stoic teaching.

[86] In the *Tripartite Tractate*, Word (Λόγος) assumes the role reserved for Wisdom in other Valentinian sources.

[87] *Tri. Trac.* 83–85.

[88] *Tri. Trac.* 89–90.

[89] This idea, in my opinion, is also the bottom line in Heracleon's interpretation of the Johannine stories of the Samaritan woman (John 4:1–42) and the son of the royal officer (John 4:46–54) (Heracleon, Fragments 17–40).

the feast will be "common to all, until all are made equal to each other and <know each other>."⁹⁰ And yet, the great equalitarian banquet ends with a renewed separation of the spirit and the soul: the spiritual elements (τὰ πνευματικά) discard the souls and proceed to the truly divine realm, where they are granted the vision of the Father. The souls remain in the Ogdoad, the region of intermediate salvation, where the wedding feast took place.⁹¹

What is striking here is the idea that before the banquet, the spiritual elements, waiting for the final consummation of salvation in the state of repose (ἀνάπαυσις), are still wearing souls as their "garments" (ἐνδύματα). In other words, Valentinians did not think of the soul and the spirit as two mutually exclusive features: the humans endowed with the spirit do have souls as well.⁹² In addition, this passage suggests that at least some Valentinians envisaged one salvation for all: the souls of the spiritual ones and those of the faithful will remain in one and the same region of intermediate salvation. Notably, it is not "the spiritual persons" (οἱ πνευματικοί) who will be summoned to the divine realm, but rather it is "the spiritual elements" (τὰ πνευματικά) that, after the eschatological banquet, will return to their place of origin.

This whole imagery of the coming together of different kinds of souls, and the following image of the final separation of the spiritual essence and the souls (of both groups!), is best understood as a theological application of the Stoic theory of blending. The spiritual essence is conceived of as something that can be mixed with the soul having the right inclination. Yet, neither the spirit nor the soul disappears or loses its distinct nature in the ensuing mixture, which means that they can be separated from each other.

Let us now return to Seneca's depiction of the gods' blending as part of their return to their original state and the image of Zeus "reposing in himself" as the result. This Stoic description of what happens at the end of a cosmic cycle is strikingly similar to the Valentinian eschatological imagery in which the spiritual beings are in the state of repose, the souls of different varieties are made equal to each other, and the spiritual element returns to the divine realm. On the basis of these affinities, it seems feasible that Stoic eschatological tradition, such as that in Seneca, may have inspired Valentinians' imagination as to what happens at the end of time.

Nevertheless, it is clear that Valentinians did not completely buy into Stoic cosmology and eschatology. One obvious disagreement is that most Valentinians ascribed to matter both a beginning and an end,⁹³ whereas the Stoics thought that

---

⁹⁰The expression "know each other" is based upon emendation of the Greek original text.
⁹¹Clement, *Exc. Theod.* 63–64.
⁹²Note also Irenaeus, *Adv. haer.* 1.7.5: the divine seed is planted in just souls (δικαίαις ψυχαῖς), so that it, through being educated in the world, becomes "worthy of perfection." However, the view about the "just souls" in this passage is different from that in Clement: these souls are those in possession of the divine seed—that is, the spiritual ones—and not the second-best group as in Clement. It is impossible to tell whether this difference is due to variety in Valentinian teaching or to Irenaeus's and Clement's different ways of interpreting Valentinian materials at their disposal.
⁹³The only possible exception among Valentinians is the heterodox teacher combated in Methodius, *On Free Will*, and identified as Valentinus in the *Dialogue on the True Faith in God*, which rehashes large parts of Methodius's dialogue. This teacher argues that the

matter is as eternal as God. Not only did Valentinians maintain that matter stems from Wisdom's emotions, but also they thought that matter will be completely destroyed in the eschatological conflagration.[94] This leaves little room for renewal of the cosmos in the Valentinian system of thought. Accordingly, Valentinians probably thought that the great eschatological blending in the Ogdoad would take place only once, not time after time.

5. Conclusion

It is plausible to assume that Valentinian teachers, who must have had some sort of philosophical education, might have known Stoic philosophy, at least in a rudimentary form. It may seem more difficult to demonstrate that their teaching was directly influenced by Stoicism. There are other options that could also explain affinities between Stoicism and Valentinianism. Although I do not think John Dillon is fair in branding "the Gnostics" as "the magpies of the intellectual world of the second century,"[95] Valentinians probably were as selective in their usage of philosophical traditions as most other early Christians who had developed taste for philosophy. Moreover, it is possible that Valentinians derived ideas that we can classify as "Stoic" from popular philosophy, or religiosity, of their time without having advanced education in Stoicism or by Stoics. Finally, it could be argued that Valentinians were familiar with a similar mixture of Platonism and Stoicism as Philo and other so-called Middle Platonists were.

Where do the examples discussed in this essay leave us in regard to these options? One could at least assume that a Stoically oriented ancient reader would have been able to see a number of reflections of, and allusions to, Stoic teaching in Valentinian texts. Perhaps this Stoic reader may even have understood certain points in these texts more readily than readers with different sorts of intellectual backgrounds. I would even go one step further and claim that a "Stoic" reading sometimes helps us make better sense of the cases discussed above than do some other approaches to them. Hence comes my assumption that Valentinians knew more than just the rudiments of Stoic philosophy and made innovative use of some ideas borrowed from that philosophy.

Unlike Philo, Valentinians did not confine themselves to the interpretation of Scripture in light of Platonic and Stoic traditions. They were more innovative in creating new mythic tales of origin and the end, in which these learned traditions play a part. In this sense of "philosophical myths," Valentinians provide us with a Christian counterpart to Hermetic writings, where we are faced with a similar

---

preexistence of matter explains the fact that the world is not perfect. Although most recent commentators are doubtful concerning the identification of the heterodox teacher with Valentinus, I have argued that a good case for this identification can indeed be made (see Dunderberg 2008, 67–72).

[94] Irenaeus, *Adv. haer.* 1.7.1.

[95] Dillon 1999, 74. On this and Dillon's other denigrating comments on Gnostics and Valentinians, see Dunderberg 2008, 17–18.

mixture of ideas derived from Platonic and Stoic philosophies, all embedded in tales of origin (e.g., *Poimandres*) or other instances of "sacred discourse."[96]

Such combinations of myth and philosophy pose intriguing questions and interpretive challenges to modern interpreters. For example: Why was mythic discourse preferred to philosophical treatises in these groups? Were these myths originally composed for religious usage? Or were they rather intended as tools for philosophical reflection? Or was the genre of myth chosen because of educational purposes? These questions are still far from being adequately addressed.

Bibliography

Buch-Hansen, G. 2007. "It Is the Spirit That Makes Alive: A Stoic Understanding of Pneûma in John." Th.D. diss., University of Copenhagen.

———. 2010. *"It Is the Spirit that Gives Life": A Stoic Understanding of Pneuma in John's Gospel*. Beihefte zur Zeitschrift für die neutestamentliche Wissenschaft und die Kunde der älteren Kirche 173. Berlin: de Gruyter.

Dillon, J. M. 1999. "Monotheism in Gnostic Tradition." Pages 69–79 in *Pagan Monotheism in Late Antiquity*. Edited by P. Athanassiadi and M. Frede. Oxford: Clarendon Press.

Dunderberg, I. 2008. *Beyond Gnosticism: Myth, Lifestyle, and Society in the School of Valentinus*. New York: Columbia University Press.

———. 2009. "Judas' Anger and the Perfect Human." Pages 201–21 in *Codex Judas Papers: Proceedings of the International Congress on the Tchacos Codex Held at Rice University, Houston, Texas, March 13–16, 2008*. Edited by A. D. DeConick. Nag Hammadi and Manichaean Studies 71. Leiden: Brill.

Engberg-Pedersen, T. 2004. "The Concept of Paraenesis." Pages 47–72 in *Early Christian Paraenesis in Context*. Edited by J. M. Starr and T. Engberg-Pedersen. Beihefte zur Zeitschrift für die neutestamentliche Wissenschaft 125. Berlin: de Gruyter.

Greer, R. 1980. "The Dog and the Mushrooms: Irenaeus's View of the Valentinians Assessed." Pages 146–71 in *The School of Valentinus*. Vol. 1 of *The Rediscovery of Gnosticism: Proceedings of the International Conference on Gnosticism at Yale, New Haven, Connecticut, March 28–31, 1978*. Edited by B. Layton. Studies in the History of Religions (Supplements to Numen) 41. Leiden: Brill.

Knuuttila, S. 2004. *Emotions in Ancient and Medieval Philosophy*. Oxford: Oxford University Press.

Lapidge, M. 1989. "Stoic Cosmology and Roman Literature, First to Third Centuries A.D." *ANRW* 36.3:1379–1429. Part 2, *Principat*, 36.3. Edited by H. Temporini and W. Haase. Berlin: de Gruyter.

Layton, B. 1987. *The Gnostic Scriptures: A New Translation with Annotations and Introductions*. Anchor Bible Reference Library. Garden City, N.Y.: Doubleday.

---

[96] The numerous allusions to Platonic and Stoic ideas in *Corpus Hermeticum* are meticulously traced in Nock and Festugiere 1945–1954.

Long, A. A., and D. N. Sedley. 1987. *The Hellenistic Philosophers*. 2 vols. Cambridge: Cambridge University Press.

Luttikhuizen, G. P. 2006. *Gnostic Revisions of Genesis Stories and Early Jesus Traditions*. Nag Hammadi and Manichaean Studies 58. Leiden: Brill.

Mansfeld, J. 1992. *Heresiography in Context: Hippolytus' Elenchos as a Source for Greek Philosophy*. Philosophia antiqua 56. Leiden: Brill.

Markschies, C. 1992. *Valentinus Gnosticus? Untersuchungen zur valentinianischen Gnosis mit einem Kommentar zu den Fragmenten Valentins*. Wissenschaftliche Untersuchungen zum Neuen Testament 65. Tübingen: Mohr Siebeck.

Meyer, M., ed. 2007. *The Nag Hammadi Scriptures: The International Edition*. New York: HarperOne.

Nock, A. D., and A.-J. Festugière, eds. 1945–1954. *Corpus Hermeticum*. 4 vols. Paris: Les Belles Lettres.

Nussbaum, M. C. 1994. *The Therapy of Desire: Theory and Practice in Hellenistic Ethics*. Princeton, N.J.: Princeton University Press.

Onuki, T. 1989. *Gnosis und Stoa: Eine Untersuchung zum Apokryphon des Johannes*. Novum Testamentum et Orbis Antiquus 9. Freiburg: Universitätsverlag; Göttingen: Vandenhoeck & Ruprecht.

Pleše, Z. 2006. *Poetics of the Gnostic Universe: Narrative and Cosmology in the Apocryphon of John*. Nag Hammadi and Manichaean Studies 52. Leiden: Brill.

Sagnard, F.-M. 1947. *La gnose valentinienne et le témoignage de Saint Irénée*. Études de philosophie médiévale 36. Paris: Vrin.

Schoedel, W. R. 1979. "Enclosing, Not Enclosed: The Early Christian Doctrine of God." Pages 75–86 in *Early Christian Literature and the Classical Intellectual Tradition*. Edited by W. R. Schoedel and R. L. Wilken. Théologie historique 53. Paris: Beauchesne.

———. 1980. "Gnostic Monism and the Gospel of Truth." Pages 379–90 in *The School of Valentinus*. Vol. 1 of *The Rediscovery of Gnosticism: Proceedings of the International Conference on Gnosticism at Yale, New Haven, Connecticut, March 28–31, 1978*. Edited by B. Layton. Studies in the History of Religions (Supplements to Numen) 41. Leiden: Brill.

Sihvola, J., and T. Engberg-Pedersen, eds. 1998. *The Emotions in Hellenistic Philosophy*. New Synthese Historical Library 46. Dordrecht: Kluwer.

Strutwolf, H. 1993. *Gnosis als System: Zur Rezeption der valentinianischen Gnosis bei Origenes*. Forschungen zur Kirchen- und Dogmengeschichte 56. Göttingen: Vandenhoeck & Ruprecht.

Thomassen, E. 2006. *The Spiritual Seed: The Church of the "Valentinians."* Nag Hammadi and Manichaean Studies 60. Leiden: Brill.

Williams, M. A. 1996. *Rethinking "Gnosticism": An Argument for Dismantling a Dubious Category*. Princeton, N.J.: Princeton University Press.

Wolfson, H. A. 1956. *Faith, Trinity, Incarnation*. Vol. 1 of *The Philosophy of the Church Fathers*. Cambridge, Mass.: Harvard University Press.

12

CRITICAL RECEPTION OF THE STOIC THEORY OF PASSIONS IN THE *APOCRYPHON OF JOHN*

Takashi Onuki
University of Tokyo

1. The Text and Specification of the Topic

The *Apocryphon of John* exists in four extant Coptic manuscripts (NHC II,1; III,1; IV,1; BG 8502,2). Two of the four, NHC II,1 and IV,1, contain a long section (II 15.29–19.12 par.) that has no parallel in either NHC III,1 or BG 8502,2.[1] This section is, in fact, a long secondary addition, which I will call "the Great Interpolation." It is part of a larger scene describing the construction of the psychic human being—itself part of the exposition of the salvation myth in the *Apocryphon of John*. It is told in the larger scene how the world-creator Yaldabaoth, together with the angels (or the rulers) of the middle region, provides the psychic human with various limbs. The Great Interpolation itself starts with a list of various organs of the psychic human being, based on ancient anatomy, and then, from II 17.32 onward, on a distinctively Stoic epistemology, with a theory of character mixture and a theory of passions being introduced, all interpreted in a pejoratively distorted way from the perspective of Gnostic demonology.

Before specifying my aim, I will present the Stoicizing part of the added section (II 17.29–19.15), divided into five passages (the first and last passages frame the specifically Stoic discussion and partially exceed the limits of the Great Interpolation):[2]

A = II 17.29–32: Anatomy of human body

Seven, 7, have power over all of these: Michael, Ouriel, Asmenedas, Saphasatoel, Aarmouriam, Richram, Amiorps.

---

[1] NHC III,1 and BG 8502,2 are often referred to as the "short recension," and NHC II,1 and IV,1 as the "long recension." However, IV,1 is so fragmentary that it is usually given little consideration in studies on the *Apocryphon of John*. I will likewise here refer only to the NHC II version in discussing the long recension.

[2] The English translation is from Waldstein and Wisse 1995. I will also mark these passages A–E for the sake of convenience. I will explain my use of italics later.

B = II 17.32–18.2: Demonization of Stoic epistemology

And the ones who are in charge over the "senses" (are) Archendekta; and he who is in charge over "perception" (is) Deitharbathas; and he who is in charge over the "imagination" (is) Oummaa; and he who is in charge over the "agre[emen]t" (is) Aachiaram; and he who is in charge over the whole impulse (is) Riaramnacho.

C = II 18.2–14: Demonization of Stoic character (mixture) theory

And the origin of the demons which are in the whole body is determined to be four: heat, cold, wetness and dryness. And the mother of all of them is matter. And he who reigns over the heat (is) Phloxopha; and he who reigns over the cold (is) Oroorrothos; and he who reigns over what is dry (is) Erimacho; and he who reigns over the wetness (is) Athuro; And the mother of all these, Onorthochrasei, stands in their midst, for it is she who is illimitable, and she mixes with all of them.

D = NHC II 18.14–19.2: Demonization of the Stoic theory of passions

And she is truly matter, for the four chief demons are nourished by her: Ephememphi who belongs to pleasure, Yoko who belongs to desire, Nenetophni who belongs to grief, Blaomen who belongs to fear. And the mother of them all (is) Esthensis-Ouch-Epi-Ptoe.

From the four demons passions came forth. And from grief (came) envy, jealousy, distress, trouble, pain, callousness, anxiety, mourning, and so on. And from pleasure much wickedness arises, and empty pride, and similar things. And from desire (comes) anger, wrath and bitter[ness and] bitter passion and unsatedness and similar things. And from fear (comes) dread, fawning, agony, and shame.

All of these are like useful things as well as evil things. But the insight into their true (character) is Ana[io], who is the head of the material soul, for it is the seven senses of Ouch-Epi-Ptoe.

E = II 19.2–15: Adam, who was unable to stand up

This is the number of the angels: together they are three hundred sixty-five. They all worked on it until limb for limb, the psychic and the material body were completed by them. Now there are other ones in charge over the remaining passions whom I did not mention to you. But if you wish to know them, it is written in the book of Zoroaster. *And all the angels* and demons *worked until they had constructed the psychic body. And their product was completely inactive and motionless for a long time.*

In this essay, I will focus on two sentences from passage D: "All of these are like useful things as well as evil things" (II 18.31–32), and "And the mother of them all (is) Esthensis-Ouch-Epi-Ptoe" (II 18.18–19), together with "for it is the seven senses of Ouch-Epi-Ptoe" (II 19.1).

The first sentence seems abrupt and out of context even in passage D itself. Just before this sentence, it was remarked that all the four chief passions—grief, pleasure, desire, fear—as well as their subordinate passions came forth from demons. Thus, it is easy to understand the conclusion that "all of these are ... evil things." However, the subsequent statement, "All of these are like useful things ...," seems to contradict this conclusion. For this reason, scholars have presented various views on the interpretation and translation of this sentence.

First, Søren Giversen, in his edition of the Codex II version of the *Apocryphon of John* (1963), revised the Coptic пєтрωαγ, which was translated in the text quoted above as "useful things," into пєтр<αт>ωαγ.³ Giversen translated the latter expression as "all these of that kind of that which is useless,"⁴ primarily to make this part coherent with the demonizing interpretation of NHC II here. With this revision, the story in the *Apocryphon of John* myth would be coherent. However, Giversen gives no particular explanation in his note on this part, nor does he make any reference to the background of the Stoic theory of passions.⁵

Giversen's emendation of the Coptic text has found few supporters in later studies. In his translation of the *Apocryphon of John*, published in *The Nag Hammadi Library in English* (1977), Frederik Wisse, using the actual, unemended Coptic text, presents the same translation as I offer above. He has also held the same view in his subsequent publications.⁶ In *Nag Hammadi Deutsch I* (2001), Michael Waldstein translates this part: "All these are in one way useful but also evil."⁷ Michel Tardieu, in his *Écrits gnostiques* (1984), likewise follows the extant Coptic text and gives the same translation as Wisse and I offer.⁸ Tardieu also adds a note on this: "It seems to me that the conclusion of the catalog of the passions wishes to say that they are 'simultaneously useful and harmful'; useful for the demiurge but harmful for the creature."⁹ This is an attempt to make a coherent interpretation of the internal plot of the salvation myth in the *Apocryphon of John*. However, for the intellectual background history of this passage, Tardieu explicitly points out its relation to the Stoic theory of passions, making the observation that the ancient Stoics admitted the usefulness of the passions as well as their harmfulness,¹⁰ though he does not successfully present any Stoic passage to demonstrate this.¹¹

Finally, in his *Gnostic Scriptures* (1987), Bentley Layton also translates the section in question according to the extant text: "Now, all these are as it were virtues and vices."¹² In his notes on the passages before and after our sentence, he repeatedly points out parallels with Stoic ethics. In fact, as is evident from his use of the terms "virtues" and "vices," his translation here has a stronger affinity with the Stoic theory of virtues than with that of passions. Therefore, his translation makes

---

³αт is a Coptic prefix, corresponding to English "in-/un-," which can be used to negate nouns and adjectives.
⁴Giversen 1963, 80. The whole of II 18.31–32 reads, "All these of that kind of that which is useless and that which is evil."
⁵Giversen 1963, 250–51.
⁶Wisse 1977, 109; 1988, 115: "All of these are like useful things as well as evil things"; Waldstein and Wisse 1995, 111.
⁷Waldstein 2001, 130: "All diese sind in einer Weise nützlich, aber auch schlecht."
⁸Tardieu 1984, 130: "Toutes ces (passions) sont utiles et nuisibles."
⁹Ibid., 315: "La conclusion du catalogue des passions veut dire, me semble-t-il, que celles-ci sont 'à la fois utiles et nuisibles,' utiles au démiurge mais nuisibles pou la créature."
¹⁰"Le thème de l'utilité des passions vient de l'ancien stoïcisme" (ibid.).
¹¹Although Tardieu (ibid., 130) refers to SVF 3.391, 400, 401, 407, 409, 414, none of these passages testifies to the usefulness of passions.
¹²Layton 1987, 43.

it difficult to discern the demonization of the Stoic theory of passions in this passage of the *Apocryphon of John*.

Scholars generally agree today that behind the "Esthensis-Ouch-Epi-Ptoe" and "Ouch-Epi-Ptoe" is a Greek phrase, αἴσθησις οὐχ ἐπὶ πτοῇ, which literally means "perception not in a state of excitement." As far as I know, the exact same expression is not used in any sources of the Stoic theory. Undoubtedly, however, the idea itself is one of the fundamental propositions of Stoic (especially the early Stoic) epistemology and of the Stoic theory of passions, which is indivisibly united with epistemology. "A state of excitement (πτοία)" will mislead perception, the misled perception will misguide cognizance, and the misguided cognizance will stir passions. Therefore, being "not in a state of excitement" is closely related to the famous Stoic ideal of "apathy"—that is, a sagacious way of life that is free from all sorts of passions and is regarded as being of positive value.[13]

On the other hand, although Gnosticism certainly is fundamentally opposed to Stoicism in its cosmology (especially to Stoic natural philosophy), determinism, and eschatology,[14] it is undeniable that passions were evaluated negatively in Gnosticism. This is demonstrated by passages B–E above, which obviously demonize passions. With such a negative view of passions, some degree of sympathy with the Stoic theory of apathy, particularly to the slogan "perception not in a state of excitement" (αἴσθησις οὐχ ἐπὶ πτοῇ), should be expected. Then why is this slogan made into a proper noun, as the name of the mother of the demons, and thus debased enormously?[15]

From the considerations above, my concern in this study can be specified by the following three sets of questions:

(1) To what degree can the ambivalent evaluation of passions, "All of these are like useful things as well as evil things," be understood on the basis of the internal data derived from the mythic plot of the *Apocryphon of John*? Furthermore, to what extent can passages B–E, including this sentence conspicuously related to Stoic thought, be dealt with at the same level as the other parts of NHC II, which do not include anything particularly Stoic? In my book *Gnosis und Stoa*, I treated the whole Great Interpolation as stemming from a single redactor. We may, however, be dealing with multiple layers of redaction here. (These issues will be dealt with in section 2 below.)

(2) What form of the Stoic theory of passions do passages B–E assume? Do they betray direct knowledge of the Stoic theory of passions (i.e., in its pure form), or are they based on Stoic thought in its compromised form after it was syncretized with other forms of philosophy in late antiquity and transformed into a sort of popular philosophy? (See sections 2 and 4 below.)

---

[13] Pohlenz 1978, 150–52.
[14] See Onuki 1989.
[15] According to Waldstein and Wisse (1995, 109, note on II 18–19; 111, note on II 19.1), NHC II misunderstands the slogan of the Stoic theory of passion, αἴσθησις οὐχ ἐπὶ πτοῇ, as a proper noun and then does a "bastardization" of it. Does this mean that the inserter failed to understand the intellectualism of the Stoic theory of passions?

(3) What is the meaning and intention of the interpolator in taking up that Stoic thought? Up to what point does the interpolator faithfully report the Stoic thought, and why does he start debasing it with his own Gnostic idea? (See section 5 below.)

2. Critical Analysis of the Text

In his analysis of passages B–E, Giversen has already pointed out an extremely interesting fact: the word "demons" (ⲛⲓⲇⲁⲓⲙⲱⲛ) appears more frequently here than in any other part of all manuscripts of the *Apocryphon of John*.[16] NHC III and BG refer to "demons" only once, in the passage on fate. Although this passage also has its parallel text in NHC II, it does not belong to the Great Interpolation:

[1] And it (= the bitter fate) is harder and stronger than she (= fate) with whom the gods united and the angels and *the demons* and all the generations until this day. (II 28.19/III 37.10/BG 72.7)

In NHC II, the word "demons" appear also at the end of the manuscript, in the self-revelation hymn of Pronoia. This hymn, like the Great Interpolation itself, belongs to NHC II's material not found in the short recension—that is, in NHC III or BG:

[2] And follow your root, which is I, the merciful One [i.e., Pronoia], and guard yourself against the angels of poverty and *the demons* of chaos and all those who ensnare you. (II 31.18)

In addition to these passages, "demons" appear in NHC II four times, all in the Great Interpolation, and notably all occurrences concentrate in passages B–E, which are my special concern here.

[3] And the origin of *the demons* which are in the whole body is determined to be four. (II 18.2 [C])

The four "origins" mentioned here are "heat," "cold," "wetness," and "dryness." Because "the demons which are in the whole body" are said to be subordinate to these origins, the latter are also regarded as demons. It is in this passage that NHC II mentions "demons" for the first time. One who has read the Great Interpolation from its beginning now realizes that "the demons which are in the whole body" are to be contextually identified with the multitudinous "angels" (II 15.24–29), named one by one. The "Mother" of the four demons who stands above them is "illimitable matter" called Onorthochrasei:

---

[16] Giversen 1963, 250.

the matter

the mother, Onorthochrasei

↓

heat	cold	wetness	dry
Phloxopha	Oroorrothos	Athuro	Erimacho
↓	↓	↓	↓
demons	demons	demons	demons

[4] ... for *the four chief demons* are nourished by her [= the matter, II 18.13]. (II 18.15 [D])

[5] From *the four demons* passions came forth. (II 18.20 [D])

Although the names of the personalized "four chief demons" are different from those given in [3] (II 18.2 [C]), these chief demons are the same as in [3]: children of "the matter," or "the mother." However, the name of the "mother" is in this case given as "Esthensis-Ouch-Epi-Ptoe." "The four chief demons" are said to have given birth to the four Stoic chief passions and their subordinate passions.

the Matter

the mother, Onorthochrasei = Esthensis-Ouch-Epi-Ptoe

pleasure	desire	grief	fear
Ephemenphi	Yoko	Nennentophni	Blaomen
much wickedness	anger	envy	dread
empty pride	wrath	jealousy	fawning
similar things	bitterness	distress	agony
	bitter passion	trouble	shame
	unsatedness	pain	
	similar things	callousness	
		anxiety	
		mourning	
		and so on	

[6] And all the angels and *demons* worked until they had constructed the psychic body. (II 19.11 [E])

These sentences describe the finishing up of the construction of all the limbs and organs of the psychic human being, a description that has continued since II 15.13–29 (III 22.18–23.14/BG 49.9–50.14). The construction of the limbs and organs, according to II 15.13–29, was started by "the multitude of the angels" (II 15.24–29). Accordingly, this passage first refers to "all the angels." However, the following words "and demons" give the inevitable impression that the passage is a secondary addition. For, as was already remarked above, when NHC II first mentions the demons in [3] (II 18.2 [C]), "the demons which are in the whole body" are already, contextually and implicitly, identified with "the multitude of the angels" mentioned in II 15.24–29. Thus, this sentence can be seen as an explicit statement of the implicit identification in II 18.2. This suggests that the frequent mentioning of "the demons" in passages B–E is a secondary addition into the story of the construction of the psychic human being, which was originally related with the "multitude of the angels" as its grammatical subject.

The same development can be found in the distribution of the word "matter" (ϩⲩⲗⲏ). The use of the term "matter" is not as much confined to NHC II as that of "the demons." In the case of "the demons," five of the six references appear only in NHC II, since even quotation [2] above is attested only in NHC II. In NHC III and BG, the word "demons" appears only once, in [1]. On the other hand, "matter" is clearly referred to in NHC III and BG, as well as in NHC II, in a story of the creation of the material human being—that is, in the stage where the constructed psychic human being is pulled down into the lower region and clothed with the body. BG even refers to "matter" three times:

[1] And when they recognized that he (Adam) was luminous, and that he could think better than they, and that he was free from wickedness, they took him and cast him down into the lowest region of all *matter*. (II 20.9/III 24.24/BG 52.17)

[2] And they brought him (Adam) into the shadow of death in order that they might form (him) again from earth and water and fire and spirit, that is, from *the matter*— which is the ignorance of darkness—and desire and the counterfeit spirit. This is the tomb of the form of the body with which the robbers had clothed the man, the fetter of forgetfulness. And he became a mortal man. This is the first one who came down and the first separation. (II 21.7/III 26.18/BG 55.7)

[3] This is the tomb of the form of the body with which they clothed the man as the fetter of *matter*. (BG 55.13 [the term "matter" is substituted with "forgetfulness" in the other manuscripts])

"The matter," or "the region of matter," exists from the very first as the opposite of Pleroma ("Fullness"). While NHC III and BG speak of matter only implicitly, NHC II alone explicitly states its existence, and it does so in the most appropriate scene for the development of the plot of the myth, namely, where the supreme God of Pleroma reveals himself (in human guise) to Yaldabaoth. In the respective parallels to this scene in NHC III and BG, there is no mention of "(the region of) matter."

> [4] And the whole aeon of the Chief Ruler (Protarchon) trembled, and the foundations of the abyss shook. And of the waters which are above *matter*, the underside was illuminated by [the appearance] of this image. (II 14.28)

In addition to the cases I have mentioned so far, NHC II refers to "matter" twice. If we take into account the adjective "material/hylic" (ὑλική/ὑλικόν), "matter" is referred to four more times in NHC II, all these occurrences being concentrated in the passages C–E:

> [5] And the mother of all of them [= the four origins of the demons which are in the whole body] is *matter*. (II 18.5 [C])

> [6] And she [= Onorthochrasei] is truly *matter*. (II 18.13 [D])

> [7] But the insight into their true (character) is Ana[io], who is the head of the *material* (ὑλική) soul. (II 18.34 [D])

> [8] They all worked on it until limb by limb, the psychic and the *material* [ὑλικόν] body were completed by them. (II 19.6 [E])

Such frequent repetition of references to "matter" in passages C–E proves that the construction of "the psychic *and* the material body" is already assumed here. This can be seen especially clearly in [8]. However, this does not fit into the development of the plot in the *Apocryphon of John*. The clothing of the psychic body with the material body is, as we have seen in [1] and [2], a theme addressed in II 19.34–21.16 (III 24.14–27.4/BG 52.1–55.18) that has not yet been mentioned. Here is an inconsistency that Bentley Layton has already pointed out.[17] The text in C–E does not take into account the theme of the construction of limbs and organs for the psychic human being, of which other parts of the Great Interpolation are strongly aware.

From all these observations regarding the distribution of the two key terms "the demons" and "the matter," we can postulate a hypothesis that passages B–E were secondarily added to the end of the Great Interpolation. It is likely that the editor tried to make his addition to the Great Interpolation fit the earlier version by modifying the original conclusion of the Great Interpolation in passage E—that is, by changing the conclusion of the story of how the psychic human being was formed by "the multitude of the angels" into a story of the creation of the "material" human (body) by "the demons."

Now, on this hypothesis, if we try to divide passage E into the part that probably belonged to the original Great Interpolation and the part that is likely to have

---

[17] Layton 1987, 43n19b (note to II 19.3): "'and material body': with this word the narrator assumes something, since the material body's creation is described at 20,28f. The present passage tells only how the "animate . . . body was completed." However, the theme of II 20.28–29, to which Layton refers, is not the creation of material human beings. Thus, there seems to be some confusion in his remark here.

been added later, it seems to me that there are two possibilities. One is to divide the text as already presented at the beginning of this essay (the original Great Interpolation is in italics):

> This is the number of the angels: together they are three hundred sixty-five. They all worked on it until limb for limb, the psychic and the material body were completed by them. Now there are other ones in charge over the remaining passions whom I did not mention to you. But if you wish to know them, it is written in the book of Zoroaster. *And all the angels and demons worked until they had constructed the psychic body. And their product was completely inactive and motionless for a long time.*

The other alternative is as follows:

> This is the number of the angels: together they are three hundred sixty-five. They all worked on it until limb for limb, the psychic and the material body were completed by them. Now there are other ones in charge over the remaining passions whom I did not mention to you. But if you wish to know them, it is written in the book of Zoroaster. And all the angels and demons worked until they had constructed the psychic body. *And their product was completely inactive and motionless for a long time.*

However, there is no serious difference between the first and the second alternative. The crucial thing is that, in either case, the passage in italics follows directly and very smoothly after passage A, presented at the beginning of this study. In other words, the text of B–D, together with the nonitalicized part of passage E, forms a secondary addition to the Great Interpolation. This conclusion follows from the philological observations presented above.

Obviously, the final redactor, who made a later addition to the Great Interpolation, had some particular interest in Stoic epistemology, in the character (mixture) theory and in the theory of passions. In passage E, the redactor comments particularly on the theory of passions:

> Now there are other ones in charge over the remaining passions whom I did not mention to you. But if you wish to know them, it is written in the book of Zoroaster. And all the angels and demons worked until they had constructed the psychic body. (NHC II 19.7–10).

The reference to the *Book of Zoroaster* shows that this author used various literary sources. How was this *Book of Zoroaster* related to the Stoic theories in question? To explore this, I begin with a review of basic principles of Stoicism, especially its theory of passions.

3. Ancient Stoic Theory of Passions

As we can see from some witnesses in the *Stoicorum Veterum Fragmenta* (*SVF*),[18] the ancient Stoic school divided the human psyche into eight parts:

---

[18] von Arnim 1968.

The Stoics say that the soul is composed of eight parts. Five of them are controlling the five senses, that is, the senses of sight, hearing, smell, taste, and touch. The sixth part controls language, and the seventh controls procreation. The eighth part is *the governing part* [τὸ ἡγεμονικόν] itself, and by this, all the other parts are governed through their attached organs. They say it is just like the intertwining of tentacles of a sea anemone.[19]

The "governing part" mentioned here is equivalent to the "governing reason" (Logos) that governs the whole universe, and the passions are explained as its perverse judgment (κρίσις/δόξα)—that is, as a sort of illness. One of the causes of such perverted judgment is "excitement" (πτοία = πτοή). We will look at two witnesses in which this relation can be seen most clearly. The first is Stobaeus, the second Plutarch.

> They [Zeno and other Stoic philosophers] say that passions [πάθος] are either overpowering impulses that do not obey the instruction of Logos, or the soul's irrational [i.e., not according to the Logos] movement against its nature, though *all the passions belong to the governing part of the soul* [ἡγεμονικόν]. Therefore, *all the excitements* [πτοία] *are also passions, or to say it the other way around, all the passions are excitements*. Then, if passions are such, it should be assumed that some of them are leading passions and the others are subordinate to those leading passions. The leading passions are desire [ἐπιθυμία], fear [φόβος], grief [λύπη] and pleasure [ἡδονή]. Among them, desire and fear come forth chronologically in advance. Desire comes forth in regard to some emerging good and fear is against some emerging evil. In contrast, pleasure and grief come forth chronologically afterwards. Pleasure comes when we have got what we desired or when we have escaped from what we feared. Grief comes when we have failed to get what we desired or when we are trapped by what we have feared.[20]

> They [Zeno, Chrysippus, and others] also think that the passionate and the irrational part of the soul is not distinguished from the rational by any difference or by its nature, but is the same part, *which, indeed, they term intelligence* [διάνοια] *and the governing part* [ἡγεμονικόν]; *it is, they say, wholly transformed and changes both during its emotional states and in the alterations brought about in accordance with an acquired disposition or condition and thus becomes both vice and virtue* [κακίαν τε γίγνεσθαι καὶ ἀρετήν]; it contains nothing irrational within itself, but is called irrational whenever, by the overmastering power of our impulses, which have become strong and prevail, it is hurried on to something outrageous which contravenes the convictions of reason. Passion, in fact, according to them, is a vicious and intemperate reason, formed from an evil and perverse judgment [κρίσις] which has acquired additional violence and strength.[21]

What is especially important to note here is the sentence "*All the excitements* [πτοία] *are also passions, and to say it the other way around, all the passions are*

---

[19] Aëtius, *De placita* 4.4.4 (Diels 1965, 390.5–13 [my translation]). See also *SVF* 1.143 on Zeno; *SVF* 2.879 on Chrysippus.

[20] *SVF* 3.378 = Stobaeus, *Anth.* 2.7.10 (= 2.88.8–21 W-H) (my translation and italics). A parallel sentence to the latter part of "all the excitements [πτοία] are also passions, and to say it the other way around, all the passions are excitements" is attributed to Zeno, the founder of the school (see *SVF* 1.206 = Stobaeus, *Anth.* 2.7.1 [= 2.37.15–39.18 W-H]).

[21] *SVF* 3.459 = Plutarch, *Virt. mor.* 441C–447A, here 441C-D (translation, Helmbold 1939; my italics).

excitements." The "excitement" of the "governing part" of the psyche, like its "ignorance," would lead to evil and perverse judgment (κρίσις), from which comes vice. Virtue is brought about when "the governing part" is completely in the opposite condition. This is the so-called radical intellectualism ("schroffe Intellektualismus") of the Stoic doctrine of passions.[22]

In the light of these witnesses, it is obvious that the slogan αἴσθησις οὐχ ἐπὶ πτοῇ behind the names "Esthensis-Ouch-Epi-Ptoe" and "Ouch-Epi-Ptoe" in passage D of the *Apocryphon of John* reflects nothing other than the Stoic theory of passions. The *Apocryphon of John* debases this by demonization, but at the end of passage D it is affirmed: "But the insight into their [= the four demonized chief passions and their subordinated passions] true (character) is Ana[io], who is the head of the material soul, for it is the seven senses of Ouch-Epi-Ptoe." It is clear that the Stoic theory of the soul's eight parts is present in the thought expressed here. "Ouch-Epi-Ptoe" is nothing but a demonization of the Stoic "governing part" (ἡγεμονικόν). The same can be said about the "Esthensis-Ouch-Epi-Ptoe" (D) and "Onorthochrasei" (C), which are contextually identified with that "Ouch-Epi-Ptoe."

Then what about "All of these are like useful things as well as evil things," which is also found in passage D? Among the aforementioned accounts about the Stoic theory of passions, the closest analogy to this statement is found in Plutarch:

> They [Zeno, Chrysippus, and others] also think that the passionate and the irrational part of the soul is not distinguished from the rational by any difference or by its nature, but is the same part, *which, indeed, they term intelligence* [διάνοια] *and the governing part* [ἡγεμονικόν]; *it is, they say, wholly transformed and changes both during its emotional states and in the alterations brought about in accordance with an acquired disposition or condition and thus becomes both vice and virtue.*[23]

Layton perhaps had this statement in mind when he translated the same sentence in passage D above as "Now, all these are as it were virtues and vices."[24] In that case, this sentence in passage D is presented as a virtual transcription of the Stoic theory of passions, particularly its theory on "the governing part."

In my judgment, however, Layton's interpretation is untenable. According to the ancient Stoics, passions and vices certainly *emerge* from the same "governing part." Passions and vices, however, are themselves always "the soul's irrational [i.e., not according to the Logos] movement against its nature." Therefore, they could never be "useful." Passions are, as it were, an "illness" of the soul's "governing part."[25] Thus, it is a Stoic sage's great task to eradicate them and attain the life of "apathy." In contrast to this ideal, passage D admits the usefulness as well as the harmfulness of the four chief passions and their subpassions, which it has listed as ruled by the demons. The difference from the Stoics' idea is too obvious not to be noticed.

---

[22] Pohlenz 1978, 144, 147; Colish 1985, 1:44.
[23] Plutarch, *Virt. mor.* 441C (translation, Helmbold 1939).
[24] Layton 1987, 43.
[25] Pohlenz 1978, 150.

Although the Stoics evaluated the passions, particularly the four chief passions, in general and in principle negatively, they also talked about "good passions." For instance, Diogenes Laertius enumerates these emotional states as follows:

> Also they say that there are three emotional states which are good [εὐπαθεῖαι], namely, joy [χαρά], caution [εὐλάβεια], and wishing [βούλη]. Joy, the counterpart of pleasure [ἡδονή], is rational elation; caution, the counterpart of fear [φόβος], rational avoidance; for though the wise man will never feel fear, he will yet use caution. And they make wishing the counterpart of desire [or 'craving,' ἐπιθυμία], inasmuch as it is rational appetency [εὔλογος ὄρεξις]. And accordingly, as under the primary passions are classed certain others subordinate to them, so too is it with the primary wishing or good emotional states. Thus under wishing they bring well-wishing or benevolence, friendliness, respect, affection; under caution, reverence and modesty; under joy, delight, mirth, cheerfulness.[26]

However, all three of these "good emotional states" are defined as the opposite of "pleasure," "fear," and "desire." Therefore, such an exceptional theory of "good emotions" cannot possibly be assumed as the background of the sentence in passage D, which is concerned with the four chief passions and with the passions subordinated to them.[27]

As has become clear by now, the usefulness of passions, which passage D admits, cannot be explained by the ancient Stoic theory of passions. Thus, I cannot agree with Tardieu, who argues for this possibility.[28] Among the philosophical schools in the Hellenistic period, it was specifically the Peripatetics who admitted the usefulness of passions. The Stoic theory of passions was always conscious of such a Peripatetic theory affirming the usefulness of passions, and intensely opposed it.[29] Should we therefore suppose the Peripatetic theory of passions as the background of passage D's affirmation of usefulness as well as the harmfulness of passions?

4. The History of Influence of the Ancient Stoic Theory of Passions

In regard to the usefulness of passions, affirmed in passage D, Tardieu refers not only to the Stoic theory of passions but also to some passages in the *Pseudo-Clementine Homilies*.[30] Among them, the following passage seems to be the most relevant one to this study:

---

[26] SVF 3.431 = Diogenes Laertius, *Vit. phil.* 7.115 (translation, Hicks 1931).

[27] In fact, "appetency" (ὄρεξις), which is mentioned in Diogenes Laertius's report, also appears often on the lists of negative passions, and therefore it is a neutral passion. Cf. SVF 3.442 (= Clement, *Strom.* 4.18.5). "Then those who understand this point well distinguish appetency [ὄρεξις] from desire [ἐπιθυμία]. They place desire as an irrational thing which directs to pleasure [ἡδονή] and self-indulgence, while regarding appetency as directing to the necessary things in nature." However, as far as I know, this is the only example that concerns both good and bad passions.

[28] "Le thème de l'utilité des passions vient de l'ancien stoïcisme" (Tardieu 1984, 315).

[29] See Cicero, *Tusc.* 4.37–57; Seneca, *Ira* 1.5.1–17.7; Milobenski 1964, 89; Pohlenz 1978, 150.

[30] Tardieu 1984, 316.

And Peter also said, "Then evil does not exist eternally, nor surely could it exist that way. For feeling pain and dying is something happening, and if we are healthy, neither of them will do harm. For what is feeling pain except that something is in discord? What is death except separation of soul from body? If there is harmony, there is no feeling pain. And neither is dying that of the total existence. For, as I have said, death is nothing but separation of soul from body. And when separation happens, the body is in nature without the ability to sense and so dissolves. And the soul, as having senses, continues to live. Therefore, where there is harmony, there is no feeling pain or dying, nor are there deadly plants or venomous reptiles, or anything which brings death at the end to human beings. Therefore, where immortality is victorious, all will appear to have come into being in a reasonable way [εὐλόγως]. And so all will be when the kingdom of Christ's peace is triumphant, and when the human being becomes immortal for the sake of justice. And when man's mixture [κρᾶσις] is in good condition and never suffers from *excessive impulses* [ὁρμάς] *and its knowledge* [γνῶσις] *is free from stumbling, so that it never takes something evil for something good*, lest it should cause pain and death."

Then Simon said, "All that you said correctly. Nevertheless, in this world, does it not seem to you that the human being is liable to all passions? I just mention *desire* [ἐπιθυμία], *anger* [ὀργή], '*pain*' [λύπη], *and other passions* [τὰ τοιοῦτα]." And then Peter said, "And such passions are also something that happens to us and not something existing eternally. But it will be found that these things happening are beneficial for the soul. For desire [ἐπιθυμία] is attached to the living things by the one who created all things beautifully. Consequently, passions for sexual intercourse fill mankind and if mankind chooses the better, a lot of things which are advantageous and suitable for eternal life will come about. In any case, without desire no one would welcome intercourse with a woman. But now, human beings are doing it to indulge themselves in pleasure, and by doing so, they are executing the purpose of that one [i.e., the Creator]. But even if someone uses this desire for lawful marriage, he is not acting impiously. If he does it from an impulse to commit adultery, however, he is acting impiously. He will be punished. For he used badly what is given for good. Likewise, anger [ὀργή] is given by God to have its proper place to occur naturally in us so that we might be led by it to defend ourselves against sin. However, if someone uses it excessively, he does injustice; while, if properly using it, he is acting to complete justice. Also, as we are susceptible to pain [λύπη], it is in order to have sympathy in regard to deaths in families, of wife or children or brothers or parents or friends. Indeed, if we did not feel such sympathy, we would be inhuman. Likewise, *all the other passions* [τὰ ἄλλα πάντα] will be found existing properly, if they are understood in the way they came about." (*Hom.* 19.20.6–19.21.7).[31]

Differing from the ancient Stoic theory of passions, this passage clearly affirms that desire and all other passions are *in themselves* useful in some circumstances when properly used.[32] Could this affirmation belong to the line of the Peripatetic theory of passions?

---

[31] Rehm 1953, 264–65 (my translation). See also the French translation in Siouville 1933, 359–60.
[32] Usually, the four chief passions are desire, grief, pleasure, and fear. However, in this case, anger replaces fear.

The *Pseudo-Clementine Homilies*, which consist of twenty books, repeatedly refer to Greek myths and Greek philosophical traditions. They do not, however, seem to exalt any single philosophical school in particular. At least, they certainly do not exalt or give any privileged position to the Stoic theory of passions. However, the italicized passages in the quotation above perhaps can be seen as being influenced by the Stoic theory of passions. The first italicized phrase reminds us of the following passage in Plutarch's report:

> [The passionate and the irrational part of the soul] is called irrational whenever, by the overmastering power of our impulses, which have become strong and prevail, it is hurried on to something outrageous which contravenes the convictions of reason. Passion, in fact, according to them, is a vicious and intemperate reason, formed from an evil and perverse judgment [κρίσις] which has acquired additional violence and strength.[33]

The "other passions" (τὰ τοιοῦτα) and "all the other passions" (τὰ ἄλλα πάντα) (the second and third italicized passages above) are typical Stoic catalog expressions, going back to the early Stoics. They are also repeatedly found in our passage D—three times, to be exact. However, all these considerations are not sufficient to place the quoted passage from the *Pseudo-Clementine Homilies* directly in the line of the Stoic theory of passions, since Peripatetic influence on it is also undeniable.[34]

Nonetheless, we have at least one text that clearly is under the influence of the Stoic theory of passions, but at the same time relativizes, or at least neutralizes, the negative evaluation of passion in the soul's "governing part." This text is the *Testament of Reuben*, one of the *Testaments of the Twelve Patriarchs*. Significantly, this text was composed under the influence of both Judaism and Christianity. The relevant passage in this text (2.1–3.7) runs as follows:

> 2:1And now hear me, my children, what things I saw concerning the seven spirits of deceit, when I repented. ²Seven spirits therefore are appointed against man, and they are the leaders in the works of youth. ³*And seven other spirits are given to him at his creation, that through them should be done every work of man.* ⁴*The first is the spirit of life, with which the constitution (of man) is created. The second is the sense of sight, with which ariseth desire.* ⁵*The third is the sense of hearing, with which cometh teaching. The fourth is the sense of smell, with which tastes are given to draw air and breath.* ⁶*The fifth is the power of speech, with which cometh knowledge.* ⁷*The sixth is the sense of taste, with which cometh the eating of meats and drinks; and by it strength is produced, for in food is the foundation of strength.* ⁸*The seventh is the power of procreation and sexual intercourse, with which through love of pleasure sins enter in.* ⁹*Wherefore it is the last in order of creation, and the first in that of youth, because it is filled with ignorance, and leadeth the youth as a blind man to a pit, and as a beast to a precipice.* 3:1*Besides all these there is an eighth spirit of sleep, with which is brought about the trance of nature and the image*

---

[33] Plutarch, *Virt. mor.* 441C–D (translation, Helmbold 1939).
[34] For a similar example of syncretism, one may refer to 4 Maccabees. The theory of passions found in this book is fundamentally based on that of the Stoics, with some additional Peripatetic influence. See von Gemünden 2003; Theißen 2007, 426n25.

of death. ²*With these spirits*³⁵ *are mingled the spirits of error.* ³First, the spirit of fornication is seated in the nature and in the senses; the second, the spirit of insatiableness, in the belly; ⁴the third, the spirit of fighting, in the liver and gall; the fourth is the spirit of obsequiousness and chicanery, that through officious attention one may be fair in seeming. ⁵The fifth is the spirit of pride, that one may be boastful and arrogant. The sixth is the spirit of lying, in perdition and jealousy to practise deceits, and concealments from kindred and friends. ⁶The seventh is the spirit of injustice, with which are thefts and acts of rapacity, that a man may fulfil the desire of his heart; for injustice worketh together with the other spirits by the taking of gifts. ⁷And with all these the spirit of sleep is joined which is (that) of error and fantasy.³⁶

It seems to have become a *communis opinio* among scholars that the italicized part of the text above is a secondary addition, and that the interpolator was under influence of the Stoic theory of passions.³⁷ I agree with this view. In my judgment, the interpolator was basically concerned with introducing the Stoic theory of passions about the "governing part" (ἡγεμονικόν) of the soul in a popularized form.

Before the addition was made, the main theme of the text was obviously "the seven spirits of deceit," as 2.1–2 manifestly states. In contrast, the editor tells of "seven other spirits" given to human beings; these spirits, listed in 2.3–9, are said to be "other spirits" than "the spirits of deceit." Except for the seventh one, "the power of procreation and sexual intercourse," these "other spirits" are evaluated as beneficent powers working for human beings.

In 3.1, the editor introduces an eighth spirit, the "spirit of sleep." Its function is, like that of the seventh spirit, negative. The eighth spirit is said to be the one "with which is brought about the trance of nature and the image of death." In fact, "the eighth spirit" is secondarily added as a negative figure again in 3.7, after the listing of the seven "spirits of deceit," according to the text before the addition was made.³⁸ The editor's purpose in introducing the eighth spirit in 3.1 and 3.7 with almost the same words is to make the number of both "the spirits of deceit" and the "other spirits" eight.

It is virtually certain that the inserter associates this "eight" with the Stoic theory of the soul consisting of eight parts. Furthermore, what is crucial is the following sentence in 3.2: "With these spirits are mingled the spirits of error." "These spirits" mentioned here are the "other spirits" *and* "the eighth spirit" listed in 2.3–3.1. These eight spirits are said to "be mingled" with the seven "other spirits" and "the eighth spirit" listed in 3.2–7. This corresponds to the Stoic theory of passions: "They also think that the passionate and the irrational part of the soul is not distinguished from the rational by any difference or by its nature, but is the same part."³⁹

---

³⁵ The Greek original has two variant readings in singular and plural. The plural reading is consistently referred to in both 2.2 and 3.3–6 (the vices), and therefore it is contextually more natural.
³⁶ Translation, Charles 1913.
³⁷ See Charles 1913, 2:297n2; Becker 1980, 33n3a.
³⁸ See Becker 1980, 33n3a, 35n7b.
³⁹ Plutarch, *Virt. mor.* 441C (translation, Helmbold 1939).

The editor substantiates, on the one hand, each of the eight parts of the soul as an independent "spirit." On the other hand, the author divides the ambivalent "governing part" (which is susceptible to an "illness" of the passions but, when it acts according to its nature, capable of working rationally) into two groups, "the spirit of deceits" and "other spirits." However, the editor thinks that these divided parts will be mingled de facto with each other. Though it must be admitted that neither the chief passions nor their subordinate passions are explicitly mentioned here, even less is their usefulness acknowledged. Nevertheless, it can be said at least that the solely negative values attributed to those passions by the ancient Stoics are beginning to be relativized.

The *Book of Zoroaster*, which was a source used by the redactor of the *Apocryphon of John* responsible for the addition to the Great Interpolation, presumably went in the same direction as the secondary addition in the *Testament of Reuben* (2.3–3.2; 3.7). Based on the Stoic theory of passions, the *Book of Zoroaster* could have also adopted the Peripatetic idea of the usefulness of passions. Moreover, the *Book of Zoroaster* depicts passions as being under the control of various angels (or demons), and such mythologization of passions goes hand in hand with the secondary insertion added to the *Testament of Reuben*.

5. Conclusion: The Theory of Passions in the *Apocryphon of John* NHC II 17.32–19.15

In conclusion, I will clarify how, from the Gnostic viewpoint, the redactor who made an addition to the Great Interpolation (B–E) evaluated the Stoic theory of passions and other similar theories when he made that insertion, which was based on the *Book of Zoroaster*.

First, one important conclusion is that the redactor is quite indifferent as to whether his addition is, in terms of the plot, consistent with the rest of the myth related in the *Apocryphon of John*. Thus, the aforementioned attempts by Giversen and Tardieu to interpret, in their respective ways, the sentence "All of these are like useful things as well as evil things" in passage D purely from the internal plot of the *Apocryphon of John* are quite inconclusive. Admittedly, for an interpretation of the myth internal to the text, the following passage, in which each of the seven rulers under Yaldabaoth is said to have two names, may prove helpful:

> They were given names according to the glory of the heavenly ones for the [destruction of the] powers. And in the names which were given to [them by] their Archigenetor there was power. But the names which were given them according to the glory of the heavenly ones mean for them destruction and powerlessness. Thus they have two names. (II 12.26–13.4/III 17.5–17/BG 40.19–41.12)

However, despite the similarity of the phraseology, there is little possibility that the person who made the addition to the Great Interpolation had this passage in mind. He simply does not have such a long perspective on storytelling. His main concern is to demonize the Stoic theory of passions and to debase it together with the Stoic epistemology and character (mixture) theory. It is for this reason that he has brought the key words "demon" and "matter" in such a concentrated way into the text of B–E, even disregarding the plot of the myth told in the *Apocryphon of John* as a whole. Of course, the development in that direction could have started in his source, the *Book of Zoroaster*. Even so, the redactor certainly has pushed the movement of demonization greatly ahead.

At the same time, it should be noted that such demonization is a severe criticism of "radical intellectualism," which is so characteristic of the Stoic theory of passions. "Perception not in a state of excitement" (αἴσθησις οὐχ ἐπὶ πτοῇ) is a proposition that has extremely positive connotations with the Stoics. This leads to the fundamental proposition of Stoic ethics: "apathy." It is, in principle, possible that the redactor who expanded the Great Interpolation in passages B–E, as a Gnostic, might have had sympathy with the Stoic eagerness to eradicate the passions. However, he has debased the Stoic proposition into the expression "Esthensis-Ouch-Epi-Ptoe" or "Ouch-Epi-Ptoe," identifying it with "matter," which for the Gnostics is the principle of evil itself, mythologically personalizing it as the mother of various demons. The redactor is not objecting to the fact that the Stoic theory of passions evaluates passions negatively, but he is strongly objecting to the fact that the Stoic theory of passions defines passions by radical intellectualism.[40]

The NHC II version of the *Apocryphon of John* had already partly identified the creator god Yaldabaoth with what the Stoics called the "governing part" before a later redactor made his addition to the Great Interpolation. With this affirmation, the *Apocryphon of John* refuted Stoic cosmology that argued that the "governing part" of the soul of the whole macrocosmos lies in the supreme region of the eighth heaven, the region of aether.[41] The person who made the final addition to passages B–E is making the same refutation in regard to the "governing part" of the soul. He does it, however, in the framework of the Stoic theory of passions that has to do with the soul of human beings, the microcosmos.

Bibliography

Becker, J. 1980. *Die Testamente der zwölf Patriarchen*. Jüdische Schriften aus hellenistisch-römischer Zeit 3/1. Gütersloh: Mohn.
Charles, R. H., ed. 1913. *The Apocrypha and Pseudepigrapha of the Old Testament in English, with Introductions and Critical and Explanatory Notes to the Several Books*. 2 vols. Oxford: Clarendon Press.
Colish, M. L. 1985. *The Stoic Tradition from Antiquity to the Early Middle Ages*. 2 vols. Studies in the History of Christian Thought 35. Leiden: Brill.
Diels, H. 1965. *Doxographi Graeci*. 4th ed. Berlin: de Gruyter.

---

[40] See Onuki 2007.
[41] See Pohlenz 1978, 95, 186; Onuki 1989, 55–74.

Giversen, S. 1963. *Apocryphon Johannis: The Coptic Text of the Apocryphon Johannis in the Nag Hammadi Codex II, with Translation, Introduction and Commentary.* Acta theologica Danica 5. Copenhagen: Munksgaard.

Helmbold, W. C. 1939. *Plutarch's Moralia.* Vol. 6. Loeb Classical Library. Cambridge, Mass.: Harvard University Press.

Hicks, R. D. 1931. *Diogenes Laertius: Lives of Eminent Philosophers.* 2 vols. Loeb Classical Library. London: Heinemann.

Layton, B. 1987. *The Gnostic Scriptures: A New Translation with Annotations and Introductions.* Anchor Bible Reference Library. Garden City, N.Y.: Doubleday.

Milobenski, E. 1964. *Der Neid in der griechischen Philosophie.* Klassisch-philologische Studien 29. Wiesbaden: Harrassowitz.

Onuki, T. 1989. *Gnosis und Stoa: Eine Untersuchung zum Apokryphon des Johannes.* Novum Testamentum et Orbis Antiquus 9. Freiburg: Universitätsverlag; Göttingen: Vandenhoeck & Ruprecht.

———. 2007. "Der Neid in der Gnosis." Pages 321–42 in *Erkennen und Erleben: Beiträge zur psychologischen Erforschung des frühen Christentums.* Edited by G. Theißen and P. von Gemünden. Gütersloh: Gütersloher Verlagshaus.

Pohlenz, M. 1978. *Die Stoa: Geschichte einer geistigen Bewegung.* Vol. 1. 5th ed. Göttingen: Vandenhoeck & Ruprecht.

Rehm, B., ed. 1953. *Die Pseudoklementinen I: Homilien.* Die griechischen christlichen Schriftsteller der ersten Jahrhunderte 42. Berlin: Akademie-Verlag.

Siouville, A. 1933. *Les homélies Clémentines.* Les textes du christianisme 11. Paris: Rieder.

Tardieu, M. 1984. *Écrits gnostiques: Codex de Berlin.* Sources gnostiques et manichéennes 1. Paris: Cerf.

Theißen, G. 2007. *Erleben und Verhalten der ersten Christen: Eine Psychologie des Urchristentums.* Gütersloh: Gütersloher Verlagshaus.

von Arnim, H. F. A., ed. 1968. *Stoicorum Veterum Fragmenta.* 4 vols. Leipzig: Teubner, 1903–1924. Repr., Stuttgart: Teubner.

von Gemünden, P. 2003. "La gestion de la colère et de l'agression dans l'antiquité et dans le Sermon sur la montage." *Henoch* 25:19–45.

Waldstein, M. 2001. "Das Apokryphon des Johannes (NHC II,1; III,1; IV,1 und BG 2)." Pages 95–150 in vol. 1 of *Nag Hammadi Deutsch.* Edited by H.-M. Schenke, H.-G. Bethge, and U. U. Kaiser. Die griechischen christlichen Schriftsteller der ersten Jahrhunderte, Neue Folge 8; Koptisch-Gnostiche Schriften 2. Berlin: de Gruyter.

Waldstein, M., and F. Wisse, eds. 1995. *The Apocryphon of John: Synopsis of Nag Hammadi Codices II,1; III,1; and IV,1 with BG 8502,2.* Nag Hammadi and Manichaean Studies 33. Leiden: Brill.

Wisse, F. 1977. "The Apocryphon of John (II,*1*, III,*1*, IV,*1* and BG 8502,*2*)." Pages 98–116 in *The Nag Hammadi Library in English.* Edited by J. M. Robinson. Leiden: Brill.

———. 1988. "The Apocryphon of John (II,*1*, III,*1*, IV,*1* and BG 8502,*2*)." Pages 104–23 in *The Nag Hammadi Library in English.* Edited by J. M. Robinson. 3rd ed. Leiden: Brill.

13

STOIC INGREDIENTS IN THE NEOPLATONIC *BEING-LIFE-MIND* TRIAD: AN ORIGINAL SECOND-CENTURY GNOSTIC INNOVATION?

Tuomas Rasimus
University of Helsinki & Université Laval

It has become customary to think that Stoicism had two founders: Zeno, the original founder of the school, and Chrysippus, the reformer and systematizer of early Stoicism. In the 1950s and 1960s, the French scholar Pierre Hadot painted a comparable picture of Neoplatonism: Porphyry, the star student of Plotinus (the traditionally credited founder of Neoplatonism), should be seen as a great innovator and reformer of Plotinus's thinking, a veritable second founder of Neoplatonism.[1] According to Hadot, Porphyry invented an array of conceptual tools, having combined the metaphysics of Plotinus and the Middle Platonic *Chaldean Oracles* in an ingenious way to solve the puzzle of how to derive multiplicity from unity, crafting such tools out of Stoic ingredients.[2] These tools, in fact, consisted of various aspects of the famous *being-life-mind* triad, which Porphyry would have systematized and of which later Neoplatonists, as well as Christian theologians defending the "orthodox" doctrine of the Trinity, made much use. In this essay, I will, on the one hand, argue that Hadot was right in suggesting that the main aspects of the being-life-mind triad can be satisfactorily explained as having been based on Stoic ideas. On the other hand, I claim that Porphyry, in the third century, could not have been the Stoic-minded innovator and/or systematizer of the triad because the triad with its "Porphyrian" aspects is already attested in Sethian/Classic Gnostic texts from the second and third centuries.[3] The present state of our knowledge, based now also on sources not yet available to Hadot (the Coptic Nag Hammadi codices—he was, however, aware of the Coptic Gnostic Berlin Codex 8502), suggests that it could indeed have been Christian Gnostics of

---

[1] Hadot 1957; 1960; 1961; 1966; 1968.
[2] For the Stoic elements, see Hadot 1968, 1:89–90n5, 109–143, 225–34, 485–88.
[3] I argue this in detail in Rasimus, forthcoming. As for Sethian or Classic Gnosticism, see Schenke 1981; Layton 1987; Pearson 1990; Turner 2001; Rasimus 2009.

a strong philosophical inclination who contributed the being-life-mind triad to the history of Platonism—with all its consequences—by creatively crafting it out of Stoic elements. In what follows, I first discuss the Neoplatonic being-life-mind triad itself, then address the question of its Stoic ingredients, and finish with the problem of the likeliest innovators of these ideas. It should be noted that this essay builds upon a more extensive and technical one on Porphyry and the Gnostics that I published elsewhere, and that the discussion here, while elaborating on the Stoic question, lacks details meant for an audience attuned to Neoplatonism.[4]

1. The Being-Life-Mind Triad

Rudimentary forms of the being-life-mind triad are already found in the Stoicizing Middle Platonic *Chaldean Oracles* as well as in Plotinus's *Enneads*.[5] According to Hadot, Porphyry introduced the *Chaldean Oracles* with their theurgic tendencies into Neoplatonism and combined their metaphysics with that of Plotinus.[6] The Plotinian One is the first, utterly transcendent principle, which is beyond being and intellect. The Intellect proper, the second principle (also called the "One-Being"), then establishes itself by proceeding out of the One and turning back to gaze at its source.[7] Plotinus sometimes spoke of "being" and "life" as somehow belonging to the Intellect,[8] but he never clearly formulated the later famous being-life-mind triad. From the *Chaldean Orcales*, Porphyry would then have found a triad of first principles, Father-power-intellect,[9] although such a triad is not attested in the surviving fragments of the *Chaldean Oracles*.[10] In any case, Porphyry, supposedly being inspired by certain triadic speculations in the *Chal-*

---

[4] See Rasimus, forthcoming.

[5] For the *Chaldean Oracles* in general, see Majercik 1989. For the triadic speculations in them, see below. For Plotinus and the being-life-mind triad, see, on the one hand Hadot 1957; Turner 2001, 407–24, and on the other, Plotinus, *Enn.* (the canonical order: being-life-mind) 1.6 [1] 7.11–12; 5.4 [7] 2.17–18; 5.4 [7] 2.43–44; 6.9 [9] 2.24; 5.6 [24] 6.20–22; 3.6 [26] 6.10–17; 3.6 [26] 6.23–24; 5.5 [32] 1.38; 6.6 [34] 9.27–29; 6.7 [38] 23.22–25; 5.3 [49] 16.38–42; 1.8 [51] 2.5–7; *Enn.* (the noncanonical order: being-mind-life) 1.6 [1] 7.12; 5.9 [5] 10; 6.9 [9] 9; 3.9 [13] 6.3–6; 6.4 [22] 3.31–35; 5.6 [24] 6.20–22; 3.6 [26] 6.23–24; 3.6 [26] 7.7–8; 3.8 [30] 8.8–12; 3.8 [30] 10.1–2; 5.5 [32] 10.12–14; 6.6 [34] 8.1–2; 6.6 [34] 8.9–10; 6.6 [34] 8.11–13; 6.6 [34] 8.15–17; 6.6 [34] 8.17–23; 6.6 [34] 9.29–32; 6.6 [34] 15.1–3; 6.6 [34] 18.35–36; 6.6 [34] 18.51–53; 6.7 [38] 13.42–43.

[6] Hadot 1968, 1:92, 482–93.

[7] Plotinus, *Enn.* 5.1 [11]; 6.7 [38] 37.18–22.

[8] See note 5 above.

[9] Hadot 1968, 1:260–72.

[10] According to Hadot, Porphyry could have deduced the triad's existence from fragments 3 and 4 (Majercik 1989), where the Father is said to have snatched himself away without sharing his fire with his intellectual power (fragment 3), and where it is stated that while the power is with the Father, the intellect is from him (fragment 4). A triadic structure of everything is also alluded to in several fragments (2, 23, 27, 28, 29, 31). Some later *testimonia* (see note 18 below) attribute such a metaphysical scheme and an interest in the *Chaldean Oracles* to Porphyry.

dean Oracles,[11] would then have arranged this Father-power-intellect triad into an ennead (three triads), where each member of the triad already contains the other two but predominates in turn; this can be expressed as follows: (1) *FATHER*-power-intellect; (2) Father-*POWER*-intellect, (3) Father-power-*INTELLECT*. Porphyry would also have applied the method of paronyms (various forms of the same word, such as "intellectuality" and "intellect") to express the differences among the predominating and predominated aspects of the members. Porphyry, Hadot continues, then identified the Father with "Existence" (ὕπαρξις), an undetermined, potential existence beyond actualized being. Finally, Porphyry would have identified the Chaldean Father-*Existence* with the Plotinian One and come up with an enneadic triad at the top of his own metaphysical system: (1) *EXISTENCE*-Life-Mind, (2) Existence-*LIFE*-Mind; (3) Existence-Life-*MIND*.[12] In this system, multiplicity is derived from its potential and undetermined existence within the first principle, the One beyond actual being (or the "One-Existence" beyond the "One-Being"), out of which it proceeds and establishes itself in three phases.

Such an innovative combination of Plotinian and Chaldean views supposedly caused Porphyry to come up with several characteristic and innovative ideas that have to do with various aspects and functions of the being-life-mind triad. They can be expressed as follows (some of the items overlap as they represent various aspects of the same ideas; for occurrences, see the synopsis below):[13] (1) use of the being-life-mind triad, especially to explain the generation (externalization) of the Intellect from the One; (2) the concept of the prefiguration or potential existence of the Intellect within the One; (3) the distinction between undetermined and determined aspects of being, life, and mind; (4) the enneadic structuring of the being-life-mind triad (and/or Father-power-intellect); (5) the use of the principles of mutual implication and relative predominance; (6) the method of paronyms; (7) the use of ὕπαρξις (Latin: *exsistentia*) to denote the undetermined being or existence; and (8) the related description of the first principle as the "non-being above being." In addition, one could mention (9) the characterization in this context of the One/God as spirit, which Hadot, however, was not ready to ascribe to Porphyry, but to the Gnostics![14]

While such ideas and such a metaphysical system are, for the most part, alluded to in the surviving genuine works of Porphyry and later *testimonia*,[15] they are found more clearly in the *Anonymous Parmenides Commentary* (although some items are missing in this work),[16] and, in abundance, in some eighty-nine sections of the theological works of the fourth-century Christian Neoplatonist

---

[11] Especially fragment 27: "For in every world shines a triad, ruled by a monad."
[12] See, for example, Hadot 1968, 1:112, 260–62, 352–75, 488–90.
[13] The list differs to some extent from the one I present in Rasimus, forthcoming, mainly due to the shift of the focus on Stoicism.
[14] Hadot 1968, 1:293–97; 1996.
[15] See the synopsis below. For a detailed discussion, see Rasimus, forthcoming.
[16] The only known manuscript of this fragmentary work was lost in a fire in 1904, but it had been already published in 1892 by Kroll. Subsequent editions and translations are based on Kroll's edition and one photograph of the original manuscript. See especially

Marius Victorinus,[17] who used these speculations to defend Christ's *homoousia* against Arians. Hadot was convinced that Victorinus could not have invented such finely tuned philosophical doctrines himself, but instead borrowed them from an earlier source, probably Porphyry's now lost *Commentary on the Chaldean Oracles*. From later *testimonia* we learn that Porphyry wrote such a work and did speculate on an enneadic triad similar to what Hadot reconstructed,[18] although the details in these *testimonia* are meager. Indeed, Hadot's reconstruction of Porphyry's metaphysics is based largely on Victorinus, and to a smaller extent on the *Anonymous Parmenides Commentary*, which Hadot also attributed to Porphyry. That Victorinus was borrowing from an earlier source is now confirmed by the Coptic manuscripts from Nag Hammadi. Two Sethian Gnostic texts in particular, *Zostrianos* (NHC VIII,1) and *Allogenes* (NHC XI,3), each describing a visionary's ascent to the highest ontological planes, contain all of the suggested "Porphyrian" innovations,[19] and Greek versions of these texts were read in Plotinus's seminars in mid-third-century Rome.[20] However, even their Coptic translations from Nag Hammadi predate Victorinus,[21] which alone proves that Victorinus did not invent these ideas. The recent debate has revolved around the question of whether it was Porphyry who influenced the Sethian Gnostics or the Sethian Gnostics who influ-

---

Hadot 1968, 2:61–113; Bechtle 1999, 17–65. For the occurrences of the listed "Porphyrian" innovations in the *Anonymous Parmenides Commentary*, see the synopsis below.

[17] The sections, or fragments, are collected in Hadot 1968, 2:13–55. Sections §§90–93 are treated separately (see Hadot 1968, 1:73). Some of the eighty-nine sections are further subdivided into several units—for example, §§36, 36a, 36b. For Hadot's methods for identifying the borrowed material from Victorinus's own text, see Hadot 1968, 1:67. The synopsis at the end of this essay gives some occurrences of the listed "Porphyrian" innovations in Victorinus and utilizes Hadot's enumeration of the sections.

[18] Lydus, *De mens.* 4.122; Augustine, *Civ.* 10.23, 29; Damascius, *De princ.* 2.1.4–2.10 (Westerink and Combès 1989 = Ruelle 1966, §43); Proclus, *In Tim.* 3.64.

[19] See the synopsis at the end of this essay, which, however, is far from being an exhaustive list of occurrences (for more, see Rasimus, forthcoming). For the editions of *Zostrianos* and *Allogenes*, see Barry et al. 2000; Funk 2004.

[20] According to Porphyry's *Vita Plotini* 16, the Gnostic *hairetikoi* in the seminars appealed to "apocalypses" of Zoroaster, Zostrianos, Nikotheos, Allogenes, Messos, and others. Plotinus, in his *Ennead* 2.9 [33]—to which Porphyry had assigned the title "Against the Gnostics," and to which he refers in *Vit. Plot.* 16—disapprovingly refers to a set of unique expressions and ideas that are found concentrated in *Zostrianos* 8–10: ἀντίτυποι, παροίκησις, μετάνοια, "image of an image," and Sophia's connection with "darkness" (*Enn.* 2.9.6.1–3; 2.9.10.19–33 [Armstrong 1966]). It seems likely that Plotinus here is paraphrasing a Greek version of the Nag Hammadi *Zostrianos*. In addition, the names "Zostrianos" and "Zoroaster" occur side by side in the colophon of the Nag Hammadi *Zostrianos*, while Allogenes and Messos are both central characters in the Nag Hammadi *Allogenes*. Thus, Porphyry's list of five Gnostic apocalypses may be not a list of five texts (perhaps only of three), but five authoritative figures mentioned in these texts. Two other Sethian texts, *The Three Steles of Seth* (NHC VII,5) and *Marsanes* (NHC X), also contain many of the suggested "Porphyrian" innovations. See Turner 2001; Rasimus, forthcoming.

[21] Fragments of letters used in the manufacturing of the covers of the Nag Hammadi codices can be dated to 309 (Codex VIII, where *Zostrianos* is found) and 348 (Codex VII). See Robinson 1976, xi; Williams 1996, 242–44. Marius Victorinus started writing his relevant theological treatises probably in the late 350s. See Hadot 1960, 1:14; Clark 1981, 4.

enced Porphyry (if Porphyry is indeed Victorinus's source).[22] I will return to this question below, and also to Sethian Gnostic metaphysics, after having dealt with the suggested Stoic background of these innovative ideas—that is, the various aspects of the being-life-mind triad.

2. The Stoic Ingredients

In this section I will go through the nine listed "Porphyrian" innovations and discuss their possible Stoic background, which in most cases was already suggested by Hadot himself.

First, the being-life-mind triad is used, especially to explain the externalization of the Intellect from the One in three phases with the help of the so-called Stability-Procession-and-Conversion scheme.[23] This scheme expresses the mechanics of the externalization and establishment of the Intellect. In the first phase, the still undetermined and potential intellect exists at stability/rest within the One. This phase is called "being" or "existence." In the second stage ("life"), the potential proceeds out of its source. However, it stops and turns around to gaze at its own source; this allows the undetermined and now externalized intellect to establish itself as the actualized and determined Intellect proper, the second One (this constitutes the third stage, "mind," also sometimes called "blessedness" by Victorinus and the Sethians).

Hadot compared this scheme to the Stoic concept of the tensile or systolic movement of the πνεῦμα, whose outward movement/expansion produces quantities and qualities (i.e., multiplicity), and whose inward movement/contraction produces unity and substance.[24] This seems to correspond rather well to the Procession and Conversion aspects of the scheme: the procession of the undetermined intellect out of the One causes quantity and quality to arise simply because something now exists outside the One;[25] and its turning and gazing back toward its source causes it to achieve substance and unity, as it is now able to establish itself as the actualized and determined Intellect (the "One-Being"). It should be noted that the outward and inward movements of the πνεῦμα are described as

---

[22] Abramowski (1983) and Majercik (1992; 2001) defend Hadot's thesis and argue that the Sethian Gnostic texts *Zostrianos* and *Allogenes* were heavily updated in light of Porphyry's criticism in Plotinus's seminars; Corrigan (2000a; 2000b) and Turner (2001) argue that the Sethian Gnostic texts in question already contained most of these ideas when Porphyry first read them. For discussion, see Rasimus, forthcoming.

[23] See Hadot 1968, 1:262-63. Compare the Sethian Gnostic triad of καλυπτός-πρωτοφανής-αὐτογενής (see, e.g., *Zostrianos* 15.6-12; 18.5-19; 58.14-16; 124.18-125.20; *Allogenes* 45.30-46.23; 51.17-26; 58.12-19), which represents the three sublevels of the second principle, Barbelo, and specifically Barbelo's procession out of the first One in three phases identified as "hidden" (καλυπτός), "first manifestation" (πρωτοφανής), and "self-constitution/self-generated" (αὐτογενής).

[24] Nemesius, *Nat. hom.* 70.6-71.4 (L-S 47J). See Hadot 1968, 1:225-34.

[25] By definition, the Neoplatonic One is devoid of quantity and quality. See, for example, Plotinus, *Enn.* 6.9 [9] 3.

simultaneous in Stoic sources,[26] and, despite the three-phase language I have used of the Stability-Procession-and-Conversion scheme, it is also a nonchronological scheme in that it takes place in eternity and its phases can be thus understood as simultaneous. However, this does not yet explain the Stability aspect of the scheme. To understand it, we must look at the Stoic theory of conflagration. During the conflagration period of the ever-recurring world cycle there exists nothing but God, or to be more precise, the world order during the conflagration exists only potentially/seminally within God, who then produces and actualizes it;[27] the πνεῦμα and its tensile movement,[28] pervading the whole world as God's instrument, itself comes into existence in this actualization process. Thus, it seems that the whole Stability-Procession-and-Conversion scheme could be explained as a Platonic adaptation of the Stoic idea of God actualizing the potentially existing world order, which is then pervaded by the tensile movement of the πνεῦμα.[29]

The Stoic idea of God producing the seminally existing world out of himself also explains item (2) in the list of "Porphyrian" innovations, namely, the prefiguration or the undetermined, potential existence of the Intellect within the One. It also partially explains item (3)—that is, that being, life, and mind have their undetermined (potential) and determined (actual) aspects. Another concept that might illuminate this third Neoplatonic idea is the Aristotelian concept of the aether, which at least some Stoics adopted in the form of God as the higher, divine and designing fire, as opposed to the lower, elemental fire.[30] This Stoic idea became meaningful in discussions of the conflagration, during which only God, the divine fire, exists and later produces the world order by condensation into the four elements, including the lower or elemental fire.[31]

As for items (4) and (5), we must look at the Stoic theory of mixture. The being-life-mind triad often was expressed as an ennead where each of the three members of the triad already contains the other two but also predominates in turn. The locus classicus of this idea is proposition 103 of the *Elements of Theology* of the fifth-century Neoplatonist Proclus,[32] but it is already found earlier, for example, in Victorinus and *Allogenes*.[33] In any case, Hadot suggested that this kind

---

[26] Alexander of Aphrodisias, *Mixt.* 224.14–26 (*SVF* 2.442; L-S 47I); Nemesius, *Nat. hom.* 70.6–71.4 (L-S 47J). See also Long and Sedley 1987, 1:288.

[27] See, for example, Aëtius, *De placita* 1.7.33 (*SVF* 2.1027; L-S 46A); Diogenes Laertius, *Vit. phil.* 7.135–136 (*SVF* 1.102; L-S 46B); Eusebius, *Praep. ev.* 15.14.2 (*SVF* 1.98; L-S 46G).

[28] Πνεῦμα consists of fire and air, and its tensile movement is a combination of the expanding force of the hot fire and the condensing force of the cold air (Long and Sedley 1987, 1:288). God is a designing fire, and as such is above the elemental fire and air, of which the πνεῦμα consists (see below).

[29] See Pleše 2006, 112–99.

[30] Stobaeus, *Anth.* 1.25.5 (= 1.213.15–21 W-H) (*SVF* 1.120; L-S 46D); Diogenes Laertius, *Vit. phil.* 7.137 (*SVF* 2.580; L-S 47B). See also Long and Sedley 1987, 1:286–87.

[31] See Diogenes Laertius, *Vit. phil.* 7.135–136, 142 (*SVF* 1.102; L-S 46B–C).

[32] "All things are in all things, but in each according to its proper nature: for in Being there is life and intelligence; in Life, being and intelligence; in Intelligence, being and life; but each of these exists upon one level intellectually, upon another vitally, and on the third existentially" (translation, Dodds 1963).

[33] For the occurrences in Victorinus and *Allogenes*, see the synopsis below.

of structuring might be based on the Stoic theory of total blending with its various applications.[34] The Stoics explained that there can be three kinds of mixtures:[35] (a) juxtaposition, where the ingredients do not penetrate each other, but rather retain their identities and can be separated afterwards, like almonds and walnuts in a bowl; (b) total fusion, where the ingredients completely penetrate each other, lose their original identities, and cannot be separated afterwards, like flour and water in dough; and (c) total blending, where the ingredients completely penetrate each other but retain their original identities and can be separated afterwards, like a mixture of water and wine (according to the Stoics, an oiled sponge dropped into a container of water and wine would be able to separate these totally interpenetrated ingredients, absorbing the water into itself—I must confess that I have never tried).[36]

The third kind of mixture, that of total blending, would seem to illuminate the principles of mutual implication and relative predominance in the being-life-mind triad, where each of the members also includes the others within itself but predominates under various circumstances; that is, the members retain their identities while being thoroughly interpenetrated with the other members. This is, in fact, how most Stoics explained the theory of virtues. All virtues are ultimately one, and a person who has one of the virtues has them all. However, under specific circumstances, one specific virtue, or, perhaps better said, a specific aspect of the one virtue, such as courage, manifests itself above the others and hence can be said to predominate.[37] This is also how the Stoic curriculum itself was explained—that is, that philosophy can be divided (for practical reasons) into logic, physics, and ethics, but that ultimately the (Stoic) philosophical system is one, a unity with three aspects.[38] Interestingly, as Hadot already showed, Philo treated the three patriarchs Abraham, Isaac, and Jacob as representing three inseparable stages of παιδεία; each aspect contains the other two but derives its specific name from its relative predominance over the other two.[39] Philo, of course, is known for having combined Stoic ideas with Platonic ones in a biblical framework.[40] In any case, it seems that the Stoic theory of total blending can well explain the "Porphyrian" concepts of the enneadic structuring of the being-life-mind triad with its principles of mutual implication and relative predominance (items 4 and 5).

The distinction between the undetermined and determined aspects of being, life, and mind (item 3) in Neoplatonic sources often was expressed with cognates of the same word—such as "to be" (εἶναι), "being" (τὸ ὄν), and "existentially"

---

[34] Hadot 1968, 1:239–46.
[35] See, for example, Alexander of Aphrodisias, *Mixt.* 216.14–218.6 (*SVF* 2.473; L-S 48C).
[36] Stobaeus, *Anth.* 1.17.4 (= 1.155.5–11 W-H) (*SVF* 2.471; L-S 48D).
[37] See, for example, Plutarch, *Virt. mor.* 440E–441D (L-S 61B); *Stoic. rep.* 1046E–F (*SVF* 3.299, 243; L-S 61F); Stobaeus, *Anth.* 2.7.5b5 (= 2.63.6–24 W-H) (*SVF* 3.280; L-S 61D). See also Long and Sedley 1987, 1:383–86.
[38] Diogenes Laertius, *Vit. phil.* 7.39–41 (L-S 26B); Sextus Empiricus, *Math.* 7.19 (L-S 26D).
[39] Hadot 1957, 123–26; 1968, 1:242–43.
[40] See Dillon 1996, 139–83.

(ὄντως)—known as the method of paronyms (item 6).⁴¹ Hadot suggested that this might also go back to the Stoics.⁴² Indeed, the Stoics used the method of paronyms to explain causal relations. For example, in order to be prudent (τὸ φρονεῖν), one must first have prudence (φρόνησις).⁴³ This, again, would seem to explain well the Neoplatonic use of paronyms.

One specific deviation from this usage is the substitution of ὕπαρξις for εἶναι in some Neoplatonic sources. Ὕπαρξις is used to denote the higher, yet undetermined and potential "being" or "existence" above the determined and actualized "being" (τὸ ὄν). According to Hadot, this would be based on Stoicism, where the use of ὕπαρξις belongs to the realm of incorporeal, and hence (for the Stoics) non-being.⁴⁴ This would indeed fit well with the "Porphyrian" usage of ὕπαρξις denoting the mere potential existence, the "non-being existence" (see below), and therefore a transposition of the term from Stoic to Neoplatonic ontology would seem a good possibility.

Another characterization of the first principle in Neoplatonic sources, including the undisputed Porphyry, Victorinus, and *Allogenes*, is the "non-being above being," where the "non-being" is equal to ὕπαρξις—that is, the not-yet-actualized being. Hadot suggested that this kind of characterization of the One/God might be inspired by Stoic ontology, namely, by its most general and highest category of "something" (τί), and its opposite, the "not-something" (οὔτι).⁴⁵ The category of "something" contains in itself both objects that exist (corporeals) and objects that do not (incorporeals); in other words, it contains in itself, but also transcends, the subcategories of "being" and "non-being." The opposite category of "not-something," on the other hand, includes mere imaginary objects that do not exist at all, such as centaurs.⁴⁶ What is more, the opposition between τί and οὔτι, according to Hadot, would correspond to a Neoplatonic idea of the soul's capacity for moving between two poles of "non-being," as it were: either toward God, who is "non-being above being," or away from God, which results in false concepts that are "absolutely non-being."⁴⁷ That the Stoic category of "something"—with

---

⁴¹ Cf. Proclus, *El. theol.* 103: "All things are in all things, but in each according to its proper nature: for in Being there is life and intelligence; in Life, being and intelligence; in Intelligence, being and life; but each of these exists upon one level intellectually, upon another vitally, and on the third existentially" (translation, Dodds 1963). See also the occurrences listed in the synopsis below.

⁴² Hadot 1968, 1:353, 364–66, 487–93.

⁴³ See, for example, Stobaeus, *Anth.* 1.13.1c (= 1.138.14–139.4 W-H) (*SVF* 1.89; 2.336; L-S 55A); and one of Hadot's examples, Simplicius, *In categ.* 216.27 (Kalbfleisch 1907), where it is stated that, for example, equality comes from being equal, and corporeality from being corporeal (ἀπὸ τοῦ ἰσῶσθαι ἰσότητα καὶ ἀπὸ τοῦ σῶμα ὑπάρχειν σωματότητα).

⁴⁴ Hadot 1968, 1:487–93.

⁴⁵ Hadot 1968, 1:147–78, esp. 174–78.

⁴⁶ The placement of the "not-something" in the Stoic ontological hierarchy is a matter of debate. Hadot (1968, 1:159–78) placed it on the highest level together with and in opposition to the "something," whereas Long and Sedley (1987, 1:163–66) suggest a somewhat lower and ambiguous placement: the "not-something" is "neither" corporeal or incorporeal, and hence, in a way, it constitutes a third subcategory of the "something."

⁴⁷ Hadot 1968, 1:176–77. Cf. Porphyry, *Sent.* 26, which uses the very expression τὸ ὑπὲρ τὸ ὂν μὴ ὄν (Victorinus: τὸ μὴ ὂν *super* τὸ ὄν [Hadot, §19]). Victorinus identified four kinds

its opposite, the "not-something"—might have inspired a Neoplatonic thinker to describe the first principle as the "non-being above being" (whose "non-being" is different from that of false concepts) is thus an attractive possibility, and it becomes even more attractive because of certain statements in the Sethian Gnostic texts *Allogenes* and the *Apocryphon of John* (NHC II,1; III,1; IV,1; BG 8502,2). In *Allogenes*, the One is described as a "non-being" (ⲁⲧⲱⲱⲡⲉ [55.30; 62.23; 65.33; 66.27]; ⲁⲧⲟⲩⲥⲓⲁ [53.31]), as well as "not one of those things that exist, but another thing (ⲕⲉⲛ̄ⲕⲁ), superior to all superlatives" (63.17–20). John Turner has speculated that the Coptic ⲕⲉⲛ̄ⲕⲁ might translate the Greek τὶ, and this certainly is a good possibility; the parallel passage in the *Apocryphon of John* has ⲁⲗⲁⲩ,which does translate τὶ.[48] In addition, elsewhere in *Allogenes* (62.28–36) and the *Apocryphon of John* (BG 24.6–25.7) the One is said to transcend what is negated of him, and this in a way structurally parallels the Stoic category "something," which in itself is not identical to the category of "being" or "non-being" but transcends and includes both; in Victorinus, one also finds formulations according to which God is both "being" and "non-being" at the same time yet transcends both categories.[49]

One final characterization of the One that requires attention is the One/God as spirit, πνεῦμα. This characterization occurs in Victorinus, and it greatly puzzled Hadot. In fact, he was already prepared to admit in the 1960s that Victorinus got this characterization from someone other than Porphyry, and in 1996—after Michel Tardieu had shown that this specific section in Victorinus is practically identical to a section in *Zostrianos* and that both probably depend on a common Middle Platonic source—he admitted that the source probably was Gnostic in origin.[50] Whatever Victorinus's source here is, the background of the concept itself surely is at home in Stoicism, where God is described as πνεῦμα.[51] Of course, God is spirit also in the Judeo-Christian tradition (e.g., John 4:24), and thus this is not problematic for Victorinus or the Sethian Gnostic authors, but given all the other

---

of "non-being": absolute and negative, according to otherness, according to power, beyond being (Hadot, §§3–6).

[48] *Ap. John* BG 24.20–25.1 parr.: "He is not something [ⲟⲩⲗⲁⲁⲩ] that exists, but something superior to them, not as being superior but as being himself." See Turner 2004, 54. For the edition of the *Apocryphon of John*, see Waldstein and Wisse 1995.

[49] See, for example, Hadot §§4, 19.

[50] See Hadot 1968, 1:293–97; 1996; Tardieu 1996, 27–45, 112–13; cf. Brisson 1999. This section in Victorinus (especially *Adv. Ar.* 1.50 [Hadot, §41]) also speaks of the One/God as "blessed" (μακάριος) and "triple-powered" (τριδύναμος > ϣⲙⲛ̄ⲧϭⲟⲙ). These characterizations occur also in *Zostrianos* (e.g., 20.15–18; *66.14–18) and *Allogenes* (e.g., 51.8–9; 60.17–31), as well as in the second-century Sethian text the *Apocryphon of John* (see notes 64–65 below). In Victorinus, *Zostrianos*, and *Allogenes*, the term μακάριος occasionally replaces "mind" in the being/existence-life-mind triad. Interestingly, according to Hadot (1968, 1:287–93), this replacement might also be based on Stoicism, because God, during the conflagration period, is said to be turned toward himself in repose and think of himself (since nothing else exists) (cf. Seneca, *Ep.* 9.16 [*SVF* 2.1065; L-S 46O]), and this state might therefore be thought of as "blessedness" (cf. Majercik 1992, 483–86). In my view, the Stoic background of the term "blessedness" is hypothetical.

[51] For example, Aëtius, *De placita* 1.7.33 (*SVF* 2.1027; L-S 46A). This characterization, however, needs to be qualified. See note 28 above.

potential and, in my estimate, quite probable Stoic ingredients in the being-life-mind triad, it is conceivable that the description of the One/God as *pneuma* here owes at least as much to Stoic ideas as to Judeo-Christian traditions.

3. Porphyry or the Gnostics?

It remains to be discussed whether Hadot was right in suggesting that it was Porphyry in the mid-third century who invented these Stoic-based Neoplatonic ideas, or, as I argue in detail elsewhere,[52] the credit should go to advocates of Sethian Gnosticism, some of whom also attended Plotinus's seminars and were drawing on texts produced in the same Sethian Gnostic movement in the second century.[53] These earlier, highly mythopoetic Sethian texts (e.g., the *Apocryphon of John*) posited a triad of first principles consisting of Father the Invisible Spirit, Mother Barbelo, and the Son Autogenes Christ. This triad likely was based on Plato's Father-Mother-Child triad (*Tim.* 48E–52D) rather than an early version of the Christian Trinity.[54] *Zostrianos* and *Allogenes* adopted this Father-Barbelo-Autogenes triad, with its mythopoetic context, but added speculations about a mediating triple-power and the being-life-mind (or, existence-life-blessedness)[55] triad in order to better explain the derivation of multiplicity from the unitary Father, the One.[56] Greek versions of these texts then circulated in Plotinus's seminars and were known to Porphyry, who, together with Plotinus and a fellow student, Amelius, refuted certain ideas contained in them.[57]

As noted above, Hadot built his case for Porphyry being the originator of the innovative Neoplatonic ideas on the assumption that Victorinus was dependent on Porphyry and that Porphyry was also the author of the *Anonymous Parmenides*

---

[52] Rasimus, forthcoming.

[53] On the literary contacts between *Allogenes* and the *Apocryphon of John*, see Turner 2001, 502–4.

[54] See ibid., 252.

[55] See note 50 above.

[56] The Invisible Spirit, using its triple-power (τριδύναμος), identified as existence-life-blessedness/mind triad in *Zostrianos* 15.18–19, externalizes the hidden (καλυπτός) potential multiplicity as the manifested (πρωτοφανής) aeon of Barbelo, whose final constituent is αὐτογενής—that is, self-constitution. The triple-power is the energy (ἐνέργεια [*Zostrianos* 79.21]) by means of which this three-stage process takes place, perhaps simply a name given to the process itself. Depending on the viewpoint, the triple-power, if it is taken as describing the whole triadic process, can then be seen as a mediating entity between the principles (*Allogenes* 45.9–46.35), or as belonging to the Invisible Spirit (*Zostrianos* 20.15–18; *Allogenes* 51.8–9; 66.33–35), or Barbelo (e.g., in the closely related *Steles Seth* 121.31–32). See Turner 2001, 512–31; Rasimus, forthcoming.

[57] The criticism in Porphyry (*Vit. Plot.* 16) and Plotinus (*Enn.* 2.9) seems to be aimed only at certain concepts appearing in some of the Gnostic "apocalypses" circulating in the seminars. The "Porphyrian" innovations contained in these texts would presumably not have been objectionable to Porphyry, and Plotinus continued to consider these Gnostics personal friends even after criticizing some of their ideas (*Enn.* 2.9.10). For discussion, see Corrigan 2000a, 24–25; Rasimus, forthcoming.

Commentary. This assumption, in turn, was based on two main arguments: first, because the suggested Porphyrian works—that is, the eighty-nine sections in Victorinus, and the *Anonymous Parmenides Commentary*—show fidelity to the Neopythagorean Numenius (on whom Plotinus lectured) and depend on Plotinus's doctrine of the One, yet are relatively simple in their metaphysics, the only suitable candidate for being their author is Porphyry;[58] second, when one compares the doctrinal content, vocabulary, and interpretative strategies of these two suggested Porphyrian works to the undisputed Porphyrian evidence (i.e., the genuine surviving works and later *testimonia*), one finds such a close correspondence that Porphyry must be their author.[59] The first argument has been challenged mainly because the metaphysics of these suggested Porphyrian works does not necessarily depend on Plotinus and thus might be Middle Platonic and pre-Plotinian (the probable common source behind Victorinus and *Zostrianos* certainly would be Middle Platonic).[60] Even if this were not the case, the Nag Hammadi finds have shown that Porphyry is not the only suitable candidate from the mid-third century: especially the Sethian texts *Zostrianos* and *Allogenes* contain all of the suggested "Porphyrian" innovations.[61]

In addition, when one takes a critical look at the undisputed Porphyrian evidence, one finds that the correspondence to the two suggested Porphyrian works (i.e., the eighty-nine sections in Victorinus, and the *Anonymous Parmenides Commentary*) is not as close as Hadot claimed, and, importantly, that the correspondence between the suggested Porphyrian works and the Sethian Gnostic texts in question is perhaps even closer, mainly because the undisputed Porphyrian evidence actually lacks some of the innovative "Porphyrian" features, with individual texts (e.g., *Sententiae*) rarely containing more than a few of these features (whereas *Zostrianos* and *Allogenes* contain all of them).[62] Furthermore, one specific Stoicizing element in the *Anonymous Parmenides Commentary* even seems to disqualify Porphyry as its author, as Kevin Corrigan has argued:[63] although Porphyry used the Stoic theory of mixture in discussing the union of *sensible* and intelligible (e.g., *Sent*. 33.5), the author of the *Anonymous Parmenides Commentary* (11-12) uses the Stoic theory of mixture as an analogy to the theory of *intelligible* participation (explaining the union of "One" and "Being" in the second principle, the "One-Being," i.e., the Intellect), and intelligible participation is specifically denied of Porphyry by later *testimonia* (Syrianus, *In Metaph*. 109; Proclus, *In Tim*. 3.32-33).

What, in my view, tips the balance in favor of seeing the Sethian Gnostics as the originators of these innovative "Porphyrian" ideas, although not necessarily the actual authors of the *Anonymous Parmenides Commentary* or Victorinus's sources, is that while all the ideas are found explicitly in *Zostrianos* and

---

[58] Hadot 1961; 1968, 1:79-98, 102-7.
[59] For example, Hadot 1968, 1:98-102, 107-43.
[60] See especially Bechtle 1999, 77-91; Corrigan 2000b; Turner 2001, 724-36; Cazelais 2005.
[61] See the synopsis on the following page.
[62] See the synopsis following; also the detailed discussion in Rasimus, forthcoming.
[63] For example, Corrigan 2000b, 153, 165-67.

A Nonexhaustive Synopsis of the Suggested "Porphyrian" Innovations Relating to the Being-Life-Mind Triad

Neoplatonic Concept	Undisputed Porphyry (surviving works and *testimonia*)
#1: being-life-mind/blessedness triad is used, especially to explain the generation of the Intellect from the One	not clearly evident; cf., however, the "non-canonical" order where mind precedes life (*Sent.* 21; 40; Proclus, *In Tim.* 3.64); and the general principle of generation (*Sent.* 41)
#2: prefiguration/potential existence of the Intellect within the One	*Sent.* 31; *Hist. phil.* 18
#3: distinction between undetermined and determined aspects of being, life, and mind	*Sent.* 10; 25–26; Proclus, *Plat. Theol.* 1.11 (Saffrey and Westerink 1968–1997, 1:51)
#4: enneadic structuring of the being-life-mind triad	Lydus, *De mens.* 4.122; Proclus, *In Tim.* 3.64
#5: use of the principles of mutual implication and relative predominance	Lydus, *De mens.* 4.122; Proclus, *In Tim.* 3.64
#6: method of paronyms	*Isagoge* 69.14–70.24; Proclus, *In Tim.* 3.64
#7: use of ὕπαρξις (Latin: *exsistentia*) to denote the undetermined being or existence	*Hist. phil.* 18
#8: description of the first principle as the "non-being above being"	*Sent.* 26.3–6
#9: God/One as πνεῦμα	

Allogenes, many of them are already found—some explicitly, others implicitly—in the second-century Sethian text[64] the *Apocryphon of John*.[65] More-

---

[64] Irenaeus paraphrased a version of the *Apocryphon of John* ca. 180, and the Greek *Vorlagen* of the four Coptic versions are customarily dated to the second century. See Tardieu 1984, 10, 37–39; Logan 1996, xx, 26–69, 191, 283; Turner 2001, 257–92; 2005; Rasimus 2009, 259–77.

[65] In the *Apocryphon of John*, the first principle is described as always existing (BG 24.2), yet his being is superior to that of others (24.20–25.1); he is also said to be life who gives life, and blessedness who gives blessedness (25.15–16). Here we seem to have implicitly not only the being/existence-life-blessedness triad (cf. item 1) (see also note 50 above), but also the idea of the prefiguration of the triad in the One, because apparently higher forms of being, life, and blessedness coincide with the One (cf. items 2–3). What is more, the second principle, Barbelo, who comes into existence out of the first one through the mediating "living" (ⲛⲱⲛϩ) water (26.18), is called "triple-powered" (BG 27.21–28.1:

Marius Victorinus (enumeration from Hadot 1968, 2:13–57)	Anonymous Parmenides Commentary	Allogenes	Zostrianos (*parallel to Victorinus)	Apocryphon of John
§§80–89	14.17–26	49.7–14; 49.26–38	20.22–24; *66.16–17; *66.23–67.2; *68.1–7; 79.10–81.20	BG 24.2–25.16
§§41, 80–89	14.17–26	47.10–14; 66.28–30	20.2–15; *65.6–7	BG 24.2–25.16; 26.15
§§65, 70, 78, 86a	12.29–35	61.32–62.2	61.32–62.2; *64.14–16	BG 24.2–25.16
§§65, 76		49.26–38	15.1–12; *66.14–20	
§§30, 41, 56, 65, 76, 88		49.26–38	15.1–12; *66.14–20	
§§10, 65, 76		49.26–38	15.1–12; *66.14–20	
§§23, 23a, 86a–89	14.6, 15, 17, 18, 23, 25; cf. 12.29–35	46.7–12; 47.25; 62.23	*66.16–19; *68.16–17; 73.1, 8; 74.8–9	
§19		53.31; 55.30; 62.23; 65.33; 66.27	*68.5–7	BG 24.20–25.1
§41		49.9–10; 51.35; 64.36	17.12–13; 20.17–18; cf. *67.20	BG 29.7–8; 23.3; 32.1–2

over, as Takashi Onuki and Zlatko Pleše have shown, the *Apocryphon of John* already draws heavily on Stoic ideas, while adopting an essentially Platonic

---

ⲧⲱⲟ[ⲙ]ⲛⲧⲉ ⲛ̄ϭⲟⲙ; III 8.2–3: [ⲧⲱⲟ]ⲙⲛ̄ⲧ ⲛ̄ⲁⲩⲏ[ⲁⲙⲓⲥ]), and her tripleness is stressed several times (BG 27.21–28.2 parr.). Finally, the third principle, the self-generated Son, who came from the Father, is also identified as "blessed" (ⲙⲁⲕⲁⲣⲓⲟⲛ [BG 30.2–3]) like the Father; and whereas the Son receives νοῦς (31.5–9 parr.), the Father is said to "contemplate" (ⲛⲟⲓ̈) himself (26.15 parr.). Thus, the seeds of the being-life-*mind* triad, together with a variant of the Two Intellect theory, may be seen here as well (cf. items 1–2). The *Apocryphon of John* also describes the One as existing above being (BG 24.20–25.1 parr.) (item 8). Moreover, the peculiar expressions from Victorinus's *Adv. Ar.* 1.50 (Hadot §41)—God as spirit, blessed, and triple-powered—not only are found here in the *Apocryphon of John* (item 9), but also occur in connection with an implicit form of the being/existence-life-blessedness/mind triad. In *Allogenes* and *Zostrianos* these speculations become explicit.

worldview.⁶⁶ In addition, the *Apocryphon of John* has some close parallels with the *Chaldean Oracles*, but, interestingly enough, these parallels in the *Apocryphon of John* that have to do with the triadic nature of the first principles appear to better explain the background of the "Porphyrian" triadic speculations than do the *Chaldean Oracles* themselves—remember that according to Hadot, such triadic speculations would be based on Porphyry's exegesis of the *Chaldean Oracles*.⁶⁷ Thus, an internal Sethian Gnostic development from implicit to explicit formulations would seem to best explain the (explicit) occurrence of the Stoic-based "Porphyrian" ideas in *Zostrianos* and *Allogenes*. How much Plotinus or even Porphyry himself contributed to this internal Sethian Gnostic development is a trickier matter. It nevertheless seems that even if Porphyry was Victorinus's main source (except for the section that characterizes the One/God as *pneuma*), Porphyry must have been at least indirectly dependent on the Sethian Gnostics, who, given our present state of knowledge, make better candidates for having been the original Stoic-minded innovators of many, if not all, of these Neoplatonic ideas.

Bibliography

Abramowski, L. 1983. "Marius Victorinus, Porphyrius und die römischen Gnostiker." *Zeitschrift für die Neutestamentliche Wissenschaft* 74:108–28.

---

⁶⁶See Onuki 1989; Onuki's essay in the present volume; Pleše 2006, 97–139, 199. Pleše has shown that the *Apocryphon of John*, in describing the Invisible Spirit and its relation to what follows, utilizes Stoic concepts. These include: (a) the first principle is described as πνεῦμα; (b) that the Invisible Spirit's *seeing* his own image in the luminous waters actualizes his first thought (Barbelo) points to Stoic influence in assigning priority to perception as an essential prerequisite for concept formation; (c) the Invisible Spirit's expansion from unity into multiplicity is partially articulated in terms of the tensile movement of the πνεῦμα, and this expansion all the way to the material realm further seems to be an articulation of the movement from tensility (εὐτονία) to slackness (ἀτονία) of the divine breath permeating all levels of reality; (d) the concept of conflagration, when the world is coextensive with the state of pure fire/πνεῦμα, seems to lie behind the notion of the Invisible Spirit's being the source of everything.

⁶⁷Both the *Apocryphon of John* and the *Chaldean Oracles* seem to assume a triad of supreme principles, of whom the first one is the Father and the middle one is a feminine power (Barbelo/δύναμις). The triad in the *Apocryphon of John* is the usual Sethian one of Father-Mother Barbelo-Son Autogenes, but the tripleness and the power nature of the middle member of the triad is stressed (see note 65 above). We do not find such a specific stress on the triple nature of the median power in the surviving fragments of the *Chaldean Oracles*. Since the *Apocryphon of John* further connects the implicit being-life-blessedness/mind triad with this triple power, it would seem that the later enneadic structuring of the triad, especially in *Allogenes*, can be explained by Sethian material alone, without having to assume a dependence on Porphyry and his exegesis of the *Chaldean Oracles*. The surviving *Chaldean Oracles* only *imply* that there is a supreme triad of Father-power-intellect; that the Father gives birth to power and intellect; that the Father somehow coincides with the power; and that there is a general triadic structure in reality. Nor does the term τριδύναμος occur in the *Chaldean Oracles*, although similar expressions, τριγλώχις and τριοῦχος (fragments 2; 26), do. For discussion, see Rasimus, forthcoming.

Armstrong, A. 1966. *Plotinus: Ennead II*. Loeb Classical Library. Cambridge, Mass.: Harvard University Press.

Barry, C., et al., eds. 2000. *Zostrien (NH VIII,1)*. Bibliothèque copte de Nag Hammadi, Section "Textes" 24. Québec: Presses de l'Université Laval; Leuven: Peeters.

Bechtle, G. 1999. *The Anonymous Commentary on Plato's "Parmenides."* Berner Reihe philosophischer Studien 22. Bern: Paul Haupt.

Brisson, L. 1999. "The Platonic Background in the *Apocalypse of Zostrianos*: Numenius and *Letter II* attributed to Plato." Pages 173–88 in *Traditions of Platonism: Essays in Honour of John Dillon*. Edited by J. Cleary. Aldershot: Ashgate.

Cazelais, S. 2005. "L'expression HO EPI PASI THEOS de l'Ancienne Académie à Origene et dans le *Commentaire* anonyme *sur le Parmenide*." *Science et Esprit* 57(3):199–214.

Clark, M. 1981. *Marius Victorinus: Theological Treatises on the Trinity*. The Fathers of the Church: A New Translation 69. Washington, D.C.: Catholic University of America Press.

Corrigan, K. 2000a. "Positive and Negative Matter in Later Platonism: The Uncovering of Plotinus's Dialogue with the Gnostics." Pages 19–56 in *Gnosticism and Later Platonism: Themes, Figures, and Texts*. Edited by J. Turner and R. Majercik. Society of Biblical Literature Symposium Series 12. Atlanta: Society of Biblical Literature.

———. 2000b. "Platonism and Gnosticism: The Anonymous Commentary on the Parmenides: Middle or Neoplatonic?" Pages 141–77 in *Gnosticism and Later Platonism: Themes, Figures, and Texts*. Edited by J. Turner and R. Majercik. Society of Biblical Literature Symposium Series 12. Atlanta: Society of Biblical Literature.

Dillon, J. M. 1996. *The Middle Platonists: 80 B.C. to A.D. 220*. Rev. ed. Ithaca, N.Y.: Cornell University Press.

Dodds, E. R. 1963. *Proclus: The Elements of Theology: A Revised Text with Translation, Introduction and Commentary*. 2d ed. Oxford: Clarendon Press.

Funk, W.-P. 2004. "Texte Copte." Pages 189–238 in *L'Allogène (NH XI,3)*. Edited by W.-P. Funk et al. Bibliothèque copte de Nag Hammadi, Section "Textes" 30. Québec: Presses de l'Université Laval; Leuven: Peeters.

Hadot, P. 1957. "Être, vie, pensée chez Plotin et avant Plotin." Pages 107–57 [discussion: pp. 142–57] in *Les Sources de Plotin*. Entretiens sur l'antiquité classique 5. Geneva: Vandoeuvers.

———. 1960. *Marius Victorinus: Traitées théologiques sur la Trinité: Texte établi par Paul Henry, introduction, traduction et notes par Pierre Hadot*. 2 vols. Sources chrétiennes 68–69. Paris: Cerf.

———. 1961. "Fragments d'un commentaire de Porphyre sur le *Parmenide*." *Revue des études grecques* 74:410–38.

———. 1966. "La métaphysique de Porphyre." Pages 127–57 [discussion: pp. 158–65] in *Porphyre*. Entretiens sur l'antiquité classique 12. Geneva: Vandoeuvers.

———. 1968. *Porphyre et Victorinus*. 2 vols. Paris: Études Augustiniennes.

———. 1996. "Porphyre et Victorinus: Questions et hypotheses." *Res Orientales* 9:115–25.
Kalbfleisch, K. 1907. *Simplicii in Aristotelis categorias commentarium*. Commentaria in Aristotelem Graeca 8. Berlin: Reimer.
Kroll, W. 1892. "Ein neuplatonischer Parmenidescommentar in einem Turiner Palimpsest." *Rheinisches Museum* 47:599–627.
Layton, B. 1987. *The Gnostic Scriptures: A New Translation with Annotations and Introductions*. Anchor Bible Reference Library. Garden City, N.Y.: Doubleday.
Logan, A. 1996. *Gnostic Truth and Christian Heresy: A Study in the History of Gnosticism*. Peabody, Mass.: Hendrickson.
Long, A., and D. Sedley. 1987. *The Hellenistic Philosophers*. 2 vols. Cambridge: Cambridge University Press.
Majercik, R. 1989. *The Chaldean Oracles: Text, Translation, and Commentary*. Studies in Greek and Roman Religion 5. Leiden: Brill.
———. 1992. "The Existence-Life-Intellect Triad in Gnosticism and Neoplatonism." *Classical Quarterly* 42:475–88.
———. 2001. "Chaldean Triads in Neoplatonic Exegesis: Some Reconsiderations." *Classical Quarterly* 51:265–96.
Onuki, T. 1989. *Gnosis und Stoa: Eine Untersuchung zum Apokryphon des Johannes*. Novum Testamentum et Orbis Antiquus 9. Freiburg: Universitätsverlag; Göttingen: Vandenhoeck & Ruprecht.
Pearson, B. A. 1990. *Gnosticism, Judaism, and Egyptian Christianity*. Studies in Antiquity and Christianity. Minneapolis: Fortress.
Pleše, Z. 2006. *Poetics of the Gnostic Universe: Narrative and Cosmology in the Apocryphon of John*. Nag Hammadi and Manichaean Studies 52. Leiden: Brill.
Rasimus, T. 2009. *Paradise Reconsidered in Gnostic Mythmaking: Rethinking Sethianism in Light of the Ophite Evidence*. Nag Hammadi and Manichaean Studies 68. Leiden: Brill.
———. Forthcoming. "Porphyry and the Gnostics: Reassessing Pierre Hadot's Thesis in Light of the Second and Third Century Sethian Material." In *Plato's Parmenides and Its Reception in Patristic, Gnostic, and Christian Neoplatonic Texts*. Edited by K. Corrigan and J. Turner. Society of Biblical Literature Writings from the Greco-Roman World. Atlanta: Society of Biblical Literature; Leiden: Brill.
Robinson, J. 1976. "Preface." Pages vii–xxi in *The Facsimile Edition of the Nag Hammadi Codices: Codex VIII*. Edited by J. Robinson et al. Leiden: Brill.
Ruelle, C., ed. 1966. *Damascii successoris dubitationes et solutiones: De primis principiis, in Platonis Parmenidem*. 2 vols. Amsterdam: Hakkert.
Saffrey, H., and L. Westerink. 1968–1997. *Proclus: Théologie platonicienne*. 6 vols. Paris: Les Belles Lettres.
Schenke, H.-M. 1981. "The Phenomenon and Significance of Gnostic Sethianism." Pages 588–616 in *Sethian Gnosticism*. Vol. 2 of *The Rediscovery of Gnosticism*. Edited by B. Layton. Studies in the History of Religions (Supplements to Numen) 41. Leiden: Brill.
Tardieu, M. 1984. *Écrits Gnostiques: Codex de Berlin*. Paris: Cerf.

———. 1996. "Recherches sur la formation de l'apocalypse de *Zostrien* et les sources de Marius Victorinus." *Res Orientales* 9:7-114.

Turner, J. 2001. *Sethian Gnosticism and the Platonic Tradition*. Bibliothèque copte de Nag Hammadi, Section "Études" 6. Québec: Presses de l'Université Laval; Leuven: Peeters.

———. 2004. "Introduction." Pages 1-188 in *L'Allogène (NH XI,3)*. Edited by W.-P. Funk et al. Bibliothèque copte de Nag Hammadi, Section "Textes" 30. Québec: Presses de l'Université Laval; Leuven: Peeters.

———. 2005. "Sethian Gnosticism and Johannine Christianity." Pages 399-433 in *Theology and Christology in the Fourth Gospel: Essays by the Members of the SNTS Johannine Writings Seminar*. Edited by G. van Belle, J. G. van der Watt, and P. Maritz. Bibliotheca Ephemeridum theologicarum Lovaniensium 184. Leuven: Leuven University Press.

Waldstein, M., and F. Wisse, eds. 1995. *The Apocryphon of John: Synopsis of Nag Hammadi Codices II,1; III,1; and IV,1 with BG 8502,2*. Nag Hammadi and Manichaean Studies 33. Leiden: Brill.

Westerink, L., and J. Combès, eds. 1989. *Damascius: De la triade et de l'unifié*. Vol. 2 of *Traité des premiers principes*. Collection des universités de France. Paris: Les Belles Lettres.

Williams, M. A. 1996. *Rethinking "Gnosticism": An Argument for Dismantling a Dubious Category*. Princeton, N.J.: Princeton University Press.

Index of Modern Authors

Abel, K., 19n24
Abramowski, L., 261n22
Adams, E., 116n4, 116n6, 117n8, 118n16, 119n20, 126n56, 129n68
Algra, K., 48, 48n32, 60n4
Allert, C. D., 176n1
Allison, D. C., 67n32
Amundsen, D. W., 193n96
André, J.-M., 2n5, 6, 6n13
Annas, J. E., 26n53, 120n22, 123n36
Arichea, D. C., 117n14
Armstrong, A., 260n20
Arya, D., 181n23
Ash, H. B., 143n2
Ashton, J., 77n3
Asmis, E., 115n1, 129n69, 211n60
Attridge, H. W., 77nn2-3, 78nn5-6, 87nn61-62, 89n69
Aune, D. E., 16n3, 101n41, 190n76

Babut, D., 8n25
Balz, H., 51n40
Banateanu, A., 70n48
Barnard, L., 176n1, 177n7
Barnes, J., 7n20
Barrett, C. K., 15n3, 81nn21-22, 88n64
Barry, C., 260n19
Bartchy, S. S., 44n21, 162n110
Barton, C., 184, 184nn34-35, 185n46, 188n65, 192, 193n92
Basore, J. W., 125n49, 149n35, 156n76, 161n105, 177n8
Bauckham, R. J., 116n2, 116n6, 118n16, 128n65, 129n67
Bechtle, G., 260n16, 267n60
Becker, J., 253nn37-38
Behm, J., 24n46
Berchman, R. M., 2n4

Bergadá, M., 153n58
Berry, P., 177n11
Berryman, S., 119n21
Betz, H. D., 25n50, 54n50, 70, 70nn51-52
Beutler, J., 82n28, 86n57
Bigg, C., 118n14
Bisel, S. L. C., 151n40
Bobzien, S., 177n10
Bonhöffer, A., 16n7, 41n10, 42nn14-15, 43n18, 45n22, 48n33, 49nn35-37, 50n39, 52n44, 52n47, 123n36
Borgen, P., 77n2
Boring, M. E., 86n58
Boulvert, G., 144n12
Bowen, A. C., 122n31
Bowersock, G. W., 184n40
Boys-Stones, G. R., 1, 1n1, 5, 10n30, 119n21
Bradley, K. R., 148, 148n26, 153n57, 162n111, 163n116
Braund, S. H., 126nn52-53
Brennan, T., 17n13, 48n34, 62n11, 68n38, 83n33, 84n43, 102n47, 104n54, 107, 107n62, 107n64, 111n82
Brisson, L., 265n50
Brooke, A. E., 97n14, 98nn16-21, 99nn23-32, 100nn33-37, 101nn39-40, 110n78
Brown, R. E., 77n3, 81n21, 81n24, 82n26, 96, 96n9, 97, 97n12, 101
Brunt, P. A., 152n53, 153n55, 157, 157n83, 162n113
Buch-Hansen, G., 78, 230n57, 232n74
Bultmann, R., 40n8, 81n23

Canarella, G., 143n3, 143n5, 146n18, 148n27, 150n37
Capasso, L., 150n39
Carlson, M. L., 192n88
Castelli, E. A., 184n40, 185, 185n44

Caulley, T. S., 116n4, 131n75
Cazelais, S., 267n60
Chaine, J., 117n12
Champeaux, J., 181n23
Chantraine, H., 144n12
Charles, J. D., 118n16, 128n64
Charles, R. H., 253nn36–37
Chilton, B., 55, 55n51
Chilton, C. W., 123n41
Christensen, J., 103n48
Clark, M., 260n21
Colish, M. L., 17n13, 18n19, 28n74, 127n59, 249n22
Collins, J. J., 117n8, 118n15, 126n56
Colpe, C., 77n2
Colson, F. H., 109n75, 110n80, 212n63
Combès, J., 260n18
Conzelmann, H., 117n11
Cooper, J., 68, 68n40
Corrigan, K., 261n22, 266n57, 267, 267n60, 267n63
Costa, C. D. N., 159n95
Cranfield, C. E. B., 15n3, 46, 46n24, 46n26, 51, 51n42, 53n49
Crego, P., 123n38
Cribiore, R., 143n7, 151n42
Crowley, T. J., 122n33, 129n67
Crum, W. E., 209n52
Culpepper, R. A., 77n1

D'Alessandro Behr, F., 125n51, 127n57
Dal Lago, E., 143n4
Daly-Denton, M., 82n28, 86n57
Danker, F., 116n5
Dautzenberg, G., 42n14
Davie, J., 159n96, 161n106
De Boer, E. A., 200n4, 204n27
DeFilippo, J. G., 124n44
De Lacy, P., 95n4
Deming, W., 34n109, 42n14
Dennis, T. J., 153n58
DesRosiers, N., 68n37
Di Domenicantonio. L., 150n39
Diels, H., 123, 123n38, 248n19
Diggle, J., 149n34
Dihle, A., 159n94, 179n14
Dillon, J. M., 1n2, 3, 3nn7–9, 5, 5nn10–11, 7nn21–22, 11, 12n35, 95n6, 108, 108nn66–72, 110, 179n16, 212n62, 236, 236n95, 263n40
Dobbin, R. F., 49n38, 156n73, 170n133
Dodd, C. H., 15n3
Dodds, E. R., 262n32, 264n41
Dods, M., 195n102

Downing, F. G., 39n4, 118n16
Droge, A. J., 117n13, 186, 186n52, 186n55, 187n57
Dubois, J.-D., 199n2
Dunderberg, I., 224n27, 226n38, 226n41, 230n57, 236n93, 236n95
Dunn, F. M., 125n50
Dunn, J. D. G., 16n3, 30nn89–90, 46n24, 46n27, 51nn42–43, 53n49
Dupont-Roc, R., 118n16

Edelstein, L., 157n77
Edgar, C. C., 169n132
Edwards, C., 19n23, 183, 183n33, 184, 184n35, 190, 190n73, 192, 192n87
Elliott, J. H., 116n2
Elliott, J. K., 148n25
Engberg-Pedersen, T., 5n12, 9nn28–29, 11nn32–34, 16nn6–7, 17n14, 18, 18n15, 19n21, 21n34, 29n83, 31nn96–97, 32n99, 34n110, 39n3, 47, 47n29, 66n30, 82n32, 107n62, 111n83, 115n1, 130n71, 159n97, 180n19, 226n40, 230n57
Engel, D. M., 211n61
Esler, P. F., 16n6, 20n30
Evans, C., 77n2

Falls, T., 176n2
Fee, G. D., 117n11
Feeney, D., 118n14
Fenoaltea, S., 143n6, 144n11, 145n13
Ferguson, J., 214nn75–76
Festugière, A.-J., 237n96
Fiasse, G., 70n47
Fiore, B., 168n131
Fitzgerald, J. T., 143n7, 147n20, 149n30, 151n42, 151n44, 157n79, 157n81, 162n109, 166n125, 170n134
Fitzmyer, J. A., 16n4, 30n90
Fornberg, T., 118n16, 128n66, 131n75
Forschner, M., 49n37
Fortenbaugh, W. W., 153n55
Foucault, M., 184, 184n41, 185, 185n43
Fox, M. V., 149n31
Fox, R. L., 184n40, 185, 185n45
Frede, D., 178n12
Frede, M., 6, 6nn15–16, 95n4, 107n62
Fredriksen, P., 70n50
Frend, W. H. C., 184n40
Fridrichsen, A., 51n41
Fuchs, E., 117n12
Fuglseth, K., 119n19
Funk, W.-P., 260n19

Furley, D., 117n8
Furnish, V. P., 30n87

Gager, J. G., 189n71
Garnsey, P., 147n19
Garver, E., 153n55
George, D. B., 126n55
Gerdmar, A., 117n12
Geytenbeek, A. C. van, 19n27
Gibson, R. J., 23n38
Gifford, E. H., 123n37
Gill, C., 2n3, 2n5, 11n32, 52n44, 84n42, 102n46, 103n47, 115n1, 119n21, 121n26, 122n32, 123n36, 130n71, 130n73
Gilmour, M. J., 117n12
Giversen, S., 241, 241nn4–5, 243, 243n16, 254
Glad, C. E., 21n33, 22n37, 33n108, 39n3
Glasson, T. F., 117n12
Göransson, T., 121n25
Gould, J. B., 120n22
Gourinat, J.-B., 117n8
Graf, F., 118n17
Graver, M. R., 67nn35–36, 71nn53–54, 72nn56–57, 73, 73nn58–59, 107n62, 108, 108n66, 108n69, 109, 109n73, 109n76–77, 120, 120n23, 121n26, 127n57, 131n74
Graves, R., 165n122
Green, M., 117n14
Greer, R., 153n61, 221n12
Griffin, M. T., 18n16, 19nn24–25, 153n57, 155, 155nn70–71, 177n8, 190n73, 191n81
Gummere, R. M., 177n8

Hadot, P., 257, 257nn1–2, 258, 258nn5–6, 258nn9–10, 259, 259n12, 259n14, 260, 260nn16–17, 260n21, 261, 261nn22–24, 262, 263, 263n34, 263n39, 264, 264nn42–47, 265, 265n47, 265nn49–50, 266, 267, 267nn58–59, 269, 269n65, 270
Haenchen, E., 81n20, 81n24
Hahm, D. E., 117n8, 123n37
Hands, A. R., 27n59
Hankinson, R. J., 161n108
Hansen, W., 154n63
Harkins, P. W., 164n120
Harmon, A. M., 149n33
Harrill, J. A., 118n15, 152n52
Hart, D. B., 153n58
Hart, V., 119n21
Hartenstein, J., 199n3, 205n28
Hatton, H. A., 117n14
Hays, R. S., 122n34
Headlam, A. C., 15n2
Heath, M., 147n21, 153n55

Heine, R. E., 97n15, 98nn18–20, 99nn23–24, 99n26–29, 110n78
Helmbold, W. C., 104n51, 107n61, 158n86, 163n117, 248n21, 249n23, 252n33, 253n39
Hense, O., 17n10, 155n65, 159n93
Hershbell, J. P., 162n113
Hershkowitz, D., 121n26, 127n57
Heseltine, M., 156n74
Hicks, R. D., 158n85, 250n26
Hock, R. F., 156n74
Hoffman, G. N., 123n41
Hooper, W. D., 143n2
Hopkins, K., 160n103
Horrell, D. G., 20n30
Hoven, R., 123n36
Hunt, A. S., 169n132
Huttunen, N., 39n2, 41n9, 52n45, 220

Inwood, B., 61n8, 119n21, 124n44, 177n10, 178n12, 192, 192n85
Irwin, T. H., 83n34, 106n58

Jewett, R., 16n3, 16n5, 26n55, 26n58, 31n98
Johnson, L. T., 25n50, 26n56, 168n131
Jones, A., 122n31
Jones, F. S., 39n4, 42n14, 44n20
Jongman, W., 160n103

Kalbfleisch, K., 264n43
Käsemann, E., 15n3, 79n13, 93n1
Katsari, C., 143n4
Kee, H. C., 117n12, 123n42
Keener, C. S., 82n29, 88n64
Kelly, J. N. D., 117n10
Kidd, I. G., 157n77, 208n47
King, J. E., 107n63
King, K. L., 200n5, 202nn15–17, 204, 204n23, 205n28, 211n57
Kirschenbaum, A., 162n113
Kitzberger, I. R., 81n25
Knust, J. W., 189n71
Knuuttila, S., 226n40
Konstan, D., 119n21
Kraut, R., 153n55
Kroll, W., 259n16
Kuss, O., 46n24, 47n28, 53n49

Lachenaud, G., 123n38
Laes, C., 143n7, 150n38, 151nn41–42, 163n115
Lang, F., 41n12
Lang, M., 79n8
Lapidge, M., 121nn27–28, 122n30, 122n35, 126n55, 129n67, 221n13

Larsen, K. B., 77, 77n4, 78n5
Lattimore, R., 181n25
Layton, B., 221, 221nn10–11, 241, 241n12, 246, 246n17, 249, 249n24, 257n3
Lee, M. V., 16n7, 28n70
Leigh, M., 126n54, 127n63
Leisegang, H., 9n26, 213n70
Lenhard, H., 116n5
Leonhardt-Balzer, J., 77n2
Lewis, E., 123n37
Lietzmann, H., 15n3
Lindars, B., 81n20, 96n7, 96n10–11, 97n13, 100n38
Lindemann, A., 41n13
Lindsay, W. M., 163n114
Loader, W., 80n17
Logan, A., 268n64
Long, A., 125n51, 127n57
Long, A. A., 5n10, 8n24, 9n27, 11n31, 17n12, 17n14, 18n15, 20n29, 34n109, 41n10, 42n15, 48n33, 49n38, 52n44, 60n4, 61n9, 63n21, 65n25, 67n34, 79n10, 83nn36–38, 84n39, 84n42, 103n50, 115n1, 117n8, 120, 120n22, 120n24, 121n26, 204, 204nn25–26, 206nn30–31, 206nn33–39, 207nn43–44, 208n46, 208n48, 209n53, 210nn54–55, 211n58, 222n17, 233n77, 262n26, 262n28, 262n30, 263n37, 264n46
Longenecker, R. N., 54n50
Lührmann, D., 199n2
Luttikhuizen, G. P., 220, 220n6
Lutz, C. E., 16n8, 20n28, 52n48
Lyman, R., 176n1

MacRae, G. W., 199n2
Majercik, R., 258n5, 258n10, 261n22, 265n50
Malherbe, A. J., 39n3, 40nn7–8, 151n43
Manning, C. E., 125n50
Mansfeld, J., 116n7, 117n8, 123n38, 123n41, 220n2
Marcovich, M., 176n2
Marcus, R., 213n73
Marjanen, A., 199n3, 200n4, 205n28
Markschies, C., 222n15, 223, 223nn21–22, 224n27
Marti, B. M., 127n63
Martin, D. B., 39n3, 44n20, 115n1, 118n15, 118n18
Masters, J., 127n63
Mayer, R., 117n14
Meeks, W. A., 22n36, 79n9, 86n58, 118n15, 189n71, 194, 194n110
Metzger, B. M., 117n10
Meyer, M., 225nn31–32

Michel, O., 15n3
Milavec, A., 116n6
Milobenski, E., , 250n29
Miranda, J. P., 86n58
Mitsis, P. T., 124n44
Mohri, E., 199n2
Moloney, F. J., 81n21, 81n25
Montini, P., 176n4
Moo, D. J., 46n24, 46n27
Morard, F., 200n7
Morford, M. P. O., 127n63
Moriarty, R., 153n59
Morris, J., 212n62
Most, G. W., 126n55
Motto, A. L., 124n47
Moxnes, H., 26n57
Munier, C., 177n7
Murphy, F. S., 116n7
Musurillo, H., 186n56, 187n59

Newmyer, S., 127n63
Newport, K., 69n42
Neyrey, J. H., 116nn3–4, 116n6, 117n10, 118n16, 128n65, 129n67, 130n72, 131n75
Nock, A. D., 237n96
North, H., 26n58
Nussbaum, M. C., 48n34, 82n32, 87n60, 88, 88n66, 88n68, 95n6, 102n45, 106n57, 107n62, 226n40

Oldfather, W. A., 42n16, 156n72
Olivier, F., 117, 117n9
Olyan, S., 63n17
O'Neil, E. N., 156n75
Onuki, T., 220, 220n5, 225, 227n42, 242n14, 255nn40–41, 269, 270n66

Pasquier, A., 199n2, 201, 201nn9–10, 202, 202nn10–14, 202nn16–17, 203, 203nn18–19, 203n22, 204, 205, 205nn28–29, 207, 207nn40–42, 207nn44–45, 208, 208n46
Paulsen, H., 117n14
Pearson, B. A., 118n16, 257n3,
Perrin, B., 154n64
Petersen, S., 199n3
Plank, K. A., 45n23
Pleše, Z., 220, 220n7, 232n75, 262n29, 269, 270n66
Pohlenz, M., 34n109, 40n7, 46n25, 51n41, 242n13, 249n22, 249n25, 250n29, 255n41
Pomeroy, A. J., 17n10, 17n13, 121n25
Pomeroy, S. B., 144n8, 145n14
Przybylski, B., 64n23

Index of Modern Authors

Rackham, H., 17n14, 204n24
Rackham, R., 145n15
Räisänen, H., 40, 40n6, 41n12
Ramelli, I., 153n58, 159n93, 160n98
Rasimus, T., 257n3, 258n4, 259n13, 259n15, 260nn19–20, 261n22, 266n52, 266nn56–57, 267n62, 268n64, 270n67
Raymer, A. J., 153n56, 160n104
Rehm, B., 251n31
Reichert, A., 22n36
Reiser, M., 29n83, 69n43
Rengstorf, K. H., 43n19
Reydams-Schils, G., 28n68, 69n45, 70n48, 84n43, 120n22, 125n50
Reymond, P., 117n12
Richter, W., 153n57, 155n68, 155n70
Riddle, D. W., 184n40
Riesner, R., 117n14
Rigsby, K. J., 162n111
Rist, J. M., 25n49, 49n37, 84n42, 178n12
Robinson, J., 260n21
Rosenmeyer, T. G., 123n42
Ruelle, C., 260n18
Runia, D. T., 118n19, 123n38, 212n62, 213, 213n66, 213n71–73
Russell, D. M., 117n12

Saffrey, H., 268
Sagnard, F.-M., 221n9
Salles, R., 178n12
Sambursky, S., 103n48
Sanday, W., 15n2
Sandbach, F. H., 19n20, 163n117, 209n51
Sanders, E. P., 39, 47n31
Scheer, R., 67n33
Scheidel, W., 160n103
Schenke, H.-M., 199n2, 202nn16–17, 205n28, 257n3
Schlier, H., 15n3
Schmithals, W., 52n46
Schnackenburg, R., 81n23, 96, 96n8
Schneemelcher, W., 178n13
Schneider, G., 51n40
Schnelle, U., 79n13
Schoedel, W. R., 221n12
Schofield, M., 65n26, 152n54, 153n55
Scholtissek, K., 87n63
Schotes, H.-A., 126n55
Schrage, W., 30n87, 45n23
Schröter, J., 200n6
Sedley, D. N., 2n3, 2n5, 6, 6n14, 6n17–18, 7, 9n27, 10n30, 34n109, 61n9, 65n25, 67n34, 83nn36–38, 84n39, 117n8, 120n22, 121n26, 206n30, 206n31, 206n34, 206nn38–39, 208n46, 208n48, 210nn54–55, 222n17, 233n77, 262n26, 262n28, 262n30, 263n37, 264n46
Seeley, D., 39n3, 177n9
Segal, C., 130n70
Sevenster, J. N., 16n7
Sharp, D. S., 41n10
Sharples, R. W., 209n51, 210n55
Sherk, R. K., 149n29
Sherwin-White, A. N., 122n34
Siegert, F., 77n2
Sihvola, J., 82n32, 226n40
Sim, D. C., 117n12
Siouville, A., 251n31
Sklenář, R., 126n55
Söding, T., 30n87
Sorabji, R., 50n39, 73n58, 82n32, 84n43, 102n46
Spanneut, M., 41n10, 177n9, 177n11, 215n80
Stalnacker, A., 115n1
Stanton, G. N., 66n28, 70n52
Stark, R., 189n71
Starr, J. M., 117n14, 128n64, 128n66
Ste. Croix, G. E. M. de, 162n111, 184n40
Steinmetz, P., 157n78, 206n31
Stibbe, M. W. G., 81n25, 93n1
Story, C. I. K., 81n20, 97n13
Stowers, S. K., 16n3, 21n32, 22n36, 40n8, 47, 47n30
Stramara, D. F., Jr., 153n58
Strange, S. K., 107n62
Straw, C., 186, 186n53, 187n60, 189, 189n70, 190, 191n77, 193, 193nn94–95
Strutwolf, H., 224n24, 224n28
Stuhlmacher, P., 16n3
Suggs, J. M., 61n7
Swete, H. B., 152n51

Tabor, J., 186n52
Tanner, R. G., 185n47
Tardieu, M., 199n2, 202nn16–17, 205n28, 241, 241nn8–11, 250, 250n28, 250n30, 254, 265, 265n50, 268n64
Terian, A., 108nn66–72
Testa, P. E., 117n12
Theißen, G., 252n34
Thiede, C. P., 117n14
Thom, J. C., 60n4, 61n6, 63n20
Thomas, R. F., 127n63
Thomassen, E., 221, 221n8, 225n31
Thompson, M., 33n107
Thorsteinsson, R. M., 16n6, 19n22, 20n31, 21n34, 22n36, 32n101, 34n111

Thyen, H., 81n20, 82n28, 86n57, 87n63, 88n64
Tieleman, T., 121n26
Till, W. C., 199n2, 202nn16–17, 203n21, 205n28
Todd, R. B., 122n31, 122n33, 206n34
Tomaske, J. A., 143n3, 143n5, 146n18, 148n27, 150n37
Tuckett, C. M., 199n2, 200n4, 202nn15–17, 203, 203nn20–21, 205n29, 208n46
Turner, J., 257n3, 258n5, 260n20, 261n22, 265, 265n48, 266nn53–54, 266n56, 267n60, 268n64

Urbainczyk, T., 151n49

Van der Horst, P. W., 116n6, 117n10, 117n14, 118n16, 126n56
van Rensburg, F. J., 151n44
van Rooy, H. F., 151n44
Van Unnik, W. C., 215n81
Van Winden, J. C. M., 176n1
Veyne, P., 177n8
Vogt, J., 162n112
Vögtle, A., 117n12
Volk, K., 122n34
Vollenweider, S., 42n14
von Allmen, D., 118n16
von Arnim, H. F. A., 178n12, 208n46, 247n18
von Gemünden, P., 252n34
Von Staden, H., 120n22
Voorwinde, S., 95n5

Wachsmuth, C., 17n10, 155n65, 159n93
Waldstein, M., 239n2, 241, 241nn6–7, 242n15, 265n48

Walker, D. D., 162n109
Walsh, P. G., 159n95, 167n127
Walzer, R., 188n67, 194n97
Wasserman, E., 121n26
Watson, F. P., 22n36
Weaver, P. R. C., 144n12
Weber, R., 40n5
Wenham, D., 116n5
Westerholm, S., 39n1
Westerink, L., 260n18, 268
Whitaker, G. H., 109n75, 110n80
White, M. J., 117n8, 121n27
Wibbing, S., 128n64
Wigodsky, M., 129n67
Wilckens, U., 46n24
Williams, F., 123n38
Williams, M. A., 220n4, 260n21
Wilson, M., 124n47
Wilson, R., 199n2
Wilson, W. T., 29n83, 30n87
Winterbottom, M., 156n74
Wirszubski, C., 179n15
Wisse, F., 239n2, 241, 241n6, 242n15, 265n48
Witherington, B., 16n3
Wolfson, H. A., 233nn76–77, 233n82
Wolters, A., 116n6
Wolterstorff, N., 82n31
Wright, N. T., 16n3

Zahn, T., 15n3
Zelnick-Abramovitz, R., 142n1
Ziesler, J., 16n3

Index of Subjects

Academy
  New Academy, 2, 3, 4, 7, 17n13
  Old Academy, 7
  See also Platonic, Platonism
aether, 222, 222n17, 223-24, 262. *See also* elements
Aëtius, 123, 206n34, 208n46, 210n55, 248n19, 262n27, 265n51
Alexander of Aphrodisias, 4, 12n36, 206n34, 229n55, 230n63, 233n78, 233n82, 234n85, 262n26, 263n35
allegorical interpretation, 41, 98, 98n22, 101, 108, 222
Antiochus of Ascalon, 3, 3n9, 7-8, 10, 204
Antipater of Tarsus, 17n10, 17n14, 156, 157n77
apatheia, 71, 80, 82n29, 84, 93, 95, 95n5, 97, 101, 102, 102n45, 104, 106-8, 156, 166n123, 191, 228, 242, 249, 255. *See also* emotion
Apollodorus, 82
appropriate action (καθῆκον), 25, 25n49, 49, 49n37, 52, 61, 61n9, 62-63, 65-67, 102, 109, 159, 159n92, 160-161, 166
Apuleius, 4, 165n122, 181, 181n24
Archedemus of Tarsus, 17n10, 62
Aristotelian(s)/Peripatetic(s), 2, 4, 6, 7, 8, 10, 12, 83-84, 87, 95, 104, 107, 118, 119n21, 121, 155, 220, 222, 222n17, 234, 250, 251, 252, 252n34, 254, 262
Aristotle, 2, 3, 4, 25n50, 95, 103, 108, 119, 121, 144n10, 145, 145n15, 147, 147nn22-23, 151, 152, 152n54, 153, 153n55, 155, 156, 158n85, 163n113, 221n12, 232-33n76, 233, 233n77, 233n82
Aristoxenus, 158n85
Arrian, 20, 20n29, 69, 122n34, 181, 181n21

assent, (συγκατάθεσις) 67, 71, 72, 73, 84, 103-5, 120, 181, 208, 227
Augustine, 74, 82, 82n31, 177, 192n88, 193, 260n18
Aulus Gellius, 120, 120n23, 160n100, 162n111

being, 258, 259, 261, 262n32, 263-64, 264n41, 265, 265n47, 267, 268, 268-69n65
  non-being, 259, 264-65, 265n47, 268
being-life-mind triad, 257, 258, 258n5, 259, 261-63, 265n50, 266, 268, 268-69n65, 270n67
blending (κρᾶσις), 206, 232, 232nn74-76, 233, 233n77, 233nn79-80, 234, 234n85, 235-36, 251, 263. *See also* fusion; juxtaposition; mixture
breath, 9, 9n26, 11, 66, 78, 93, 95, 103, 103n50, 120-21, 125, 155, 206, 209, 213, 222, 225, 252, 261-62, 262n28, 265-66, 268, 270, 270n66

Calcidius, 205-6
Cato (the Elder), 67, 143, 143n2, 154, 168n130
Cato (the Younger), 126, 126n54, 127, 127n57, 190-92
Christ, 5, 9, 19, 20, 21, 22, 23, 26-27, 31, 32, 33, 46, 93n1, 100, 111, 130, 163, 186, 189, 226, 228, 228n51, 229, 266. *See also* Jesus; Son of Man
Chrysippus, 17nn9-10, 19n21, 49, 61, 65, 79, 95n4, 102, 102n46, 103n49, 105, 120, 121, 122, 122n31, 123, 130n73, 155, 155n68, 155n70, 232, 248, 248n19, 249, 257
Cicero, 2, 3, 4, 7n22, 17, 17n11, 17nn13-14, 18, 18nn15-16, 18n18, 19n21, 23n40, 24n42, 28n69, 28n71, 29n78, 34n109,

40n7, 49n36, 60n3, 62, 62n11, 63n20, 67, 67n34, 102, 102n42, 104n52, 107, 107n63, 109, 110n81, 111n82, 122n29, 122n34, 123n36, 125n50, 153, 156, 156n72, 159n92, 159n95, 167n127, 184, 184nn36–37, 204, 204n26, 250n29

Cleanthes, 17nn9–10, 61, 86, 121, 123

Clement of Alexandria, 3, 3n8, 192, 192n90, 214, 214nn75–78, 215, 215nn79–80, 216, 225n34, 226n39, 227n44, 228n49, 228n51, 229n54, 229n56, 230n65, 233, 233n81, 234, 235nn91–92, 250n27

Cleomedes, 122, 122n31

conflagration (ἐκπύρωσις), 78, 115–16, 116n2, 117, 117n13, 118–19, 119n20, 121–27, 127n59, 128–29, 131–32, 176, 206, 233, 233n79, 236, 262, 265n50, 270n66

corporeal
  corporeality, 9n27, 103n50, 120, 124, 127, 131, 205, 233, 264, 264n43, 264n46
  cosmic body, 103, 200, 208, 209
  human body, 9, 10, 11, 21, 24, 25, 26, 27, 42, 43, 51, 53, 54, 98, 99, 101, 101n41, 103, 104, 119, 120, 121, 123, 130, 147, 149n33, 150, 157, 158, 158n88, 159, 163n113, 167, 179, 183, 201, 208, 210, 211, 214, 220n4, 228n51, 233, 234, 239, 240, 243, 245, 246, 246n17, 247, 251
  incorporeal, 228, 264, 264n46
  mind/body dualism, 16n3, 73n61, 103n50, 123

covenantal nomism, 39, 47, 55

creation
  of humanity, 226, 245, 246, 246n17, 252
  recreation, (παλιγγενεσία) 60, 60n5, 78, 115, 117, 121, 122, 124, 125, 126, 126n54, 127, 129, 131, 177, 233n79, 236, 262. See also conflagration
  of the world, 60, 69, 115, 118n19, 128, 129, 200n4, 206, 209, 212, 213, 214, 215, 215n81, 216, 226, 227, 228

Cynic(s), Cynicism, 40, 40n7, 86n58, 190
Cynic (Demetrius), 186
Cyprian, 186, 186n50, 187, 187n59, 187n64

determinism, 12, 161, 161n108, 177–78, 178n12, 179, 181, 193, 229–30, 242. See also fate

Diogenes of Babylon, 17n14, 122
Diogenes Laertius, 17, 17n10, 17nn13–14, 18n15, 23n40, 61, 62n13, 63n14, 66n27, 79, 79n12, 79n14, 80, 80nn15–16, 82, 82n29, 83, 84n40, 88, 88nn65–66, 102nn43–44, 103n49, 104n53, 106, 106n59, 107n63, 109n74, 110n81, 111n82, 122n34, 123, 123nn39–40, 152n50, 155, 156n75, 158, 158n85, 161n107, 163n113, 206n32, 206n34, 208n46, 210n55, 222n18, 227n42, 227n45, 233n82, 250, 250nn26–27, 262n27, 262nn30–31, 263n38

Diogenes of Oenoanda, 123, 123n41

Early Stoicism. See Old Stoa

elements (στοιχεῖα), 78, 116–17, 125, 127n59, 129, 129n67, 132, 207, 210–11, 222, 222n17, 223–24, 224n26, 262, 262n28

fifth element. See aether

emotion, 32, 48, 48n34, 49–50, 52–54, 60n3, 67, 70, 71, 72, 73, 80–81, 81n18, 82, 82n29, 83, 83n36, 84–89, 93, 93n1, 94–95, 95nn4–5, 96–102, 102–3n47, 104–6, 107–8, 108n69, 109, 110n79, 111, 111n83, 112, 121, 130, 130n73, 155–57, 157n79, 158n90, 160, 163, 166n123, 178–79, 183–85, 190, 190n76, 191–92, 194, 200–201, 205, 205n29, 208, 208n46, 208n48, 209–11, 211n58, 212, 212nn63–64, 213–16, 225–26, 226n38, 226n40, 227, 227n42, 227n45, 228, 228n51, 229, 236, 239, 240, 241, 241nn8–11, 242, 242n15, 244, 247–48, 248n20, 249–50, 250nn27–28, 251, 251n32, 252, 252n34, 253–55. See also apatheia; good emotions; metriopatheia; preemotion

appetite/desire/craving/lust (ἐπιθυμία), 42, 48, 50–54, 67, 67n34, 67n36, 83, 88–89, 101, 101n41, 107–9, 128, 179, 192, 208, 211, 211n58, 214–15, 225–27, 240, 244–45, 248, 250, 250n27, 251, 251n32, 252–53

distress/grief/pain (λύπη), 32, 32n100, 48–49, 67, 70–73, 73n58, 81–84, 86–88, 88n64, 89, 95, 95n4, 96–97, 100–102, 106–8, 108n69, 109–12, 208, 211, 225–28, 240, 244, 248, 251, 251n32

fear (φόβος), 48, 67, 71–72, 82–84, 86–88, 88n64, 89, 98–100, 105, 107–8, 111, 126, 144–45, 160, 163–68, 182–83, 185, 187n60, 190, 208, 225–27, 227n42, 227n45, 228, 240, 244, 248, 250, 251n32

Index of Subjects 283

pleasure/delight (ἡδονή), 48, 52, 61, 83, 88, 107–9, 111, 208, 225–27, 240, 244, 248, 250, 250n27, 251, 251n32, 252
  therapy of, 84, 87, 89, 105, 124, 124n47, 226, 228
Epictetus, 4, 8, 8n24, 10, 11, 16n4, 17–20, 23, 23nn40–41, 24nn42–43, 24n47, 25nn51–52, 27–28, 28n67, 28nn75–77, 29, 29nn79–80, 29n84, 30, 30n86, 30n88, 32nn99–100, 32n102, 33, 33nn105–6, 34, 34n109, 40–41, 41n9, 42, 42nn15–16, 43, 43n17, 44–49, 49n37, 50, 50n39, 51–55, 63n20, 69, 69n41, 73n61, 82n29, 84n41, 85n47, 86, 86nn53–56, 86n58, 147n19, 149n28, 151n47, 155–56, 156nn72–73, 157, 157n82, 158n88, 158n90, 161n107, 162n111, 163, 166n124, 170, 177n10, 179–80, 180n18, 180n20, 181, 209, 209n51, 211n58, 228n48, 230n61, 231n69
Epicureans, 2, 4, 49, 82n29, 116n4, 118–19, 119n21, 123, 158n85, 190
Epiphanius of Salamis, 123, 227n45, 232n72
error (ἁμάρτημα), 25n49, 29, 63, 157
ethics
  Johannine, 79
  Matthean, 59–60, 66, 70, 74, 74n62
  Pauline, 20–22, 26, 30n87, 33n108, 51
  Stoic, 2, 2n6, 15, 17, 17nn13–14, 18, 18n15, 18n18, 19, 19n21, 20, 20n30, 23, 25, 25n49, 27–29, 34, 48, 55, 59–60, 62, 66–67, 71, 73–74, 82, 102, 104, 108, 119, 119n21, 120–21, 124n44, 129, 131, 179–80, 241, 255, 263
  Valentinian, 230, 231n71, 232
Eudorus of Alexandria, 3, 11
Eusebius, 123n37, 191, 191n80, 193, 193n93, 206n38, 262n27
evil, 30, 30n86, 31, 34, 48, 63n18, 64, 67, 69–71, 73–74, 79, 99–101, 104, 106–7, 110, 149n31, 152, 157, 164–65, 179, 182, 199, 208, 210, 212–13, 213nn72–73, 214–16, 227, 232, 240–41, 241n4, 241nn6–7, 242, 248–49, 251–52, 254–55

fate, 121, 124, 129, 156n74, 161, 161n108, 165, 177–81, 184, 186–87, 189–90, 193, 200, 202, 204, 223, 243. See also determinism
fire, 74n62, 115–16, 116n6, 117, 117n8, 117n10, 118–19, 119n20, 121–27, 127n59, 128–29, 131–32, 176–77, 206,

210–11, 222–23, 245, 258n10, 262, 262n28, 270n66
Fortuna, 181, 181n23, 181n25, 182, 184, 187–88, 191
free will, 43, 153, 177, 179, 179n14, 183–86, 186n52, 235n93
fusion (σύγχυσις), 232, 233n79, 234, 263. See also blending; juxtaposition; mixture

Galen, 95n4, 149n32, 157n80, 164, 188, 194, 194n97, 209n51
Gentiles, 21, 39–40, 46–47, 51–55, 118n19
  Gentile Christians, 22, 22n36
Gnostic, 199–200, 200nn4–5, 201–2, 204–5, 205n29, 207–8, 214–16, 236, 236n95, 239, 242–43, 254–55, 257, 257n3, 258–60, 260n20, 261, 261nn22–23, 265–66, 266n57, 267, 270
God
  biblical, 11, 21, 23–24, 25n49, 26, 30–31, 33–34, 41–42, 44, 45, 46, 47, 50–51, 53–54, 55, 60, 61, 62, 63, 63n16, 63nn18–19, 64n23, 65, 66, 68, 68n39, 69, 70, 71, 72, 73, 74, 94, 98, 101, 109, 110, 115–16, 128, 129, 163, 166, 168, 169, 178–79, 180, 181, 185, 186, 187, 187n60, 200, 202, 211, 212, 212n63, 213, 213n72, 214, 216, 220, 221, 224n26, 225n30, 225n34, 245, 251, 255, 259, 265, 265n50, 266, 268, 269n65, 270
  Stoic, 11, 23–24, 28, 42–44, 45, 46, 47, 48–50, 53, 54, 55, 60, 61, 62, 63, 68, 69, 69n41, 70, 71, 74, 80, 103, 120, 125, 155–56, 176, 178–79, 182, 186, 200, 206, 208n46, 209, 221, 222, 229, 233, 235–36, 259, 262, 262n28, 264, 265, 265n50, 266, 268
good emotions (εὐπάθειαι), 32n99, 70–73, 73n58, 88, 95, 106–7, 107n62, 108–12, 227, 250
  caution/precaution (εὐλάβεια), 72, 88, 106–8, 250
  "fourth eupatheia," 95, 107–8, 110–11
  joy/happiness (χαρά), 32, 32nn99–100, 65, 70–71, 73, 88–89, 95n4, 106–8, 111, 191, 211, 226–27, 250
  subspecies of, 70, 72, 110n79
  volition/wishing (βούλη, βούλησις), 88, 106, 110n79, 193, 250
Gregory of Nyssa, 153

Hellenistic
  culture, 118, 119, 131n75

doxographers, 111
Judaism, 77, 78n7, 95n5, 126
medicine, 120
moralists, 157, 160, 162, 165
period, 1–2, 82, 84, 250
philosophy/thought, 3, 97, 101, 106, 117–18, 118n15, 131, 157, 161n108, 204, 216
Hermetism, 221n12, 236–237, 237n96
homosexuality, 50–54

Ignatius of Antioch, 185, 185n47
impression (φαντασία), 67, 71, 73, 84–87, 89, 103, 105, 120, 210–11, 211n58
impulse (ὁρμή), 52, 83, 83n36, 84, 84n40, 85, 102–4, 104n53, 105, 120–21, 227–28, 240, 248, 251–52
indifferent, 31, 33–34, 34n109, 42–46, 48, 55, 65–66, 68n38, 73, 89, 152, 182–83. *See also* value
preferred indifferent, 73, 152

Jesus, 23, 31, 33, 59, 59n1, 60–62, 62n12, 63, 63n19, 64, 64n23, 65–72, 72n55, 73, 73n58, 78–81, 81n18, 82–84, 86–88, 88n64, 89, 93, 93n1, 94–95, 95n5, 96–97, 97n12, 98–101, 104–7, 111–12, 130, 157, 164–66, 189, 214–16, 228n51, 233. *See also* Christ; Son of Man
Jews, Judaism, 1–3, 8–12, 30, 32, 39–41, 41n9, 47, 47n31, 55, 61, 63, 63n16, 64n23, 69, 71, 72, 74, 78, 79n11, 95, 112, 117–18, 126, 131, 131n75, 158, 177, 190n76, 200, 212, 212n62, 214–15, 215n81, 216, 224, 252
Jewish-Christians, 22, 22n36, 96
Jewish Law, 32, 40. *See also* law; Torah
Jews in the Fourth Gospel, 81, 93–98
Jewish Scriptures, writings, 30, 50, 60, 126
John Chrysostom, 187, 187n58
Judas, 94, 97, 99
Judas, Gospel of, 230n57
Justin Martyr, 117n13, 176, 176nn1–5, 177, 177nn6–7, 178–80, 185, 190, 190nn74–75, 191, 194, 194n99, 195, 195nn101–2
juxtaposition (παράθεσις), 232, 234, 263. *See also* blending; fusion; mixture

Late Stoicism. *See* Neostoicism
law
  biblical, 32, 39–41, 46–47, 54, 59–62, 64, 67–68, 74, 180, 232. *See also* Torah

concerning slavery, 144n8, 149, 154n62, 162n113
Stoic, 24, 42–43, 45–50, 54, 60, 61, 71, 124–25, 156, 186
universal, 60, 61, 71
Lazarus, 81, 87, 94, 96–97, 97n13, 98
logic, 18, 102, 263
logos/reason
  biblical, 77–78, 93, 98, 116, 128, 128n65, 129, 176, 207, 213, 231, 234, 234n86
  reasonable worship, 15n3, 21, 23
  Stoic, 23–24, 28, 28n68, 61, 61n9, 62, 63n16, 69–71, 73, 79, 83–84, 84n36, 84n40, 88–89, 102–7, 110n79, 119–22, 124, 126, 131, 147, 151, 155–56, 166n123, 176, 202, 206–7, 207nn43–44, 209–13, 230, 248–54
love, 21, 22, 23, 27, 28, 28n68, 29, 29n78, 29n83, 30, 30n87, 31, 32, 32n100, 33, 34, 41, 46, 54, 59, 64, 65, 66, 69, 70, 71, 73, 74, 79, 87, 88, 97, 99, 102n45, 111, 128, 130, 131, 165n122, 167, 191, 215, 225, 227, 252

Marcus Aurelius, 4–6, 11, 11n32, 18n17, 23n40, 24n47, 28n68, 40, 69, 122n34, 188, 194, 194n98
martyr, martyrdom, 177–78, 183–84, 184n40, 185–86, 186n52, 187–88, 190, 190n76, 191–95
Mary of Bethany, 81, 83, 94, 96, 97
Mary Magdalene, 78, 199, 204, 210–212, 216
Mary the mother of Jesus, 80
matter, 78, 103, 103n50, 125, 199–206, 206n31, 207, 207n43, 208, 208n46, 209–10, 212–13, 213n73, 214–16, 228–30, 232, 235–36, 236n93, 240, 243–46, 255
Methodius, 235n93
metriopatheia, 95, 107–8
Middle Stoicism, 1, 2, 6, 10
mind (νοῦς), 16n3, 24–25, 25n49, 52, 60, 66, 73n61, 85, 105, 151, 156, 206, 208, 211n56, 213n65, 223, 257–58, 258n5, 259, 261–63, 265n50, 266, 266n56, 268, 269n65, 270n67
Minucius Felix, 187, 187n62, 192n88
mixture, 201, 206–7, 207n43, 210, 212–15, 232–33, 233n76, 234–37, 239–40, 247, 251, 255, 262–63, 267. *See also* blending; fusion; juxtaposition
Moses, 62, 78, 106–8, 118n19, 212n62, 231
Musonius Rufus, 4, 16n8, 18–20, 20n28, 24, 24n42, 24n44, 25n52, 26n54, 29,

Index of Subjects 285

29n79, 29n85, 30, 30n86, 31, 31n91, 32n100, 33n105, 34, 52, 157n83, 161n107, 170

natural law, 46–48, 54, 124, 124n44
natural theology, 46, 50–51, 54–55
Nature, 28–29, 32, 49–50, 52–54, 61, 65, 83, 83n36, 84, 89, 102–3, 103nn49–50, 104, 120, 124–25, 128, 152, 155–56, 184, 188, 191–92, 200–205, 205n29, 206–7, 207nn43–44, 208–12, 212n64, 213–16, 223, 229, 229n56, 231, 233, 233n77, 233n79, 234–35, 248–49, 250n27, 251–54, 262n32, 264n41
   in accordance with Nature (κατὰ φύσιν), 49–50, 83, 84, 89, 102, 103n49, 120, 206–7, 254
   contrary to Nature (παρὰ φύσιν), 52–53, 83n36, 152, 192, 200–201, 205, 205n29, 206–12, 214–15
Neopythagoreanism, 3, 221, 267
Neostoicism, 2, 4, 10, 11, 15n3, 19, 40, 70n47
Numenius, 4, 267

Oikeiōsis, 62, 65, 70, 73, 109, 130, 159, 160, 229, 230, 230n57, 231
Old Stoa, 19, 19n20, 73n58, 102, 105, 155, 179, 242, 252, 257
Onesimus, 153, 168. See also slaves, slavery
Origen of Alexandria, vii, 3, 72, 72n56, 73n58, 74, 95–97, 97nn12–13, 98, 98n17, 98n22, 99–101, 105–6, 109–12, 117n13, 162n111, 186, 186n51, 224, 224n24

Panaetius, 2, 5–8, 10, 17n10, 62, 79n10, 122, 159n92
pantheism, 48, 54, 60, 221
passion. See emotion
Paul, 5, 8–9, 11, 15, 15n2–3, 16, 16n3, 16n7, 17–21, 21n35, 22, 22n36, 23, 23n39, 24–26, 26n55, 27, 29–30, 30n87, 30nn89–90, 31–34, 34n109, 35, 39–42, 44, 44n21, 45–51, 51n41, 52–55, 59, 59n1, 62, 96, 111, 111n83, 112, 115, 117, 152, 152n52, 153, 153n61, 163, 163n113, 166, 168–69, 177, 177n11, 180, 180n19, 189, 223, 224n26
perfect action (κατόρθωμα), 49n37, 61, 62
Peter, 116, 118n14, 129–30, 132, 200, 208, 211–12, 251
Philo of Alexandria, 3, 3n8, 8–9, 9n26, 11, 40–41, 61–62, 62n10, 72, 72n56, 73, 78, 78n7, 79n11, 95–96, 106–8,

108n65, 109, 109nn74–75, 110, 110nn79–80, 111–12, 118n19, 122n29, 150n36, 155, 212, 212nn62–64, 213, 213nn65–70, 213nn72–73, 214, 214n74, 216, 221n12, 223, 223n23, 224, 230n61, 231, 231n69, 236, 263
Philo of Larissa, 3, 7
physics, 2, 7, 18, 78, 102–3, 103n48, 104, 119–20, 129, 131–32, 155n71, 204, 222, 222n17, 228, 233, 263
Plato, 2–3, 5, 7, 9, 9n27, 10, 43n17, 46, 50–52, 73n61, 102n45, 103, 106, 106n57, 109, 119, 186–87, 220, 220n3, 266
Platonic, Platonism, vii, 1–3, 3n8, 4–13, 46–47, 51n41, 52, 54, 73n61, 78, 83–84, 87n60, 95, 108, 119, 119n21, 121, 125n50, 179, 190, 204, 212n62, 215, 220, 220nn3–4, 221, 236–37, 258, 262–63, 269. See also Academy
   Middle Platonism, vii, 1, 3, 4, 11, 165, 179, 200, 205, 208, 212n62, 214–15, 236, 257–58, 265, 267
   Neoplatonism, 1, 3, 257–59, 261n25, 262–66, 268, 270
Plotinus, 257–58, 258n5, 258n7, 260, 260n20, 261n22, 261n25, 266, 266n57, 267, 270
Plutarch, 4, 8, 12, 26n54, 60n3, 103, 104n51, 106, 106n60, 107n61, 109, 116n4, 122n34, 123n36, 146n17, 147n20, 151nn45–46, 154, 154n64, 158n86, 160n100, 160n102, 161n105, 163, 163n117, 164n119, 165, 168n130, 180, 180n17, 230nn59–61, 233n80, 233n82, 248, 248n21, 249, 249n23, 252, 252n33, 253n39, 263n37
pneuma. See breath
Porphyry, 160nn98–99, 257–58, 258n10, 259–60, 260nn16–17, 260n20, 261, 261n22, 262–64, 264n47, 265–66, 266n57, 267–68, 270, 270n67
Posidonius of Apamea, 2, 5–8, 10, 47, 84, 84n42, 122, 156–57, 157nn77–78, 209, 209n51
preconception (πρόληψις), 86
preemotion (προπάθεια), 57, 72, 72n56, 73, 73n58, 82–87, 89, 100–101, 105–7, 108n69, 109, 110, 112, 228
providence, 50, 69, 74, 116, 116n4, 178–79, 187
   Pronoia (Gnostic), 243
Pythagoras, 158n85, 212n62, 220

Q-source, 60, 62n12, 63, 66, 69, 74

sage, 29, 60–62, 62n12, 63, 63n21, 65–66, 68, 70–73, 79–80, 83–85, 89, 95, 101–2, 104, 106–7, 109–10, 110n81, 111–12, 119n21, 120, 127–28, 131, 156, 182–84, 186, 188, 191, 230–231
Satan, 97, 97n12, 99–101, 106, 110, 112
Seneca, 4, 5, 8, 10, 15nn2–3, 16nn3–4, 18–19, 19n24, 23n40, 24, 24n42, 24n45, 24nn47–48, 25, 25nn51–52, 26n54, 27, 27nn60–66, 28, 28n69, 28nn71–73, 29, 29n78, 29n81, 29n85, 30, 30n86, 31, 31nn92–96, 32, 32n99, 32n103, 33, 33nn104–5, 34, 34n109, 47, 66n27, 69, 73, 73n58, 73nn60–61, 79n10, 83, 83n35, 85, 85nn44–52, 86–87, 87n60, 88, 88n67, 95–96, 104, 104nn55–56, 105–6, 109, 117n8, 122, 122n34, 123, 123n42, 124, 124n43, 124nn45–48, 125, 125nn49–50, 131, 149, 153–55, 155n65, 155n67, 156, 156n76, 157, 157n78, 159, 159n91, 159nn95–96, 160, 160nn101–3, 161, 161n105, 161n107, 163–64, 166n126, 167–68, 170, 176–77, 177n8, 177nn10–11, 178–79, 182, 182nn26–30, 183, 183n32, 184, 184n35, 184nn38–39, 186, 186n54, 188, 188n65, 188n68, 189, 189n69, 191, 191n78, 192, 192nn82–84, 192n86, 192n91, 206, 206n37, 208, 208n49, 209n51, 228n47, 229n55, 230n62, 232–33, 233n79, 235, 250n29, 265n50
Seneca the Elder, 156n74
Sermon on the Mount, 59, 63, 64n23, 69, 70, 73, 74n62, 157
Sethian, 220, 220nn4–5, 225, 232n75, 257, 257n3, 260, 260n20, 261, 261nn22–23, 265, 265n50, 266–68, 270, 270n67
Sextus Empiricus, 7n21, 122n34, 123n36, 263n38
slaves, slavery, 43, 44, 44nn20–21, 45, 49, 54, 79, 129, 141–43, 143n4, 144–45, 145n13, 146–47, 147n19, 147nn21–22, 148–49, 149n29, 149nn32–34, 150, 150nn37–38, 151, 151n45, 152, 152nn52–54, 153, 153n55, 154, 154n62, 155, 155n65, 155n71, 156, 156n74, 157, 157n83, 158, 158n89, 159, 159nn95–96, 160, 160nn100–101, 160nn103–4, 161, 161n105, 161n107, 162, 162nn110–13, 163, 163n113, 164–65, 165n122, 166, 166n123, 166n126, 167–70, 180–81, 183–84, 189, 192

Epictetus as a slave, 4, 20, 40, 162n111, 180
freedman, 44, 162n111, 180
imperial slaves, 144, 144n12
manumission, 44–45, 142, 142n1, 145, 150, 152n52, 153, 154n62
symbolic slavery, 44, 152, 155–57, 160, 180, 183, 193
treatment of, 141–170
Socrates, 10, 33, 43, 62, 65, 69, 73n61, 109, 119n21, 120, 143, 145–46, 158n85, 166, 182, 186–87, 190, 195
something (τὶ), 264, 264n46, 265, 265n48
not-something (οὔτι), 264, 264n46, 265
Son of Man, 71, 74n62, 93, 94, 199, 209, 211, 211n57, 212. *See also* Christ; Jesus
Sophia, 205n29, 226–27, 227n42, 227n45, 228–29, 233, 234n86, 236, 260n20; cf. 11
soul, 27, 28n68, 29, 52–53, 64, 66, 73n61, 81–83, 83n36, 84, 86–87, 94–95, 95n4, 99–101, 101n41, 103, 103n50, 104–8, 110, 112, 116, 119, 119n21, 120–21, 123–25, 131, 147, 157, 183, 193, 201, 206, 210–11, 213–15, 222–24, 224n26, 225, 225n34, 227, 229, 233–35, 235n92, 240, 246, 248–49, 251–55, 264
ascent of, 199, 199n4, 210–11, 213
chilled mind, 223–26
faculties of, 103, 210, 211, 247–48, 249, 253–54
fall of, 101, 201, 225
governing part of (ἡγεμονικόν), 83n36, 84, 95, 95n4, 103, 103n50, 104, 119, 213, 248–49, 252–55
and impulses, 84, 105, 210, 227
of Jesus, 81–82, 86–87, 94–95, 99–100
Platonic doctrine of, 52–53, 73n61, 83, 103–4, 106, 119, 121
unity of, 52–53, 83, 103, 119
Valentinian doctrine of, 229–37
Stobaeus, 17, 17n10, 23n40, 26n54, 63n14, 65, 83nn36–38, 84n39, 121n25, 155n65, 159n93, 208n48, 209n50, 210n54, 223n20, 227n42, 227n45, 228n47, 230n58, 233n82, 248, 248n20, 262n30, 263nn36–37, 264n43

tension (τόνος), 65, 95, 103, 119–21, 125
slackness/weak tension (ἀτονία), 120, 127, 127n60, 129, 270n66
strong tension (εὐτονία), 120, 270n66
Tertullian, 177, 187, 187n63, 189, 189n72, 192, 192n89, 220n3
Theodoret of Cyrus, 123

Theodoret of Mopsuestia, 152, 152n51, 153, 153n61, 168, 168n129, 169
Torah, 39–41, 44, 46–47, 53, 55, 78, 118n19, 212, 212n62, 214. *See also* law

Valentinian, 220n3, 221, 221n12, 222n14, 224, 224n26, 225, 225n34, 226, 226n38, 227–28, 228n51, 229, 229n56, 230–31, 231n67, 232, 232n72, 232n74, 233–34, 234nn85–86, 235, 235nn92–93, 236, 236n95
Valentinus, 220, 220n3, 222, 222n14, 223–24, 224nn26–27, 225n34, 234, 235–36n93
value, 42, 44, 45, 48, 49, 50, 55, 53, 65, 66, 67, 68n38, 71, 79, 102, 104, 254
vice, 46–47, 48–55, 61, 69, 71, 104, 109, 110, 119, 121, 132, 144, 156n76, 178–79, 191, 211, 230, 241, 248–49, 252, 253n35
virtue
  Christian
    display of, 188, 190–94
  Johannine, 98
  Matthean, 59, 64, 64n23, 66, 68, 69
  Pauline, 22, 25, 111
  Petrine, 128

Philonic, 108, 110–12
Stoic, 26–27, 29, 32, 61, 64, 64n23, 65–68, 68n38, 70–72, 86, 89, 110, 119–20, 128n64, 157, 162, 182, 191, 230, 241, 248–49, 263
  cardinal, 26–27, 32–33
  courage (ἀνδρεία), 26, 27, 184, 191, 193, 263
  justice (δικαιοσύνη), 26, 64–65, 69, 157–60, 251
  moderation/self-control (σωφροσύνη), 26, 26n58, 27, 33, 121, 188, 191, 194
  prudence (φρόνησις), 26, 32–33, 264
  unity of, 65–66, 230, 263

Word. *See* logos

Zeno, 17n9, 79, 83, 155–61, 161n107, 205, 248, 248nn19–20, 249, 257
Zeus, 24, 48, 51, 60–63, 68, 86, 125, 145–46, 156, 206, 222, 233, 235
Zoroaster, apocalypse of, 260n20
Zoroaster, book of, 240, 247, 254–55

Index of Ancient Sources

Old Testament

Genesis
1   129
1:2   225n30
2:17   46
6:9   63n18
9:3   108
17:1   63n18
23:2   73

Exodus
2:23   109
5:13   52
21:20   150
21:21   150
21:26–27   150
36:1   52

Leviticus
19:2   63
19:18   32, 41, 64, 69
20:26   63
25:8–55   154n62
25:44–46   154n62

Numbers
22:21–35   131n75

Deuteronomy
15:12   154n62
15:13–14   154n62
15:18   154n62
32:35   30n89

1 Samuel
15:33   164n121

2 Samuel
22:3   169

1 Kings
3:16–28   164n119

Job
1:1   63n18

Psalms
3:4 [3:3 ET]   169
17:3 [18:2 ET]   169
19   50
29   50
37:6 LXX   158n88
41:10 [42:9 ET]   169
42 [41]   72, 82
42:5   82
42:6 [41:6]   71
42:11   82
43   82
43:5   82
45:8 [46:7 ET]   169
69:9   81

Proverbs
19:25   149
21:11   149n31
22:3   149n31

Song of Songs
5:7   158n87

Isaiah
13:9–13   115
42:1   158n89
42:1–9   158n89
43:10   158n89
44:1–2   158n89
44:21   158n89
49:1–7   158n89
49:3   158n89
50:4–11   158n89
52:13   158n89
52:13–53:12   158n89
53:5 LXX   158
66:5–14   88

Daniel
11:30   81n21

Malachi
3:2–4   116n6

Old Testament Apocrypha

2 Maccabees
6:18–28   186n51

Sirach
23:10   158
28:17   158
32:23   41

Wisdom of Solomon
6:18   41
13–14   47

Old Testament Pseudepigrapha

3 Baruch
16.3   164

Life of Adam and Eve
49.3   126n56

Sibylline Oracles
3.75–92   126n56
5.515–531   126n56

Testament of Dan
4:7   82n29

Testament of Job
36:3/4–5   82n29

Testament of Reuben
2.1–2   253
2.1–3.7   252–3
2.2   253n35
2.3–3.1   253

Index of Ancient Sources 289

2.3–3.2 254
2.3–9 253
3.1 253
3.2–7 253
3.3–6 253n35
3.7 253, 254

New Testament
  Matthew
3:12 74n62
3:15 64n23, 72n55
5:6 64n23
5:7–9 66
5:10 64n23
5:17–20 64
5:18 60n5, 115
5:20 64, 64n23, 74n62, 157
5:21–22 67
5:22 70, 74n62, 157
5:27–28 67
5:33–37 67
5:43 69
5:44–46 69
5:45 69
5:48 63, 65, 69
6:1 64n23
6:1–17 69
6:10 68n39
6:12 166
6:14–15 166
6:18 69
6:33 64n23, 70
7:11 64
7:11–12 64n22
7:12 64
7:13 64
7:13–14 74n62
7:21 68n39
7:21–23 63n19, 74n62
7:24 63
7:24–27 63n19
7:25–34 69
8:12 74n62, 165
8:29 74n62
9:30 81
10:15 74n62
10:26–28 74n62
10:29–31 69
11:20–24 74n62
12:41 74n62
12:50 68n39
13:42 74n62, 165
13:50 74n62, 165
16:27 74n62

18:3 74n62
18:10 74n62
18:14 68n39
18:23–35 165
18:24–25 165
18:25 165
18:26–27 165
18:27 166n123
18:28–31 165
18:30 165
18:32–34 165
18:34 165
18:35 166
19:16–22 64
19:28 60n5, 115
21:12–13 70
21:32 64n23
22:13 74n62, 165
23 69
23:5–6 69
23:17 70
23:23 69
23:25 69
24:35 60n5
24:45–47 164
24:45–51 164
24:48–51 164
24:51 74n62, 164n118, 165
25:14–30 164
25:21 164
25:23 164
25:26 164
25:28–30 165
25:30 74n62, 164, 165, 166
25:46 165
26:37 72
26:37–38 70
26:41 73n61
26:42 68n39, 73
27:4 72n55
27:19 64n23, 72n55

  Mark
1:43 81
10:17–31 64
13:24–31 115

  Luke
1:54 168
6:20–26 66
6:35 154n64
6:46–49 63
13:23–24 74n62
16:17 115

  John
2:3–5 80
2:12–16 81
2:17 81
4:1–42 234
4:7 93n1
4:24 93, 265
4:34 80, 86n59
4:46–54 234
5:18 93
5:23–24 86n59
5:30 80, 86n59
5:37 86n59
6:38–39 86n59
7:16 80, 86n59
7:28 86n59
7:33 86n59
8 97n15
8:12 59
8:16 86n59
8:18 86n59
8:26 86n59
8:29 86n59
8:32 79
8:44 80
8:59 93
9:4 80, 86n59
10:6 80
10:16 80
10:18 186
10:31 93
10:32 80
10:38 80
10:40 94
11 82, 83, 86, 87, 96, 97, 97n15
11–13 112
11:2 94n3, 98n22
11:3 94, 94n3, 96, 98n22
11:4 94n3, 98n22
11:4–6 94
11:5 96
11:6 94n3, 98n22
11:11 96
11:21 94
11:23 87
11:24 87
11:25–26 87
11:31 81
11:32 81, 94
11:33 81n18, 82n29, 94, 96–97, 99–101, 104
11:33–35 86, 96
11:34 94, 97–98

11:35 81, 87, 94, 96–97, 101, 104
11:36 94, 96
11:38 81, 87, 94, 96–97, 100, 104
11:39 97, 97n15
12 82–83, 86–87, 97, 98, 100
12:23 87, 94
12:27 81, 86, 94, 98, 104
12:27–28 100
12:28 86
12:49 80
13 97, 97n15, 98
13:1 87
13:2 97
13:15 87
13:21 94, 97–99, 104
13:30 94
13:33 97n15
13:34 87
14 83
14:1 82, 94
14:2 88
14:6 89
14:27 82n27, 94
15:4 87
15:11 88
15:12 59, 87
15:13 87
16:20–23 88
17 80
18:33–38 79
19:30 80
20:20 89

Acts
17:28–29 156
20:35 168
21:39 39
22:3 39
27:5 149n29

Romans
1 46, 47, 52, 53, 54, 55
1–2 20, 46, 47n31
1–11 21
1:9 23n39
1:18 51
1:18–32 21, 41, 46, 47, 55
1:19–20 46
1:20 51
1:21 51
1:21–22 51
1:21–24 51
1:23 51
1:24 51, 53
1:25 52
1:25–27 51
1:26 52
1:26–27 52, 53
1:27 51
1:28 25, 25n49, 52, 54, 62n10
1:28–31 25, 52
1:28–32 51
1:29 53
1:29–31 46, 52
1:31 53
1:32 46, 47, 52, 53, 54, 55
2 55
2:4 154n64
2:14 46, 47, 54
2:14–15 46
2:28–29 41
3:12 154n64
5:12 47
6–7 20
6:16 180
6:18 180
6:22 180
7 52n45
7:3 180
8:1–2 180
8:15 163
8:18–25 115
9:4 23n39
11:22 154n64
12 15
12–13 21, 22
12–15 15, 15n3, 16, 16nn3–4, 16nn6–7, 20, 21, 23, 25, 34, 35
12:1 15n3, 24
12:1–2 15n3, 16n3, 20, 23, 25, 26
12:2 24, 33, 34
12:3 25, 26, 32, 33
12:3–8 22
12:3–12 21
12:3–15:14 21
12:4–5 26
12:6–8 26
12:9 32
12:9–21 29
12:10 32
12:13 21
12:14 21, 29, 30
12:15 21n35, 32
12:16 21, 33
12:17 30, 31
12:17–18 21
12:17b 30, 30n87
12:18 30n87, 31
12:19 30
12:19–21 21
12:20 30, 30n90
12:20a 29
12:21 31
13 31
13:1–7 16n3, 21, 30, 31, 31n96, 32
13:8–10 21, 31, 32
13:9 41
13:11–14 31
13:13 31n98
13:14 23, 33
14 22n36
14–15 21, 22, 23, 33, 33n108
14:1 22
14:1–15:14 22
14:2 33
14:5 33, 34n109
14:6 33
14:6–8 34n109
14:13 22
14:14 23, 33
14:14–17 34n109
14:15 34
14:17 23, 33
14:19 23, 34
14:20 23, 33, 34n109
15:1 22, 33
15:2 33, 34
15:5 33
15:5–6 34
15:5–7 23
15:13 21n33
15:14 21n33, 22
15:23–29 20

1 Corinthians
1:25 187n58
2:14–15 224n26
3:15 117
6:19–20 44
7 44, 55
7:10 59n1
7:17–24 41, 44, 45, 46
7:19 41, 44, 45, 46, 55
7:21 44, 45, 152n52
7:21–24 152

9:14   59n1
9:26   163n113
9:27   163n113
12:28   168
14:37-38   98n17
15   9

2 Corinthians
2:1-2   111
2:1-11   111
2:3-4   96, 111
2:5   111
4-5   11
4:16-5:5   9
4:18   9
6:6   154n64

Galatians
3:28   189
5:14   41
5:15   54
5:22   154n64

Ephesians
2:7   154n64
4:32   154n64
5:21   168
6   167
6:5   167
6:7   167
6:8   167
6:8-9   166
6:9   167

Philippians
3:3   23n39
3:20   194n99

Colossians
3:12   154n64
4:1   166

1 Thessalonians
1:10   115
4:13-5:10   115
4:15   59n1

2 Thessalonians
2:1-12   115

1 Timothy
2:9-10   169
6:1-2   170
6:1   169
6:2   168, 169
6:17-18   169

Titus
2:9-11   170

Hebrews
2:15   87n62
7:10   209n52
11:37   164n121

1 Peter
1:7   116n6
2:2   23n39
2:3   154n64
2:18   162
2:18-25   170
2:24   158

2 Peter
1:4   128
1:5-7   128, 128n64
1:7   130
1:10   130
1:12-15   116, 130
1:16   131
1:19   130
2:1-3   129
2:4-10   129
2:12   130
2:14   131
2:15-16   131
2:17   130, 132
2:18   130
2:22   131
3   119
3:1-2   116
3:3-4   116
3:5-7   116, 128
3:7   116, 117, 129
3:8-9   129
3:10   117, 129
3:10-11   116
3:10-12   116
3:10-13   116
3:12   129, 132
3:13   132
3:13-14   116, 119
3:14   129
3:16   116, 131, 132
3:17   129
3:17-18   130

1 John
4:18   167

Jude
11   131

Revelation
6:13-14   115
21:1   115

Apostolic Fathers

Barnabas
21.6   116n6

1 Clement
20   215n81
59.4   169

2 Clement
16.3   116n6

Didache
16.5   115

Diognetus
5-6   194n99

Shepherd of Hermas
Mandate
1.1   221n12

Ignatius
To the Romans
4   185n47

Martyrdom of Polycarp
2.1   187n61
10.1   185n42

New Testament Apocrypha and Pseudepigrapha

Acts of Thomas
83   148n25

Gospel of the Egyptians (apud Clement, Strom.)
3.63.1   214n75
3.64.1   214n75

Pseudo-Clementines
Homilies
19.20.6-21.7   251
Recognitions
12.3-4   178n13

Nag Hammadi and Related Coptic Codices

Allogenes (NHC XI,3)
45.9-46.35   266n56
45.30-46.23   261n23
46.7-12   269
47.10-14   269
47.25   269
49.7-14   269
49.9-10   269
49.26-38   269
51.8-9   265n50, 266n56
51.17-26   261n23
51.35   269

53.31   265, 269
55.30   265, 269
58.12–19   261n23
60.17–31   265n50
61.32–62.2   269
62.23   265, 269
62.28–36   265
63.17–20   265
64.36   269
65.33   265, 269
66.27   265, 269
66.28–30   269
66.33–35   266n56

Apocryphon of John (NHC II,1; III,1; BG 8502,2)

NHC II,1
12.26–13.4   254
14.28   246
15.13–29   245
15.24–29   243, 245
15.29–19.12   239
17.29–32   239
17.29–19.15   239
17.32   239
17.32–18.2   240
17.32–19.15   254
18   225n36
18–19   242n15
18.2   243, 244, 245
18.2–14   240
18.5   246
18.13   244, 246
18.14–19.2   240
18.15   244
18.18–19   240
18.20   244
18.31–32   240, 241n4
18.34   246
19.1   240, 242n15
19.2–15   240
19.3   246n17
19.6   246
19.7–10   247
19.11   245
19.34–21.16   246
20.9   245
20.28–29   246n17
21.7   245
28.19   243
21   220n4
31   220n4
31.18   243

NHC III,1
8.2–3   269n65
17.5–17   254
22.18–23.14   245
24.14–27.4   246
24.24   245
26.18   245
37.10   243

BG 8502,2
23.3   269
24.2   268n65
24.2–25.16   269
24.6–25.7   265
24.20–25.1   265n48, 268n65, 269, 269n65
25.15–16   268n65
26.15   269, 269n65
26.18   268n65
27.21–28.1   268n65
27.21–28.2   269n65
29.7–8   269
30.2–3   269n65
31.5–9   269n65
32.1–2   269
40.19–41.12   254
49.9–50.14   245
52.1–55.18   246
52.17   245
55.7   245
55.13   245
72.7   243

Gospel of Mary (BG 8502,1)
7   204, 207, 210
7.1–5   207
7.1–19   204
7.1–8.11   199, 200, 201, 204, 207, 215
7.3   202, 205, 207
7.3–7   203
7.3–8   203, 210
7.4   210
7.12–13   203
7.13–16   205
7.15–16   208
7.17   211
7.18–19   202, 205, 207
7.18–20   203
8.1–4   204
8.2   205
8.2–4   205, 208, 209
8.2–6   208, 210
8.2–7   208

8.4   205
8.7   214
8.7–10   201n8
8.8   214
8.9–10   214
8.15–19   209
8.15–21   211n56
8.21–22   204
9.6–11   208
9.13–19   200n7
9.16   213n69
9.20   212, 213n70
9.20–23   211n56, 213n65
9.21–23   211
10.8   204
10.13   213n69
10.14–23   211n56
10.20–21   213n68
15.1–17.7   200n4, 211, 213n67
15.1–17.9   210
17.10–15   211
18.1–5   208
18.14–21   204

Gospel of Philip (NHC II,3)
§§7–8 (52)   225n33
§59 (64)   225n35
§109 (77)   225n32

Gospel of Truth (NHC I,3)
16   227n43
34   224n29
34–35   225n31

Interpretation of Knowledge (NHC XI,1)
9.27–37   231n71
16.32   231n68
16.34–35   231n70

Three Steles of Seth (NHC VII,5)
121.31–32   266n56

Tripartite Tractate (NHC I,5)
83–85   234n87
89–90   234n88

Zostrianos (NHC VIII,1)
8–10   260n20
15.1–12   269
15.6–12   261n23
15.18–19   266n56
17.12–13   269
18.5–19   261n23

Index of Ancient Sources

20.2–15   269
20.15–18   265n50, 266n56
20.17–18   269
20.22–24   269
58.14–16   261n23
61.32–62.2   269
64.14–16   269
65.6–7   269
66.14–18   265n50
66.14–20   269
66.16–17   269
66.16–19   269
66.23–67.2   269
67.20   269
68.1–7   269
68.5–7   269
68.16–17   269
73.1   269
73.8   269
74.8–9   269
79.10–81.20   269
79.21   266n56
124.18–125.20   261n23

Papyri
London
23   169
Oxyrhynchus
3525   199n2
3525.13   211n56, 213n65
Rylands
263   199n2

Other Ancient Sources
Aeschylus
 Seven against Thebes
96n10
Aëtius
 De placita
1.3.25   208n46
1.7.33   206n34, 262n27, 265n51
4.4.4   248n19
4.21.1–4   210n55
Alexander of Aphrodisias
 De fato
199.14–22   230n63
 De mixtione
216.14–218.6   233n78, 233n82, 263n35
224.14–26   262n26
225.1   229n55
225.1–2   206n34

Andronicus, see
 Pseudo-Andronicus
Anonymous Parmenides Commentary
11–12   267
12.29–35   269
14.6   269
14.15   269
14.17   269
14.17–26   269
14.18   269
14.23   269
14.25   269
Antipater of Tarsus
 On Anger
156–7
Apuleius
 Metamorphoses
8.22   165n122
11.15   181n24
Aristotle
 De generatione et corruptione
I 5.321a–312b   233n82
I 5.322a   233n82
I 10.327b   233n77
I 10.328a   233n82
I 10.328a29–31   233n76
 Ethica nichomachea
3.5   121
7.5.6   147n22
7.6.1   144n10
10.6   147n23
 Politica
1.1.5   152n54
1.2.1   153n55
1.2.3   152
1.2.4–6   147
1.2.13   147
1.2.14   147
1.2.15   153n55
1.2.18   153n55
1.2.19   153n55
1.2.20   153n55
1.2.21   151
1.3.8   147
1.5.6   147
1.5.11   147, 151
3.5.10   147
3.9.3   152n54
7.9.9   145

Arius Didymus
 Epitomai
 apud Eusebius, Praep. ev.
15.20.6   123n37
 apud Stobaeus, Anth.
2.7.5–12   (W-H
  2.57.13–116.18)   17n10
2.7.5a–5b7   (W-H
  2.57.18–65.6)   26n54
2.7.5b13   (W-H
  2.68.18–23)   121n25
2.7.8   (W-H
  2.85.13–86.4)   63n14
Arrian
 Epicteti dissertationes
3.13.4–5   122n34
3.22.54   69
4.1.6–14   181n21
Athenaeus
 Deipnosophistae
6.267B   155n66
14.629F   122n34
14.643F   157n77
Augustinus
 De civitate Dei
5.18   192n88
10.23   260n18
10.29   260n18
15–24   192n88
Aulus Gellius
 Noctes atticae
1.26.4–9   160n100
2.18.1–10   162n111
7.2.6–7   120n23
Calcidius
 In Timaeum
292   206
Cato the Elder
 De agricultura
2.2   143
2.5   143
2.7   143
Chaldean Oracles (frg. [ed. Majercik 1989])
2   258n10, 270n67
3   258n10
4   258n10
23   258n10

26   270n67
27   258n10, 259n11
28   258n10
29   258n10
31   258n10

Cicero

Academica posteriora
1.26–30   204n26
1.27   204

De finibus
3   17n14, 18n15
3.3–5   18n16
3.6   18n18
3.22   24n42
3.32   67n34, 104n52
3.41   60n3
3.50–58   34n109
3.62–63   28n71
3.64   28n69
3.65   29n78

De legibus
1.6.18   62n11
1.24   156, 156n72
58–59   63n20

De natura deorum
1.39   23n40
1.41   159n95
2.19–92   122n34
2.24   167n127
2.118–119   122

De officiis
1.128   40n7
2.1–8   17n13
3.102   49n36

De republica
3.37   153
6.9–26   125n50
6.23–24   122n34

Pro Murena
61   60n3

Tusculanae disputationes
1.77–78   123n36
2   184
2.17.41   184nn36–37
3.12–13   60n3
3.30   102n42
4.6.14   107n63
4.11.25   110n81
4.14   111n82
4.37–57   250n29
4.43–57   60n3
5.32   60n3
5.120   60n3

Cleanthes

Hymn to Zeus
24–29   61
33   61

Clement of Alexandria

Excerpta ex Theodoto
17.1   233n81
45.1–2   228n49
55–56   230n65
56   229n56
61.7   228n51
63–64   235n91
67.2   226n39, 229n54
78.2   227n44

Stromata
2.114.3–6   225n34
3.45.1   214n77
3.63.1   214nn75–76, 215n79
3.64.1   214n75
3.104.4   214n78
4.18.5   250n27
4.19   192n90

Cornutus

Epidrome
17.2–4   122n34

Crates

Epistle
34   82n29

Cyprian

De lapsis
8   186n50

Epistle
10.2–3   187n64
60.2.3   187n59

Damascius

De principiis
2.1.4–2.10   260n18

Dio Cassius

Historia Romana
61.3–4   19n24

Dio Chrysostom

Orationes
1.42–49   122n34
36.40–61   122n34

Diogenes Laertius

Vitae philosophorum
1.118   158n85
2.11   158n85

2.63   158n85
2.110   158n85
5.35   158n85
5.70   158n85
6.5   158n85
6.73   158n85
6.75   158n85
6.77   158n85
6.78   158n85
6.80   158n85
6.89   163n113
7.23   156n75, 161n107
7.36   158n85
7.39–41   263n38
7.41   158n85
7.86   84n40, 104n53
7.87   102n44
7.87–88   23n40, 61
7.87–88D   103n49
7.88   62n13
7.103   66n27
7.104   152n50
7.107   63n14
7.111   83
7.112   102n43, 227n42, 227n45
7.115   250n26
7.116   88n65
7.117   80n15, 88n66, 106n59, 109n74
7.118   82, 107n63, 111n82
7.119   79n14, 80n16
7.121   158n85
7.121–122   79n12
7.123   110n81
7.133–143   122n34
7.134   23n40
7.134.1   208n46
7.135   206n32
7.135–136   206n34, 262n27, 262n31
7.135.6   210n55
7.137   262n30
7.137.2   222n18
7.142   206n34, 262n31
7.147   23n40
7.151   123n40, 233n82
7.156–157   122n34, 123n39
8.14   158n85
9.7–9   122n34
9.33   122n34
9.67   158n85
9.106   158n85
10.9   158n85

Index of Ancient Sources

10.12 158n85
10.85 82n29
10.144.17 82n29

Diogenes of Oenoanda
Fragment
3 123n41

Epictetus
Dissertationes
1.1 211n58
1.3.1–3 23n40
1.3.3 156n73
1.4 84n41, 230n61, 231n69
1.4.32 48
1.6.1 48
1.6.9 50, 53
1.6.24 48, 51
1.9.23–24 43n17
1.9.29 162n111
1.9.29–30 170
1.11 32n102
1.12.1–7 47
1.12.7 47
1.12.32 48
1.13.3–4 156
1.13.5 24n43, 156
1.16.7 48
1.16.15–19 23n41
1.16.20–21 23n41
1.18 85n47, 157, 157n82
1.19.12–13 29n79
1.19.13 28n77
1.19.21 162n111
1.19.22 166n124
1.20.7 86n53
1.23.1 29n79
1.25.3–6 24n43
1.26.1–2 49
1.27.6 86n54
1.27.7–10 86n55
1.28 157
1.28.25 86n56
1.29.2 42
1.29.4 24n43
1.29.5–7 42
1.29.13 24n43
1.29.46 44
1.29.49 44
1.29.59–63 163
1.30 34n109, 69
1.30.4–5 24n42
2.1.39 44
2.5.1 42
2.5.2 82n29
2.5.22 43
2.5.23 32n100
2.5.26 47
2.6 34n109
2.6.24 180n18
2.8 211n58
2.8.2–3 23n40
2.8.11–14 23n40, 209n51
2.8.14 49
2.9.15 34n109
2.9.19–21 41, 41n9
2.10 50
2.10.4 28n67, 50, 53
2.10.17 50
2.10.23 28n77, 29n79
2.11.24–25 25n52
2.14.11 69n41
2.14.12–13 24n42
2.16 42
2.16.24 42
2.16.27–28 24n43
2.16.28 43, 45
2.16.42 43
2.17.23–25 24n42
2.18.11 158n88, 158n90
2.18.19–21 24n47
2.19.13 34n109
2.19.26–27 24n42
2.20.6 29n79
2.20.23–25 48
2.26.5 147n19
3.26.37 161n107
3.1.19–20 43n17
3.1.25 23n40
3.1.37 49
3.2 84n41
3.3 211n58
3.7.27 29n79
3.8 211n58
3.12 211n58
3.13.5 28n75, 29n79
3.14.11–13 63n20
3.21.1–7 25n51
3.22.2 49
3.22.23–25 86n58
3.22.54 29n84, 33n105
3.24 43, 48
3.24.12 29n79
3.24.22–24 32n99
3.24.37 49
3.24.41 49
3.24.41–43 54
3.24.42 24n43
3.24.42–43 49
3.24.43 49
3.24.64 33n105
3.24.64–65 29n84
3.24.65 24n42
3.24.95–97 43
3.24.95–102 24n42
3.24.98 43
3.24.98–99 43
3.24.110 24n42
3.24.114 44
3.25.9–10 149n28
3.26.1 151n47
3.26.29 24n42
3.26.29–30 23n41
4.1.122 28n76, 30n86
4.1.167 30n86
4.3.9–10 43
4.3.12 24n43
4.5.24 30n88
4.7 180
4.7.6 41, 41n9
4.7.8 29n79
4.7.17 24n43
4.7.20 24n42
4.8.27 82n29
4.10.12 28n77, 29n79
4.11.1 29n79
4.12.19 29n80

Encheiridion
1.1 42
11 43
43 30n86
51.3 33n106

Fragment
7 29n85
9 228n48

Epiphanius of Salamis
De fide
9.40 123

Panarion
31.9–32 227n45
33.5.10–12 232n73
33.5.13 232n72

Eusebius
Historia ecclesiastica
8.9.5 191n80
8.12.3–4 193n93

Praeparatio evangelica
15.14.2 206n38, 262n27
15.18.2 206n38
15.20.6 123n37

Galen
De affectuum dignotione
1.4   149n32, 164
De placitis Hippocratis et Platonis
3.7.3   95n4
5.6.1   157n80
448.11–12   209n51

Heracleon (Valentinian)
Fragment
17–40   234n89

Herodotus
Historiae
2.139   164n121
3.13   164n121
7.39   164n121

Hierocles
On Appropriate Acts (apud Stobaeus, Anth.)
1.3.53   (W-H 1.63.6–7)   155n65
3.39.34   (W-H 3.730.17)   155n65
4.27.20   (W-H 4.660.16–661.6)   159n93
4.27.23   (W-H 4.671.3)   155n65

Hippolytus of Rome
Refutatio omnium haeresium
6, praef.   220n3
6.21.1–3   220n3
6.22.1–3   220n3
6.29.1   220n3
6.32.5   226n41
6.32.5–6   228n53
6.34.6   225n34
6.37.1   220n3
6.37.5–6   220n3
6.37.7   222n14
10.13.4   224n27

Homer
Iliad
8.19   222

Horace
Epistulae
1.1.106–108   60n3
Satirae
1.3.76–142   60n3
2.3.40–46   60n3

Irenaeus of Lyons
Adversus haereses
1   227n45
1.2.1   227n46
1.2.2   227n45, 228n50
1.2.3   226n41
1.4.1   226n41, 228n52
1.4.3   226n37
1.4.5   228n53
1.6.1–2   229n56
1.6.2   233nn83–84
1.6.3   231n66
1.6.4   230n64
1.7.1   236n94
1.7.5   235n92
1.13.5.3–5   231n66
2.14.3–4   220n3
2.33.2   220n3
3.15.2   231n67

Joannes Lydus
De mensibus
4.122   260n18, 268

John Chrysostom
Homiliae in epistulam i ad Corinthios
4.7 (on 1 Cor 1:25)   187n58

Josephus
Antiquitates judaicae
1.70   126n56
8.31   164n119

Justin Martyr
Apologia i
1   195n101
11   194n99
19.5   176n5
20.1–2   176n5
20.4   176n5
60.8–9   117n13
Apologia ii
7   177nn6–7
8.3   176n5
10.5   190n74
12.1   190n75
Dialogus cum Tryphone
1.5   176n5
2.1–2   176n3

Life of Aesop
109   154, 169

Lucan
Bellum civile
1.67–81   126n52
1.71–84   122n34
2.4–11   122n34
2.289–292   126n53
4.48–120   127n58
5.75–96   122n34
5.176–182   122n34
5.504–677   127n58
6.611–616   122n34
8.777–9.18   127n63
9.319–347   127n58, 127n60
9.381   127n61
9.445–492   127n58
9.463–465   127n61
9.734–838   127n62
9.942–945   126n54

Lucian
Menippus
20   81n21
Philopseudes
20   149n33
Vitarum auctio
14   122n34

Lucretius
De rerum natura
1.215–250   122n34

Manilius
Astronomica
1.121–146   122n34
2.63–81   122n34
2.82–83   23n40
2.105–127   23n40

Marcus Aurelius
Meditations
2.5   24n47
3.3.1   122n34
4.4   23n40
5.27   23n40
7.31   69
10.7.2   122n34
11.1   28n68
11.3   194n98

Marius Victorinus
Adversus Arium
1.50   265n50, 269, 269n65

Martyrdom of Montanus, Lucius and Flavian
19.6   187n59

Martyrs of Lyons and Vienne
3–6   185n42

Minucius Felix
Octavius
37.1–2   187n62
37.3–6   192n88

Musonius Rufus
Dissertationes
2.38.1–3   29n79
2.38.12–14   29n79
4.44.10–35   26n54
4.48.1–14   26n54
5.50.32–52.4   25n52
8.64.14   24n42
10.78.26–28   30n86
10.78.31–33   31n91
12   157n83
14.92.29–33   33n105
14.94.5–8   32n100
16.104.35–36   24n44
17.108.8–18   24n42, 29n79
18a   161n107
Fragment
32   52
41.136   29n85

Nemesius
De natura hominis
70.6–71.4   261n24, 262n26

Origen of Alexandria
Commentary on
St. John's Gospel
BOOK
19–20   97n15
28   97n15, 97–98, 98nn18–20, 110n78
32   97n15, 98, 99nn23–24, 99nn26–29
FRAGMENT
83   97, 98, 98nn16–17, 98n21, 101n40
84   97, 100n37, 101n39
88   98, 99n25, 99nn31–32, 100nn33–36
100   97, 98, 99n30
Contra Celsum
4.68–69   117n13
7.53   162n111
De principiis
2.8.3   224n24

Exhortatio ad martyrium
22   186n51

Ovid
Metamorphoses
1.253–261   122n34
2.201–234   122n34

Passion of Perpetua
6.1   191n79
6.4   185n42
18.5   185n48
20.7   186n49
21.8–10   186n49
21.9–10   188n66

Petronius
Satyricon
71   156n74

Philo of Alexandria
De aeternitate mundi
8–9   118n19
76–77   122n29
83–103   118n19
120–129   118n19
De cherubim
14–15   62n10
De confusione linguarum
84–103   213n67
85   212n63
De congressu eruditionis gratia
60   213n69
De ebrietate
1–3   118n19
198–205   118n19
De fuga et inventione
9   213n73
12   212n64
De migratione Abrahami
89–93   41
148–150   213n69
156   110n80
De opificio mundi
72–75   213n72
151–156   213n66
De plantatione
106   110n79
140–177   118n19
De somniis
1.31   223n23
2.228   213n67, 213n69
2.267   213n70

De specialibus legibus
2.53   212n63
2.69   155
2.122   155, 155n68
3.201–202   150n36
De virtutibus
187–188   213n65
De vita Mosis
2.288   78
Legum allegoriae
1.31–32   213n68
1.37–38   213n68
3.134   108n65
3.159   230n61, 231n69
3.211   109
3.211–213   109n75
Quaestiones et solutiones in Exodum
1.23   213n72, 214n74
Quaestiones et solutiones in Genesin
1.79   73
2.57   108
Quod Deus sit immutabilis
151–167   213n67

Plato
Apologia
28E–29A   43n17
De legibus
636C   52
836C–841D   52
890D   46
Phaedrus
253C–256D   52
Republic
II–III   106n57
IV.434D–441C   52
VI.507B   51
Timaeus
47B–C   50
48E–52D   266

Pliny the Elder
Naturalis historia
2.22   181n22
2.240–241   122n34
7.73   122n34
Epistulae
6.20.15   122n34

Plotinus
  Ennead
1.6 [1] 7.11–12   258n5
1.6 [1] 7.12   258n5
1.8 [51] 2.5–7   258n5
2.9 [33]   260n20, 266n57
2.9 [33] 6.1–3   260n20
2.9 [33] 10   266n57
2.9 [33] 10.19–33   260n20
3.6 [26] 6.10–17   258n5
3.6 [26] 6.23–24   258n5
3.6 [26] 7.7–8   258n5
3.8 [30] 8.8–12   258n5
3.8 [30] 10.1–2   258n5
3.9 [13] 6.3–6   258n5
5.1 [11]   258n7
5.3 [49] 16.38–42   258n5
5.4 [7] 2.17–18   258n5
5.4 [7] 2.43–44   258n5
5.5 [32] 1.38   258n5
5.5 [32] 10.12–14   258n5
5.6 [24] 6.20–22   258n5
5.9 [5] 10   258n5
6.4 [22] 3.31–35   258n5
6.6 [34] 8.1–2   258n5
6.6 [34] 8.9–10   258n5
6.6 [34] 8.11–13   258n5
6.6 [34] 8.15–17   258n5
6.6 [34] 8.17–23   258n5
6.6 [34] 9.27–29   258n5
6.6 [34] 9.29–32   258n5
6.6 [34] 15.1–3   258n5
6.6 [34] 18.35–36   258n5
6.6 [34] 18.51–53   258n5
6.7 [38] 13.42–43   258n5
6.7 [38] 23.22–25   258n5
6.7 [38] 37.18–22   258n7
6.9 [9] 2.24   258n5
6.9 [9] 3   258n5, 261n25

Plutarch
  Cato Major
5.1   154
5.2   154n64
5.5   154
6.3   168n130
  De cohibenda ira
459A   160n102
459B   146n17
459C   147n20
459C–D   161n105
459D   151n46
459D–E   160n100
459E   151n45

462A   163
463A–B   158n86
  De communibus notitiis
  contra Stoicos
1063A–B   230n61
1063B   230n60
1078B–D   233n80
1078E   233n82
  De Stoicorum
  repugnatiis
1034C   26n54
1056D   180n17
1046E–F   230n59, 263n37
  Moralia
389C   122n34
415F–416A   122n34
548B–568A   116n4
926D–928D   122n34
950D–951B   122n34
955E–F   122n34
1052C–1053E   122n34
1074E–1076A   122n34
1077A–E   122n34
1107B   123n36
  On Calumny
  FRAGMENT
153   163n117
  Pyrrhus
24.3   164n119
  De virtute morali
440E–441D   26n54, 263n37
441B–D   104n51
441C   249n23, 253n39
441C–D   248n21, 252n33
441C–447A   248n21
449A   107n61
449B   106n60

Porphyry
  De abstinentia
3.19   160n98
  Historia philosophiae
18   268
  Isagoge
69.14–70.24   268
  Sententiae ad intelligi-
  bilia ducentes
10   268
21   268
25–26   268
25.3–6   268
26   264n47

31   268
33.5   267
40   268
41   268
  Vita Plotini
16   260n20, 266n57

Posidonius
  Fragment
36   157n77
155   157n77

Proclus
  Elementa theologiae
103   262, 264n41
  In Platonis Timaeum
  commentaria
3.32–33   267
3.64   260n18, 268
  Theologia Platonica
1.11   268

Pseudo-Andronicus
  De passionibus
1   83n37
3   227n42, 227n45
6   70n46, 72, 110n79

Pseudo-Demetrius
  Epistolary Types
7   151n43

Pseudo-Plutarch
  Placita philosophorum
4.7.3   123

Ptolemaeus
  Letter to Flora (apud
  Epiphanius, Panarion)
33.5.10–12   232n73
33.5.13   232n72

Seneca (the Younger)
  Ad Helviam
1.24   161n107
  Ad Marciam de
  consolatione
25.1–2   124n48
26.5–7   122n34, 125n49
  Ad Polybium de
  consolatione
1.1–2   122n34
  De beneficiis
1.6.1–3   29n81
1.6.3   24n45
2.17.4   29n81

3.18–28   166n126
3.18.2   29n81
3.22–27   166n126
3.22.1   155n67
4.3.1   27n66
4.6.2–3   122n34
4.6.21–22   122n34
4.25.1   24n47
4.26   69
7.1.3   25n52
7.1.7   29n78
7.19.9   28n69
7.31.1   29n85, 31n95
7.31.5   29n85

De clementia
1.1–4   31n96
1.3.2   27n62, 29n78
1.4   122n34
1.4.3   27n65
1.5.1   27n65
1.11.2   27n64, 33n105
1.13.4   27n64
1.18.1   159n91
1.18.2   149, 159n96, 160n101
1.19.6   27n64
1.21.4   27n63
2.2.1   27n65
2.5.3   33n105
2.6.2–3   32n99

De Constantia sapientiis
5   191n78
8.3   182nn26–27

De ira
1.1.3–4   83n35
1.1.5   156n76
1.5.1–17.7   250n29
1.5.3   32n104
1.9.2   87n60
1.14.3   30n87, 31n93
1.16.1   30n86
1.17.1   87n60
2.1.3–4.2   157n78
2.2.4–5   85n44
2.2.5   86
2.3.1   85n45
2.3.1–2   104n55, 228n47
2.3.1–2.4   208n49
2.3.5   85n46
2.4.1–2   104n56
2.9.1–2   85n47
2.10.6   79n10
2.10.6–7   31n94

2.13.1   87n60
2.19–21   85n48, 157n78
2.22.2   85n49
2.28.4   29n85, 31n94
2.28.5–8   85n50
2.31.7   28n72
2.32.2   31n94
2.34   69
2.34.5   31n94
3.1.2   85n51
3.3.1   87n60
3.4.4   160n102
3.5.4   85n52
3.24.2   161n105
3.27.1   31n94
3.32.1–2   161
3.32.2   164
3.35.2   161n105
3.40.2–5   160n101

De otio
1.4   29n85, 31n92, 69
8.2   29n85

De providentia
2.10   192n86
3.1   28n69
3.9   192n91
4.12   176
4.12–13   182n28
5.4.6   186n54

De tranquillitate animi
11.5   188n65
11.1–6   184nn38–39
16.4   32n99

De vita beata
15   69
15.5   24n42
20.5   29n85

Epistulae morales
1.2   182n30
2.4   182n28
5.4   27n61
6.1–3   25n51
6.5   25n52
9.16   206, 233n79, 265n50
9.17   122n34
16.5   24n42, 69
20.2   25n52
22.5–6   192n82
23.4   88n67
26.10   192nn83–84
27.4–8   160n103
41.2   209n51
47   153, 159n95, 167

47.1   156, 167
47.2   167
47.5   160
47.10   155
47.11   155, 159, 163
47.13   167
47.16   167
47.17   167
47.18   167, 168
47.19   160, 167
48.2   29n78, 32n103
51.9   182n29
58   10
65   10
65.2   206, 229n55
65.21–22   183n32
66.12   23n40
66.21   31n94
70   188, 188n68
70.14   192n84
70.19–21   189n69
70.23   189n69
71.12–14   122n34
73.16   123n42
76.9–10   23n40
82.10–12   34n109
85.2   26n54
88.29–30   27n60
90   47
90.40   27n66
90.46   26n54
91   123
91.1–21   122n34
91.11–12   124n43
91.13   124n46
91.15–16   124n45
92.1–2   23n40
92.11   34n109
92.27   23n40
94   230n62
94.1   155n65
94.47–48   25n51
95.33   28n73
95.47–50   24n47
95.51–52   27n66, 28n71
95.52   32n103
99   73n60
102.18   29n78
102.22   10
115.5   24n48
116.5   79n10
118.11   66n27
120.4   206n37
120.10   29n85

120.11   26n54
124.23   23n40
  Hercules furens
940–952   122n34
  Hercules Oetaeus
1101–1127   122n34
  Naturales quaestiones
1, Pref. 14   23n40
3.13   122n34
3.27–30   122n34
  Thyestes
789–884   122n34

Seneca the Elder
  Controversiae
7.6.18   156n74

Sextus Empiricus
  Adversus mathematicos
7.19   263n38
9.70–74   123n36
9.78–85   123n36
  Pyrrhoniae hypotyposes
1.212   122n34

Simplicius
  In Aristotelis categorias commentarium
216.27   264n43

Stobaeus
  Anthologium
1.3.53   (W-H 1.63.6–7)   155n65
1.10.16c   (W-H 1.129.2–130.13)   223n20
1.13.1c   (W-H 1.138.14–139.4)   264n43
1.17.4   (W-H 1.155.5–11)   233n82, 263n36
1.25.5   (W-H 1.213.15–21)   262n30
2.7.1   (W-H 2.37.15–39.18)   248n20
2.7.5–12   (W-H 2.57.13–116.18)   17n10
2.7.5a–5b7   (W-H 2.57.18–65.6)   26n54
2.7.5b5   (W-H 2.63.6–24)   263n37
2.7.5b10   (W-H 2.66.14–67.4)   230n58
2.7.5b13   (W-H 2.68.18–23)   121n25
2.7.6   (W-H 2.75.7–78.17)   23n40
2.7.8   (W-H 2.85.13–86.4)   63n14
2.7.9b   (W-H 2.88.2–6)   84n39
2.7.10   (W-H 2.88.8–21)   248n20
2.7.10   (W-H 2.88.8–10)   210n54
2.7.10–10a   (W-H 2.88.8–90.6)   83nn36–37, 228n47
2.7.10b   (W-H 2.90.19–91.9)   83n38, 208n48
2.7.10c   (W-H 2.92.1–6)   227n42, 227n45
2.7.10e   (W-H 2.93.1–13)   209n50
2.31.123   (W-H 2.235.23–239.29)   26n54
3.39.34   (W-H 3.730.17)   155n65
4.27.20   (W-H 4.660.16–661.6)   159n93
4.27.23   (W-H 4.671.3)   155n65
4.39.22   (W-H 5.906.18–907.5)   65

Suetonius
  Divus Claudius
25   49
  Gaius Caligula
27   164n121

Syrianus
  In Aristotelis Metaphysica commentaria
109   267

Tacitus
  Agricola
46   123n36
  Annales
13.2   19n24
14.42–45   151n48
15.60–64   183n31

Tertullian
  Ad martyras
3   187n63
4.1.4–9   192n89
  Apologia
50.7–8   192n89
  De carne Christi
20   220n3
  De spectaculis
27   189n72

Themistius
  In Aristotelis physica paraphrasis
104.9–19   233n80

Theodore of Mopsuestia
  Commentariorum in epistulam ad Philemonem liber
1:182.15–183.21   168
2:259.2–4   168
2:259.4   168n129
2:260.7   168n129
2:260.8–10   168
2:262.25–263.7   152n51
2:264.8–14   153
2:269.12   168n129
2:272.7   168n129
2:273.10   168n129
2:275.1   168n129
2:278.15   168n129
2:278.15–16   168
2:278.17   168n129
2:280.8–9   168
2:281.8   168n129
2:281.9   168
2:283.10   168
2:283.16   168
  Commentariorum in epistulam i ad Timotheum liber
2:174.18–19   169
2:175.1–2   169
2:175.2–4   169

Theodoret of Cyrus
  Graecarum affectionum curatio
5.23–24   123

Theophrastus
  Characteres
12   149n34

Valentinus
  Fragment
2   225n34
11   224n27

Harvest (apud Hippolytus, Refutatio)
6.37.7   222n14

Xenophon
Memorabilia
1.4   50
4.3   50

Oeconomicus
5.15   144n8
5.16   145
7.37   146
7.41   144n9, 146
9.5   145, 146
9.11–13   145
9.12   146
9.14   144n8

12.5–7   146
12.6–7   166
12.9   145
12.15   145
13.6–8   148
13.9   145, 148, 148n24
13.10   145, 146
13.11–12   148
21.12   145n16

www.ingramcontent.com/pod-product-compliance
Lightning Source LLC
Chambersburg PA
CBHW032222010526
44113CB00032B/208